THE THEORY OF FINANCE
FINANCE
Evidence
and
Applications

THE THEORY OF FINANCE
Evidence
and
Applications

John D. Martin
University of Texas at Austin

Samuel H. Cox, Jr.
University of Nebraska–Lincoln

Richard D. MacMinn
University of Texas at Austin

The Dryden Press
Chicago   New York   San Francisco   Philadelphia
Montreal   Toronto   London   Sydney   Tokyo

Acquisitions Editor: Ann Heath
Developmental Editor: Judy Sarwark
Project Editor: Paula Ransdell
Production Manager: Barb Bahnsen
Permissions Editor: Doris Milligan
Director of Editing, Design, and Production: Jane Perkins

Text and Cover Designer: Alan Wendt
Copy Editor: Nancy Maybloom
Compositor: Beacon Graphics
Text Type: Times Roman

Library of Congress Cataloging-in-Publication Data

Martin, John D.
    The theory of finance.

    Includes index.
    1. Finance. I. Cox, Sam. II. MacMinn, Richard.
III. Title.
HG173.M353   1988   332'.01   87-496
ISBN 0-03-063854-2

Printed in the United States of America
789-038-987654321

Address orders:
111 Fifth Avenue
New York, NY 10003

Address editorial correspondence:
One Salt Creek Lane
Hinsdale, IL 60521

The Dryden Press
Holt, Rinehart and Winston
Saunders College Publishing

The Dryden Press Series in Finance

Preface

In this text, we have attempted to gather and synthesize the principal theoretical results in the finance literature. In addition, we have surveyed the seminal elements of the supporting body of empirical tests and reviewed the present state of the art in applying its basic tenets to financial choices. In short, we have attempted to write a text that spans financial theory, its empirical tests, and its applications to real-world financial problems.

For doctoral students, the book provides a conceptual knowledge base from which they can build their future study. For the M.B.A. and advanced undergraduate, the book offers an in-depth overview of financial theory, evidence, and practice. Our aim is to give users enough educational background to put them in command of the most recent developments in the theory of finance and its applications. Although some of the subject matter appears complex, the problems confronted in modern-day financial management are equally challenging. Today's practicing financial manager regularly encounters complex issues, such as valuation of options and futures contracts and the use of asset pricing theories, that require a highly sophisticated knowledge base to master. We hope that this text will prepare the user to operate effectively in this environment.

Intended Market

Our objective in this text is to provide an introduction to the theory of financial decisionmaking that is *accessible* to a broad audience of finance students. A financial theory course used to be considered a luxury for all but Ph.D. candidates. We believe, however, that the increasing complexity of the financial environment makes this material mandatory at all levels of instruction.[1] We have used the manuscript to teach at three very different levels: a senior finance elective, a second-year M.B.A. course, and a first-year Ph.D. course. No text can be all things to all users, and we certainly make no such claim. However, we have made an earnest attempt to provide a text that is as accessible as possible and, with careful selection of material, conducive to use by advanced undergraduates interested in financial theory up through first-year Ph.D. students.

Special Features and Use of the Text

We have endeavored to offer enough flexibility to accommodate the divergent backgrounds and interests of students at these three levels of instruction. To this end, we have partitioned the text by degree of analytical rigor. Specifically, we have made it understandable to the broadest group of users by presenting "parallel" discussions of technical material where possible. For more advanced students, we have included *Mathematical Overviews* of many topics covered in the book; these treat selected financial theory problems in more depth and with greater rigor than in the text presentation. Further, we offer two additional types of mathematical aids. First, *Mathematical Reviews* of math concepts used in the text provide a quick and convenient review of the underlying concepts. Second, the *Mathematical Compendium* at the end of the book details the mathematical concepts now common throughout the finance literature. Thus, the Compendium serves as both a background reference for the mathematics utilized in the text and a guide to some of the more sophisticated mathematical concepts prevalent in the theory of finance. With these different forms of presentation, we hope to provide a flexible teaching/learning instrument.

 We also include a generous number of end-of-chapter questions and problems. Detailed solutions to these are provided in the *Instructor's Manual* along with a set of alternative course outlines, sample examinations, and selected lecture notes. Further, a number of chapters contain in-text *Exercises* and detailed solutions. These are distinct from the flow of the chapter material to avoid interrupting the reader's train of thought.

 In teaching the undergraduate (senior elective) and M.B.A. (second-year elective) courses, we generally omit the Mathematical Reviews and Overviews. This allows us to teach the material in an "intuitive" format, using graphs and some algebra but avoiding calculus. If this format is adopted, we strongly suggest that students be told early in the semester that they are not responsible for the mathematics presented in the Reviews and Overviews — this will greatly reduce user stress! In addition, the end-of-chapter study problems that require calculus or are particularly challenging are identified with an asterisk (*).

---

[1] One need only survey the growing list of finance Ph.D.s lured to Wall Street investment banking firms to find evidence of the demand for increased knowledge of financial theory in the day-to-day world of financial decisionmaking.

In general, the minimal background requirements for text users include algebra and elementary calculus,[2] basic statistics, microeconomics, and an understanding of basic financial statements. A prior introduction to the subject of finance, although useful, is not a prerequisite. It has been our experience, however, that undergraduate and M.B.A. users find the text much more useful after they have been introduced to financial management in a traditional applications-oriented text. Previous exposure to the subject matter of finance frequently leaves students with a wide range of unanswered questions about the standard "prescriptions" for financial problems.

We do not think that the treatment of financial theory should ignore the real-world problems that gave rise to its development. In this regard, we present both empirical evidence and applications of financial theories. Part IV is devoted to the tests and applications of financial theory developed in recent years. In addition, the *Institutional Notes* scattered throughout the text bridge the gap between the theory being discussed and the real world.

Overview of the Book

Our objective is to provide a coherent treatment of the evolving theory of finance. Part I consists of Chapter 1, which surveys the fundamental underpinnings of financial theory. Here we define positive and normative theories, relate financial theory to the various subfields of economics, and discuss the goal of owner wealth maximization in financial decisionmaking.

Part II (Chapters 2 through 6) considers the case of complete certainty of future outcomes. This material is based on the seminal work of Fisher (1930) and the valuable extensions made by Hirshleifer (1970). The assumption of certainty of future outcomes obviously is unrealistic; however, this simplistic setting offers a great deal of insight into the theoretical underpinnings of finance. Specifically, we note three advantages in introducing the theory of financial decisionmaking under certainty. First, it greatly simplifies the analysis. Second, this order of presentation follows the chronological development of the theory. Third, there generally exist straightforward counterparts to the theoretical results obtained under certainty when the analysis is extended to include uncertainty. Therefore, as we proceed through the development of the theory of finance under certainty, keep in mind that these results will, in most cases, continue to hold (albeit in a modified form) when uncertainty is introduced.

Chapter 2 overviews the economic theory of choice as applied to the consumer's decisions on how to allocate available wealth between consumption and savings. Here we establish the benefits to society that capital markets provide and the theoretical rationale for using the net present value rule in financial decisionmaking. Chapter 2 treats the single-period case. Appendix 2A extends the analysis

---

[2]As we just noted, the text can be used without the Mathematical Reviews and Overviews, which along with careful end-of-chapter problem selection, can preclude the necessity for using calculus. In a sense the text is two books in one, with parallel discussions of many of the topics covered using verbal and graphic descriptions along with mathematical descriptions.

to multiple periods to permit consideration for the term structure of interest rates. Appendix 2B contains an overview of the basic tenets of utility theory.

Chapter 3 introduces the corporate form of business organization. The corporation is found to pose two potential sources of difficulty for the financial theorist. First, a corporation can have multiple owners; thus, there arises the question of whether to consider "group preferences" in developing a theory of financial decisionmaking. Second, a corporation may be managed by individuals who are not themselves owners of the firm (or, at least, do not own all of its assets). Thus, managers act as agents for the owners (principals). This situation creates a potential conflict of interest between them, which can lead to decisions that will benefit one party to the detriment of the other. In addition, Chapter 3 addresses the impact of the firm's financing and dividend policy decisions on its value under conditions of certainty. Here we develop the Modigliani and Miller capital structure irrelevance propositions, which we extend in Chapters 11 and 12.

Chapter 4 discusses the valuation of a firm's securities under conditions of certainty. This material is a straightforward extension of the theory presented in Chapter 3, where securities provide cash flows over multiple time periods. We consider the valuation of bonds, preferred stock, and common stock as well as the concept of duration.

Chapter 5 introduces capital budgeting as an application of the theory of choice developed in Chapter 2. Here we consider the capital investment decision in terms of two broad types of investment problems: capital widening (the optimal level of productive activity) and capital deepening (the optimal term of investment). We also examine the role of diminishing returns to scale to determine the shape of the investment opportunity set the firm faces.

Chapter 6 extends Chapter 5's discussion of capital budgeting to consider problems unique to the measurement of cash flows. Specifically, we consider the definition of project cash flows and their relationship to accounting profits, the role of inflation in capital budgeting, and the relationship between positive net present value investment opportunities and monopoly rents. This last concept has become standard in many recent corporate finance texts and serves to focus the analyst's attention on the source of positive net present values.[3]

Part III (Chapters 7 through 10) extends the analysis to consider uncertainty. This discussion owes much to the work of Markowitz (1952, 1959), who pioneered the use of mean-variance analysis in finance. In addition, we consider the capital asset pricing model, the arbitrage pricing model, and the efficient market hypothesis.

Chapter 7 introduces the theory of finance under conditions of uncertainty. Here we first develop the expected utility paradigm as the basis for characterizing individuals' choices under uncertainty. Specifically, we examine two basic types of analyses: stochastic dominance and mean-variance analysis. In the first case we develop first-, second-, and third-degree stochastic dominance rules as a straightforward application of the expected utility maximization paradigm. In the second,

---

[3]For example, see Brealey and Myers (1985), Chapter 11, and Franks, Broyles, and Carleton (1985), Chapter 6.

we develop the conditions under which mean-variance-based decisions are consistent with expected utility maximization.

Chapter 8 considers mean-variance analysis in detail. This chapter is largely "rudimentary" in that it reviews the computation of portfolio means and variances and the selection of the optimal portfolio of risky assets. In the latter case, we refer to the identification of the mean-variance efficient set comprised of the set of portfolios that offer the maximum expected return for a given variance.

Chapter 9 explores the implications of mean-variance analysis for capital market equilibrium. Specifically, we develop the original capital asset pricing model and its zero-beta version. In addition, we develop the arbitrage pricing model as a more general representation of the relationship among expected rates of return on risky assets where the basic assumption is that riskless arbitrage profits are eliminated from the capital market.

Chapter 10 discusses the meaning and implications for finance of "efficient" capital markets. We examine the efficient market hypothesis and describe the various empirical tests using Fama's (1970) three-part classification scheme (weak-, semistrong-, and strong-form). We also review a sample of recent empirical literature that provides anomalous evidence regarding market efficiency, including the "size effect," low price/earnings ratio trading strategy, "unexpected" earnings announcements, and seasonality in security returns (the weekend and January effects).

Part IV (Chapters 11 through 21) discusses the implications of the theory of finance for financial decisionmaking. Here we consider its normative implications for a firm's investment, financing, and dividend policy decisions. In addition, we review some of the empirical evidence on tests of these implications.

Chapter 11 discusses corporate financial policy issues, empirical evidence, and applications. Here we discuss the capital budgeting decision under conditions of uncertainty, specifically the use of the capital asset pricing model in a single-period context when evaluating capital expenditures. In addition, we discuss the implications of the principal-agent relationship between the firm's owners (shareholders) and managers for the firm's investment decisions.

Chapter 12 reviews capital structure theory under conditions of uncertainty, including the analysis of tax considerations and the costs of financial distress. Specifically, we survey and synthesize the words of Modigliani and Miller (1958, 1963), Miller (1977), and DeAngelo and Masulis (1980). These theories are referred to as *frictionless market* theories of the capital structure problem, for they assume no transactions costs associated with trading in the capital market. We also discuss the managerial hypothesis of the firm's capital structure decision as well as the role of transactions costs, agency costs, and asymmetric information.

Chapter 13 surveys the empirical evidence on tests of capital structure theory as well as the theory's normative implications. We present selected papers from each of the many subsets of financial research dealing with the capital structure issue.

Chapter 14 discusses the theory of dividend policy and reviews empirical tests on these theories. We synthesize this literature into two parts: frictionless theories of dividend policy and theories that consider transactions costs, agency costs, and asymmetric information.

Chapter 15 develops the theory underlying the valuation of options. Here we use the binomial option pricing model to describe in simple terms the "spanning" type of argument that has been used to arrive at a valuation expression for an option. We then generalize this model to illustrate its relationship to the well-known Black/Scholes (1973) option pricing model as well as several others.

Chapter 16 reviews the tests of various option pricing theories and the application of option pricing technology to corporate finance problems. We discover that the original Black/Scholes (1973) model is surprisingly robust compared to its more recent theoretical counterparts. Further, we demonstrate how the firm's bond and equity can be characterized as "contingent claims" or options written on the firm's present and future asset investments.

Chapter 17 reviews the valuation of futures contracts and the institutional considerations surrounding this relatively new form of traded security. Specifically, we note the speculative and hedging uses of this type of financial contract.

Chapter 18 surveys merger theory and evidence. First we review the fundamental theoretical results in this literature, including the irrelevance proposition whereby investors can diversify their personal portfolios costlessly to achieve the same returns as those provided by the merged firm. We also discuss mergers and acquisitions as a means for disciplining firms via the capital market when those firms are not managed so as to achieve the highest possible value of their assets. This concept frequently is discussed under the rubric of the "market for corporate control." Finally, we discuss the empirical evidence on the impact of mergers and acquisitions on the wealth of the acquiring and acquired firm's security holders.

Chapter 19 discusses the theory underlying the analysis of financial leases. This topic has perplexed financial theorists and practitioners for years, due largely to the fact that the analysis of the lease versus purchase problem entails elements of both the investment and financing decisions. Further, by being forced to consider both these elements in the same problem, we recognize our inadequate knowledge of how these elements impact on shareholder wealth. In fact, many of the lease versus purchase models appearing in the finance literature are solely normative in nature, lacking any sound footing in positive theory simply because there has been none to draw upon.[4]

Chapters 20 and 21 survey the theory and evidence regarding the international ramifications of financial decisionmaking. Here we review the fundamental paradigms of international finance, including the purchasing power and interest rate parity theorems. Further, we discuss the empirical tests of those theories as well as tests of the value of international portfolio diversification.

---

[4]Positive theories are distinguished from normative theories in that their purpose is to explain "what is" as opposed to "what should be." Note that the predictions of positive theory frequently provide the basis for prescriptive action or normative theories in financial management. The problem encountered in the lease versus purchase decision is that although no *generally accepted* positive theory yet exists, analysts must daily confront the problems that the leasing option creates. It is in this environment that normative theories of leasing have been proposed for aiding in the analysis. We return to the distinction between positive and normative theory in Chapter 1, for it is an important issue in the "applied discipline" of finance.

Acknowledgments

A large number of people have donated generous amounts of time and energy to the development of this text. First, three classes of students who used the manuscript in its various stages contributed invaluable comments and criticisms. One student deserves special thanks in this regard: Bonyul Koo, Ph.D. candidate at the University of Texas at Austin, tirelessly read and reread every chapter of the manuscript and prepared, checked, and rechecked solutions to the end-of-chapter problems.

We extend special thanks to our peer reviewers for their candid comments. They include Professors Nasser Arshadi, University of Missouri; Giovanni Barone-Adesi, University of Alberta; Kerry Cooper, Texas A&M University; Richard DeMong, University of Virginia; Richard Dowen, Northern Illinois University; John Ezzell, The Pennsylvania State University; Bruce Fredrikson, Syracuse University; J. P. Giles, Claremont Graduate School; William Jean, University of Alabama; John Kensinger, University of Texas; Cheng-few Lee, University of Illinois; Terry Maness, Baylor University; Kerry Mann, University of New Mexico; Edward Saunders, Northeastern University; Lemma Senbet, University of Wisconsin; A. J. Senchack, University of Texas; and Leslie Young, University of Texas at Austin.

No preface would be complete without a disclaimer for any text errors. Even after our exhaustive efforts to search them out, there undoubtedly will be some errors remaining for which we take full responsibility. To quote George Mackey, in his preface to *Mathematical Foundations of Quantum Mechanics* (1963), "If the reader feels a sign should be changed, he is probably right." We are extremely interested in hearing from our readers about anything (error or praise) concerning their experience with the text. Please send comments to John Martin at the Graduate School of Business, Finance Department, University of Texas, Austin, Texas 78712.

John D. Martin

Samuel H. Cox, Jr.

Richard D. MacMinn

References

A. Barnea, R. Haugen, and L. Senbet, *Agency Problems and Financial Contracting* (Englewood Cliffs, N.J.: Prentice-Hall, 1984).

W. Beranek, "Research Directions in Finance," *Quarterly Journal of Economics and Business* 21 (1981): 6–24.

F. Black and M. Scholes, "The Pricing of Options and Corporate Liabilities," *Journal of Political Economy* (May/June 1973): 637–659.

R. Brealey and S. Myers, *Principles of Corporate Finance*, 2d ed. (New York: McGraw-Hill, 1985).

T. Copeland and J. Weston, *Financial Theory and Corporate Policy* (Reading, Mass.: Addison-Wesley, 1983).

R. M. Cyert and J. G. March, *A Behavioral Theory of the Firm* (Englewood Cliffs, N.J.: Prentice-Hall, 1963).

H. DeAngelo and R. Masulis, "Optimal Capital Structure under Corporate and Personal Taxation," *Journal of Financial Economics* (March 1980): 3–30.

E. Fama, "Efficient Capital Markets: A Review of Theory and Empirical Work," *Journal of Finance* (May 1970): 383–417.

————— and M. Miller, *The Theory of Finance* (New York: Holt, Rinehart and Winston, 1972).

I. Fisher, *The Rate of Interest* (New York: Macmillan, 1907).

—————, *The Theory of Interest* (New York: Macmillan, 1930).

J. Franks, J. Broyles, and W. Carleton, *Corporate Finance: Concepts and Applications* (Boston: Kent, 1985).

C. Haley and L. Schall, *The Theory of Financial Decisions* (New York: McGraw-Hill, 1979).

J. Hirshleifer, *Investment, Interest, and Capital* (Englewood Cliffs, N.J.: Prentice-Hall, 1970).

W. Jean, *The Analytical Theory of Finance* (New York: Holt, Rinehart and Winston, 1972).

C. F. Lee and Junkus, "Financial Analysis and Planning: An Overview," *Journal of Economics and Business* 35 (1983): 259–279.

F. Lutz, "Inflation and Security Returns," *Journal of Finance* (May 1975): 259–280.

F. Machlup, "Theories of the Firm: Marginalist, Behavioral, Managerial," *American Economic Review* (March 1967): 1–33.

H. Markowitz, "Portfolio Selection," *Journal of Finance* (March 1952): 77–91.

—————, *Portfolio Selection: Efficient Diversification of Investments* (New York: Wiley, 1959).

M. Miller, "Debt and Taxes," *Journal of Finance* (May 1977): 261–275.

F. Modigliani and M. Miller, "Corporation Income Taxes and the Cost of Capital: A Correction," *American Economic Review* (June 1963): 433–443.

—————, "The Cost of Capital, Corporation Finance, and Theory of Investment," *American Economic Review* (June 1958): 261–297.

J. Mossin, *Theory of Financial Markets* (Englewood Cliffs, N.J.: Prentice-Hall, 1973).

P. A. Samuelson, *Foundations of Economic Analysis*, rev. ed. (Cambridge, Mass.: Harvard University Press, 1983).

W. Sharpe, *Portfolio Theory and Capital Markets* (New York: McGraw-Hill, 1970).

E. Solomon, *The Theory of Financial Management* (New York: Columbia University Press, 1963).

L. H. Summers, "On Economics and Finance," *Journal of Finance* (July 1985): 633–636.

About the Authors

John D. Martin, Ph.D. (Texas Tech University) is professor of finance in the Graduate School of Business at the University of Texas at Austin. Dr. Martin has published widely in the areas of financial management and investments. His articles have appeared in a wide variety of academic publications including the *Journal of Finance, Journal of Financial and Quantitative Analysis, Advances in Financial Planning and Forecasting, Research in Finance, Journal of Monetary Economics, Journal of Business, Advances in Quantitative Analysis of Finance and Accounting,* and *Financial Management*. He has also written a number of papers to professional audiences that have appeared in the *Financial Analysts Journal*, the *Journal of Portfolio Management*, and the *Midland Corporate Finance Journal*. In addition to *The Theory of Finance: Applications and Evidence*, Dr. Martin has coauthored several other textbooks, including *Basic Financial Management*, 4th edition, *Cases in Finance, Readings in Financial Management*, and *Guide to Financial Analysis*. Dr. Martin has served as finance editor for the *Journal of Business Research* and on the editorial boards of the *Financial Review, Journal of Financial Research, Journal of Business Research*, and *Advances in Financial Planning and Forecasting*. For two years Dr. Martin served as Finance Ph.D. Program Advisor for the University of Texas and Chairman of the Graduate Studies Committee. It was due in part to his experiences during this period that this text was written. He chaired a committee that revised the Ph.D. program curriculum and has taught an introduction to theory of finance course using the notes that eventually became this text.

Samuel H. Cox, Jr., Ph.D. (Louisiana State University) is a professor in the Actuarial Science Program and the Department of Finance at the University of Nebraska–Lincoln. He holds B.A. and M.S. degrees from Texas Christian University. Most recently, Dr. Cox was an actuary with The Wyatt Company in Dallas, Texas. Dr. Cox has taught at the University of California at Los Angeles, the University of Puerto Rico, and the University of Texas at Austin, where he was also Director of the Actuarial Science Program for five years. Dr. Cox is a Fellow of the Society of Actuaries and Member of the American Academy of Actuaries. He serves on the Research Committee and the Education and Examination Committee of the Society of Actuaries. Dr. Cox's research articles have appeared in the *Transactions of the American Mathematical Society, Transactions of the Society of Actuaries, Journal of Risk and Insurance, Scandinavian Actuarial Journal,* and *Journal of Economics and Business.*

Richard D. MacMinn, Ph.D. (University of Illinois) is an associate professor and graduate advisor in the Department of Finance at the University of Texas at Austin. He holds degrees from UCLA (B.A.) and the University of Illinois (M.A.P.A. and Ph.D.). Dr. MacMinn has taught at the State University of New York–Binghamton, as well as the University of Texas. Dr. MacMinn holds the business school's Ambassador Edward A. Clark Fellowship and has won numerous university and business school research awards. At the Ph.D. level his teaching specialty is in the area of risk and uncertainty. Dr. MacMinn's research papers have appeared in the *Journal of Political Economy, Quarterly Journal of Economics, Journal of Finance, Information Economics and Policy,* and *Geneva Papers on Risk Insurance.* His research interests include the theory of decisionmaking under risk and uncertainty, information economics, and the theory of search.

Contents in Brief

Contents

I

Introduction to Financial Theory

In this section, we discuss the basic tenets on which the theory of finance is
built. Specifically, we link the study of financial theory to the much older
discipline of economics, including macro-, micro-, and managerial economics; in
fact, some now regard the theory of finance as a branch of economics known as
financial economics. We define the boundaries of the study of finance and how
its scope has broadened over time.

The role of theory in financial decisionmaking sometimes has been
controversial. We present the "positivist" notion of theory as the basis for
abstract model building in the study of financial problems. Finally, we review
the various alternatives offered as "the" goal for financial decisionmaking and
show why the goal of owner wealth maximization is the generally accepted choice.

Chapter 1

Overview of Financial Theory

A Historical Overview of the Theory of Finance

The study of finance as an independent subject of inquiry is relatively recent, its roots tracing back to the turn of this century. The theory of finance in its present-day form originated in the 1950s with the work of Markowitz (1952) and Modigliani and Miller (1958), among others.

Unlike many other areas of study in business and economics, the theory of finance is in its infancy. This observation is supported by the fact that the major theoretical paradigms that we can claim for finance have all been established during the last 60 years. In fact, the contributions to the theory of finance made by individuals whose primary research focus is finance or financial economics are even more recent. These contributions span the last 30 years, beginning with the writing of Modigliani and Miller (1958).

The development of a theory of finance began in the 1920s as an offshoot of the study of the theory of the firm in microeconomics. However, two major differences exist between the microeconomist's study of the firm and the financial theorist's. First, microeconomists traditionally have focused on the relationship between profits and the volume of output while holding the amount of capital invested constant. Financial theorists, on the other hand, have long been interested in the amount of capital used, as the vast literature on capital budgeting will attest. Second, the theory of finance has developed largely under conditions of uncertainty and in the presence of risk-averse behavior. This contrasts with the study of microeconomics, where the inclusion of materials on uncertainty in standard microeconomics texts is of relatively recent origin.[1]

At the risk of offending by omission, we provide a brief summary of the history of finance by identifying the following ten prominent contributions to the theory of finance.[2]

1. *Fisher's (1930) diagrammatical characterization of the individual's intertemporal consumption/savings and investment decisions.*[3] Hirshleifer (1970) expanded this analysis to provide a coherent theory of financial decisionmaking under certainty. The subject matter of Part II of this book is based on this literature.

2. *Williams' (1938) formulation of the principle of the conservation of investment value.* Lintner (1975) noted that this work, although not rigorously developed, provided the essence of Modigliani and Miller's (1958) rigorous treatment of the impact of a firm's financing decision on firm value.

3. *Hicks's (1939) and Lutz's (1940) development of theories of the term structure of interest rates based on expectations of future rates.* This insight into the interrelationship between interest rates on bonds differing only in terms of their term to maturity provides the basis for our discussion of the term structure under certainty in Appendix 2A.

4. *Markowitz's (1952) analysis of the individual's investment decision under conditions of uncertainty using mean-variance analysis.* His 1959 text still serves as a cogent treatment of the individual's decision problem under uncertainty. This approach to the decision problem under uncertainty has pervaded much of modern-day financial theory and serves as the theoretical foundation for the materials presented in Chapters 7, 8, and 9.

5. *Modigliani and Miller's (1958, 1961, 1963) treatment of the impact of a firm's financing choices on equity valuation.* Here we also include Miller's (1977) extension of this analysis to a more general bond market equilibrium setting. This body of literature has been referred to by Myers (1984) as the

---

[1]For example, see Layard and Walters' (1978) text, in which Chapter 13 is devoted to the analysis of uncertainty, or Varian's (1982) text.

[2]In his presidential address to the American Finance Association in December 1974, Lintner (1975) provided a brief but cogent historical overview of the study of finance. His basic premise is

Progress in academic disciplines has typically been marked by a series of seminal conceptual breakthroughs, followed by often long periods of consolidation, refinement, testing, and implementation. The grand insights which have fundamentally restructured our understanding of major areas of concern have very often been a response to pressing new conditions or needs which overwhelmingly demonstrated the inadequacy of earlier analytical models. (p. 259)

It would appear that in academics, like other fields of endeavor, "Necessity is the mother of invention."

[3]One could also argue that Fisher's *Nature of Capital and Income* (1906) deserves inclusion in this list, for it contains cogent discussions of the determination of income and the valuation of earning assets. The student interested in the history of financial thought should definitely take the opportunity to pull this text off the library shelf. It is surprisingly modern, underscoring the rich history of finance, albeit under the name of political economy.

"static tradeoff theory of the capital structure." We review this approach to the theory of capital structure in Chapter 12.

6. *Sharpe's (1964) derivation of the capital asset pricing model as an extension of Markowitz's mean-variance analysis to a market equilibrium setting.* Here we should also give credit to the independent efforts of Lintner (1965) and Mossin (1966), as well as Fama (1968), for providing a synthesis of the Sharpe and Lintner models. The asset pricing theory literature constitutes what is probably the largest single contribution to the theoretical literature in finance during the last 25 years. Many variations on the original Sharpe capital asset pricing model have been developed, including the Black (1972) zero-beta model. This literature is discussed in Chapter 9.

7. *The evolution of the efficient capital markets literature, synthesized by Fama (1970).* The efficient markets literature has provided finance with its own research methodology, the "event study." Using this technique, financial researchers have studied the stock and bond markets' reaction to countless "events," including earnings announcements, stock splits, and merger announcements. The methodology itself has been the subject of careful scrutiny in the now classic Brown and Warner (1980) paper and its sequel (1985). We review a sample of this empirical literature in Chapter 10 as well as in many of the chapters in Part IV, which reviews empirical studies in finance.

8. *The derivation of a pricing model for options on common stocks by Black and Scholes (1973).* Perhaps no other theoretical development in the finance literature has been followed so quickly by an institutional innovation as this one. One of the most significant institutional innovations of this decade has been the creation of options markets where options on a wide range of individual shares of common stock as well as portfolios of stock (such as stock market indexes) are now freely traded. We discuss option pricing theory in Chapter 15 and applications of this theory to corporate finance in Chapter 16.

9. *The introduction of agency costs and the attendant property rights issues that were introduced into the finance literature by Jensen and Meckling (1976).* This paper marks the beginning of a growing body of literature on financial theory and constitutes a clever insight on the part of its authors. They recognized the applicability of a strain of literature in economics concerning the theory of the firm, including work spanning Coase (1937) and Alchian and Demsetz (1972), to financial decisionmaking. We discuss this literature and its application to the general manager-shareholder relationship in the corporation in Chapter 3, to the investment decision in Chapter 11, to financing decisions in Chapter 12, and to mergers and acquisitions in Chapter 18.

10. *Ross's (1977) derivation of the arbitrage pricing model.* Ross provided the finance literature with a general representation of market equilibrium. Simply put, market equilibrium exists when there are no opportunities to make riskless arbitrage profits in that market. The beauty of the model is its generality, for it is actually consistent with a host of asset pricing theories. We discuss this model in Chapter 9.

Much, if not most, of the published work on the theory of finance can be traced to one or more of the aforementioned papers.[4] Our intent in listing these contributions is simply to highlight what we feel are turning points in the development of the theory of finance. The ideas presented in virtually all these papers represent an attempt by the authors to reach outside the confines of the study of finance and bring in a novel way to address a recognized problem in finance. Therefore, our listing of seminal works represents a set of historical markers in the study of the theory of finance.

Economics and Finance

The theoretical foundation for modern finance represents an amalgam of the various subfields of economics. To foster an appreciation for the roots of finance in the study of economics, we will summarize the broad categories of economic theory that have contributed to the evolution of the theory of finance, or what some now refer to as *financial economics*.

Macroeconomics is the branch of economics that seeks to explain economy-wide aggregates such as the level of aggregate production, income, prices, interest rates, and employment. The primary tool of analysis used in this field is the *general equilibrium* model of the economy as a whole. Here the theorist seeks to demonstrate the interrelationships among factors such as total productive output, level of employment of factors of production, individuals' savings decisions, and investment firms' decisions. The level of disaggregation involved in the study of macroeconomic problems characteristically is quite low—that is, the principal "players" are government (generally all levels of government units combined), businesses (entities that employ resources to produce goods and services), and consumers (entities that save, spend, and supply labor services).

Microeconomics seeks to explain the determination of production levels (and consequent levels of employment of labor and capital) and prices of both input factors and outputs within "industry groups." Of particular concern here is the influence of various competitive circumstances on the production and pricing of output by firms. The level of disaggregation involved in the study of microeconomics—as the term implies—is greater than in the case of macroeconomics. However, its focus of inquiry generally is much narrower; the traditional study of microeconomics treats economywide factors such as the level of interest rates and factor prices as "givens" and consequently involves *partial equilibrium* types of analyses. The primary players here are firms that make production decisions and indi-

---

[4]The finance literature is dynamic and ever evolving; thus, our attempt to identify the seminal papers in the discipline is necessarily incomplete. In addition, many of the papers listed above had their impact on the finance literature many years after they were written. For example, Markowitz's original paper on mean-variance portfolio analysis appeared in the early 1950s but was incorporated into the finance literature over ten years later. Thus, we offer our apologies to those researchers whose work merits inclusion in the above list but was omitted.

viduals who make savings/investment choices. Note that here the term *firm* refers to a "producing unit" or, more formally, "a collection of resources gathered under the common control of an entrepreneur for the purpose of producing goods or services." The traditional microeconomist's conception of the firm is not, however, sufficiently detailed to explain the "organizational structure" of the firm and its internal workings. In other words, in traditional microeconomic analysis the firm is simply an entity that contracts in product, factor, and financial markets to acquire the resources necessary for producing and selling a product or service. Note that this mode of inquiry *excludes* the fact that firms actually enter into long-term discretionary contracts wherein their management becomes involved in allocating resources (over which they have discretionary contractual control) without the direct influence of the factor or financial markets — that is, once a firm contracts in the financial markets for, say, $100 million for use in financing its operations for 10 years, the actual uses to which it puts those funds are left to its management (within the confines of the contractual agreement, of course).

Managerial economics attempts to apply the basic tenets of both micro- and macroeconomics to the internal organization and operation of the business enterprise. Once again we see that the power of the "theoretical microscope" has been increased to allow us to focus on the internal workings of the business firm. Much of the literature concerns the development and use of more sophisticated tools for analyzing data with which to support decisionmaking at the sub-firm level. The issues addressed here are the evaluation of product or output mix, production level, and input mix. In this subset of economics, firms begin to take on attributes that distinguish them in terms of the product demand they face, the production technology they have developed, and the set of inputs over which they have contractual control.

As we noted earlier, *financial economics* represents an amalgam of the aforementioned subfields of economics. Specifically, financial economics incorporates the general equilibrium type of analysis that characterizes macroeconomics into an expanded view of the theory of the firm as studied in microeconomics to include the existence of transactions costs and individuals' property rights. Note that the study of finance has grown up in an applied or "professional" environment where prescriptions for financial decisionmaking have been developed even though the analysis dealt with circumstances outside the purview of existing theory. Thus, financial economics shares a heritage with managerial economics in that it has inspired a body of literature aimed at solving specific financial problems and incompletely integrated into a single, unified theory of finance. Yet another important attribute is the fact that, like managerial economics, it attempts to look into the firm and explain its internal workings. In fact, within the study of financial economics the firm can be defined as a collection of resources that is under the discretionary control of an entrepreneur who may (depending on the organizational form chosen) be represented by a management team. This very "disaggregated" or detailed definition of the firm allows the financial economist to observe and theorize about the internal workings of the firm. But at the same time this level of disaggregation poses a very difficult problem when the theorist attempts to aggregate the effects of all individuals' and firms' actions in order to analyze market equilibrium in the entire economy.

In this brief survey of the various subareas of economics, we have attempted to place the study of financial theory in perspective.[5] Although some may disagree with the details of financial theory's basis in economics as discussed here, few will dispute its fundamental heritage in that discipline. Some may argue, however, that this heritage has restricted the development of the study of finance. For example, both Carleton (1978) and Andrews (1979) have criticized the "body" of financial theory for ignoring what they feel are the problems of financial management. Carleton suggests that "most contemporary theory and research in corporate finance do not even deal with what in the abstract are the central problems in corporate finance" (p. 7). Andrews criticizes the current body of finance literature as follows: "People in the real world have the habit of not listening to their academic brethren in corporate financial management for the simple reason that the product of academic labors is too infrequently addressed to real problems" (p. 7). He goes on to call for a theory of "dynamic states in capital management." Both authors recommend expansion of the theoretical base of knowledge into areas as yet undeveloped. The following quotation by Keynes (1890) puts the issues raised by these authors in perspective:

As regards the scope of political economy, no question is more important, or in a way more difficult, than its relation to practical problems. Does it treat of the actual or of the ideal? Is it a positive science concerned exclusively with the investigation of uniformities, or is it an art having for its object the determination of practical rules of action?

It would be presumptuous for us to try to resolve the issue Keynes raised so long ago; however, we will endeavor to present the body of knowledge that has come to be known as the theory of finance. In the next section, we consider the scope of the study of finance as it has evolved during this century.

The Scope of the Study of Finance

How broad is the scope of the study of finance? The answer obtained from the finance literature varies greatly with the time frame involved. For example, had this question been posed in the 1920s, the answer might have been: "Finance is concerned with raising and administering funds." This functional definition of finance is quite narrow and focuses on the procurement of funds. The study of finance typically was dominated by discussions of financial instruments (securities), institutions, and markets.[6] More recently, the study of finance has been broadened to

---

[5]Although omitted from our discussion of financial economics, there are other areas of academic inquiry in the field of economics that have been incorporated into the study of finance. The area of *industrial organizations*, which deals with market structure, behavior of market participants, and performance evaluation of markets, has been incorporated into the analysis of mergers and acquisitions and the market for corporate control. The field of *law and economics*, particularly the subfield of property rights, has been used to analyze the firm as a set of contracts among owners, creditors, suppliers, and customers. The study of agency theory, now so prevalent in the theory of finance, stems largely from the property rights literature.

[6]Dewing's (1920) finance text reflects this approach to the study of finance and remained the dominant text in the field through the 1940s.

include both the procurement and allocation of funds within the firm. In addition, the point of view has shifted from that of the outsider looking in (that is, from the perspective of an investment banker or someone outside the firm) to the viewpoint of the insider looking out (those concerned with the financial management of the firm's internal affairs). Thus, the study of finance has come to consider the acquisition of funds, their investment, and their return to the original suppliers — in other words, financing, investment, and dividend policy decisions. Fama and Miller (1972) incorporated all these decisions in their definition of financial theory: "The theory of finance is concerned with how individuals and firms allocate resources through time." This broader scope of finance is the one we adopt in this text. Consequently, our study of finance incorporates issues such as (1) what assets should be acquired (capital budgeting) and (2) how funds should be raised to finance the acquisition of those assets (financing and dividend policy). We now turn to the role of theory in the study and practice of financial decisionmaking.

The Role of Theoretical Models in the Study of Finance[7]

Why theorize about financial decisions? Indeed, why construct abstract models based on sets of assumptions that frequently appear to bear little resemblance to the world in which financial choices are made? This may seem an unorthodox way to introduce a text whose objective is to provide an introduction to the theory of finance. However, it is exactly where such a discussion should begin and a question common to the study of theoretical models that transcends all disciplines. Our answer is a very general one that is as applicable to physics and sociology as it is to finance. Specifically, the world is very complex and its complete description difficult, if not impossible. Thus, theory represents an attempt to capture the "essence" of our complex environment by abstracting from reality via simplifying assumptions. The use of theoretical models pervades the physical and social sciences; for example, physicists use the concept of a perfect vacuum to permit the study of real-world phenomena in a simplified setting, and anthropologists use the concept of culture to characterize the elements of a society. Microeconomists use the concept of market structure to analyze the behavior of economic players under very idealized sets of assumptions about individuals and firms. Thus, theory represents an effort to simplify a complex situation to permit study of its essential elements.

   If theoretical models are abstractions from reality, how do we know whether we have a good theory? This question relates to the verification of a theory, for which there are two basic approaches. The first involves assessing the validity of the basic assumptions underlying the model. However, if we define a theoretical model as a simplification of reality, any theory is almost sure to fail this test. The

---

[7]Webster's *New Collegiate Dictionary* offers a number of definitions for the term *theory:* "(1) the analysis of a set of facts in their relation to one another; (2) a belief, policy, or procedure proposed or followed as the basis of action; (3) the general or abstract principles of a body of fact, a science, or an art; (4) a plausible or scientifically acceptable general principle or body of principles offered to explain phenomena; (5) a hypothesis assumed for the sake of argument or investigation; an unproved assumption; a body of theorems presenting a concise systematic view of a subject; or (6) abstract thought."

second approach involves testing the accuracy of the theory's predictions concerning the real-world environment it was developed to describe. This is generally referred to as the *positive approach,* and its chief modern-day proponent is Milton Friedman (1953).[8] This approach provides the predominant rationale underlying the verification of financial theory. One of its key features is the crucial role it provides for empirical research. In fact, the main element of the positivist's verification procedure is the empirical testing of the model's predictions, making theory and empirical evidence essentially inseparable.[9]

Thus, our answer to the basic question of why we study theoretical models in finance can be summarized by two crucial points. First, the real world is extremely complex, and theoretical models offer a tool for simplifying to permit observation of important relationships between decision variables and the environment. Second, we "check" our abstract theories by subjecting their predictions to tests of real-world accuracy. Without this check, no theory that significantly abstracts from the real world can be trusted to provide useful insight.

Positive and Normative Theories

The distinction between positive and normative theory is simple but important. A *positive theory* attempts to explain "what is," while a *normative theory* purports to explain "what should be." The former is frequently considered "scientific" in that it seeks to discover the nature of the environment; the latter attempts to determine how to manipulate that environment in light of a predetermined set of notions (moral positions) about how something should be done. Suffice it to say at this point that the theory of finance has both positive and normative components.[10]

Beranek (1981) defines positive financial theories as those that seek to describe what is and are characterized by an effort to describe financial relationships by developing axiom sets that will yield valid groups of generalizations. In contrast, he defines normative financial theories as those that seek to develop deci-

---

[8]Keynes (1890) defined positive and normative theory as follows:
A positive science may be defined as a body of systematized knowledge concerning what is; a normative or regulative science as a body of systematized knowledge relating to criteria of what ought to be, and concerned therefore with the ideal as distinguished from the actual; and are as a system of rules for the attainment of a given end. (p. 35)

[9]Some believe the finance literature is comprised of theory and empiricism and refer to its contributors as either "theorists" or "empiricists." This dichotomy, although perhaps valuable in some contexts, can be misleading, as Keynes (1890) noted:
It may be said without qualification that political economy, whether having recourse to the deductive method or not, must both begin with observation and end with observation. As already pointed out, there is a tendency to forget that the deductive method in its complete form consists of three stages, only one of which is actually deductive, the two others being the inductive determination of premises, and the inductive verification of conclusions. (p. 227)

[10]One need attend only one meeting of the American Finance Association, Financial Management Association, or other professional finance organization to observe the near evangelical zeal with which financial researchers present and defend their research. If we are not guilty of normative bias in our prescriptions for business practice, we almost certainly are in terms of our research.

sionmaking models by investors-consumers, financial managers of institutions, and administrators of government agencies. Of course, the two types of theory are related; for example, positive theory provides predictions that form the basis for many normative theories.

A debate has arisen in the finance literature over extending positive theories to areas of financial decisionmaking in which they are as yet unverified. Beranek argues that under these circumstances, normative theories that fit the conditions of the firm and provide the ultimate decisionmaker with a manageable range of conditional statements should be developed. On the other side of the debate are theorists who shun normative models that reflect the perceived conditions faced by the decisionmaker in favor of the dictum implied by a positive theory.[11]

In this text, we present elements of both types of theories. Parts II and III have a predominantly positive orientation. Part IV, which discusses applications for which positive financial theory is only partially verified, offers normative theories for dealing with those issues.

The Objective in Financial Decisionmaking[12]

In a normative sense, theory provides the basis for establishing "prescriptions" for rational behavior or decisionmaking. However, before one can develop guides for rational choice, one must clearly identify a goal. In economics, this goal generally has been "profit maximization." However, we will see that this goal cannot capture the full ramifications of financial decisions in the context in which the theory of finance has evolved. In other words, financial decisionmaking takes place under conditions of uncertainty, financial decisions frequently affect revenues and expenses for many future periods, and financial choices are frequently made within corporations whose managers act as agents for the firms' owners. We will briefly review the goal of profit maximization and its specific shortcomings as a goal for financial decisionmaking before we present the generally accepted goal in the theory of finance — *owner wealth maximization*.

In the simplistic setting in which the traditional microeconomic theory of the firm has evolved, profit maximization can be defended as a goal for decisionmaking — that is, in a world of complete certainty where decisions are made by entrepreneurs who reap the rewards of their own decisions in a single-period setting (in which the quantity of capital employed is fixed), profit maximization is directly related to the decisionmaker's well-being. The profit-maximizing choice is also the decision that maximizes its favorable impact on the entrepreneur's economic wealth. However, when the quantity of capital employed varies, total profits can be increased simply by raising additional funds and employing them to earn returns that are higher than their out-of-pocket cost. However, this may *not* be

---

[11]The reader interested in this debate should refer to Carleton (1978), Andrews (1979), and Weston (1981).

[12]The discussion in this section is based on Chapter 2 of the classic text by Ezra Solomon (1963).

consistent with maximizing the owner's economic well-being. For example, consider the case where a corporation issues common stock on which there is no explicit out-of-pocket cost reflected in the determination of the firm's profits. If the firm's manager simply issues stock and invests the proceeds in low-yielding U.S. Treasury securities, the firm's profits will rise. Is this consistent with the best interests of the firm's owners? Perhaps not, for although total profits have risen, profits per share may have declined. Alternatively, consider the case where the firm faces a choice between two alternative investments. The first offers an increase in profits for three years by $X per year (where X > 0), while the second increases profits in the next year by only $2X. Profit maximization may dictate choosing the second alternative, while the first may have a more favorable impact on the owner's wealth. Finally, suppose the firm has one risky investment opportunity that offers an expected year-end profit of $Y and another that offers a certain profit of $Y/2. Profit maximization dictates selection of the risky project even though this may not be in the owners' best interests. Thus, profit maximization per se does not consider the impact of financial decisions on a per-share basis, the timing of profits, or the uncertainty of future outcomes. We therefore need an objective for financial decisionmaking that encompasses all of these factors.

The basic response to this dilemma has been the use of *utility maximization,* in which utility is used as an index of "well-being" (Appendix 2B briefly reviews the basic axioms underlying the use of utility theory). We further simplify the problem by assuming that an individual's utility function has but one argument, wealth. Further, as we will see in Parts II and III, financial theorists have painstakingly established the conditions under which maximization of the utility of wealth is consistent with wealth maximization. Thus, they have chosen wealth maximization as the goal for financial decisionmaking, in which wealth is defined as present monetary value. Monetary value, in turn, is determined by a combination of the amount, timing, and riskiness of the cash flows involved in the investment and financing decisions facing a business enterprise.

Here we have justified maximizing owner wealth based on the interests of the firm's stockholders. However, we can do the same from the perspective of society as a whole. Specifically, where financial choices are made in a manner consistent with owner wealth maximization, resources will be allocated to those uses where their value is greatest.[13] This is analogous to the "invisible hand" allocation of resources that characterizes a competitive market economy. However, from management's perspective, owner wealth maximization may not always be optimal. In an uncertain world where managers acting as agents make decisions for owners (principals), there arise situations in which owner and manager interests come into conflict. For example, a manager may tend to take on fewer risky

---

[13]This point has been the subject of debate in the finance literature, beginning with the work of Diamond (1967) and continuing with papers by Leland (1972), Jensen and Long (1972), Fama (1972), and Merton and Subrahmanyam (1974). The basic issue is important and can be stated as follows: Does following the objective of share value maximization lead to the optimal allocation of resources in the economy? The answer is a qualified yes. Particularly under conditions of perfectly competitive product and capital markets, share value maximization does lead to an optimal allocation from the perspective of society as a whole.

investments than the owner may prefer. This could be due to the fact that the value of the manager's human capital is largely tied to the firm's fortunes while the owner may be well diversified and hold stock in a wide variety of firms. There are many other instances in which managers' well-being may conflict with owners'. These problems are relatively recent in finance. However, they are becoming increasingly important, for they help explain much of the "institutional" structure of firms and markets as well as the managerial behavior we observe in reality.

In summary, the theory of finance is founded on the goal of owner wealth maximization. This goal can be viewed as a logical "mutation" of the traditional goal of profit maximization utilized in neoclassical microeconomics in light of the richer set of environmental assumptions addressed in the theory of finance. Specifically, the world is an uncertain place wherein choices must be made by managers who exercise their own discretion in selecting investments and financing alternatives (that is, managers have a degree of autonomy from the owners whose funds they manage). In addition, these choices may impact on owner wealth long into an uncertain future.

Overview of the Book

For convenience, this text divides the study of financial theory into three major segments. Part II contains an overview of the theory of finance in a world in which all future outcomes are known with certainty. The basic theoretical tool used in this section is the Fisher two-period consumption model, which we introduce in Chapter 2. This relatively simple model can be used to explain much of the theoretical foundation for financial decisionmaking that is covered in an introductory course in financial management. Part III discusses the theory of finance under conditions of uncertainty. This treatment allows us to consider how the theory of choice used to develop financial theory under certainty is affected by relaxing the requirement of complete certainty. Here we consider the notion of individuals' risk aversion, the desirability of diversification, and the valuation of securities in market equilibrium. Part IV discusses the application of financial theory to financial management problems, including the capital budgeting decision, the financing decision, and dividend policy. We consider the application of option pricing theory to the theory of corporate finance, the analysis of mergers and acquisitions, and implications of the existence of trade across international boundaries. Part IV presents empirical evidence from tests of a number of theories.

Summary

In this chapter we reviewed the foundations of the study of financial theory. Specifically, the theory of finance was founded on the basic tenets of economics, including elements of macroeconomics, microeconomics, and managerial economics; in fact, the term *financial economics* is sometimes used as a surrogate for the body of knowledge referred to here as *financial theory*. We also observed that financial theorists' reliance on economics has not been without criticism. Detractors argue that the study of finance should be guided by real-world problems, which require explicit consideration for the dynamic nature of the world (for which the body of economic theory offers little guidance). Related to this criticism are the notions of positive and normative theory, the former dealing with "what is" and the latter with "what should be." Here we observe that financial theory is a mixture of both positive and normative theories. The former tend to emanate from theorists who favor the approach taken in economics, namely constructing abstract models and testing their implications to validate the theories they derive.

We discussed the various objectives that might be adopted in developing theories of financial decisionmaking. The neoclassical microeconomist's goal of profit maximization has been found to be lacking when applied to corporate enterprises. In the study of finance, financial decisions are made within the context of multiowner firms, which make financial choices under conditions of uncertainty whose consequences extend far into the future. In these circumstances, the goal of profit maximization has proven too simplistic; thus, the goal of owner wealth maximization has come to be the standard in financial theory.

Study Questions

1.1 "Empirical tests play a unique role in the study of the theory of finance." Discuss.

1.2 "Profit maximization has long been the objective used in the traditional study of microeconomics. However, this goal is limited as a goal for financial decisionmaking." Discuss.

1.3 Consider the following firms and their corresponding cash flow streams. Which one would you select for investment? Why?

Year	Firm A	Firm B	Firm C	Firm D[a]
1	$2,000	$ 0	$3,000	$3,000
2	2,000	0	3,000	3,000
3	2,000	0	3,000	3,000
4	2,000	12,000	3,000	3,000

[a]Firm D's cash flows are risky and reflect a 0.5 probability of a $6,000 cash flow and a 0.5 probability of a $0 payoff. The cash flows of the other firms are known with certainty.

1.4 Distinguish between "positive" and "normative" theories. Why are positive theories sometimes referred to as "scientific" theories? What is the role of normative theory in the study of finance?

References

A. Alchian and H. Demsetz, "Production, Information Costs, and Economics Organization," *American Economic Review* (1972): 777–795.

V. Andrews, "Sterile Premises in Corporate Capital Theory," *Financial Management* (Winter 1979): 7–11.

W. Beranek, "Research Directions in Finance," *Quarterly Journal of Economics and Business* 21 (1981): 6–24.

F. Black, "Capital Market Equilibrium with Restricted Borrowing," *Journal of Business* 45 (July 1972): 444–455.

——— and M. Scholes, "The Pricing of Options and Corporate Liabilities," *Journal of Political Economy* (May/June 1973): 637–659.

S. J. Brown and J. B. Warner, "Measuring Security Price Performance," *Journal of Financial Economics* (September 1980): 205–258.

———, "Using Daily Stock Returns in Event Studies," *Journal of Financial Economics* (March 1985): 3–31.

W. T. Carleton, "An Agenda for More Effective Research in Corporate Finance," *Financial Management* (Winter 1978): 7–9.

R. H. Coase, "The Nature of the Firm," *Econometrica* (November 1937): 386–405.

T. Copeland and J. Weston, *Financial Theory and Corporate Policy,* 2d ed. (Reading, Mass.: Addison-Wesley, 1983), Chapter 1.

R. M. Cyert and J. G. March, *A Behavioral Theory of the Firm* (Englewood Cliffs, N.J.: Prentice-Hall, 1963).

A. S. Dewing, *The Financial Policy of Corporations* (New York: Ronald Press, 1920, and successive editions).

P. Diamond, "The Role of a Stock Market in a General Equilibrium Model with Technological Uncertainty," *American Economic Review* (September 1967): 759–776.

E. Fama, "Efficient Capital Markets: A Review of Theory and Empirical Work," *Journal of Finance* (May 1970): 383–417.

———, "Perfect Competition and Optimal Production Decisions under Uncertainty," *Bell Journal of Economics* 7 (Autumn 1972): 509–530.

———, "Risk, Return, and Equilibrium: Some Clarifying Comments," *Journal of Finance* (1968): 29–39.

E. Fama and M. Miller, *The Theory of Finance* (New York: Holt, Rinehart and Winston, 1972), Chapter 1.

I. Fisher, *The Nature of Capital and Income* (New York: Macmillan, 1906).

———, *The Theory of Interest* (New York: Macmillan, 1930).

M. Friedman, *Essays in Positive Economics* (Chicago: University of Chicago Press, 1953), Chapter 1.

C. Haley and L. Schall, *The Theory of Financial Decisions* (New York: McGraw-Hill, 1979).

J. R. Hicks, *Value and Capital* (Oxford, England: Oxford University Press, 1939).

J. Hirshleifer, *Investment, Interest and Capital* (Englewood Cliffs, N.J.: Prentice-Hall, 1970).

W. Jean, *The Analytical Theory of Finance* (New York: Holt, Rinehart and Winston, 1972).

M. Jensen and J. Long, "Corporate Investment under Uncertainty and Pareto Optimality in the Capital Markets," *Bell Journal of Economics* (Spring 1972): 151–174.

M. Jensen and W. Meckling, "Theory of the Firm: Managerial Behavior, Agency Costs and Ownership Structure," *Journal of Financial Economics* (October 1976): 305–360.

J. N. Keynes, *The Scope and Method of Political Economy* (New York: Kelley and Millman, 1955, first edition 1890).

P. R. G. Layard and A. A. Walters, *Microeconomic Theory* (New York: McGraw-Hill, 1978).

H. E. Leland, "Theory of the Firm Facing Uncertain Demand," *American Economic Review* 62 (June 1972): 278–291.

J. Lintner, "Inflation and Security Returns," *Journal of Finance* (May 1975): 259–280.

———, "Security Prices, Risk and Maximal Gains from Diversification," *Journal of Finance* (December 1965): 587–615.

F. Lutz, "The Structure of Interest Rates," *Quarterly Journal of Economics* (November 1940): 36–63.

H. Markowitz, *Portfolio Selection: Efficient Diversification of Investments* (New York: Wiley, 1959).

———, "Portfolio Selection," *Journal of Finance* (March 1952): 77–91.

R. Merton and M. Subrahmanyam, "The Optimality of a Competitive Stock Market," *Bell Journal of Economics* (Spring 1974): 145–170.

M. Miller, "Debt and Taxes," *Journal of Finance* (May 1977): 261–275.

—— and F. Modigliani, "Dividend Policy, Growth, and the Valuation of Shares," *Journal of Business* (October 1961): 411–433.

F. Modigliani and M. Miller, "Corporation Income Taxes and the Cost of Capital: A Correction," *American Economic Review* (June 1963): 433–443.

——, "The Cost of Capital, Corporation Finance, and Theory of Investment," *American Economic Review* (June 1958): 261–297.

J. Mossin, "Equilibrium in a Capital Asset Market," *Econometrica* (1966): 768–783.

——, *Theory of Financial Markets* (Englewood Cliffs, N.J.: Prentice-Hall, 1973).

S. Myers, "The Capital Structure Puzzle," *Journal of Finance* (July 1984): 575–592.

W. Nicholson, *Microeconomic Theory: Basic Principles and Extensions*, 3d ed. (Hinsdale, Ill.: Dryden Press, 1985), Chapter 1.

S. Ross, "The Arbitrage Theory of Capital Asset Pricing," *Journal of Economic Theory* (December 1976): 343–362.

W. Sharpe, "Capital Asset Prices: A Theory of Market Equilibrium under Conditions of Risk," *Journal of Finance* (September 1964): 425–442.

——, *Portfolio Theory and Capital Markets* (New York: McGraw-Hill, 1970), preface.

E. Solomon, *The Theory of Financial Management* (New York: Columbia University Press, 1963).

L. H. Summers, "On Economics and Finance," *Journal of Finance* (July 1985): 633–636.

H. Varian, *Microeconomic Analysis* (New York: Norton, 1982).

J. F. Weston, "Developments in Finance Theory," *Financial Management* (Tenth Anniversary Issue, 1981): 5–22.

J. B. Williams, *Theory of Investment Value* (Cambridge, Mass.: Harvard University Press, 1938).

II

The Theory of Finance under Certainty

The basic issues studied in finance pertain to the valuation of investments, firms, and the securities they issue. Included in these analyses is the study of capital budgeting, the financing decision, and dividend policy. We will introduce each of these topics in the simplest possible setting: a certain world where all things, past and future, are assumed to be known with certainty. This approach is not only the easiest but also follows the chronological development of financial theory. As noted in the preface, much of the financial theory prior to Markowitz's introduction of portfolio theory in 1952 was couched in a certain world. Also, the initial attempts to incorporate uncertainty into financial theory essentially eliminated it from consideration due to the way they structured problems to be addressed. For example, Modigliani and Miller (1958) analyzed the impact of financial structure on firm value in an uncertain world but assumed that the firms being analyzed (with respect to the impact of their capital structure on firm value) were all in the same "risk class." This allowed the authors to compare levered and unlevered firm values without further consideration of the impact of risk on their analysis. This is not a criticism of their approach — on the contrary, had they not used the equivalent risk class assumption and attempted to incorporate risk differences directly into their analysis, they would have considerably complicated matters without enhancing their results. In fact, it was not until the development of the capital asset pricing model in the early 1960s that financial theorists began to incorporate uncertainty into the development of financial theory. Hence, the extent to which the fundamental tenets of financial theory can be captured in a certain world should not be surprising.

In Chapter 2, we develop the basic structure of the Fisher intertemporal consumption model that has served as the primary tool for analysis of financial theory in a certain world. This model provides a very powerful means of analyzing individuals' consumption/savings decisions, the optimal investment in productive assets, and the role of capital markets. Perhaps the key element in Chapter 2 is the Fisher separation theorem, which provides the theoretical basis for analyzing firms' investment decisions independently of the preferences (utility) of their owners. In Chapter 3, we consider the special problems arising from the corporate form of business organization. Here we find that the Fisher separation theorem provides the basis for much corporate finance theory. In Chapter 4, we explore the valuation of investments and securities under conditions of certainty. This material is comprised of present value formulae, since the value of an asset under conditions of certainty is simply the present value "equivalent" of the future cash flows to which the asset owner is entitled. Chapters 5 and 6 offer an overview of the firm's investment decision. In Chapter 5, we address the "mechanical" aspects of the capital budgeting problem by reviewing the net present value and internal rate of return rules for making investment decisions. In Chapter 6, we consider the cash flow issues that arise in making capital budgeting decisions. Specifically, we consider the roles of taxes, accounting profits versus cash flow, inflation, and market structure (competition) in determining project cash flows.

Chapter 2

Financial Decisions and the Theory of Choice

The foundation of the theory of finance under certainty relies largely on the theory of choice as applied to the individual's decision on how to allocate expenditures for consumption over time. This problem is generally referred to as the *intertemporal consumption choice problem.*[1]

Our analysis of the consumer choice problem will extensively utilize graphics in order to illustrate the principles as simply as possible. The basic model used is the Fisher consumer choice diagram. Learning to "read" the diagram may take some time; however, given its status as the theoretical base for a broad range of finance issues, the time will be well spent.

Our discussion of the theory of choice is based on four very important assumptions:

1. Capital markets are competitive in the sense that individuals' actions do not affect market prices.

2. Transactions can be made instantaneously and without cost.

3. There is complete certainty regarding present and future consumption possibilities (choices).

4. There are no taxes.

---

[1]Fisher (1930) generally is credited with providing the first synthesis of this material.

We retain assumption 1 throughout the text but relax assumptions 2 through 4 as we progress. We introduce income taxes in Chapter 6. In Part III, we relax the certainty assumption to consider the choice problem under uncertainty. In Part IV, we discuss the implications of transactions costs and their important role in the management of the firm's financial affairs.

Although we restrict our analysis throughout Part II to the case of complete certainty, we are able to develop a number of propositions essential to both the theory and practice of financial management:

1.   We demonstrate the "benefits" derived from the existence of capital markets that effectively "uncouple" the individual's savings and investment choices.

2.   We derive the net present value rule for investment analysis and demonstrate its consistency with the goal of wealth maximization that pervades the theory of finance.

3.   We examine the crucial role of the Fisher separation theorem in the theory of finance.

In this chapter, we discuss in detail the individual's choice between current and future consumption. This also involves his or her savings/investment decision, since any money not spent on current consumption should be saved and invested to increase the level of future consumption opportunities. These savings and investment decisions constitute the theoretical basis for the study of finance under certainty. First we treat the individual's consumption problem assuming that borrowing and lending are the only means by which money wealth can be transferred from one period to another. Then we introduce *real investments,* which provide the opportunity to exchange current for future dollars by both investing in productive assets and by borrowing/lending in the capital market. In this setting we are able to define the traditional tools used in capital expenditure analysis: *internal rate of return (IRR)* and *net present value (NPV).* In addition, we discuss the Fisher separation theorem (in the case of zero transactions costs) and its ramifications in financial decisionmaking. Finally, we note the importance of transactions costs in capital markets and the resultant loss of Fisher separation. In Appendix 2A, we extend the analysis to multiple periods. In that context, we both define the term structure of interest rates and demonstrate the generality of the two-period results of this chapter. Appendix 2B contains an overview of the basic tenets of utility theory. Here we develop the concept of indifference curves that we use throughout the text.

The Individual's Consumption/Savings Decision

To simplify the exposition, we initially consider a two-period model: the current period and one future period, where an individual must make only one consumption/savings decision. Therefore, if the individual has *current wealth* of w_0 dollars and the objective of selecting an optimal time pattern of consumption, he or she must decide how much of w_0 to spend on consumption now (c_0 dollars) and, consequently, how much to save ($w_0 - c_0$ dollars) in order to support the next period's consumption of c_1 dollars.

We solve the choice problem as follows. First, we define the consumption opportunities available to the individual. Second, we describe preferences for current versus future consumption using indifference curves. An indifference curve reflects the utility, or satisfaction, derived from consumption; specifically, it represents a set of consumption bundles that offer the individual the *same* level of utility. Finally, we identify the optimal consumption savings choice as the utility-maximizing decision.

The Consumption Opportunity Set

Let r denote the market rate of interest (for borrowing or lending) in the capital market. Then $(1 + r)$ represents the *terms of trade* in the capital market — that is, if you borrow \$1 you will have to repay $\$(1 + r)$ one year hence and, alternatively, $\$(1 + r)$ one year hence can be converted into \$1 today. The terms of trade are also referred to as the *marginal rate of transformation (MRT)* in the capital market: An individual can "transform" current into future dollars, and vice versa, by borrowing and lending in the capital market.

The following equation describes the individual's current and future consumption opportunities:

$$c_1 = (1 + r)(w_0 - c_0),$$

or

(2.1)
$$c_0 + \left[\frac{c_1}{(1 + r)} \right] = w_0.$$

The left-hand side of Equation 2.1 is the present value of current and future consumption; the right-hand side is present or current wealth. The *trading line,* or the set of consumption opportunities provided by the capital market, appears in Figure 2.1. The trading line represents the set of consumption bundles (c_0, c_1) that are

Figure 2.1   Consumption Opportunities/Trading Line

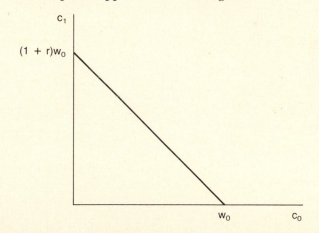

feasible given the individual's wealth level (w_0) and the rate of interest (r). For example, if the individual consumes all wealth in the current period, he or she will consume w_0 now and nothing next period; if the individual consumes nothing in the current period, he or she can consume $(1 + r)w_0$ next period. Note that the slope of the trading line is the derivative of c_1 with respect to c_0, which equals $-(1 + r)$. Hence, by reducing consumption in the current period by \$1, the individual may increase future consumption by \$$(1 + r)$.

A Mathematical Review of Constrained Optimization

The general form of the constrained optimization problem that we will be solving in this chapter is as follows:

maximize the objective function $u(x_0, x_1) = x_0^2 x_1$

subject to

$$x_1 = (100 - x_0)(1 + .10)$$

and

$$x_0 \geq 0, \qquad x_1 \geq 0.$$

Before we solve this optimization problem analytically, let us first visualize the shape of the objective function. The following three-dimensional diagram depicts the general shape of the objective function with $u(x_0, x_1)$ rising with x_0 and x_1. Note that we have "sliced" the surface representing the objective function with the two shaded planes that are parallel to the floor of the diagram. The lower plane corresponds to a value of $u(x_0, x_1) = c$, where c is a constant, while the higher plane corresponds to a value of $u(x_0, x_1) = 3c$. Note that the semicircles traced on the surface of the objective function by the planes represent indifference curves, as found in Figures 2.2 and 2.3. We can visualize this observation if we look down into the figure from above the $u(x_0, x_1)$ axis. The indifference curves appearing in the upper right-hand corner of the diagram represent higher levels of the objective function.

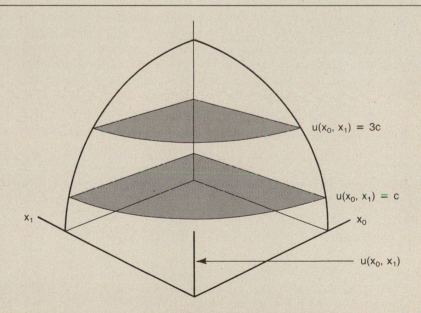

The optimization problem posed here is constrained by limits placed on x_0 and x_1. Thus, we seek to reach the maximum height on the $u(x_0, x_1)$ surface and not exceed the constraint placed on x_0 and x_1. The type of constraint placed on the problem is linear, and it can be superimposed on the two-dimensional or indifference curve view of the optimization problem in the following manner:

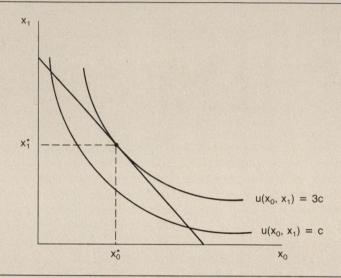

Thus, the maximum level of $u(x_0, x_1)$ that can be achieved given the constraint placed on x_0 and x_1 is 3C. We now investigate the analytical solution to this constrained optimization problem.

To solve this problem analytically, we use the Lagrange multiplier method (named after the French mathematician J. L. Lagrange). This method involves replacing the original problem with an equivalent one having a more complicated objective function than $u(x_0, x_1)$ but a less complicated set of constraints. Here we introduce a new variable, λ, called the *Lagrange multiplier* of the problem. It multiplies the equality constraint, and the product is added to the function to be maximized. The resulting function is called the *Lagrangian* of the problem, denoted as follows:

$$L(x_0, x_1, \lambda) = x_0^2 x_1 + \lambda(x_1 - 110 + 1.10x_0).$$

Next, we calculate the partial derivatives of L with respect to x_0, x_1, and λ and set them equal to zero:

(i) $$\frac{\partial L}{\partial x_0} = 2x_0 x_1 + \lambda(1.10) = 0.$$

(ii) $$\frac{\partial L}{\partial x_1} = x_0^2 + \lambda = 0.$$

(iii)
$$\frac{\partial L}{\partial \lambda} = x_1 - 110 + 1.10x_0 = 0.$$

We now solve this system of equations for x_0 and x_1. Solving (i) and (ii) for λ and equating the results produce the following:

$$\frac{2x_0x_1}{1.10} = x_0^2$$

or

$$x_0 = \frac{2x_1}{1.10}.$$

Substituting this expression for x_0 in (iii) produces the following:

$$x_1^* = 110 - 1.10\left(\frac{2x_1^*}{1.10}\right)$$

(iv)

$$x_1^* = 36.67.$$

Substituting this value into (iv), we solve for x_0^*:

$$x_0^* = \frac{2(36.67)}{1.10} = 66.67.$$

Graphically, the problem we have just solved appears as follows:

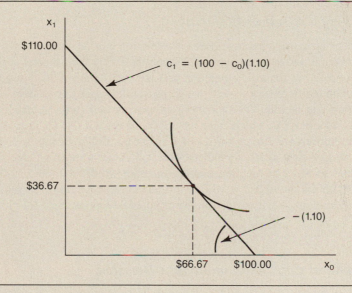

A more complete discussion of this method is found in the Mathematical Compendium at the end of the text.

Figure 2.2   Indifference Curves

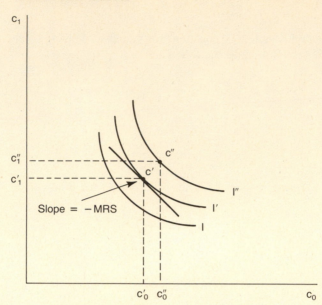

Describing Consumer Preferences

Preferences for current versus future consumption can be represented by *indifference curves,* as shown in Figure 2.2 (Appendix 2B contains a brief review of the axioms underlying the utility function and the indifference curves used to represent it.) The indifference curve I', which passes through (c_0', c_1'), represents the set of consumption bundles (combinations of current and future consumption) that yield the same level of satisfaction, or utility, as (c_0', c_1'). As the consumer moves to higher indifference curves (such as I''), his or her utility increases. Note too that the line tangent to I' at (c_0', c_1') indicates the individual's *marginal rate of substitution (MRS)* at that consumption bundle. In other words, the MRS is the interest rate at which the individual is willing to trade current for future consumption and remain indifferent—that is, total utility from consumption does not change.

The Optimal Consumption/Savings Decision

Recall that the individual's problem is to select an optimal time pattern of consumption. To do this, he or she selects that consumption bundle (on the trading line) to which no other is preferred. As shown in Figure 2.3, this optimal bundle,

Figure 2.3   Optimal Consumption Choice

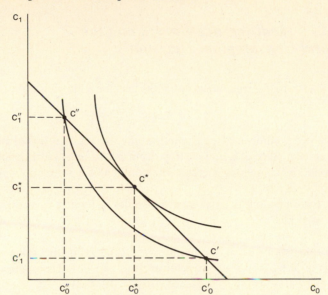

$c* = (c_0^*, c_1^*)$, is that bundle on the trading line that is also on the highest attainable indifference curve — that is, that bundle has maximum utility. Equivalently, it is the bundle for which $MRS* = (1 + r)$.[2]

To see why $c*$ is the optimal bundle in Figure 2.3, suppose the individual has the bundle $c' = (c_0', c_1')$. For this consumption bundle, MRS' is less than $(1 + r)$; thus, the rate at which the individual is willing to acquire future consumption by sacrificing current consumption and remain indifferent (that is, MRS') is less than the rate at which he or she can obtain future consumption by lending $(1 + r)$. The individual therefore can increase satisfaction by forgoing present consumption in the amount of $(c_0' - c_0^*)$ and loaning it to receive a rate of return of r.

---

[2]The MRS at a particular point on an indifference curve is defined as follows:

$$MRS(c_0, c_1) = -\frac{dc_1}{dc_0}.$$

Thus, the MRS is the slope of the tangent line to $u(c_0, c_1)$ at (c_0, c_1), neglecting the negative sign. When $MRS* = (1 + r)$, the slope of the indifference curve just equals the terms of trade in the capital market.

Exercise 2.1:   Indifference Curves and the Intertemporal Consumption Decision

Betty McDeal, with initial wealth (w_0) of \$100, has the following utility function:

$$u(c_0, c_1) = c_0^3 c_1^2 .$$

She is considering a number of consumption alternatives. Unlimited borrowing and lending can take place at a rate of 10 percent per annum. Let I denote the indifference curve (set) containing the consumption bundle $c = (c_0, c_1) = (60, 44)$.

1. Find the c_1 corresponding to consumption bundles in I where $c_0 = 40$, $c_0 = 50$, $c_0 = 70$, and $c_0 = 80$.

Solution.   I consists of all those bundles (c_0, c_1) having the same utility as $(60, 44)$ — that is, $u(60, 44) = u(c_0, c_1)$ for each (c_0, c_1) in I. Using the definition of u, we see that $(60)^3(44)^2 = c_0^3 c_1^2$. Hence, if $c_0 = 40$, then

$$c_1^2 = \frac{(60)^3(44)^2}{(40)^3}$$

and

$$c_1 = \left(\frac{60}{40}\right)^{3/2} (44) = 80.83 .$$

The remaining values are calculated similarly.

2. Find the value of the marginal rate of substitution (MRS) at each of the bundles found in question 1.

Solution.   Along indifference curve I, the MRS is, by definition, the negative of the derivative of c_1 with respect to c_0 — that is,

$$\text{MRS at } (c_0, c_1) = -\frac{dc_1}{dc_0}.$$

For each point (c_0, c_1) on I where the level of utility is constant, $u(c_0, c_1) = c_0^3 c_1^2 = (60)^3(44)^2$. Thus, solving for c_1 we get the following:

$$c_1 = \frac{(60)^{3/2}(44)}{c_0^{3/2}} = (60)^{3/2}(44)c_0^{-3/2}.$$

Differentiating with respect to c_0 gives

$$\frac{dc_1}{dc_0} = (60)^{3/2}(44) \left(\frac{-3}{2}\right) c_0^{-5/2};$$

thus,

$$MRS = (60)^{3/2}(44)\left(\frac{3}{2}\right)c_0^{-5/2}.$$

For example, for the bundle $(20, 228.63)$,

$$MRS = \frac{(60)^{3/2}(44)\left(\dfrac{3}{2}\right)}{(20)^{5/2}} = \frac{30{,}674}{(20)^{5/2}} = 17.15.$$

Similar calculations produce these values of MRS:

c_0	c_1	MRS
40	80.83	3.03
50	57.84	1.74
60	44.00	1.10
70	34.92	.75
80	28.58	.54

3. Draw the graph of I and the graph of trading line $c_1 = (1.10)(100 - c_0)$.

Solution

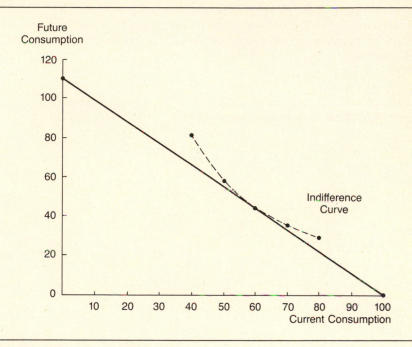

4. Find the optimal consumption bundle.

Solution. $(60, 44)$ is optimal, since for this bundle $MRS = (1 + r) = (1.10)$. Note too that $c = (60, 44)$ is feasible with an initial wealth $w_0 = 100$.

The Investment Decision

Real/Productive Investment Opportunities

We will now consider the individual with *only* real investment opportunities, that is, capital markets in which lending and borrowing do not exist. As before, let w_0 denote the individual's initial wealth. In this case, the individual can transform current consumption into future consumption only via real investment undertaken now. The *real investment opportunity frontier (F)* shown in Figure 2.4 represents the set of consumption feasible pairs (x_0, x_1). The frontier F is concave, exhibiting "diminishing returns to scale," or a declining marginal rate of return as the level of real investment increases. By making a real investment of $w_0 - x_0'$, the individual obtains the consumption bundle $x' = (x_0', x_1')$. The absolute value of the slope of the frontier represents the rate at which the investor can transfer current to future dollars via investment in real (productive) assets, as opposed to capital market notes, and is called the *marginal rate of transformation (MRT)* — that is,

$$MRT = -\left(\frac{dx_1}{dx_0}\right).$$

Alternatively, we may think of MRT as $(1 + i)$, where i is the real rate of return on the marginal dollar investment at a particular investment level. Note that i decreases where the level of investment in real assets increases such that the real investment frontier is concave to the origin and the MRT declines with increasing real investment.

Figure 2.4   Real Investment Opportunities

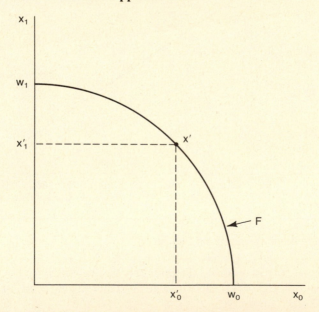

The Consumer Choice Problem: A Mathematical Overview

The axioms of choice provided in Appendix 2B guarantee the existence of a utility function $u(c_0, c_1)$ that may be used to represent the individual's preferences. The individual selects (c_0, c_1) to

$$\text{maximize } u(c_0, c_1)$$

subject to

$$c_0 + \left[\frac{c_1}{(1 + r)}\right] = w_0,$$

or, equivalently,

$$\text{maximize } L(c_0, c_1, \lambda)$$

where λ is the Lagrange multiplier and

$$L(c_0, c_1, \lambda) = u(c_0, c_1) + \lambda\left[w_0 - c_0 - \frac{c_1}{(1 + r)}\right].$$

The first-order conditions are

(i) $$D_1L = D_1u - \lambda = 0.$$

(ii) $$D_2L = D_2u - \left[\frac{1}{(1 + r)}\right]\lambda = 0.$$

(iii) $$D_3L = w_0 - c_0 - \left[\frac{1}{(1 + r)}\right]c_1 = 0.$$

Conditions (i) and (ii) may equivalently be expressed as

$$\text{MRS} = \frac{D_1u}{D_2u} = (1 + r).$$

(Note: D_1L denotes $\partial L/\partial c_0$, or the partial derivative of L with respect to the first argument in the Lagrangian. Correspondingly, D_2L is the derivative of L with respect to the second argument, c_1, and so forth.)

Diminishing Returns and the Internal Rate of Return

Frontier F in Figure 2.4 is concave from the origin and thus represents diminishing returns to further investment. Equivalently, MRT and i decrease as the investor moves along the frontier from the initial position $(w_0, 0)$ toward $(0, w_1)$. The shape of the frontier also indicates a decreasing average return on further investment or,

Figure 2.5 Internal Rate of Return

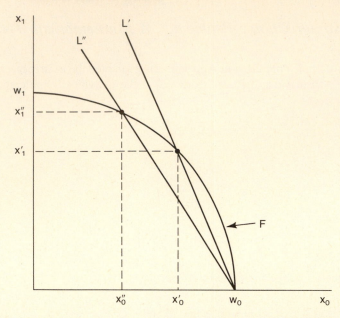

equivalently, a decreasing internal rate of return, denoted by IRR. To see this, note that the IRR, or average return on the investment of $w_0 - x_0'$ shown in Figure 2.4, is

$$\frac{x_1'}{(w_0 - x_0')} = -\frac{x_1'}{(x_0' - w_0)}.$$

Thus, $(1 + IRR')$ is the absolute value of the slope of line L′ shown in Figure 2.5; similarly, $(1 + IRR'')$ is the absolute value of the slope of line L″.

The Optimal Investment Decision

As before, the individual's problem is to select an optimal time pattern of consumption. With only real investment opportunities, the individual must select a pair (x_0, x_1) on F to which no other is preferred. In this case, the investor will select an $x^* = (x_0^*, x_1^*)$ as shown in Figure 2.6. Note that at the optimum position, x^*, $MRT^* = MRS^*$. To see why this is so, suppose the individual selects $x' = (x_0', x_1')$ as shown in Figure 2.6. Then $MRS' < MRT'$; thus, the rate at which the individual is willing to acquire future consumption by sacrificing current consumption and remain indifferent is less than the rate at which he or she can transform current into future dollars for consumption. Thus, the individual can increase his or her level of satisfaction by moving up the frontier toward x^*. The converse of this argument holds at x'', where $MRS'' > MRT''$.

Figure 2.6   Optimal Real Investment Decision with No Capital Market

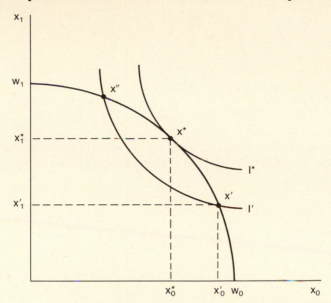

Exercise 2.2:   Real/Productive Investments and the Intertemporal Consumption Decision

Abe Turner's feasible consumption bundles resulting from his real investment opportunities (x_0, x_1) are given by $F(x_0, x_1) = 0$, where

$$F(x_0, x_1) = 100{,}000 - x_1 - \left(\frac{1.25}{3}\right)x_0 - \left(\frac{1.25}{120{,}000}\right)x_0^2.$$

In addition, his utility for bundle (x_0, x_1) is given by

$$u(x_0, x_1) = x_0^{3/4}x_1^{1/2}.$$

Find his optimal choice (x_0^*, x_1^*).

Solution.   Figure 2.6 provides a graphic representation of the solution to the general problem faced by Turner. Analytically, Abe Turner seeks to maximize $u(x_0, x_1)$ subject to the constraint $F(x_0, x_1) = 0$. The Lagrangian for this problem is

$$L(x_0, x_1, \lambda) = x_0^{3/4}x_1^{1/2} + \lambda\left[100{,}000 - x_1 - \left(\frac{1.25}{3}\right)x_0 - \left(\frac{1.25}{120{,}000}\right)x_0^2\right].$$

Note that both the constraint *and* the objective function are nonlinear in this problem.

The first-order condition is given by the following partial derivatives:

(i) $D_1L = \dfrac{3}{4}x_0^{-1/4}x_1^{1/2} - \lambda\left[\dfrac{1.25}{3} + \left(\dfrac{1.25}{60,000}\right)x_0\right] = 0$.

(ii) $D_2L = \dfrac{1}{2}x_0^{3/4}x_1^{-1/2} - \lambda = 0$.

(iii) $D_3L = 100,000 - x_1 - \left(\dfrac{1.25}{3}\right)x_0 - \left(\dfrac{1.25}{120,000}\right)x_0^2 = 0$.

Now we must solve for x_0 and x_1 using the above three partial derivatives; in this case, we use substitution to solve them simultaneously. First, we solve (ii) for

$$\lambda = \left(\frac{1}{2}\right)x_0^{3/4}x_1^{-1/2},$$

then solve (i) for

$$x_1 = \left(\frac{1.25}{4.5}\right)x_0 + \left(\frac{1.25}{90,000}\right)x_0^2,$$

and substitute into (iii) to get a single equation in x_0 alone:

(iv) $100,000 - \left(\dfrac{1.25}{4.5}\right)x_0 - \left(\dfrac{1.25}{90,000}\right)x_0^2 - \left(\dfrac{1.25}{3}\right)x_0 - \left(\dfrac{1.25}{120,000}\right)x_0^2 = 0$.

Collecting terms, we obtain

(v) $100,000 - \left(\dfrac{1.25 + 1.875}{4.5}\right)x_0 - \left(\dfrac{5 + 3.75}{360,000}\right)x_0^2 = 0$.

Finally, simplifying terms, (v) reduces to

$$.07x_0^2 + 2,000x_0 - 288,000,000 = 0.$$

Solving for x_0 using the quadratic equation gives

$$x_0 = \frac{-2,000 \pm [(2,000)^2 + 4(.07)(288,000,000)]^{1/2}}{(2)(.07)} = \frac{(-2,000 \pm 9,200)}{(.14)}.$$

Hence,

$$x_0^* = \$51,428.$$

Substituting this value of x_0^* into (iii), we get

$$x_1^* = \left(\frac{1.25}{4.5}\right)(51,428) + \left(\frac{1.25}{90,000}\right)(51,428)^2 = \$51,020.$$

The solution to Turner's investment and consumption problem involves his consuming \$51,428 in the current period and \$51,020 next period. Since he began with \$100,000, we see that he has invested \$48,572 = \$100,000 − \$51,428 in real assets, which provides him with an end-of-period return of \$51,020 or with an average rate of return of approximately 5 percent. Note that Turner's savings decision is tied directly to his investment decision—he consumes \$51,428 and saves \$48,572. The decision about how much to consume and save was made at the same time as the investment decision. The reason for this is simple: There are no capital markets in which Turner can borrow and lend; thus, all the monies needed to finance his investment must come from his own savings.

The Consumer Choice Problem with Both Real/Productive Investment Opportunities and Capital Markets

Defining the Opportunity Set. Up to this point, we have allowed the individual to have only one means of transferring wealth from the current period to the next: either the capital market or real investment. In this section, we assume the individual has both means available. We further assume that the interest rate in the capital market is a constant, r, that is independent of the individual's choice of whether to borrow or lend.

The introduction of a capital market has important implications for the behavior of the individual who invests in real/productive assets. Without capital markets, the individual's optimal investment decision ($w_0 - x_0^*$ in Figure 2.6) was shown to be equivalent to the savings decision. In other words, in this hypothetical world, an individual's optimal investment choice ($w_0 - x_0^*$) equaled his or her optimal savings choice ($x_0^* = c_0^*$). However, with the introduction of a capital market, saving need no longer function as the surrogate of investment, and vice versa. If the individual selects a position on the investment frontier such as x' in Figure 2.7, he or she may either lend more of the remaining current wealth (x_0') or borrow against the next-period investment return of x_1'. Given the investment decision that yields the pair (x_0', x_1'), the individual may select any pair (c_0, c_1) such that its present value is no greater than that of the pair (x_0', x_1'), that is,

$$c_0 + \left[\frac{1}{(1 + r)}\right]c_1 \leq x_0' + \left[\frac{1}{(1 + r)}\right]x_1'.$$

Since the individual prefers more consumption to less, we may restrict our attention to the pairs (c_0, c_1) such that

$$c_0 + \left[\frac{1}{(1 + r)}\right]c_1 = x_0' + \left[\frac{1}{(1 + r)}\right]x_1.$$

In other words, we assume that the present value of the individual's current plus future consumption equals the present value of his or her current and future income (wealth). This means that the individual's consumption choice will lie on the

Figure 2.7   Optimal Investment in Real Assets with Capital Markets

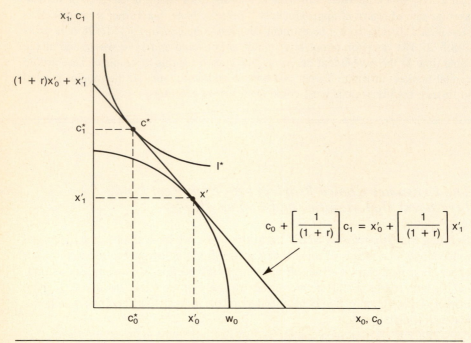

market trading line containing income (x_0, x_1) as depicted in Figure 2.7. Note that after investment, when $c_1 = 0$,

$$c_0 = x_0' + \left[\frac{x_1'}{(1 + r)}\right].$$

Fisher Separation Theorem.   The individual's problem still is to select an optimal time pattern of consumption; however, now there is an investment decision to be made that will determine the trading possibilities in the capital market. Note, as Fisher (1930) did, that the individual selects that point on the frontier having the greatest present value. This choice is made *independently* of the individual's time preferences for consumption because it permits more current *and* future consumption than any other, as the example in Figure 2.8 demonstrates. This result — that the investment decision is separate from the consumption decision — is known as the *Fisher separation theorem.*

Figure 2.8   The Fisher Separation Theorem and the NPV Rule

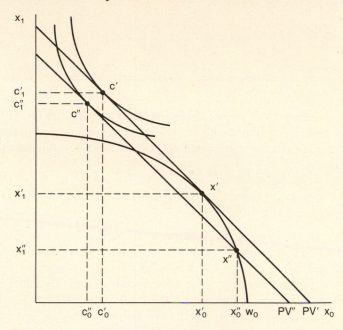

The Optimal Investment in Real Assets: A Mathematical Overview

In this section, the individual's problem may be specified as

maximize $u(x_0, x_1)$
subject to $F(x_0, x_1) = 0$

where $u(x_0, x_1)$ is the utility for current versus future consumption and $F(x_0, x_1) = 0$ implicitly defines the frontier F in Figures 2.4 through 2.6. Equivalently, the individual may select (x_0, x_1) by maximizing

$$L(x_0, x_1, \lambda) = u(x_0, x_1) - \lambda F(x_0, x_1),$$

where λ is the Lagrange multiplier. The first-order conditions are

(i) $D_1 L = D_1 u - \lambda D_1 F = 0,$

(ii) $D_2 L = D_2 u - \lambda D_2 F = 0,$

(iii) $D_3 L = F(x_0, x_1) = 0,$

where $D_1L = \partial L/\partial x_0, D_2L = \partial L/\partial x_2$, and $D_3L = \partial L/\partial \lambda$. Conditions (i) and (ii) may be equivalently expressed as

$$MRS = \frac{D_1u}{D_2u} = \frac{D_1F}{D_2F} = MRT.$$

Net Present Value (NPV) versus Internal Rate of Return (IRR).   In Figure 2.8, the present value of current wealth resulting from investing $w_0 - x_0''$ dollars equals PV'' and is less than the corresponding present value resulting from investing $w_0 - x_0'$; that is,

$$PV'' = x_0'' + \left[\frac{1}{(1 + r)}\right]x_1'' < x_0' + \left[\frac{1}{(1 + r)}\right]x_1' = PV'.$$

Also, $c' = (c_0', c_1')$ yields more current and future consumption than does $c'' = (c_0'', c_1'')$ — that is, $c_0' > c_0''$ and $c_1' > c_1''$. At the optimum positions in Figure 2.8 we have $MRT' = 1 + r = MRS'$; in other words, the first equality holds at x' and the second at c'. (The interpretation of these equalities is the same as that discussed earlier for Figures 2.3 and 2.6.) Since $MRT' = 1 + i'$, the first equality is equivalent to $i' = r$, which says that *the individual will invest to the point at which the real rate of return on the last dollar of investment, i', equals the rate of interest in the capital market, r.* Note that the optimal investment level is determined where the *marginal* rate of return earned, i', equals r and *not* where the average rate of return or the internal rate of return equals r. In fact, the IRR for the optimal investment level in Figure 2.8 is determined, as noted earlier, by the absolute value of the slope of a line passing through w_0 and x'; the slope of this line is $-(1 + IRR)$. Since i declines with increasing investment, IRR (which is the average rate of return) also decreases. Hence we cannot find the optimal investment level by maximizing IRR (which is greatest for the first dollar invested where the investment exhibits diminishing returns).

    If we denote the level of real investment by $I_0 = w_0 - x_0$ and recall that i decreases as I_0 increases, we will see in Figure 2.9 an alternative way of selecting the optimal investment. Note too that the net present value (NPV) of the investment is

$$NPV = -I_0 + \left[\frac{x_1}{(1 + r)}\right]$$

$$= x_0 - w_0 + \left[\frac{x_1}{(1 + r)}\right]$$

$$= PV - w_0.$$

Hence the investment level I', at which $i' = r$, is the level at which the individual maximizes net present value. This may be directly observed in Figure 2.8, since $NPV' = PV' - w_0 > NPV'' = PV'' - w_0$.

Figure 2.9 An Alternative Way to Represent Optimal Investment in Real Assets

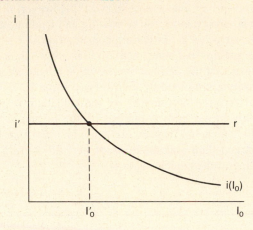

To summarize, where the Fisher separation theorem holds, the optimal investment decision is the one that maximizes the investment's NPV. This choice also maximizes the individual's present wealth, which means that it also provides the individual with the largest possible set of consumption opportunities.

Benefits Provided by Capital Markets. The gain to consumers provided by the existence of capital markets is illustrated in Figure 2.10. Where capital markets

Figure 2.10 Benefits Derived from Capital Markets

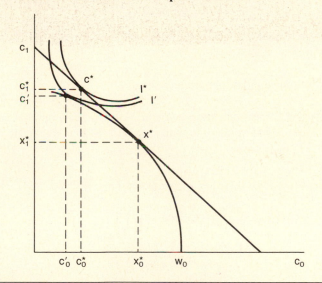

exist, the individual will invest $(w_0 - x_0^*)$ and lend $(x_0^* - c_0^*)$ from x_0^* so as to consume the bundle $c^* = (c_0^*, c_1^*)$. This consumption bundle provides the individual with utility represented by indifference curve I*. However, if there are no capital markets and thus no opportunities for borrowing and lending, the individual will find it optimal to invest $w_0 - x_0'$, providing consumption of $c' = (c_0', c_1')$. In this case, the individual's savings and investment (in real assets) choices are necessarily the same. The result is that the optimal consumption bundle allows the individual to reach only the utility represented by indifference curve I'. Hence, the presence of capital markets effectively "uncouples" the individual's investment and savings decisions. As we saw in our earlier analysis of the Fisher separation theorem, the individual can (when capital markets are available) make an NPV-maximizing investment decision and then maximize his or her utility from consumption by borrowing and lending in the capital markets.

Exercise 2.3:   The Consumption Decision with Both Real Investments and Capital Markets

In Exercise 2.2, the real investment frontier Abe Turner faced was $F(x_0, x_1) = 0$ where

$$F(x_0, x_1) = x_1 - 100{,}000 + \left(\frac{1.25}{3}\right)x_0 + \left(\frac{1.25}{120{,}000}\right)x_0^2$$

and his utility function was

$$u(c_0, c_1) = c_0^{3/4} c_1^{1/2}.$$

We now modify Turner's consumption problem by allowing him to borrow and lend at a rate of $r = 10\%$.

1. Describe the consumption opportunity set.

Solution.   By the Fisher separation theorem, Abe Turner's optimal consumption bundles (c_0, c_1) are found on the line with slope -1.10 that is tangent to the curve $F(x_0, x_1) = 0$. On this curve

$$x_1 = 100{,}000 - \left(\frac{1.25}{3}\right)x_0 - \left(\frac{1.25}{120{,}000}\right)x_0^2.$$

Thus, at (x_0, x_1) we solve $dx_1/dx_0 = -(1 + r)$ for (x_0, x_1):

$$-\left(\frac{1.25}{3}\right) - \left(\frac{1.25}{60{,}000}\right)x_0^* = -1.10$$

such that

$$x_0^* = \$32,800.$$

Substituting for x_0 in $F(x_0, x_1)$ and solving for x_1^*,

$$x_1^* = 100,000 - \left[\left(\frac{1.25}{3}\right)(32,800)\right] - \left[\left(\frac{1.25}{120,000}\right)(32,800)^2\right].$$

$$= 100,000 - 13,667 - 11,207$$

$$= \$75,126.$$

Hence the optimal real/productive investment is $(x_0^*, x_1^*) = (32,800; 75,126)$. Note that given the nature of the investment opportunity, F, and the market rate of interest, r, this is optimal for *all* investors. This, of course, is the essence of the Fisher separation theorem. We now know that the consumption opportunity set is the market trading line passing through $(32,800; 75,126)$ with slope -1.10. Its equation is

$$\frac{(c_1 - 75,126)}{(c_0 - 32,800)} = -1.10$$

or

$$c_1 = 75,126 - 1.10(c_0 - 32,800).$$

2. Find the optimal consumption bundle for Turner.

Solution.   Abe Turner's utility function is $u(c_0, c_1) = c_0^{3/4}c_1^{1/2}$. He should choose the bundle (c_0^*, c_1^*) in the opportunity set for which $MRS = 1.10$. He seeks to maximize $u(c_0, c_1)$ subject to the constraint $c_1 = 75,126 - 1.10\ (c_0 - 32,800)$, which is the consumption opportunity set. The Lagrangian for this problem is

$$L(c_0, c_1, \lambda) = c_0^{3/4}c_1^{1/2} + \lambda[75,126 - c_1 - 1.10(c_0 - 32,800)].$$

The first-order conditions are

(i) $$D_1L = \frac{3}{4}c_0^{-1/4}c_1^{1/2} - 1.1\lambda = 0.$$

(ii) $$D_2L = \frac{1}{2}c_0^{3/4}c_1^{-1/2} - \lambda = 0.$$

(iii) $$D_3L = 75,126 - c_1 - 1.10(c_0 - 32,800) = 0.$$

Dividing (i) by (ii), we get

$$1.5\left(\frac{c_1^*}{c_0^*}\right) = 1.1$$

or

(iv)
$$c_0^* = \left(\frac{1.5}{1.1}\right)c_1^* .$$

Substituting c_0^* into (iii), we obtain

$$-c_1^* + 75,126 - 1.10\left[\left(\frac{1.5}{1.1}\right)c_1^* - 32,800\right] = 0$$

or

$$111,206 - 2.5c_1^* = 0$$

$$c_1^* = \$44,482 .$$

Substituting the value of c_1^* into (iv), we get

$$c_0^* = \$60,657 .$$

In Exercise 2.2, when we solved for the optimal investment and consumption bundle for Abe Turner, we solved both problems simultaneously. This resulted from the fact that there was no capital market in which he could borrow and lend to adjust his consumption/savings decision. The optimal consumption bundle found in Exercise 2.2 was ($51,428; $51,020), which, given Turner's utility function, has a total utility of 771,383. However, in this exercise, where Turner can separate his investment and consumption decisions by borrowing and lending in the capital market, we find that he will consume the bundle ($60,657; $44,482), which has a utility level of 815,179. The increase in utility is a direct result of Turner's access to the capital market. Specifically, with a capital market he invests $67,200 = $100,000 − $32,800; however, he then borrows the $27,857 needed to restore his current income to the desired consumption for the current period of $60,657.

Transactions Costs and the Loss of the Fisher Separation Theorem

The Fisher separation theorem allows us to determine the consumer's optimal investment choice without regard for his or her preferences for current versus future consumption. As we have seen, this result follows by noting that selecting the investment level such that MRT = $(1 + r)$ or $(1 + i)$ = $(1 + r)$ maximizes the present value of income. Note that since NPV = PV − w_0, NPV is also maximized. Once invested at this level, the consumer may borrow or lend at the rate r to obtain the preferred current versus future consumption position. Alternatively, if r < i, the investor may enhance his or her consumption opportunities further by increasing real investment than by investing in the capital market; then the investor may borrow at r < i to increase current consumption, if desired. Hence, with no transactions costs the optimal investment will satisfy the condition i = r.

Figure 2.11   Transactions Costs and the Optimal Investment/Consumption Choice

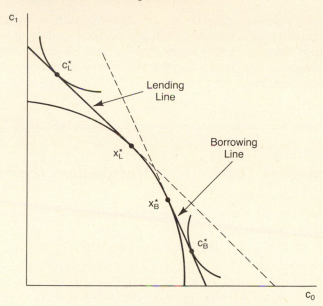

When transactions costs are recognized in using capital markets to borrow and lend, the Fisher separation theorem breaks down. Here transactions costs refer to the costs incurred when buying notes (lending) or selling notes (borrowing) in the capital market. These costs consist of commissions and fees paid to *financial intermediaries,* such as investment bankers and commercial banks. Their net result is to make borrowing more costly than lending. For example, if a consumer is willing to loan money at 12 percent and a financial intermediary charges a 2 percent fee for its services in bringing borrower and lender together, the borrowing rate is really 14 percent.

Figure 2.11 contains an example in which the borrowing rate, r_B, exceeds the lending rate, r_L. The slope of the trading line through x_B^* is $-(1 + r_B)$ while the slope of the trading line through x_L^* is $-(1 + r_L)$. Consumer B invests to the point at which $i = r_B$ and then borrows to obtain the consumption pair $c_B^* = (c_{B0}^*, c_{B1}^*)$. Consumer L invests to the point at which $i = r_L$ and lends to obtain the consumption pair $c_L^* = (c_{L0}^*, c_{L1}^*)$. Since i decreases as the investment level increases and $r_B > r_L$, consumer B prefers a smaller investment level than consumer L. The key point here is that it is in the borrower's and lender's self-interests to make *different* investment choices. This means that the optimal investment decision is *contingent* on consumer preferences for current versus future consumption. Hence, the Fisher separation theorem no longer holds. Note that the presence of capital markets is still beneficial since both borrowers and lenders can achieve higher consumption levels, and thus higher utility, than they could with real investment opportunities

alone. However, we can no longer use the NPV rule to select the optimal investment choice for *all* individuals, regardless of their particular time preferences for
consumption.

     Loss of the separation property as a result of transactions costs makes the
solution to the individual's optimal investment decision contingent on personal
preferences with regard to current versus future consumption. However, for the
rest of this chapter we will assume that the Fisher separation theorem holds as a
reasonable approximation.

Fisher Separation Theorem: A Mathematical Overview

The Fisher separation theorem may be obtained directly by noting that the individual's consumption problem is

$$\text{maximize } u(c_0, c_1)$$

  subject to

$$c_0 + \left[\frac{1}{(1 + r)}\right]c_1 = x_0 + \left[\frac{1}{(1 + r)}\right]x_1$$

  and

$$F(x_0, x_1) = 0,$$

or, equivalently,

$$\text{maximize } L(c_0, c_1, x_0, x_1, \lambda_1, \lambda_2) = L(c, x, \lambda)$$

  where

$$L(c, x, \lambda) = u(c_0, c_1) + \lambda_1\left(x_0 + \left[\frac{x_1}{(1 + r)}\right] - c_0 - \left[\frac{c_1}{(1 + r)}\right]\right) + \lambda_2 F(x_0, x_1).$$

Then the first-order condition states the following:

(i) $D_1 L = D_1 u - \lambda_1 = 0.$

(ii) $D_2 L = D_2 u - \left[\frac{1}{(1 + r)}\right]\lambda_1 = 0.$

(iii) $D_3 L = \lambda_1 + \lambda_2 D_1 F = 0.$

(iv) $D_4 L = \left[\frac{1}{(1 + r)}\right]\lambda_1 + \lambda_2 D_2 F = 0.$

(v) $D_5 L = x_0 + \left[\frac{x_1}{(1 + r)}\right] - c_0 - \left[\frac{c_1}{(1 + r)}\right] = 0.$

(vi) $D_6 L = F(x_0, x_1) = 0.$

It follows from (i) and (ii) that

$$MRS = \frac{D_1u}{D_2u} = (1 + r)$$

and from (iii) and (iv) that

$$MRT = \frac{D_1F}{D_2F} = (1 + r).$$

Hence, MRS = MRT.

Summary

The theory of finance relies heavily on the theory of consumer choice. This chapter discussed the choice of an optimal time pattern of consumption for the two-period (one-decision) case, where all decisions are made under conditions of complete certainty. A great deal of insight was gained by considering the simple two-period certainty case.

Specifically, in this chapter we

1.   Demonstrated the "benefits" derived from the existence of capital markets that effectively "uncouple" the saving and investment choices of the individual.

2.   Derived the net present value rule for investment analysis and demonstrated its consistency with wealth maximization.

3.   Noted the crucial role of the Fisher separation theorem in the theory of finance.

Solving the individual's consumption choice problem was found to involve a three-step process:

▪   *Step 1: Identify the elements of the consumption opportunity set.* This set consists of real investment opportunities as well as borrowing and lending opportunities in the capital market.

▪   *Step 2: Describe consumer preferences for current versus future consumption.* The traditional approach to this problem involves the use of a "utility function" supported by a set of *axioms* or assumptions about individuals and their behavior.

▪   *Step 3: Select the element of the consumption opportunity set that maximizes the individual's utility derived from consumption.*

Step 3 involved both an investment and a consumption decision. The investment choice was found to be independent of consumption preferences where the Fisher separation theorem held. This theorem states that the optimal investment choice is the same regardless of the individual's specific time preferences for consumption.

This very important theorem holds, however, only where there are no transactions costs associated with borrowing and lending in the capital market. Thus, the Fisher separation property generally does not characterize the consumption choices individuals face. Its saving grace is that transactions costs usually are considered so small as to cause very minor differences in borrowing and lending rates such that the theorem produces a reasonable first approximation. This point will prove very important when we consider the investment decisions that must be made by nonowner corporation managers for their stockholders.

Study Questions

2.1   What is the role of the Fisher separation theorem in the theory of the intertemporal consumption choice problem?

2.2   How does a decline in the interest rate affect consumers' "well-being"?

2.3   How does the presence of a capital market make consumers better off? Demonstrate using an example.

2.4   How do transactions costs affect the individual's investment choice problem?

2.5   How, if at all, is the internal rate of return related to the MRT of real assets?

Study Problems

2.1   An individual has initial wealth (w_0) of $100, and the market rate of interest (r) on borrowing and lending is 10 percent. Alternative consumption bundles are ranked using the following function:

$$u(c_0, c_1) = c_0^{1/2} c_1^{1/3}$$

where the bundle (c_0, c_1) is preferred to the bundles (a_0, a_1) if $c_0^{1/2} c_1^{1/3} > a_0^{1/2} a_1^{1/3}$. Finally, let I denote the indifference set containing the consumption bundle $(60, 44)$.
a. Find c_1 for the bundles in I having $c_0 = 20$, $c_0 = 80$, and $c_0 = 100$.
b. Find the marginal rate of substitution (MRS) for each bundle in part a.
c. Draw the graphs of I and the consumption opportunities $[(c_0, c_1): w_0 = c_0 + c_1(1 + r)^{-1}]$.

2.2   As in Problem 2.1, an individual has $w_0 = 100 and $r = 10\%$. However, the appropriate utility function now becomes

$$u(c_0, c_1) = c_0^{1/2} c_1^{1/4}$$

where I is the indifference curve containing the current and future consumption bundle $(60, 44)$.
a. Same as part a in 2.1.
b. Same as part b in 2.1.
c. Same as part c in 2.1.
d. Explain why $(60, 44)$ is not the optimal consumption bundle.
e. Find a bundle that is both feasible and better than $(60, 44)$.

*2.3   Using the information contained in Problem 2.2 but substituting $r = 11\%$, solve for the optimal consumption bundle.

*2.4   Modify Problem 2.2 such that $u(c_0, c_1) = \log(c_0 c_1)$. What is the optimal level of current consumption (c_0)?

2.5   Consider two income streams, (y_0', y_1') and (y_0'', y_1''). At what interest rates will an individual be indifferent between the two streams (if there are any)?

*2.6   The R. Crusoe Farming Corporation faces the following real/productive investment opportunity set:

$$F(x_0, x_1) = (100 - x_0)(1.07 + .0003 x_0) - x_1$$
$$0 \le x_0 \le 100$$

where x_0 represents current-period dollars and x_1 corresponds to end-of-year dollars resulting from the investment in its farming operation. There is no capital market; however, R. Crusoe has assessed his utility for current and future consumption, which is as follows:

$$u(x_0, x_1) = x_0^2 x_1 .$$

Solve for the optimal level of real investment for R. Crusoe. [Hint: R. Crusoe's current wealth is found by solving $F(x_0, x_1)$ for x_0 where $x_1 = 0$.]

*2.7   Using the same real investment opportunity set $[F(x_0, x_1)]$ and utility function $[u(x_0, x_1)]$ as in Problem 2.6, solve for the optimal level of real investment and the optimal level of consumption where capital markets exist and the borrowing and lending rate equals 7.5 percent. Compare your answer to that obtained in Problem 2.6.

*2.8   Solve Problem 2.6 where $u(x_0, x_1) = x_0 x_1^2$.

*2.9   Solve Problem 2.6 with a borrowing and lending rate of 6.5 percent.

*2.10   Solve for the optimal level(s) of real investment using the real/productive opportunity set given in Problem 2.6 with a borrowing rate (r_B) of 7.5 percent and a lending rate (r_L) of 6.5 percent. Also, describe the consumption opportunity set that is available under these circumstances.

2.11   Construct a graph that demonstrates the Fisher separation theorem. Include consideration for diminishing marginal rates of return from investing in real assets and equal borrowing/lending rates.

2.12   Graph an investment opportunity set that offers a constant 20 percent rate of return on any level of real investment. If the borrowing/lending rate is 10 percent and the individual's current wealth is $100, what is the optimal level of real investment? (Hint: There is no limit on how much the individual can borrow at 10 percent.)

---

*Problems denoted with an asterisk(*) involve the use of calculus.

2.13   Graphically analyze the impact of an increase in the interest rate on the real/productive investment and consumption decisions of a borrower and a lender where there are no transactions costs. How is borrowers' and lenders' utility affected?

2.14   If the marginal rate of transformation of future for current consumption through investing in real assets is 1.24 (that is, the investor must forgo $1.24 in future consumption for $1.00 of current consumption), what is the rate of return earned on real investment? In general, what is the relationship between the rate of return earned on investment and the marginal rate of transformation?

2.15   "The use of the net present value method is consistent with maximizing consumer wealth." True or false? Explain.

*2.16   Show that NPV > 0 if and only if IRR > r.

*2.17   Let F denote the investment frontier [that is, $y_1 = F(y_0)$ denotes the dollar return next period]. Let $1 + r = F'(y_0)$ and $1 + IRR = F(y_0)/(w_0 - y_0)$ where w_0 is the initial wealth position in the current period. Show that if F is strictly concave (as in Figure 2.4), IRR > i. Use this to show that the investor will always select an investment level such that IRR > r.

2.18   The following figure reflects two real investment opportunities. The first alternative offers a rate of return i_1; the second has a rate of return of i_2.

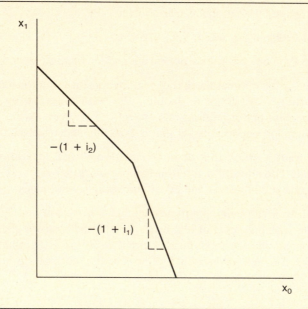

If $i_2 < r < i_1$, what is the optimal investment? What is IRR for that investment? For larger investments?

*2.19   Note that in the following figure,

$$\int_0^{I^*} i(I)\, dI > \int_0^{I^*} r\, dI .$$

Use this to explain why I* is the optimal investment level.

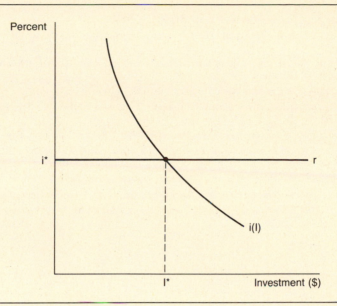

2.20   Let $I' = w_0 - x_0'$ and $I'' = w_0 - x_0''$. Observe that $NPV' = NPV''$, and use this to show that $NPV(I)$ first increases and then decreases with I (see the following figures).

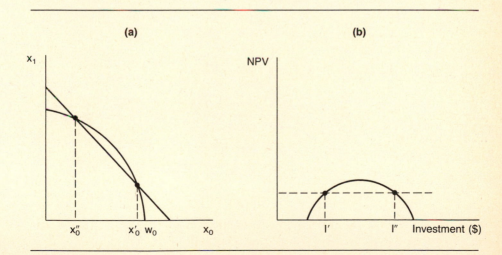

References

J. W. Conard, *Introduction to the Theory of Interest* (Berkeley, Calif.: University of California Press, 1959).

T. E. Copeland and J. F. Weston, *Financial Theory and Corporate Policy* (Reading, Mass.: Addison-Wesley, 1983), Chapter 1.

E. F. Fama and M. H. Miller, *The Theory of Finance* (New York: Holt, Rinehart and Winston, 1972), Chapter 1.

I. Fisher, *The Theory of Interest* (New York: Macmillan, 1930).

C. W. Haley and Lawrence D. Schall, *The Theory of Financial Decisions* (New York: McGraw-Hill, 1979), Chapter 2.

W. B. Hickman, *The Term Structure of Interest Rates: An Exploratory Analysis* (New York: National Bureau of Economic Research, 1943).

J. R. Hicks, *Value and Capital* (Oxford, England: Oxford University Press, 1939).

J. Hirshleifer, *Investment, Interest Rates and Capital* (Englewood Cliffs, N.J.: Prentice-Hall, 1970), Chapters 2, 3.

S. Homer, *A History of Interest Rates* (New Brunswick, N.J.: Rutgers University Press, 1963).

R. Kessel, *The Cyclical Behavior of the Term Structure of Interest Rates,* Occasional Paper 91 (New York: National Bureau of Economic Research, 1965).

F. Lutz, "The Structure of Interest Rates," *Quarterly Journal of Economics* (1940).

B. G. Malkiel, *The Term Structure of Interest Rates* (Princeton, N. J.: Princeton University Press, 1966).

D. Meiselman, *The Term Structure of Interest Rates* (Englewood Cliffs, N.J.: Prentice-Hall, 1962).

Appendix 2A

Financial Decisions and the Theory of Choice: Multiple Periods

In this appendix, we extend the simple two-period trading model to three or more periods. Our objective is to analyze the individual's consumption/savings decision in a multiperiod setting. This extension provides the basis for two important results. First, the individual's consumption/savings problem is solved in exactly the same way as it was for the two-period case, although the solution's analytical complexity increases; that is, with more periods the individual has several ways to transfer present wealth to a future date. The optimal consumption/savings decision, then, must consider all these possibilities. Second, the presence of multiple periods means that there are as many capital market interest rates as there are individual time periods. Thus, the presence of multiple periods provides an opportunity to investigate the relationships among interest rates on capital market notes of different maturities — the term structure of interest rates.

In our analysis we retain the same basic assumptions as in the two-period model: (1) complete certainty, (2) competitive capital markets, and (3) no transactions costs. The extension of our analysis from two to three or more periods poses no additional problems for the consumer if preferences for consumption now and in future periods are well defined. In other words, we assume the existence of a utility function $u(c_0, c_1, \ldots, c_T)$ that specifies the individual's preferences over each choice $(c_0, c_1, \ldots, c_T)$ where c_t denotes consumption in period t and t = $0, 1, \ldots, T$. Further, the indifference curve in the two-period case now generalizes to an indifference *surface* for the T-period case.

Capital Market Trading Opportunities and the Term Structure of Interest Rates

The Multiperiod Trading Plane

The trading line used to describe consumption opportunities created by the capital market with two periods generalizes to a trading plane as shown in Figure 2A.1 (or a hyperplane if $T > 2$). This generalization poses no new difficulties, but it does provide some new insight—for now there is more than one way in which to transfer wealth from the present to future periods. For example, the individual may transfer wealth directly from the present to period 2 or indirectly by transferring it first to period 1 and then to period 2. Where borrowing and lending rates are equal (there are no transactions costs), we let $r_{01} = r_{10}$ denote the borrowing and lending rates between period 0 and 1 and 1 and 0, respectively. Also, we define $r_{02} = r_{20}$ and $r_{12} = r_{21}$. If the consumer chooses to transfer one dollar from period 0 to period 2 by purchasing a two-year capital market note, he or she obtains $(1 + r_{02})^2$ at the end of year 2. Alternatively, if the individual transfers one dollar from period 0 to period 1 and then from 1 to 2, he or she obtains $(1 + r_{01})(1 + r_{12})$. In a well-functioning capital market under conditions of certainty, these two strategies should provide the same end-of-year-2 wealth. This "result" is the basis for the "pure expectations" hypothesis of the term structure, which we consider next.

The Pure Expectations Hypothesis

We use *term structure of interest rates* to describe the series of interest rates that correspond to different maturities existing at a given point in time; that is, the term structure of interest rates is simply the collection of rates $r_{01}, r_{02}, r_{03}, \ldots, r_{0T}$. Under certainty there is a relationship that must exist among all rates in the term structure

---

Figure 2A.1   Trading Plane

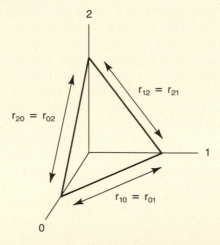

Figure 2A.2   Pure Expectations Hypothesis of the Term Structure

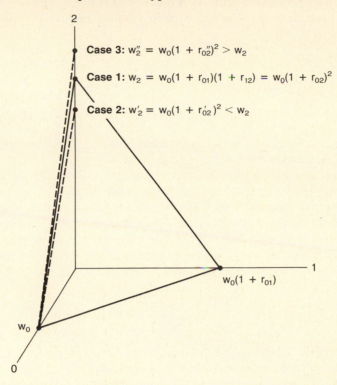

2

Case 3: $w_2'' = w_0(1 + r_{02}'')^2 > w_2$

Case 1: $w_2 = w_0(1 + r_{01})(1 + r_{12}) = w_0(1 + r_{02})^2$

Case 2: $w_2' = w_0(1 + r_{02}')^2 < w_2$

$w_0(1 + r_{01})$

w_0

0

so as to eliminate opportunities to make certain or riskless profits, called *arbitrage opportunities*. In other words, to eliminate arbitrage opportunities the rates in the term structure must satisfy the condition $(1 + r_{01})(1 + r_{12}) = (1 + r_{02})^2$.[1] This relationship characterizes what we will call the *pure expectations hypothesis* of the term structure of interest rates.[2] We refer to this theory as the "pure expectations theory" because investors' expectations of the level of future interest rates are the sole factor used to explain the term structure.[3] We will now demonstrate how expectations are captured in the term structure.

We can easily show that the pure expectations hypothesis must characterize the term structure using Figure 2A.2. With initial wealth w_0, the individual can transfer his or her wealth to period 2 in one of two ways: (1) purchase two con-

---

[1] Of course, if the term structure of interest rates is flat—if $r_{st} = r$ for $s = 0, 1$ and $t = 1, 2$—this condition is obviously satisfied.

[2] Hicks (1939) and Lutz (1940) developed unique theories of the term structure based on investor expectations of the pattern of future short-term interest rates.

[3] The pure expectations theory of the term structure technically applies to a world in which future interest rates are uncertain. However, we introduce it here under certainty since the basic concept is the same.

secutive one-year notes earning r_{01} and r_{12} for periods 1 and 2, respectively, producing end-of-period-2 wealth $w_2 = w_0(1 + r_{01})(1 + r_{12})$ or (2) purchase a two-period note earning r_{02}, in which case end-of-period-2 wealth will be one of the following:

Case 1: $\quad w_2 = w_0(1 + r_{02})^2 = w_2 \quad$ if $(1 + r_{02})^2 = (1 + r_{01})(1 + r_{12})$.

Case 2: $\quad w_2' = w_0(1 + r_{02}')^2 < w_2 \quad$ if $(1 + r_{02}')^2 < (1 + r_{01})(1 + r_{12})$.

Case 3: $\quad w_2'' = w_0(1 + r_{02}'')^2 > w_2 \quad$ if $(1 + r_{02}'')^2 > (1 + r_{01})(1 + r_{12})$.

Only Case 1 is consistent with no arbitrage profits and the pure expectations hypothesis of the term structure.

If Case 2 exists, the individual can enhance his or her wealth by issuing two-period notes (borrowing at r_{02}') and purchasing a combination of one-period notes (lending via two consecutive single-period notes at rates r_{01} and r_{12}, respectively). With each replication of the scheme, the individual can reap a certain (arbitrage) profit equal to $w_2 - w_2' = w_0[(1 + r_{01})(1 + r_{12}) - (1 + r_{02}')^2]$, where the amount of each transaction equals w_0 dollars to receive $w_2' = w_0(1 + r_{02}')^2$ two periods hence. The net present value of each such investment is

$$NPV = \left[\frac{w_0(1 + r_{01})(1 + r_{12})}{(1 + r_{02}')^2}\right] - w_0.$$

Therefore, NPV is positive only where $(1 + r_{02}')^2 < (1 + r_{01})(1 + r_{12})$, that is, where the pure expectations hypothesis does not hold.

If Case 3 arises, the individual will find it advantageous to issue two single-period notes at r_{01} and r_{12} and use the proceeds to purchase two-period notes yielding r_{02}''. The net present value of each such transaction involving w_0 dollars will be

$$NPV = \left[\frac{w_0(1 + r_{02}'')^2}{(1 + r_{01})(1 + r_{12})}\right] - w_0.$$

This relationship will be positive only where $(1 + r_{02}'')^2 > (1 + r_{01})(1 + r_{12})$, which, of course, is a case where the pure expectations hypothesis does not hold.

Only in Case 1 will arbitrage not be possible. This case is depicted in Figure 2A.2 as the trading plane. Here the net present values of either of the arbitrage strategies successful in Cases 2 and 3—also depicted in Figure 2A.2—will be zero. *Therefore, the pure expectations hypothesis describes conditions under which nonzero (positive or negative) net present values cannot be earned by buying and selling securities traded in the capital market.*

To summarize, the multiperiod trading plane—which is consistent with the pure expectations hypothesis—is that set of consumption bundles such that the present value of all future consumption opportunities equals current wealth:

$$c_0 + \left[\frac{c_1}{(1 + r_{01})}\right] + \left[\frac{c_2}{(1 + r_{02})^2}\right] = w_0.$$

Figure 2A.3   Optimal Multiperiod Consumption Choice

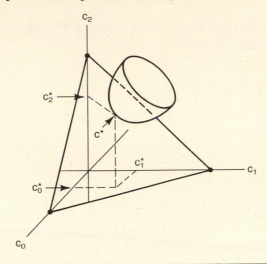

More generally, in higher dimensions the trading hyperplane is the set of consumption bundles $(c_0, c_1, \ldots, c_T)$ such that

$$\sum_{t=0}^{T} \frac{c_t}{(1 + r_{0t})^t} = w_0.$$

As before, the individual's consumption/savings problem is to select the optimal consumption path. This is done by selecting the bundle (c_0, c_1, c_2) on the trading plane to which no other is preferred, or, equivalently, by selecting the bundle (c_0, c_1, c_2) on the highest indifference surface as shown in Figure 2A.3. Let MRS_{0t} $(t = 1, 2)$ denote the consumer's marginal rate of substitution for consumption between periods 0 and t. Recall too that one dollar sacrificed now yields $(1 + r_{02})^2$ dollars in period 2 and thus represents the terms of trade. Hence, at the optimal point $c^* = (c_0^*, c_1^*, c_2^*)$ shown in Figure 2A.3, it must be true that $\text{MRS}_{01} = (1 + r_{01})$ and $\text{MRS}_{02} = (1 + r_{02})^2$; otherwise the rate at which the consumer would be willing to trade consumption in one period for that in another and remain indifferent would differ from the terms of trade and would allow him or her to attain a higher indifference surface.

The Multiple-Period Consumer Choice Problem:
A Mathematical Overview

The consumer's multiple-period consumption problem may be expressed as
$$\text{maximize } u(c_0, c_1, \ldots, c_T)$$
subject to

$$\sum_{t=0}^{T} \frac{c_t}{(1 + r_{0t})^t} = w_0$$

$$c_t \geq 0, \qquad t = 0, \ldots, T$$

or, equivalently (assuming an interior solution),
$$\text{maximize } L(c, \lambda)$$
where $c = (c_0, c_1, \ldots, c_T)$ is the Lagrange multiplier and the function is defined by

$$L(c, \lambda) = u(c) + \lambda \left[\sum_{t=0}^{T} \frac{c_t}{(1 + r_{0t})^t} - w_0 \right].$$

Then the first-order conditions are

(i)
$$D_t u(c) + \lambda \left[\frac{1}{(1 + r_{0t})^t} \right] = 0 \quad \text{for } t = 0, \ldots, T.$$

(ii)
$$\sum_{t=0}^{T} \frac{c_t}{(1 + r_{0t})^t} - w_0 = 0.$$

Equivalently,

$$\frac{D_0 u(c)}{D_t u(c)} = (1 + r_{0t})^t$$

where the left-hand side is the MRS_{0t} and the right-hand side is the rate at which dollars now can be transferred to dollars in period t. More generally,

$$\frac{D_s u(c)}{D_t u(c)} = \frac{(1 + r_{0t})^t}{(1 + r_{0s})^s}$$

$$= \frac{(1 + r_{01}) \ldots (1 + r_{t-1\,t})}{(1 + r_{01}) \ldots (1 + r_{s-1\,s})}$$

$$= (1 + r_{st})$$

where the left-hand side is MRS_{st}.

Real/Productive Investment Opportunities

Next we will consider the individual's investment frontier as shown in Figure 2A.4. As with the trading plane, the increased dimension of the problem introduces no new complications, but it does allow the individual more options — that is, by making an investment now, the individual may obtain a return in either period 1, period 2, or both. As before, let w_0 denote the individual's initial wealth. Then, by making an investment now of $w_0 - x_0'$, the individual may obtain any of the pairs (x_1, x_2) shown in Figure 2A.5. In other words, each investment decision now yields a range of choices for returns in periods 1 and 2. The absolute value of the slope of the frontier in Figure 2A.5 is the marginal rate of transformation between periods 1 and 2. It is denoted $MRT_{12} = (1 + i_{12})$, where i_{12} is the real rate of return. Similarly, MRT_{01} and MRT_{02} represent the rates at which income may be transferred (via investment in real/productive assets) from the current period to periods 1 and 2, respectively.

The frontier F in Figure 2A.5 is concave from the origin, as are all two-dimensional slices of it. This represents generalized diminishing returns to further investment. Equivalently, both MRT and i decrease as the investor moves in any direction along the frontier away from the initial position $(w_0, 0, 0)$.

The Optimal Investment/Consumption Decision

Now the individual's problem is to select an investment level that yields cash flows (x_0, x_1, x_2). The x_t $(t = 0, 1, 2)$ represents dollars available for consumption or saving in period t. The individual can then borrow or lend against the present

---

Figure 2A.4   Multiperiod Real/Productive Investment Frontier

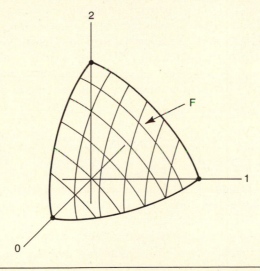

Figure 2A.5   Two-Dimensional "Slice" of the Multiperiod Real/Productive Investment Opportunity Set

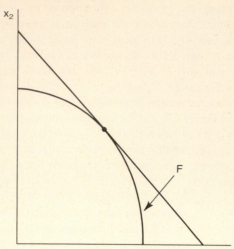

value of this income stream to obtain an optimal time pattern of consumption (c_0, c_1, c_2). Just as in the preceding two-period analysis, it is easy to see that these decisions are separable — that is, the individual will first select the (x_0, x_1, x_2) with the maximum net present value, since this choice allows more consumption now and later. Let $x^* = (x_0^*, x_1^*, x_2^*)$ denote the optimal position on the real investment frontier F as shown in Figure 2A.6. At this point, it must be true that $MRT_{01} = 1 + r_{01}$, $i_{02} = r_{02}$, and $i_{12} = r_{12}$. These conditions simply express the notion that at the margin the individual cannot restructure the investment choice to make a larger gain via real investment than via the capital markets. Graphically this means that $x^* = (x_0^*, x_1^*, x_2^*)$ is on the plane tangent to the frontier F at x^* as shown in Figure 2A.6. Finally, the individual selects the optimal time pattern of consumption $c^* = (c_0^*, c_1^*, c_2^*)$ by choosing the position on the tangent plane, that is, the set of (c_0, c_1, c_2) such that

$$c_0 + \left[\frac{c_1}{(1 + r_{01})} \right] + \left[\frac{c_2}{(1 + r_{02})^2} \right] = x_0^* + \left[\frac{x_1^*}{(1 + r_{01})} \right] + \left[\frac{x_2^*}{(1 + r_{02})^2} \right].$$

This constraint simply requires that the individual consume within his or her means; in other words, the present value of consumption must equal the individual's present wealth.

Just as was the case in the two-period problem, the solution to the multiperiod consumption problem will be a consumption bundle $c^* = (c_0^*, c_1^*, c_2^*)$ such

Figure 2A.6   Optimal Multiperiod Investment Decision

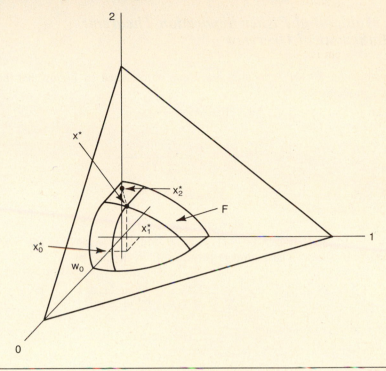

that $MRS_{01}^* = (1 + r_{01})$, $MRS_{02}^* = (1 + r_{02})^2$, and $MRS_{12}^* = (1 + r_{12})$. It follows that the optimum conditions may be equivalently expressed as

$$MRT_{01}^* = (1 + r_{01}) = MRS_{01}^*.$$

$$MRT_{02}^* = (1 + r_{02})^2 = MRS_{02}^*.$$

$$MRT_{12}^* = (1 + r_{12}) = MRS_{12}^*.$$

The Multiperiod Fisher Separation Theorem: A Mathematical Overview

The multiperiod Fisher separation result can be obtained by noting that the individual's problem is

$$\text{maximize } u(c_0, c_1, \ldots, c_T)$$

subject to

$$\sum_{t=0}^{T} \frac{c_t}{(1 + r_{0t})^t} = \sum_{t=0}^{T} \frac{x_t}{(1 + r_{0t})^t}$$

and
$$F(x_0, \ldots, x_T) = 0$$

or, equivalently,

$$\text{maximize } L(c, x, \lambda)$$

where $c = (c_0, \ldots, c_T)$, $x = (x_0, \ldots, x_T)$, and $\lambda = (\lambda_1, \lambda_2)$ is the vector of Lagrange multipliers. The Lagrange function, L, is defined by

$$L(c, x, \lambda) = u(c) + \lambda_1 \left[\sum_{t=0}^{T} \frac{x_t}{(1 + r_{0t})^t} - \sum_{t=0}^{T} \frac{c_t}{(1 + r_{0t})^t} \right] + \lambda_2 F(x).$$

The first-order conditions are:

For $t = 0, 1, \ldots, T$

(i)
$$D_t u(c^*) - \lambda_1 \left[\frac{1}{(1 + r_{0t})^t} \right] = 0.$$

For $t = 0, 1, \ldots, T$

(ii)
$$\lambda_1 \left[\frac{1}{(1 + r_{0t})^t} \right] + \lambda_2 D_t F(x^*) = 0.$$

(iii)
$$\sum_{t=0}^{T} \frac{x_t}{(1 + r_{0t})^t} - \sum_{t=0}^{T} \frac{c_t}{(1 + r_{0t})^t} = 0.$$

(iv)
$$F(x) = 0.$$

From (i) it follows that

$$MRS_{st}^* = \frac{D_s u(c^*)}{D_t u(c^*)} = \frac{(1 + r_{0t})^t}{(1 + r_{0s})^s} = (1 + r_{st}).$$

From (ii) it follows that

$$MRT_{st}^* = \frac{D_s F(x^*)}{D_t F(x^*)} = \frac{(1 + r_{0t})^t}{(1 + r_{0s})^s} = (1 + r_{st}).$$

Therefore,

$$MRS_{st}^* = (1 + r_{st}) = MRT_{st}^* \quad \text{for } t, s = 0, 1, \ldots, T \text{ and } t \neq s.$$

Summary

This appendix concludes our review of the theory of the consumer choice problem as applied to the consumption/savings problem. In Chapter 2, we restricted our attention to the two-period case, and the individual made a consumption/savings choice for the present period only. In this appendix, we extended the two-period model to a more general, multiperiod setting. This provided no problems for the theory other than a need to extend the capital market trading line to its multiperiod trading plane equivalent. This trading plane then provided the basis for defining the relationship that must describe interest rates in the term structure where arbitrage profits are not possible.

References

J. R. Hicks, *Value and Capital* (Oxford, England: Oxford University Press, 1939).

F. Lutz, "The Structure of Interest Rates," *Quarterly Journal of Economics* (1940).

Appendix 2B

Axioms of Choice and Utility Maximization

In this appendix, we present four fundamental axioms concerning how individuals make choices and develop a representation of a utility function using indifference curves.[1] The axioms of choice actually are assumptions about the way choices are made that are believed to be "self-evident truths" or "acceptable without verification or proof." The discussion is made as simple as possible in keeping with our need for this material in Chapter 2. We will return to this subject when we introduce uncertainty and add some more axioms needed to support the expected utility maximization principle.

---

[1]Utility theory entered the economics literature over a century ago as a means of explaining consumer behavior. In its early development economists thought utility was, at least in principle, measurable. That is, they believed that a definite number of units of utility could be attached to the consumption of a given quantity of goods or services. Perhaps the most profound statement of this early view of utility theory was *Mathematical Psychics*, by Francis Y. Edgeworth (1881). Latter-day economists have abandoned much of the earlier utility theory doctrine and now use it to explain the behavior of a rational consumer. Specifically, economists no longer suggest that utility is measurable or that comparisons of utilities can be made among different people. Neither do they use utility arguments to support public policy statements. The interested reader will find Stigler's (1966) Chapter 4 an excellent overview of the basic tenets of utility theory and its use in describing a rational consumer.

The axioms of choice that we will need are as follows:[2]

A1. *Comparability:* The decisionmaker is both able and willing to compare and make choices among all available alternatives.

A2. *Transitivity:* This requires the decisionmaker to be consistent in his or her preferences — that is, if A is preferred to B and B is preferred to C, A is also preferred to C if the individual's preferences are transitive.

A3. *Nonsatiety:* This axiom states that, other things equal, an individual always prefers more of any given commodity to less.

A4. *Diminishing marginal utility:* Here we make the commonsense assumption that, other things equal, the more one has of any commodity, the less each successive unit adds to one's total utility or satisfaction.

The first two axioms are in themselves sufficient to enable us to "characterize" an individual's preferences in terms of the maximization of a utility function. Note that the individual need not actually maximize a utility function but only make choices "as if" utility were being maximized.

We will represent an individual's utility function using indifference curves. An *indifference curve* is simply a set of "bundles" of commodities (from which a choice is to be made) that offer the same total utility. Figure 2B.1 contains a "typical" set of indifference curves that in turn are consistent with our four axioms of choice. Each axiom provides the basis for defining the shapes and interpretations of the curves. For example, Axiom A1 (comparability) means that the entire choice space (the upper-right-hand quadrant) technically is filled with indifference curves; that is, the comparability axiom requires that the individual be willing and able to compare *all* possible alternatives. Thus, we can find no point in the choice space that is not on some indifference curve.

Note that as we move up and to the right in Figure 2B.1 (along the arrow), we increase the levels of both c_0 and c_1. According to the Axiom A3 (nonsatiety), this means that utility is increasing as we move in this direction. Thus, as we move away from the origin the level of utility is increasing with each successive indifference curve we intersect.

Axiom A2 (transitivity) rules out the possibility of indifference curves intersecting. Consider the two indifference curves in Figure 2B.2. Observe that the individual is indifferent between consumption bundles A and B and also between

---

[2]In addition to the axioms stated here, a technical assumption regarding continuity is frequently included. This assumption can be stated as follows: For all bundles a in the consumption set, the set of bundles c such that c is preferred or indifferent to a and the set of bundles a such that a is preferred or indifferent to c are closed. That is, these sets include their boundary points. This assumption is technical but also intuitive, because it says that if a is preferred to c, any bundle b sufficiently close to a is also preferred to c.

Figure 2B.1   Indifference Curves

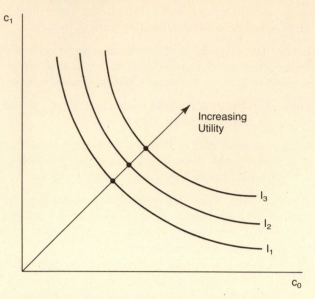

Figure 2B.2   Transitivity and Nonintersecting Indifference Curves

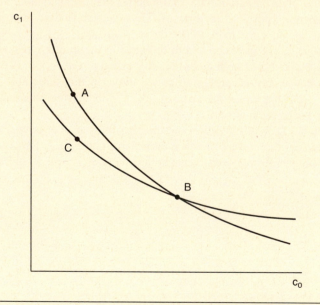

Figure 2B.3   Diminishing Marginal Utility

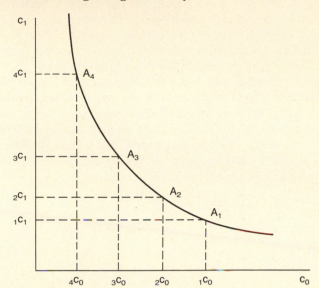

B and C; therefore, if the individual's choices are transitive, he or she should be indifferent between A and C. We see that where the indifference curves intersect the choices are not transitive, for the individual actually prefers consumption bundle A to C.

Next, consider the indifference curve in Figure 2B.3. This figure illustrates the convexity of the indifference curves, which in turn reflects diminishing marginal utility. Diminishing marginal utility occurs where the increased consumption of a good or service (that is, current consumption) provides the individual with smaller and smaller increases in total satisfaction or utility. Note that as the individual moves from consumption bundle A_1 to A_2 to A_3, equal amounts of current consumption are being substituted for increasing amounts of future consumption in order to maintain the same level of utility. This phenomenon reflects the fact that total current consumption is declining and thus becoming more "dear," while future consumption is increasing and, due to diminishing marginal utility, becoming less dear.

In closing this brief overview of the axioms underlying the utility maximization principle, let us note the following caveats. First, we have presented an axiomatic set sufficient to define an "ordinal" utility function. In other words, the indifference curves we have developed using the four axioms of choice allow us to rank choices (bundle A is preferred to B, which is preferred to C, and so forth), but they do not permit us to say by how *much* one bundle is better than another to which it is preferred. To use an analogy, if we had an "ordinal" road map of the state of Texas, we would be able to determine that Dallas is further from Austin than Waco. However, we would be unable to say that it is roughly twice as far; this would require a "cardinal" map. For our purposes here, an ordinal function is sufficient. Note that for mathematical tractability we have used cardinal utility functions in the example problems in Chapter 2 (such as $u(c_0, c_1) = c_0^2 c_1$). This leads us directly to our second caveat, which relates to the need for additional axioms for dealing with the problem of choice under uncertainty. Where outcomes are not known with certainty, the utility of the final outcome cannot be known at the time the choice is made. In this instance, we add a set of axioms to those discussed here that will allow us to characterize an individual's choices under uncertainty "as if" he or she were maximizing the "expected utility of the outcomes." We review the choice problem under uncertainty in Chapter 7.

Chapter 3

Corporate Financial Decisionmaking

Businesses can be organized in a variety of ways, including sole proprietorship, general partnership, limited partnership, joint venture, and corporation. However, the corporate form is by far the most important in terms of the total dollar value of assets involved. For this reason we devote this chapter to introducing the special problems of "corporate" finance. Throughout this and all subsequent chapters, the terms *firm* and *business* will refer to a corporation when used without reference to a specific organizational form.

Before we proceed further, we should note that although we do identify the problems of corporate finance in this chapter, we also show that in a world of certainty, where markets are competitive, transactions are costless, and there are no taxes, many of these problems simply do not arise. Specifically, we demonstrate that in the ideal setting used here the corporation's financing decisions do not affect its value. Hence, financing decisions are irrelevant where the objective in choosing among financing alternatives is to maximize the value of the firm's equity (that is, the owners' wealth). This means that when we discuss, for example, the choice of value-maximizing debt/equity financing mix or the determination of the optimal dividend payout ratio, we will find that neither choice is of any consequence to the firm's stockholders. We study these *irrelevance results* not because they provide the final word on the importance of the financing choices faced by every business firm but because they offer a theoretical structure that we can later expand to include uncertainty, taxes, and transactions costs. In doing so, we will find that these "unproblems" in a certain world are indeed worthy of consideration in the milieu in which firms actually operate.

The Corporate Form of Organization

A corporation, in the words of Chief Justice Marshall, "is an artificial being, invisible, intangible, and existing only in the contemplation of the law."[1] Thus, the corporation exists as a legal entity that is separate and apart from its owners. In brief, the corporate form of organization has the following important attributes:

1.   Corporations can have many owners.

2.   The owner's legal liability is limited to the amount of the investment in the corporation.

3.   Ownership rights can be transferred.

4.   The corporation is regarded as a separate legal person.

5.   Corporations may be managed by individuals who are not owners themselves but act as agents for the owners.

Thus, a corporation is a separate legal entity that raises money by selling shares of stock to investors, who become the legal owners of the firm, and by borrowing money from creditors via the sale of bonds. Professional — frequently nonowner — managers direct the corporation's financial affairs by (1) selecting the real/productive investments it undertakes (the investment decision), (2) determining the mix of bonds and stock that it should sell in order to finance its investments (the financing decision), and (3) setting the firm's policy with regard to the payment of dividends to its owners (the dividend policy decision).

At this point, we note the fundamental issues that arise in the theory of corporate finance. The first relates to the fact that corporations are owned by many shareholders, each of whom has individual time preferences for consumption. Thus, a potential problem in corporate decisionmaking is that decisions must be "unanimously" preferred by all owners. We will show that the Fisher separation theorem and value maximization play key roles in the solution to this problem. Second, corporations, especially large ones, are generally *not* managed by their owners. This gives rise to what financial theorists call a *principal-agent problem*. In other words, managers (agents) must make decisions about which investments to undertake and how to finance them. Presumably they make these choices in the best interests of the firm's owners (principals). However, the fact that their own best interests may not always coincide with the owners' means that they have an incentive not to make the choices preferred by the owners. Third, as we noted in Chapter 2, the Fisher separation theorem states that present value or wealth-maximizing choices will be preferred by all individuals regardless of their specific time preferences for consumption. Thus, the third fundamental problem we address in the theory of corporate finance involves evaluating the impact of the firm's investment, financing, and dividend policy decisions on its value, that is, the value of the owners' and creditors' interests in the firm. Finally, since shares of a corporation's stock as well as its bonds can be sold or transferred, we will ad-

---

[1]Chief Justice John Marshall set forth the legal definition of a corporation in *The Trustees of Dartmouth College v. Woodward*, 4 Wheaton 636 (1819).

dress the basic issues involved in security valuation. In Chapter 4, we expand this discussion to a multiperiod setting but retain the basic assumptions made in the previous two chapters: competitive capital markets, no transactions costs, no taxes, and certainty.

Organization of This Chapter

Our discussion progresses as follows: First, we treat the multiple-owner or group utility function problem that frequently arises with the corporate form of organization. Next, we overview the principal-agent problem as it pertains to the corporation. Then we discuss the financing and investment choices corporate managers make in the context of the single-period choice model developed earlier.

Optimal Financial Decisions with Multiple Owners

In our earlier discussion of the consumer choice problem, we described the consumption decision as that of selecting, from among alternative intertemporal consumption opportunities, the one to which no other is preferred, that is, the one that maximizes the decisionmaker's utility for present and future consumption. With the corporate form of organization, however, there are potentially many owners, each having his or her own set of intertemporal consumption preferences. If these preferences could somehow be combined into a single utility function, we could use the same procedure as in Chapter 2 to determine the optimal set of real investment decisions and an optimal time pattern of consumption for a single individual. However, as we next demonstrate, combining individual preferences to obtain a group preference or utility function generally is not possible.

Describing Group Preferences: The Problem[2]

Some serious difficulties arise when we attempt to construct group utility functions (commonly referred to as *welfare functions*). Consider the following example. The Alpha Corporation is owned by three individuals, A, B, and C, each of whom controls one-third of its common stock. The firm currently has three investment opportunities, X, Y, and Z, from which it can select only one. Each owner has been asked to rank the three choices in order of his or her own preference:

	A	B	C
Choice 1	X	Y	Z
Choice 2	Y	Z	X

---

[2]For a more complete discussion, see Arrow (1963), who addresses this problem in the context of his "impossibility theorem." Very simply, Arrow provided a fundamental result of social choice theory: Any social decision rule must violate at least one of the axioms of rational choice that he set forth. The voting paradox was known in the eighteenth century. It was developed by the Marquis de Condorcet in his *Essai sur l'application de l'analyze à la probabilité des décisions rendues à la pluralité des voix* (Paris, 1785).

Management is now left with the problem of assimilating these preferences and arriving at a single selection that will best reflect the desires of the three owners. They might, for example, decide to follow a majority rule on project acceptance. Thus, in comparing project X with project Y, both A and C prefer X to Y. In comparing X with Z, both B and C prefer Z to X. If the owners' preferences are consistent—that is, transitive—we would expect the following: Since X is preferred to Y and Z is preferred to X, Z should be preferred to Y. However, when Y and Z are compared using the majority rule, it appears that the rankings are inconsistent: Both A and B state that they prefer Y to Z, whereas the inference from majority rule would be that Z is preferred to Y.

To summarize, there is no easy way to combine individuals' preferences into a global utility function that can be used to make decisions in the *best* interests of all concerned.[3] As we shall see, however, the investment and consumption decisions can, where the Fisher separation theorem holds, be partitioned into two components, allowing the problem of multiple owners to be avoided.

The Fisher Separation Theorem and the Market Value Principle (NPV Rule): The Solution

One solution to the multiple-owner/group utility function problem involves the use of the market value principle, or net present value (NPV) rule, where Fisher separation holds: When capital markets are competitive and there are no transactions costs (such that borrowing and lending rates are the same), we can prescribe a decision rule whose choices will be unanimously preferred by all shareholders. This is true even though the owners' intertemporal consumption preferences may be quite different. We will demonstrate this result with an example.

The Corporate Investment Decision with Multiple Owners: An Example.
Consider the real investment opportunities faced by Bangles Corporation, depicted in Figure 3.1. Bangles has $w_0 = \$100,000$ available to invest in the current period and faces a set of investments offering diminishing marginal rates of return, as evidenced in the concave investment opportunity set. If this were the investment choice problem faced by an individual, the Fisher separation theorem would indicate that $20,000 should be invested in real assets. This investment choice would serve to maximize the NPV of real investment, which in turn would maximize the individual's set of available consumption opportunities (w_0^*, w_1^*). In the example in Figure 3.1, $(w_0^*, w_1^*) = (\$127,000, \$139,700)$. The same is true with multiple owners, and it is this fact that allows us to "circumvent" the group utility function problem.

Assume that Bangles Corporation has only two shareholders, A and B, each of whom owns one-half of its stock. Thus, the investment decision made by Bangles' manager using the net present value rule provides a *wealth increment* to each stockholder equal to $(w_0^* - w_0)/2$, or $(\$127,000 - \$100,000)/2 = \$13,500$, such that each one's *current wealth* equals $\$127,000/2 = \$63,500$. Since the in-

---

[3]There are circumstances under which this problem can be solved; for example see Wilson (1968).

Figure 3.1   Real Investment Opportunity Set Faced by Bangles Corporation
Borrowing = Lending rate = 10%.
Initial endowment = w_0 = $100,000.

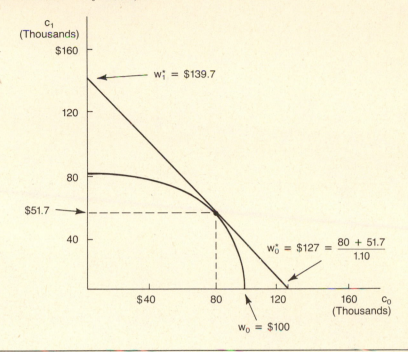

vestment choice maximizes the NPV available from real investment, it also maximizes the increment to shareholder wealth provided by investing in real assets. In other words, the NPV of the optimal investment decision equals $(w_0^* - w_0)$, which in turn is the largest such increment to shareholder wealth that can be attained by engaging in real investment. After the NPV-maximizing investment decision has been made, each stockholder can seek to maximize his or her own utility for consumption by using the capital market to borrow or lend. The reason for this is the following: By making the value-maximizing investment choice, the individual's wealth (ability to consume) is maximized. The key element here is the "separability" of the investment and consumption decisions, or the Fisher separation theorem.

Figure 3.2 depicts the optimal consumption choices for A and B. A's preference for current consumption (panel a) is such that he chooses to consume $40,000 today, leaving $25,850 = ($63,500 − $40,000)(1.10) for next year's consumption. B's optimal consumption choice (panel b) will entail consuming $20,000 in the current period and $47,900 in the next. The beauty of this solution to the consumer choice problem is that *one* investment choice provides both investors with the maximum set of consumption opportunities. Thus, the individual consumption preferences of Bangles Corporation's shareholders has had *no* bearing on the optimal investment choice. Recall, however, that this solution to the multiple-owner problem requires that Fisher separation hold. This, in turn, re-

Figure 3.2   Consumption Choices for the Owners of Bangles Corporation

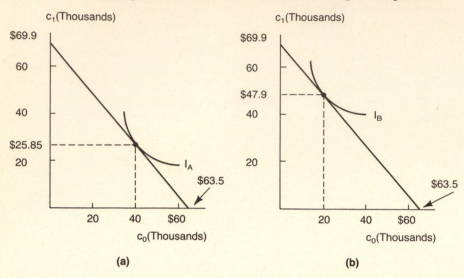

(a)   (b)

quires that there be no transactions costs — in effect, equal borrowing and lending rates — and competitive capital markets.

As a practical matter, the optimal investment choice is unlikely to change drastically with the presence of transactions costs. Thus, although Fisher separation does not hold exactly, it may provide a reasonable approximation.

Nonowner Managers and the Principal-Agent Problem

Earlier in this chapter, we alluded to the possibility that owners and managers of corporations may not always agree on which investments to undertake and which methods to use to finance them. In this setting, the owner is the principal and the manager acts as her agent. If the manager is a utility-maximizing individual and his personal utility is affected by an investment/financing choice in a different way than the owner's utility, then, to the extent that the manager is free to deviate from owner preferences, he will do so. This is the commonsense notion behind the principal-agent problem. Jensen and Meckling (1976) summarize this problem as follows:

We define an agency relationship as a contract under which one or more persons (the principal[s]) engage another person (the agent) to perform some service on their behalf which involves delegating some decision making authority to the agent. If both parties to the relationship are utility maximizers there is good reason to believe that the agent will not always act in the best interests of the principal. (p. 308)

To alleviate this agency problem, the owner must engage in monitoring activities designed to limit the manager/agent's ability to deviate from owner-utility-maximizing decisions. Note, however, that in a world of complete certainty and no transactions costs, the owner can costlessly monitor agent activity. This means that the agent is *not* free to vary his choices from those that would maximize the owner's utility. Thus, the principal-agent issue does not arise in the theory of corporate finance under certainty.

We will return to the principal-agent problem again in Part IV after we have introduced uncertainty. Specifically, we will consider the impact of the principal-agent problem on the firm's investment (Chapter 16) and financing decisions (Chapters 12 through 14) in general and specifically with respect to mergers and acquisitions (Chapter 18) and lease financing (Chapter 19). We will conclude this brief overview of the issue by again noting that in a world of certainty, where everyone — managers and owners alike — is fully aware of one another's actions as well as their consequences, owners can "costlessly" monitor agent behavior. Therefore, *in a world of complete certainty,* agents can be costlessly compelled to make owner-utility-maximizing (present-value-maximizing) investment and financing decisions.[4]

---

[4]A corollary to this inference from a world of perfect information was made by Fama (1980). He proposed that properly functioning labor markets for managers would minimize agency costs. Once again this requires reliable information about manager performance. To the extent that this information is expensive to obtain, Fama's labor market argument is restricted.

An Institutional Note: Master Limited Partnerships As an Alternative to the Corporation

The corporate form of organization has long been dominant in the U.S. economy. The advantages of the corporation include limited liability for the owners, continuity of life, and transferability of ownership. These advantages have served to outweigh the significant disadvantage of two tax layers associated with the corporation: taxes on its income and personal taxes paid by the stockholders on dividends received and on any capital gains from the sale of their shares.[a] Recently, however, a new form of organization has come into being which offers many of the advantages of the corporation but not its disadvantage of double layers of taxation: the master limited partnership (MLP). The MLP offers limited liability and easy trans-

---

[a]An excellent discussion of the tax advantages of the MLP over the corporation can be found in Collins and Bey (1986).

fer of partnership units, which are frequently traded on major stock exchanges.[b] Beginning with the formation of the Apache Petroleum MLP in 1981, more than 90 such organizations have been formed, predominantly by oil and gas firms. The primary explanation of this phenomenon has been the removal of the corporate layer of taxation and corresponding increase in cash flow to the investors. However, the motives for forming MLPs may be more than simple tax reduction. By "spinning off" or "selling off" a productive asset, the parent firm may achieve a higher value for the asset than could be achieved by retaining it under the corporate umbrella.[c] To understand the rationale for this statement we must delve into the "theory of the firm" literature, which addresses the issues surrounding the choice of an organizational form.

In the modern theory of the firm literature, a firm is defined as a "nexus of contracts." These contracts define the relationships among the various stakeholders involved in the firm, including the owners, creditors, suppliers, employees, and various government units.[d] Thus, one organizational form can be distinguished from another by the general parameters of the contracts among the participants. For example, in the corporate form of organization, managers are given broad discretion over operating matters and the decision to retain and reinvest or pay out corporate cash flow to the stockholders. With the MLP, however, management's discretionary control over the assets of the partnership is restricted and in some cases virtually eliminated.[e]

---

[b]Active trading of limited partnership units need not necessarily jeopardize the tax status of the partnership. The tax code allows a duly constituted limited partnership to be treated as such, as long as it does not have more of the characteristics of a corporation than of a partnership. Specifically, the determination is made based on the following four questions (see 26CFR 301.7701–2):

- Does the partnership have continuity of life?
- Is there centralization of management in the partnership?
- Is there limited liability for all members of the partnership?
- Do all partners have free transferability of partnership interests?

If the answer is yes to more than two of the above questions, the partnership is taxed as a corporation. Note that the favored tax treatment of MLPs has not gone unchallenged. In 1984 the Treasury Department proposed that all partnerships with more than 35 partners be treated as a corporation for tax purposes. The proposal was not included in either the 1985 or 1986 tax bills.

[c]In a "spinoff," the assets placed in the MLP are *given* to the shareholders of the firm forming the MLP, whereas in a "selloff," the formation of the MLP constitutes a divestiture of the assets used to form the MLP. The selloff therefore involves the sale of a portion of the firm's interest in the MLP's assets to a new set of investors, thereby replacing the assets used to form the MLP with the cash proceeds generated by the sale of limited partnership units. MLPs have been both spinoffs and selloffs. For a review of the spinoff literature see Schipper and Smith (1983) and Hite and Owers (1983). A review of the selloff or divestiture literature can be found in Alexander, Benson, and Kampmeyer (1984).

[d]This notion of the firm was formulated by Williamson (1981).

[e]Management of the MLP can have widely different degrees of discretionary control over the cash flows of the partnership. For example, in Mesa Limited Partners II the general partner, Mesa Petroleum, was able to use the cash flows of the partnership to acquire shares of stock in other companies, including Unocal and later KN Energy, in takeover attempts. At the other end of the spectrum is McCormick Oil and Gas and Petroleum Investments, which are contractually committed to paying 100 percent of their cash flow out to their limited partners. For the 12 MLPs analyzed in Stanger (1985), the average cash distribution was 86 percent, including only two firms that were contractually committed to paying out all of their cash flow.

What distinguishes this view of the firm from the traditional (neoclassical) microeconomist's view is the "discretionary control" that the manager of the firm exercises over its assets. The traditional notion of the firm is constructed using assumptions that effectively reduce the role of management to that of an automaton that instantly and costlessly responds to market forces with optimal (profit maximizing) choices. The neoclassical theory of the firm assumes the use of "classical" contracts, which Williamson defines as "fully specified" for the rights and obligations of all the parties involved, in all future states of the world, and which can be costlessly written, monitored, and enforced. If we add to this scenario the assumption that managers can costlessly acquire information needed to make their decisions, the role of the manager/entrepreneur is merely to "solve" for the optimal resource combinations to use in each production/marketing opportunity encountered. This means that the firm has no need to contract in advance for resources or to carry inventories of raw materials or financial resources. In short, the firm is merely a set of costlessly monitored and enforced performance contracts.

The world is obviously more complex than is suggested by the neoclassical theory of the firm. Information must be gathered at a cost and processed by professional managers. Contracts must specify the rights and duties of all parties (if only incompletely), and contract performance is sometimes left to the court system when irreconcilable differences arise. The decision about the choice of the best organizational form must be made in this more complicated environment, and the corporation must be compared to the MLP in it as well.[f]

Jensen (1986) has posited a theory of mergers and acquisitions based on managerial discretion over corporate cash flows.[g] He argues that managerial discretion over the firm's cash flows in the corporation provides a potential source of conflict of interest between the firm's stockholders and management. In fact, when management utilizes its discretion to allocate those cash flows to uses that are not in the shareholder's best interest, there arises a motive for a takeover or challenge to the corporate control. However, the same end can be accomplished by spinning off the cash-producing assets of the firm into an MLP, wherein managerial discretion over cash flow is restricted contractually, such that the shareholders receive them and reinvest them when and where they please. Thus, it can be argued that the formation of MLPs can effectively eliminate the agency cost from managerial discretion over the firm's free cash flow. Consequently the MLP can be an alternative to the takeover market as a means of restructuring the corporation.

MLPs traded on public exchanges in the United States control total assets valued in excess of $10 billion.[h] To date, these organizations have been predomi-

---

[f]The cost of contracting notion of the firm is not new. This approach is credited to Coase (1937). More recently, Hirsch (1979) identifies three basic sources of contracting costs: (1) information-gathering related to discovering potential contracting partners, (2) negotiating and contract-writing, and (3) monitoring compliance with contract terms. These factors provide the basis for "managerial discretion" over the portfolio of assets gathered under the control of the firm by the nexus of contracts that define the firm.

[g]See Jensen (Summer 1986) and (May 1986).

[h]This includes $8.4 billion in oil and gas MLPs and $2.4 billion in real estate MLPs (see Stanger, 1986).

nantly in the oil and gas industry. However, with the current revision of the U.S. tax code, the incentives are now in place for a more widespread use of the MLP as an alternative to the corporation, and, in the case of real estate, MLPs may replace some traditional non-traded limited partnerships.[i] Specifically, the provisions of the 1986 tax law contain three different implications for the use of MLPs:[j]

- The bill eliminates the favorable treatment of capital gains and thus increases the tax liability of the corporation at the time of the transfer of the asset to the MLP. The impact is minimized, however, by virtue of the reduction of the maximum corporate tax rate from 46 percent to 34 percent. Thus, although the alternative capital gains tax rate of 28 percent is no longer applicable, any gain realized at the time of the conversion to the MLP is taxed at a maximum of 34 percent.

- The tax code tightens the tax deductibility of partnership losses; they can only be used (except in limited cases) to offset other "passive" investment income and cannot be used to offset personal income. This could pose a problem for newly formed MLPs, which provide substantial tax writeoffs for the limited partners, who must seek other passive income against which to offset those losses or carry them forward to offset future partnership income. This certainly would reduce the value of some MLPs and reduce the tax advantage of forming some. However, for those cases where the assets involved in the MLP provide relatively large cash flows, and consequently taxable income, this provision of the tax code is of little consequence.

- The third change in the tax law with importance for the desirability of forming an MLP is the reduction of personal and corporate taxes and, more importantly, the reduction of the maximum personal tax rate (28 percent) below the maximum corporate tax rate (34 percent). What this means is that the corporation would not be able to distribute the same aftertax cash flow to its shareholders that they could as limited partners in an MLP managing the same assets.

With respect to this last point, Collins and Bey (1986) note that the cash flow from a corporation and an MLP are equal only if the following condition holds:

$$\frac{\text{RE}}{\text{EBT}} = \frac{t_c}{t_p}(1 - t_p),$$

where RE represents the earnings retained and reinvested either by the corporation or the limited partner, EBT is earnings before taxes, t_c is the corporate tax rate,

---

[i]MLPs have been formed using assets spanning such diverse areas as equipment leasing (Airlease Ltd.) to cattle feeding (Win-Tex II Cattle Feeders).

[j]In the discussion that follows we will ignore the "transition rules" for tax rates applicable to 1987 and refer instead to the rates applicable to 1988, when the tax revision becomes fully effective (see *Summary of Conference Agreement on H.R. 3838* (Tax Reform Act of 1986) prepared by the staff of the Joint Committee on Taxation, August 29, 1986, U.S. Government Printing Office).

and t_p is the personal tax rate. Consequently, with a maximum corporate tax rate of 34 percent and a maximum personal tax rate of 28 percent, the corporate form of organization will provide the same cash flow to its stockholders as the MLP does to its unit holders if the ratio of RE to EBT equals 87.43 percent. However, since the corporation retains aftertax dollars, it must pay 34 percent of its EBT in taxes, leaving a maximum of 66 percent of its EBT available for retention. Consequently, under the circumstance where the maximum corporate tax rate exceeds the maximum personal tax rate, the MLP offers the maximum aftertax cash flow.

Value-Maximizing Corporate Financing Decisions

Corporations finance their investments via the sale of shares of common stock (equity) to investors, who then become its owners, and of bonds (debt) to investors, who then become its creditors. In this section we will demonstrate that in a world of certainty, with a competitive capital market and no transactions costs, the corporation's choice of debt/equity financing mix has *no* effect on the present value of its investments (the value of the firm) or on the wealth of its shareholders (the value of the firm's common shares). Thus, the corporation's financing decisions are irrelevant under these conditions.

We have shown that under the conditions in which Fisher separation holds, the corporation's investment decision can be separated from its owners' consumption choices: The optimal investment decision for all the firm's owners is the one that maximizes the net present value of the firm's investment. This result has allowed us to state the goal of the corporation as one of "maximizing net present value." We will now show that the solution to the firm's investment problem is unaffected by the firm's choice of financing mix for that optimal level of investment. However, before doing this we must introduce the fundamentals of security valuation.

Security Valuation

In general, the value of a security, whether a bond or a share of common stock, equals the present dollar amount that its holder would exchange *today* for the *future* cash flow receipts to which he or she is entitled. Thus, in a certain world, the value of a security is simply the present value of the future cash flow it provides discounted at the risk-free rate, r.

In Figure 3.2, we assumed that A and B each own one-half of the Bangles Corporation. The value of their individual ownership shares of Bangles therefore equals the present dollar sum $63,500 = $69,850/1.10 that they would be willing to exchange for the future dollar sum to which their ownership in Bangles entitles them, that is, ½ × $139,700 = $69,850. Hence, in a world where all future cash flows (dividends) to which owners are entitled is certain, their value can be determined by discounting them back to the present using the risk-free interest rate.

To illustrate firm and security valuation, consider the XYZ Corporation depicted in Figure 3.3. XYZ raises k_0 dollars in equity (through the sale of common

Figure 3.3   XYZ Corporation's Real/Productive Investment Opportunities

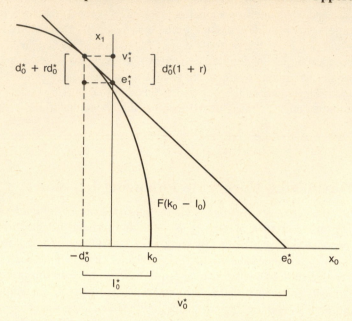

stock) and then d_0 in debt to finance an investment requiring $I_0 = k_0 + d_0$ dollars of funding. Let $x_1 = F(x_0)$ denote the investment frontier for real/productive assets, as shown in Figure 3.3. The firm selects I_0 so as to maximize the present value of the consumption opportunities created by the investment. In Figure 3.3, we see that by investing $I_0^* = k_0 + d_0^*$ dollars the firm receives an end-of-year cash flow of v_1^* dollars. Thus, the present value of the cash flows provided by the firm's optimal investment (v_0^*) is simply

$$v_0^* = \frac{v_1^*}{(1 + r)}.$$

However, since d_0^* dollars plus rd_0^* in interest must be repaid at year's end, the *owners* can look forward to an end-of-year cash flow, e_1^*, equal to

$$e_1^* = v_1^* - (1 + r)d_0^*.$$

Thus, the present value of the cash flow produced by the firm's investment that accrues to the owners is

$$e_0^* = \frac{[v_1^* - d_0^*(1 + r)]}{(1 + r)}$$

or

$$e_0^* = v_0^* - d_0^*.$$

Figure 3.4   Capital Structure Irrelevance

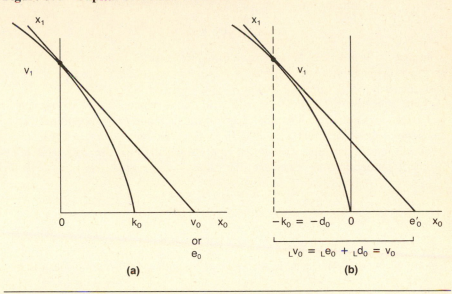

Thus, the value of the firm's equity (e_0^*) equals total firm value (v_0^*) less the value of the firm's debt (d_0^*).

The Debt/Equity Financing Decision

The irrelevance of the firm's financing decision can be demonstrated by showing that maximizing the value of the firm and its equity depends *only* on the investment opportunities it faces and the market rate of interest. Specifically, under the assumptions used here neither total firm value nor equity value is in any way influenced by the particular mix of debt and equity financing the firm selects to finance its optimal level of investment in real assets.

To illustrate, consider the firm depicted in panel a of Figure 3.4. Note that the firm has raised equity funds (k_0) equal to its optimal investment in real assets; that is, $k_0 = I_0^*$. If the firm invests its k_0 dollars in real assets, it will receive an end-of-period cash flow of v_1 dollars. Hence, the value of this *all-equity-financed* or *unlevered* firm is

$$v_0 = \frac{v_1}{(1 + r)},$$

which also equals its equity value, e_0, since it has no debt.

Now consider the following scenario. The firm in panel a of Figure 3.4 decides to finance its investment in real assets with debt rather than equity. To accomplish this, the firm issues $d_0 = k_0$ dollars in capital market notes requiring an end-of-period payment of $(1 + r)d_0$. The firm then pays a cash dividend of k_0 dollars to its common stockholders. The unlevered firm in panel a has now been transformed into the levered firm depicted in panel b. The value of the "levered" firm $(_LV_0)$ is as follows:

$$_LV_0 = {}_Le_0 + d_0.$$

Note that the firm's need to issue capital market notes to finance its k_0^* dollars in real investment "shifts" the vertical (x_1) axis $k_0 = d_0$ dollars to the right. Otherwise, panel b is the same as panel a.

  In brief, the firm's decision to use all debt financing for its investment in real assets does not affect either the shape of the real investment opportunity set or the slope of the capital market trading line. Thus, the optimal level of real investment will remain the same, as with all equity financing, and the total value of the firm will not be affected. Therefore, the value of the levered firm is

$$_LV_0 = {}_Le_0 + d_0$$

$$= \frac{v_1}{(1 + r)},$$

which, of course, is the same as the value of the unlevered firm $(v_0 = e_0)$; that is,

(3.1) $$_LV_0 = v_0 = e_0.$$

Note that since the value of the levered firm equals the value of the equity of an unlevered firm $(_LV_0 = e_0)$ and also the sum of the levered equity value and the value of the firm's debt $(_LV_0 = {}_Le_0 + d_0)$, $e_0 > {}_Le_0$. Does this mean that the shareholders of the unlevered firm are "better off" than they would be if the firm were levered? The answer is no, since the levered firm's owners not only have shares worth $_Le_0$ dollars but also receive a cash dividend of $k_0 = d_0$ dollars. Thus, regardless of how the firm's real investments are financed, the shareholders have the same current wealth — that is, $e_0 = {}_Le_0 + k_0 = {}_Le_0 + d_0 = {}_LV_0$ — and consequently face the same set of consumption opportunities. For the unlevered firm, the consumption opportunity set is as follows:

$$c_1 = (e_0 - c_0)(1 + r);$$

correspondingly, for the levered firm it is

$$_Lc_1 = (_Le_0 + k_0 - c_0)(1 + r).$$

But since $e_0 = {}_Le_0 + k_0$,

$$_Lc_1 = c_1.$$

Thus, shareholders are indeed "indifferent" as to how the firm finances its investment in real assets.

Value-Maximizing Corporate Dividend Policy

Using an analysis very similar to that in the previous section, we can assess the impact of a firm's dividend policy on firm value and, consequently, on the present value of the owners' consumption opportunity set. We will find that the payment

Figure 3.5   Corporate Dividend Policy and Firm Value

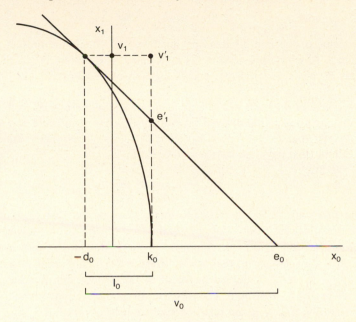

of a cash dividend in the current period neither enhances nor detracts from that set of consumption opportunities; hence, dividend policy is irrelevant.

In a single-period model, the corporate dividend decision involves determining what portion of the firm's available equity resources (k_0) should be paid to its shareholders in dividends and, consequently, what portion should be retained and used to help finance its optimal investment in real assets.

Dividend Irrelevance: Theory

Once again let k_0 represent the resources supplied to the firm by its owners and let the firm's optimal investment outlay be $I_0 = d_0 + k_0$ as depicted in Figure 3.5. First, suppose that the firm pays no dividend. In this case d_0 dollars must be raised from sources outside the firm, since k_0 is available from reinvested earnings within the firm and $d_0 = I_0 - k_0$. Debt was used in the previous example; however, since financing mix does not impact on firm value, either debt or equity could be used. The value of the non-dividend-paying firm is, therefore,

$$v_0 = \frac{v_1}{(1 + r)}$$

or, equivalently,

$$v_0 = \frac{v_1 - e_1}{(1 + r)} + \frac{e_1}{(1 + r)},$$

which we recognize as simply

$$v_0 = d_0 + e_0.$$

Thus, the value of the non-dividend-paying firm (v_0) equals the present value of the future cash flow (v_1) provided by its investment of I_0 dollars in real/productive assets. This in turn, by definition, equals the sum of its equity (e_0) and debt (d_0) values.

Now consider the case where a dividend of k_0 dollars is paid to the current shareholders. To finance the optimal investment (I_0), the firm must now raise the entire I_0 dollars (that is, $I_0 = d_0 + k_0$) from outside sources. These funds, once raised, will require a payment next period equal to

(3.2) $(1 + r)(d_0 + k_0) = v_1' - e_1';$

that is, the difference in the investment's total end-of-period cash flow of v_1' dollars and the residual cash flow that goes to the firm's current (old) owners (e_1') is, *by definition,* the sum paid to the suppliers of the I_0 dollars in funds used to finance the firm's investment in real assets. If the entire I_0 dollars is raised via the sale of equity, the end-of-period payment to these new shareholders will be $(1 + r)I_0$. Note that in a world of complete certainty, the new shareholders will be content to earn the risk-free rate just like bondholders.

Solving for v_1' in Equation 3.2 and then present valuing it to find v_0', we obtain

$$v_0' = d_0 + k_0 + \frac{e_1'}{(1 + r)}.$$

Noting in Figure 3.5 that $e_1'/(1 + r)$ is the increase in equity value resulting from the firm's investment in real assets (that is, $e_0 - k_0$),

$$v_0' = d_0 + k_0 + e_0 - k_0.$$

Hence,

$$v_0' = d_0 + e_0$$

or

$$v_0' = v_0.$$

Therefore, the value of the firm that paid no dividends (v_0) equals the value of the dividend-paying firm (v_0'), and dividend policy does not affect its value. Note too that the shareholder's current wealth given no dividend is e_0 while it is $[k_0 + (e_0 - k_0)]$ given a k_0 dollar dividend and a capital gain (appreciation in equity value resulting from the optimal investment decision) of $e_0 - k_0$.

Stated very simply, the reason dividend policy does not affect firm value and shareholder wealth is as follows: *For every dollar paid in dividends today, the firm must raise a dollar from the sale of stock. These new shares of stock require a future payment of $(1 + r)$ dollars per dollar of equity issued. Thus, when the firm's ini-*

tial stockholders receive $1 in dividends, they give up $(1 + r) in end-of-period cash flow that has a present value of $1.

Exercise 3.1: Irrelevance of Corporate Dividend Policy— The Case of No Cash Dividends

Recall from Figure 3.1 that the Bangles Corporation, with an initial endowment of $100,000, determined that its optimal investment in real assets consisted of $20,000, offering a net present value to its two stockholders (A and B) of $27,000. Consider now the consequences of Bangles paying *no* cash dividends to its two stockholders in the current period.

Given Bangles Corporation's investment decision and its dividend policy, what are the consumption opportunities provided to each of the firm's shareholders (they each own half the firm's stock), where borrowing and lending can take place in the capital market at a rate of 10 percent?

Solution. If Bangles Corporation pays no cash dividends, it will invest $20,000 in real assets and $80,000 in capital market notes (buy bonds) earning 10 percent. This means that Bangles will provide its owners with a total of $139,700 = $51,700 + $88,000 in consumption opportunities *next* period and zero this period. However, assume that A wants to consume *all* of his wealth in the current period. This poses no problem, since the capital market can be used to convert future income into current income, and vice versa. A can do one of two things: He can borrow, using his share of the corporation's income next period to repay the loan, or he can sell his ownership interest in Bangles to someone else. In a world in which all present and future cash flows are known with complete certainty, A can produce the same current consumption opportunity in either case; that is, if he borrows using his share of the corporation's next-period cash flow ($69,850 = $139,700/2) for repayment, he can borrow a total of $63,500 = $69,850/1.10. Note that A can borrow at the risk-free rate of 10 percent, since in a world with complete certainty the future cash flow earned by Bangles is *risk free*. Thus, even where Bangles decides to pay zero dividends, A can enjoy the same set of consumption opportunities.

Alternatively, A can choose to sell his stock in Bangles. The question then arises as to how much he can expect to receive for his one-half interest in the firm. Since the firm provides a *certain* cash flow of $139,700 and the holder of 50 percent of the firm receives one-half of that cash flow *with certainty*, A should accept nothing less than the present value of that certain cash flow discounted at the risk-free rate. Hence, the value of A's shares is $63,500 = $69,850/1.10. An important observation here is that under the assumptions we have made (including complete certainty and no transactions costs), equity and debt securities are perfect substitutes and therefore should command the same rate of return (that is, the risk-free rate).

Exercise 3.2: Irrelevance of Corporate Dividend Policy— The Case of Cash Dividend Payments

The Bangles Corporation determined its optimal investment in real assets to be $20,000 (Figure 3.1). Given the firm's initial endowment of $100,000, this left $80,000 that was not invested in real assets. In Exercise 3.1 we assumed that this $80,000 was invested in capital market notes. Consider now the possibility of paying an immediate cash dividend to the firm's two stockholders (A and B—each owns one-half the firm's stock) totaling $80,000.

1. What are the consumption opportunities provided by Bangles to its stockholders?

Solution.   Recall that Bangles' $20,000 investment in real assets provides its shareholders with the same $51,700 in next-period cash flow. This cash flow has a present value of $47,000 = $51,700/1.10, providing a net present value of $27,000 = $47,000 − 20,000. In addition, Bangles' shareholders now receive an $80,000 cash dividend, producing a total firm value—that is, a total contribution to shareholder wealth—of $127,000. Hence, it is no surprise that A and B, who can borrow and lend at the risk-free rate of 10 percent, can reproduce the same consumption opportunity sets that they faced with zero dividends. In other words, A can consume $63,500 = $127,000/2 today, or any fraction thereof, in conjunction with lending (buying bonds) the remainder to produce the same consumption opportunities set depicted in Figure 3.2 as well as the set that was produced where no dividends were paid (Exercise 3.1).

2. Discuss why corporate dividend policy does not affect shareholders' consumption opportunities.

Solution.   Under the assumptions of no transactions costs, competitive markets, and certainty, we have found that firm dividend policy is of little concern to shareholders. This resulted from the simple fact that shareholders can *costlessly* produce any pattern of cash payments (pseudo–cash dividends) they desire by buying or selling capital market notes or perfect substitutes in the form of equity shares.

Summary

The corporate form of organization is the most prominent business form in the theory of finance. The corporation is unique in that it is a legal entity separate and distinct from its many owners, issues bonds and stock that are transferable from one individual to another, and is managed by professionals who are not necessarily owners. These attributes shape the study of "corporate" finance. The problems associated with the corporate form of organization include (1) choosing a decision rule that is unanimously preferred by all owners, (2) providing a set of incentives for corporate managers to make decisions consistent with the owners' best interests, and (3) determining the value of the corporation's securities.

In this chapter we introduced and discussed the fundamental issues in the theory of corporate finance under conditions of certainty, competitive capital markets, no taxes, and no transactions costs. This overview helped define the issues in the simplest of settings. The results of our introductory analysis can be summarized as follows:

1. Where Fisher separation holds, net present value (or value) maximization provides a decision rule that is unanimously preferred by all stockholders.

2. In a world of certainty, the actions of corporate managers are apparent to everyone, including stockholders, thus obligating management to make NPV-maximizing decisions.

3. Neither the firm's financing nor its dividend policy decisions has any impact on shareholder well-being; that is, both are nonissues in the theory of corporate finance under certainty.

4. The value of a corporation's securities is the present value of the anticipated cash payments to the security holders discounted at the risk-free rate of interest.

Study Questions

3.1 "Corporations, by their unique characteristics, pose a unique set of problems for the financial theorist." Discuss.

3.2 The principal-agent problem does not arise in the theory of corporate finance under certainty and where there are no transactions costs. Why?

3.3 Illustrate the irrelevance of corporate financial structure using a two-period consumption model.

3.4 Firm X has equity valued at $200,000 after making the optimal investment decision, as depicted in the following figure:

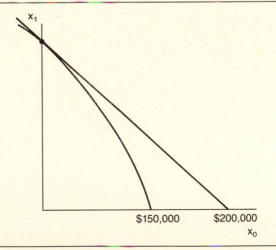

Firm Y's investment opportunities are identical to firm X's, and it too has $150,000 in cash. However, firm Y pays its shareholders a cash dividend of $100,000. What is the value of firm Y's equity? Which set of stockholders is better off?

3.5   Firm Z faces the same set of investment opportunities as firms X and Y in Question 3.4. However, it pays a cash dividend of $150,000 to its shareholders and borrows the $150,000 needed to finance its real investments at an interest rate of r. What is the value of firm Z? What is the value of its equity?

Study Problems

3.1   Using the diagram below, identify each of the following items:
  a. The optimal (utility-maximizing) level of real investment, I_0^*
  b. The future cash flow from real investment, x_1^*
  c. The present value of the optimal real investment cash flow
  d. The net present value of the optimal real investment level
  e. The internal rate of return for the optimal real investment level
  f. The marginal rate of return on the last dollar invested in real assets
  g. The increase in wealth due to the real/productive investment decision
  h. The optimal consumption pair, c^*

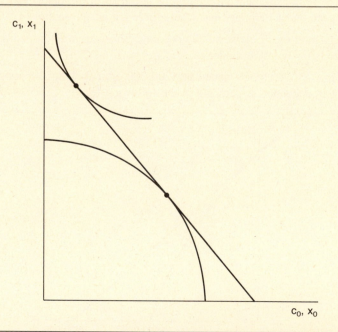

*3.2   ABC Corporation has \$100,000 in cash to invest in various projects. The outcome (in thousands), x_1, next period that results from investing $100 - x_0$ (in thousands) this period is given by $x_1 = 108 - 1.04x_0 - .0004x_0^2$. All investors can borrow or lend freely at a rate of 6 percent per period.

  a. Find the optimal level of investment for ABC Corporation.

  b. Find the current value of ABC.

  c. The utility function of ABC's owner is given by $u(c_0, c_1) = c_0c_1$, where c_i denotes consumption in period i. Find the owner's optimal consumption bundle (c_0^*, c_1^*).

3.3   Assume that the investment in Problem 3.1 is undertaken by a corporation with no cash on hand (new, startup firm) that finances it entirely with borrowed funds on which it must pay interest at a rate of r. What is the value of the "post-investment" firm? Of its equity? If the investment were financed by a new equity issue, would your answer be altered? If so, how?

3.4   Alpha Corporation has k_0 dollars in earnings available at the present time. Show that if the firm pays $k_0/2$ in dividends now, the current shareholders' consumption opportunities will be the same as they would if zero dividends were paid.

*3.5   XYZ Corporation has the same amount of cash and the same investment opportunity set as ABC Corporation in Problem 3.2. However, XYZ decides to pay \$50,000 in dividends this period. It will still invest the optimal amount in real assets. Any financing required will be at 6 percent. What amount will XYZ be able to return to its owner next period? Find the current value of XYZ.

3.6   Ambling Manufacturing Company has a real/productive investment opportunity set that exhibits diminishing marginal rates of return. The firm currently has w_0 dollars in funds with which to finance new investment and can borrow and lend at the market rate of r. The company is wholly owned by three sisters who inherited it from their father, who had founded it around 1900. Each fall the firm's management addresses the owners as to their investment and financing plans for the coming year. This year is unique, because the owners have decided to dissolve the firm after one more year of operations. Management has suggested that the firm invest all its available funds in real assets and borrow no more funds since the company will be liquidated in one year. Emmy Ambling disagrees with this plan, stating that "We are going to liquidate the company next year anyway, so let's put all our money in the capital market now so that the firm will automatically dissolve when the notes mature in one year." Ethel Ambling is not sure that the firm should invest any money in

_____

*Problems denoted with an asterisk (*) involve the use of calculus.

assets yielding an internal rate of return lower than the market rate; she suggests that the company's investment in real assets be guided by the IRR rule (that is, invest in that amount of real assets for which IRR = r). Annie Ambling is the youngest of the three sisters and has never really cared much for leaving her inheritance in the business. In fact, she suggests that the firm simply pay out all its cash in dividends today and discontinue operations immediately.

a. Construct a diagram with an investment opportunity set and market rate of interest for which management's recommended investment policy will maximize owner welfare.

b. Construct a diagram similar to that in part a in which Emmy's recommendation will maximize owner welfare.

c. Can Annie's suggestion be followed without reducing the welfare of all three sisters? If so, how?

d. Analyze Ethel's investment policy recommendation.

References

G. Alexander, G. Benson, and J. Kampmeyer, "Investigating the Valuation Effects of Announcements of Voluntary Corporate Selloffs," *Journal of Finance* (June 1984): 303–316.

K. Arrow, *Social Choice and Individual Values,* 2d ed. (New York: Wiley, 1963).

R. H. Coase, "The Nature of the Firm," *Econometrica* (November 1937): 386–485.

J. M. Collins and R. P. Bey, "The Master Limited Partnership As an Alternative to the Corporation," *Financial Management* (Winter 1986).

R. M. Cyert and J. G. March, *A Behavioral Theory of the Firm* (Englewood Cliffs, N.J.: Prentice-Hall, 1963).

E. G. Fama, "Agency Problems and the Theory of the Firm," *Journal of Political Economy* 88 (April 1980): 288–307.

———, "Dividends, Earnings, and Stock Prices," *Review of Economics and Statistics* (May 1959): 99–105.

M. Gordon, *The Investment Financing and Valuation of the Corporation* (Homewood, Ill: Irwin, 1962).

D. G. Heckerman, "Motivating Managers to Make Investment Decisions," *Journal of Financial Economics* (September 1975): 273–292.

W. Hirsch, *Law and Economics: An Introductory Analysis* (New York: Academic Press, 1979).

G. Hite and J. Owers, "Security Price Reactions around Corporate Spin-off Announcements," *Journal of Financial Economics* 12 (1983): 409–436.

M. C. Jensen, "The Takeover Controversy: Analysis and Evidence," *Midland Corporate Finance Journal* 4 (Summer 1986): 6–33.

———, "Agency Costs of Free Cash Flow, Corporate Finance and Takeovers," *American Economic Review* (May 1986).

M. Jensen and W. Meckling, "Theory of the Firm: Managerial Behavior, Agency Costs and Ownership Structure," *Journal of Financial Economics* (October 1976): 305–360.

M. Miller and F. Modigliani, "Dividend Policy, Growth, and the Valuation of Shares," *Journal of Business* 34 (October 1961): 411–433.

———, "Corporate Income Taxes and the Cost of Capital: A Correction," *American Economic Review* 53 (June 1963): 433–443.

F. Modigliani and M. Miller, "The Cost of Capital, Corporation Finance and the Theory of Investment," *American Economic Review* 48 (June 1958): 261–297.

K. Schipper and A. Smith, "Effects of Recontracting on Shareholder Wealth: The Case of Voluntary Spin-offs," *Journal of Financial Economics* 12 (1983): 437–467.

W. R. Scott, "Group Preference Ordering for Audit and Valuation Alternatives: The Single Peakedness Condition," *Journal of Accounting Research* 15 (Spring 1977): 120–137.

The Stanger Report™ VII (June 1985): 3.

The Stanger Report™ VIII (September 1986): 2.

O. E. Williamson, "The Modern Corporation: Origins, Evolutions, Attributes," *Journal of Economic Literature* (December 1981): 1537–1568.

———, *The Economics of Discretionary Behavior: Managerial Objectives in a Theory of the Firm* (Englewood Cliffs, N.J.: Prentice-Hall, 1964).

R. Wilson, "The Theory of Syndicates," *Econometrica* (January 1968): 119–132.

Chapter 4

Valuation under Certainty

In Chapter 3, we defined the value of a security as the present dollar amount that the holder would be willing to exchange *today* for the *future* cash flow receipts to which he or she is entitled. Therefore, we found that in a certain world the value of a security is simply the present value of its future cash flow(s) discounted to the present using the risk-free interest rate. In this chapter, we will investigate security valuation where there are multiple future periods but retain the assumptions used in Chapters 2 and 3: competitive capital markets, no taxes, and no transactions costs. Specifically, we will consider the valuation of each basic type of security corporations issue: bonds, preferred stock, and common stock. We will also investigate the concept of a security's duration, which reflects the interest rate elasticity of the security's market value. First we will consider a general formula for determining the present value of a series of future cash flows. Then we will use this model to characterize the values of bonds, preferred stock, and common stock.

The Mechanics of Multiperiod Security Valuation

In this section, our objective is to extend the single-period valuation equations developed in Chapter 3 to a multiperiod setting. This involves a rather straightforward conceptual step and some rudimentary algebraic transformations.

A General Model for Security Valuation

Earlier we noted that the value of a security equals the present dollar sum that the holder would be willing to exchange for the future cash flow(s) to which he or she is entitled. In a multiperiod setting (and still under conditions of certainty), this statement translates into the following valuation model:

$$v = \left[\frac{c_1}{(1 + r_1)}\right] + \left[\frac{c_2}{(1 + r_1)(1 + r_2)}\right] + \ldots + \left[\frac{c_N}{(1 + r_1)(1 + r_2)\ldots(1 + r_N)}\right]$$

or

$$v = \sum_{t=1}^{N} \left[\frac{c_t}{\Pi_{j=1}^{t}(1 + r_j)}\right],$$

where v is the present value of all future cash flows, c_t, to be received over the next N years and r_j ($j = 1, 2, \ldots, N$) is the corresponding single-period risk-free rate. For simplicity we will assume that the term structure of risk-free rates of return is *flat*, that is, $r_i = r_j$ for all $i, j = 1, \ldots, N$.[1] In this case, the general valuation model reduces to the following:

$$v = \left[\frac{c_1}{(1 + r)^1}\right] + \left[\frac{c_2}{(1 + r)^2}\right] + \ldots + \left[\frac{c_N}{(1 + r)^N}\right]$$

or

(4.1)
$$v = \sum_{t=1}^{N} \frac{c_t}{(1 + r)^t}.$$

We will use this general valuation model in defining the value of both bonds and stocks.

An Institutional Note: Zero Coupon Bonds

The *zero coupon bond* is of relatively recent origin, with a flurry of issues appearing since 1980. The concept is quite simple: The issuer sells a "pure discount" bond that pays no interest or principal until it matures. If, for example, a $1,000 face value bond with a 5-year maturity were sold to yield 12 percent, its issue price (ignoring flotation costs) would be $567.42. Under current tax law, the issuer would realize an annual tax-deductible interest expense per bond issued equal to ($1,000 − 567.42)/5 = $86.52. The bondholder, in turn, would realize tax-

---

[1]The term structure of interest rates under conditions of complete certainty was discussed in Appendix 2A.

able income of $86.52 per bond each year. This would hold even though no interest would be either paid or received until the bond matured.

One major attraction of zero coupon bonds is the "locked-in" reinvestment return — that is, where no coupon interest payments are received, the investor need not be concerned about a decline in future interest rates that would reduce the earned yield. Zero coupon bonds come in three basic forms. Treasury issues are offered in the form of "stripped" Treasury bonds whose coupon payments are removed from the issue. The other two forms are taxable corporate zero coupon bonds and nontaxable municipal bonds.

Bond Valuation

A *bond* is a simple security that entitles the holder to future interest and principal payments in accordance with an agreement, known as the *bond indenture*, between the issuing corporation and the bondholder. The bondholder generally receives a fixed interest payment equal to the product of the issue's "stated" or "coupon" rate of interest and the face or principal amount of the bond at maturity. Corporations generally issue bonds with principal amounts in multiples of $1,000 and pay interest semiannually. Thus, if a $1,000 bond has a coupon interest rate of 10 percent and pays interest semiannually, each interest payment equals $1,000 \times 0.10 \times \frac{1}{2} = $50 per bond. If the market rate of interest is 12 percent per annum (assuming a flat term structure in which all future short-term rates are equal (see Appendix 2A for a discussion of the term structure of interest rates) and the bondholder receives interest for 10 years and a return of principal at the end of the tenth year, the current value of the bond, by Equation 4.1, equals

$$d_0 = \sum_{t=1}^{20} \frac{\$50}{\left(1 + \dfrac{0.12}{2}\right)^t} + \frac{\$1,000}{\left(1 + \dfrac{0.12}{2}\right)^{20}}$$

$$= \$573.50 + \$311.80$$

$$= \$885.30.$$

Note that the above bond is an "interest-only" bond. Bonds are frequently more complex. For example, they are sometimes convertible into a prescribed number of common shares in accordance with a conversion ratio set forth in the bond indenture. These bonds are called *convertibles*; their valuation requires knowledge of equity valuation, since the conversion option actually makes this type of bond a hybrid security with both debt and equity attributes.

Bond prices change as the interest rate on comparable bonds changes. For example, a rise in the interest rate will lead to a decline in bond prices, other things equal. Malkiel (1962) summarizes the mathematics of bond price movements using five theorems. These provide a brief but efficient method for summarizing the mechanics of bond price variations. We enumerate these theorems here without proof; however, the proofs are relatively straightforward and can be found in both Malkiel (1962) and Malkiel (1966).

- *Theorem 1:* Bond prices move inversely to bond yields.

- *Theorem 2:* For a given change in yield from the nominal yield, changes in bond prices are greater the longer the term to maturity (N).

- *Theorem 3:* The percentage price changes described in Theorem 2 increase at a diminishing rate as N increases.

- *Theorem 4:* Price movements resulting from equal absolute (or equal proportionate) increases or decreases in yield are asymmetric; that is, a decrease in yields raises bond prices more than a similar increase in yields lowers prices.

- *Theorem 5:* The higher the coupon carried by the bond, the smaller will be the percentage price fluctuation for a given percentage change in yield, except for one-year securities and consols (bonds with infinite maturities).

Some of the theorems are more widely recognized than others; for example, Theorem 1 is very familiar, while Theorem 4 perhaps is less widely known. It should also be recognized that these theorems were derived for a coupon bond — that is, they assume that the bond pays a fixed coupon interest payment periodically until its maturity, when its face amount becomes due and payable. Further, Malkiel uses the term "nominal yield" in a very specific way. This concept is defined as the ratio of the coupon interest payment divided by the face value of the bond. The "market yield" or "yield to maturity," on the other hand, is defined in the traditional manner: the yield to maturity or internal rate of return that would be earned if the bond were purchased at its current market price and held until maturity. We will encounter Theorem 2 again when we discuss the concept of "duration."

Standard Bond Valuation Formulas: A Mathematical Overview

While the valuation model in Equation 4.1 is valid for bonds, a separate set of symbols has been developed for bond formulas. P is used instead of v for the value one period before the first coupon. The coupons are denoted rF, where F is the face amount of the bond and r is the coupon rate per coupon period, and C is the redemption value. In terms of Equation 4.1, we have

$$c_j = rF \qquad j = 1, \ldots, N - 1$$

$$c_N = C + rF.$$

The yield to maturity (YTM) earned by purchasing the bond at its current market price is denoted i (instead of r), and N is the number of coupon payments. The bond valuation in terms of the standard bond symbols is, therefore,

$$P = \frac{rF}{(1 + i)} + \frac{rF}{(1 + i)^2} + \ldots + \frac{(rF + C)}{(1 + i)^N}.$$

Recall that a geometric series of the form $a + ax + ax^2 + \ldots + ax^N$ sums to

$$\frac{a - ax^{N+1}}{1 - x};$$

that is, if $x \neq 0$,

$$\frac{a - ax^{N+1}}{1 - x} = a + ax + \ldots + ax^N.$$

Here is the derivation:
  Let

$$S = a + ax + \ldots + ax^N;$$

then

$$xS = ax + ax^2 + \ldots + ax^{N+1}$$

Now subtract:

$$S - xS = a + ax + \ldots + ax^N - ax - ax^2 - \ldots - ax^{N+1} = a - ax^{N+1}$$

Therefore,

$$S(1 - x) = a - ax^{N+1}$$

$$S = \frac{a - ax^{N+1}}{(1 - x)}.$$

Applying the above formula with $a = rF/(1 + i)$ and $x = 1/(1 + i)$, we get

$$P = a + ax + ax^2 + \ldots + ax^{N-1} + Cx^N$$

$$= \frac{a - ax^N}{(1 - x)} + Cx^N$$

$$= \frac{\dfrac{rF}{(1 + i)} - \left[\dfrac{rF}{(1 + i)}\right]\left[\dfrac{1}{(1 + i)^N}\right]}{1 - \left[\dfrac{1}{(1 + i)}\right]} + \frac{C}{(1 + i)^N}$$

$$= \frac{rF[1 - (1 + i)^{-N}]}{i} + C(1 + i)^{-N}$$

$$= rFa_{\overline{N}|} + C(1 + i)^{-N},$$

where

$$a_{\overline{N}|} = \frac{1 - (1 + i)^{-N}}{i}$$

is the value of an annuity of \$1 per period for N periods, present valued at i percent per period. This is known as the standard formula.

We can also express the above bond valuation formula in the following equivalent forms. First,

$$P = \frac{rF}{i} + \left[C - \left(\frac{rF}{i} \right) \right] (1 + i)^{-N}.$$

This is known as the alternate formula. Finally, we can write

$$P = (rF - iC)a_{\overline{N}|} + C.$$

This is Makeham's formula (named for a famous nineteenth-century British actuary). These formulas are summarized in Table 4.1.

If the price is known, one can determine the yield for a given bond by solving one of the equations for i. For a bond with three or more coupons, it is usually easier to solve for i using some iterative procedure than by trying to find an explicit formula for i. However, a convenient explicit approximation for i has been developed, and it provides a good starting point for an iterative procedure. The approximation is called the *bond salesman's formula*:

$$i = rF + \left[\frac{\frac{1}{N}(C - P)}{\left(\frac{P + C}{2} \right)} \right].$$

Table 4.1   Summary of Bond Price Formulas

$P = rFa_{\overline{N}|} + Cv^N$ Standard

$$P = \frac{rF}{i} + \left[C - \left(\frac{rF}{i} \right) \right] v^N \quad \text{Alternate}$$

$P = C + (rF - iC)a_{\overline{N}|}$ Makeham's

where $a_{\overline{N}|} = \dfrac{1 - v^N}{i}$

$v = \dfrac{1}{(1 + i)}$

P = price on coupon period before the first coupon

C = redemption value

F = face amount

r = coupon rate per coupon period

i = yield rate per coupon period

The numerator is the sum of the periodic coupon and one-Nth of the difference in the current price and redemption value. This formula recognizes that if the bond sells at a discount ($P < C$), the gain in principal upon maturity should be spread over all N coupon periods. Similarly, if the bond sells at a premium ($P > C$), the average decrease in principal $(1/N)(P - C)$ is deducted from the coupon to estimate the periodic yield. The denominator approximates the average principal over the life of the bond.

Common and Preferred Stock Valuation

The firm's common stockholders are entitled to receive its declared cash dividends as well as the proceeds from the sale of their shares. Thus, adapting the general valuation model in Equation 4.1, the value of a firm's common stock can be stated as follows:

$$e_0 = \sum_{t=1}^{N} \frac{div_t}{(1 + r)^t} + \frac{e_N}{(1 + r)^N},$$

where div_t is the dividend per share paid to the firm's stockholders in year t and the stock is held for N years, at which time it is sold for e_N dollars. Note, however, that e_N is simply the value of those dividends, beginning with div_{N+1}, that accrue to the individual who purchases the stock in year N. Therefore, given the fact that common stock has no maturity (as does a bond, for example), we will assume that it has an infinite life. In general, the value of a common share can be written as follows:

(4.2)
$$e_0 = \sum_{t=1}^{\infty} \frac{div_t}{(1 + r)^t},$$

where all future dividends again are assumed to be known with certainty and the term structure is flat such that the per period interest rate is r for all periods. Note that in a certain world the valuations of a bond and a share of stock look very similar. The only real difference lies in the specification given to the cash flows accruing to the security holder; that is, for a bond the periodic payments are set via an agreement (the bond indenture) and the term of the payments is usually finite, neither of which characterizes a share of common stock.

Valuing No-Growth Common (and Preferred) Stock.   Since the dividends paid to common stockholders are not set in any agreement between the stockholders and the issuing corporation, a number of valuation models for common stock have been developed for various "popular" (that is, tractable) time patterns of dividends. For example, where dividends are the same dollar amount each year, Equation 4.2 reduces to the following (perpetuity form):

(4.3)
$$e_0 = div/r.$$

Since we will again use the general form of the proof of this valuation formula, we will describe it briefly here. Where a constant dividend, div, is paid each year, we can write Equation 4.2 as follows:

$$e_0 = \frac{div}{(1 + r)^1} + \frac{div}{(1 + r)^2} + \ldots$$

Now let $a = div/(1 + r)$ and $x = 1/(1 + r)$ such that

(i) $e_0 = a(1 + x + x^2 + \ldots)$.

Multiplying through both sides by x, we obtain

(ii) $e_0 x = a(x + x^2 + \ldots)$.

Subtracting (ii) from (i) produces the following result:

$$e_0(1 - x) = a .$$

Substituting for a and x and rearranging terms gives us Equation 4.3:

$$e_0 = div/r .$$

Hence, for a no-growth stock the value of the shares equals the level dividend divided by the rate of interest.

Exercise 4.1:   Bond Valuation

(Note that this exercise uses the notation found in the Mathematical Overview of bond valuation.) For example from the "Treasury Issues" column of *The Wall Street Journal* (WSJ) in 1988, we might read

    14 1/2s   1994 July   112.19   112.27 . . . 11.48

This denotes a Treasury bond with an annual coupon rate of $14\frac{1}{2}$ percent, maturing in July 1994, bid price 112.19, asked price 112.27, and a yield of 11.48 percent per year. Almost all U.S. Treasury and corporate bonds have semi-annual coupons. Hence,

$$r = 0.145/2 = 0.0725$$

$$N = 6 \times 2 = 12$$

$$i = 0.1148/2 = 0.0574$$

Using the standard, alternate, and Makeham's formulas, and using F = 100, find the value of these Treasury bonds (per $100 of face value).

Solution.   Using the standard formula, we get

$$P = 7.25[(1 - (1.0574)^{-12})/0.0574] + 100(1.0574)^{-12}$$

$$= 7.25[(1 - 0.5118)/0.0574] + 100(0.5118)$$

$$= 61.66 + 51.18$$

$$= 112.84$$

Using the alternate formula, we obtain

$$P = (7.25/5.74)100 + 100(1 - 7.25/5.74)(0.5118)$$

$$= 126.31 + (-26.31)(0.5118)$$

$$= 112.84.$$

Using Makeham's formula, we get

$$P = (7.25 - 5.74)[(1 - 0.5118)/0.0574] + 100$$

$$= (1.51)(8.5052) + 100$$

$$= 112.84.$$

The WSJ reports prices per $100 of face value in units of one-thirty-second. Our price of $112.84 equals $112 + (.84)(32)/32 = 112$ and 27/32. The WSJ lists this as 112.27 since it uses a period to separate the thirty-seconds.

At this point we note that Equation 4.3 can also be used to describe the value of a share of preferred stock, since preferred shares generally pay a fixed dividend each period and the security has an infinite maturity. A preferred share differs from a common share in important ways, however. A preferred shareholder receives dividends before any common dividends can be paid. In addition, should the firm be dissolved, the preferred shareholders' claims will be senior to the common shareholders'. Finally, preferred shares generally are cumulative such that dividends not paid in any given year must be paid in the future before any common dividends.

Valuing Constant (Non-Zero) Growth Common Stock.   Still another popular common stock valuation model assumes that dividends grow at a constant rate, g, which is less than r, forever. This general valuation model can be written as follows:

$$e_0 = \frac{div_0(1 + g)^1}{(1 + r)^1} + \frac{div_0(1 + g)^2}{(1 + r)^2} + \dots.$$

Using the same method of proof just applied to the level perpetuity (constant dividend) case and letting a = $div_0(1 + g)/(1 + r)$ and x = $(1 + g)/(1 + r)$ produce the following valuation model, provided r > g:

$$(4.4) \qquad e_0 = \frac{div_0(1 + g)}{r - g}.$$

The constant growth rate model has gained a very prominent position in the finance literature and is generally referred to as the *Gordon growth model*.[2] It has been used to place a value on common stock and as the basis for evaluating the investor's required rate of return. In the latter case, the stock's market price is assumed to be the same as its value. Here a stock's observed market value, p_0, is substituted into Equation 4.4 for e_0, an estimate of the growth rate of dividends is substituted for g, and the current dividend per share is substituted for div_0. The required rate of return for the stock is then found by solving for r:

$$r = \frac{div_0(1 + g)}{p_0} + g.$$

Of course, in a certain world r must equal the risk-free rate, and in an uncertain environment this would not be true. This model has been widely used to estimate required rates of return on equity, which in turn are used to set rates for public utilities and other regulated enterprises.

Valuing a Common Stock's Growth Opportunities. The growth stock valuation model found in Equation 4.4 can be reformulated to reflect those portions of the stock's value that are attributable to its existing asset investments and that portion that is due to the firm's anticipated growth opportunities. A growth opportunity is simply an investment offering a rate of return on equity, ROE, that is greater than the market rate of interest, r. The resulting model can be generalized as follows:

$$(4.4a) \qquad e_0 = \frac{EPS_0}{r} + PVGO,$$

where PVGO is the present value of the firm's growth opportunities.

We can provide some intuition for the meaning of the PVGO term as follows. First, let ROE be the rate of return earned on reinvested (equity) funds and let b represent the fraction of a firm's earnings that is reinvested (that is, $div_0 = (1 - b)EPS_0$). Further, assume that both ROE and b are constants such that the firm faces the same set of investment opportunities and reinvests the same fraction of its earnings each year. Finally, assume the investment of $bEPS_1$ yields a cash flow of $bEPS_1ROE$ per year, indefinitely. That is, suppose each investment yields a perpetuity. Under these circumstances, the result of the firm's reinvesting $bEPS_1$ dollars next year is the following NPV_1:

---

[2]See Gordon (1959).

$$NPV_1 = \left(\frac{bEPS_1 ROE}{r}\right) - (bEPS_1),$$

where r is the market rate of interest and NPV_1 is stated in Year 1 dollars. Note that the reinvested funds earn a perpetual rate of ROE; thus, the present value of the added earnings is simply those earnings divided by r. Similarly, for Year 2 the NPV_2 created by reinvesting $bEPS_2$ is defined as follows:

$$NPV_2 = \left(\frac{bEPS_2 ROE}{r}\right) - (bEPS_2),$$

where NPV_2 is stated in Year 2 dollars. The PVGO is the present value of the NPVs. We get the PVGO as follows:

$$PVGO = \sum_{t=1}^{\infty} \frac{NPV_t}{(1 + r)^t}.$$

Note that EPS_2 can be rewritten in terms of EPS_1 as follows:

$$EPS_2 = EPS_1 + EPS_1 b(ROE) = EPS_1(1 + bROE).$$

Therefore, bROE = g where g is the growth rate in the firm's earnings. Then $EPS_t = EPS_1(1 + g)^t$ where g = bROE < r. It follows that

$$NPV_t = -b(1 + g)EPS_{t-1} + \frac{bROE(1 + g)EPS_{t-1}}{r}$$

$$= (1 + g)NPV_{t-1}$$

$$= (1 + g)^{t-1}NPV_1.$$

Thus PVGO reduces to the following:

$$PVGO = \sum_{t=1}^{\infty} \frac{(1 + g)^{t-1}NPV_1}{(1 + r)^t} = \frac{NPV_1}{r - g}.$$

Thus, the value added to the firm by its growth opportunities where ROE is greater than r is an increasing function of the rate of return it can earn on its reinvested funds (ROE), the fraction of its earnings it chooses to reinvest (b), and the level of its current earnings (EPS_1). In fact, in this circumstance (where ROE is a positive constant greater than r) the optimal dividend policy (1 − b) is zero or the optimal retention rate is b = 1. Note too that where b = 1 the firm is retaining all its earnings and paying no dividends, yet the equity has value! The reason is, of course, that the shares are growing in value as earnings are being retained and reinvested. The shareholder can realize this value at any time simply by selling his or her shares.

Thus, the PVGO formulation for equity value found in Equation 4.4a can be summarized as follows: The value of a growth stock equals the present value of the stream of cash flows provided by its "assets in place" plus present value of the NPVs resulting from the reinvestment of future earnings to provide earnings at a rate of ROE > r.

An Institutional Note: Adjustable-Rate Preferred Stock

New varieties of securities are created almost continuously to meet the real or perceived needs of security holders. One such example is the adjustable-rate preferred stock (ARPS) issue. Floating- or adjustable-rate preferred stock issues are a relatively recent phenomenon, having come into use in May 1982. The concept is quite simple and has been widely adopted by a variety of corporate issuers (see Winger et al. [1986]).

A floating-rate preferred stock issue is one whose dividend is adjusted quarterly in accordance with a specified spread from the highest of the 91-day Treasury bill rate, the 10-year Treasury note rate, or the 20-year Treasury bond rate. In addition, the dividend rate is bounded at both the low and high end, that is, 6 to 12 percent.

This new security has proven quite attractive to corporate cash managers who seek relatively short-term investments for temporarily idle cash balances. The underlying reasons for its attractiveness include the following. First, if a corporation holds the stock for at least 46 days, 80 percent of the dividends received will not be taxed. Thus, compared to holding short-term debt securities whose interest is fully subject to the corporate income tax, the ARPS holder pays tax on only 20 percent of the dividend income received. Second, the dividend rate on an ARPS issue fluctuates with the general level of interest rates and is pegged to the highest of the short-, intermediate-, and long-term interest rate. This means that corporate cash managers need no longer be concerned about the impact of maturity on their investments' yields. Further, since the dividend rate floats with the current level of interest rates, the stock price should remain fairly close to its issue price, thus eliminating the "interest rate risk" (fluctuations in stock price due to interest rate variations) attendant to investing in long-term securities with fixed-rate returns.

Corporate issuers of ARPS find it attractive for three reasons. First, ARPS provides the issuer with a permanent source of equity capital without the potential dilution effect of a common stock offering. This feature was particularly important when ARPSs were first issued in 1982. At that time the issuers were large bank holding companies whose stock prices were depressed as a result of problems stemming from their international loan commitments. Thus, the sale of common stock at this time would have been at severely depressed prices that the banks felt were a temporary phenomenon. Second, the call provisions for ARPS issues have been much less costly to issuers than comparable fixed-rate issues. For example, the call premiums on some early issues were as low as 3 percent, whereas for fixed-rate preferred issues they were as high as 12 percent or more. This difference reflects the fact that the refunding of a floating-rate issue does not offer the potential cost savings when rates decline as does the refunding of a fixed-rate preferred stock issue. Finally, the ARPS issuer need not worry about being caught with a high-cost source of financing when interest rates decline as would be the case with preferred stock.

Duration of a Security

The subject of this entire chapter has been the valuation of securities that provide multiple future cash flows. In some cases, the number of cash flows is fixed, for example, being comprised of principal and interest payments to bondholders. In other instances the number of payments is not fixed but goes on indefinitely, as is the case with preferred or common stock. Many years ago financial theorists recognized a need to be able to measure and compare two securities' cash flow patterns.[3] Out of this need arose the concept of duration.

The concept of duration was first introduced by Macaulay (1938) as a measure of the "length" of a loan. We deliberately use the term *duration* here rather than *maturity,* for the latter concept indicates only the time up until the last loan payment is received. Duration, on the other hand, incorporates consideration not only for the maturity or term over which cash flows are received but also for the time pattern of interim cash flows. Specifically, duration is a weighted average time to maturity in which the weight attached to each year in which a security provides a cash payment is the present value of the cash flow for that year.

Consider the following example. Bond A is a "pure discount bond" that has a current value of $62.09 and provides the holder with a single cash flow of $100 at the end of five years; this represents a 10 percent rate of return to the bondholder. Bond B is an installment bond having a current market value of $62.09 and paying the holder $16.38 each year for five years; the holder of this bond also receives a 10 percent rate of return. Both bonds have the same current value, the same maturity, and earn the same rate of return. However, bond A has the longer duration, since it provides only one cash flow and the cash flow is not received for five years. In contrast, bond B provides the holder with annual cash flows each year of its five-year term to maturity. In fact, the duration of bond A is the same as its maturity, or 5 years, while the duration of bond B is only 2.81 years (we will derive a measure of duration shortly).

Duration has yet another important interpretation, which we will find useful both in an analytical sense and as the basis for deriving a measure of it. Hicks (1939) recognized that the duration of a cash flow stream is also the absolute value of the interest rate elasticity of its present value. For example, we know that bond value and interest rates vary inversely. In informal terms, the duration of a bond is simply a measure of the "responsiveness of its price to a change in the interest rate." The greater the relative percentage change in bond price in response to a given percentage change in the interest rate, the longer the duration.

---

[3]For example, a pension fund might have a set of retirement benefits, which it must pay each year over the next 30 years. The firm receives payments from working employees that must be invested to earn the promised pension benefits. One way to manage the pension fund's investments so as to assure that funds will be available when needed is to "match" the cash flow stream resulting from its investments with that of its pension liabilities. To do this requires that both the amount and timing of the two cash flow streams be "measured." Duration provides such a measure.

We can represent duration as a measure of a bond's interest rate elasticity as follows:[4]

(4.5a)
$$D_i = -\left(\frac{\dfrac{dB_i}{B_i}}{\dfrac{dR}{R}}\right),$$

which can also be written as

(4.5b)
$$D_i = -\left(\frac{\dfrac{dB_i}{B_i}}{\dfrac{dr}{r}}\right)\left(\frac{R}{r}\right),$$

where D_i = duration of the ith bond

B_i = price of the ith bond (that is, present value of all future payments to the bondholder discounted at the market rate of interest, r)

R = 1 + r

r = "yield to maturity" on the bond

Note that in a world of certainty r is the same for all bonds and equals the risk-free rate.

Duration is technically a measure of bond price elasticity with respect to changes in *1 plus the rate of interest*. However, there is a simple analog (defined in Equation 4.5b) for D_i in terms of changes in the interest rate. Note too that the above measure of duration is valid only for very small changes in interest rates. Where dR is large, the measure of duration that we derive from Equation 4.5a is no longer exact.

Deriving a Measure of the Duration of a Coupon Bond

Dropping the "i" subscript, we develop a measure of duration by first defining a bond's current value or price (B) as follows:

(4.6)
$$B = \frac{I_1}{R} + \frac{I_2}{R^2} + \ldots + \frac{I_N}{R^N} + \frac{F}{R^N},$$

where I_t = interest paid in year t

R = 1 + r

F = face or principal amount of bond

N = bond's term to maturity

Solving for the derivative of B with respect to R,

$$\frac{dB}{dR} = -\frac{I_1}{R^2} - \frac{2I_2}{R^3} - \frac{3I_3}{R^4} - \ldots - \frac{NF}{R^{N+1}}.$$

---

[4]Equation 4.5a can be rewritten $D_i = -(dB_i/dR)(R/B)$.

Dividing both sides of the above by B/R—that is, multiplying through by R/B—we obtain the following:

$$\frac{\dfrac{dB}{B}}{\dfrac{dR}{R}} = \frac{-\dfrac{I_1}{R^1} - \dfrac{2I_2}{R^2} - \cdots - \dfrac{NI_N}{R^N} - \dfrac{NF}{R^N}}{B}.$$

When we let C_t represent the cash flow received in year t and multiply through by -1, we can reduce the above to the following definition of duration:

(4.7)
$$D = \frac{1\left(\dfrac{C_1}{R}\right) + 2\left(\dfrac{C_2}{R^2}\right) + \cdots + N\left(\dfrac{C_N}{R^N}\right)}{B}.$$

Therefore, the duration of a cash flow stream is simply the weighted average time to maturity where each year t is weighted by the ratio $(C_t/R^t)/B$. Note that the sum of the weights is unity; that is,

$$\frac{\dfrac{C_1}{R} + \dfrac{C_2}{R^2} + \cdots + \dfrac{C_N}{R^N}}{B} = 1,$$

because

$$\frac{C_1}{R} + \frac{C_2}{R^2} + \cdots + \frac{C_N}{R^N} = B.$$

   Although we have used the cash flow stream of a bond to derive our measure of duration, the concept is equally well suited to any cash flow stream. We will now consider some special cases frequently encountered in the valuation of financial claims or securities.

Duration of a Zero Coupon Bond (Point Input–Point Output)

A *zero coupon bond* pays no interest or principal until it matures; it therefore provides only one payment, which occurs at maturity (C_N). Thus, appropriately modifying Equation 4.7 we obtain the following measure of duration:

(4.8)
$$D_{zero} = \frac{\dfrac{NC_N}{R^N}}{B_{zero}} = N.$$

In this case, as we mentioned at the beginning of this section, the maturity (N years) and duration of the cash flow stream are the same. However, this is the only case for which this is true, as we will see in the ensuing examples.

Duration of a Level Perpetuity

The present value of a level payment perpetuity is simply C/r where the perpetuity cash flow is C dollars per year and the term structure is flat and equal to a rate r for all maturities. Thus, using the second definition of duration found in Equation 4.5b, which defines duration in terms of the interest rate elasticity of the bond price, we obtain the following:

$$(4.9) \qquad D_{level} = 1\left[\frac{(1 + r)}{r}\right] = \frac{(1 + r)}{r}.$$

Note that as r increases, duration declines. Hence, when the interest rate is at a relatively modest or low level, duration is longer than when it is at higher levels.

Duration of an Installment Note (Annuity)

In the case of an installment note or annuity, the cash flow stream constitutes a level payment annuity of C dollars per year for each of N years. The present value of the installment note (B) is given by the following:

$$B = C\left[\frac{1 - (1 + r)^{-N}}{r}\right].$$

Using the duration Equation 4.5b, we find that the duration of this cash flow stream is given by the following:

$$(4.10) \qquad D_{install} = \left[\frac{(1 + r)}{r}\right] - \left[\frac{N}{(1 + r)^N - 1}\right].$$

Note that we can think of the duration of a level payment annuity as the duration of a level perpetuity (the first term in the above expression) less an adjustment for a finite maturity (the second term).

Duration of a Growing Perpetuity

For the case of a perpetuity that grows at a rate g per annum for g < r, we can derive the following definition of duration:

$$(4.11) \qquad D_{grow} = \frac{(1 + r)}{(r - g)}.$$

We used this type of cash flow stream in Equation 4.4 to characterize the dividend payments on a share of common stock. Once again duration declines with increasing r, *ceteris paribus*. Also, note that the duration of such a cash flow stream is longer than that of a perpetual bond, which in turn is longer than that of a fixed-maturity bond.

Summary

In this chapter we investigated the valuation of a corporation's securities in a multiperiod setting. Specifically, we developed valuation models for bonds, preferred stock, and common stock. The basic principle underlying the valuation of all these types of securities is that the value of a future cash flow stream equals the present sum to which the owner of the stream is indifferent. Thus, in a certain world the value of a security is simply the present value of the future cash flows to which the security owner is entitled discounted using the market or risk-free interest rate. In addition, we discussed the concept of duration of a cash flow stream. This notion was first introduced by Macaulay in 1938 as a measure of the length of a loan but was quickly recognized as also representing a measure of interest rate elasticity by Hicks in 1939.

In Part III, we will again discuss the valuation of corporate securities. However, there we will focus on the impact of uncertainty on security valuation. We use the capital asset pricing model and arbitrage pricing theory as alternative models for describing how the capital market values securities under conditions of uncertain future cash flows. However, the mechanical aspects of multiperiod valuation discussed here will continue to be useful when we broaden our scope to consider these same issues in a more realistic setting.

Study Questions

4.1   How is the value of a security related to an individual's consumption opportunities?

4.2   "Other things equal, the longer the term to maturity of a bond, the greater the fluctuations in its price in response to changes in the interest rate." True or false? Explain.

4.3   The values of a no-growth common stock and a preferred stock are the same. True or false? Explain.

4.4   Define the duration of a cash flow stream. Can duration be interpreted as a "risk" measure? If so, how?

Study Problems

4.1   Company X's bonds have a par value of $1,000, mature in 20 years, and pay a coupon interest rate of 10 percent (with interest payable semiannually). The market rate of interest on the bond is 8 percent (compounded annually). At what price should the bond sell?

4.2   Brewers, Inc. has $1,000 par value bonds with a 9 percent coupon (paid semiannually). The appropriate interest rate is 10 percent (compounded annually). The bonds mature five years from today. What is the market price today?

4.3   Commonwealth Company has 100 bonds outstanding (maturity value = $1,000 each). The current required rate of return on these bonds is 10 percent. If interest is paid semiannually and the bonds mature in five years, what should the coupon rate be if the market value is $760 per bond?

4.4   Show that

$$e_0 = \sum_{t=1}^{\infty} \frac{div_0(1 + g)^t}{(1 + r)^t}$$

reduces to

$$e_0 = \frac{div_0(1 + g)}{(r - g)}$$

where $r > g$.

4.5   Develop a stock valuation model for a firm whose dividends are expected to grow at a rate g for N years, after which time they will grow at the same rate as the market as a whole, g_M. In addition, at the end of N years the firm's stock is expected to sell at the same price/earnings ratio as the market, P/E_M, and the firm plans to pay out a constant fraction, b, of its earnings in dividends.

4.6   Demonstrate the relationship among the dividend growth rate, earnings, and book value for a stock that is expected to grow at a constant rate of g forever.

4.7   The stock of Witherspoon Manufacturing Company has a value of $20. The dividend paid last year was $1.50, and the market rate of interest is 10 percent. What constant dividend growth rate is consistent with the $20 value? What value should Witherspoon's stock have if the anticipated growth rate is 12 percent?

4.8   An issue of XYZ Corporation bonds matures July 31, 1998. The bonds pay semiannual coupons at a rate of 14 percent per year. What is the price on July 31, 1983, that will insure a yield to maturity of 11.25 percent per annum?

4.9   U.S. Treasury 14s maturing in July 1991 are priced at 112 in July 1983. What is the implied yield to maturity?

4.10   The ABC Corporation's latest dividend per share was $12.50. ABC pays only annual dividends. Investors agree that ABC's dividend growth rate is a constant 5 percent per year and that the current value of one share is $75. What rate of return are investors requiring on their investment in ABC?

4.11   Under what circumstances is the following common stock valuation equation appropriate?

$$e_0 = EPS_0/r,$$

where e_0 = value of common stock

EPS_0 = last period's earnings per common share

r = market (risk-free) interest rate

4.12   Show that the present value of a stream of N cash flows of C dollars each period equals the following:

$$\left(\frac{C}{r}\right)\left[1 - \frac{1}{(1 + r)^N}\right],$$

where r is the interest rate.

4.13   In the context of the constant growth common stock valuation model, $e_0 = div_0(1 + g)/(r - g)$, why do different stocks have different price/earnings ratios? (Hint: The growth rate in dividends, g, equals the product of the retention ratio and the rate of return earned on stockholders' equity, ROE.)

4.14   The trust department of the Texas Bank recently was approached by one of its customers for help in valuating a note that he wishes to sell. The note has a face amount of $330,000. The potential purchaser has offered to buy it at a price that will yield a 14 percent annual percentage rate (APR). The note carries a 10.5 percent coupon rate and pays $18,168.31 every six months (this represents a 30-year amortization of the face amount of the note with a 10.5 percent nominal annual rate). However, the note is due in seven years and entails a balloon payment equal to the sum of the principal amount due at that time. The note is now 3 years old. What price should the bank's customer expect to receive for the note?

*4.15   Derive a measure of duration for each of the following cash flow streams:
a. A level perpetuity
b. A growing perpetuity with a growth rate of $g < r$
c. A zero coupon bond
d. A level payment installment note

4.16   For each of the cash flow streams in Problem 4.15, estimate the impact of a 10 percent relative change in $(1 + r)$ on its value (that is, if r' is the new rate and r the old rate, $(1 + r')/(1 + r) - 1 = 0.10$).

*4.17   Evaluate how each of your duration measures from Problem 4.15 varies with the interest rate level (r).

4.18   Calculate the durations for each of the following installment notes where N is the maturity and r is the interest rate (yield):
a. $N = 10$ and $r = 0.15$
b. $N = 20$ and $r = 0.15$

---

*Problems denoted with an asterisk (*) involve the use of calculus.

        c. N = 30 and r = 0.15
        d. N = 10 and r = 0.20
        e. N = 10 and r = 0.25

4.19   The XYZ Life Insurance Company just purchased a level payment installment note yielding 10 percent and having a duration of 10 years.
    a. What is the maturity of the note?
    b. If the interest rate rose to 12 percent, what would be the note's duration?

4.20   The J. P. Minzee Company just acquired an installment note that pays 6.25 percent interest compounded annually. The note has a current market value of $1,000 and provides equal annual installments of $137.48 per year over the next 10 years. The firm knows that it will need to sell the note in five years to meet a financial commitment equal to $1,000.
    a. What is the duration of the note?
    b. If interest rates rise such that the note yields 8 percent, what will be the note's market value (assuming that rates change immediately following the purchase)? What rate of return should the firm expect to realize over the five-year holding period assuming that all interim payments are reinvested to earn 8 percent? What is the duration of the note following the rate change?
    c. If the firm sells the note after only two years given the interest rate change in part b, what rate of return will it receive on its $1,000 investment?

References

L. Fisher and R. L. Weil, "Coping with the Risk of Interest Rate Fluctuations: Returns of Bondholders from Naive and Optimal Strategies," *Journal of Business* (October 1971): 408–431.

———, "Dividends, Earnings, and Stock Prices," *Review of Economics and Statistics* (May 1959): 99–105.

M. Gordon, *The Investment Financing and Valuation of the Corporation* (Homewood, Ill.: Irwin, 1962).

R. A. Haugen and D. W. Wichern, "The Elasticity of Financial Assets," *Journal of Finance* (September 1974): 1229–1240.

J. R. Hicks, *Value and Capital* (Oxford, England: Clarendon Press, 1939; 2d ed., 1946).

M. H. Hopewell and G. G. Kaufman, "Bond Price Volatility and Term to Maturity: A Generalized Respecification," *American Economic Review* (September 1973): 749–753.

S. G. Kellison, *The Theory of Interest* (Homewood, Ill.: Irwin, 1970).

F. R. Macaulay, *Some Theoretical Problems Suggested by the Movements of Interest Rates, Bond Yields, and Stock Prices Since 1856* (New York: National Bureau of Economic Research, 1938).

B. G. Malkiel, "Expectations, Bond Prices, and the Term Structure of Interest Rates," *Quarterly Journal of Economics* 76 (May 1962): 197–218.

———, *The Term Structure of Interest Rates* (Princeton, N.J.: Princeton University Press, 1966), Chapter 3.

R. L. Weil, "Macaulay's Duration: An Appreciation," *Journal of Business* (October 1973): 589–592.

B. J. Winger, C. R. Chen, J. D. Martin, et al., "Adjustable Rate Preferred Stock," *Financial Management* (Spring 1986): 48–57.

Chapter 5

Capital Budgeting:
Single and Multiple Periods

This is the first of two chapters dealing with capital budgeting under certainty. This chapter addresses the fundamental issues of "how much to invest" (referred to here as the capital widening decision) and "how long to invest" (hereafter referred to as the capital deepening decision). Specifically we discuss the following: (1) the traditional tools of capital budgeting analysis, including net present value (NPV), profitability index (PI), payback, average rate of return, and internal rate of return (IRR); (2) the ranking differences that can arise between NPV and IRR;[1] (3) the types of capital expenditure decisions the firm encounters, including independent, mutually exclusive, and mutually inclusive projects; (4) the optimal investment term for a project; and (5) the abandonment value problem in capital budgeting. In Chapter 6, we consider the cash flows relevant to an analysis of a capital expenditure proposal. This discussion focuses on the difference between accounting profits and project cash flows, the impact of inflation on project cash flows, and the role of competition on positive net present value projects.

We will assume throughout the same ideal set of circumstances as in the previous chapters: certain cash flows, no transactions costs, and perfectly competitive

---

[1]The NPV criterion has won the popularity contest in the finance literature, largely due to the reasoning provided by Fisher (1930) and presented earlier in Chapter 2. However, the IRR method also has its proponents, including a wide base of industrial users and a number of theorists, such as Keynes (1936). Dorfman (1981) provides an excellent overview of these two criteria for capital budgeting choices.

capital markets. Likewise, we will defer consideration of taxes until the next chapter.[2] As noted above, the present discussion will be organized around the two primary issues encountered in the economic analysis of capital expenditures: capital widening and capital deepening.[3] As we shall soon see, the topics normally discussed in traditional presentations of the capital budgeting problem—the analysis of independent and dependent investment proposals and the abandonment decision—can be addressed as special cases of the more general classification scheme consisting of capital widening/deepening.

Capital widening deals with the optimal amount for a firm to invest in a proposed capital project. Introductory discussions of the capital budgeting problem frequently overlook this issue or implicitly assume that only one investment outlay is feasible. In this case, the capital widening decision reduces to a simple accept/reject decision based on the given, fixed level of investment and the corresponding project cash flows. *Capital deepening* deals with the analysis of the optimal term over which to hold an asset. This issue therefore arises only in the context of multiperiod investments. A corollary issue considered here is that of how frequently an asset should be replaced or recycled. Introductory discussions of the capital budgeting problem frequently overlook the capital deepening issue by assuming either that no optimal investment term exists or that if one exists it is already known, thus reducing the capital budgeting analysis to an accept/reject decision based on a single investment term.

In addition to these two basic capital expenditure issues, we will address the problems encountered in analyzing independent and dependent (that is, mutually inclusive or mutually exclusive) investment proposals. To simplify the discussion, we will address each of these in the context of single-period investments—invest now to earn a single cash flow one period hence. We will also analyze the decision to abandon an asset, an issue that turns out to be the mirror image of the capital deepening problem.

The order of the discussion will be as follows. First, we look at capital budgeting in a single-period context, where we consider the use of the net present value criterion to evaluate independent, mutually inclusive, and mutually exclusive investments as special cases of the capital widening problem. Second, we examine the multiple-period case; here we consider the capital deepening issue with respect to both investments, which either can or cannot be replicated through time. In this discussion we also address the abandonment problem in capital budgeting, that is, how to determine the optimal time to divest of an asset.

---

[2]In Chapter 11 we evaluate the capital budgeting problem under uncertainty. However, the fundamental elements of the analysis described here under certainty provide the background necessary for a full understanding of capital budgeting under uncertainty.

[3]This terminology is synonymous with that of Hirshleifer (1970).

An Institutional Note: Capital Budgeting Techniques and Corporate Practice

The methods used to evaluate capital expenditures in corporate practice vary widely. In recent decades, there has been a growing trend toward use of what academics call *discounted cash flow techniques*. Here we briefly review the definitions of some popular capital budgeting techniques. In addition, we summarize the results of a number of surveys of industry practice with respect to their use.

A Quick Review of Capital Budgeting Techniques

We will review the definitions for five commonly used capital budgeting techniques. These include three discounted cash flow (DCF) models—net present value, profitability index, and internal rate of return—and two non-DCF models—payback and average rate of return.

The *net present value* of an investment can be defined as follows:

$$NPV = \sum_{t=1}^{N} \frac{NCF_t}{(1 + r)^t} - I,$$

where NCF_t = annual net cash flow provided by the project in year t (we discuss the determination of this quantity in detail in Chapter 6)

r = project's required rate of return

N = number of years project will be held

I = investment outlay for the project

Thus, NPV equals the present value of a project's cash flows less the amount of funds invested in the project. If $NPV > 0$, the project should be undertaken.

Although infrequently cited in the finance literature, the uniform annual equivalent (UAE)—sometimes referred to as the annualized worth method—is widely used in industry and engineering. This measure of project worth is simply the annual annuity equivalent of NPV; that is,

$$UAE = \frac{NPV}{\sum_{t=1}^{N} (1 + r)^{-t}}.$$

Obviously the UAE and NPV methods will yield the same accept/reject decisions, since when $NPV > 0$, UAE will also be positive, and vice versa. However, the project rankings the two criteria provide can differ for mutually exclusive projects (discussed later in the chapter). For this reason, the NPV criterion is the preferred ranking method.

A project's *profitability index (PI)*, or benefit/cost ratio, is closely related to NPV in that it uses the same inputs. Specifically,

$$PI = \frac{\sum_{t=1}^{N} \dfrac{NCF_t}{(1 + r)^t}}{I}.$$

With this tool, a project is worthwhile if $PI > 1$; that is, the project will increase shareholder wealth where the present value of its benefits (NCF_t) exceeds its cost. The *project IRR* for a multiple-period investment can be defined as follows:

$$\sum_{t=1}^{N} \frac{NCF_t}{(1 + IRR)^t} - I = 0.$$

This measure signals that a project should be undertaken where the calculated IRR exceeds the opportunity cost of funds (r).

Two popular non-DCF techniques are the payback and average rate of return methods. A project's *payback* is simply the number of years it takes to cover the project's initial cost. For example, if a project requires a $100,000 initial investment and produces $25,000 per year in cash flow, its payback will be 4 years.

In the *average rate of return (AROR) method*,

$$AROR = \frac{\dfrac{\sum_{t=1}^{N} NI_t}{N}}{\left(\dfrac{\text{Initial investment} + \text{Salvage value}}{2}\right)},$$

where NI_t = accounting net income for year t

N = project life

Salvage value = project's year N resale value

Thus, the AROR equals the ratio of the average annual accounting profit produced by the project over its life divided by the average investment in the project over its life.

Neither non-DCF technique has any basis in financial theory, but both have gained widespread use by practitioners, as we now discuss.

Survey of Industry Capital Budgeting Practice

Table 5.1 summarizes the results of seven surveys of industry capital budgeting practice. One prominent feature of these results is the shift away from non-DCF techniques toward DCF methods. Note too the prevalence of the use of two techniques as opposed to relying on a single metric. For example, in the Kim et al. (1986) survey the most frequently used *primary* method was the IRR (49 percent of the survey respondents), while the most popular *secondary* method was payback (35 percent).

Table 5.1   Surveys of Capital Budgeting Practice

Capital Budgeting Technique	Klammer, 1959	Klammer, 1964	Klammer, 1970	Petty et al., 1972	Gitman and Forrester, 1976	Kim and Farragher, 1979	Kim et al., 1986
Primary method:							
NPV }	19%	38%	57%	15%	13%	19%	21%
IRR }				41	53	49	49
Payback	34	24	12	11	9	12	19
AROR	34	30	26	31	25	8	8
Secondary method:							
NPV				14	28	8	24
IRR				19	14	8	15
Payback				37	44	39	35
AROR				24	14	3	19

Sources: Thomas Klammer, "Empirical Evidence of the Adoption of Sophisticated Capital Budgeting Techniques," *Journal of Business* (July 1972): 387–397; J. William Petty, David F. Scott, Jr., and Monroe M. Bird, "The Capital Expenditure Decision-Making Process of Large Corporations," *Engineering Economist* (Spring 1975): 159–172; S. H. Kim, T. Crick, and S. H. Kim, "Do Executives Practice What They Preach?" *Management Accounting* (November 1986): 49–52; Lawrence J. Gitman and John R. Forrester, Jr., "A Survey of Capital Budgeting Techniques Used by Major U.S. Firms," *Financial Management* (Fall 1977): 66–71; S. H. Kim and E. J. Farragher, "Current Capital Budgeting Practices," *Management Accounting* (June 1981): 26–30.

Ross (1986) used personal interviews and field research to survey in depth the capital budgeting practices of 12 large manufacturers. His findings give insight into the nuts and bolts of capital investment decisionmaking not possible from mail questionnaires like the ones summarized above. Ross first notes that the procedures used to evaluate new projects vary with the nature of the investment. Projects are broadly classified as either "mandatory" (for example, regulatory or contractual requirements or replacement of antiquated equipment) or "discretionary" (for example, assets required to reach expanded markets). Although Ross concentrated on discretionary investments, he noted that the type of analysis used frequently varied with a project's classification as mandatory or discretionary. A second key factor in determining the type of analysis used for a new project proposal was the dollar investment involved. The key difference is at what level in the firm's managerial hierarchy the decisionmaking authority was located. For example, decisions regarding very small projects (up to $100,000) were generally made at the plant level, and decisions regarding large projects (greater than $10 million) were generally made by the CEO and board. In general the level of detail in the project analysis varied directly with the amount of funds being sought. The largest projects received detailed discounted cash flow analysis, including sensitivity analyses of key economic variables. Very small projects, on the other hand, were evaluated on the basis of a single quantitative measure, such as the internal rate of return or payback.

Single-Period Analysis of Capital Budgeting

Capital Widening

The *capital widening* decision aims at determining the optimal scale of an investment, that is, the amount of outlay for the investment that will maximize its impact on investor wealth.

The "Simple" Accept/Reject Capital Budgeting Problem.   Before we proceed with our discussion of capital widening, let us first consider a simple accept/reject capital budgeting proposal, where there is only one feasible investment outlay. Figure 5.1 illustrates such a case. In panel a, the entrepreneur begins with initial wealth w_0 and has an opportunity to invest $I_0^* = w_0 - x_0^*$ in a project that will

Figure 5.1   A Simple Accept/Reject Capital Budgeting Proposal

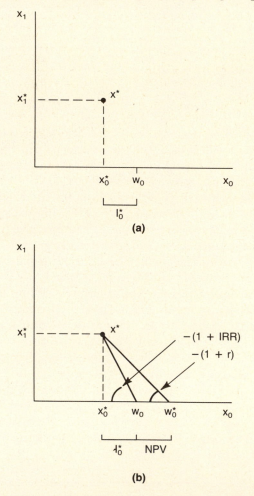

produce a cash flow next period of x_1^*. In panel b, the net present value of the investment is shown as $w_0^* - w_0$, which is positive, indicating that the investment should be undertaken. Note too that $-(1 + IRR)$ is the slope of the line passing through x^* and w_0 in panel b. Since $-(1 + IRR) < -(1 + r)$, then $(1 + IRR) > (1 + r)$—the internal rate of return is greater than the interest rate[4]—which also suggests that the project should be undertaken.

This agreement between the net present value and the internal rate of return criteria occurs here only because there is just one feasible investment outlay. In addition, since we do not have to select the optimal level of the investment outlay, we can simply evaluate whether $IRR > r$ for the one feasible case. We will soon discover, though, that this agreement between IRR and NPV does not always occur when we consider mutually exclusive investments. Net present value, on the other hand, always measures the increase in current wealth resulting from an investment. Thus, where a conflict arises we will utilize net present value, since our objective is to maximize the current consumption opportunities an investment creates, which, by the Fisher separation theorem, corresponds directly to current wealth maximization.

The General Capital Widening Problem.   Capital widening expands the traditional, simple presentation of the capital budgeting problem—illustrated in Figure 5.1—to include consideration for the "optimal," that is, wealth-maximizing, level of the initial investment outlay. In fact, the accept/reject decision for an investment opportunity is a special case of the capital widening problem, where a reject decision corresponds to an optimal investment equal to zero and an accept decision means that some positive investment in the asset will increase shareholder wealth.

To simplify our discussion of capital widening, we will assume that investment proposals are completely divisible. This means that projects can be undertaken at levels ranging from zero up to the total available supply of the asset in question. Thus, the consumption possibilities created by investing in such a project will form a smooth curve, such as that in panel a of Figure 5.2, rather than a discontinuous investment frontier, depicted in panel b. In the latter case, real investment opportunities occur in discrete lumps of $(w_0 - x_0')$ dollars, which earns a marginal rate of return i_1, $(x_0' - x_0'')$ dollars, which earns i_2, and $(x_0'' - 0)$, which earns i_3.

Independent Investment Opportunities

If an investment alternative can be accepted or rejected without regard for the acceptance or rejection of any other projects under consideration, it is an *independent* capital budgeting proposal. An example of a set of independent proposals

---

[4]Note that in a world characterized by perfectly competitive markets, no transactions costs, and certainty, there should be no cases where $IRR > r$ in equilibrium. We return to this point in Chapter 6, where we discuss monopoly rents as the source of positive NPVs.

Figure 5.2   Divisibility of Capital Investments

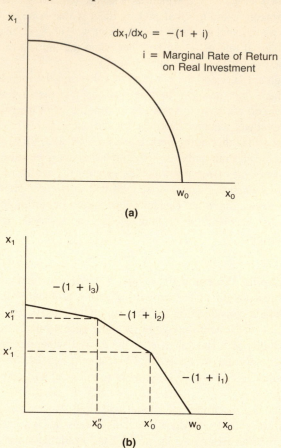

(a)

(b)

might include the acquisition of a new data processing system, the renovation of a conveyor belt drive, and the purchase of a company plane. These projects are independent in the sense that any combination of them (from none to all three) conceivably could be undertaken. Thus, independent capital expenditure proposals can be analyzed individually, or "independently."[5]

Figure 5.3 contains the consumption possibilities created by two independent investment opportunities designated A and B. Note that using the net present value rule, the optimal level of investment in project A is I_0^* dollars, which pro-

[5]Technically, two projects are said to be independent if the value to the firm of the combined project cash flows equals the sum of the projects' values taken individually. For example, if we let NCF_x and NCF_y be the end-of-period net cash flows for projects x and y, respectively, these projects are independent where the value of both projects (x + y) to the firm equals $V(x + y) = V(x) + V(y) = NCF_x/(1 + r) + NCF_y/(1 + r)$. If the two projects are dependent, $V(x + y) \neq V(x) + V(y)$ since the value of each project in combination would "depend" on whether the other has been accepted or rejected.

Figure 5.3   Independent Capital Investment Proposals

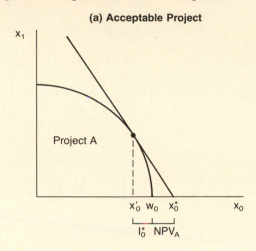

(a) Acceptable Project

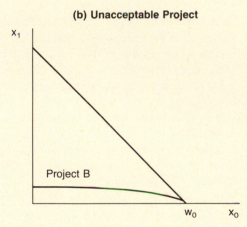

(b) Unacceptable Project

vides an increase in current shareholder wealth of NPV_A dollars. Project B, however, provides such low returns on all dollars invested that the optimal level of investment in that proposal is zero — that is, the borrowing/lending rate (r) in capital markets exceeds the rate of return earned on even the smallest investment in project B. In analyzing projects A and B, note that we determined the optimal level of investment in each project; in other words, we simultaneously solved the capital widening problem *and* determined whether to accept or reject each project.

We can summarize the accept/reject criteria for independent investment proposals as follows:

Decision	Optimal Initial Outlay	NPV	IRR
Accept	> 0	> 0	> r
Reject	= 0	< 0	< r

Note first that these accept/reject criteria correspond to the value-maximizing investment (that is, the one for which NPV is maximized). Further, for the optimal level of investment (I_0^* in panel a of Figure 5.3), the internal rate of return exceeds the risk-free interest rate. Recall, however, that we cannot determine the optimal level of real investment using the IRR.

Given that the Fisher separation theorem holds, the solution to the capital widening problem involves maximizing the present value of the wealth created by the investment project, or solving the following optimization problem:

$$\text{Max } w_0^* = x_0 + \frac{F(x_0)}{(1 + r)},$$

where $F(x_0)$ is a function describing the project's cash flows. We can rewrite this function to include the investment outlay, I_0, explicitly by noting that $x_0 = w_0 - I_0$. In this case, the objective function becomes

(5.1) $$\text{Max } w_0^* = w_0 - I_0 + \frac{F(w_0 - I_0)}{(1 + r)},$$

where

w_0^* = current wealth of the post-investment entrepreneur (or equity value, e_0, in the case of a corporation)

w_0 = current wealth of the pre-investment entrepreneur (or the initial equity endowment, k_0, of a corporation)

$w_0^* - w_0$ = net present value, or wealth increment resulting from the investment

I_0 = size of investment outlay in the project, the object of the analysis

$F(w_0 - I_0)$ = function describing how dollars invested in a real/productive asset are converted into end-of-period cash flow (consumption possibilities), x_1

r = market-determined interest rate for borrowing and lending

Thus, the first-order condition (that is, the first derivative set equal to zero) for the wealth-maximizing investment decision is the following:

$$\frac{dw_0^*}{dI} = -1 - \left[\frac{F'(w_0 - I_0)}{(1 + r)} \right] = 0,$$

which can be rewritten as follows:

$$-F'(w_0 - I_0) = (1 + r),$$

or, where we recognize that $x_0 = (w_0 - I_0)$,

(5.2) $$F'(x_0) = -(1 + r).$$

Thus, the optimal level of investment in a project occurs where the marginal rate at which a dollar invested in it produces future wealth just equals the rate at which that same dollar would produce future wealth if used to buy capital market notes. Analytically, the optimal investment level occurs when $-F'(w_0 - I_0)$, the marginal rate of transformation provided by real investment, equals $(1 + r)$, the marginal rate of transformation in the capital market. Recall that $F'(w_0 - I_0) < 0$ such that $-F'(w_0 - I_0) > 0$.

Exercise 5.1: A Capital Widening Problem

Consider an entrepreneur who has $40,000 in current wealth and is analyzing an investment opportunity that provides the following future consumption possibilities (in thousands of dollars):

$$F(x_0) = F(w_0 - I_0) = 60 + 0.10(w_0 - I_0) - 0.04(w_0 - I_0)^2,$$

where $F(x_0) = F(w_0 - I_0)$ describes the functional relationship between investment today and cash flow one period hence (provided by the investment being considered); w_0 equals $40,000; and the market rate of interest is 10 percent. What is the optimal level of real investment?

Solution. Using the first-order condition stated in Equation 5.2, we find the optimal level of $x_0 = x_0^*$ and, consequently, the optimal investment level $I_0^* = (w_0 - x_0^*)$ where

$$F'(x_0^*) = -(1 + r).$$

Note that $F'(x_0) = 0.10 - 0.08x_0$ and $r = 0.10$ such that substituting into Equation 5.2 produces

$$0.10 - 0.08x_0^* = -1.10$$

or

$$x_0^* = \$15 \text{ (thousand)}.$$

Solving for $I_0^* = (w_0 - x_0^*)$, we determine the optimal investment outlay in the project to be $25,000. Substituting this investment level back into $F(w_0 - I)$ gives us the future cash flow provided by investing in the project, which equals $52,500. This, in turn, translates into additional current wealth of $52,500/(1.10) = $47,727.27 (see Figure 5.4).

To summarize, the entrepreneur started with an initial wealth endowment (w_0) of $40,000 and invested $25,000 in the project, leaving $15,000 of present wealth uninvested; the investment produced current wealth of $47,727.27; and this increased his current consumption power or wealth from $w_0 = $40,000 to $w_0^* = $47,727.27 + $15,000 = $62,727.27, which represents an increase in current wealth of $22,727.27. Hence, the net present value of the investment is $47,727.27 - $25,000 = $22,727.27, which equals (not by chance) the increase in present wealth due to real investment.

Figure 5.4   Example: Optimal Investment Outlay

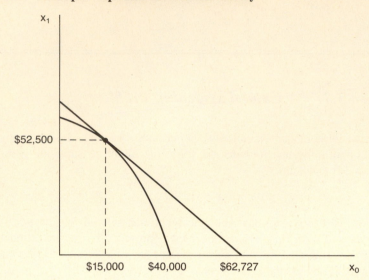

Dependent Investment Opportunities

A set of investment opportunities is said to be *dependent* if the acceptance or re-jection of any member thereof is in any way contingent on the prior acceptance or rejection of another member. Therefore, dependence can take one of two forms: mutually *inclusive* investment opportunities, in which the acceptability of one pro-ject is contingent on the prior acceptance of another, and mutually *exclusive* op-portunities, in which the acceptance of one depends on the prior rejection of another.

Mutually Inclusive Investments.   An example of *mutually inclusive* dependence would be an investment in a new product line that involves first a test market pro-gram and then a national marketing campaign. Figure 5.5 contains an example of such an investment. In this case, the test market will produce a positive net present value of NPV_{test}; however, the national marketing effort will produce an even larger net present value equal to $NPV_{national}$. Note that NPV_{test} need not have been positive for the project to be undertaken, since $NPV_{national}$ was positive. The dependence here relates to the *necessity* of the test market program (much like re-search and development) for the national marketing campaign's success.

Once again the net present value rule provides the correct choice of invest-ment outlay. However, the first-order condition in Equation 5.2 does not identify a unique investment outlay. There are three investment levels (X_A, X_B, and X_C) that satisfy the first-order condition. Thus, to identify the current wealth-maximizing choice, the net present values of all three investment levels identified in step 2 must be evaluated and the largest selected.

Figure 5.5   Mutually Inclusive Project Dependence

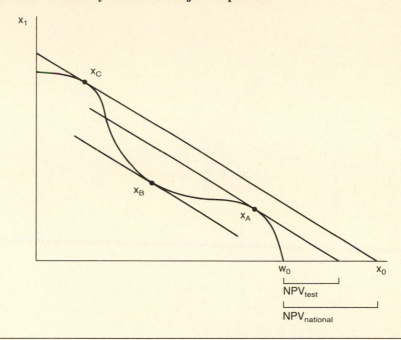

Mutually Exclusive Investments.   A set of investment opportunities is said to be *mutually exclusive* when only one or a limited number of members can be chosen. For example, consider a firm that is analyzing two conveyor belt systems for possible installation in its plant. Only one of the systems is needed. Figure 5.6 depicts the investment opportunities posed by the conveyor belt choices. In this case, the net present value rule easily provides the basis for the decision. We simply identify the optimal level of investment in each system and then use its corresponding net present value to select the alternative having the greatest positive impact on current wealth.

Recalling that $-(1 + IRR)$ for system I in Figure 5.6 is the slope of a line passing through x' and w_0, we observe that IRR_I is less than IRR_{II}. Hence, using the IRR criterion, system II is preferred to system I. This disagreement between the IRR and NPV rankings of these mutually exclusive projects results from the *disparity in the sizes* of the optimal investment outlays for them. Thus, although system II offers the higher IRR, the optimal investment outlay for I_{II} is so much less than that for I_I that NPV_I exceeds NPV_{II}. Note that both systems produce NPVs that are greater than zero — that is, each $IRR > r$. Note too that we determined the optimal investment level by maximizing NPV; only then could we calculate the appropriate IRRs for the two alternatives. In other words, we did *not* use the IRR as the basis for determining the optimal scale of investment.

Figure 5.6   Mutually Exclusive Investment Opportunities

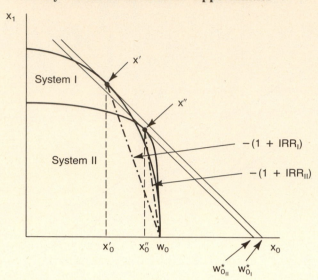

Summary of Capital Widening

Solving the capital widening problem entails finding the optimal level of investment for a capital budgeting proposal. The optimal investment level is that which maximizes the owner's present and future consumption opportunities. We have seen that where the Fisher separation theorem holds, this optimal investment level is found by maximizing the owner's current wealth or, in the case of a corporate owner, the present value of the corporation's equity. Since the net present value of an investment equals the change in current wealth resulting from an asset's acquisition, it also serves as an appropriate basis for determining the optimal investment outlay. Further, the internal rate of return criterion cannot be used to assess the appropriate level of investment outlay, because it does not *directly* measure the impact of an asset's acquisition on current wealth. Although the internal rate of return and net present value methods may *agree* with respect to accept/reject signals for *a particular investment level,* they will frequently *disagree* as to the rankings of two or more mutually exclusive proposals. When disagreement occurs, the net present value ranking is preferred since it ranks projects by their impact on current wealth rather than by the average rate of return earned per dollar invested in each asset. We will have more to say about the flaws of the internal rate of return method when we discuss the multiperiod capital deepening problem.

Continuous Compounding: A Mathematical Overview

Multiple Compounding Periods per Year

Where interest is compounded annually, the year T future value, $S(T)$, of a present amount, $S(0)$, is given by

(i) $$S(T) = S(0)(1 + i)^T,$$

where i is the annual interest rate. When interest is compounded m times per year, there are mT compounding periods in a T-year period, and i/m becomes the per period interest rate. Thus, the future value of $S(0)$ dollars in T years (and mT compounding periods) is

(ii) $$S(T) = S(0)\left(1 + \frac{i}{m}\right)^{mT}.$$

Note that i is now the nominal annual interest rate, which is less than the true or effective annual interest rate actually being earned. To see this, let i^* be an annually compounded rate equivalent to—that is, providing the same future value as—the nominal annual rate i with m compounding periods per year. Since i^* provides the same future value, $S(T)$, with annual compounding as does a rate i with m compounding periods per year,

$$S(T) = S(0)(1 + i^*)^T$$

$$= S(0)\left(1 + \frac{i}{m}\right)^{mT}.$$

Setting the above equations equal to each other and solving for i^* produces the following:

(iii) $$i^* = \left(1 + \frac{i}{m}\right)^m - 1.$$

The term "annual percentage rate," or "APR," is frequently used when referring to i^*. We see that i^* equals i only when m equals 1, that is, in the case of annual compounding. Where m is greater than 1, i^* is greater than i; for example, where $m = 12$ and $i = 18\%$,

$$i^* = \left(1 + \frac{0.18}{12}\right)^{12} - 1$$

$$= .1956, \text{ or } 19.56\%.$$

Continuous Compounding for a Single Cash Flow

To compound interest continuously, we "conceptually" allow the number of compounding periods within a year to go to infinity. The result is the following:

(iv) $$S(T) = S(0)e^{iT},$$

where e = 2.718 . . . and i is the interest rate paid if compounding occurs continuously.

The derivation of (iv) follows directly from (ii), which is restated as follows:

$$S(T) = S(0)\left(1 + \frac{i}{m}\right)^{mT}.$$

Multiplying the exponent mT by i/i, we can rewrite as mT = (m/i)(iT). Substituting for mT in (ii) produces the following result:

$$S(T) = S(0)\left[\left(1 + \frac{i}{m}\right)^{m/i}\right]^{iT}.$$

Letting g = m/i, we can rewrite the above equation as follows:

(v) $$S(T) = S(0)\left[\left(1 + \frac{1}{g}\right)^{g}\right]^{iT}.$$

Note that as the number of compounding periods, m, increases, g = m/i gets larger such that, in the limit, the term in brackets in (v) approaches the value e = 2.718 . . . ; that is,

$$e \equiv \lim_{g \to \infty}\left(1 + \frac{1}{g}\right)^{g}.$$

Hence, for continuous compounding we substitute e for the term in brackets in (v) to get (iv).

For example, let i = 18%, S(0) = $100, and T = 5. With interest compounded continuously, we can use (iv) to calculate

$$S(5) = \$100e^{(0.18)(5)} = \$245.96.$$

If interest were compounded annually, by (i) future value would be as follows:

$$S(5) = \$100(1 + 0.18)^5 = \$228.78.$$

The effect of more frequent compounding is evident in the two future values quoted here.

Continuous Compounding of a Stream of Cash Flows

Let z(t) be the continuous function denoting cash flow in dollars per year from t = 0 through t = T. Note that cash flow is assumed to be received continuously over time. The present value, z_T, of this cash flow stream is given by the following integral:

(vi)
$$z_T = \int_0^T z(t)e^{-it}\,dt.$$

Finally, note that for the special case where $z(t)$ is equal to a constant, a, (vi) reduces to the following:

(vii)
$$z_T = a\left[\frac{(1 - e^{-iT})}{i}\right].$$

Multiperiod Capital Budgeting

Capital Deepening

The introduction of the prospect of cash flows generated for multiple periods adds another dimension to the capital budgeting problem. The analyst must determine not only "how much to invest" but also "how long to hold the asset" (or "when to replace the asset" in the event its productive capacity deteriorates with use over time). This issue is referred to as the *capital deepening* problem. To simplify the analysis, we will assume that the capital widening problem has been solved—that is, the optimal scale of investment has been determined, and this level does not vary with the term of investment or holding period. This assumption will allow us to solve the capital deepening problem without explicitly considering the question of how much to invest in the project.

Investing in a Single Asset (No Replications)

In this first case, we will determine the optimal holding period for a single asset; that is, no replication of the investment is contemplated when the first terminates.

Consider an entrepreneur who is analyzing the possible acquisition of an asset. The optimal scale of the investment is known to require an investment of I_0 dollars today; in other words, the capital widening decision has been made, and the optimal investment in the asset is independent of the holding period. The entrepreneur now wants to determine whether or not to acquire the asset based on its anticipated impact on his or her present wealth.

To begin, we will assume that cash flows are continuous. This is a simplifying assumption, for it will permit us to use calculus in solving the optimization problem encountered in capital deepening. However, once we have solved the problem for continuous time, we will summarize what happens when cash flows are discrete, which is the usual case. The adjustment is straightforward and natural given the underlying results exposed in the continuous case.

First we note that the asset being analyzed is expected to generate a continuous net cash flow stream at a rate of z(t) dollars at time t; for example, if z(t) = \$50, cash flow is realized at a constant rate such that the cumulated cash per annum is \$50. This cash flow equals cash revenues net of all cash expenses and corresponds to the optimal scale of investment represented by the initial cash outlay of I_0 dollars. Thus, we can think of z(t) as a function that describes how net cash flows vary with time. In addition, the asset is expected to provide a salvage or abandonment cash flow equal to S(T) dollars if the investment is terminated in year T; S(T) is a function that describes how salvage value changes with time. Finally, the entrepreneur estimates that the opportunity cost of funds invested in the asset is a continuously compounded rate, r, for all T. Thus, the entrepreneur's problem is to determine the investment period (T) for which the asset will provide a maximum net present value, NPV(T). Note that NPV is now a function of time that we denote as NPV(T), where T is the holding period for which we will evaluate NPV. If the optimal NPV(T) > 0, the asset should be acquired. In addition, for mutually exclusive investments the entrepreneur seeks the maximum NPV(T) for each alternative to use in selecting the one that offers the largest expected wealth increment, or the largest NPV(T).

Where cash flows are assumed to be received and compounded continuously (we will treat the discrete cash flow case later), the objective can be stated analytically as follows:

(5.3) $$\text{Max NPV(T)} = \int_0^T z(t)e^{-rt}\,dt + S(T)e^{-rt} - I,$$

where the first term represents the present value of all net revenues, z(t), realized over the T periods in which the asset is held and the second equals the present value of the asset's salvage or residual value when sold in year T. Recall that to simplify the solution to the optimization problem we assumed continuous project cash flows, z(t), and used continuous compounding, where e^{-rt} is the present value of \$1 received in year t and discounted at rate r (see "Continuous Compounding: A Mathematical Overview" on page 125). We then find the optimal term over which to hold the investment by maximizing NPV(T) with respect to T.

If S(T) is differentiable and z(t) is continuous, NPV(T) is differentiable; thus, NPV(T) is maximized by finding the zeros of NPV'(T) where

$$\text{NPV}'(T) = e^{-rT}[z(T) + S'(T) - rS(T)]$$

and the prime (′) refers to the derivative taken with respect to T. The first-order condition for maximizing NPV(T) requires that for the optimal T, NPV'(T) = 0, which in turn implies the following:

(5.4) $$z(T) + S'(T) = rS(T).$$

Thus, at the optimal time for abandoning or divesting of the asset, the rate of cash flow generated by holding the asset, z(T), plus the rate of decrease or increase in the asset's salvage value, S'(T), just equals the return the entrepreneur would realize by investing the asset's current abandonment value, S(T), to earn the opportunity cost of funds, r. Alternatively, the optimum value of T is found where the marginal benefit of holding the asset for one more instant of time $[z(T) + S'(T)]$ just equals the marginal cost of holding it for one more instant of time $[rS(T)]$.[6]

Note that the NPV(T) model presented in Equation 5.3 omitted any *explicit* consideration of the reinvestment of funds upon termination of the investment. This formulation is consistent with an assumption that the reinvestment opportunity rate in year T equals the opportunity cost of funds, r. This particular reinvestment assumption is appropriate in a *competitive* real asset market where positive net present value investment opportunities *cannot* continue to exist in the long run since new firms enter to capitalize on them. In fact, the impact of competitive forces in the product market over time should be reflected in the $z(t)$ and $S(t)$ functions. (We will further discuss project cash flows and competitive forces later in this chapter and in Chapter 6, where we examine the source of positive NPV investments.)

The solution to the capital deepening problem is demonstrated graphically in Figure 5.7. To simplify the illustration, we have chosen the situation where an investment of I dollars is made today and the total cash realized from it is received when the asset is sold for $S(T)$ dollars in year T. Thus, in our example $z(t) = 0$ for all t. For obvious reasons this is often referred to as a point-input, point-output investment problem. The $S(T)$ function varies from $S(0)$ up to a maximum of $S(T')$ at $t = T'$. We might think of $S(T)$ as the net cash proceeds resulting from the sale of a barrel of wine in year T. Note that $S(T)$ is negative in the early years, indicating that the costs of marketing the wine in these years exceed its market value; thus, a net negative cash flow results. Our objective is to select that year (T) for which the present value of the wine's net proceeds, $S(T)e^{-rT}$, is greatest. Using the iso-present value curve $V_0^*V^*(t)$, we determine that the optimal time to sell the wine is T*. Note that all the points along $V_0^*V^*(t)$ share the same present value when discounted at r — hence the term *iso-present value curve*. Further, given the function describing the wine's future net sales proceeds, $S(T)$, the maximum attainable present value, V_0^*, occurs at $t = T^*$. In addition, the slope of $V^*(t) = V_0^*e^{rt}$ at T*, which equals $rV_0^*e^{rT^*} = rS(T^*)$, equals the slope of the $S(T)$ function, which equals the following:

$$rS(T^*) = S'(T^*).$$

---

[6]The second-order condition for a maximum NPV(T) insures that the marginal benefit function reflecting the present value benefits derived from holding the asset for one more instant of time will intersect the marginal cost function from above. In the simplest case, where there is no replication, the second-order condition appears as follows:

$$NPV''(T) < 0,$$

which equals

$$e^{-rT}[z'(T) - rS'(T) + S''(T)] - rNPV'(T) < 0.$$

Noting that $e^{-rT} > 0$ and that $NPV'(T) = 0$ by the first-order condition, the second-order condition holds where

$$Z'(T) + S''(T) < rS'(T),$$

which, of course, is true where the slope of the marginal benefit function (the left-hand side) is less than the slope of the marginal cost of holding function (the right-hand side).

Figure 5.7   The Capital Deepening Problem (No Replications)

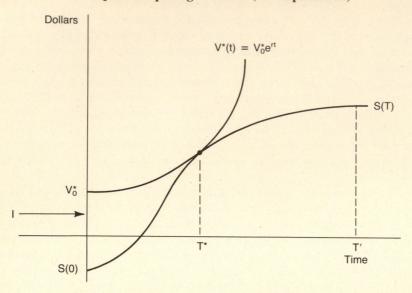

We recognize this as an abbreviation of the first-order condition stated in Equation 5.4 where there are no interim cash flows, that is, $z(t) = 0$ for all t.

Investing in a Sequence of Assets

Constant Scale Replication (Replacement Chain).   Now assume that the entrepreneur has an opportunity to invest I dollars in an asset that produces NPV(T) for a T-year holding period and can repeat the investment for an unlimited number of periods. In other words, the entrepreneur can invest I dollars in an asset every T years as many times as desired to earn the same rate of return. He or she will then receive a stream of cash flows equivalent to NPV(T) every T years.

In this case, the investment problem becomes one of maximizing the *sum* of the present values of all future NPV(T)s. The solution, then, is for the optimal time interval (T) between replications. Let $NPV_c(T)$ denote the net present value of the sequence of investments, where the subscript c refers to *constant scale replication* — this refers to the fact that the project's initial outlay (the scale of the investment) is the same for all future replications. The investment problem can then be stated as follows:

$$(5.5) \qquad \text{Max } NPV_c(T) = \sum_{j=0}^{\infty} NPV(T)e^{-jTr}.$$

Note that the right-hand side of Equation 5.5 is simply the present value of an infinite series of NPVs realized every T years.

With constant scale replication over an indefinite number of years, and where each replication of the investment earns the same rate of return, that is, NPV(T) is the same for all future replications, the investment objective in Equation 5.5 reduces to the following:

$$\text{Max NPV}_c(T) = \frac{\text{NPV(T)}}{(1 - e^{-rT})}.$$

Differentiating $\text{NPV}_c(T)$ with respect to T and substituting for $\text{NPV}'(T)$ using the equation leading to Equation 5.4 found on page 128, the first-order condition for the optimal T can be stated as follows:

(5.6)
$$z(T) + S'(T) = rS(T) + r\left[\frac{\text{NPV(T)}}{(1 - e^{-rT})}\right]$$

$$= rS(T) + r\text{NPV}_c(T).$$

Note that this condition differs from the corresponding first-order condition for the nonreplicated asset (Equation 5.4) only by the inclusion of r times the annualized net present value of the asset, reflected in the last term on the right-hand side of Equation 5.6. This means that for projects with positive NPV(T), $\text{NPV}_c(T) >$ NPV(T); consequently, the opportunity cost of not terminating the project in any year T, expressed by the right-hand side of Equation 5.6, is higher than was the same opportunity cost for the nonreplicated case, the right-hand side of Equation 5.4. Since the left-hand side of 5.6 is decreasing in T while the right-hand side is increasing, the optimal T is shorter for the constant scale replication case than for the single-asset case, that is, no replications. However, where NPV(T) equals zero, the optimal abandonment time is the same for both the nonreplicated and constant scale replicated investment opportunities. The case in which NPV(T) = 0 is consistent with the notion of long-run perfect competition.

At this point, a comment concerning the impact of competitive market conditions on project net present value is in order. In order for a firm to face an endless stream of investments in a positive net present value project, there must be some barrier to the free entry of competitive firms. If there were free entry, the forces of competition would drive the supply price of the investment up and/or its net cash proceeds down to the point where there would be no incentive for further investment — that is, NPV(T) = 0 for the optimal T. Thus, it makes sense to evaluate capital budgeting proposals using $\text{NPV}_c(T)$ only where the firm has some reason to believe that competitive forces will not drive the NPV(T) of future replications to zero. An example of such a situation occurs when the firm holds a patent on a particular product or productive process that it believes cannot be infringed upon. However, even in this case an "infinite" replication of the positive net present value is probably not warranted. The point here is that the decision to maximize $\text{NPV}_c(T)$ rather than NPV(T) should be based on a careful evaluation of the competitive circumstances surrounding future replications of the investment. In Chapter 6, we consider an example where the firm's monopoly access to a new productive process results in a positive net present value investment. However, the firm's monopoly power over the process is expected to disappear after a few years, and this has an important impact on the investment's net present value.

Replication with a Proportional Growth in the Scale of Investment. In this formulation of the asset abandonment problem, the firm faces the opportunity to replicate the investment through time to earn the same rate of return *and* can increase the scale or amount of the investment by a constant proportion, p, with each replication. Once again the economic circumstance for which this model would be applicable is that where barriers to competition are present such that positive net present values are expected to continue ad infinitum. The increase in scale of the optimal investment might, for example, result from an expansion in market size over time. The basic problem here is again one of selecting a replication period, T, that will maximize the sum of the present values of the $NPV_j(T)$, where j refers to the net present value of the jth replication; that is,

$$NPV_j(T) = NPV_0(T)e^{jpT},$$

where the zero subscript refers to the net present value of the first investment outlay. Since the scale of the investment is growing at a rate p through time and the rate of return on it is assumed invariant with the scale, $NPV_j(T)$ grows at the same rate as the initial investment outlay; that is, $I_j = I_0e^{jpT}$. The investment objective can now be restated as follows:

(5.7)
$$\text{Max } NPV_p(T) = NPV_0(T) \sum_{j=0}^{N} e^{jT(p-r)}.$$

Note, however, that the geometric series in Equation 5.7 converges to a finite sum only when the rate of growth in the scale of investment, p, is less than the opportunity cost of funds, r. For all $p \geq r$, the investment opportunity offers infinite wealth for all values of T offering a positive net present value. This is the proverbial "money machine."

For the case where $p < r$, the investment objective reduces to

$$\text{Max } NPV_p(T) = \frac{NPV_0(T)}{1 - e^{(p-r)T}}$$

and the corresponding first-order condition is

(5.8)
$$z(T) + S'(T) = rS(T) + \frac{[(r - p)e^{Tp}NPV_0(T)]}{1 - e^{(p-r)T}}.$$

Using Equation 5.8, we can see that where $NPV_0(T) > 0$ (for all T) and $0 < p < r$, the opportunity cost of retaining the asset per unit of time — that is, the right-hand side of Equation 5.8 — exceeds the opportunity cost of retention in both

Equations 5.4 and 5.6. Thus, in this situation the optimal replication interval would be shorter than either the nonreplicated or the constant scale replication cases. This results from the previously noted fact that the left-hand side of Equation 5.8 declines over time. Thus, where the right-hand side is greater than its counterpart in Equations 5.4 and 5.6, the optimal T from 5.8 will be smaller, *ceteris paribus*.

   Note once again that in order for this solution to the capital deepening problem to be useful, there must exist barriers to competitors' entry over time — that is, the investor cannot reasonably expect to continue earning growing positive net present values ad infinitum on asset investment replications unless there are effective barriers to competition. Further, as we have noted, a proportionately increasing scale of investment makes sense only when the growth rate in the scale of investment — perhaps due to growth in market size for a monopolist — is less than the opportunity cost of funds.

Summary of Capital Deepening

We have analyzed the basic issue of "how long to hold an investment," or the "capital deepening" problem, and offered possible solutions to three alternative specifications of the problem. In each case we derived different numerical answers. The solution appropriate in each case was shown to hinge upon the economic environment within which the investment decision is made. Particularly important here is the potential intrusion of competitors who could drive the net present value of an investment's future replications to zero. Thus, the usefulness of the models based on replication with constant scale and with proportionally increasing scale of investment depends on the existence of effective barriers to competition and, consequently, the continued presence of constant rate of return investment opportunities offering positive net present values.

   The three alternative solutions to the capital deepening problem offer *systematically* different solutions, as shown in Figure 5.8. This figure contains the marginal conditions (from the first-order conditions) for an optimal holding period for a positive net present value investment. In the case of both an asset whose value appreciates with time (panel a) and one that depreciates (panel b), we see that the optimal holding period is the shortest for the proportional scale growth case, followed by the constant scale replication case and finally the nonreplicated case. As noted above, however, the appropriate method of solution depends on the competitive environment in which the investment is being made.

Figure 5.8   Summary of Alternative Solutions to the Capital Deepening Problem

$X = r[NPV(T)/(1 - e^{-rT})]$.

$Y = [(r - p)e^{-pT}NPV_0(T)]/[1 - e^{T(p-r)}]$.

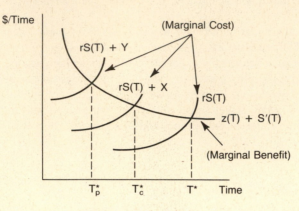

(a) Appreciating Asset

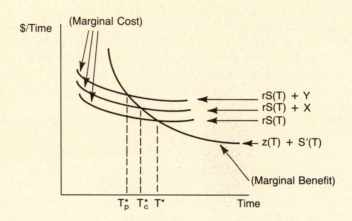

(b) Depreciating Asset

Exercise 5.2: Determining When to Harvest Timber— A Basic Capital Deepening Problem

The T. L. Ramos Corporation owns a tract of land on which it periodically plants and harvests timber. The firm estimates that the value of the timber at harvest time, S(T), varies with its age as follows:

$$S(T) = \$100,000(1 + T)^{0.5}.$$

In addition, Ramos estimates the cost of each planting as \$140,000. If the firm's opportunity cost of funds, r, is a constant 10 percent per year and if there are no interim cash revenues or expenditures associated with the timber investment, what is the optimal investment period for Ramos?

Solution 1: Single Investment with No Replications.   In this case, we solve for the optimal holding period by maximizing NPV(T) just as we did in Equation 5.3, with one small difference: Here the z(t), or interim cash flows, are zero such that the first-order condition becomes

$$S'(T) = rS(T).$$

Substituting for the appropriate terms, we obtain

$$\$50,000(1 + T)^{-0.5} = (0.10)\$100,000(1 + T)^{0.5}.$$

Multiplying through by $(1 + T)^{0.5}$ and simplifying gives

$$\$50,000 = \$10,000(1 + T)$$

$$T = 4 \text{ years.}$$

Therefore, in this case the optimal holding period for the timber is 4 years. The net present value corresponding to the optimal holding period is found by substituting into NPV(T) where T = 4:

$$NPV(4) = \$100,000(1 + 4)^{0.5}e^{-0.1(4)} - \$140,000$$

$$= \$9,888.11.$$

Thus, the timber investment has a positive wealth increment of \$9,888.11 and should be undertaken.

Solution 2: Constant Scale Replications.   In this formulation of the problem, the T. L. Ramos Corporation is assumed to face an infinite stream of replications of the timber investment where the initial cost of planting, scale of investment, and rate of return on investment are assumed to remain constant over time. The appropriate first-order condition is found in Equation 5.6 with one difference: Once again z(t) is zero for Ramos' investment. The first-order condition, then, is the following:

$$S'(T) = rS(T) + r\left[\frac{NPV(T)}{(1 - e^{-rT})}\right].$$

Solving for T by trial and error produces an optimal asset life of approximately 3.32 years, which provides a net present value, $NPV_c(T)$, of \$32,306.30.

Solution 3: Proportionate Scale Replications.   This formulation of the problem assumes that the scale of investment in each planting of trees grows at a constant rate, p. If this growth rate is less than the opportunity cost of funds, $NPV_p(T)$ is finite and finding the optimal T involves solving Equation 5.8 for T. If the growth in the scale of investment is 5 percent per replication and the other project information is unchanged, the optimal T is approximately 3.28 years. Once again a trial-and-error solution has been used to solve Equation 5.8 for the optimal T. The net present value corresponding to this asset life is \$59,689.41.

Summary

The solutions to the optimal economic life of the tree-cutting problem are summarized in Table 5.2. The proportionate scale replication solution produced the highest net present value and the shortest optimal investment period. This does *not* mean however, that this solution is preferred to the other two methods. *The preferred solution to the optimal investment term problem depends on the economic environment in which the decision is being made.* Thus, the proportionate scale replication solution is "appropriate" only where the firm making the tree-cutting investment can continually reinvest in a *growing* scale project (growing at rate p < r) with a constant rate of return earned on each dollar invested. In a competitive environment, for example, one might expect to be able to invest only once in a project earning a positive net present value; in this case, the "no replication" solution would be the appropriate model for evaluating the investment.

Table 5.2   Optimal Investment Term for Tree-Cutting Problem

Solution	Method	Optimal Life (Years)	Net Present Value
1	No replications	4	\$ 9,888.11
2	Constant scale replications	3.32	32,306.30
3	Proportionate scale replications	3.28	59,698.41

Internal Rate of Return Criteria and the Multiple Rate of Return Problem

Up to this point, our discussion of the capital deepening problem has focused entirely on the use of net present value. There is, however, another problem that arises with the use of the internal rate of return investment criterion in a multiperiod setting. Specifically, we show that in a multiperiod setting the internal rate of return may not be unique; that is, certain cash flow streams may have more than one internal rate of return.[7] Consider the following set of project cash flows:[8]

Year	0	1	2
Cash flow	−$1,600	$10,000	−$10,000

This example involves the replacement of an existing pump with a newer, more efficient model. The internal rate of return for this problem is calculated by solving the following equation for IRR:

$$NPV = -\$1,600 + \frac{\$10,000}{(1 + IRR)} - \frac{\$10,000}{(1 + IRR)^2} = 0.$$

---

[7]For a complete discussion of this problem, see Teichroew et al. (1965).

[8]This example was first used in the classic paper by Lorie and Savage (1955).

The Capital Deepening Problem with Discrete Cash Flows: A Mathematical Overview

Here we evaluate the capital deepening problem where cash flows are received and paid at discrete points in time. We define i as the annual interest rate, paid or compounded once per year. In terms of the continuous compounding case, $(1 + i) = e^r$, where r is the annual interest rate paid or compounded continuously. In addition, we redefine $z(t)$ as the cash flow received at the end of period t (in this case, t = years).

Single Asset with No Replication Case

In this case, the optimal economic life of an asset (that is, the optimal time to abandon) is found by maximizing the following function:

$$NPV(T) = z(1)v + z(2)v^2 + \ldots + z(T)v^T + S(T)v^T - I,$$

where $v = 1/(1 + i)$. The appropriate decision rule is: *Abandon at T if NPV(T + 1)* $\leq$ *NPV(T)*, or *hold past T if NPV(T + 1)* > *NPV(T)*. Letting

$$\Delta NPV(T) = NPV(T + 1) - NPV(T),$$

we can operationalize the decision rule for abandonment as follows: *Continue to hold the asset for year T so long as the change in NPV(T) is positive*, that is,

$$\Delta NPV(T) = z(T + 1)v^{T+1} + S(T + 1)v^{T+1} - S(T)v^T > 0$$

or

$$\Delta NPV(T) = v^{T+1}[z(T + 1) + S(T + 1) - S(T)(1 + i)] > 0$$

$$= v^{T+1}[z(T + 1) + \Delta S(T) - iS(T)] > 0,$$

where $\Delta S(T)$ is the change in the asset's residual value from year T to T + 1. This is the discrete time analog of the first-order condition found in Equation 5.4 and can also be written as

$$z(T + 1) + \Delta S(T) > iS(T).$$

Constant Scale Replication Case

For this case, we seek to maximize the following function:

$$NPV_c(T) = NPV(T) + NPV(T)v^T + NPV(T)v^{2T} + \ldots.$$

Recall that $v = 1/(1 + i)$ such that the above series can be rewritten as follows:

$$= \frac{NPV(T)}{(1 - v^T)}.$$

Again we hold the asset past year T if $NPV_c(T + 1) > NPV_c(T)$, or, equivalently, $\Delta NPV_c(T) > 0$; that is,

$$\Delta NPV_c(T) = \frac{NPV(T + 1)}{(1 - v^{T+1})} - \frac{NPV(T)}{(1 - v^T)}$$

$$= \frac{NPV(T + 1)(1 - v^T) - NPV(T)(1 - v^{T+1})}{(1 - v^T)(1 - v^{T+1})}$$

$$= \frac{\Delta NPV(T)(1 - v^{T+1}) - v^{T+1}iNPV(T+1)}{(1 - v^{T+1})(1 - v^T)}.$$

Hence, $\Delta NPV_c(T) > 0$ if

$$(1 - v^{T+1})\Delta NPV(T) > v^{T+1}iNPV(T + 1)$$

or

$$\Delta NPV(T) > \frac{v^{T+1}iNPV(T + 1)}{1 - v^{T+1}}.$$

Since $\Delta NPV(T) = v^{T+1}[z(T + 1) + \Delta S(T) - iS(T)]$, this gives

$$z(T + 1) + \Delta S(T) > iS(T) + \frac{iNPV(T + 1)}{1 - v^{T+1}} \, .$$

This is the discrete time analog to Equation 5.6 and has the same interpretation.

Replication with Proportionate Growth in Scale

First, we observe that the NPV of the jth investment replication can be defined as follows (where the growth in scale of investment occurs at a rate p):

$$NPV_j(T) = NPV_0(T)(1 + p)^{jT}.$$

Note that $j = 0$ for the initial investment and NPV_0 is the NPV of that investment. The objective function for this case can then be written as follows:

$$
\begin{aligned}
NPV_p(T) &= \sum_{j \geq 0} NPV_j(T) \\
&= NPV_0(T)(1 + w^T + w^{2T} + \ldots),
\end{aligned}
$$

where $w = [(1 + p)/(1 + i)]$. Provided that $p < i$ such that $w < 1$, we can rewrite the above expression as follows:

$$NPV_p(T) = \frac{NPV_0(T)}{1 - w^T} \, .$$

The decision rule, then, is: *Hold past year T if $\Delta NPV_p(T) > 0$.* In this case, we define $\Delta NPV_p(T)$ as follows:

$$\Delta NPV_p(T) = \Delta NPV_0(T)(1 - w^{T+1}) - \frac{w^{T+1}kNPV_0(T + 1)}{(1 - w^{T+1})(1 - w^T)},$$

where $k = (1/w) - 1 = [(1 + i)/(1 + p)] - 1 = [(i - p)/(1 + p)]$. Further, $\Delta NPV_p > 0$ if and only if

$$z(T + 1) + \Delta S(T) > iS(T) + \frac{[kw^{T+1}NPV_0(T + 1)]}{1 - w^{T+1}} \, .$$

This is analogous to Equation 5.8 and has the same interpretation.

Summary

In closing, we should note that the criteria developed here for evaluating the optimal economic life/abandonment problem with discrete cash flows are necessary but insufficient conditions for an optimum — that is, these criteria correspond to the first-order conditions for a maximum. In other words, $\Delta NPV(T)$ is the change in $NPV(T)$ for a one-unit change in T and, as such, is the discrete time equivalent of the derivative of $NPV(T)$ with respect to T. Therefore, finding $\Delta NPV(T)$ equal to zero does not insure that we will have a maximum rather than a minimum or point of inflection or that there will not be multiple local maxima. Further, even if the criteria could identify a global maximum, we would still have to evaluate whether the corresponding net present value was positive. Thus, to solve the abandonment problem in discrete time involves the following:

- *Step 1:* Evaluate ΔNPV(T) for all feasible values of T and T + 1.
- *Step 2:* Calculate NPV(T) for all instances where ΔNPV(T) < 0.
- *Step 3:* Select the year T in which to abandon for which NPV(T) > 0 and is the largest.

However, two values of IRR satisfy this equality: 25 percent and 400 percent. Graphically, we can observe how NPV behaves as we increase the rate used to discount the project cash flows in Figure 5.9. Typically, NPV declines monotonically as the interest rate used to discount cash flows increases. However, where the sign on the incremental cash flows changes more than once (for example, in the pump problem there were two sign changes in the cash flows), the possibility of multiple internal rates of return arises. In this case, NPV does not decline monotonically with increasing discount rates. In general, Descartes' "rule of signs" tells us that there can be as many different solutions to a polynomial equation — such as the one used to solve for the internal rate of return — as there are changes in the terms' signs. Hence, where there are two sign changes in the incremental cash flows of a proposed capital expenditure (as was the case with the pump ex-

Figure 5.9   Multiple Internal Rates of Return

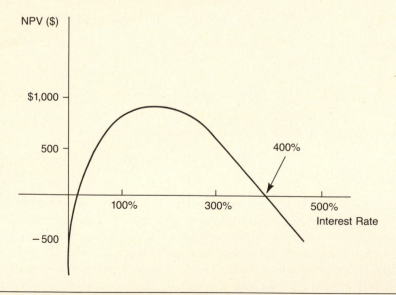

ample), there *potentially* are two different interest rates that will satisfy the internal rate of return equation.

Should the internal rate of return criterion be used in evaluating multiple-period capital budgeting proposals? The answer is a conditional yes — that is, it can be used *only* where a unique IRR exists and where an accept/reject decision is being made for a *given* level of investment outlay and a *given* investment holding period. The qualifications of a "given" investment level and holding period result from the fact that the internal rate of return cannot be used to find the optimal level of investment or the investment term that will maximize current wealth. However, recall that where capital budgeting choices are made so as to maximize current wealth, the net present value criterion provides a direct measure of a project's wealth impact. Therefore, use of the internal rate of return criterion generally is appropriate only when it provides answers that are consistent with the net present value criterion.

Exercise 5.3:   Evaluating an Investment with Multiple Internal Rates of Return

The incremental cash flows resulting from the replacement of a machine assembly station in an auto plant are as follows:

Year	0	1	2	3
Cash flow	$-$2,000	$12,000	$-$22,000	$12,000

Determine the internal rate(s) of return for the proposed expenditure. For what interest rate(s) will the investment produce a positive net present value?

Solution
0%:

$$NPV = -\$2,000 + \frac{\$12,000}{(1 + 0)^1} - \frac{\$22,000}{(1 + 0)^2} + \frac{\$12,000}{(1 + 0)^3}$$

$$= 0.$$

100%:

$$NPV = -\$2,000 + \frac{\$12,000}{(1 + 1)^1} - \frac{\$22,000}{(1 + 1)^2} + \frac{\$12,000}{(1 + 1)^3}$$

$$= 0.$$

200%:

$$NPV = -\$2,000 + \frac{\$12,000}{(1 + 2)^1} - \frac{\$22,000}{(1 + 2)^2} + \frac{\$12,000}{(1 + 2)^3}$$

$$= 0.$$

Figure 5.10 Net Present Value Function for Exercise 5.3

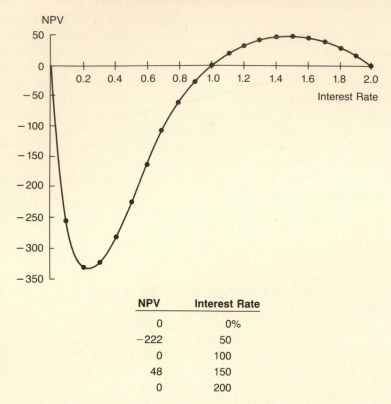

NPV	Interest Rate
0	0%
-222	50
0	100
48	150
0	200

The graph of NPV for different interest rates appears as in Figure 5.10. The range of interest rates for which the project will produce a positive net present value is 100 to 200 percent. Hence, even though the project produces two very large internal rates of return, it will provide a positive net present value (wealth increment) only where the opportunity cost of funds lies between 100 and 200 percent.

Summary

The capital budgeting problem holds a very prominent place in both the theory and practice of corporate finance. Our primary objective in this chapter was to illuminate the two fundamental aspects of any such analysis: "how much to invest" and "how long to plan to hold the investment" (or its corollary, "how long will the investment last?"). Both issues are central to the analysis of any capital budgeting problem but are frequently overlooked in introductory discussions of this topic. This simplification presumably is an attempt to reduce the analysis to a simple accept/reject decision based on a single investment outlay and a single investment period. While this type of analysis obviously simplifies the exposition, it also masks the true complexity of the capital budgeting task and the critical issues involved in determining the optimal amount to invest and the optimal term of investment.

Within the context of the capital widening problem, we analyzed the special cases of independent, mutually inclusive, and mutually exclusive investment proposals. Further, while discussing the capital deepening problem, we noted that the abandonment or divestiture problem is merely a special case of the capital deepening or optimal investment term problem.

We retained the assumption of certainty throughout our analysis because a great deal of insight into the critical dimensions of the capital budgeting problem can initially be gained without adding the complexities attendant on uncertainty. We will introduce these more realistic conditions in Part III and apply them specifically to the capital budgeting problem in Chapter 10.

In Chapter 6, we examine the cash flows that are "relevant" for project evaluation. Specifically, we (1) contrast project cash flow and accounting profits, (2) discuss the impact of inflation on project value, and (3) analyze the source of positive net present value projects.

Study Questions

5.1   Compare and contrast the capital widening and capital deepening problems in capital budgeting.

5.2   In the context of the capital widening decision, define what we mean when we refer to independent and dependent investment opportunities.

5.3   "The abandonment problem is a special case of the capital deepening problem." Discuss.

5.4   Discuss the conditions under which the single-asset, constant scale replication, and proportionate growth in scale replication solutions to the capital deepening problem are appropriate.

5.5   "The three solutions offered to the capital deepening problem produce not only different NPV estimates but also different optimal investment periods." Discuss.

5.6   The discrete time solution to the capital deepening problem looks very similar to the continuous time solution; however, the procedure used is quite different. Describe the discrete time procedure.

5.7   "The multiperiod setting gives rise to yet another flaw in the IRR methodology for evaluating proposed capital expenditures." Discuss.

Study Problems

*5.1 The Zepher Company, Inc. faces the following real/productive investment opportunity:

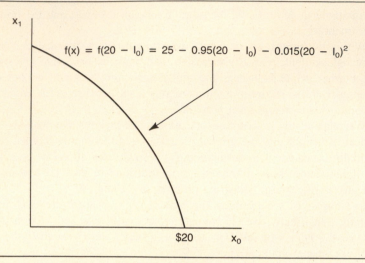

$$f(x) = f(20 - I_0) = 25 - 0.95(20 - I_0) - 0.015(20 - I_0)^2$$

However, Zepher has only $20 of owner funds and does not want to sell any new shares of stock (for reasons known only to the eccentric owner, L.D. Zepher).

a. If the market rate of interest is 10 percent, what amount of debt should Zepher issue in order to raise the funds for the optimal investment level? What will be the total value of the Zepher Company after it accepts the optimal investment level? What will be the total value of Zepher's stock?

b. What would be your answer to part a if Zepher had $30 in equity funds available? Would the investment decision change?

c. Answer part a where the interest rate is 20 percent.

*5.2 Fledgling Microchip, Inc. is faced with the following investment problem. The firm's newly patented microcomputer is now ready for marketing, and the firm's owners have a total of $50,000 to commit to the venture. The end-of-period cash flow from the investment is described by the following function:

$$f(x_0) = 60 - 1.12857x_0 - 0.0014286x_0^2.$$

The firm can borrow or lend at a rate of 10 percent.

a. What is the optimal level of investment in the venture for Fledgling?

---

*Problems denoted with an asterisk (*) involve the use of calculus.

b. Some of Fledgling's owners have been working for years on the promised monetary rewards from the venture. If Fledgling should sell its patent to someone else to manufacture and market, how much should they expect to receive?

*5.3   The Stephen P. Witt Manufacturing Company is a textile firm located in Spartensburg, South Carolina. The firm manufactures fabric used in making sheets, bedspreads, tablecloths, and towels. The company has been in business for over 50 years and is still using the basic weaving equipment originally installed in the plant. Although the equipment has been well maintained, current technology has made it obsolete, and the firm is now prepared to replace it. There are two competing lines of equipment under consideration, which, for simplicity, we will call Alpha and Beta. Although both pieces of equipment are viable alternatives, their operating characteristics are quite different. The production frontier (cash flows) for each are as follows (in millions of dollars):

$$F(100 - I_0)_{Alpha} = F(x_0)_{Alpha} = 150 - 0.7(x_0) - 0.008(x_0^2).$$

$$F(100 - I_0)_{Beta} = F(x_0)_{Beta} = 76.8 - 0.52e^{0.05x_0}.$$

Note that both pieces of equipment offer completely divisible investment opportunities. In addition, the opportunity rate of interest in the capital market equals 10 percent and w_0 is $100.
a. Assuming that $F(w_0 - I_0)$ represents net cash flows realized or received next period from investing I_0 dollars in the project, what is the optimal level of capital outlay for each piece of equipment?
b. What are the NPV and IRR for the optimal investment level in each piece of equipment?
c. Which alternative should the firm adopt? How would your answer be affected by an increase in the interest rate to 20 percent?

5.4   In March 1986, J. P. Worthington Company was considering the construction of a new warehouse facility. Two alternatives are now under evaluation. The first warehouse is smaller than the second but is sufficient to meet the firm's present needs and could be expanded later as required; its cost would be $0.8 million. The second warehouse is substantially larger and would cost $1.2 million. The smaller warehouse would have to be expanded in N years to the size of the larger alternative. Under what conditions should the firm proceed to construct the larger warehouse today?

5.5   Calculate the internal rate(s) of return for the following set of cash flows:

Year	Net Cash Flow
0	−$ 7,500
1	15,000
2	− 4,500

If the opportunity cost of funds is 10 percent, should the investment be undertaken? Discuss.

*5.6   The Y. B. Abrams Company of San Luis, California, is a vintage winery. For years the firm has bottled and sold its wine after allowing it to age for five years. Recently it has come under increased pressure to shorten the aging period to reduce its rather large investment in inventories and improve its cash flow position. In an effort to evaluate the implications of changing its policies, Abrams has engaged a marketing consulting firm. The consultants estimate that the market value of each bottle of wine has the following relationship to time (T):

$$\text{Market value (T)} = -10 + 50T - 4T^2.$$

In addition, Abrams estimates its opportunity cost of funds invested in wine aging as 12 percent, the investment outlay per bottle is $20, and it costs $1.00 per year (per bottle) in other out-of-pocket costs to monitor and insure the process.
a. What is the optimal aging period for Abrams where no future replications are anticipated? (Hint: You can perform your analysis on a per bottle basis.)
b. Given your answer to part a, what is the maximum net present value Abrams can realize per bottle?
c. Solve parts a and b again assuming constant scale replication.
d. Solve for parts a and b assuming a proportionate growth rate in the investment of 5 percent.

*5.7   The A. L. Craig Equipment Company was in the midst of analyzing the acquisition of a laser welding fabricator. Craig manufactures light- to heavy-duty forklift trucks and has been automating its production facilities so as to maintain its competitive position in the face of increasing foreign competition (particularly from Japan). The fabricator will cost $500,000 and produce cash at an annual rate described by the following function of time (t):

$$\text{ACF(t)} = \$80,000 - 4,000t \quad (\text{i.e., } \$/\text{year}).$$

The fabricator's scrap value will decline over time according to the following relationship:

$$S(T) = \$500,000 - \$38,000T.$$

a. If the market rate of interest is 6 percent, what is the optimal holding period for the new fabricator? (Assume no replications.)
b. What would be the fabricator's net present value if held for the optimal period calculated in part a?
c. Answer parts a and b where the investment is to be replicated at a constant scale indefinitely.
d. Discuss the economic implications of constant scale replications (replacement chains).

*5.8   The J. M. Evans Winery of San Pedro, California, is concerned about its policies regarding the aging and sale of wines. In particular, the firm is engaged in analyzing the optimal aging for its Bordeaux #1. This is one of Evans' more expensive wines, and its final selling price varies directly with the wine's age. The sales price of the wine is estimated as follows:

$$S(T) = 10T^{1/2},$$

where $S(T)$ is sales price and T represents the number of years until sold. The initial cost of the wine is \$4, and a cost of \$2 per year is incurred to store and insure it. The interest rate is 6 percent per annum (that is, there is a flat term structure).

a. What is the optimal investment period over which to hold the wine? What is the present value of the wine investment for this period?

b. What impact would a rise in the interest rate to 8 percent have on your answer in part a?

References

H. Bierman, Jr., and S. Smidt, *The Capital Budgeting Decision,* 6th ed. (New York: Macmillan, 1984).

J. Dean, *Capital Budgeting* (New York: Columbia University Press, 1951).

R. Dorfman, "The Meaning of Internal Rates of Return," *Journal of Finance* (December 1981): 1011–1021.

I. Fisher, *The Theory of Interest* (New York: Macmillan, 1930).

L. J. Gitman and J. R. Forrester, Jr., "A Survey of Capital Budgeting Techniques Used by Major U.S. Firms," *Financial Management* (Fall 1977): 66–71.

J. Hirshleifer, *Investment, Interest and Capital* (Englewood Cliffs, N.J.: Prentice-Hall, 1970), Chapters 3, 6, 7.

J. M. Keynes, *The General Theory of Employment, Interest, and Money* (New York: Harcourt Brace, 1936).

S. H. Kim and E. J. Farragher, "Capital Budgeting Practices in Large Industrial Firms," *Baylor Business Studies* (November 1976): 19–25.

———, "Current Capital Budgeting Practices," *Management Accounting* (June 1981): 26–30.

T. Klammer, "Empirical Evidence of the Adoption of Sophisticated Capital Budgeting Techniques," *Journal of Business* (July 1972): 387–397.

H. Levy and M. Sarnat, *Capital Investment and Financial Decisions* (London: Prentice Hall-International, 1982), Chapters 3–6.

J. H. Lorie and L. J. Savage, "Three Problems in Rationing Capital," *Journal of Business* 28 (October 1955): 229–239.

J. S. Osteryoung, *Capital Budgeting: Long-Term Asset Selection,* 2d ed. (Columbus, Ohio: Grid, 1979).

J. W. Petty, D. F. Scott, and M. M. Bird, "The Capital Expenditure Decision-Making Process of Large Corporations," *Engineering Economist* (Spring 1975): 159–172.

G. D. Quirin and J. C. Wiginton, *Analyzing Capital Expenditures: Private and Public Perspectives* (Homewood, Ill.: Irwin, 1981), Chapters 3, 4.

M. Ross, "Capital Budgeting Practices of Twelve Large Manufacturing Firms," *Financial Management* (Winter 1986): 15–22.

S. A. Ross and C. S. Spatt, "Present Values and Internal Rates of Return," *Journal of Economic Theory* 23 (1980): 66–81.

D. Teichroew, A. A. Robickek, and M. Montalbano, "An Analysis of Criteria for Investment and Financing Decisions under Certainty," *Management Science* (November 1965): 151–179.

Chapter 6

Cash Flows in Capital Budgeting

In Chapter 5, we analyzed the mechanical aspects of capital budgeting, specifically "how much to invest" (the capital widening issue) and "how long to invest" (the capital deepening issue). There we considered the mechanical problems arising in the calculation of project net present value and internal rate of return. In this chapter, we analyze the cash flows that are "relevant" to the evaluation of a capital budgeting proposal. In doing so we will discover that the analysis of project cash flows is at the very heart of the capital budgeting problem: We must come to grips not only with *what* a project's cash flows are but also with *why* they arise. In the latter case, we must address the impact of competition (or lack thereof) on project cash flows over time. Simply stated, the problem is: "Where do positive net present value projects come from?" The issues discussed here have a heavy accounting flavor, since the language used is derived from financial accounting, where the study of income measurement is paramount. However, we will temper our analysis by carefully considering opportunity costs in capital budgeting.

In addition, we address the impact of two unavoidable economic factors on project cash flows: taxes and inflation. With respect to taxes, we focus on the different treatment accorded interest payments on debt and dividends to stockholders. With regard to inflation, we examine its impact on both project cash flows and interest rates. The key methodological point of these discussions is the need for consistency when dealing with these factors in net present value calculations.

We will retain the simplifying assumptions that have characterized our discussion thus far: (1) competitive capital markets, (2) zero transactions costs, and

(3) certainty about all future events. For analytical convenience we will also assume a flat term structure, that is, that the interest rates for all future periods are equal.[1]

This chapter is organized as follows. First we discuss the composition of capital budgeting cash flows, including the impact of federal income taxes. Next we consider inflation and its impact on cash flows and net present value and in particular the accounting treatment of capital investment expenditures for purposes of calculating taxable income. Finally, we illustrate, using a case study, the relationship between positive net present value investments and monopoly rents.

Accounting Profits, Income Taxes, and Capital Budgeting Cash Flows

Relevant Cash Flows

Earlier we determined that it is cash flow that impacts on investor wealth and, consequently, provides the proper basis for valuing a firm's securities. The same is true for the capital budgeting decision, where we seek to place a value on a firm's investment in a productive asset and then compare it to the asset's cost to calculate its net present value.

Cash flow is relatively simple to define: dollars received less dollars spent. However, in capital budgeting analyses, determining the "relevant" cash flows for use in evaluating an investment proposal can be a complex task. Our objective in this section is to provide guidelines for evaluating the relevant cash flows of a capital budgeting project.

There are two basic principles to follow when evaluating the costs and benefits of a proposed capital expenditure:

1.   *Cash,* not accounting profit, provides the proper basis for valuing an investment proposal.

2.   Only *incremental* cash flows specifically attributable to the proposed investment are relevant.

Cash Flow versus Accounting Profit

The notion of accounting profit differs from that of cash flow in two important respects. First, the *accounting profit* for a particular period is defined as

$$Revenues - Expenses,$$

where revenues are "recognized" in the period in which they are *earned* and not necessarily when cash is actually received. For example, sales made on credit during December are recognized as revenues for December even though the cash col-

---

[1]The term structure of interest rates was reviewed in Appendix 2A.

lections from those sales may not be received until January. Further, expenses for December represent only those costs incurred in the process of generating December's revenues; thus, expenses are "matched" with December revenues. As an illustration, assume that firm X sells an item on credit for $100 on terms that allow payment in the following calendar year. Assume too that firm X had bought and paid for the item four years prior to the sale for $60. Note that no cash was received or spent during the current year; however, accounting profit for the year would equal $100 − 60 = $40, while actual cash flow would be zero.

The second basis for the difference between accounting profit and cash flow relates to the sorting of expenditures into two basic categories for accounting and income tax purposes. First, *current expenditures* for things like wages, salaries, raw materials purchases, and utilities are matched with the revenues they help generate. These expenditures are deducted *in full* from that period's revenues. However, expenditures made to acquire assets that last many years (called *capital expenditures*) are not fully expensed in the period of their acquisition; rather, their cost is "allocated" over the asset's life against revenues they (presumably) help to generate. This allocation takes many forms, one of the more important being depreciation of plant and equipment.

The distinction between cash flow and accounting profit is of more than academic interest, since income taxes, which constitute a cash flow, are based on accounting profits. Thus, when analyzing a proposed capital expenditure, it is necessary to estimate the accounting profit attributable to the project so that the income tax consequences of the investment can be properly evaluated and entered into the cash flow calculation.

The annual after-tax cash flow (ACF) for a capital budgeting proposal can be defined as follows:

(6.1) $ACF \equiv (Rev_c - VC_c - F_c) - T(Rev_a - VC_a - F_a - Depr)$,

where the "c" subscript refers to "cash" and the "a" refers to "accounting-based profits." Rev is revenues; VC is variable operating expenses; F is fixed operating expenses; T is the marginal tax rate on the accounting profits generated by the project; and Depr is the depreciation expense, that is, the annual cost recovery representing the allocation of a portion of the asset's cost to current-period expenses.[2] Equation 6.1 simply means that after-tax cash flows consist of the net period cash flows minus the taxes on accounting profits for the same period.

Where both "cash" and "accounting" revenues and operating expenses (other than depreciation) equal each other, we can reduce the annual cash flow expression to the following:

(6.2a) $ACF = (Rev - VC - F - Depr)(1 - T) + Depr$

or

(6.2b) $ACF = (Rev - VC - F)(1 - T) + (T)Depr$.

---

[2]Congress instituted the accelerated cost recovery system to replace the depreciation cost system in the Tax Act of 1981. Basically, the ACRS provided for simpler depreciation rules and a more rapid expensing of plant and equipment.

Note that ACF represents the *total* cash flow accruing from the entire investment in the project and not simply the return earned on the stockholders' equity. Specifically, note that it does *not* reflect the deduction of the interest paid on any funds borrowed to help finance the asset's purchase. The reason for excluding financial expenses is that we are trying to value the entire investment in the asset and not just the equity that was used to finance its acquisition.[3]

Estimating Incremental Cash Flows

The only cash flows that affect the value of a proposed investment are those that the investment creates. This principle is far easier to state than to implement, due to the necessity of considering not only observable cash receipts and disbursements but also *opportunity* revenues and costs associated with the investment. For example, the incremental cost of acquiring a machine includes not only the observable out-of-pocket costs of purchasing, shipping, and installing it — all the costs of placing the machine in full working order — but also the opportunity costs of searching and contracting for it in the first place. In addition, if the purchase of the machine means that an older machine must be sold, the cash proceeds, net of any tax consequences of the sale, will constitute a direct offset to the observable cost of the investment. Further, if the new machine requires that a larger stock of raw materials be carried to support an increase in productive capacity over the old one, the added investment in inventory will also be part of the opportunity cost of acquisition.

Although difficult to evaluate when analyzing a project's annual cash flows, the present value of any "future investment opportunities" or "options" created by the investment should be considered — as opportunity revenues. For example, if the new machine above will enable the firm to produce a new product line, the incremental value of the potential sales of that line will be relevant to the evaluation of the purchase. The evaluation of such "options" is not an easy task; nonetheless, where present, they do enhance an asset's worth.

Another example of a valuable "option" is the option to abandon an investment. Consider a firm that is analyzing two machines that can be used to perform the same task. One is a highly specialized piece of equipment that is useful to this

---

[3]As we saw earlier, project NPV measures the change in the value of the firm's equity resulting from an investment. However, the traditional method used to define NPV (which we utilize here) utilizes the following approach:

$$NPV = \Delta V - I_0,$$

where ΔV is the total value of the asset being acquired, which in turn equals the present value of the total cash flows produced by the asset or the sum of the value of the equity (ΔS) and debt (ΔD) invested in the project, and I_0 is the cost or initial outlay paid for the project. If we let $\Delta S'$ represent the equity component of the initial investment outlay,

$$I_0 = \Delta S' + \Delta D.$$

Substituting this relationship for I_0 reduces NPV to the following:

$$NPV = \Delta S - \Delta S';$$

that is, net present value indeed reflects the change in equity value resulting from the investment. The traditional NPV model, however, uses Equations 6.2a and 6.2b to estimate total investment cash flow, which is then used to "value" the total investment (see Chapter 13 for further discussion).

firm but of little use to anyone else. The other is somewhat less well adapted to the firm's specific application but has much greater resale value should the firm decide to sell it before it wears out. Evaluation of both machines should include consideration for their respective "abandonment" options. Since the abandonment option is of primary concern under uncertainty, we will return to its evaluation in Chapter 16.

The following list summarizes the factors to consider when evaluating the relevant cash flows of a proposed capital expenditure:

1. Opportunity cash flows associated with the project as well as direct and explicit cash flows incremental to it.

2. The value of any "options" created by the proposed investment.

3. The possible impact of the project on the firm's investment in "other" assets, such as inventories and accounts receivable.

4. The irrelevance of sunk costs. This item is actually redundant; see item 1, which states that only "incremental" costs should be considered. However, the problem of sunk costs or expenditures that are *not* affected by the decision to accept or reject a project is so important (and difficult to deal with) that it bears repeating.

Exercise 6.1: *Evaluating Relevant Cash Flows*

The Vandel Manufacturing Company has 5,000 square feet of factory space that cost $10 per square foot to construct and has an estimated useful life of 25 years. The annual out-of-pocket cash expenses for property taxes, heat, lighting, maintenance, and insurance is $0.50 per square foot regardless of whether the space is being used. The interest rate is 10 percent. What cost per square foot should be assigned to the evaluation of project Alpha (which involves using the factory space) under each of the following sets of conditions?

Situation 1. At present, Vandel is not using the space and sees no alternative for its utilization during the period project Alpha would need it.

Solution. In this instance, the opportunity cost of using the space is zero, since the $0.50-per-square-foot cost will be incurred regardless of whether project Alpha uses it.

Situation 2. The space is currently being used by project Beta. However, this project could be moved to another location costing $2 per square foot per annum.

Solution. Here the opportunity cost of using the space for project Alpha becomes the cost incurred in moving project Beta, or $2 per square foot per year.

Situation 3.   The space currently is not being used, but plans exist for its use at the end of three years. If project Alpha is undertaken, the planned project requiring 5,000 square feet of factory space, which can be leased for $2 per square foot per year, will have to be located elsewhere three years hence. The displaced project will require an additional 5,000 square feet for years 6 through 10, that is, beginning six years hence. This added square footage also can be acquired for $2 per square foot per year.

Solution.   In this case, the space that project Alpha would occupy will eventually be needed by the planned project; in fact, the planned project will need the space in 3 years, plus an additional 5,000 square feet beginning 6 years hence. If project Alpha is undertaken, the date when the added space will be needed will be moved from the end of year 6 to the end of year 3. At $2 per square foot, this will cost Vandel (in present value terms) the following:

$$\$2(5,000 \text{ sq. ft.}) \left[\sum_{t=4}^{6} (1 + 0.10)^{-t} \right]$$

$$\$10,000(1.8684) = \$18,684 .$$

Thus, by taking on project Alpha the firm will be forced to acquire an added 5,000 square feet of factory space at $2 per year for years 3 through 5 (with payments made at the end of the year) that it otherwise would not need.

Inflation and Capital Budgeting

Inflation, Depreciation (Annual Cost Recovery), and Real Cash Flows

The fact that the annual cost recovery or depreciation system used by firms for income tax calculations — that is, for allocating the cost of a fixed asset over its life — is based on historical costs can, in a period of rising prices, have a very detrimental effect on firms' real after-tax cash flows. Consider the project cash flows for a machine costing $40,000 and having a useful life of 4 years, shown in Table 6.1. From these calculations we see that the asset is expected to generate annual net cash flows of $22,000. In the absence of inflation, these are *real* as well as nominal cash flows. By *real* we mean that the purchasing power of the $22,000 received in period 1 is the same as that of the $22,000 received in period 2, and so forth. Correspondingly, nominal cash flows are *not* adjusted to reflect constant purchasing power.

Now consider the impact of a 10 percent rate of inflation in the expected cash flows. The resulting net cash flows are shown in Table 6.2.

Table 6.1 Project Cash Flows with No Inflation

Year	(1) Net Revenue before Depreciation and Taxes[a]	(2) Annual Cost Recovery	(3) Taxes (40%) $0.4 \times [(1) - (2)]$	(4) Annual Cash Flow (ACF) $(1) - (3)$
1	$30,000	$10,000	$8,000	$22,000
2	30,000	10,000	8,000	22,000
3	30,000	10,000	8,000	22,000
4	30,000	10,000	8,000	22,000

[a]In terms of Equation 6.2b, this column equals (Rev − VC − F).

Table 6.2 Project Cash Flows with 10 Percent Inflation

Year (t)	(1) Before Depreciation and Taxes	(2) Annual Cost Recovery	(3) Taxes (40%) $0.4 \times [(1) - (2)]$	(4) Nominal Annual Cash Flow $(1) - (3)$	(5) Real Annual Cash Flow[a] $(4)/[1.1]^t$
1	$33,000	$10,000	$ 9,200	$23,800	$21,636
2	36,300	10,000	10,520	25,780	21,306
3	39,930	10,000	11,972	27,958	21,005
4	43,923	10,000	13,569	30,354	20,732

[a]Real annual cash flow (t) = [Nominal annual cash flow (t)] $(1 + i)^{-t}$, where i is the inflation rate for the economy as a whole.

Exercise 6.2: *Evaluating Sunk Costs*

In the spring of 1987, Marvel Enterprises, a computer leasing firm, purchased a medium-sized computer system for $158,000. Marvel planned to lease the computer for rentals valued at $165,000. However, within two months after the purchase and before the machine could be leased, the manufacturer introduced a new model that would perform the same functions at roughly two-thirds the cost.

The disposition of the computer poses a real dilemma for Marvel's management. The company president does not want to sell the machine unless its original purchase price can be realized (this also equals the present value of the lease benefits). The chief accountant believes that even that is insufficient since the machine has been occupying needed warehouse space for six months. He suggests that the full cost of purchase plus inventory or carrying costs of $2,400 is the minimum Marvel should accept for the computer. Given the need for the warehouse space for the new computer model, the accountant feels the old machine should be disposed of as soon as possible since its inventory cost, and thus its minimum acceptable selling price, is increasing daily. What should Marvel do?

Solution.   The $158,000 purchase price of the computer clearly is a sunk cost. No matter what course of action Marvel decides to take, these funds have been spent and will remain spent. At this point, the only cash or out-of-pocket cost associated with keeping and leasing the machine is its market value, which is probably no more than $2/3 \times \$158,000 = \$105,333$. If the machine can be leased to earn present value rental payments greater than $105,333, it should be kept; otherwise it should be sold. (This analysis, of course, assumes that the machine's actual resale value is indeed $105,333.) As for the accountant's conjecture concerning storage or inventory costs, these also are sunk costs at this point. If, however, the firm decides to keep the machine and try to lease it at a later date, any "cash" expenses or opportunity costs due to displacement of other inventory accruing until the lessee actually takes delivery of the machine should be deducted from the present value of the machine rentals.

Note that although the nominal cash flows for each year under inflation *exceed* those of the zero-inflation case, the opposite is true for the *real* cash flows; that is, the current purchasing power of inflation-adjusted cash flows is less. The reason is that with a positive inflation rate, the revenue stream is rising but the annual cost recovery or depreciation expense for income tax calculation purposes is not. Thus, an increasing fraction of the firm's net revenues before depreciation and taxes is being taxed. The result is that real cash flows actually decline with inflation. This is directly attributable to the fact that for tax purposes the annual depreciation expense is based on the asset's historical cost and therefore is fixed over the asset's life, despite the fact that the asset's replacement cost may be rising. Thus, a complete analysis of a capital expenditure proposal requires that inflation be directly incorporated, as we now demonstrate.

A Simple Illustration

To see the impact of inflation on the capital budgeting decision, consider the following example. J. B. Burks is considering whether to invest his $1,000 in current wealth in a new business. There is only one commodity that can be purchased, and it costs $1 per unit at today's price. However, in one year, when the investment returns will be realized, the price of that commodity will be $1.10 per unit. In addition, because Burks is giving up the opportunity to consume the 1,000 units of commodity he could purchase today for a period of one year, he wants to increase his ability to consume from 1,000 to 1,050 units as compensation. This simplified setting illustrates the problem inflation poses to an individual who invests or lends a portion of his or her present wealth. Now let's solve the problem to determine those circumstances under which investment should be undertaken.

What future cash return would entice Burks to invest his $1,000? This question can be answered by considering the dollars needed to purchase the number of commodity units Burks requires one year hence. First, if the commodity costs $1.10 per unit one year from now, Burks must receive

$$1,000 \text{ units} \times \$1.10/\text{unit} = \$1,100$$

from his investment just to maintain his current purchasing power, that is, his ability to consume. If Burks also requires a 50-unit, or 5 percent, increase in purchasing power, he must realize a cash flow of

$$1,000 \text{ units} \times \$1.10/\text{unit} \times 1.05 = \$1,155.$$

To summarize, Burks requires a 10 percent rate of return on his investment in order to maintain his current level of purchasing power, plus a 5 percent increase in purchasing power as compensation for "deferring" his consumption for one year. In total, Burks requires a nominal return, K, such that

$$\frac{\$1,155}{(1 + K)} = \$1,000.$$

Therefore,

$$K = 0.155, \text{ or } 15.5\%.$$

The fact that 10 percent plus 5 percent does not sum to the 15.5 percent required return is explained by Burks' desire for a 5 percent increase in purchasing power *after* prices have risen by 10 percent; thus, his nominal required return, K, is calculated as follows:

$$K = (1 + 0.10)(1 + 0.05) - 1$$

$$= 0.155,$$

or, in general,

(6.3)
$$K = (1 + i)(1 + r) - 1$$

$$= i + r + ir,$$

where i is the inflation rate and r is the desired increase in purchasing power, or the "real" rate of interest. Therefore, the rate of return used as the opportunity cost of investment can be thought of as a composite of the inflation rate and the real interest rate as contained in Equation 6.3.

Inflation and Project NPV

A number of models for incorporating the influence of inflation into the calculation of project NPV have been proposed. Rappaport and Taggart (1982), for example, identify three basic inflation-adjusted NPV models and demonstrate the conditions under which they provide equivalent results: the gross profit per unit model, the nominal cash flow model, and the real cash flow model.

The *gross profit per unit model* is based on the fundamental assumption that the project's gross profit per unit ($p_0 - c_0$) remains constant over the project's life. Specifically, project NPV is formulated as follows:

$$NPV_{GP} = \left[\sum_{t=1}^{N} \frac{(p_0 - c_0)Q_t(1 - T) + TD_t}{(1 + r)^t} \right] - I_0,$$

where p_0 is the per unit selling price at time 0, c_0 is the average cost per unit of output at time 0, Q_t is the number of units of output from the project at time t, T is the firm's tax rate on income from the project, D_t is the year t depreciation expense for the project, r is the real interest rate (which is assumed to be the same for each year of the project's life), and N is the project's life. The key assumption here is that ($p_0 - c_0$) is constant over the project's entire life. If this is a reasonable assumption, the above inflation-adjusted NPV model is appropriate. Note that the cash flows are denominated in real or constant time 0 dollars, since the project's gross profit per unit is assumed to be unaffected by inflation. Thus, we discount real cash flows back to the present using the real interest rate, r.

In the *nominal cash flow model*, future price and cost changes are incorporated directly into the revenue and cost estimates. The resulting "inflated" or nominal cash flow estimates are then discounted back to the present using an inflation-adjusted interest rate (as in Equation 6.3). This NPV model appears as follows:

$$NPV_{NC} = \left[\sum_{t=1}^{N} \frac{(R_t - C_t)(1 - T) + TD_t}{(1 + r)^t(1 + i)^t} \right] - I_0,$$

where R_t is the nominal or inflation-adjusted cash operating receipts from the project in year t, C_t is the nominal cash operating expenditures for year t, i is the yearly inflation rate (which is assumed to be constant over the project's entire life), and the remaining terms retain their previous definitions. Note that in this model the revenues and expenses are *allowed* to have individual inflation rates. For example, we might think of R_t as $R_0(1 + i_p)^t$, where i_p is the estimated annual inflation rate in price per unit of output. Similarly, operating expenditures for year t might be defined as follows: $C_0(1 + i_c)^t$, where i_c is the inflation rate in the project's per unit production costs.

The *real cash flow model* represents a straightforward variation of the nominal cash flow model, as follows:

$$NPV_{RC} = \left[\sum_{t=1}^{N} \frac{\dfrac{NCF_t}{(1 + i)^t}}{(1 + r)^t} \right] - I_0,$$

where NCF_t is the net cash flow produced by the nominal cash flow model, converted to its real cash flow equivalent by dividing it by $(1 + i)^t$ and then discounting the result at the real interest rate, r.

The nominal and real cash flow models offer the greatest appeal because they allow the user the flexibility of selecting a different inflation rate for the revenue and expense categories of project cash flow and do not require these rates to be the same as is impounded in the returns of securities in the capital market, i. Thus, in the following example, we will use the nominal cash flow model when analyzing the impact of inflation on project NPV.

A More Realistic Example

When evaluating an investment alternative, the rate of return used as the opportunity cost of investing includes consideration for the inflation rate (as demonstrated in Equation 6.3). In addition, the cash flow from the investment will reflect the inflation rate(s)' impact on its various components, each of which, as the next example demonstrates, should be included in the analysis.

Suppose that the H. P. Bing Company is considering investing in a machine that produces bowling balls and costs $200,000. Production by year during the machine's 5-year life is expected to be 10,000, 16,000, 24,000, 20,000, and 12,000 units. As a result of a declining interest in bowling, management believes that the price of bowling balls will increase by only 2 percent per year compared to a general inflation rate of 5 percent. In addition, the price of bowling balls in the first year of the machine's use will be $20. The plastic used to produce bowling balls is becoming increasingly expensive as a direct result of rising petroleum prices. Because of this, production expenses are expected to grow at 10 percent per year beginning with the first-year production costs of $10 per unit. Depreciation of the machine will be straight line for 5 years, after which its salvage value will be zero. The company's tax rate is 40 percent, and its opportunity cost of funds for the investment — reflecting the general inflation rate — is 15 percent. Should the project be undertaken?

This problem setting is more realistic than the J. B. Burks example in that the inflation rate differs for each component of the cash flows produced by the investment and there is some "average" or "composite" inflation rate that affects the entrepreneur's opportunity cost of funds. The inflation-adjusted net present value for such a project can be calculated using the following variant of the nominal cash flow NPV model:

$$(6.4) \quad NPV = \sum_{t=1}^{N} \frac{[p_1(1 + i_p)^{(t-1)}Q_t - c_1Q_t(1 + i_c)^{(t-1)} - D_t](1 - T) + D_t}{(1 + K)^t}$$

$$+ \frac{S_N}{(1 + K)^N} - I_0,$$

where NPV = net present value for investment[4]

p_1 = initial price per unit at end of year 1

---

[4]Note that this is a *nominal* cash flow NPV model in that observed or inflated cash flows are evaluated using a nominal required rate of return. An equivalent *real* cash flow NPV model could be used; however, one must evaluate the impact of anticipated inflation in either case.

Table 6.3   Calculating the Inflation-Adjusted NPV for the H. P. Bing Company

Year (t)	Quantity (Q_t)	Price ($p_{t-1}[1.02]$)	Cost/Unit ($c_{t-1}[1.10]$)	Revenue (p_tQ_t)	Depreciation (D_t)	Total Cost ($c_tQ_t + D_t$)
1	10,000	$20.00	$10.00	$200,000	$40,000	$140,000
2	16,000	20.40	11.00	326,400	40,000	216,000
3	24,000	20.81	12.10	499,440	40,000	330,400
4	20,000	21.22	13.31	424,400	40,000	306,200
5	12,000	21.65	14.64	259,800	40,000	215,680

Year (t)	Earnings before Taxes (EBT) ($p_tQ_t - c_tQ_t - D_t$)	Taxes ($T \times EBT_t$)	NI (EBT_t − Taxes)	NCF ($NI_t + D_t$)	Discount Factor (15%) ($[1 + K]^{-t}$)	Present Value (PV_t)
1	$ 60,000	$24,000	$ 36,000	$ 76,000	0.8696	$66,090
2	110,400	44,160	66,240	106,240	0.7561	80,328
3	169,040	67,616	101,424	141,424	0.6575	92,986
4	118,200	47,280	70,920	110,920	0.5718	63,424
5	44,120	17,648	26,472	66,472	0.4972	33,050

NPV = $335,878 − 200,000 = $135,878

i_p and i_c = inflation rates for selling price and cost per unit, respectively

Q_t = number of units sold in year t

N = project life in years

T = firm's marginal tax rate

D_t = depreciation expense for year t

c_1 = cost per unit in year 1

K = opportunity cost of investing in project [reflecting general inflation rate, or $(1 + r)(1 + i) - 1$]

S_N = after-tax salvage value of investment in year N

The key element here is that different inflation rates are allowed to impact on project net present value. The solution to the H. P. Bing Company problem can now be found using Equation 6.4. Calculations are presented in Table 6.3, where the inflation-adjusted NPV is found to be a positive $135,878. Thus, the asset should be acquired.

Monopoly Rents and Positive Net Present Value Investments

Monopoly Rents Defined

The term *quasi-rent* refers to the difference between the revenue and variable cost of an investment in a particular period. The term *monopoly rent* refers to that portion of the quasi-rent in excess of the annualized capital cost.[5] In a world of certainty, an investment that generates quasi-rents greater than or equal to the annualized capital costs in all periods has a non-negative net present value. If the investment generates quasi-rents strictly greater than the annualized capital costs in some periods, the investment has a positive net present value, and we show that the net present value may be represented as the present value of the monopoly rents.

Recalling a little microeconomics, we note that in competitive markets positive monopoly rents are a short-run phenomenon; the pressures of competition will drive these monopoly rents to zero in the long run. Thus, positive net present value investments will be temporary phenomena in those cases in which the potential for competition exists.

A Comprehensive Capital Budgeting Case Study

The following problem illustrates one of the complexities added to capital expenditure evaluations when a new technology is discovered and also demonstrates the relationships between monopoly rents and positive net present values. To simplify the exposition, we will assume there are no income taxes, that all investment is equity financed, and the interest rate, which is also the required return on equity under certainty, is 25 percent. We will also assume that assets have perpetual lives and thus need not be replaced; depreciation expense is therefore zero.

Our example involves the KPG Manufacturing Company, which engages in high-technology product development for the defense industry. A recent byproduct of its research and development efforts has been the discovery of a method for manufacturing industrial-grade crystals that are widely used in the manufacture of radios and other items utilizing microcircuitry. The new process entails the expenditure of $28 in capital investment for each unit of annual productive capacity; that is, to produce one "manmade" crystal per year, KPG must make a one-time expenditure of $28 on plant and equipment. In addition, the variable manufacturing cost per unit is $8; this compares with capital costs — that is, capital investment — of $20 and $40, plus manufacturing costs of $15 and $10, for the existing V_1 and V_2 vintages of technology, respectively. The costs and capacities of the two existing technologies plus the new V_3 technology are summarized in Table 6.4.

KPG feels it can meet the capital investment (capital cost) and manufacturing costs for a 100 million–unit plant. In addition, KPG will have exclusive rights to the new technology for only five years, after which everyone in the industry can use it. Thus, in the numerical example considered here we have given the technological leader (KPG) a discrete choice: to either invest or not invest in the fixed (100 million–unit) capacity. The question addressed is whether or not the monopoly power, due to the exclusive control of the new technology, will be exercapital is ($19 − 10)/32 = 28.125 percent. Since both rates exceed 25 percent, no capital of either vintage is scrapped, and the demand faced by KPG is the

---

[5]The origin of the use of the term *rent* in this context probably goes back to the discussion of the fees paid for the use of land. For example, in *The Wealth of Nations* (1776), Adam Smith defined rent as "the produce which is over what is necessary to pay the farmer ordinary profit" (p. 161). Alfred Marshall originated the term *quasi-rent*.

**Table 6.4   Summary of Cost Information
                for Crystal Production Technologies**

Technology	Capacity (Millions)	Manufacturing Cost Unit	Capital Cost Unit	Scrap Value Unit
V_1	100	$15	$20	$12
V_2	200	10	40	32
V_3	100	8	28	

cised. The question of the degree of monopoly control, while interesting, is not considered in the analysis.[6]

The annual demand for the crystals has been stable for several years and will remain so in the future. The annual demand function for the crystals (in millions of units) is described by the function $Q = 10(50 - \text{price})$. Figure 6.1 depicts the annual industry demand for crystals and the short-run industry supply. Note that this supply is only appropriate prior to the entry of the firm with monopoly control of the V_3 technology. The short-run supply is perfectly elastic at $10 until the V_2 technology reaches capacity; the supply is also perfectly elastic at $15 until the V_1 technology reaches capacity. Of course, the supply is perfectly inelastic once industry capacity is reached, that is, at 300 million units. The shaded areas A and B in Figure 6.1 represent the quasi-rents generated by technologies V_2 and V_1, respectively:

$$(\text{Price} - \text{Unit manufacturing cost}) \times \text{Vintage capacity}.$$

Given the two technologies' fixed capacities, manufacturing costs, and capital costs (which are assumed to remain constant over time), the equilibrium market price is $20 per crystal.

Note that the capital costs of the two technologies reflect their differential manufacturing costs. This means that the net present values of the V_1 and V_2 technology capital are the same; both equal zero at the current market equilibrium price of $20 per crystal. The "per unit" net present value of each technology can be calculated as follows:

$$\text{NPV}_{V_1} = -\$20 + \frac{(\$20 - 15)}{0.25} = 0$$

and

$$\text{NPV}_{V_2} = -\$40 + \frac{(\$20 - 10)}{0.25} = 0.$$

---

[6]As we will soon see, some constraint on the availability of the new V_3 technology's productive capacity is necessary to ensure that KPG cannot drive out all competitors during the five years over which it has monopoly rights. When the technological leader — the firm with exclusive rights to the new technology for T years — may determine the scale of investment in the new technology, however, the analysis is more complex. The technological leader must now determine how the firms in the industry with the older technologies will react to its capacity choice. Although this more general question is interesting, the added complexity attendant on its analysis would obscure the point we are attempting to make here.

Figure 6.1   Annual Demand for and Supply of "Manmade" Crystals (Before Introduction of V_3 Technology)

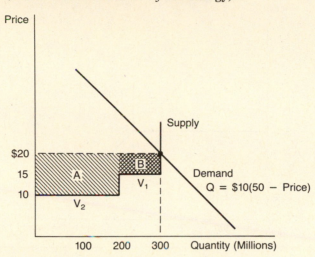

Recall that the capital costs of V_1 and V_2 equipment are not the same; thus, there is no incentive for any firms in the industry to exchange V_1 productive capacity for V_2, or vice versa. In terms of capital widening, the marginal benefit of investing one more dollar in *either* V_1 or V_2 productive assets exactly equals that dollar's incremental or marginal cost (in this case, $0.25). The short-run supply in Figure 6.1 may be respecified in its long-run form by including the marginal required return on invested capital — the interest rate times the unit capital cost, as shown in Figure 6.2. Note that the resulting per unit cost of output for the two technologies is exactly $20:

Technology	Manufacturing Cost	Capital Cost/Year (0.25 × Capital Cost)		Marginal Cost
V_1	$15	0.25 × $20	=	$20
V_2	10	0.25 × 40	=	20

In this form it is clear that the equilibrium price is $20 and the quantity produced will be 300 million units.

KPG now must evaluate whether to enter into crystal production through the expenditure of $28 × 100 million = $2,800 million. The investment's ultimate desirability hinges on the new equilibrium market price of crystals following KPG's entry into the market. Figure 6.3 shows the price impact that KPG's capacity choice has on the market price. The figure depicts KPG's leadership demand D_L during the period that KPG has exclusive rights to the new technology.

KPG determines its leadership demand by considering the circumstances under which firms with the older technologies will scrap capacity. If KPG sets a price of $19, the rate of return on V_1 capital is ($19 − 15)/12 = 33.333 percent (where the scrap value of V_1 capacity is $12 per unit) and the rate of return on V_2

Figure 6.2   Annual Demand for and Supply of Crystals

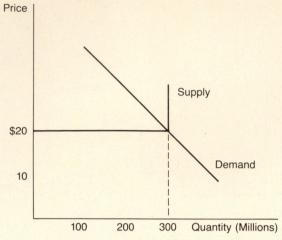

Figure 6.3   Market Equilibrium after KPG's Entry, Years 1 through 5

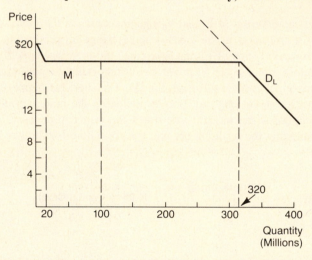

capital is $(\$19 - 10)/32 = 28.125$ percent. Since both rates exceed 25 percent, no capital of either vintage is scrapped, and the demand faced by KPG is the market demand minus 300 units. If KPG sets a price of $15, the rate of return on V_1 capital is $(\$15 - 15)/12 = 0$ percent, and the rate of return on V_2 capital is $(\$15 - 10)/32 = 15.625$ percent. Since both rates are less than 25 percent, capital of both vintages is scrapped and KPG has the entire market demand. If KPG sets a price of $18, the rates on V_1 and V_2 capital are both 25 percent, and the firms with those vintages are indifferent between scrapping and continuing to use the vintage. It follows that for a price of $18, every unit of V_3 capacity introduced will be associated with a unit of V_1 or V_2 capacity scrapped.

Now, note that the long-run marginal cost of V_3 is $8 + (0.25)\$28 = \$15$ per million units. Of course, this is also the new long-run equilibrium market price when KPG's exclusive rights to V_3 lapse. It follows that, given the 100 million capacity, KPG will exercise its monopoly control and set a price of $18. At this price, 320 million units are sold. Since KPG sells 100 million units, the output of the older vintages is reduced by 80 million units; that is, 80 million units of capacity in the older vintages are scrapped.

Area M in Figure 6.3 depicts the monopoly rent generated per period of control, and $M = (\$18 - 15)100 = \$300$ million. Finally, we have restricted KPG to a 100 million unit capacity, and from Figure 6.3 it is clear that KPG is not fully exploiting its monopoly power. Institutional constraints that prevent full exploitation may not be reflected in the leadership demand. In the absence of such constraints, KPG should expand capacity to 320 million units and temporarily drive all its competition out of the market. The most important point here, however, is that KPG has the ability to generate monopoly rents for five years.

At the end of the five years, all firms have an opportunity to invest in the V_3 technology, and the market is again competitive. Investment in the V_3 technology occurs until the long-run price equals the long-run marginal cost of $15. The new long-run supply is shown in Figure 6.4. As noted above, V_1 and V_2 are scrapped, because the rates of return generated by keeping V_1 and V_2 for another period are 0 percent and 15.625 percent, respectively; both are less than the rate of return on alternative investments, 25 percent. Therefore, 250 million units of V_3 capacity are added.

We can now evaluate the net present value (in millions of dollars) of KPG's investment in the "manmade" crystal industry as follows:

Figure 6.4   Market Equilibrium after KPG's Entry, Years 6 through 10

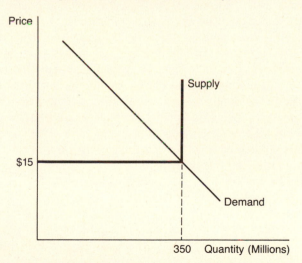

$$\text{NPV} = -\$2,800 + \sum_{t=1}^{5} \frac{100(\$18 - \$8)}{1.25^t} + \left(\frac{100(\$15 - \$8)}{0.25}\right)\left(\frac{1}{1.25^5}\right)$$

$$= -\$2,800 + \$2,689.28 + \$917.50$$

$$= \$806.78 .$$

Note that KPG expects to earn a positive net present value of $806.78 million if it makes the investment. This positive net present value is a direct result of the fact that KPG can produce crystals for a marginal cost of $15 while receiving $18 per unit for the 100 million units it produces in each of the next five years. Thus, the positive net present value of $806.78 million results directly from these five years of monopoly rents (see Figure 6.3). The present value of these monopoly rents *is* the net present value of the investment, as follows:

$$\text{NPV} = \sum_{t=1}^{5} \frac{100(\$18 - \$15)}{1.25^t} = \$806.78 .$$

The key point here is that positive net present values represent investment opportunities earning rates of return *larger* than that justified by the investment's inherent risks. In the certainty case, this means rates of return greater than the risk-free rate. In addition, where the pressure of competition is ever-present, positive net present values are temporary phenomena.

An Institutional Note on Product Pricing Strategies

Firms entering a market for the first time face a choice of pricing strategies. If a firm has some degree of monopoly power (for instance, it is the first producer of a new product), it must take into account the strength of potential rivals. One strategy that can be followed is *limit pricing*. This strategy entails placing a limit on the price charged in order to deter or at least slow down the rate of entry of competitors. Limit pricing may decrease early profits but sustain future profits over a long period of time, because competition is deterred from entering the market. For example, in the microchip industry Japanese firms have been accused of selling newly developed products at or below their actual production cost in the early stages of the product's life cycle to deter the entry of competition. Manufacturers who follow such a strategy hope to deter others from entering the market while their production costs decline because of increased efficiency in production and economies of scale from higher sales volume.

An alternative pricing strategy is *predatory pricing*. As the name implies, this pricing strategy involves "predatory behavior" by the firm. Specifically, predatory pricing entails driving competitors from the market by pricing the firm's product below the competitor's average total cost of production just long enough to drive it out of the market. Price wars can be viewed as evidence of predatory pricing behavior by the participant firms. When firms engage in predatory pricing in another country, it is frequently referred to as "dumping," since the firm effectively dumps its product on the other country at a very low price (below production cost).

Summary

In this final chapter on capital budgeting under certainty, we evaluated project cash flows, inflation, and income taxes. Through the use of a case study we discussed the relationship between positive net present values and monopoly rents, that is, excess profits. The latter issue frequently is underemphasized in finance and is the source of potentially gross errors in judgment. An obvious case in point is the extrapolation of positive net present value investments into the distant future. For example, during the late 1970s and early 1980s, many oil companies invested in drilling and exploration based on the expectation that energy prices would continue to rise throughout the eighties. These firms did not properly account for major structural changes in the demand for energy related to conservation. This, in turn, left them with investments requiring $35 per barrel of oil in a time when oil prices were dropping well below $20 per barrel. The consequences are now history.

Study Questions

6.1   "Accounting profit is calculated on an 'accrual' rather than cash basis and thus does not equal net cash flow." Explain.

6.2   Net cash flow provides the appropriate basis for evaluating a proposed capital expenditure; however, we still must estimate accounting income or profits. Why?

6.3   Evaluate the statement "Sunk costs don't matter" in the context of a capital budgeting analysis.

6.4   "Inflation causes both revenues and expenses to increase; thus, it should have no impact on project NPV." True or false? Explain.

6.5   Define monopoly rents, and relate this concept to a project's NPV.

Study Problems

6.1   The J-Set Manufacturing Company is attempting to determine the breakeven level of productive output (that is, total costs = total revenue) for a new manufacturing plant. The relevant information is as follows:

Annual depreciation expense	$30,000,000
Annual fixed operating costs	$60,000,000
Total investment outlay (current)	$300,000,000

Unit variable cost	$3,000
Unit selling price	$3,750
Opportunity cost of funds	10%
Marginal tax rate	50%
Estimated investment life	10 years

a. Calculate the breakeven number of units J-Set must sell in order to cover all its costs. (Hint: Include the $30 million depreciation as the annual cost associated with recovering the initial cash investment of $300 million.)

b. Calculate the investment's net present value where the level of productive activity equals the breakeven level identified in part a.

c. Defining breakeven output (Q*) as that level for which $NPV_{Q^*} = 0$, solve for Q*.

d. Why does your answer to part c differ from that to part a?

6.2   The J. M. Ramey Bottling Company has invested $2 million and 5 years in the development of a new soft drink. The drink is both caffeine-free and sugar-free but lacks the after-taste problem that has plagued other sugar-free soft drinks (including the firm's present sugar-free offering, "Tubs"). The key to the new product's success lies in a special blending process that Ramey has patented. However, Ramey's management is aware that its primary competitors are only three years away from developing and marketing a similar product offering.

The capital budgeting staff has prepared the following cost estimates for producing and marketing the new soft drink.

New blending and bottling machinery	$12,000,000
Expanded plant facility	4,000,000

In addition, the staff recognizes that inventories of the product and increased accounts receivable resulting from its sales will constitute a $2 million investment. However, since these funds will never leave the firm, it is felt that these expenditures are irrelevant to the investment decision.

The annual after-tax cash flows for the project's five-year estimated investment life are $5 million. However, these figures include the loss of $2 million in cash flow due to lost sales of "Tubs." Some staff members have expressed concern that sales lost to another product are inappropriate here; they believe the new project should be evaluated completely independently of Ramey's other investments. In other words, the project should "stand or fall on its own merit."

a. What initial outlay should be used in evaluating the proposed investment?

b. What annual cash flows should Ramey attribute to the new investment?

c. If the interest rate is 10 percent, should the investment be made?

d. If Ramey had an offer to sell its patent for $2 million in exchange for agreeing not to produce a similar product for five years, would this affect your evaluation of the proposed investment? If so, how?

6.3   Harrison Manufacturing Company is evaluating a proposed investment in mechanical pencils. The pencils use 0.5-mm lead and are used by professional accountants and draftspeople. The firm's analysts estimate that 1,000 units per year could be sold for each of the next 5 years. The pencils would be packaged in an attractive gift case and initially sold for $11 per unit. In addition, the price of each pencil is expected to rise by 10 percent each year due to inflation.

Harrison's analysts estimate that the investment in manufacturing equipment required for starting production is $10,000. For tax purposes, the equipment will be depreciated over 5 years using respective annual cost recovery factors of 0.15, 0.22, 0.21, 0.21, and 0.21. The analysts estimate that Harrison will incur fixed cash operating expenses totaling $2,000 per year and variable cash operating expenses of $5.40 per unit in year 1. The variable cost per unit is expected to rise by 8 percent each year over the project's life.

For investment analyses, Harrison uses a 40 percent marginal income tax rate, estimates salvage values to be zero, and requires a 15 percent (inflation-adjusted) required rate of return.

a. Under the above circumstances, what is the pencil project's net present value?

b. How would your analysis be affected by an upward revision in the general inflation rate such that the required return on investment rose to 18 percent? Would the project be acceptable?

6.4   Kathy and Allen Kelly have a 10-year-old daughter, Justine. They are upper-middle-class professionals and want to send Justine to one of the better Ivy League colleges when she is 17 and for this purpose wish to begin saving as soon as possible. They estimate that the current cost of such an education, including tuition, room and board, books, and holiday travel is $15,000 per year. However, for the foreseeable future they expect inflation to rise by 5 percent per year and college expenses to increase accordingly. The Kellys want to know how much they should save each year for the next 7 years in order to afford her 4-year college expenses. Savings will be made once each year (beginning one year from today) and will be invested to earn an average of 10 percent per year. Withdrawals will be made annually at the beginning of each college year. How much should the Kellys plan to set aside for Justine's college education?

Note: Problems 6.5 through 6.8 relate to the KPG Manufacturing Company example.

6.5   Suppose that m_3 is KPG's unit production cost, k_3 its unit capital cost, and x_3 its capacity choice. If KPG maintains monopoly control of the V_3 technology for T years, P_3 is the new long-run equilibrium price, and P is the temporary equilibrium price, set up an expression for the NPV of the firm's investment and show that it reduces to

$$NPV = (P - P_3)x_3 d_T,$$

where d_T is the T-year annuity discount factor.

6.6   Consider a competing firm with V_2 equipment. Let m_2 and s_2 denote the unit production cost and unit scrap value, respectively, for this equipment and r the interest rate in the capital market. Explain why some of the V_2 equipment should be scrapped if

$$(P - m_2)/s_2 < r,$$

where P is the temporary equilibrium price of the firm's output.

6.7   Suppose only V_1 capital is in use and that it must be replaced every T years. Show that the long-run competitive equilibrium price is

$$P_1 = m_1 + \frac{k_1}{d_T},$$

where m_1 = variable cost per unit of output
         k_1 = capital investment required to produce 1 unit per year
         d_T = annuity present value factor for the risk-free rate and T years

6.8   Suppose a monopolist has a demand of $P = a - bQ$ in each period, and let m_1 and k_1 denote the unit production and capital costs, respectively. Derive and interpret the condition for a maximum of the monopolist's NPV.

6.9   The Momar Manufacturing Company has recently perfected the technology for producing a commercially viable laser disk for use with desktop computers. The new laser disk operates as a random access memory (RAM) device as opposed to the read only memory (ROM) disks currently sold. The advantage of the RAM disk is that the user can store his or her own data on it, whereas the ROM disk, which has been available for over a year, can be used only to access data already stored there by someone else. Momar is considering two possible pricing strategies: (1) a short-run strategy that involves initially pricing the disk very high to take full advantage of the firm's monopoly advantage, followed by a period of declining prices as competitors enter the market (as expected), and (2) a long-run strategy aimed at keeping the price near the firm's cost so as to discourage competitors' entry (frequently referred to as a *limit-pricing* strategy). The estimated net cash flows to Momar from pursuing each strategy over the next 10 years are as follows:

Estimated Annual Net Cash Flows (Millions)

Year	Short-Run Pricing	Limit Pricing
1	$60	$35
2	50	35
3	45	35
4	40	35
5	35	34
6	30	33
7	25	32

8	25	32
9	25	31
10	25	30

a. Which strategy is better if the required rate of return is 10 percent?

b. Under what opportunity cost of funds will the firm be indifferent between the two strategies?

References

D. Bodenhorn, "A Cash-Flow Concept of Profit," *Journal of Finance* (March 1964): 16–31.

R. Brealey and S. Myers, *Principles of Corporate Finance* (New York: McGraw-Hill, 1984), Chapters 9–12.

P. L. Cooley, R. L. Roenfeldt, and I. K. Chew, "Capital Budgeting Procedures Under Inflation," *Financial Management* (Winter 1975): 18–27.

E. Fama, "Inflation Uncertainty and Expected Returns on Treasury Bills," *Journal of Political Economy* (June 1976): 427–448.

M. C. Findlay and A. W. Frankle, "Capital Budgeting Procedures under Inflation," *Financial Management* (Autumn 1976): 83–90.

H. Levy and M. Sarnat, *Capital Investment and Financial Decisions* (London: Prentice-Hall International, 1982), Chapters 5–7.

D. Mehta, M. Curley, and H. Fung, "Inflation, Cost of Capital, and Capital Budgeting Procedures," *Financial Management* (Winter 1984): 48–54.

J. S. Osteryoung, *Capital Budgeting: Long-Term Asset Selection,* 2d ed. (Columbus, Ohio: Grid, 1979), Chapter 2.

G. D. Quirin and J. C. Wiginton, *Analyzing Capital Expenditures: Private and Public Perspectives* (Homewood, Ill.: Irwin, 1981), Chapter 10.

A. Rappaport and R. Taggart, Jr., "Evaluation of Capital Expenditure Proposals under Inflation," *Financial Management* (Spring 1982): 5–13.

A. Smith, *An Inquiry into the Nature and Causes of the Wealth of Nations* (originally published in 1776), edited by Edwin Cannan (University of Chicago Press, 1976).

J. C. Van Horne, "A Note on Biases on Capital Budgeting Introduced by Inflation," *Journal of Financial and Quantitative Analysis* (January 1971): 653–658.

III

The Theory of Finance under Uncertainty

In this section, we introduce the theory of financial decisionmaking under conditions in which future outcomes cannot be known at the time choices are being made. The dominant approach to this problem in the finance literature relies on the mean-variance model — that is, higher mean returns and lower variances are preferred. This approach generally is defended in terms of its theoretical ties to the maximization of expected utility. Thus, in Chapter 7 we consider the expected utility paradigm and the conditions under which mean-variance analysis is consistent with expected utility maximization. In Chapter 8, we analyze the "mechanics" of portfolio analysis using mean-variance analysis. This material has become routine at all levels of finance instruction and for the student who is skimming over this material it will serve as a refresher. In Chapter 9, we extend the mean-variance model to conditions describing capital market equilibrium. Here we derive the capital asset pricing model in both its original form (with risk-free borrowing and lending) and the zero-beta version. In addition, we characterize a "no-arbitrage-profit" capital market and, in so doing, derive the arbitrage pricing model. In Chapter 10, we explore the theory and evidence regarding the efficient market hypothesis, a concept of the capital market that has pervaded much of the finance literature over the last two decades.

In studying this section, the reader will be constructing the building blocks on which Part IV rests. A good working knowledge of the theory and concepts presented in this section will greatly enhance the student's understanding of the applications material in Part IV.

Chapter 7

Decisionmaking under Uncertainty

Up to this point, we have analyzed choices among alternatives that offered *known* outcomes or returns. However, an important attribute of real-world decision-making is the uncertainty of future outcomes. In this chapter we overview the problem uncertainty poses and present one possible method for dealing with it. Specifically, we develop the *expected utility theorem,* which states that:

Individuals choose among risky investments as if they were maximizing the expected value of their utility.[1]

In addition, we discuss the circumstances under which mean-variance analysis — maximizing the expected return for a given variance or minimizing the variance in return for a given expected return — is consistent with the expected utility paradigm. This is particularly important given the prominence of mean-variance analysis in the theory of finance.

This chapter is organized as follows. First we discuss the axioms underlying the expected utility theorem. Next we briefly examine the expected utility paradigm itself. We then discuss the relationship between risk aversion and the cost

---

[1]A caveat is in order here. We will use the notion of expected utility maximization to "characterize" individuals' choices under uncertainty. However, this is not to suggest that individuals actually calculate the expected utility of alternatives. We posit *only* that if individuals' behavior is consistent with a set of axioms, their decisions will be *consistent* with expected utility maximization. In fact, a more careful and formal statement of the expected utility theorem would be,

Under the axioms of choice, there exists a real-valued utility function such that one risk is preferred to another if and only if it yields higher expected utility.

of risk and derive measures of both absolute and relative risk aversion. Next we examine the basic elements of stochastic dominance, which serves as a "general" tool for evaluating preferences for risky assets; here we find that while stochastic dominance provides a very general approach to choice under uncertainty, it has very onerous information requirements. Finally, we discuss the relationship between mean-variance analysis and expected utility maximization. Here we discover a relatively simple and apparently powerful tool for analyzing choices among risky assets. At the same time, however, we find that it makes some rather dubious assumptions about either the individual's utility function or the nature of the probability distributions of the risky assets from which choices are made. Nevertheless, recent empirical studies have shown that mean-variance-based choices may be "reasonable" approximations of expected utility-maximizing decisions when used to select from among a set of observed return distributions for common stock portfolios. Appendix 7A overviews the time state preference model.

Axioms of Rational Choice

In Appendix 2B, we discussed a set of basic axioms concerning individuals' preferences under conditions of certainty about all future outcomes. In their classic work, von Neumann and Morgenstern (1947) showed that under certain circumstances it is possible to construct a utility function for use in predicting an individual's choices under uncertainty. Our objective here is to summarize those conditions that are stated as axioms of individual choice behavior. The interested reader will find Chapter 1 of von Neumann and Morgenstern particularly useful.

It is possible to construct an index of utility for use in predicting consumer choices under uncertainty when rankings over uncertain alternatives have the following attributes (in addition to those discussed in Appendix 2B):

A1. *Complete ordering:* For any set of alternatives, the individual must be willing and able to compare and rank all members. For example, for two alternatives, A and B, one of the following must be true: A is preferred to B, B is preferred to A, or the individual is indifferent between the two.

A2. *Transitivity:* If A is preferred to B and B is preferred to C, A is also preferred to C.

A3. *Continuity:* Consider three alternatives, A, B, and C, where A is preferred to B, B is preferred to C, and (by transitivity) A is also preferred to C. The continuity axiom requires that there exist some probability P $(0 < P < 1)$ such that the individual is indifferent between outcome B with certainty and a lottery composed of alternatives A (with probability P) and C (with probability $[1 - P]$).

A4. *Independence:* Assume that there are three alternatives, A, B, and C, among which the individual is indifferent; in other words, the individual does not prefer any one alternative to any other. If we construct one lottery consisting of alternatives A and C with probabilities P and $(1 - P)$, respectively, and a second consisting of alternatives B and C with the same respective probabilities, the individual, according to the independence axiom, will be indifferent between the lotteries; similarly, if the individual is assumed to prefer A to B, he or she will prefer the first lottery to the second.

A5. *Unequal probability:* Consider two lotteries composed of outcomes A and B where A is preferred to B. The first offers outcome A with probability P_1 and outcome B with probability $(1 - P_1)$; the second offers the same two outcomes but with probabilities P_2 and $(1 - P_2)$, respectively. By the unequal-probability axiom, lottery 1 is preferred to lottery 2 when $P_1 > P_2$.

A6. *Compound lottery:* The individual evaluates risky alternatives or lotteries only in terms of the probabilities of obtaining the prizes and not in terms of how many times he or she is exposed to the chance mechanism.

These axioms generally are thought to reflect individuals' choice behavior. However, there do exist some types of "plausible" choice behavior that these axioms rule out. These "paradoxes" have been widely noted in the economics literature and will not be discussed here. The interested reader will find the first essay in Arrow (1971) particularly useful in this regard.

The Expected Utility Paradigm

For an individual who makes choices that are consistent with the axioms discussed above, we can calculate an index or utility function that we can use to *describe* his or her preferences. The *expected utility paradigm* states that the individual will choose those alternatives *as if* he or she were maximizing *expected* utility.[2]

We can define the expected utility of a risky asset's impact on wealth as follows:

$$(7.1) \qquad\qquad E[u(w)] = \sum_{i=1}^{N} \psi_i u(w_i) ,$$

where $u(w_i)$ is the utility of the end-of-period wealth corresponding to the ith state of the world ($i = 1, 2, \ldots, N$) for a particular individual and ψ_i is the probability associated with the ith state.

The following example illustrates the concept of expected utility. Table 7.1 describes two risky assets. For each of the three possible states of the world, it includes the corresponding end-of-period wealth for each asset as well as the probability of occurrence of each state. It also gives the utility of the outcome of each state, calculated by means of the following (quadratic) utility function:

$$u(w) = 0.004w - 0.000004w^2.$$

---

[2]Voluminous literature suggests that the expected utility paradigm may not model individual choice behavior as well as do some alternative models. See Schoemaker (1982) for a very thorough and well-documented review of this literature.

Table 7.1   Calculating Expected Utility

	State (i)	Probability (ψ_i)	Wealth (w_i)	Utility $(u[w_i])$
Asset A	1	0.20	100	0.36
	2	0.60	100	0.36
	3	0.20	100	0.36
Asset B	1	0.20	50	0.19
	2	0.60	150	0.51
	3	0.20	250	0.75

The expected utility of each risky asset's returns can now be calculated as follows:

$$E[u(w_A)] = 0.2(0.36) + 0.6(0.36) + 0.2(0.36) = 0.36$$

$$E[u(w_B)] = 0.2(0.19) + 0.6(0.51) + 0.2(0.75) = 0.494.$$

Hence, risky asset B is preferred to A even though A is a risk-free asset.

A Mathematical Review of Taylor Series Expansions

Any smooth function can be approximated using a polynomial equation. The method we discuss here was suggested by Brook Taylor, an eighteenth-century mathematician.

Suppose the values of a function $F(x)$ and its derivatives are known for one value of x, say, $x = x_0$; an example is the function $F(x) = (1 + x)^k$ for $x = 10\%$. How can we use this information to approximate the values of $F(x)$ for values of x near x_0? If we restrict ourselves by using none of the derivatives, we might use

$$F(x) \approx a_0 \quad \text{where } a_0 = F(x_0).$$

Geometrically, this amounts to approximating the graph of $y = F(x)$ with the line $y = a_0$, which passes through the point (x_0, a_0) on the graph of $y = F(x)$. This is illustrated in Figure 7.1a. The error is the distance between the graphs of $y = F(x)$ and $y = p_0(x) = a_0$.

This would be satisfactory only if x were very near x_0. For example, to approximate $(1.101)^{24}$ it may be reasonable, for some purposes, to use the tabulated value $(1.10)^{24}$. However, it is hard to imagine that $(1.10)^{24}$ would ever be an acceptable approximation to $(1.11)^{24}$.

More useful approximations are obtained by using the known values of the derivatives as well as those of the function. Using just one derivative, we might use

$$F(x) \approx a_0 + a_1(x - x_0),$$

where $a_0 = F(x_0)$ and $a_1 = F'(x_0)$, because the graph of $p(x) = a_0 + a_1(x - x_0)$ is tangent to the graph of $F(x)$ at $x = x_0$. This means that the linear function $p(x)$ has the same value as $F(x)$ at x_0, as do their respective derivatives,

$$p(x_0) = F(x_0)$$

and

$$p'(x_0) = F'(x_0).$$

Since a linear function is uniquely characterized by a point on its graph and its slope at that point, $p(x)$ is the only linear function that satisfies these equations. This is illustrated in Figure 7.1b. The error is the distance between the graphs of $y = F(x)$ and the Taylor polynomial $p_1(x) = a_0 + a_1(x - x_0)$.

For example, to approximate $(1.11)^{24}$ using one derivative, we would use

$$(1.11)^{24} \approx (1.10)^{24} + 24(1.10)^{23}(0.11 - 0.10)$$

because

$$F(x) = (1 + x)^{24} \quad \text{so} \quad a_0 = (1.10)^{24}$$

Figure 7.1

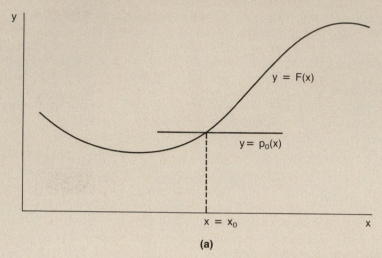

(a)

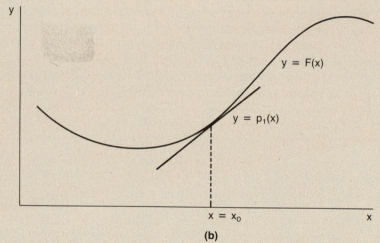

(b)

and

$$F'(x) = 24(1 + x)^{23} \quad \text{so} \quad a_1 = 24(1.10)^{23}.$$

The right-hand side of the above expression can be considered a function of x; as such, it is the simplest function having the same value at x_0, as F has the same derivative as it has at x_0. If we wish to incorporate the value of $F''(x_0)$, it is natural to seek the simplest function $p(x)$ that agrees with F at x_0 and whose first two derivatives are the same as F. The three conditions are

(i) $$p(x_0) = F(x_0)$$

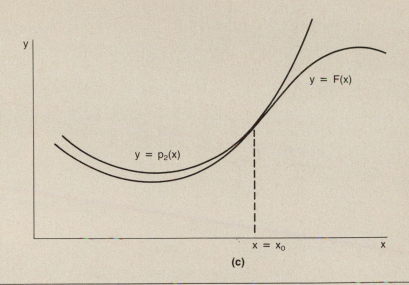

(c)

(ii) $$p'(x_0) = F'(x_0)$$

(iii) $$p''(x_0) = F''(x_0).$$

These three equations will determine the coefficients of a quadratic,

$$p(x) = a_0 + a_1(x - x_0) + a_2(x - x_0)^2,$$

as follows:

$$p(x_0) = a_0 \Rightarrow a_0 = F(x_0)$$

$$p'(x) = 2a_2(x - x_0) + a_1 \Rightarrow p'(x_0) = a_1 \Rightarrow a_1 = F'(x_0)$$

$$p''(x) = 2a_2 \Rightarrow a_2 = \frac{F''(x_0)}{2}.$$

Therefore, a natural choice with which to approximate F(x) for x near x_0 using two derivatives at x_0 is

$$p(x) = F(x_0) + F'(x_0)(x - x_0) + \left[\frac{F''(x_0)}{2}\right](x - x_0)^2.$$

In other words, it would be natural to use

$$F(x) \approx F(x_0) + F'(x_0)(x - x_0) + \left[\frac{F''(x_0)}{2}\right](x - x_0)^2.$$

For example,

$$(1.11)^{24} \approx (1.10)^{24} + 24(1.10)^{23}(0.11 - 0.10) + \left[\frac{(24)(23)(1.10)^{22}}{2}\right](0.11 - 0.10)^2$$

because

$$F(x) = (1 + x)^{24}, \; F'(x) = 24(1 + x)^{23}, \; \text{and} \; F''(x) = (24)(23)(1 + x)^{22}.$$

This is called the *Taylor series expansion of F* (or approximation) *of order two* (because two derivatives are used) at x_0. It has not only the same value as F at x_0 and the same slope at x_0 as F but also the same concavity; that is, near x_0 the graphs of F and the second-order Taylor polynomial have the same height, slope, and concavity (see Figure 7.1c). The error is the distance between the graphs of $y = F(x)$ and

$$p_2(x) = a_0 + a_1(x - x_0) + a_2(x - x_0)^2.$$

The general approximation using n derivatives is

$$F(x) \approx F(x_0) + F'(x_0)(x - x_0) + \left[\frac{F''(x_0)}{2}\right](x - x_0)^2 + \left[\frac{F'''(x_0)}{3!}\right](x - x_0)^3$$

$$+ \ldots + \left[\frac{F^{(n)}(x_0)}{n!}\right](x - x_0)^n.$$

The approximating function is the polynomial of degree n, which mimics the behavior of F at x_0, at least through n derivatives. Typically, the higher the order n, the better the approximation. The error $E(x)$ in the approximation depends on x (and, of course, x_0). Generally, the closer x is to x_0, the better the approximation. The most important fact about the error is that there is a value ξ between x_0 and x for which the error has the form

$$\left[\frac{F^{(n+1)}(x_0)}{n!}\right](\xi - x_0)^{n+1};$$

that is,

$$F(x) = F(x_0) + F'(x_0)(x - x_0) + \left[\frac{F''(x_0)}{2}\right](x - x_0)^2 + \left[\frac{F'''(x_0)}{3!}\right](x - x_0)^3$$

$$+ \ldots + \left[\frac{F^{(n)}(x_0)}{n!}\right](x - x_0)^n + \left[\frac{F^{(n+1)}(x_0)}{n!}\right](\xi - x_0)^{n+1}$$

for some ξ between x_0 and x. This is called *Taylor's formula with remainder* (or *error*) *term*. For example, in the approximation

$$(1.11)^{24} \approx (1.10)^{24} + 24(1.10)^{23}(0.11 - 0.10) + \left[\frac{(24)(23)(1.10)^{22}}{2}\right](0.11 - 0.10)^2,$$

the error is of the form

$$\left[\frac{(24)\,(23)\,(22)\,(1.10)^{21}}{6}\right](\xi - 0.10)^3$$

where $0.10 \le \xi \le 0.11$ because

$$F'''(x) = (24)\,(23)\,(22)\,(1 + x)^{21}.$$

In this example, the error in the approximation is positive (the approximation is less than the true value) but less than

$$\left[\frac{(24)\,(23)\,(22)\,(1.10)^{21}}{6}\right](0.11 - 0.10)^3$$

because ξ is less than 0.11.

Risk Aversion and the Cost of Risk (Risk Premium)

An individual who refuses to take a fair bet is *risk averse* — that is, if the expected payoff of a gamble is $50 (say, 0.5 probability of a $100 payoff and 0.5 probability of a $0 payoff) and an individual is willing to pay only, say, $35, that individual is exhibiting risk-averse behavior. This aversion to assuming risk gives rise to the notion of a "cost of risk," which we now investigate.

The *cost of risk* or *risk premium* can be viewed in terms of how much wealth or return one would give up in order to eliminate risk altogether; that is, the cost of risk is the difference between the expected return from a risky asset $(E[w] = \mu)$ and the investor's certainty equivalent return. For example, if offered a lottery that returns $100 with probability 0.5 or 0 with probability 0.5, an individual might consider a certain return of $30 equivalent to the lottery. In this case, the cost of risk is $20 = $50 - $30, where $50 represents the expected return from the lottery. Thus, designating the cost of risk as C, we note the following relationship for any risky asset:

(7.2) $$u(\mu - C) \equiv E[u(w)] = \Sigma\, \psi_i u(w_i)\,,$$

where ψ_i is the probability associated with the *i*th event. In other words, the utility of the certainty equivalent return, $u(\mu - C)$, is by definition equal to the expected utility of the risky asset's returns (see Figure 7.2).

We can solve for C as follows. First we use a Taylor series expansion for the left-hand side of Equation 7.2:

$$u(\mu - C) = u(\mu) + u'(\mu)(\mu - C - \mu) + \frac{u''(\mu)(\mu - C - \mu)^2}{2!}$$

$$+ \frac{u'''(\mu)(\mu - C - \mu)^3}{3!} + \ldots.$$

Figure 7.2   The Cost of Risk

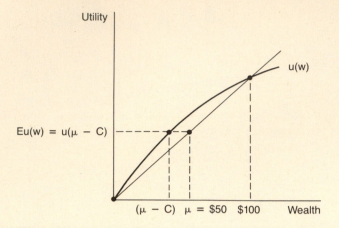

If the series converges, then, provided that C is very small, we can approximate $u(\mu - C)$ with a linear utility function by ignoring the second- and higher-order terms. Thus, we can approximate the utility of the certain equivalent return as follows:

$$u(\mu - C) \simeq u(\mu) - u'(\mu)C.$$

Next, we take a Taylor series expansion of the right-hand side of Equation 7.2. This time we use a quadratic approximation by retaining the second-order term but dropping all higher-order terms. In this instance we eschew a linear approximation of the utility function to allow for the possibility of wide variation in w. The resulting Taylor series expansion of the right-hand side of 7.2 is thus

$$\Sigma\,\psi_i u(w_i) \simeq u(\mu)\,\Sigma\,\psi_i + u'(\mu)\,\Sigma\,\psi_i(w_i - \mu) + \frac{1}{2!}u''(\mu)\Sigma\,\psi_i(w_i - \mu)^2.$$

Simplifying terms, we get

$$\Sigma\,\psi_i u(w_i) \simeq u(\mu) + \frac{1}{2!}u''(\mu)\sigma^2(w),$$

where $\sigma^2(w)$ is the variance in returns for the risky asset. Substituting both Taylor series approximations for the terms in Equation 7.2 produces the following:

$$u(\mu) - u'(\mu)C \simeq u(\mu) + \frac{1}{2!}u''(\mu)\sigma^2(w).$$

Solving for C, we obtain the following approximation for the cost of risk:

(7.3)
$$C \simeq \frac{1}{2}\sigma^2(w)\left[\frac{-u''(\mu)}{u'(\mu)}\right].$$

Using our approximations, then, the cost of risk is found to be proportional to the variance in wealth provided that both C and the variance are reasonably small. Where risk is measured by the variance, the cost assigned by the individual per unit of risk is

(7.4)
$$a(\mu) = \frac{-u''(\mu)}{u'(\mu)},$$

where $a(\mu)$ can be referred to as a *local measure of absolute risk aversion* for a wealth level μ. Note that $u'(\mu) > 0$ due to nonsatiety and $u''(\mu) < 0$ to reflect risk aversion. Thus, for risk-averse individuals $a(w) > 0$.

Since $a(w)$ is potentially different for each level of w, it constitutes a "local" measure of risk aversion. However, in some utility functions $a(w)$ is a constant, c; for example,

$$u(w) \simeq w \qquad \text{if } a(w) = c = 0$$

$$u(w) \simeq 1 - e^{-cw} \quad \text{if } a(w) = c > 0$$

$$u(w) \simeq e^{-cw} - 1 \quad \text{if } a(w) = c < 0.$$

Graphically, the shapes of these three utility functions are, respectively, linear, strictly concave, and strictly convex. Figure 7.3 depicts each of these functions. Note that $c = 0$ reflects risk-neutral behavior, $c > 0$ reflects risk aversion, and $c < 0$ reflects risk-seeking behavior.

We can also define a measure of *relative* risk aversion by dividing Equation 7.3 by mean wealth (μ). Hence,

(7.5)
$$\frac{C}{\mu} \simeq \frac{1}{2}\sigma^2(w)\left[\frac{-u''(\mu)}{u'(\mu)\mu}\right] \simeq -\left[\frac{u''(\mu)\mu}{2u'(\mu)}\right]\left[\frac{\sigma^2(w)}{\mu^2}\right].$$

Thus, the relative cost of risk — that is, relative to the mean wealth or return of the risky asset — equals C/μ. Further, the relative cost of risk is — for small variances — proportional to the square of the coefficient of variation, σ^2/μ^2.

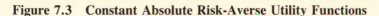

Figure 7.3   Constant Absolute Risk-Averse Utility Functions

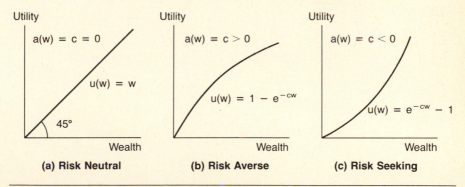

Stochastic Dominance and Expected Utility

Earlier we evaluated an individual's preference for risky assets in terms of each asset's expected utility. This required us to know not only all possible outcomes and their associated probabilities but also the mathematical function that characterizes the individual's utility function. In other words, we had to know whether the utility function was quadratic, exponential, or whatever, as well as its parameters, in order to estimate the utility of each possible outcome and, consequently, the expected utility of the return from each asset. *Stochastic dominance* criteria provide the analyst with a set of "rules" for making choices among risky assets consistent with the preferences of broad "classes" of utility functions *without* having to know the utility's precise functional characterization. For example, the first-degree stochastic dominance (FSD) rule provides the basis for ranking risky assets for all individuals who simply prefer more wealth to less, that is, who satisfy the nonsatiety axiom discussed in Appendix 2B. Second-degree stochastic dominance (SSD) provides a rule for ranking risky assets for all individuals who *both* prefer more wealth to less and are not risk seekers, that is, who are either risk neutral or risk averse. Third-degree stochastic dominance (TSD) provides a similar rank-ordering rule but for another, more restricted group of individuals, that is, those whose preferences share the restrictions of those caused by FSD and SSD but have additional restrictions that are less easily or intuitively identified.[3]

---

[3]Although we will not discuss them here, Meyer (1977a) has developed another set of stochastic dominance criteria. He has created rules for ranking risky asset distributions for investor "classes" where such classes are defined using upper and lower bounds on an individual's absolute risk aversion. This method, although little used to date in financial research, promises to be a very useful tool of performance analysis. See, for example, Meyer (1977b) and Martin and Petty (1983).

A Mathematical Review of Integration by Parts

The integration by parts formula provides a means for restating the integral of the product of two functions in what may be an easier form to solve. This formula can be derived from the product rule for differentiation. Specifically, if we let u(x) and F(x) represent two differentiable functions, the derivative of the product u(x)F(x) is as follows:

(i) $$[u(x)F(x)]' = u(x)F'(x) + u'(x)F(x),$$

where the primes (') signify the derivative of the function with respect to x. Solving (i) for u(x)F'(x) produces the following:

(ii) $$u(x)F'(x) = [F(x)u(x)]' - u'(x)F(x).$$

The corresponding indefinite integrals of both sides of (ii) must also be equal such that

(iii) $$\int u(x)F'(x)\, dx = \int [u(x)F(x)]'\, dx - \int u'(x)F(x)\, dx.$$

Recognizing that

$$\int [u(x)F(x)]'\, dx = u(x)F(x) + C,$$

where C is a constant, we can now rewrite (iii) as the integration by parts formula:

(iv) $$\int u(x)F'(x)\, dx = u(x)F(x) - \int u'(x)F(x)\, dx.$$

Note that (iv) involves integrals on both sides; thus, there is no need to display the constant of integration with the term u(x)F(x).

To summarize, the integration by parts formula provides a means for integrating products of the form

$$u(x)F'(x).$$

Of course, this formula is useful only where the restated integral on the right-hand side of (iv) is easier to solve than the original form on the left-hand side.

We find an immediate use for this formula when we derive the stochastic dominance theorems. In this application, we will be using definite integrals. The corresponding integration by parts formula in this case is

(v) $$\int_a^b u(x)F'(x)\, dx = u(x)F(x)\Big|_a^b - \int_a^b u'(x)F(x)\, dx,$$

where a and b are the limits of integration and $u(x)F(x)\big|_a^b = u(x)F(b) - u(x)F(a)$.

First-Degree Stochastic Dominance

Before we develop the *first-degree stochastic dominance (FSD)* rule, let us define some of the terms and symbols we will be using. Let F and G represent the cumulative probability distributions of the returns for risky assets A and B, respectively; that is, F(w) = prob (return on A $\leq$ w) and G(w) = prob (return on B $\leq$ w). Analytically,

$$F(x) = \int_0^x f(w)\,dw$$

and

$$G(x) = \int_0^x g(w)\,dw,$$

where f and g are the density functions corresponding to F and G, respectively. We will continue to use u(w) to refer to the utility of w dollars of wealth and will assume, for convenience, that u(w) is defined on the interval (0, 1).

FSD provides us with a rule for rank-ordering risky assets in a manner consistent with the preferences of *all individuals who prefer more wealth to less.* Note that this group of individuals includes risk seekers, risk averters, and those who are risk neutral. Given the breadth of the group, one would not expect to find many cases in which there is "unanimity" of preference; this has, in fact, been the result of empirical studies that have attempted to use FSD to rank order empirical return distributions of risky assets. Technically, we seek a rule for ranking uncertain prospects for all those individuals who have increasing utility functions, for that is what it means to "prefer more wealth to less." Symbolically, u(w) is increasing if $w_1 < w_2$ implies $u(w_1) < u(w_2)$. Note that this implies that at a point, w, at which an individual's utility function, u(w), is differentiable, we must have a positive first derivative, $u'(w) > 0$. If we were considering only differentiable utility functions, the condition $w_1 < w_2$ would imply that $u(w_1) < u(w_2)$ would be equivalent to $u'(w) > 0$ for all w.

FSD using the cumulative probability distributions is demonstrated graphically in Figure 7.4. Thus, A dominates B by FSD where the probability of any given return (w* or lower) for the dominated asset (B) is either equal to or greater than that for the undominated asset (A). Note that the only attribute of the individual's utility function that we need to know is that he or she "prefers more wealth to less." However, we must know the entire cumulative probability distribution of asset returns over which a choice is to be made.

Figure 7.4   First-Degree Stochastic Dominance

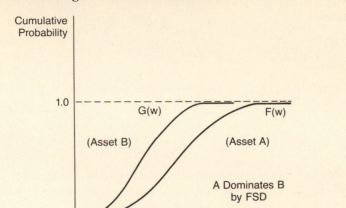

Derivation of the FSD Rule: A Mathematical Overview

We will develop the FSD rule by comparing the expected utility of risky assets A and B. Specifically, risky asset A is said to dominate risky asset B by FSD if

$$E_F[u(w)] \geq E_G[u(w)]$$

for all increasing utility functions. We use $E_F[u(w)]$ and $E_G[u(w)]$ to refer to the expected utility of the returns from risky asset A and B, respectively. To develop the FSD rule, we substitute for the expected utility of assets A and B as follows:

$$E_F[u(w)] = \int_0^1 u(w)\,dF(w)$$

and

$$E_G[u(w)] = \int_0^1 u(w)\,dG(w)$$

so that we can state the FSD rule as follows:

(7.6) $$\int_0^1 u(w)\,dF(w) > \int_0^1 u(w)\,dG(w),$$

where the limits of integration are 0 and 1. Note that this is simply a restatement of the FSD requirement that in order for asset A to dominate B it must have a greater expected utility of wealth. Integrating both sides of Equation 7.6 by parts (see "A Mathematical Review of Integration by Parts"), we can rewrite the expression as follows:

$$u(1)F(1) - \int_0^1 F(w)\,du(w) \geq u(1)G(1) - \int_0^1 G(w)\,du(w)$$

or, noting that $u(1)F(1) = u(1)G(1)$, we can rewrite the above expression as follows:

$$\int_0^1 [G(w) - F(w)]\,du(w) \geq 0.$$

The only case for which this condition is unambiguously satisfied for all increasing utility functions $u(w)$ defined on $(0, 1)$ is that in which $G(w) \geq F(w)$ for all w contained in that set. Therefore, asset A dominates asset B by FSD if and only if

$$G(w) \geq F(w)$$

for all w in $(0, 1)$.

The proof of the FSD rule is as follows. We have just seen that A dominates B if and only if, for all increasing utility functions $u(w)$,

$$\int_0^1 [G(w) - F(w)]\,du(w) \geq 0.$$

Thus, we must show that this reformulation is equivalent to $F(w) \leq G(w)$ for all w in $(0, 1)$. Certainly, if $F \leq G$, then

$$\int_0^1 [G(w) - F(w)]\,du(w) \geq 0$$

for all increasing utility functions. Therefore, A dominates B.

Stating the converse requires some care, however: For w in $(0, 1)$ we must show that $F(w) \leq G(w)$. Corresponding to w^*, a point of $(0, 1)$ on which we focus, we define a utility function $u^*(w) = 1$ if $w \geq w^*$ and $u^*(w) = 0$ if $w < w^*$. Clearly $u(w)$ is increasing so that

$$E_F[u^*(w)] \geq E_G[u^*(w)].$$

This is because A dominates B and $u^*(w)$ is an increasing utility function. However,

$$E_F[u^*(w)] = \int_0^1 u^*(w)\,dF(w)$$

$$= \int_{w^*}^1 dF(w)$$

$$= F(1) - F(w^*) = 1 - F(w^*),$$

and, similarly,

$$E_G[u^*(w)] = 1 - G(w^*).$$

Thus, $[1 - F(w^*)] \geq [1 - G(w^*)]$, or, equivalently, $F(w^*) \leq G(w^*)$. As this is true for any point w^*, the proof is complete.

Second-Degree Stochastic Dominance

Second-degree stochastic dominance (SSD), developed by Hadar and Russell (1969), provides us with a rule for rank ordering risky assets in a manner consistent with the preferences of (1) *all individuals who prefer more wealth to less* and (2) *all individuals who are either risk neutral or risk averse*. Thus, we seek a ranking device that will enable us to evaluate the unanimous preferences of all individuals with increasing and concave utility functions. Note that now the proposition "A dominates B" means that $E_A[u(w)] \geq E_B[u(w)]$ for all increasing concave (down) utility functions. If we are dealing with twice-differentiable utility functions, $u'(w) > 0$ and $u''(w) < 0$ for all w.

Derivation of the SSD Rule: A Mathematical Overview

Recall that when we developed the FSD theorem we integrated Equation 7.6 by parts, which produced an expression that was a function of the cumulative probability distributions of both the risky assets and $u(w)$. One way to develop the SSD theorem is to again integrate by parts; we can do this conveniently where $u(w)$ is twice differentiable. Thus, integrating Equation 7.6 by parts twice produces the following result for asset A:

$$
\begin{aligned}
E_A[u(w)] &= \int_0^1 u(w)\, dF(w) \\
&= u(w)F(w)\Big|_0^1 - \int_0^1 F(w)\, du(w) \\
&= u(1) - \int_0^1 F(w)u'(w)\, dw \\
&= u(1) - \left[u'(w)\int_0^w F(z)\, dz \right]\Big|_0^1 + \int_0^1 u''(w)\int_0^w F(z)\, dz\, dw \\
&= u(1) - u'(1) + \int_0^1 \int_0^w u''(w)F(z)\, dz\, dw.
\end{aligned}
$$

Similarly, for asset B,

$$E_B[u(w)] = u(1) - u'(1) + \int_0^1 \int_0^w u''(w)G(z)\, dz\, dw.$$

Hence, A dominates B if and only if

$$\int_0^1 \int_0^w u''(w)[F(z) - G(z)]\, dz\, dw \geq 0,$$

where $u'(w) \geq 0$ and $u''(w) \leq 0$ for all w. This condition will hold for all wealth levels where

$$\int_0^w [F(z) - G(z)]\, dz \leq 0$$

for all w in the set $(0, 1)$, and this is the SSD rule.

As in the proof of the FSD rule, the proof of this last assertion involves constructing a utility function, but this time it must be twice differentiable.

Figure 7.5 illustrates SSD using risky assets A and B. Note that the two cumulative probability distributions intersect at w' so that neither asset dominates the other by FSD. However, since the cumulative "difference" in the cumulative probability distributions is always positive — that is, $\int_0^w [G(z) - F(z)]\, dz \geq 0$ for all w — asset A dominates asset B by SSD (see "Derivation of the SSD Rule: A Mathematical Overview"). Note that asset A did not dominate B by FSD as the two cumulative probability distributions intersected because $G(w)$ was not always greater than $F(w)$ for all levels of w. Hence, we had to place an additional restriction on the class of utility functions considered — $u''(w) \leq 0$ — in order to obtain a preference ordering of the two alternatives.

Figure 7.5   Second-Degree Stochastic Dominance

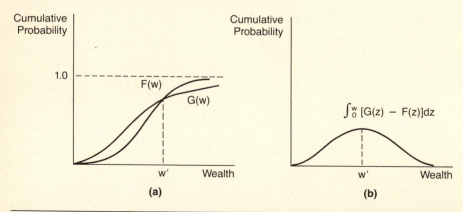

Third-Degree Stochastic Dominance

Third-degree stochastic dominance (TSD), developed by Whitmore (1970), provides the basis for ranking risky assets for that set of individuals whose preferences or utility functions — which we suppose to be thrice differentiable — have the following attributes:

1. $u'(w) > 0$ for all w

2. $u''(w) < 0$ for all w

3. $u'''(w) > 0$ for all w

Note that each set of restrictions corresponds to the three levels of stochastic dominance: FSD requires only 1, SSD requires 1 and 2, and TSD requires 1, 2, and 3. Hence, the TSD rule applies to the smallest set of investors thus far. Unfortunately, its requirement that $u'''(w)$ always be positive does not have the intuitive meaning that accompanies $u'(w) > 0$ (nonsatiety) and $u''(w) < 0$ (risk aversion). However, we do know that the set of individuals who fall into the third-degree dominance group includes those who exhibit a *decreasing absolute aversion to risk as their wealth rises*. Many believe this group includes most individuals. Thus, if asset A were found to dominate asset B by TSD, all those individuals who became less risk averse as their wealth increased would also prefer A over B.[4]

Summary

Stochastic dominance offers a very general preference-ordering tool in that the restrictions placed on individual preferences are few and not very limiting. For example, second-degree stochastic dominance provides a tool for assessing the preferences of all individuals who prefer more wealth to less and exhibit risk-averse behavior. These are not terribly restrictive assumptions, as most individuals probably fulfill them anyway.

Unfortunately, stochastic dominance has two very important limitations as a tool for financial decisionmaking under uncertainty. First, the information requirements for its use are great. We need to know the entire cumulative probability function for the alternatives being compared; in contrast, with mean-variance analysis we need estimate only two parameters of the probability distribution. Second, there are no algorithms for forming optimal portfolios in a stochastic dominance sense. For example, combining two risky assets together, such as ⅓ A and ⅔ B, may produce a cumulative probability distribution that would dominate A, B, or

---

[4]To derive the TSD rule, we integrate Equation 7.6 by parts yet a third time, producing the following result:

$$\int_0^x \int_0^y [G(w) - F(w)]\, dw\, dy \geq 0$$

for all x contained in the set $(0, 1)$ and

$$E_A[u(w)] \geq E_B[u(w)],$$

with the strict inequality holding for at least one level of w.

any other single asset or portfolio. However, there exist no algorithms for discovering this dominant portfolio. This too contrasts with mean-variance analysis, where efficient portfolio construction algorithms have long been available (as we will discuss in Chapter 8).

Expected Utility and Mean-Variance Analysis

Overview

In the preceding section, we developed some very general rules for assessing individual preferences with regard to risky assets. However, we found that in order to implement these rules we had to know the entire cumulative probability distribution of returns for each asset. In this section we will consider yet another method for ranking risky assets, which is based on the mean and variance of the probability distribution of asset returns rather than on the entire cumulative distribution. The appeal of such a methodology is its reduced information requirement and the mathematical tractability of the mean and variance. However, as we now demonstrate, this "gain" does not come without a price, for the assumptions needed in order to make mean-variance rankings consistent with expected utility maximization are quite restrictive.

The Quadratic Utility Function and Mean-Variance Analysis

In the example used to illustrate the expected utility paradigm, the utility function used was quadratic. That is, $u(w)$ in Equation 7.1 was of the following general form:

(7.7) $$u(w) = a + bw + cw^2,$$

where a, b, and c are the parameters of $u(w)$. This *quadratic utility function* is of particular interest in financial theory because it allows us to calculate the expected utility of the returns on a risky asset as a function of the mean and variance of their probability distribution. We can easily see this by taking the expectation of the quadratic utility function in Equation 7.7,

$$E[u(w)] = a + bE[w] + cE[w^2],$$

and recalling that the variance can be written $\sigma^2(w) = E[w^2] - E[w]^2$ such that

$$E[u(w)] = a + bE[w] + c[\sigma^2(w) + E(w)^2].$$

Thus, to calculate the expected utility of wealth for a risky asset where the individual's utility can be represented by a quadratic function, we need know only the mean and variance of the asset's wealth distribution (and, of course, the parameters of the quadratic utility function, a, b, and c).

The quadratic utility function is one of two possible bases on which the theorist can justify the analysis of risky assets using only the mean and variance of their respective probability distributions of returns. However, before we discuss

Figure 7.6 Quadratic Utility Function

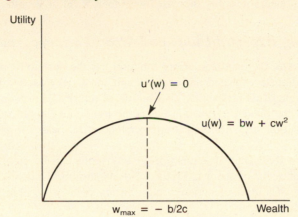

the second, let us enumerate the shortcomings of the quadratic function as a representation of an individual's utility function.

The quadratic form is not a completely satisfactory utility index for two reasons. First, a quadratic function eventually reaches a maximum and turns down, as shown in Figure 7.6. The maximum occurs where $u'(w) = 0$ or where $w = -b/2c$. This creates a problem, since $u'(w) \leq 0$ violates the nonsatiety axiom underlying the expected utility paradigm, which demands that $u'(w) \geq 0$ for all wealth levels. One possible solution to this problem is to limit our use of the quadratic function to that segment for which $u'(w) \geq 0$, that is, the segment where $w < w_{max} = -b/2c$.

The second deficiency of the quadratic function relates to the fact that it exhibits "increasing absolute risk aversion"—that is, as the wealth level increases, the individual with quadratic utility becomes increasingly more risk averse, which clashes with the generally held belief that risk-averse individuals exhibit *decreasing* risk aversion as their wealth increases. We can demonstrate this disturbing attribute of the quadratic utility function by noting how the Arrow-Pratt measure of absolute risk aversion varies with increasing wealth. Absolute risk aversion for a particular level of wealth was defined earlier in Equation 7.4 as follows:

(7.4)
$$a(w) = \frac{-u''(w)}{u'(w)}.$$

For the quadratic utility function, the measure of absolute risk aversion is

$$a(w) = \frac{-2c}{b + 2cw}.$$

Correspondingly, $a'(w)$ for the quadratic utility function is as follows:

$$a'(w) = \frac{4c^2}{(b + 2cw)^2} > 0.$$

Hence, $a'(w) > 0$ for all levels of wealth such that the absolute risk aversion of individuals with quadratic utility increases with their level of wealth.

Approximating Expected Utility and Mean-Variance Analysis

As we noted above, the quadratic utility function has the desirable property of allowing us to calculate expected utility of wealth for a risky asset using only the mean and variance of its probability distribution of returns. However, as we have just discovered, the quadratic function has some important limitations as a utility index. In this section we will note yet another theoretical basis for mean-variance analysis.

Recall that the value of a function at any point can be estimated to any desired degree of accuracy using a Taylor series expansion. Thus, taking a Taylor series expansion of a utility function at an arbitrary point w^* within the range of possible outcomes, we get

(7.8) $$u(w) = u(w^*) + u'(w^*)(w - w^*) + \frac{u''(w^*)(w - w^*)^2}{2!}$$

$$+ \frac{u'''(w^*)(w - w^*)^3}{3!} + \dots$$

Since the values of $u(w^*)$ and each derivative are constants, we can substitute for them as follows:

(7.9) $$u(w) = \alpha_0 + \alpha_1(w - w^*) + \alpha_2(w - w^*)^2 + \alpha_3(w - w^*)^3 + \dots,$$

where $\alpha_0 = u(w^*)$, $\alpha_1 = u'(w^*)$, $\alpha_2 = u''(w^*)/2!$, $\alpha_3 = u'''(w^*)/3!$, and so forth.

Now let w^* equal zero such that Equation 7.9 can be rewritten as follows:

$$E[u(w)] = \alpha_1 E(w) + \alpha_2 E(w^2) + \alpha_3 E(w^3) + \dots$$

provided that the series converges where $w = w^*$. In this form, it is obvious that expected utility can be expressed as a function of the moments of the probability distribution of returns from a risky asset. Thus, if the probability distribution of wealth is normal and therefore can be described in terms of the first two moments — the mean and the variance — expected utility can be calculated using only the mean and variance even though the utility function is not quadratic! In addition, even if the probability distribution is only approximately normal, expected utility may be "approximated" using the mean and variance of the distribution of asset returns.

Although normally distributed asset returns will salvage mean-variance analysis (in the absence of a quadratic utility function), there is yet another "fly in the ointment." When risky assets, such as common stock, are characterized by "limited liability," their return distributions are, by definition, truncated on the lower tail. For example, if you purchase a share of common stock for $110, the very worst that can happen is that you will lose your $110 investment. Your liability is effectively limited to the amount of your investment. Thus, unlike the normal probability distribution, which is unbounded from above or below, the distribution of returns to risky assets with limited liability is bounded and, consequently, cannot be normal. We will further consider the probability distribution of common stocks when we discuss the empirical work on this problem in conjunction with the efficient capital market hypothesis in Chapter 10. At this point, we note only that the normal distribution assumption can be used to justify mean-variance analysis only as a rough approximation to choices involving risky assets with limited liability.

Summary of Mean Variance Analysis

Mean-variance analysis has become the primary vehicle through which to analyze decisionmaking under uncertainty. The rationale underlying its use is the expected utility paradigm, which in turn is based on a set of fundamental axioms concerning individual behavior. Here we have shown that mean-variance analysis is indeed consistent with the expected utility paradigm in one of three cases:

1.   The individual's utility function is quadratic.

2.   The probability distribution of asset returns is normal.

3.   The probability distribution is approximately normal so that the mean and variance provide the basis for an "acceptable" approximation of expected utility.

Of course, the last approximation argument is not a hard and fast justification but merely an assertion that although mean-variance analysis may not be completely consistent with expected utility maximization, it is sufficiently accurate in its predictions to provide valuable insight into decisionmaking under uncertainty.

Recent studies by Levy and Markowitz (1979) and Kroll, Levy, and Markowitz (1984) have provided empirical evidence of the reasonableness of mean-variance analysis. Using a wide variety of mathematical forms to represent the utility function, these studies employed historical rates of return on mutual funds and common stocks, respectively, to test whether mean-variance rankings were significantly different from the expected utility-maximizing choices. The earlier paper found that out of the 149 mutual fund portfolios studied, the mean-variance-efficient portfolio frequently was the one that maximized expected utility or at least approached optimum expected utility. These studies attest to the "robustness" of mean-variance analysis even when its assumptions are not entirely acceptable.[5] For the "positivist," these papers provide empirical verification of the mean-variance paradigm.

---

[5]Meyer (1985) has shown that mean–standard deviation rankings of risky assets will be consistent with expected utility maximization where the probability distributions of asset returns satisfy a "consistency" condition. This condition is the following: The cumulative distribution functions for the assets in the choice set may differ from one another only by location parameters. Note that there is no restriction placed on the functional form of any particular cumulative density function. Thus, a given asset's returns can be distributed in any fashion as long as the random payoffs of the assets to which it is being compared are similarly distributed.

Summary

The theory of decisionmaking under uncertainty occupies a prominent position in the theory of finance because it provides a basis for understanding the real world. Choices must be made today that will provide the decisionmaker with a spectrum of possible outcomes. An investor who acquires a share of stock cannot know what the future holds for the firm in which he or she has invested; therefore, the payoff from that investment is random, since it depends on several factors whose values are unknown at the time the investment decision is made.

The dominant approach to the theory of decisionmaking under uncertainty in both economics and finance relies on the utility theory work of von Neumann and Morgenstern. These studies established the possibility of constructing and using a utility function to predict individuals' choices under conditions of uncertainty by maximizing the expected utility of the available alternatives. However, we further refined the choice problem by developing rules that restrict the types of utility functions and thereby rank order sets of alternatives. For example, first-, second-, and third-degree stochastic dominance rules permit the ranking of risky assets for individuals who simply prefer more wealth to less (first-degree stochastic dominance), who both prefer more wealth to less and are not risk seeking (second-degree stochastic dominance), and who have both attributes of second-degree dominance and utility functions of which the third derivative is everywhere positive (third-degree stochastic dominance).

We also found that mean-variance analysis provides a means of ranking risky alternatives. Where individual utility functions are quadratic or where the probability distributions of the assets being ranked are normal, all we need know about the risky asset's probability distribution are its mean and variance. Although the conditions under which mean-variance analysis is theoretically consistent with the maximization of expected utility are quite restrictive and unrealistic, recent empirical studies have shown this approach to be quite robust. As we will discover throughout the balance of our discussion of decisionmaking under uncertainty, mean-variance analysis has become the dominant paradigm in financial theory. It is the basis for modern portfolio theory as well as for the capital asset pricing model, which we will develop in the following chapters.

Study Questions

7.1   For the expected utility theorem to apply to individuals, do they have to actually calculate it when making choices? Explain.

7.2   How does risk aversion help explain an individual's willingness to buy insurance?

7.3   Mean-variance analysis has pervaded financial theory for over 30 years despite its theoretical shortcomings. Discuss the problems underlying its use.

Study Problems

7.1   Consider the following utility function:

$$u(w) = w - kw^2,$$

where w corresponds to money wealth and k is a constant.
a. Sketch this utility function.
b. Sketch the function

$$a(w) = \frac{-u''(w)}{u'(w)}.$$

c. Discuss the risk aversion attributes of this utility function as wealth increases.

7.2   Answer Problem 7.1 using the following utility function:

$$u(w) = 1 - e^{-aw}$$

where a is a positive constant.

7.3   Jim Rogers has the following utility function:

$$u(w) = e^{-aw} - 1,$$

where $a = -2$.
a. Evaluate Rogers' expected utility for the following gamble:

Probability	Payoff (w)
0.5	$2
0.5	1

b. What is the certain equivalent of the above gamble for Rogers?
c. How much would Rogers be willing to pay to eliminate the uncertainty associated with the above gamble such that it would produce a certain return of $1.50?

7.4   James Richard's utility of wealth function is defined by the following function:

$$u(w) = a + bw + cw^2,$$

where $b > 0, c < 0$, and for all relevant values of $w, b + 2cw > 0$.
a. Show that $u'(w) > 0$ and $u''(w) < 0$ for all relevant values of w.
b. Show that if w is a random variable, $E[u(w)]$ is a quadratic function of $E(w)$ and σ_w^2.
c. Demonstrate the relationship between Richard's preferences with respect to $E(w)$ and σ_w^2.

7.5   Illustrate graphically the increasing absolute risk-averse behavior of individuals with quadratic utility. What does this attribute imply with regard to individuals' desire to purchase insurance as their wealth increases?

7.6   The Richardson brothers, Prodigal and Miser, are "almost-identical" twins; however, their utility "genes" were quite different at birth. Miser has been able to amass and hold a fortune consisting of $15 in cash and a home worth $10, while his poor brother Prodigal owns only a $10 house inherited from their father. Prodigal has recently undergone a major change in priorities and decided to "straighten up and fly right" like his brother. This means that both now share the same utility for wealth, that is,

$$u(w) = 60w - w^2.$$

Prodigal has learned that all is not great when one decides to covet rather than squander one's wealth and that the risk of its loss is one of the unfortunate facts of life. For Prodigal this means that there is, say, a 0.5 probability of losing his home to fire next year. Prodigal has been advised by his brother to buy fire insurance.

a. How much would Prodigal be willing to pay to insure against the prospect of losing the house to a fire?

b. How much would Miser be willing to pay for the same coverage?

c. Graph Prodigal's and Miser's utility functions, and illustrate graphically your answers to parts a and b.

7.7   Answer Problem 7.6 where the Richardson brothers' utility for wealth function is given by the following:

a. $u(w) = 1 - e^{-aw}$, where a = 0.3.

b. $u(w) = e^{-aw} - 1$, where a = −0.3.

References

A. A. Alchian, "The Meaning of Utility Measurement," *American Economic Review* 42 (1953): 26–50.

K. J. Arrow, *Essays in the Theory of Risk Bearing* (Amsterdam, Netherlands: North Holland, 1971).

D. Bernoulli, "Exposition of a New Theory on the Measurement of Risk," *Econometrica* 22 (1954): 23–37.

P. C. Fishburn, *Decision and Value Theory* (New York: Wiley, 1964).

M. Friedman and L. J. Savage, "The Utility Analysis of Choices Involving Risk," *Journal of Political Economy* 56 (1948): 279–304.

J. Hadar and W. R. Russell, "Rules for Ordering Uncertain Prospects," *American Economic Review* (March 1969): 25–34.

C. Haley and L. Schall, *The Theory of Financial Decisions* (New York: McGraw-Hill, 1982), Chapter 5.

J. M. Henderson and R. E. Quandt, *Microeconomic Theory: A Mathematical Approach* (New York: McGraw-Hill, 1980), Chapter 3.

K. Kroll, H. Levy, and H. M. Markowitz, "Mean-Variance versus Direct Utility Maximization," *Journal of Finance* 39 (1984): 47–61.

P. R. G. Layard and A. A. Walters, *Microeconomic Theory* (New York: McGraw-Hill, 1980), Chapter 13.

H. Levy and H. M. Markowitz, "Approximating Expected Utility by a Function of Mean and Variance," *American Economic Review* 69 (1979): 308–317.

R. D. Luce and H. Raiffa, *Games and Decisions* (New York: Wiley, 1957).

H. M. Markowitz, *Portfolio Selection: Efficient Diversification of Investments* (New York: Wiley, 1959; New Haven, Conn.: Yale University Press, 1970).

J. D. Martin, L. Blose, and J. W. Petty, "An Analysis of the Use of ARPS Funds in Corporate Cash Management" (Forthcoming, *Advances in Quantitative Analysis of Finance and Accounting,* 1987).

J. D. Martin and J. W. Petty, "An Analysis of the Performance of Publicly Traded Venture Capital Companies," *Journal of Financial and Quantitative Analysis* (September 1983): 401–410.

J. Meyer, "Choice among Distributions," *Journal of Economic Theory* 14 (1977a): 235–242.

——— , "Further Applications of Stochastic Dominance to Mutual Fund Performance," *Journal of Financial and Quantitative Analysis* (June 1977b): 235–242.

——— , "Two Moment Decision and Expected Utility Maximization" (Working paper, Michigan State University, September 1985).

J. W. Pratt, "Risk Aversion in the Small and in the Large," *Econometrica* 32 (1964): 122–137.

L. M. Pulley, "A General Mean-Variance Approximation to Expected Utility for Short Holding Periods," *Journal of Financial and Quantitative Analysis* 16 (1981): 361–375.

J. P. Quirk and R. Saposnik, "Admissibility and Measurable Utility Functions," *Review of Economic Studies* 20 (1962): 140–147.

P. J. H. Schoemaker, "The Expected Utility Model: Its Variants, Purposes, Evidence and Limitations," *Journal of Economic Literature* XX (June 1982): 529–563.

H. R. Varian, *Microeconomic Analysis* (New York: Norton, 1978), Chapter 3.

J. von Neumann and O. Morgenstern, *Theory of Games and Economic Behavior,* 2d ed. (Princeton, N.J.: Princeton University Press, 1947).

G. A. Whitmore, "Third-Degree Stochastic Dominance," *American Economic Review* (June 1970): 457–459.

Appendix 7A

The Time State Preference Model

The time state preference (TSP) model provides a useful way of thinking about the problem of choice in the presence of uncertain outcomes. As the name implies, individuals are assumed to have preferences that are sensitive to both *when* a dollar is received and the particular circumstances, or *state of nature,* in which it is received. This means, for example, that the utility of a $1 payoff received in 4 years will reflect both the fact that the payoff was 4 years in coming and the state of nature that produced the payoff (such as whether the economy was in recession or boom).

Stated very simply, in the time state preference model assets provide returns (payoffs) in each period in accordance with the existing state of nature. Individuals then evaluate the desirability of buying an asset by determining the expected value of the utility of the asset's returns in each period. We now define the essential elements of the time state preference model: (1) states of nature, (2) payoffs, and (3) utility.

Basic Elements of the Time State Preference Model

The fundamental element of the time state preference model is the concept of *states* or *states of nature.* Each individual is assumed to know the possible states of nature at each point in time. These states can be classified very broadly, such as:

- *State 1:* Expanding economic conditions

■   *State 2:* Stationary economic conditions

■   *State 3:* Contracting economic conditions

On the other hand they can be very detailed, for example,

■   *State 488:* Gross national product rising at 6 to 8 percent per year, a Republican Congress, and a 4 to 6 percent rate of inflation

The key consideration here is that individuals utilize the concept of states of nature to characterize an uncertain future.

In addition, states of the world are assumed to be both "exhaustive" and "mutually exclusive"; that is, the individual is assumed to ascribe states of nature to all possible outcomes, and only one state can occur at any point in time. Each state has a positive probability of occurrence. The sum of the state probabilities at any time is one, because the states are both exhaustive and mutually exclusive; that is, letting ψ_{st} denote the probability of state s at time t, $\Sigma_{s \in S} \psi_{st} = 1$.

The second basic element of the time state preference model is the *payoff,* or return, for each time period and state of nature. Note that it is the particular state of nature that will occur, *not* the payoff associated with it, that is uncertain. For example, a risky asset may provide the following distribution of payoffs:

State	Payoff	Probability
Boom	$100	0.70
Recession	30	0.30

Both the states of nature (boom and recession) and their corresponding payoffs are assumed to be known. However, the particular state that will occur is not known.

The third element of the TSP model is the individual's *utility function.* In our earlier discussions of an individual's utility function, we denoted the utility of wealth, or equivalently, consumption, as u(w). In a one-period setting with a fixed saving decision, this function is appropriate. With the TSP model, this function must be generalized to consider both the time t and the state s associated with the payoff being evaluated. Much like our earlier work on the Fisher model, the utility function appropriate in the TSP model assigns value to consumption levels now and at each point in the future. Unlike our earlier work on the Fisher model, the TSP model incorporates uncertainty, and the utility function must assign value to consumption levels now and at each time and state in the future.

For example, if there are two periods and three dates, the consumer must assess the utility of the possible consumption at t = 0, consumption at t = 1 in state r, and consumption at t = 2 in state s, for all possible states at dates one and two. Letting (c_0, c_{1r}, c_{2s}) denote those consumption levels, the utility function is of the form $u(c_0, c_{1r}, c_{2s})$, where c_0 is consumption now, c_{1r} is consumption next period if state r occurs, and, similarly, c_{2s} is future consumption if state s occurs. The form of this utility function reflects the individual's preferences for consumption at each date in each state. The individual is then assumed to make decisions that maximize the expected utility of the alternatives considered. This is obviously more complicated than the expected utility maximization discussed in Chapter 7, but it is a natural generalization of both the expected utility discussed there and the notion of utility discussed in connection with the Fisher model in Chapter 2.

Note that individuals are assumed to agree about the number of possible states of the world and the payoffs in each state. However, they may disagree about the probability of the states' occurrence. Hence, the TSP model incorporates heterogeneous beliefs via the individuals' subjective probability beliefs.

Security Market Valuation

Although we will not discuss the process by which market equilibrium is attained in the context of a TSP model, we will investigate the relationship among the security prices that must prevail in market equilibrium. In particular, we will explore the relationship between the equilibrium prices of risky assets and their payoff structures (that is, the states in which the assets provide their holders with payoffs).

Definitions

Before we proceed further, we must define some terms that are critical to the discussion of a TSP equilibrium, namely a pure or primitive security, a complex security, and a complete market.

A *pure* or *primitive* security can be thought of as a "state-contingent claim" in that it pays one dollar at the end of the period if a given state of nature occurs and nothing otherwise. These securities are sometimes called *Arrow-Debreu securities* after Arrow (1964) and Debreu (1959), who first utilized the concept. A *complex security* is merely a combination of pure securities. For example, a risky asset that produces a payoff in two or more states of nature is a complex security. The essential insight provided by a TSP market equilibrium is that risky assets can be valued as a linear combination of the values of the pure securities that make it up (we will return to this point shortly). A *complete market* is one in which there are as many linearly independent securities as there are states of nature at each date. One important implication of a complete market is that any pattern of payoffs (defined by the times and states of nature in which they are received) can be created using a linear combination (portfolio) of existing securities; that is, in a complete market any desired complex or pure security can be created using a portfolio of existing securities. Another implication is that uncertainty about one's future wealth at a particular time can be "theoretically" reduced to zero by dividing one's current wealth among a portfolio of securities such that the payoff will be the same across all possible states of nature. This latter strategy is equivalent to investing equal amounts in each of the pure securities corresponding to all possible states of nature on the date in question.

Complete Markets and the Fisher Model:
A Mathematical Overview

In a complete market model there are a finite number of states of nature, and there are an equal number of assets which yield \$1 in state s and \$0 otherwise. Let p_s denote the price now of an asset that pays \$1 in the event that state s occurs then. The price p_s may be equivalently interpreted as a risk-adjusted discount factor. The consumer has an income now of m_0 and an income m_{1s} then, in the event that state s occurs, where s $= 1, 2, \ldots, S$. Let ψ_s denote the consumer's subjective probability assessment that state s will occur then, where

$$\sum_{s=1}^{S} \psi_s = 1 .$$

Let c_0 denote the dollar consumption level now and c_{1s} denote the dollar consumption level then, in the event state s occurs. Then, letting u denote the consumer's utility function, expected utility is

$$\sum_{s=1}^{S} u(c_0, c_{1s}) \, \psi_s .$$

The consumer selects a consumption plan that specifies a consumption level now and a consumption level for each state of nature then. In its classic form, the problem is stated as a constrained maximization problem. Due to the uncertainty concerning consumption then, the consumer maximizes expected utility subject to the budget constraint. Hence the problem may be stated as follows:
   maximize

$$\sum_{s=1}^{S} u(c_0, c_{1s}) \psi_s$$

   subject to

$$c_0 + \sum_{s=1}^{S} p_s c_{1s} = m_0 + \sum_{s=1}^{S} p_s m_{1s} ,$$

where the LHS of the constraint is the present value of consumption and the RHS is the present value of income. Note that m_0 is current income or wealth, and m_{1s} is next period's income if state s occurs. The budget constraint is shown in the following figure.

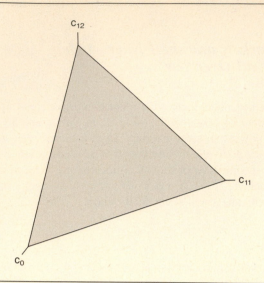

Using the Lagrange function $L(c_0, c_{11}, \ldots, c_{1S}, \lambda)$, the maximization problem may be expressed as follows:

   maximize

$$L(c_0, c_{11}, \ldots, c_{1S}, \lambda),$$

   where

$$L(c_0, c_{11}, \ldots, c_{1S}, \lambda) = \sum_{s=1}^{S} u(c_0, c_{1s})\psi_s - \lambda\left(c_0 + \sum_{s=1}^{S} p_s c_{1s} - m_0 - \sum_{s=1}^{S} p_s m_{1s}\right).$$

Then the first-order conditions for an optimal consumption plan, in the case where there are only two future states, $s = 1, 2$, are

(i)
$$D_1 L = \sum_{s=1}^{S} D_1 u \psi_s - \lambda = 0$$

(ii)
$$D_2 L = D_2 u \psi_1 - \lambda p_1 = 0$$

(iii)
$$D_3 L = D_2 u \psi_2 - \lambda p_2 = 0$$

(iv)
$$D_4 L = m_0 + \sum_{s=1}^{S} p_s m_{1s} - c_0 - \sum_{s=1}^{S} p_s c_{1s} = 0$$

Note that the first of the two conditions simply says that the Lagrange multiplier λ equals the expected marginal utility of consumption now. Also observe that, using (i), (ii) may be equivalently expressed as

$$p_1 = \frac{D_2 u \psi_1}{\displaystyle\sum_{s=1}^{S} D_1 u \psi_s},$$

which says that the consumer will purchase state 1 claims until its price equals the marginal rate of substitution; that is, the rate at which the consumer is willing to sacrifice consumption now for more consumption in state 1 equals the price now of consumption in state 1.[a] Similarly, using the conditions in (ii) and (iii),

$$\frac{p_1}{p_2} = \frac{D_2 u \psi_1}{D_2 u \psi_2},$$

which says that the consumer will purchase state 2 claims until the marginal rate of substitution, that is, of state 2 for state 1 consumption, is equal to the price ratio. Therefore, we find that the Fisher model generalizes nicely to an uncertainty model, and the same type of conditions are generated to describe the optimal consumption plan.

---

[a]To see that the RHS is the marginal rate of substitution, take the differential of the expected utility function, set it equal to 0, let $dc_{1s} = 0$ for $s \neq 1$, and note that this yields

$$\left(\sum_{s=1}^{S} D_1 u \psi_s \right) dc_0 + (D_2 u \psi_1) \, dc_{11} = 0 \iff -\frac{dc_0}{dc_{11}} = \frac{D_2 u \psi_1}{\sum_{s=1}^{S} D_1 u \psi_s}.$$

A Single-Period Example of Market Equilibrium

To demonstrate the relationship that must exist among security prices in market equilibrium, we will utilize a simple two-date model, that is, one with two periods — now and later. Securities offer an uncertain payoff at the end of the period depending on which state of nature occurs. In the context of this simple setup, one possible representation of a complete market is one in which pure securities are traded for every possible state of nature. We will begin our discussion with this setting and then expand to the case where all the necessary pure securities do not exist but their payoffs can be created using a portfolio of existing risky assets.

Consider a simple one-period model with four possible states of nature. In our initial complete market setting, we assume that the values of each of the pure securities corresponding to the four possible states of nature are known. The payoffs of these securities are shown in Table 7A.1. We now assume that the capital market is perfect in the sense that there are no transactions costs involved in trading securities, information about security prices is freely available to everyone, there are no restrictions on trading (such as unlimited short selling), and no buyer or seller is so large that his or her actions can impact on market prices. In a perfectly competitive and complete capital market, equilibrium would be characterized by the following condition: An individual would be unable to make riskless arbitrage profits by buying and selling existing securities. For example, consider complex security Alpha. Alpha has a market price of $0.95 and provides a payoff of $1 if states A or D occur. (Note that riskless arbitrage is possible in this case

Table 7A.1   Pure Security Prices in Market Equilibrium

	State of Nature				
Pure Security	A	B	C	D	Market Value
1	$1	$0	$0	$0	$0.45
2	0	1	0	0	0.23
3	0	0	1	0	0.30
4	0	0	0	1	0.45

because an individual can costlessly issue [short] one share of Alpha for $0.95 and simultaneously acquire pure securities 1 and 4 for $0.90.) At the end of period 1, the security holder will receive $1 if state A or D occurs (as would have been the case with holding Alpha) but will have invested only $0.90 and realized a $0.05 arbitrage profit on each arbitrage trade. Thus, arbitrage profits will continue as long as the value of complex securities differs from that of a portfolio of the pure securities that make up the complex securities. In general, the value of complex security XYZ can (in equilibrium) be defined as follows:

$$(7A.1) \qquad\qquad V_{XYZ} = \sum_{s=1}^{S} q_s p_s ,$$

where there are S possible states of nature, q_s is the number of pure security payoffs provided by complex security XYZ, and p_s is the price of pure security s.

In our previous example (Table 7A.1), we assumed that pure securities were traded for all possible states of nature. However, this is not the only form that a complete market can take as we now demonstrate. Suppose again that there are four possible states of the world but only three pure securities traded corresponding to payoffs in states A, B, and C. However, now assume a risky asset, Beta, exists and offers a $1 payoff if either state B or state D occurs and its market price is $0.68. Using Equation 7A.1,

$$V_{Beta} = 1p_B + 1p_D = 1(0.23) + 1p_D = \$0.68$$

$$p_D = \$0.45 .$$

In this case, pure security 4 is not traded in the market, but the market "spans" its payoff—that is, pure security D's payoff can be created from a portfolio of existing and traded securities and thus its value can be determined. Here the market is not complete in the sense that a pure security is traded for every possible state of the world but is complete in that all such securities can be created as a linear combination of existing securities. Security D is "spanned" by the market.

Consider a more complex example of spanning. Assume now that only pure securities 1 and 3 are traded. Further, there exist two complex securities, Big and Little. Big has a payoff of $20 if state B occurs and $10 if state D occurs; Little offers a $3 payoff if state B occurs and $5 if state D occurs. Big sells for $9.10 (recall that we are assuming the prices of pure securities 2 and 4 are not known or observed directly since they are not traded), and Little sells for $2.94. Using Equation 7A.1, we can now express the values of each security as follows:

$$V_{Big} = 20p_2 + 10p_4 = \$9.10$$

$$V_{Little} = 3p_2 + 5p_4 = \$2.94 \, .$$

Here we have two linear equations in two unknowns; thus, we can solve for p_2 and p_4. The resulting values are $0.23 and $0.45, respectively. Hence, in equilibrium it is not necessary that every pure security be traded for the market to be complete, as long as the set of traded securities "spans" the set of all possible pure securities. Once the values of all pure securities are known, the value of any complex security can be determined using Equation 7A.1, and consequently the market is complete.

Complete Markets and Fisher Separation: A Mathematical Overview

Here we consider whether the Fisher separation result holds under uncertainty for the publicly held and traded corporation. The manager of the corporation makes two decisions. First, like other investors, the manager selects a portfolio of assets that determines consumption both now and then. Second, unlike other investors, the manager selects the investment level and stock issue for the corporation. Of course, the manager could use retained earnings or bonds rather than stock to finance the investment, but the source and type of funds used do not affect corporate value.[a]

As before, let $s = 1, 2, \ldots, S$ denote the set of states of nature and p_s denote the price of the asset that pays $1 in state s and $0 otherwise. Now, let p_f and N_f denote the share price and number of shares issued for corporation f. Suppose the manager issues enough shares to finance an investment expenditure of I_f dollars now. Suppose too, that the payoff on the investment is $[\Pi_{f1}(I_f), \ldots, \Pi_{fS}(I_f)]$, so the payoff depends on the investment level and the state.[b] Let Π_{fs} be increasing and concave in I_f for all s. Let V_f denote the stock market value of the corporation. Clearly,

$$V_f = p_f N_f = \sum_{s=1}^{S} p_s \Pi_{fs}(I_f)$$

and the risk-adjusted net present value of the investment is $V_f - I_f$. By analogy to the certainty version of the Fisher separation result, we should find that all managers select the same investment level, and that it is the investment level which maximizes the risk-adjusted net present value of the corporation.

Now consider an unconstrained version of the manager's maximization problem. To do this, define consumption now and then in terms of the financial assets. Let x_s be the number of pure or primitive securities for state s purchased and let n_f be the number of shares of firm f purchased by the manager. Alternatively, we may note that $N_f - n_f$ is the manager's net supply of shares to the market. The manager's consumption now and then may be represented as

(i)
$$c_0 = m_0 - \sum_{s=1}^{S} p_s x_s + p_f(N_f - n_f) - I_f$$

and

(ii)
$$c_{1s} = m_{1s} + x_s + n_f\left(\frac{\Pi_{fs}}{N_f}\right), \qquad s = 1, 2, \ldots, S.$$

The manager makes the investment and portfolio choices to maximize expected utility; the manager's expected utility is

$$\sum_{s=1}^{S} u(c_0, c_{1s})\psi_s,$$

where the consumption pairs are defined by (i) and (ii). Maximizing expected utility with respect to x_s, n_f, and I_f, respectively, yields the following first-order conditions:

(iii)
$$-p_s\left[\sum_{j=1}^{S} D_1 u\psi_j\right] + D_2 u\psi_s = 0 \text{ for all S}$$

(iv)
$$\sum_{s=1}^{S}\left[-p_f D_1 u + D_2 u\left(\frac{\Pi_{fs}}{N_f}\right)\right]\psi_s = 0$$

(v)
$$\sum_{s=1}^{S}\left\{D_1 u[p_f'(N_f - n_f) - 1] + D_2 u\left(\frac{n_f}{N_f}\right)\Pi_{fs}'\right\}\psi_s = 0.$$

Using (iii), we note that

(vi)
$$p_s = \frac{D_2 u\psi_s}{\displaystyle\sum_{j=1}^{S} D_1 u\psi_j},$$

as previously. Then, using (iv) and (vi), we note that the firm's share price is

(vii)
$$p_f = \sum_{s=1}^{S} p_s\left(\frac{\Pi_{fs}}{N_f}\right).$$

Of course, it follows that the stock market value of corporation f is

$$V_f = p_f N_f = \sum_{s=1}^{S} p_s\Pi_{fs}.$$

Observe, too, that the firm's share price is a function of the firm's investment level. By (vii), we have

(viii)
$$p_f' = \left(\frac{1}{N_f}\right)\sum_{s=1}^{S} p_s\Pi_{fs}' > 0,$$

since $\Pi'_{fs}(I_f) > 0$ for all s by hypothesis. Finally, using (v), (vi), and (viii), we obtain

$$\sum_{s=1}^{S}\left\{D_1 u\left[\left(\frac{N_f - n_f}{N_f}\right)\sum_{s=1}^{S} p_s\Pi'_{fs} - 1\right] + D_2 u\left(\frac{n_f}{N_f}\right)\Pi'_{fs}\right\}\psi_s = 0$$

$$\Leftrightarrow \left[\left(\frac{N_f - n_f}{N_f}\right)\sum_{s=1}^{S} p_s\Pi'_{fs} - 1\right]\sum_{s=1}^{S} D_1 u\psi_s + \left(\frac{n_f}{N_f}\right)\sum_{s=1}^{S} D_2 u\Pi'_{fs}\psi_s = 0$$

$$\Leftrightarrow \left(\frac{N_f - n_f}{N_f}\right)\sum_{s=1}^{S} p_s\Pi'_{fs} + \left(\frac{n_f}{N_f}\right)\sum_{s=1}^{S} p_s\Pi'_{fs} = 1$$

$$\Leftrightarrow \sum_{s=1}^{S} p_s\Pi'_{fs} = 1.$$

Therefore we have the Fisher separation result, because the choice of investment level depends on neither the manager's consumption preferences nor the manager's probability beliefs. In addition, the manager selects the investment level that maximizes the net present value of the corporation; that is, $V_f - I_f$.

---

[a]This is a consequence of the Modigliani and Miller (1958) theorem and the Miller and Modigliani (1961) theorem. Both results will be discussed in subsequent chapters.

[b]Note that this is equivalent to assuming that the payoff on the investment is a function defined in $\mathbf{R}$ with values in $\mathbf{R}^N$, that is, $\Pi_f: \mathbf{R} \rightarrow \mathbf{R}^N$. Note that the function Π_f can be regarded as a curve in the space $\mathbf{R}^N$ and the derivative of Π_f yields a tangent vector to the curve.

Summary

The time state preference model offers a very general way to conceptualize the decisionmaking problem under uncertainty. It assumes that individuals visualize the future in terms of a set of states of nature to which they ascribe payoffs and probabilities of occurrence. The states are required to be both exhaustive and mutually exclusive—that is, the individual is assumed to be able to describe all possible future outcomes in terms of states, and the sum of the probabilities associated with these states for a given time period is unity.

When using the time state preference model to consider market equilibrium, we found it necessary to require all individuals to agree as to the possible states of nature and associated security payoffs. However, heterogeneous expectations could be accommodated by including individuals' beliefs concerning the probability of the occurrence of each state. We described the relationship that must hold between security prices in market equilibrium where the market is perfectly competitive and complete. Under these conditions, market equilibrium implies the absence of riskless arbitrage profits, which in turn means that the value of a security equals the weighted average of the values of the pure securities that its payoff comprises.

We return to the time state preference model in Chapter 15, where we discuss option pricing theory. There we will envision an option as a security that has a payoff in those states of nature with a stock price greater than the option's exercise price and $0 otherwise. We will then use a spanning-type argument to place an equilibrium value on the option.

References

K. J. Arrow, "The Role of Securities in the Optimal Allocation of Risk Bearing," *Review of Economic Studies* (April 1964): 91–96.

T. E. Copeland and J. F. Weston, *Financial Theory and Corporate Policy,* 2d ed. (Reading, Mass.: Addison-Wesley, 1983), Chapter 5.

G. Debreu, *Theory of Value* (New York: Wiley, 1959), Chapter 7.

P. Diamond, "The Role of a Stock Market in a General Equilibrium Model with Technological Uncertainty," *American Economic Review* (September 1967): 759–786.

C. W. Haley and L. D. Schall, *The Theory of Financial Decisions,* 2d ed. (New York: McGraw-Hill, 1979), Chapter 9.

J. Hirshleifer, "Investment Decision under Uncertainty: Applications of the State-Preference Approach," *Quarterly Journal of Economics* (May 1966): 252–277.

———, *Investment, Interest and Capital* (London: Prentice-Hall International, 1970), Chapter 8.

A. Kraus and R. Litzenberger, "A State-Preference Model of Optimal Financial Leverage," *Journal of Finance* (September 1973): 141–183.

S. F. LeRoy and L. D. Singell, Jr., "Knight on Risk and Uncertainty," *Journal of Political Economy* 95, no. 2 (1987).

S. C. Myers, "Time-State Preference Model of Security Valuation," *Journal of Financial and Quantitative Analysis* (March 1968): 1–34.

———, "Procedures for Capital Budgeting under Uncertainty," *Industrial Management Review* (Spring 1968): 1–15.

W. F. Sharpe, *Portfolio Theory and Capital Markets* (New York: McGraw-Hill, 1970), Chapter 10.

Chapter 8

Uncertainty: Portfolio Choice in a Mean-Variance Framework

In this chapter, we extend our discussion of mean-variance analysis. Here we address some of the technical issues encountered in decisionmaking under uncertainty using the mean-variance model; these issues revolve around expected return and variance in return as the basis for making choices. This material is frequently referred to as *portfolio analysis,* for it involves the calculation and analysis of the means and variances of portfolio returns. In Chapter 9, we extend our use of mean-variance analysis to a securities market equilibrium setting wherein we derive the capital asset pricing model.

This chapter is organized as follows. First we define the rate of return earned on investing in an asset or a security. Here we note the fundamental link between an investor's wealth and the rate of return earned on an investment. In addition, we use the "expectations operator" to define the concepts of expected return and variance in return of a risky investment. Then we analyze the risk and return attributes of portfolios and consider the effects of diversifying portfolios. Finally, we discuss optimal portfolios of risky assets, where "optimal" refers to the maximum expected return for a given variance or minimum variance for a given expected return.

Risk and Return for a Single Asset

Rate of Return on Investment and Wealth

Individuals make investments with the expectation of increasing their wealth. For example, consider the purchase of 100 shares of Binsent Oil Company stock. If the stock is purchased for a price of p_0, pays an annual cash dividend of d_1 dollars,[1] and has a share price of P_1 dollars one year hence,[2] the shareholder's rate of return from investing in the stock, R, is defined as follows:

(8.1)
$$R = \frac{P_1 + d_1 - p_0}{p_0}.$$

In addition, the contribution of the stock investment to the investor's wealth one year hence, W_1, is defined as follows:

$$W_1 = P_1 + d_1 = p_0(1 + R),$$

or, stated in terms of present wealth,

$$w_0 = \frac{P_1 + d_1}{1 + R}.$$

Therefore, the rate of return, R, earned by investing in a risky asset serves as the link between current or future wealth and the net cash flows the asset provides for its owner. In the following discussions, we will use Equation 8.1 to define "rate of return" and continue to refer to a "single-period" return, which for convenience is assumed to be one year.

Expected Rate of Return

The *expected rate of return* is simply the expected value of the random or probabilistic rate of return, R. To calculate an expected value for R, we simply sum the products of the possible values that R can assume and the probability of their occurrence. The requisite information for Binsent Oil Company is provided in Table 8.1. The expected rate of return is, therefore, calculated as follows:

(8.2)
$$E(R) = \sum_{j=1}^{N} \psi_j R_j = u_B,$$

where ψ_j = probability of occurrence of the jth event.[3] For notational convenience,

---

[1]To simplify our discussion at this stage, we will assume that the cash dividend is known with certainty.

[2]We will follow the convention of using capital letters to indicate a random or probabilistic variable. For example, the price of Binsent's stock one year hence, P_1, cannot be known with certainty since it depends on a large number of factors, such as the state of the economy, the level of hostilities in the Middle East, and so forth. Lowercase letters are used to identify known variables such as the current price of Binsent's common stock, which is identified by the symbol p_0.

[3]The continuous distribution analog is the following:

$$E(R) = \int R(x)\psi(x)\,dx,$$

where $\psi(x)$ is the probability density function for returns.

Table 8.1   Sample Prices and Dividends for Binsent Oil Company

Probability (P_i)	End-of-Year Price[a] (P_{1_i})	Cash Dividend (d_1)	Rate of Return (R_i)
0.1	$ 7.00	$1.00	−0.20
0.2	9.00	1.00	0
0.4	10.00	1.00	0.10
0.2	11.00	1.00	0.20
0.1	12.00	1.00	0.30

[a]The price of Binsent's stock at the beginning of the period is $10.

we will use "u" to denote the expected rate of return. Calculating the expected rate of return for Binsent produces the following result:

$$u_B = 0.1(-0.20) + 0.2(0) + 0.4(0.10) + 0.2(0.20) + 0.1(0.30)$$

$$= 0.09, \text{ or } 9\%.$$

Thus, the expected value of the one-year investment return for Binsent stock is 9 percent.

The expected value is known as a measure of *location* and is only one of several such measures. Other commonly used measures of location include the median and the mode. Since we will not be using any location measures other than the expected value, we will not discuss these alternatives here; interested readers will find a description of them in the Mathematical Compendium in conjunction with a review of probability and statistics.

Variance in the Rate of Return

So far we have determined that the expected rate of return on Binsent's common stock is 9 percent. However, we observe from Table 8.1 that the return may be as low as −20 percent or as high as 30 percent. This "dispersion" in returns can be measured using the *variance,* which is the expected value of the squared deviation from the expected return; that is, using $\sigma^2(R)$ to designate the variance in returns,

$$\sigma^2(R) = \sum_{i=1}^{N} \psi_i [R_i - E(R)]^2.$$

For notational convenience, we will use σ_j^2 to refer to the variance in returns of the jth asset. We can calculate the σ_B^2 for Binsent using the return data provided in Table 8.1 as follows:

$$\sigma_B^2 = 0.10(-0.20 - 0.09)^2 + 0.20(0 - 0.09)^2$$

$$+ 0.40(0.10 - 0.09)^2 + 0.20(0.2 - 0.09)^2 + 0.10(0.30 - 0.09)^2$$

$$= 0.00841 + 0.00162 + 0.00004 + 0.00242 + 0.00441$$

$$= 0.0169.$$

The variance in Binsent Oil Company's returns is, therefore, 0.0169. Note that the units of measure for the variance are "squared" deviations from the expected return. Thus, we *cannot* interpret σ_B^2 in terms of rates of return. However, the square root of the variance, which we refer to as the *standard deviation, is* measured in terms of rates of return and can be interpreted accordingly. For Binsent we calculate the standard deviation, σ_B, as follows:

$$\sigma_B = (0.0169)^{1/2} = 0.13, \text{ or } 13\% \, .$$

There are a number of alternative measures of "dispersion" that we could use. However, for the purposes in this chapter, we will use the variance (and its square root, the standard deviation) exclusively. Refer to the review of probability and statistics in the Mathematical Compendium for further details.

A Mathematical Review of Operations Involving Expected Values and Variances

- **Property 1:** The expected value of the product of a constant (a) and a random variable (X) equals the product of the constant times the expected value of the random variable:

$$E(aX) = aE(X).$$

- **Property 2:** The expected value of the two random variables $(X + Y)$ equals the sum of their respective expected values:

$$E(X + Y) = E(X) + E(Y).$$

- **Property 3:** The variance of the sum of a random variable (X) plus a constant (a) equals the variance of the random variable:

$$\sigma^2(X + a) = \sigma^2(X).$$

- **Property 4:** The variance of the product of a constant (a) and a random variable (X) equals the constant squared times the variance of the random variable:

$$\sigma^2(aX) = a^2\sigma^2(X).$$

- **Property 5:** The variance of the sum of two or more random variables $(X + Y + Z)$ equals the sum of their respective variances plus 2 times the covariance between all *different* pairs of the random variables:

$$\sigma^2(X + Y + Z) = \sigma_X^2 + \sigma_Y^2 + \sigma_Z^2 + 2\sigma_{XY} + 2\sigma_{XZ} + 2\sigma_{YZ}.$$

- **Property 6:** The covariance between a pair of products of a constant and a random variable equals the product of the two constants multiplied by the covariance between the two random variables:

$$Cov(aX, bY) = abCov(X, Y).$$

Portfolio Risk and Return

Portfolio Expected Return

A *portfolio* is merely a collection of assets. Therefore, the expected return on a portfolio is the weighted average of the expected rates of return of the assets it contains. For a two-asset portfolio containing securities 1 and 2, the expected portfolio return is defined as follows:

$$E(R_p) = E(A_1R_1 + A_2R_2) = u_p,$$

where R_p is the portfolio return, A_1 is the proportion of the portfolio invested in asset 1, and $A_2 = [1 - A_1]$ is the proportion placed in asset 2. Using properties 1 and 2 of the expectations operator (see "A Mathematical Review of Operations with Expected Values and Variances"), we see that

$$u_p = A_1E(R_1) + A_2E(R_2)$$

or, for the N-asset case,

(8.3) $$u_p = \sum_{j=1}^{N} A_jE(R_j).$$

Exercise 8.1:   Calculating Portfolio Expected Return

The portfolio of common stocks held by J. E. Peddy consists of the following:

Stock	Investment Proportions	Expected Returns
A	0.5	0.20
B	0.5	0.14

The expected portfolio return for his portfolio, then, is

$$u_p = 0.5(0.20) + 0.5(0.14) = 0.17.$$

If Peddy adds a third stock to his portfolio with investment equal to that in stocks A and B and an expected return of 21 percent, what will be his expected portfolio return?

Solution

$$u_p = \frac{1}{3}(0.20) + \frac{1}{3}(0.14) + \frac{1}{3}(0.21)$$

$$= 0.1833, \text{ or } 18.33\%.$$

Portfolio Variance

The variance of a portfolio is the variance of its rate of return. The *portfolio rate of return* is simply a weighted average of the random rates of return of the assets in the portfolio (R_i), and the weights are the proportions invested in each asset

(A_i). Using Properties 4 through 6 of the expectations operator, we define the variance of a two-asset portfolio as follows:

(8.4)
$$\sigma_p^2 = A_1^2 \sigma_1^2 + A_2^2 \sigma_2^2 + 2A_1 A_2 \sigma_{12}.$$

Since the covariance of a random variable with itself (σ_{XX}) is simply its variance, we can rewrite Equation 8.4 for the N-security case as follows:

$$\sigma_p^2 = \sum_{i=1}^{N} \sum_{j=1}^{N} A_i A_j \sigma_{ij}$$

or

(8.5)
$$\sigma_p^2 = \sum_{i=1}^{N} A_i^2 \sigma_i^2 + 2 \sum_{i=1}^{N-1} \sum_{j=i+1}^{N} A_i A_j \sigma_{ij}.$$

Exercise 8.2:   Calculating Portfolio Variance

The variances and covariances of the securities contained in J. E. Peddy's portfolio are as follows:

Stock	Investment Proportions	Variance
A	0.5	0.020
B	0.5	0.015

$$\sigma_{AB} = \text{Cov}(R_A, R_B) = 0.0052$$

1. Calculate the variance in Peddy's portfolio.

Solution.   Using Equation 8.4,

$$\sigma_p^2 = 0.5^2(0.02) + 0.5^2(0.015) + 2(0.5)(0.5)(0.0052)$$

$$= 0.005 + 0.00375 + 0.0026$$

$$= 0.01135.$$

2. Calculate the standard deviation in Peddy's portfolio return.

Solution

$$\sigma_p = (0.01135)^{1/2} = 0.1065, \text{ or } 10.65\%.$$

3. Peddy plans to add a third security to his portfolio. The variance of the security is 0.022; its covariance with security A is 0.0146 and with security B, 0.0036. What is the variance in the revised portfolio if an equal investment in each security is made?

Solution

$$\sigma_p^2 = (\tfrac{1}{3})^2(0.02) + (\tfrac{1}{3})^2(0.015) + (\tfrac{1}{3})^2(0.022)$$

$$+ 2(\tfrac{1}{3})(\tfrac{1}{3})(0.0052) + 2(\tfrac{1}{3})(\tfrac{1}{3})(0.0146)$$

$$+ 2(\tfrac{1}{3})(\tfrac{1}{3})(0.0036)$$

$$= 0.00222 + 0.00167 + 0.00244 + 0.00116 + 0.00324 + 0.00080$$

$$= 0.01153,$$

and

$$\sigma_p = 0.1074, \text{ or } 10.74\%.$$

Covariance and the Benefits of Diversification.   The *covariance* between two random variables, X and Y, can be defined as follows:

(8.6) $$\sigma_{XY} = \text{Cov}(X, Y) = E\{[X - E(X)][Y - E(Y)]\},$$

where E{ } denotes the expectation of the term in braces. Thus, intuitively the covariance between two random variables is a measure of the *degree to which the variables move together, or covary.* For example, if when X is above its expected value, Y tends to be above its expected value, X and Y are said to covary with each other positively ($\sigma_{XY} > 0$). On the other hand, where X generally is below E(X) when Y is above E(Y)—or vice versa—X and Y covary negatively, or inversely ($\sigma_{XY} < 0$). The importance of the sign on the covariance between the rates of return on two risky assets contained in a portfolio becomes apparent when we look at the σ_{ij} term in Equation 8.5 for σ_p^2.

A positive covariance, other things equal, makes σ_p^2 larger, while a negative covariance reduces σ_p^2. The point here is that the sign and magnitude of the covariance term in σ_p^2 largely determine the magnitude of the benefits derived from diversification.

Consider an example where equal investments are made in each of two securities from the following set:

Security	Variance of R
A	0.02
B	0.02
C	0.02

Covariances	
$\sigma_{AB} =$	0.02
$\sigma_{AC} =$	-0.02

When securities A and B are combined into a portfolio (with equal investment in each), the portfolio variance is as follows:

$$\sigma^2[(\tfrac{1}{2})R_A + (\tfrac{1}{2})R_B] = (\tfrac{1}{2})^2 0.02 + (\tfrac{1}{2})^2 0.02 + 2(\tfrac{1}{2})(\tfrac{1}{2})(0.02)$$

$$= 0.005 + 0.005 + 0.01$$

$$= 0.02 .$$

However, when securities A and C are combined, the portfolio variance (again using equal investment in each) is

$$\sigma^2[(\tfrac{1}{2})R_A + (\tfrac{1}{2})R_c] = (\tfrac{1}{2})^2 0.02 + (\tfrac{1}{2})^2 0.02 + 2(\tfrac{1}{2})(\tfrac{1}{2})(-0.02)$$

$$= 0.005 + 0.005 - 0.01$$

$$= 0.0 .$$

Thus, in the latter case the diversification benefit derived from putting securities A and C together is such that the portfolio's variance is actually reduced to zero. As we now discover, this results from the fact that the returns of assets A and C are perfectly negatively correlated.

The Correlation Coefficient. If we standardize the covariance by dividing it by the product of the standard deviations of the respective random variables, we obtain the *correlation coefficient*. Thus, the correlation coefficient between the returns of two assets, X and Y (denoted r_{XY}), is defined as follows:

(8.7)
$$r_{XY} = \frac{\sigma_{XY}}{\sigma_X \sigma_Y} .$$

If we substitute the expectation forms for the terms in r_{XY}, we find that

$$r_{XY} = \frac{E\{[R_X - E(R_X)][R_Y - E(R_Y)]\}}{\{E[R_X - E(R_X)]^2\}^{1/2}\{E[R_Y - E(R_Y)]^2\}^{1/2}} .$$

In this form, we can see that when R_X and R_Y are the same — that is, $Y = X$ such that we calculate the correlation of a random variable with itself — $r_{XY} = \sigma_X^2/\sigma_X^2 = 1$. Also, where $R_X = -R_Y$, then $r_{XY} = -1$. In general, if $R_X = C(R_Y)$, where C is some nonzero constant, $r_{XY} = 1$, with the sign depending on the sign of C. Therefore, the correlation coefficient ranges in value from -1 to $+1$, that is, $-1 \le r_{XY} \le +1$.

Solving Equation 8.7 for σ_{XY}, we can now define the variance of an N-security portfolio found in Equation 8.5 as follows:

$$\sigma_p^2 = \sum_{i=1}^{N} \sum_{j=1}^{N} A_i A_j r_{ij} \sigma_i \sigma_j ,$$

or

$$\sigma_p^2 = \sum_{i=1}^{N} A_i^2 \sigma_i^2 + 2 \sum_{i=1}^{N-1} \sum_{j=i+1}^{N} A_i A_j r_{ij} \sigma_i \sigma_j .$$

The Limits of Diversification. We now consider the critical role the correlation coefficient plays in determining the potential benefits from diversification. Consider the portfolio problem faced by Frances Hanna. Hanna presently is fully invested in the stock of company 1. However, she is considering realigning her investment to include two security issues — security 1 plus her choice of securities 2, 3, or 4. The expected returns, standard deviations, and correlation coefficients among returns for the securities are shown in Table 8.2. The portfolio risk and return attributes for each possible combination are sketched in Table 8.3.

The impact of the correlation coefficient on diversification is shown graphically in Figure 8.1. For example, we can summarize Hanna's portfolio diversifica-

Table 8.2   Security Data for Frances Hanna's Portfolio Problem

Security	Expected Return	Standard Deviation
1	0.15	0.10
2	0.20	0.15
3	0.25	0.20
4	0.30	0.25

| | Correlation Coefficients | | |
	Security 2	Security 3	Security 4
Security 1	1.0	0.0	−1.0

Table 8.3   Portfolio Risk and Return for Frances Hanna

Percent of Portfolio in Security 1	Percent of Portfolio in Security 2	Portfolio Return	Portfolio Standard Deviation
A. Portfolio Containing Securities 1 and 2 ($r_{12} = +1.0$)			
1.0^a	0.0	0.1500	0.1000
0.5	0.5	0.1750	0.1250
0.25	0.75	0.1875	0.1375
0.0^a	1.0	0.2000	0.1500
B. Portfolio Containing Securities 1 and 3 ($r_{13} = 0.0$)			
1.0^a	0.0	0.1500	0.1000
0.5	0.5	0.2000	0.1118
0.25	0.75	0.2250	0.1521
0.0^a	1.0	0.2500	0.2000
C. Portfolio Containing Securities 1 and 4 ($r_{14} = -1.0$)			
1.0^a	0.0	0.1500	0.1000
0.5	0.5	0.2250	0.0750
0.25	0.75	0.2625	0.1625
0.0^a	1.0	0.3000	0.2500

[a]Technically this portfolio is unacceptable to Hanna but is included here to help demonstrate the impact of diversification on portfolio risk and return.

Figure 8.1   Diversification and Correlation
for Frances Hanna's Portfolio Problem[a]

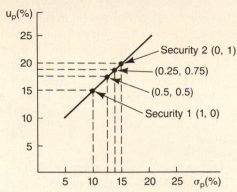

(a) r_{12} = +1.0: Portfolio of Securities 1 and 2

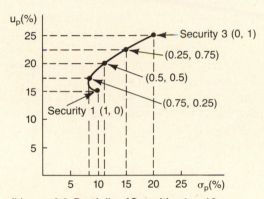

(b) r_{13} = 0.0: Portfolio of Securities 1 and 3

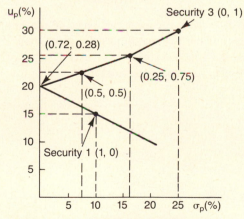

(c) r_{14} = −1.0: Portfolio of Securities 1 and 4

[a]Each pair of numbers in parentheses represents the proportions of the portfolio invested in security 1 and 2, respectively.

tion opportunities as follows. In panel c of Figure 8.1, we observe that a portfolio consisting of securities 1 and 4 (which are perfectly negatively correlated) offers the greatest diversification benefits; in fact, a zero-variance portfolio can be formed where approximately 72 percent of the portfolio is invested in security 1 and 28 percent in security 4. Combining securities 1 and 3 offers some diversification benefits, as shown in panel b; a portfolio comprised of 75 percent security 1 and 25 percent security 3 produces a portfolio standard deviation of 9.01 percent, which is smaller than that of security 1, while offering an expected return of 17.5 percent, which is higher than that of security 1. In panel a, we see that there are no benefits to diversification since securities 1 and 2 are perfectly positively correlated.

The Mean-Variance Opportunity Set Comprised of Two Risky Assets: A Primer on Mean-Variance Efficient Set Mathematics.   In this section, we analyze the concepts presented in Figure 8.1. This "characterization" of the mean-variance portfolio problem was first popularized by Roll (1977) in the appendix to his paper criticizing prior tests of the capital asset pricing model. Specifically, we note that the opportunity set of risky assets comprises a parabola. Using this fact, we can utilize the well-defined mathematics of the parabola to solve mean-variance portfolio problems. As we will demonstrate in Chapter 9, this includes the derivation of the capital asset pricing model.

To simplify the exposition at this point, we will analyze the mean-variance opportunity set comprised of only two risky assets; however, the results can easily be generalized to the case of N risky assets. Recall that we have adopted the following notational conventions:

$$u_i = E(R_i)$$

$$\sigma_i^2 = \sigma^2(R_i)$$

$$\sigma_{ij} = Cov(R_i, R_j)\,.$$

Letting $u_p = A_1 u_1 + A_2 u_2$ represent the expected return on a portfolio comprised of an investment of the fraction A_1 in risky asset 1 and A_2 in risky asset 2, where $A_1 + A_2 = 1$ (and hence $A_2 = 1 - A_1$) and $u_1 \neq u_2$, we can solve for A_1 and A_2 as a function of u_1, u_2, and u_p as follows:

(i)
$$A_1 = \frac{u_p - u_2}{u_1 - u_2}\,.$$

(ii)
$$A_2 = \frac{u_1 - u_p}{u_1 - u_2} = 1 - A_1\,.$$

Next, we let $\sigma_p^2 = \sigma^2(A_1 R_1 + A_2 R_2)$ such that

$$\sigma_p^2 = A_1^2 \sigma_1^2 + 2A_1 A_2 \sigma_{12} + A_2^2 \sigma_2^2\,.$$

Substituting for A_1 and A_2 using (i) and (ii) produces the following:

$$\sigma_p^2 = \left(\frac{u_p - u_2}{u_1 - u_2}\right)^2 \sigma_1^2 + \left(\frac{u_1 - u_p}{u_1 - u_2}\right)^2 \sigma_2^2 + \left[\frac{2(u_p - u_2)(u_1 - u_p)}{(u_1 - u_2)^2}\right]\sigma_{12}.$$

Collecting terms with u_p^2 and u_p produces

$$= \left[\frac{1}{(u_1 - u_2)^2}\right][u_p^2(\sigma_1^2 + \sigma_2^2 - 2\sigma_{12})$$

$$- 2u_p(u_2\sigma_1^2 + u_1\sigma_2^2 - u_2\sigma_{12} - u_1\sigma_{12})$$

$$+ (u_2^2\sigma_1^2 + u_1^2\sigma_2^2 - 2u_1u_2\sigma_{12})].$$

Hence, the opportunity set created by investing in a portfolio of two risky assets (that is, "spanned by two risky assets") is simply the graph of the following equation:

(8.8)
$$\sigma_p^2 = au_p^2 + bu_p + c,$$

where

$$a = \frac{(\sigma_1^2 + \sigma_2^2 - 2\sigma_{12})}{(u_1 - u_2)^2},$$

$$b = \frac{-2(u_2\sigma_1^2 + u_1\sigma_2^2 - u_2\sigma_{12} - u_1\sigma_{12})}{(u_1 - u_2)^2},$$

and

$$c = \frac{(u_2^2\sigma_1^2 + u_1^2\sigma_2^2 - 2u_1u_2\sigma_{12})}{(u_1 - u_2)^2}.$$

We now have an "explicit" equation for the opportunity set spanned by two risky assets. This equation is that of a parabola with coefficients a, b, and c defined above.

The Minimum-Variance Portfolio.   We can use Equation 8.8 to find the investment proportions for the minimum-variance portfolio as follows. First, differentiating σ_p^2 in Equation 8.8 with respect to u_p produces the following:

$$\frac{d\sigma_p^2}{du_p} = 2au_p + b.$$

The first-order condition for the minimum-variance portfolio is therefore

$$2au_p^* + b = 0,$$

or, solving for u_p^* (the mean return for the minimum-variance portfolio), we obtain

(8.9)
$$u_p^* = \frac{-b}{2a}.$$

Note that the second-order condition for a minimum ($d^2\sigma_p^2/du_p^2 > 0$) is also satisfied as a > 0. We can also solve for the investment proportions (A_1^* and $A_2^* = 1 - A_1^*$) for the minimum-variance portfolio by recalling that

$$u_p^* = A_1^* u_1 + A_2^* u_2 = A_1^* u_1 + (1 - A_1^*) u_2 .$$

Thus, substituting the latter expression for u_p^* in the first-order condition (Equation 8.9) and solving for A_1^* produces the following:

(8.10)
$$A_1^* = \frac{(\sigma_2^2 - \sigma_{12})}{(\sigma_1^2 - 2\sigma_{12} + \sigma_2^2)} .$$

The minimum-variance portfolio comprised of two risky assets, therefore, involves investing A_1^* (defined by Equation 8.10) in asset 1 and $A_2^* = 1 - A_1^*$ in asset 2.

Exercise 8.3:   Calculating the u_p and σ_p^2 of the Minimum-Variance Portfolio

Consider the following pair of securities:

Security	Expected Return	Standard Deviation
1	0.20	0.15
2	0.10	0.08

1.   Given that $r_{12} = 0.30$, what are the expected return and variance of the minimum-variance portfolio?

Solution

▪   *Step 1:* Using Equation 8.10, we solve for A* where A* is the proportion invested in security 1 and $1 - A^*$ is that invested in security 2:

$$A^* = \frac{0.08^2 - 0.30(0.15)(0.08)}{0.15^2 - 2(0.30)(0.15)(0.08) + 0.08^2}$$

$$= 0.0028/0.0217 = 0.129 .$$

Therefore, the minimum-variance portfolio is comprised of 12.9 percent invested in security 1 and $1 - 0.129 = 87.1$ percent invested in security 2.

▪   *Step 2:* Using the minimum-variance portfolio investment proportions, the expected portfolio return is calculated as follows:

$$u_p = A*E(R_1) + (1 - A*)E(R_2)$$

$$= 0.129(0.20) + (0.871)0.10$$

$$= 0.0258 + 0.0871$$

$$= \underline{0.1129}.$$

Portfolio variance for the minimum-variance portfolio is calculated as follows:

$$\sigma_p^2 = (A*)^2\sigma^2(R_1) + 2A*(1 - A*)r_{12}\sigma(R_1)\sigma(R_2) + (1 - A*)^2\sigma^2(R_2)$$

$$= (0.129)^2(0.15)^2 + 2(0.129)(0.871)(0.3)(0.15)(0.08) + (0.871)^2(0.08)^2$$

$$\sigma_p^{2*} = \underline{0.00604}$$

or

$$\sigma_p = \underline{0.0777}.$$

2.   Calculate the expected return and variance of the minimum-variance portfolio where $r_{12} = -0.30$.

Solution

- *Step 1:*

$$A* = \frac{0.08^2 + 0.30(0.15)(0.08)}{0.15^2 + 2(0.30)(0.15)(0.08) + 0.08^2}$$

$$= 0.01/0.0361 = 0.277$$

and

$$(1 - A*) = 0.723.$$

- *Step 2:*

$$u_p = 0.277(0.2) + 0.723(0.1)$$

$$= 0.1277, \text{ or } \underline{12.77\%}$$

$$\sigma_p^2 = (0.277)^2(0.15)^2 + 2(0.277)(0.723)(-0.3)(0.15)(0.08)$$

$$+ (0.723)^2(0.08)^2$$

$$= \underline{0.00363}.$$

Therefore,

$$\sigma_p = \underline{0.0602, \text{ or } 6.02\%}.$$

Optimal Portfolio Choice

Opportunity Set and Efficient Frontier with N Risky Assets

The opportunity set consisting of many risky assets is depicted in Figure 8.2. Note first that only risky assets are contained in the set of portfolios included in the opportunity set, since no portfolio or asset has a zero σ. In addition, portfolio A is the minimum-variance portfolio.

Portfolios B, C, and D are all feasible or attainable portfolios, that is, members of the opportunity set. The feasible portfolios — each represented by a mean-variance point — are contained in the shaded region of Figure 8.2. However, some portfolios are "preferred" to others. For example, consider portfolios B and C. Portfolio B offers the same risk (σ) but has a substantially higher expected return. Thus, in this comparison portfolio B is preferred. When we compare portfolios B and D, we arrive at a similar conclusion: B again offers more return and less risk. A different result occurs, however, when we compare portfolios A and B. Here it is not clear which portfolio is preferred; A offers less risk but also less return than B. In this case, neither A nor B "dominates" the other *for all risk-averse investors;* in fact, all possible pairs of portfolios on the outer surface of the opportunity set above point A, the minimum-variance portfolio, share this attribute. These "undominated" portfolios define the "efficient set" or "efficient frontier" of *risky assets.*

Figure 8.2   Opportunity Set of N Risky Assets

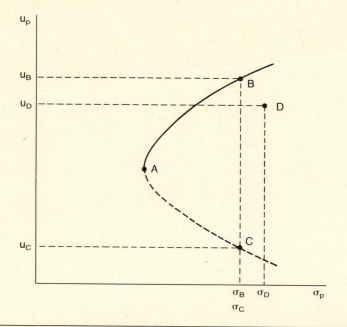

Figure 8.3   Efficient Set of Risky Assets

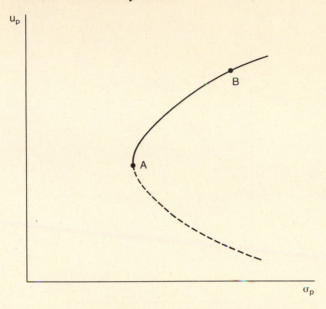

Figure 8.3 represents an efficient set of risky assets. Note that the solid line is the efficient set and the dashed line represent dominated assets or portfolios. (Solving for the efficient set is a constrained optimization problem that is fully discussed in the Mathematical Compendium.) As we will see in the next section, the efficient set is altered significantly when a risk-free asset is included in the opportunity set.

Efficient Frontier of Risky and Risk-Free Assets

When a risk-free asset is combined with a risky asset or portfolio, the resulting portfolio has risk-return characteristics that are linear in u_p and σ_p space.[4] Figure 8.4

---

[4]Proof of this proposition is straightforward. Note that for this case,

(i)
$$u_p = Ar_F + (1 - A)u_M$$

and

(ii)
$$\sigma(R_p) = (1 - A)\sigma_M .$$

Next, solving (i) and (ii) for A and equating the results, we get the following:

$$\frac{u_p - u_M}{r_F - u_M} = \frac{\sigma_M - \sigma_p}{\sigma_M} .$$

Solving for u_p, we get

$$u_p = r_F + \left(\frac{u_M - r_F}{\sigma_M}\right)\sigma_p .$$

Alternatively, we could have substituted into Equation 8.8 and obtained the same result.

Figure 8.4   Portfolios of Risky and Risk-Free Assets

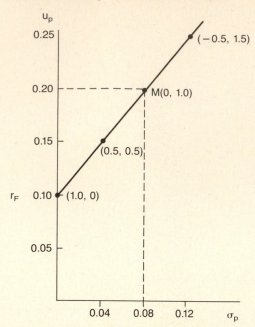

illustrates the portfolios that can be formed by combining a risk-free asset (with a return, r_F, equal to 10 percent) with a risky asset, M, that has an expected return of 20 percent and a standard deviation of 8 percent. The risk and return calculations for these portfolios are made using the following equations:

(8.11) $u_p = Ar_F + (1 - A)u_M$

$$\sigma_p = [A^2\sigma^2(r_F) + 2A(1 - A)r_{FM}\sigma(r_F)\sigma_M + (1 - A)^2\sigma^2(R_M)]^{1/2},$$

or, since $\sigma^2(r_F)$ and σ_{FM} are zero,

(8.12) $\sigma(R_p) = (1 - A)\sigma_M .$

Table 8.4 contains the expected return and standard deviation calculations for four possible portfolios. Portfolios 1, 2, and 3 involve positive or zero investments in the risk-free and risky assets. However, portfolio 4 entails short selling the risk-free asset. Note that here short selling involves selling risk-free assets or issuing risk-free bonds and investing the proceeds in the risky asset.

Let us now consider the possibility of combining the risk-free asset with different risky assets. Consider the two sets of portfolios comprised of the risk-free asset and either risky asset M or N in Figure 8.5. Clearly the set of portfolios resulting from risky asset M and the risk-free asset is preferred to that involving the risk-free asset and risky asset N. This can be shown by applying the dominance criterion used earlier to identify the efficient set of risky assets: For any given σ_p,

Table 8.4   Risk and Return for Portfolios Comprised of Risky and Risk-Free Assets

| Portfolio | Investment Proportions | | Expected Return | Standard Deviation |
	Risk-Free Asset	Risky Asset		
1	1.0	0.0	0.10	0.00
2	0.5	0.5	0.15	0.04
3	0.0	1.0	0.20	0.08
4	−0.5	1.5	0.25	0.12

Figure 8.5   Optimal Portfolio of Risky and Risk-Free Assets

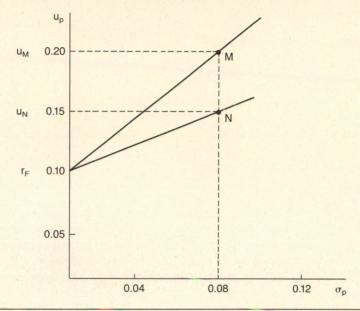

the corresponding u_p is greater for portfolios comprised of the risk-free asset and risky asset M than for portfolios consisting of the risk-free asset and risky asset N.

If we now extend our analysis to include all portfolios of risky assets in combination with the risk-free asset, we will see that the risky asset portfolio that provides the "best" risk-return investment opportunities lies on the efficient frontier of risky assets and is the one just tangent to a line passing through the risk-free return. Figure 8.6 depicts the newly defined efficient set or efficient frontier comprised of portfolios of both the risk-free asset and all risky assets. Note that all portfolios lying to the left of M on the line passing through the risk-free return involve either zero or positive investment in both the risk-free asset and asset M. Points along the efficient frontier of risky and risk-free assets to the right of M involve borrowing at a rate of r_F or short selling the risk-free asset and investing the proceeds in risky asset M.

Figure 8.6   Efficient Set of Risky and Risk-Free Assets

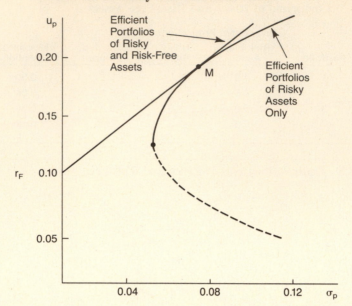

Summary

In this chapter we discussed the mechanics of mean-variance analysis. We demonstrated how this type of analysis can be used as a tool for analyzing portfolios consisting of both risky and risk-free assets. The theoretical foundation of this approach lies in the expected utility paradigm developed in Chapter 7. The primary purpose of this chapter was to flesh out this theory by sketching its technical, mathematical application to the mean-variance portfolio problem. This entailed (1) defining the expected rate of return and standard deviation for single assets and portfolios, (2) analyzing the impact of the correlation of asset returns on portfolio risk, and (3) defining the opportunity set and efficient frontier for risky assets alone and for combinations of risky assets and a risk-free asset.

The mean-variance mechanics developed in this chapter will be applied directly to the analysis of capital market equilibrium in Chapter 9. These mechanics therefore provide the background necessary for a thorough grasp of the remainder of this text.

Study Questions

8.1   Portfolio analysis generally is discussed in terms of rates of return. However, individuals spend dollars (that is, wealth), not "rates." How can we reconcile this apparent dilemma?

8.2   When is diversification beneficial? (Discuss in terms of the mean and variance.)

8.3   Figure 8.3 depicts the efficient set of risky assets. Describe the attributes of an "efficient" portfolio. Why is the dashed segment below point A not a part of the efficient set?

8.4   If an investor wished to evaluate the efficient set of portfolios comprised of 20 risky assets and a risk-free asset, what information would he or she need?

Study Problems

8.1   The current market price of JBC Corporation stock is $100, and the firm pays no cash dividends. The end-of-period price for the firm's stock one year hence has the following probability distribution:

Probability	Price
0.25	$ 80
0.25	100
0.25	120
0.25	140

a. Calculate the expected end-of-year price of JBC's stock.
b. What are the variance and standard deviation in the price of JBC's stock?
c. Using your answers to parts a and b and the properties of expected values, calculate the expected rate of return from investing in JBC's stock and the standard deviation in that rate of return.
d. Calculate the expected rates of return and standard deviations for portfolios comprised of JBC stock and a risk-free asset offering a 5 percent certain return using the following investment proportions:

	Investment Proportions			
Risk-free asset	1.0	0.50	0.0	−0.5
JBC stock	0.0	0.50	1.0	1.5

e. The expected rate of return earned by investing in Baylor, Inc. stock is 12 percent, and the standard deviation is 15 percent. Which of the following sets of portfolios would be preferred in a mean-standard deviation sense: (1) the risk-free asset from part d plus JBC stock or (2) the risk-free asset and Baylor stock? Explain.

8.2   The expected rate of return and standard deviation for three firms' stocks are as follows:

Firm	Expected Return	Standard Deviation
1	0.20	0.10
2	0.15	0.08
3	0.25	0.12

In addition, the correlation coefficients among their respective returns are as follows:

	1	2	3
1	1.0	0.5	−0.2
2	0.5	1.0	0.1
3	−0.2	0.1	1.0

a. Calculate the expected rate of return and standard deviations for the following portfolios:

	Portfolio Investment Proportions				
Firm	1	2	3	4	5
1	1.0	0.5	0.5	0.0	0.33
2	0.0	0.0	0.5	0.5	0.33
3	0.0	0.5	0.0	0.5	0.33

b. Which of the portfolios evaluated in part a is preferred? Explain.
c. If a risk-free asset earning 0.10 were available, what would the *efficient* set of risky and risk-free assets consist of? Define the function mathematically. (Hint: Assume that the five portfolios evaluated in part a are the only *feasible members* of the investment opportunity set.)

8.3   In cases where equal investment proportions are maintained in a portfolio, demonstrate the effects of increasing the number of risky assets in a portfolio from 1 to N. You may assume that the standard deviations for all assets are the same and that the correlation between all pairs of different asset returns equals a nonzero constant.

8.4   I. Q. Investor is analyzing his set of investment alternatives. He can invest in any combination of N risky assets, which are uncorrelated with one another and share identical expected returns and standard deviations. What is the composition of his optimal portfolio? (There is no risk-free asset.)

8.5   The expected returns and standard deviations for two securities, A and B, are as follows:

	Expected Return	Standard Deviation
A	0.20	0.08
B	0.10	0.06

a. Solve for the investment proportions for the minimum variance portfolio where the correlation between the two assets is −1.0. Also calculate the expected return and standard deviation for the portfolio.
b. Answer part a above for each of the following correlations between the two assets' returns: 0.0, 0.5, and 1.0.

8.6 Reduce Equation 8.8 to its simplest form where $r_{12} = -1, 0,$ and $+1$.

8.7 Consider the situation in which an investor can construct a portfolio from any combination of two risky securities plus a risk-free security. Let u_1 and u_2 denote the expected rates of return on the risky securities and r_F the risk-free return. In addition, let σ_{11} and σ_{22} represent the variances in their respective rates of return and $\sigma_{12} = \sigma_{21}$ the covariance. Further, let $u_1 > r_F$ and $u_2 > r_F$, where r_F is the risk-free interest rate. The investor's problem, then, involves solving the following problem:

$$\text{Minimize} \quad \sum_{i=1}^{2} \sum_{j=1}^{2} A_i A_j \sigma_{ij}$$

$$\text{subject to} \quad \sum_{j=1}^{2} A_j [E(R_j) - r_F] = C,$$

where C is a constant.

a. Show that for any value of C the solution to this problem lies on a line $A_2 = kA_1$, where k is a constant. Interpret this result.

b. Determine k in terms of the parameters $E(R_1)$, $E(R_2)$, r_F, and the variance-covariance matrix.

c. Under what conditions on the variance-covariance matrix will an investor be willing to sell asset 1 short (that is, $A_1 < 0$)?

8.8 In general, when is it possible to construct a zero-variance portfolio comprised of two risky assets? Discuss.

References

E. J. Elton and M. J. Gruber, *Modern Portfolio Theory and Investment Analysis* (New York: Wiley, 1984).

E. F. Fama, *Foundations of Finance* (New York: Basic Books, 1976).

J. C. Francis and S. H. Archer, *Portfolio Analysis*, 2d ed. (Englewood Cliffs, N. J.: Prentice-Hall, 1979), Chapters 2, 3, 5, 6.

H. M. Markowitz, *Portfolio Selection: Efficient Diversification of Investment*, Cowles Foundation Monograph 16 (New Haven, Conn.: Yale University Press, 1959), Chapters 2–8.

R. Merton, "An Analytical Derivation of the Efficient Set," *Journal of Financial and Quantitative Analysis* (September 1972): 1851–1872.

R. Roll, "A Critique of the Asset Pricing Theory's Tests," *Journal of Financial Economics* 4 (March 1977): 129–176.

W. F. Sharpe, *Portfolio Theory and Capital Markets* (New York: McGraw-Hill, 1970), Chapters 2–4.

———, "A Simplified Model for Portfolio Analysis," *Management Science* (January 1963): 277–293.

J. Tobin, "Liquidity Preference as Behavior Towards Risk," *Review of Economics Studies* (February 1958): 65–86.

Chapter 9

Capital Market Equilibrium

Capital market theory attempts to explain how investors place dollar values on securities traded in the capital markets. "Equilibrium" theories of capital markets endeavor to explain these values given investor satisfaction, that is, in the case where there is no incentive for further trading. In this chapter we will discuss the capital asset pricing model (CAPM) and the arbitrage pricing model (APM), two theories of security valuation.

As we will see, the CAPM and, perhaps to a lesser extent, the APM are derived under restrictive and unrealistic sets of assumptions about investor behavior and financial markets. The basic justification for this type of theorizing comes from *positive economics,* which posits the following:

The realism of the assumptions underlying the theory is unimportant so long as the implications, i.e., the predictions, of the theory are consistent with observed phenomena.[1]

Thus, although the underlying assumptions of the CAPM and APM may not be particularly palatable or realistic, their worth, according to the positivist view, stems from their ability to empower the models to make reasonable, empirically accurate predictions about the pricing of securities in the capital market.

This chapter is organized as follows. First, we enumerate the assumptions underlying the CAPM and then derive the model itself. Next, we develop a pric-

---

[1]The modern-day spokesperson for positive economics is Milton Friedman (1955); however, as we pointed out in Chapter 1, the concept is quite old (for example, see Keynes [1890]).

ing relationship for risky assets using the CAPM and explore the impact of relaxing the assumption that a risk-free asset exists. Finally, we derive the APM.

Assumptions Underlying the CAPM

The basic assumptions underlying the CAPM include the following:[2]

1.   Investors behave so as to maximize the expected utility of their wealth at the end of a single period.

2.   Investors choose among alternative portfolios according to expected return and variance (or standard deviation) in return.

3.   Borrowing and lending are unlimited and take place at an exogenously determined risk-free rate.

4.   All investors share identical subjective estimates of the means, variances, and covariances of return of all assets.

5.   Assets are completely divisible and perfectly liquid, with no transactions costs incurred in their purchase or sale.

6.   All investors are price takers,[3] there are no taxes, and the quantities of all assets are fixed.

Later we will relax the assumption that a risk-free asset exists and show that the basic character of the CAPM remains intact, albeit in slightly different form.

The investor's decision problem can be characterized as follows. At the current time the investor has a wealth level, w_0, that can be allocated to current consumption, c_0, or invested in risky and risk-free assets in the amount $w_0 - c_0$. At the end of the period, the investor will have a portfolio with a value of w_1 that can be used to support next period's consumption.[4] The investor's problem, then, is to allocate $w_0 - c_0$ dollars among the available assets in such a way as to maximize his or her utility of terminal wealth. The CAPM reports the "equilibrium" relationships among asset values given the assumptions just listed.

Deriving the CAPM

The Capital Market Line

Sharpe's (1964) derivation of the CAPM is highly intuitive and builds on our discussion of mean-variance mechanics in Chapter 8.[5] Recall from the preceding sec-

---

[2]A number of methods have been used to enumerate these basic assumptions. This presentation follows Jensen (1972).

[3]In a perfectly competitive market, no individual's decisions to buy or sell will affect the market price; hence, individuals must simply accept the market price when they trade—that is, they are price takers, not price makers.

[4]The determination of c_0 generally is omitted in the derivation of the CAPM. This "separation" of the individual's consumption and portfolio (investment) decisions is made possible in the mean-variance CAPM framework as a result of the assumptions made in structuring the problem. For a complete discussion of the conditions under which this separation result holds, see Cass and Stiglitz (1970).

[5]Lintner (1965) offers an alternative derivation of the CAPM.

Figure 9.1   Mean-Variance Efficient Set with Riskless Borrowing and Lending

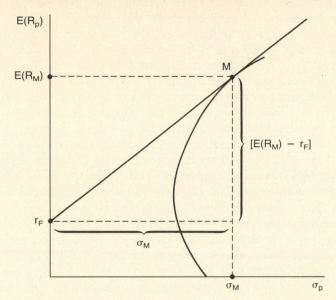

tion that all investors are assumed to share a set of beliefs regarding means, variances, and covariances. This means that all share the same belief about the set of efficient portfolios of risky and risk-free assets available to them. This set would appear as depicted in Figure 9.1. Further, everyone can—and will—select the market portfolio (portfolio M in Figure 9.1) when choosing the optimal mix of risky securities to combine with the risk-free asset.

Simply put, when everyone solves the same problem—that is, finds the optimal combination of risky and risk-free assets using the same inputs or estimates—all will arrive at the same answer. The optimal set of assets consists of those portfolios made up of the risk-free asset earning a rate r_F and the risky market portfolio, M. This set of portfolios is, as discussed in Chapter 8, a straight line passing through r_F and M. This line is referred to as the *capital market line (CML)*.

The equation for the CML can be derived as follows. First, note that the expected return on any portfolio lying on the CML is defined by

$$E(R_p) = Ar_F + (1 - A)E(R_M),$$

where A is the proportion invested in the risk-free security. The standard deviation of any portfolio on the CML is defined by

$$\sigma(R_p) = (1 - A)\sigma_M.$$

Solving both $E(R_p)$ and $\sigma(R_p)$ for A and equating the results, we obtain the following equation for the CML:

(9.1)
$$E(R_p) = r_F + \left[\frac{E(R_M) - r_F}{\sigma_M}\right]\sigma_p,$$

where the intercept of the CML is the risk-free rate and its slope equals $[E(R_M) - r_F]/\sigma_M$ (or, in terms of Figure 9.1, the "rise" over the "run").

Note that the capital market line tells us the relationship between the expected rate of return on an "efficient portfolio" — that is, one comprised of the risk-free asset and the market portfolio — and that portfolio's risk (σ_p). Hence, the slope of the CML is the universal or marketwide "risk premium" per unit of risk. Note that the measure of risk for an efficient portfolio is σ_p. Thus, for every unit of σ_p in an efficient portfolio, the investor would expect to receive an additional $[E(R_M) - r_F]/\sigma_M$ units of return over and above r_F. Alternatively, this risk premium is the marketwide "price of risk" for an efficient portfolio.

Note that we have assumed there are no transactions costs imposed on individuals and that all investors have homogeneous beliefs, which implies, among other things, equal access to information. This means that every individual can costlessly determine the expected return and variance of portfolio M and make his or her own choice of portfolio comprised of r_F and M. In such a world there is no advantage to hiring someone to make this decision for you, such as a mutual fund, pension fund, or trust department of a commercial bank. Hence, the very existence of financial intermediaries can be attributed to the relaxation of the fundamental assumptions we have made here. In particular, financial intermediaries arise when investors face transactions costs in information gathering and processing and when there are economies of scale in buying and selling securities.

Note too that the capital market line reflects investor "expectations" about means, variances, and covariances and is therefore an ex ante theory of asset pricing. Hence, one would not expect the parameters of the CML — that is, the risk-free rate and the market risk premium — to be the same for all time periods or ex post, or realized rates of return, to match expectations exactly. We will further examine the testable implications of the theory when we discuss capital market efficiency in Chapter 10.

Security Market Line

The *security market line (SML)* depicts the relationship between expected returns and risk for individual securities or assets *under conditions of market equilibrium*. The derivation of the SML is shown in Figure 9.2. Note that the market portfolio is denoted M and the curve iMi' characterizes portfolios comprised of security i and the market portfolio. The shape of iMi' depends, as you will recall from Figure 8.1, on the correlation between security i's return and that of the market portfolio. Note too that since M is the market portfolio it contains some of asset i. In other words, in equilibrium all assets must, by definition, be held by someone and, consequently, are included in the market portfolio.

To analyze the contribution of security i to the risk-return attributes of the market portfolio and, consequently, develop an expression for the SML, we will use the following procedure. First, note that at point M the slope of the CML equals the slope of the efficient frontier of risky assets (MM'), which also equals the slope of the set of portfolios containing security i and M. The slope of the CML is found by taking the derivative of Equation 9.1 with respect to σ_p; that is,

Figure 9.2   Deriving the Security Market Line

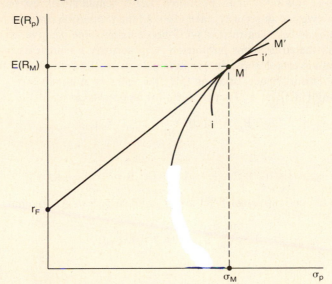

$$(9.2) \qquad \frac{dE(R_p)}{d\sigma_p} = \frac{E(R_M) - r_F}{\sigma_M}.$$

Finding the slope of the efficient frontier of risky assets (MM′) is slightly more complex, because we do not know the explicit functional relationship between $E(R_p)$ and σ_p. However, we do know that each of these variables is a function of the proportions invested in each risky asset, that is, A_i:

$$E(R_p) = \sum_{i=1}^{N} A_i E(R_i),$$

where N   = number of risky assets in the portfolio
       A_i = proportion of the portfolio invested in asset i
    $E(R_i)$ = expected rate of return for the ith asset

Further,

$$\sigma_p = \left[\sum_{i=1}^{N} \sum_{j=1}^{N} A_i A_j \mathrm{Cov}(R_i, R_j) \right]^{1/2}.$$

Thus, using the chain rule for differentiation we can solve for $dE(R_p)/d\sigma_p$ as follows:

$$(9.3) \qquad \frac{dE(R_p)}{d\sigma_p} = \left[\frac{dE(R_p)}{dA_i} \right] \left[\frac{dA_i}{d\sigma_p} \right].$$

Since the slope of MM′ equals the slope of iMi′ at point M, we will solve for the slope of this set of risky portfolios. Let A denote the excess proportion of the portfolio invested in security i and $(1 - A)$ the proportion invested in M. Note one important caveat: The market portfolio contains some positive investment in asset i; thus, the investment proportion A in security i represents an "excess" investment in i over and above its proportionate share of portfolio M in the state of market equilibrium. Hence, at M on iMi′, the value of A equals *zero*.

Defining E(R) and σ_p for the portfolios along iMi′ as

$$E(R_p) = AE(R_i) + (1 - A)E(R_M)$$

and

$$\sigma_p = [A^2\sigma_i^2 + 2A(1 - A)\text{Cov}(R_i, R_M) + (1 - A)^2\sigma_M^2],$$

we can take the derivatives of E(R) and σ_p with respect to A, obtaining

$$\frac{dE(R_p)}{dA} = E(R_i) - E(R_M)$$

and

$$\frac{d\sigma_p}{dA} = \frac{A[\sigma_i^2 + \sigma_M^2 - 2\text{Cov}(R_i, R_M)] + \text{Cov}(R_i, R_M) - \sigma_M^2}{\sigma_p}.$$

Substituting these derivatives into Equation 9.3, noting that A equals 0 at point M, and equating the result with the slope of the capital market line in Equation 9.2 produces the following:

$$\frac{[E(R_i) - E(R_M)]\sigma_M}{\text{Cov}(R_i, R_M) - \sigma_M^2} = \frac{E(R_M) - r_F}{\sigma_M}.$$

Solving this expression for E(R$_i$) produces the equation for the security market line:

(9.4)
$$E(R_i) = r_F + \left[\frac{E(R_M) - r_F}{\sigma_M^2}\right]\text{Cov}(R_i, R_M).$$

Noting that

$$\beta_i = \frac{\text{Cov}(R_i, R_M)}{\sigma_M^2},$$

where β_i is referred to as the *beta coefficient* for asset i, we can rewrite Equation 9.4 as follows:

(9.5)
$$E(R_i) = r_F + [E(R_M) - r_F]\beta_i.$$

This, then, is the familiar form of the CAPM.

Yet another formulation of the security market line can be defined using the market price of risk identified earlier with respect to the CML:

(9.6) $$E(R_i) = r_F + \left[\frac{E(R_M) - r_F}{\sigma_M}\right]\left[\frac{Cov(R_i, R_M)}{\sigma_M}\right].$$

We can see that in this form the market risk premium per unit of risk is the same as that observed in the CML. However, the risk of a security is not its standard deviation but its contribution to the risk of the market portfolio, which in turn equals $Cov(R_i, R_M)/\sigma_M$. Thus, the risk of a security or an inefficient portfolio (one not lying on the mean-variance efficient frontier) is a function of the covariance between its returns and those of the market portfolio.

Note that the SML relationship must hold for all assets contained in M *only* when the market is in equilibrium. Conversely, when the market is in equilibrium the linear SML relationship between security risk and expected return must be true. Thus, the linearity of the SML equation is a mathematical tautology wherein the market portfolio is mean-variance efficient. Consequently, one could not evaluate the appropriateness of the CAPM as a description of how security returns are determined by simply testing whether returns are a linear function of security betas.[6] We will return to this point in Chapter 10, where we discuss capital market efficiency and tests of the CAPM.

---

[6]This point was made very forcefully by Roll (1977) and has had a profound effect on subsequent tests of asset pricing models.

Derivation of the Capital Asset Pricing Model Using Efficient Set Mathematics: A Mathematical Overview

Our objective here is to use the mean-variance efficient set mathematics developed in the preceding chapter to derive the CAPM. The derivation is simplified so that we can use the equation for the mean-variance efficient frontier of risky assets (which, as we demonstrated earlier, is a parabola). This means that we no longer need use the chain rule to solve for $d\sigma_p/dE(R_p)$. Otherwise, the derivation follows the same logic that was used in the text.

In the following derivation, we use the following definitions and notational conventions:

1.   There exist N risky assets with random rates of return R_i, where $i = 1, 2, \ldots, N$.

2.   For any risky asset i, let $u_i = E(R_i)$, $\sigma_i^2 = \sigma^2(R_i)$, and $\sigma_{ij} = Cov(R_i, R_j)$.

3.   Let M designate the market portfolio of all risky assets such that $\sigma_M^2 = \sigma^2(A_1R_1 + \ldots + A_NR_N)$; $R_M = (A_1R_1 + \ldots + A_NR_N)$; $u_M = (A_1u_1 + $

$\ldots + A_N u_N$); and $A_1 + \ldots + A_N = 1$, where A_i = the proportion of the investor's total funds that is invested in asset i.

Now consider a particular risky asset with return R_i. We know from the review of mean-variance efficient set mathematics in the previous chapter that the opportunity set spanned by the market portfolio (R_M) and any risky asset (R_i) is a parabola with the following equation:

$$\sigma_p^2 = a u_p^2 + b u_p + c,$$

where σ_p^2 is the variance of a portfolio containing R_i and R_M and u_p is the expected return of that portfolio. Further, recall that

$$a = \frac{\sigma_M^2 + \sigma_i^2 - 2\sigma_{Mi}}{(u_M - u_i)^2}$$

$$b = \frac{-2(u_i \sigma_M^2 + u_M \sigma_i^2 - u_i \sigma_{Mi} - u_M \sigma_{Mi})}{(u_M - u_i)^2}$$

$$c = \frac{u_i^2 \sigma_M^2 + u_M^2 \sigma_i^2 - 2u_M u_i \sigma_{Mi}}{(u_M - u_i)^2}.$$

Next, paralleling our text discussion of the CAPM derivation, we recall that in equilibrium there is no excess investment in any risky asset i beyond the proportion of the market portfolio that it comprises (that is, investors hold some combination of the market portfolio and the risk-free asset in equilibrium). Thus, in equilibrium

(i)
$$\left. \frac{d\sigma_p}{du_p} \right|_{u_p = u_M} = \frac{\sigma_M^2 - \sigma_{Mi}}{\sigma_M(u_M - u_i)}$$

or

$$\frac{du_p}{d\sigma_p} = \frac{\sigma_M(u_M - u_i)}{\sigma_M^2 - \sigma_{Mi}}.$$

Recall from the text presentation that the slope of the capital market line is

$$\frac{u_M - r_F}{\sigma_M},$$

where r_F is the risk-free interest rate. Further, we know that the slope of the efficient frontier — found in (i) — must equal the slope of the capital market line at (σ_M, u_M). Therefore, equating the slopes of these two functions gives us the following:

$$\frac{u_M - r_F}{\sigma_M} = \frac{\sigma_M(u_M - u_i)}{\sigma_M^2 - \sigma_{Mi}}.$$

Solving for u_i produces the CAPM, that is,

$$u_i = r_F + \left(\frac{\sigma_{Mi}}{\sigma_M^2}\right)(u_M - r_F)$$

or, noting that

$$\beta_i = \left(\frac{\sigma_{Mi}}{\sigma_M^2}\right),$$

(ii) $$u_i = r_F + \beta_i(u_M - r_F).$$

Capital Asset Pricing Model

The equation for the SML frequently is referred to as the *capital asset pricing model*. Actually the SML does not tell us about prices or risky asset values directly. To derive a pricing relationship from the SML, we must recall the definition of the rate of return given in Chapter 8:

$$R_i = \frac{P_{i1} - P_{i0}}{P_{i0}} = \frac{P_{i1}}{P_{i0}} - 1,$$

where P_{i1} is the random price or value of the ith asset at the end of one year and p_{i0} is the current value of the asset, which we wish to define in terms of the SML relationship. Substituting $(P_{i1}/p_{i0} - 1)$ for R_i in Equation 9.6, we obtain the following pricing equation:[7]

(9.7) $$p_{i0} = \frac{E(P_{i1})}{1 + r_F} - \frac{\left[\dfrac{E(R_M) - r_F}{\sigma_M}\right]\left[\dfrac{Cov(P_{i1}, R_M)}{\sigma_M}\right]}{1 + r_F}.$$

Thus, the equilibrium price today for asset i, p_{i0}, equals the expected value of its price one year hence discounted at the risk-free rate minus the present value of the market risk premium. The riskiness of the asset equals $Cov(P_{i1}, R_M)/\sigma_M$, and the market risk premium per unit of risk retains its previous definition.

Equation 9.7 provides us with an explicit "pricing" equation derived directly from the equilibrium relationship represented by the SML. This pricing relationship is frequently referred to as the *certainty equivalent* form of the CAPM. The reason for this becomes apparent when we place Equation 9.7 over a common denominator equal to $(1 + r_F)$:

---

[7]Note that since $1/p_{i0}$ is a constant, $Cov[(P_{i1}/p_{i0} - 1), R_M] = (1/p_{i0})Cov(P_{i1}, R_M)$.

(9.8)
$$p_{i0} = \frac{E(P_{i1}) - \left[\dfrac{[E(R_M) - r_F]}{\sigma_M}\right]\left[\dfrac{Cov(P_{i1}, R_M)}{\sigma_M}\right]}{1 + r_F};$$

that is, the value of asset i equals the present value of its expected risky end-of-period value, $E(P_{i1})$, minus a risk premium. Thus, the numerator of Equation 9.8 is a certainty equivalent cash flow, which in turn is discounted at the risk-free rate to determine p_{i0}.

Exercise 9.1:   Valuing a Security Using the CAPM

The following information relates to the common stock of the A. B. Bing Corporation:

$$E(P_1) = \$100$$

$$Cov(P_1, R_M) = 5.25.$$

In addition, the expected rate of return on the market portfolio is 16 percent, the risk-free rate is 7 percent, and the standard deviation in the return on the market portfolio is 14 percent.

1.   What is the per share value of Bing's stock according to the CAPM?

Solution.   Using Equation 9.8, we solve for Bing's stock value as follows:

$$p_0 = \frac{\$100 - \left(\dfrac{0.16 - 0.07}{0.14}\right)\left(\dfrac{5.25}{0.14}\right)}{1.07} = \frac{\$75.89}{1.07} = \$70.93.$$

2.   What is the expected rate of return on Bing's stock using the CAPM?

Solution.   The most direct method for obtaining E(R) involves using the stock price from question 1 and the rate of return formula:

$$E(R) = \frac{E(P_1) - p_0}{p_0}$$

$$= \frac{\$100 - 70.93}{70.93}$$

$$= 0.41, \text{ or } 41 \text{ percent}.$$

However, we can obtain the answer using the SML relationship in Equation 9.6 where

$$\text{Cov}(R, R_M) = \left(\frac{1}{p_0}\right)\text{Cov}(P_1, R_M)$$

$$= 0.074027.$$

Hence, using Equation 9.6,

$$E(R) = 0.07 + \left(\frac{0.16 - 0.07}{0.14}\right)\left(\frac{0.074027}{0.14}\right)$$

$$= 0.41, \text{ or } 41 \text{ percent.}$$

Zero-Beta CAPM

Black (1972) relaxed the assumption of a risk-free asset for borrowing and lending and derived an asset pricing model very similar in form to the CAPM. In this model, the risk-free asset is replaced by a portfolio of risky assets that is uncorrelated with the market portfolio. This uncorrelated portfolio is called the *zero-beta portfolio,* since a zero covariance implies a zero beta.[8]

Figure 9.3 depicts the relationships used in developing the zero-beta CAPM, or CAPM$_z$. Note that we retain all the assumptions used in deriving the CAPM enumerated earlier *except* for the existence of a risk-free asset. Therefore, investors still agree about the shape of the efficient set of risky assets: the parabola passing through z and M in Figure 9.3. Note that this is their *only* agreement; with no risk-free asset, there is no basis for assuming that they will all invest in the same portfolio of risky assets. We will further discuss this attribute of the CAPM$_z$ later. For now we will analyze the case where portfolio M is selected as the portfolio of risky assets for the investor to hold. In addition, we will assume that there exists a set of feasible portfolios lying along line segment zz′ whose returns are uncorrelated with portfolio M's. The minimum-variance portfolio in this set is portfolio z and is identified as the zero-beta portfolio in the ensuing discussion.

To identify the new zero-beta CML, or CML$_z$, we follow a procedure similar to that used earlier in identifying the CML and SML. Specifically, we evaluate the slope of the efficient frontier of risky assets at point M, where all of the investor's funds are invested in M and none in z. To evaluate $dE(R)/d\sigma$ for the efficient frontier, we again use the chain rule for differentiation:

---

[8]Recall that beta for asset z is defined as follows:

$$\beta_z = \frac{\text{Cov}(R_z, R_M)}{\sigma_M^2}.$$

If the covariance term is zero, so is β_z.

Figure 9.3 Zero-Beta Capital Market Line

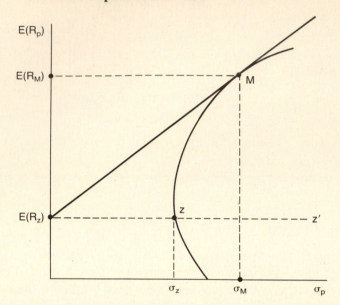

$$\frac{dE(R)}{d\sigma} = \frac{\dfrac{dE(R)}{dA}}{\dfrac{d\sigma}{dA}},$$

where A is the proportion of the portfolio invested in the market portfolio, M, and $(1 - A)$ is invested in portfolio z. Noting that

$$E(R_p) = AE(R_M) + (1 - A)E(R_z)$$

and

$$\sigma_p = [A^2\sigma_M^2 + 2A(1 - A)\text{Cov}(R_z, R_M) + (1 - A)^2\sigma_z^2]^{1/2},$$

the partials with respect to A (where, by definition, $\text{Cov}(R_z, R_M) = 0$) are as follows:

$$\frac{dE(R_p)}{dA} = E(R_M) - E(R_z)$$

and

$$\frac{d\sigma_p}{dA} = \frac{1}{2}[A^2\sigma_M^2 + (1 - A)^2\sigma_z^2]^{-1/2}[2A\sigma_M^2 - 2\sigma_z^2 + 2A\sigma_z^2].$$

Evaluating the ratio of the above partials at portfolio M (where $A = 1$) produces the following result:

(9.9)
$$\left.\frac{dE(R_p)}{d\sigma_p}\right|_{A=1} = \frac{E(R_M) - E(R_z)}{\sigma_M}.$$

Note that at M this slope differs from the slope of the CML only in the substitution of $E(R_z)$ for r_F. Considering the slope in Equation 9.9 and the fact that a straight line with this slope that passes through M will have an intercept equal to $E(R_z)$, we can define the CML$_z$ equation as follows:

(9.10)
$$E(R_p) = E(R_z) + \left[\frac{E(R_M) - E(R_z)}{\sigma_M}\right]\sigma_p.$$

The zero-beta version of the SML or SML$_z$ is found in a manner analogous to that used to find the SML earlier. However, this time $E(R_z)$ replaces r_F, with the following result:

(9.11)
$$E(R_i) = E(R_z) + \left[\frac{E(R_M) - E(R_z)}{\sigma_M}\right]\left[\frac{Cov(R_i, R_M)}{\sigma_M}\right].$$

Expressions similar to those derived earlier for the SML can easily be derived. The only difference in their form and that of the SML$_z$ is the substitution of $E(R_z)$ for r_F.

Since SML$_z$ incorporates the two portfolios of risky assets, z and M, it is frequently referred to as a *two–(risky) factor model*. The zero-beta model allows us to *represent* the expected return of all risky assets contained in M as a linear function of the beta of the asset calculated with respect to M, that is, using $Cov(R_i, R_M)$. However, there are as many such SMLs as there are mean-variance efficient portfolios and corresponding zero-beta portfolios. Thus, although we can still write an equation for equilibrium security expected rates of return as a function of their systematic risk, the beta coefficients and zero-beta portfolio expected rates of return will no longer be the same for all investors but will differ depending on the particular mean-variance efficient portfolios of risky assets that they select.

Earlier we noted that when no risk-free asset exists we cannot identify *the* market portfolio of risky assets. This is a very important point. Figure 9.4 contains the efficient frontier of risky assets that, because of our homogeneous beliefs assumption, all investors agree on. Note, however, that there are two portfolios of risky assets (M and M′) that have been selected by two different investors. For risky portfolio M there is a minimum-risk zero-beta portfolio z, and for portfolio M′ there is z′. The equations for the SML$_z$s corresponding to each investor's risky portfolio are

$$E(R_i) = E(R_z) + \beta_i[E(R_M) - E(R_z)]$$

and

$$E(R_i) = E(R_z') + \beta_i'[E(R_M') - E(R_z')].$$

Note that in both instances security i's expected rate of return is a linear function of its beta coefficient. However, the security's beta coefficient is unique to the

Figure 9.4   Absence of a Unique Market Portfolio in the Zero-Beta CAPM

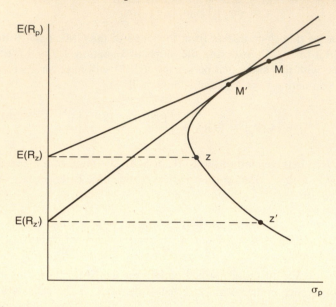

particular portfolio of risky assets used in the analysis. Thus, there are as many beta coefficients for a security as there are mean-variance efficient portfolios. This lack of uniqueness of beta for a security is the problem alluded to earlier when we noted that without a riskless asset we have no basis for identifying *the* market portfolio of risky assets. Each individual will select a portfolio lying along the efficient frontier of risky assets based on his or her own willingness to tolerate risk. Once this portfolio choice has been made, we can *represent* that investor's expected return on each asset in the market as a linear function of its beta coefficient, where the beta is measured according to the investor's chosen portfolio of risky assets. We emphasize the term "represent" since the SML_z is no longer unique but can differ for each investor depending on the portfolio of risky assets selected from those lying on the mean-variance efficient frontier of risky assets.

To conclude our discussion of the two-factor CAPM, we note that its primary contribution has been its revelation of an important property of the mean-variance efficient frontier of risky assets: The expected returns of all risky assets contained in the market portfolio can be represented as a linear function of the beta coefficients corresponding to the particular mean-variance efficient portfolio of risky assets that the investor selects. However, there are many such linear representations — in fact, as many as there are mean-variance efficient portfolios (and corresponding zero-beta portfolios). In a sense, the Sharpe-Lintner CAPM is a special case of Black's $CAPM_z$ where $E(R_z) = r_F$. Some would argue that the Black model is therefore less restrictive than the Sharpe-Lintner CAPM. Note, however, that with the Sharpe-Lintner CAPM everyone owns a nonzero portion of every risky asset. Thus, no short selling is required in order to achieve equilibrium as it is with the zero-beta model, where everyone potentially holds a different portfolio of risky assets. In this sense, the Black CAPM requires unlimited short selling in risky assets, whereas the Sharpe-Lintner model does not. Thus, it is not completely true that the Black model is less restrictive; in reality, the two models simply exhibit different sets of restrictions.

Arbitrage Pricing Model

Ross (1976) proposed an equilibrium model of asset (security) pricing that has the CAPM as a special case. The underlying rationale on which the theory is constructed is very simple:

In equilibrium, a portfolio of securities that entails a zero net investment and that has no risk should have a zero expected rate of return.

Using this "characterization" of market equilibrium, Ross developed a linear model that can be used to relate the expected rate of return on any risky asset to the fundamental economic influences on the rates of return earned on any asset investment. The method of proof simply involves mathematically defining what is meant by a riskless arbitrage portfolio. In nonmathematical terms, a *riskless arbitrage portfolio* is one that entails *no* net investment of wealth and involves *no* risk. In equilibrium, these two attributes imply that such a portfolio will earn a zero expected rate of return (if this were not the case, riskless arbitrage profits would be possible). Thus, the linear model, called the *arbitrage pricing model (APM),* is actually a mathematical *consequence* of the fundamental attribute of market equilibrium — the absence of riskless arbitrage profits. The model is so named because it is "derived" under conditions in which no riskless arbitrage profits can be earned.

Assumptions Underlying the Arbitrage Pricing Model

The basic assumptions underlying the APM are as follows:

1.   Capital markets are competitive and frictionless — that is, there are no transactions costs and individual investors' actions do not impact on market prices.

2.   All investors share homogeneous beliefs.

3.   There exist K factors common to the returns from all securities, and all investors agree on the identity of these factors.

4.   The number of securities (N) is greater than the number of common factors (K).

Given these assumptions, we can express the returns for the ith security using the following "return-generating model":

(9.12) $R_i = m_i + b_{i1}f_1 + b_{i2}f_2 + \ldots + b_{iK}f_K + e_i,$

where R_i = random rate of return on the ith security
         m_i = expected rate of return on the ith security

K   = number of factors underlying the common variance in security
      returns (assumed to be known by all investors due to our
      homogeneous beliefs assumption)

f_j = jth common factor, which has $E(f_j) = 0$ and $Cov(f_h, f_j)$
      $= 0$ for all $h \neq j$[9]

b_{ij} = $Cov(R_i, f_j)$ = sensitivity of the ith security's return to the jth factor

e_i = security-specific portion of security i's return

The K factors explain as much of the variation in the asset's returns as possible
in that

$$m_i + b_{i1}f_1 + \ldots + b_{iK}f_K$$

is an optimal linear estimator of R_i in terms of $f_1, \ldots, f_K$. In other words, it can be
shown that under the assumptions of the APM, any other linear estimate of Equation 9.12, such as

$$m_i' + b_{i1}'f_1 + \ldots + b_{iK}'f_K,$$

(with $b_{ij}' \neq Cov[R_i, R_j]$) will have a greater expected square error than $E(e^2)$.

Note that these assumptions say nothing about where the factors come from.
One might choose a set of asset returns, observe them for some time to estimate
their joint distribution, and use factor analysis to extract a set of linear combinations of these asset returns that will satisfy the assumptions of the APM.[10] Then, to
forecast the return R_i on a given asset i, one would need to estimate $Cov(R_i, f_j)$ for
$j = 1, \ldots, K$ and forecast f_j for $j = 1, \ldots, K$. In practice, K appears to be small
(for example, $K \leq 3$); thus, this involves less work than it might otherwise. We
do not imply that using the APM to evaluate expected security returns is a trivial
matter, however, for we must first identify the important economic influences on
security returns and then estimate them.

Deriving the Arbitrage Pricing Model

Derivation of the APM involves characterizing a zero-risk arbitrage portfolio as
one that involves a zero wealth investment and, under conditions of market equilibrium, earns a zero expected rate of return. By "characterizing" we mean developing formal mathematical representations of the portfolio's zero wealth, risk, and
expected return attributes. From the equations and assumptions stated earlier, the
APM is a necessary implication.

To simplify our development of the APM, we assume that there is but one
factor common to the pricing of all risky assets. Thus, we assume that security
returns are generated by the following model:

---

[9]Note that h and j are simply counters used to identify the hth and jth factors, respectively.

[10]*Factor analysis* is a generic term that refers to a set of mathematical methods that can be used to
examine the underlying relationships for a large number of variables and to simplify complex relationships by uncovering common dimensions or factors. Therefore, the purpose of factor analysis is
data reduction and summarization of large variable sets without a loss of information.

(9.13) $R_i = m_i + b_i f + e_i$.

Using this single-factor model allows us to use a graphical depiction of the APM relationship. Therefore, in the following discussion we drop the subscript from the risky factor (f) and the second subscript from its coefficient (b_{ij}); hence, b_i now refers to the coefficient of the ith risky asset on the *one* risky factor.

Recall again our definition of market equilibrium: *A portfolio with zero net investment and no risk should earn a zero expected return*. Thus, our method of proof will be to define a portfolio with zero investment and zero risk. We will then add the constraint that such a portfolio must have a zero expected return in market equilibrium.

To define the investment proportions in an arbitrage portfolio, let x_i be the proportion of an individual's wealth that is invested in the ith security. Thus, the zero investment attribute of an arbitrage portfolio means that

$$\sum_{i=1}^{N} x_i = 0. \qquad \textbf{(Zero investment)}$$

The particular arbitrage portfolio that we wish to analyze has zero risk. The reason for selecting this portfolio is that its expected return must be zero in market equilibrium. The variance of our arbitrage portfolio will be zero when the following conditions hold:

$$\sum_{i=1}^{N} x_i b_i = 0 \qquad \textbf{(Zero systematic risk)}$$

and the portfolio is sufficiently well diversified to eliminate the firm-specific component of portfolio risk:

$$\sum_{i=1}^{N} x_i^2 \sigma^2(e_i) = 0. \qquad \textbf{(Zero nonsystematic risk)}$$

In equilibrium, the arbitrage portfolio described by the above zero investment and zero risk conditions will have an expected return of zero:

$$\sum_{i=1}^{N} x_i m_i = 0. \qquad \textbf{(Zero expected return)}$$

To summarize, we define an arbitrage portfolio as one having zero investment and zero risk. In market equilibrium, such a portfolio must have a zero expected return. To complete the derivation, we simply restate each of the above attributes of a riskless arbitrage portfolio using their linear algebra equivalents and utilize a basic theorem in linear algebra:

$$X^T U = 0, \qquad \textbf{(Zero investment)}$$

where X is a column vector containing the proportions invested in each asset in the portfolio, that is,

$$X^T = (x_1, x_2, \ldots, x_N),$$

U is a column vector of ones, that is,

$$U = (1, 1, \ldots, 1)^T,$$

and

$$X^T B = 0, \qquad \qquad \textbf{(Zero systematic risk)}$$

where B is a column vector containing the b_i for the assets contained in the portfolio, that is,

$$B = (b_1, b_2, \ldots, b_N)^T.$$

Finally, the above conditions imply (in market equilibrium) that

$$X^T M = 0, \quad \textbf{(Zero expected portfolio return)}$$

where M is a column vector containing the expected returns on the assets in the arbitrage portfolio, that is,

$$M = (m_1, m_2, \ldots, m_N)^T.$$

Thus, mathematically the zero investment requirement states that the vector of investment proportions (X) is orthogonal to a vector of ones (U). Likewise, the zero systematic risk requirement states that the vector of betas (B) is orthogonal to the vector of investment proportions (X). Finally, the zero expected return requirement means that the vector of investment proportions (X) is orthogonal to the vector of asset expected returns (M). Thus, geometrically these relations mean that it is impossible to construct a vector X that is orthogonal to the plane spanned by U and B, without also being perpendicular to M. Hence, M must lie in the plane spanned by U and B. For the case used here, where there is only one common factor (K = 1 such that there is a single vector $B = [b_1, \ldots, b_N]^T$), this geometric representation appears as follows:

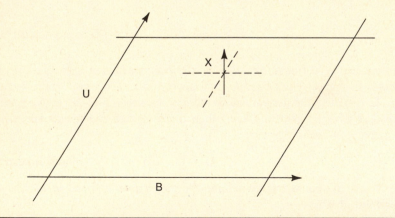

In addition, the zero expected return requirement tells us that X is also perpendicular to the mean return vector, M:

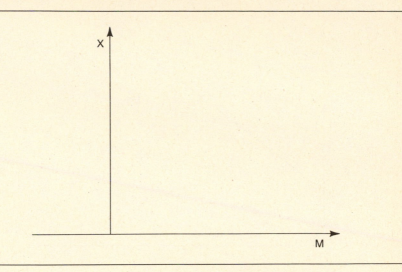

From this we conclude (see the Mathematical Compendium for proof) that M must lie on the plane defined by U and B. Since this plane consists of all linear combinations of the form $y_0 U + y_1 B$, we can express the mean return vector (M) as a linear function of the unit vector (U) and the covariance vector (B); that is, for the single-factor case,

$$M = y_0 + y_1 B$$

or, in terms of individual securities,

(9.14) $m_i = y_0 + y_1 b_i \qquad (i = 1, \ldots, N)$.

If we let y_0 equal the risk-free rate, r_F, we can interpret $y_1 b_i$ as the excess return of security i over the risk-free rate:

$$m_i = r_F + y_1 b_i .$$

This linear relationship is represented graphically in Figure 9.5. If the single factor corresponds to the market portfolio, as is the case with the CAPM, then $y_1 = [E(R_M) - r_F]$ and the APM reduces to the CAPM.

In general, there can be many factors $f_1, \ldots, f_K$. Each is assumed to be uncorrelated with the others, and all have zero expected values and unit variance. In this multifactor world, the expected rate of return on a security can be expressed as follows:

$$m_i = y_0 + y_1 b_{i1} + y_2 b_{i2} + \ldots + y_K b_{iK}.$$

In this setting, we recall that the b_{ij} (j = 1, 2, \ldots, K) represents the response coefficient for the return on the ith asset to the jth factor. If y_0 is the risk-free interest

Figure 9.5   Single-Factor APM

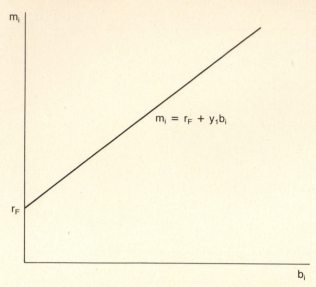

$$m_i = r_F + y_1 b_i$$

rate, the y_j ($j = 1, 2, \ldots, K$) can be thought of as the excess of the expected rate of return on the jth factor over the risk-free rate. Thus, the multifactor arbitrage pricing model can be considered a straightforward counterpart to the single-factor CAPM.

Summary

The APM provides us with a very general representation of expected returns in equilibrium based on the simple notion that arbitrage opportunities should not exist in market equilibrium. In contrast to that of the CAPM, the derivation of the APM makes no assumptions about either the probability distributions of risky assets (such as normality) or individuals' preferences (such as quadratic utility). Further, the APM permits multiple economic influences (factors) that influence the determination of security returns. However, it does not tell us what those factors represent. Recall that we assumed there were K return factors that were *known* by all investors and that they explained the common variance in security returns. The APM is simply a "representation" of market equilibrium in the case where the above assumption (among others) holds. It therefore should not be surprising to find that the APM does not *identify* the factors underlying security returns — after all, we have *assumed* that they are known by all investors. What the model does, however, is provide a general mathematical form for the equilibrium relationship between expected returns and multiple independent factors. If this indeed is a reasonable approximation of reality, the identification of the specific factors underlying security returns becomes an important empirical issue.

A number of empirical tests have attempted to identify the basic factors underlying security valuation (for example, Gehr [1978], Roll and Ross [1980],

Reinganum [1981], and Dhrymes, Friend, and Gultekin [1984]). In general, these studies point to the existence of at least three or four significant factors. Specifically, Chen, Roll, and Ross (1986) note unanticipated changes in (1) inflation, (2) industrial production, (3) risk premiums (as measured by the yield spread between low-grade and high-grade bonds), and (4) the slope of the yield curve. Thus, in order to evaluate the expected rate of return on a security, one must estimate the sensitivity of that security's expected return to each factor.

Exercise 9.2:   Security Market Equilibrium with the Arbitrage Pricing Model

Assume that the expected rates of return on securities can be described by the following two-factor (index) model:

$$E(R_i) = \lambda_0 + b_{i1}\lambda_1 + b_{i2}\lambda_2,$$

where the b_{ij} terms are the coefficients of the model specific to each security and the λ_j terms represent the risk premiums for each factor's underlying security returns. We also know that securities A, B, and C have the following risk and return information:

Security	$E(R_i)$	b_{i1}	b_{i2}
A	0.145	1.5	1.0
B	0.130	1.0	1.0
C	0.109	0.8	0.7

1. Based on the above risk and return information, what are the equilibrium values for the λ_j's?

Solution.   The following equations relate expected security returns to the λ_j's and three unknowns:

$$E(R_A) = \lambda_0 + 1.5\lambda_1 + 1.0\lambda_2 = 0.145$$

$$E(R_B) = \lambda_0 + 1.0\lambda_1 + 1.0\lambda_2 = 0.130$$

$$E(R_C) = \lambda_0 + 0.8\lambda_1 + 0.7\lambda_2 = 0.109.$$

Solving these equations simultaneously gives us the following values for $\lambda_0, \lambda_1,$ and λ_2:

$$\lambda_0 = 0.05$$

$$\lambda_1 = 0.03$$

$$\lambda_2 = 0.05.$$

2. What would be the expected rate of return on a portfolio comprised of one-quarter security A, one-quarter security B, and one-half security C?

Solution.   By investing the above proportions in each of the three securities, the b_{ij}'s for the portfolio would be the following:

$$b_{p1} = (\tfrac{1}{4})(1.5) + (\tfrac{1}{4})(1.0) + (\tfrac{1}{2})(0.8) = 1.025$$

$$b_{p2} = (\tfrac{1}{4})(1.0) + (\tfrac{1}{4})(1.0) + (\tfrac{1}{2})(0.7) = 0.85.$$

Thus, the expected portfolio return can be calculated as follows:

$$E(R_p) = 0.05 + 1.025(0.03) + 0.85(0.05) = 0.12325.$$

Note that the expected return for the portfolio can also be calculated from the expected rates of return for the individual securities; that is,

$$E(R_p) = 0.145(\tfrac{1}{4}) + 0.13(\tfrac{1}{4}) + 0.109(\tfrac{1}{2}) = 0.12325.$$

Summary

In this chapter we discussed the valuation of securities under conditions of competitive capital market equilibrium. Two theories were presented—the CAPM and the APM—each based on a unique set of assumptions about investor behavior and the factor(s) underlying the determination of security prices. We found neither the CAPM nor the APM to be totally satisfactory explanations of security valuation. The CAPM presumes that all investors hold a common portfolio of risky securities and that the market portfolio provides the *only* source of risk to security ownership. The APM provides a multifactor rationale for security valuation but gives us no hint on what these factors are. Thus, the current state of the art in capital market theory is as yet unsettled. The next step toward developing a more satisfactory theory, especially with respect to the APM, must be the empirical *identification* of the sources of common covariation among security rates of return and, consequently, the sources of nondiversifiable risk that are "priced" in determining a security's value.

Study Questions

9.1   The set of assumptions used to derive the CAPM and APM are quite unrealistic. What justification can we find for using such seemingly impractical assumptions when modeling the pricing of assets in the capital market?

9.2   Distinguish between the concepts of the capital market line and the security market line. What are the counterparts of these concepts in the context of the Black zero-beta model?

9.3   Describe verbally the basis for the derivation of the arbitrage pricing model.

9.4   "The arbitrage pricing model does not identify the factors underlying the pricing of securities, but the CAPM does." Explain.

Study Problems

9.1   The returns of the common stock of J. Bean Corporation are perfectly positively correlated with those of the market portfolio. In addition, the equilibrium rate of return for Bean's stock is 24 percent and the market's expected rate of return is 16 percent. If the risk-free rate is 11 percent and the standard deviation in the market return is 12 percent, what is the standard deviation in the returns of Bean's stock? What is the beta coefficient for Bean's stock?

9.2   The market portfolio has an expected rate of return of 19 percent and a standard deviation of 8 percent, and the risk-free rate is 10 percent. The Maxrate Investment Company is considering the acquisition of two stocks. Company A's stock has a beta of 1.2; company B's beta is only 0.80.
a. What rate of return should Maxrate expect on each stock investment?
b. If the price of both A's and B's stock for the next year is expected to be $100 and neither pays an interim cash dividend, what is the value of each stock today?

9.3   The systematic risk (beta coefficients) and standard deviations for two securities are as follows:

Security	Beta	Standard Deviation
1	1.2	0.16
2	0.8	0.10

In addition, the expected rate of return on the market portfolio of all risky assets is 18 percent, its variance is 0.01, and the risk-free interest rate is 8 percent.
a. What are the expected rates of return for the two securities according to the CAPM?
b. Calculate the correlation coefficients between the securities' and market's returns. What are the respective covariances between each security and the market?
c. Assuming there is no limit on short selling in the risk-free asset, what is the optimal portfolio of assets for achieving an expected return of 25 percent?
d. Use the above information to define the equation for the security market line.
e. If the expected next-period prices of both securities are $50, what are their respective current prices?

9.4   François Truffle Company's equity has a current market value of $20 million, and the beta for its (levered) equity is 2.0. If the risk premium for the market portfolio of risky assets is 8 percent, the risk-free rate is 6 percent, and the company's cost of capital is 14 percent, what is the market value of the firm's debt?

9.5   Jean Christopher is a talented musician but is not particularly good with numbers. She has $8,000 that she wants to invest in a stock portfolio promising a return of 15 percent and a standard deviation of 20 percent. A local banker who has heard Jean's music has offered to loan her $22,000 at a rate of 8 percent. Jean plans to invest the total of $30,000 in the stock portfolio. What would be the expected rate of return and standard deviation of Jean's levered portfolio?

9.6   Let Z_j be a random variable denoting the earnings per share for firm j and p_j the share price.
a. Show that in the context of the CAPM,

$$p_j = \frac{E(Z_j)}{1 + r_F + \beta_j(E(R_M) - r_F)},$$

and explain the right-hand side.
b. If $E(Z_K) = E(Z_j)$ and $\beta_K > \beta_j$, show that $p_K < p_j$.

9.7   Let Z_j be a random variable denoting the total earnings of firm j. Further, let S_j and D_j denote the value of the firm's equity and debt, respectively. Use $(1 + R_j) = [Z_j - (1 + r_F)D_j]/S_j$ to show that

$$S_j = \frac{E(Z_j)}{1 + r_F} - \frac{\lambda Cov(Z_j, R_M)}{1 + r_F} - D_j,$$

where

$$\lambda = \frac{E(R_m) - r_F}{\sigma_M^2}.$$

Note that

$$\frac{dS_j}{dD_j} = -1.$$

9.8   If asset A_j includes a proportion D_j/V_j of the risk-free asset and a proportion of S_j/V_j of risky asset j, that is, if

$$R_{Aj} = \left(\frac{D_j}{V_j}\right)r_F + \left(\frac{S_j}{V_j}\right)R_j,$$

show that

$$\beta_{Aj} = \left(\frac{S_j}{V_j}\right)\beta_j$$

and

$$E(R_{Aj}) = r_F + \beta_{Aj}[E(R_M) - r_F].$$

Interpret this result.

9.9   Assume that the expected rates of return on securities can be described by the following two-factor (index) model:

$$E(R_i) = \lambda_0 + b_{i1}\lambda_1 + b_{i2}\lambda_2,$$

where the b_{ij} terms are the coefficients of the model specific to each security and the λ_j's represent the risk premiums for each of the factor's underlying security returns. We also know that securities A, B, and C have the following risk and return information:

Security	$E(R_i)$	b_{i1}	b_{i2}
A	0.180	0.5	2.0
B	0.160	2.0	1.0
C	0.128	0.8	1.2

a. Based on the above risk and return information, what are the equilibrium values for the λ_j's?

b. What would be the expected rate of return on a portfolio comprised of one-third security A, one-third security B, and one-third security C?

References

F. Black, "Capital Market Equilibrium with Restricted Borrowing," *Journal of Business* (July 1972): 444–455.

D. Bower, R. S. Bower, and D. E. Logue, "Arbitrage Pricing Theory and Utility Stock Returns," *Journal of Finance* (September 1984): 1041–1054.

D. Cass and J. E. Stieglitz, "The Structure of Investor Preferences and Asset Returns and Separability in Portfolio Allocation: A Contribution to the Pure Theory of Mutual Funds," *Journal of Economic Theory* 2 (1970): 122–160.

Nai-Fu Chen, R. Roll, and S. A. Ross, "Economic Forces and the Stock Market," *Journal of Business* 59, no. 3 (July 1986): 383–403.

G. Constantinides, "Capital Market Equilibrium with Transaction Costs," *Journal of Political Economy* 94, no. 4 (1986).

P. Dhrymes, I. Friend, and B. Gultekin, "A Critical Reexamination of Empirical Evidence on the Arbitrage Pricing Theory," *Journal of Finance* (June 1984): 323–346.

W. Dillon and M. Goldstein, *Multivariate Analysis* (New York: Wiley, 1984).

P. H. Dybvig and S. A. Ross, "Yes, The APT is Testable," *Journal of Finance* (September 1985): 1173–1189.

M. Friedman, *Essays in Positive Economics* (Chicago: University of Chicago Press, 1955).

A. Gehr, "Some Tests of the Arbitrage Pricing Theory," *Journal of the Midwest Finance Association* (1978): 91–105.

H. H. Harman, *Modern Factor Analysis*, 3d ed. (Chicago: University of Chicago Press, 1976).

M. Jensen, "The Foundations and Current State of Capital Market Theory," in M. Jensen, ed., *Studies in the Theory of Capital Markets* (New York: Praeger, 1972).

J. N. Keynes, *The Scope and Method of Political Economy* (New York: Kelley and Millman, 1955, first edition 1890).

J. Lintner, "The Valuation of Risky Assets and the Selection of Risky Investments in Stock Portfolios and Capital Budgets," *Review of Economics and Statistics* (February 1965): 13–37.

J. Mossin, "Equilibrium in a Capital Asset Market," *Econometrica* (October 1966): 768–783.

M. Reinganum, "The Arbitrage Pricing Theory: Some Empirical Results," *Journal of Finance* (May 1981): 313–321.

R. Roll, "A Critique of the Asset Pricing Theory's Tests; Part I: On Past and Potential Testability of the Theory," *Journal of Financial Economics* 4, no. 2 (March 1977): 129–176.

R. Roll and S. A. Ross, "The Arbitrage Pricing Theory Approach to Strategic Planning," *Financial Analysts Journal* (May/June 1984), 14–26.

————, "An Empirical Investigation of Arbitrage Pricing Theory," *Journal of Finance* (December 1980): 1073–1103.

————, "Regulation, the Capital Asset Pricing Model, and the Arbitrage Pricing Theory," *Public Utilities Fortnightly,* May 26, 1983, 22–29.

S. A. Ross, "The Arbitrage Pricing Theory of Asset Pricing," *Journal of Economic Theory* 13 (1976): 341–360.

————, "Arbitrage and Martingales with Taxation," *Journal of Political Economy* 95, no. 2 (1987).

J. Shanken, "Multi-Beta CAPM or Equilibrium APT?" *Journal of Finance* (September 1985): 1189–1196.

W. F. Sharpe, "Capital Asset Prices: A Theory of Market Equilibrium under Risk," *Journal of Finance* (September 1964): 425–442.

————, "Factors in New York Stock Exchange Returns, 1931–1979," *Journal of Portfolio Management* 8 (Summer 1982): 5–19.

Chapter 10

Efficient Capital Markets

The term *efficient market* as used in finance refers to a market in which prices fully and correctly reflect all available information at all times. In this context, its importance to society at large cannot be overstated. The basis for this definition is the role that market prices play in the resource allocation function of capital markets; that is, security prices determine the terms under which funds are made available to various competing firms in the capital markets. If those security prices "fully reflect" all available information about these firms, financial resources will be "properly" allocated to those firms having the "most productive use" for them. Thus, a market that is efficient in the information sense used here is, by definition, an *allocationally efficient* market.[1]

Market efficiency can also be judged based on the costs involved in performing the resource allocation function (that is, market transactions costs). This notion of market efficiency is termed *operational efficiency*. Although this aspect of the capital markets has received relatively little attention compared to allocational efficiency, it is an important concern in the field of finance. In general, the transactions costs incurred when buying and selling securities add to the cost of

---

[1]Economists have long debated whether stock prices rationally reflect the intrinsic factors that characterize the issuing companies. As we will see later in the chapter, the empirical evidence offered by finance scholars suggests that the capital markets are efficient. However, Keynes (1936) and a number of economists since his time suggest that speculative markets are little more than casinos for transferring wealth from the unlucky to the lucky. Shiller's (1981a, 1981b) work constitutes a modern-day extension of this theme.

funds, thus reducing the level of productive investment in the economy. Note that in a world where information is not costless, financial intermediaries (such as commerical banks and investment bankers) provide a valuable service for their fees — specifically, they bring buyers and sellers together. The point here is that in an operationally efficient market this service is provided at the lowest possible cost. Recent innovations in computerization of financial transactions and shelf registration of prospective security offerings are examples in which the costs of using capital markets have been reduced.[2] In addition, it has long been recognized that due to the economies of scale involved in issuing securities in the capital markets, small firms frequently find it prohibitively expensive to make public offerings of their securities. Thus, the operational efficiency of capital markets is an important concern in the theory and practice of finance.

The chapter is organized as follows. First, we examine a formal definition of capital market efficiency that focuses on the information reflected in security prices. Next, we consider the problems attendant to the testing of market efficiency; here we review a broad spectrum of test methods, including investment simulation experiments such as filter rule strategies and the event study methodology that has become standard in both financial and accounting research. Finally, we survey the empirical evidence regarding capital market efficiency.

---

[2]Shelf registration allows a firm to "register" multiple security offerings with the Securities and Exchange Commission with one filing. This offers potential savings in the filing of security offerings and increases the speed with which a new offering can be brought to the market.

A Mathematical Review of Conditional Expectations

In this chapter we present a financial market model that uses the terms "securities" and "information" without giving either a precise mathematical definition. Securities are sequences of random variables defined on a probability space $\{\Omega, \Phi, \Psi\}$.[a] The price at time t is denoted P_t for $t = 0, 1, 2, \ldots$. If we must discuss two or more securities at the same time, we will use an additional subscript; for example, $P_{j,t}$ will denote the price of the jth security at time t. Thus, the rigorous definition of a *security* is simply a sequence of random variables $P_t : \Omega \to [0, \infty)$ defined on the probability space $\{\Omega, \Phi, \Psi\}$.

The σ-algebra Φ has all the information necessary for dealing with the security at any time since, by the definition of a random variable, each of the sets $[\omega \; \varepsilon \; \Omega \,|\, b \le P_t(\omega) \le a]$ must be an event in the σ-algebra Φ for all a and b, $-\infty \le b < a \le \infty$, and for all $t = 0, 1, 2, \ldots$. Indeed, the rigorous definition of *information* as used here must be given in terms of σ-algebras. The information available at time t is a σ-algebra $\Phi_t \subset \Phi$ that contains all events that might occur at times $0, 1, \ldots, t$ and affect the price of some security; that is, Φ_t is the σ-algebra generated by the random variables $P_{j,s}$, where $s \le t$ and $j = 1, 2, \ldots$.

The σ-algebra $_m\Phi_t$ of market information used in calculating expectations of future values (such as the expected value of P_{t+1}) is a subset of Φ_t. In some models, it may be appropriate to distinguish market information from full information; thus, in general, $_m\Phi_t \ne \Phi_t$. To distinguish values based on this information, we would write $E(P_{t+1} \,|\, _m\Phi_t)$ rather than $E(P_{t+1} \,|\, \Phi_t)$. However, in this chapter we usually assume that $_m\Phi_t = \Phi_t$.

The key properties of the information σ-algebras, or information sets, Φ_t, are as follows:

1. $\Phi_0 \subset \Phi_1 \subset \Phi_2 \subset \ldots \subset \Phi$

   This means that as time goes on more events can take place, no information is lost, and Φ contains all the information.

2. $\Phi = \Phi_0 \cup \Phi_1 \cup \Phi_2 \cup \ldots$

   This means that Φ contains no superfluous information.

3. P_t is measurable with respect to Φ_t for all $t = 0, 1, \ldots$.

   This means that the information available at time t is sufficient to determine the probability of any events of the form $P_t \le a$.

In general, conditioning a random variable P on a set of information, or σ-algebra Y, focuses all of the randomness of P on the events of Y. Thus, if Y is a huge set, conditioning on Y affects P very little. If Y is small, conditioning restricts the outcomes of P and could greatly affect its values. The expected value of P conditioned on Y typically is a random variable denoted $E(P \,|\, Y)$. The only ran-

---

[a] The battle for the symbol P has been won by the security's "price." We will use P for security prices and Ψ for the probability of an event.

domness remaining after calculating $E(P|Y)$ is that associated with Y. The variance of P conditioned on Y, $Var(P|Y)$, also is generally a random variable.

In the context of the financial market model, $E(P_s|\Phi_t)$ for $s \geq t$, the expectation of P_s conditioned on the information at time t is just as random as Φ_t. Thus, at time t it is not random at all, since whatever events in Φ_t are to occur will be known by that time.

The properties of the expectations operator $E[X]$ reviewed in Chapter 8 carry over to conditional expectations. These are discussed in greater detail in the Mathematics Compendium; for a complete discussion, the reader should refer to a probability theory text.

Properties of Conditional Expectations

The random variables P_0, P_1, . . . are defined on the same probability space (Ω, Φ, Ψ), have finite expectations, and are related to the sequence of σ-algebras $\Phi_0 \subset \Phi_1 \subset \Phi_2 \subset \ldots \subset \Phi$ as described earlier.

1.   Since P_t is Φ_t-measurable,

$$E(P_t|\Phi_t) = P_t.$$

(Since Φ_t contains all the relevant information on P_t, conditioning on Φ_t does not change P_t.)

2. $E(aX + bY|Y) = aE(X|\Phi_t) + bE(Y|\Phi_t)$.
(In general, the conditional expectations operator has the same linearity property as the usual expectations operator.)

3.   Since P_t is Φ_t-measurable, for $s > t$,

$$E(P_tP_s|\Phi_t) = P_tE(P_s|\Phi_t).$$

(Again, since Φ_t contains all the relevant information on P_t, conditioning on Φ_t does not change P_t.)

4.   Since $\Phi_t \subset \Phi_s \subset \Phi$ for $t < s$, for all $t < s < r$,

$$E(P_r|\Phi_t) = E[E(P_r|\Phi_t)|\Phi_s] = E[E(P_r|\Phi_s)|\Phi_t].$$

A Formal Definition of Market Efficiency[3]

We have defined an efficient capital market as one in which all available information at a point in time (we refer to this information set as Φ_t) is *fully* and *correctly* reflected in security prices. Thus, formally, the price of security j at time $t + 1$ is

[3]This presentation follows that of Fama (1976).

said to fully reflect Φ_t where (1) the information utilized by the market in determining its expected value, $E(P_{j,t+1})$, is the set of *all* available information (that is, $_m\Phi_t = \Phi_t$ where the subscript m refers to the market) and (2) that information is used correctly. In other words, for all securities "full reflection" of information implies that

(10.1) $$f_m(P_{1,t+1}, \ldots, P_{n,t+1} \mid _m\Phi_t) = f(P_{1,t+1}, \ldots, P_{n,t+1} \mid \Phi_t),$$

where $f_m(\ )$ is the joint probability distribution over *market* prices of securities at time t + 1 conditioned on the information set available to investors at time t and the right-hand side reflects the same set of prices based on "*full* and *correct* reflection" of *all* available information.

Although the formal characterization of an efficient market in Equation 10.1 is definitionally complete, it provides no basis for testing market efficiency since "informationally" efficient prices (the right-hand side of Equation 10.1) are not observable. In fact, some model of market equilibrium, such as the CAPM or APM, is needed to assess these hypothetical values. Hence, tests of market efficiency are, by their very nature, joint tests of two hypotheses: (1) the efficiency of the market and (2) the theory of market equilibrium used in assessing security market prices that fully reflect all available information. This means, for example, that when a test provides *no* evidence of market "inefficiency" it also fails to refute the validity of the assumptions made concerning market equilibrium. On the other hand, if test results show evidence of inefficiency, we face the dilemma of determining whether the market is truly inefficient, or the assumptions made about the nature of market equilibrium were inappropriate, or both.

Fortunately, we need not *fully* identify the equilibrium theory underlying the determination of security prices in order to make the efficient market hypothesis (EMH) testable. For example, the simple assumption that expected equilibrium rates of return are positive (an assumption that is wholly consistent with rational asset pricing, where positive returns are anticipated as rewards for deferring consumption and assuming risk) has provided the basis for a number of empirical assessments of market efficiency. More restrictive assumptions, such as (1) expected rates of return on securities are constant over time or (2) expected returns conform to some specific asset pricing model, have paved the way for even more tests. We will discuss each of these propositions in turn in the next section, where we consider the *empirical evidence* concerning the efficient market hypothesis as applied to the capital markets.

Testing Market Efficiency

Tests of the efficient market hypothesis (namely that security prices fully reflect all available information at any point in time) require that some specification be given to the equilibrium model that determines security prices. We will consider three specifications or assumptions that have been used in this regard:

1.   Expected rates of return are positive.

2.   Expected rates of return are constant over time.

3.   Expected rates of return are based on some variant of the capital asset pricing model.

Expected Rates of Return Are Positive

The assumption that expected rates of return are positive over time is the simplest and least restrictive assumption used to describe the equilibrium model that determines security prices in testing market efficiency. This characterization of the equilibrium pricing of a security simply says that

$$E(R_{j,t+1} | \Phi_t) > 0,$$

where $R_{j,t+1} = \dfrac{P_{j,t+1} - P_{jt}}{P_{jt}}$

$E(P_{j,t+1} | \Phi_t)$ = expected price of the jth firm's stock for period $t + 1$
conditioned on the information set Φ_t
P_{jt} = current (period = t) price of security j

Note that we have not specified exactly how the current market price of security j is determined (that is, the particular model of capital market equilibrium that is assumed to be used to determine P_{jt}). All we have assumed is that *whatever* the equilibrium model is, the expected future price is greater than the current price such that $E(R_{j,t+1} | \Phi_t) > 0$. Note that this does not preclude the possibility that for a given time interval the realized $P_{j,t+1}$ could be less than P_{jt} such that $R_{j,t+1}$ would be negative. What is required is that P_{jt} be determined by some model of market equilibrium such that $E(P_{j,t+1} | \Phi_t) > P_{jt}$ or, equivalently, $E(R_{j,t+1} | \Phi_t) > 0$.

If $E(R_{j,t+1} | \Phi_t) > 0$ and markets are efficient — that is, $f_m(P_{j,t+1} |_m\Phi_t) = f(P_{j,t+1} | \Phi_t)$ — one would not expect to utilize available information to devise a trading strategy that would produce a rate of return larger than that which would be earned by following a simple buy-and-hold strategy.[4] This is because a buy-and-hold strategy would produce an expected return of $E(R_{j,t+1} | \Phi_t) = [E(P_{j,t+1} | \Phi_t) - P_{jt}]/P_{jt}$. This particular implication of an efficient market has been used as the basis for testing capital market efficiency with respect to the information contained in past security prices.

At this point, it is worth noting that tests of market efficiency generally are based on a particular subset of the total set of information available to market participants. Fama (1970) utilized three broad categories for tests of market efficiency based on the "relative availability" of the subset of information underlying the tests.[5] Tests based on the past history of prices and volume of security trading were referred to as *weak-form* tests of the efficient market hypothesis. Those based on the broad subset of "all generally available" information were deemed *semistrong-form* tests. Tests based on *insider* or restricted-access information were categorized as *strong-form* tests.

---

[4]A *buy-and-hold strategy* simply involves purchasing and holding a security or portfolio. This strategy is in contrast to a trading strategy, whereby the individual alters the content of his or her portfolio based on a strategy designed to improve the portfolio's performance.

[5]This classification scheme was first proposed by Roberts (1959).

Using this classification scheme, tests of market efficiency based on the information contained in past security prices and using the positive expected return assumption are weak-form tests. "Chartists"—particularly "technical analysts"—advocate the use of price histories as a source of information in predicting future price movements. Of course, if the capital market fully reflected all available information (including any potential information contained in past prices), one would not expect a chartist to be able to devise a trading strategy that would produce expected returns larger than that of a buy-and-hold method. A number of tests have been executed in an effort to determine whether trading strategies successful in providing excess returns over a buy-and-hold strategy might be devised. These tests generally have involved some sort of *filter rule,* such as the following: If the price of a security goes up by Y percent, one should purchase it (take a long position) and hold it until the price goes down by Y percent from a subsequent high, at which time one should simultaneously sell the security and take a short position. The short position is maintained until the price rises by Y percent from a subsequent low, at which time the short position is covered and a long position is taken. This trading strategy is called a *Y percent filter,* where Y can take on any value the trader wishes. Alexander (1961, 1964) utilized a Y percent trading filter in an extensive set of tests using daily price indexes for the period 1897 to 1959. After comparing the results of the filter strategies tested with a simple buy-and-hold method, Alexander concluded that even minimal commissions would eliminate any evidence of excess returns (over a buy-and-hold strategy) resulting from use of his trading filters. Fama and Blume (1966) performed a similar set of tests on the individual stocks comprising the Dow Jones Industrial Average and reached a similar conclusion.

At this point, we should note that these tests certainly are not exhaustive and do not preclude the existence of more sophisticated trading strategies that provide the trader with superior returns. The fact that no such evidence has been published is consistent with the hypothesis that none exists or that such a scheme, if known, is being used by an ever wealthier trader who is concealing his or her secret. Three points are in order here. First, the efficient market hypothesis, like any other testable hypothesis, *cannot be proven*. We can either refute it (that is, find evidence of market inefficiency) or "fail" to refute it, for we can never devise a completely exhaustive test of all possibilities. Second, of all the possible trading strategies that might be devised, only a small subset have actually been tested. In addition, no allowance has been made for strategy changes based on other information. Even chartists do not limit their trading activities to blindly using a single scheme. Third, regardless of how limited the available evidence with respect to the many and varied forms of technical analysis, traders should be at least somewhat skeptical of the "quick riches" promised by the use of commercial charting information services.

The fundamental lesson of an efficient market is simply that market prices reflect what is known. Thus, with respect to past prices—which are an essentially free source of information available to everyone—we should be very surprised indeed if excess returns (over a buy-and-hold strategy) could be achieved using those data alone.

Expected Rates of Return Are Constant over Time

In the previous section, we discussed tests of the efficient market hypothesis that were based on the simple assumption that the expected rate of return is positive. In this section, we assume that the expected return is *constant over time*. Each asset may have its unique expected rate of return that reflects its riskiness. However, this expected return is assumed to remain stable over time. If the market is efficient (that is, current prices reflect all available information) and expected rates of return are constant, there is no way that information available at time t can be used to arrive at a correct assessment of next period's expected return for any security j other than the constant rate $E(R_j)$. Note that $E(R_j)$ carries no time subscript as it is assumed to be constant over time. Technically, we assume the following:

$$E(R_{j, t+1} | \Phi_t) = E_m(R_{j, t+1} |_m \Phi_t) = E(R_j),$$

which means that the expected rate of return based on the true information set Φ_t equals the expected rate of return reflected in current market prices based on information utilized by the market, which in turn equals a constant expected return for all periods.

Combining the constant expected rate of return assumption with an efficient market produces the following testable implication:

If the temporal distribution of rates of return exhibits a constant mean rate of return, knowledge of the past pattern of rates of return (the information content of which is fully reflected in current prices in an efficient market) will not alter the constant expected rate of return.

Thus, in an efficient market the realized rates of return over time should be independent of one another. If significant dependence exists—say, over a one-month lag between monthly rates of return—knowledge of last period's return will be useful in predicting next period's. Since realized rates of return vary over time, the "predicted" future return will not be a constant, as posited by the assumption given here. Thus, we test this particular hypothesis by assessing the autocorrelation among historical returns for various possible time lags.[6]

A number of studies have tested for autocorrelation in securities' historical rates of return. They vary in terms of the set of securities from which the test sample was drawn, the length of the time interval over which rates of return were calculated (daily, monthly, and so forth), and the historical period over which the test was conducted. The following basic conclusion has been reached: Although some "statistically significant" autocorrelations have been observed for very short lags (such as one or two past returns) and for very short trading intervals (intra-day or transaction-to-transaction returns and day-to-day returns), their "practical" significance is nil; that is, given the transactions costs entailed in trading, the "net" returns realized from exploiting the observed autocorrelation in security returns are inconsequential. Four studies stand out in this literature: (1) Fama (1965), who provided a very extensive study of stock price behavior; (2) Niederhoffer and

---

[6]*Autocorrelation* results when a random variable is correlated with its own past values; that is, a random variable X evidences autocorrelation when $Cov(X_t, X_{t-k}) \neq 0$ for $k > 0$.

Osborne (1966), who investigated the autocorrelation structure of transaction-to-transaction security price changes (observing a significant "reversal" process or negative autocorrelation); (3) Granger and Morgenstern (1970), who conducted an exhaustive study of the random character of stock price changes using spectral analysis; and (4) Roll (1970), who extended the analysis to include the market for new Treasury bills.

These tests of market efficiency, like those discussed earlier, deal only with the information content of past prices. Using Fama's classification scheme, these are weak-form tests of the efficient market hypothesis. In the next section, we consider methods used to perform semistrong and strong-form tests of market efficiency.

Expected Rates of Return Are Generated by an Equilibrium Theory of Asset Pricing

In this section, we postulate that expected security returns are generated by an equilibrium theory of asset pricing. The most commonly used theory is the capital asset pricing model.

The general class of studies conducted with this basic methodology is called *event studies*. Their objective is to identify the timing and magnitude of securities' price responses to the revelation of a particular piece of information. If the information is available to all investors, the study constitutes a semistrong-form test of market efficiency. Similarly, if the information "event" involves restricted-access information, the study involves a strong-form test. The predominant purpose of such event studies has been to evaluate the revelation of "publicly available" information—hence, semistrong-form tests of market efficiency. Their objective is to identify "abnormal" security price behavior attributable to a specific information event, such as an earnings or merger announcement. In order to identify "abnormal" price performance, the researcher must first evaluate what is "normal" or expected given the usual influences on security prices; thus, it is necessary to begin with a model that generates *normal* returns.

Brown and Warner (1980) have suggested three general models for use in identifying normal or ex ante expected returns: (1) mean-adjusted return, (2) market-adjusted return, and (3) market-and-risk-adjusted return. For each model, the abnormal return for a given security at time t is defined as the difference between the observed ex post return and the estimated or predicted return.

The most widely used form in financial research has been the market-and-risk-adjusted return model. However, through a very extensive set of tests utilizing a simulation experiment, Brown and Warner found that the greatest power—that is, ability to identify truly abnormal performance—actually resides with the simplest of the test methodologies. Specifically, Brown and Warner found that the mean-adjusted return model performed well under a wide variety of circumstances and, in some situations, was as powerful as any other model tested and even more so than the complex types of market-and-risk-adjusted methodologies some researchers (such as Fama and MacBeth [1973]) had used. Brown and Warner summarized their results as follows:

A "bottom line" that emerges from our study is this: beyond a simple, one-factor market model, there is no evidence that more complicated methodologies convey

any benefit. In fact, we have presented evidence that more complicated method-
ologies can actually make the researcher worse off, both compared to the market
model and to even simpler methods, like Mean Adjusted Returns, which make no
explicit risk adjustment. (p. 249)

Briefly, the *mean-adjusted return* methodology involves calculating expected
returns as a simple arithmetic average of past observed security returns. This
method assumes that the expected return for a given security i is a constant
$E(R_i) = K_i$ over time but can differ across securities. Thus, the abnormal return
for security i in period $t(_1A_{it})$ is simply

$$_1A_{it} = R_{it} - K_i,$$

where R_{it} is the observed return for security i in period t and K_i is the normal or
expected rate of return estimated by averaging security returns over several periods prior to the event month, t. Cornell (1979) notes that the mean-adjusted return
methodology is consistent with *any* equilibrium theory of asset pricing so long as
the parameters used remain unchanged over the time period under study. However, Brown and Warner provide an even stronger justification for using this model
with their simulation experiment. By randomly selecting 250 samples of securities, each with a randomly assigned event month, and "inducing" an event effect
on security returns, these authors discovered that the simple mean-adjusted return
methodology was as powerful as any other in detecting abnormal performance.

In the *market-adjusted return* method, abnormal return for security i in
period $t(_2A_{it})$ is identified as follows:

$$_2A_{it} = R_{it} - \overline{R}_{mt},$$

where $\overline{R}_{mt}$ is the mean rate of return for all risky assets for period t. Since the
market is a composite of all securities, its beta is one. Note, however, that the expected or normal return on a security may differ systematically from the expected
market return where the security's risk is different from that of the market.

The *market-and-risk-adjusted return* model is actually a whole "class" of
models in which normal or expected returns are estimated. Only two of these
models are discussed here, since they are the forms most used in financial research: the market model and the Fama-MacBeth (1973) model.

The *market model* is used to estimate the abnormal return for the ith security
in period $t(_3A_{it})$ as follows:

$$_3A_{it} = R_{it} - (a_i + b_iR_{mt}),$$

where the normal or expected return is the term in parentheses. The coefficients
of the linear market model contained in parentheses (a_i and b_i) are estimated by
regressing observed rates of return for security i on the corresponding rates of return
for a market index (which serves as a proxy for the market portfolio). This regression utilizes observed returns for a time period prior to the "event period" so as not
to contaminate their estimation with the impact of the event under study. This model
served as the basis for the pioneering event study conducted by Fama, Fisher,
Jensen, and Roll (1969) on the impact of announced stock splits on stock returns.
Further, Brown and Warner found that this simple model was more powerful in

terms of its ability to identify abnormal performance than any of the other, more complex risk-adjusted models available.

The *Fama-MacBeth model* has been widely used in financial research. Here the abnormal return for the ith security in period $t(_4A_{it})$ is estimated as follows:

$$_4A_{it} = R_{it} - (y_0 + y_1b_i),$$

where the term in parentheses is the estimated normal return for the ith security in period t. Normal or expected security returns are predicted according to the cross-sectional relationship estimated using the term in parentheses. The y_0 and y_1 coefficients are estimated by regressing average portfolio returns on average portfolio betas to make them reflect the nature of the equilibrium relationship between risk and return. To summarize, given the beta coefficient (b_i, estimated using the market model) for the ith security, the normal or expected return is calculated using the cross-sectional relationship contained in parentheses. Note, however, that the Brown and Warner study suggested that the extra time and effort required to estimate the Fama-MacBeth abnormal returns does not increase the power of the tests used to identify significant abnormal performance. In fact, the model's added complexity may actually induce error into the test procedure, thereby *reducing* its power.

In a more recent paper, Brown and Warner (1985) performed a similar set of simulation experiments on the use of daily returns in event studies. Their findings there differed only slightly from those in the 1980 study with respect to monthly returns. They found that for daily returns the mean-adjusted return and market-model-adjusted return methodologies were most successful in identifying abnormal performance. Again they observed that using complex adjustments to parameter estimates (such as beta estimates) did not improve the performance of the simpler methodologies.

Evidence: Semistrong-Form Tests

The finance and accounting literature is replete with studies of the reaction of the capital market to the revelation of information. Semistrong-form tests of market efficiency comprise a subset of that literature dealing with information announcements made to the general investing public. One might logically argue that in general information announcements are revealed sequentially such that it is "insider" or restricted-access information before it becomes available to the investing public. Thus, strong- and semistrong-form tests of capital market efficiency differ in terms of the calendar time at which the information "event" is examined rather than of the particular type or source. For example, information concerning a firm's quarterly earnings comprises "insider" or strong-form test information prior to the date on which those earnings are announced to the general public, after which time it becomes semistrong-form test information.

In the following sections, we will summarize the evidence on a number of semistrong-form tests of market efficiency, including announcements of stock splits, earnings announcements, and the listing of a firm's shares on an exchange. We will also discuss certain anomalous evidence regarding capital market efficiency that began appearing in the finance literature following the publication of a special issue of the *Journal of Financial Economics* in June 1978. This evidence relates to the observed seasonality in stock prices (the January effect), the propensity for small firms to outperform large ones (the small-firm effect), the abnormal returns earned by investing in low price/earnings ratio stocks, and the tendency for Monday returns to be negative and Friday returns positive (the weekend effect). In later chapters we will review the results of still more efficient market research related to capital structure (Chapter 13), dividend policy (Chapter 14), and mergers and acquisitions (Chapter 18).

Stock Splits

One of the earliest semistrong-form tests of the efficient market hypothesis was conducted by Fama, Fisher, Jensen, and Roll (1969), hereafter called FFJR, and dealt with stock splits.[7] The study sought to determine the timing and magnitude of the capital market's reaction to a firm's decision to engage in a stock split. Since a split has no economic impact in and of itself, the efficient market hypothesis would suggest that there should be no market reaction to its announcement. However, market folklore suggests that stock splits give rise to an increase in share value. FFJR then sought (1) to determine whether any abnormal price behavior did occur around the split date and (2) to explain a reaction, if observed, in terms of real economic phenomena coinciding with the split date.

The methodology used to identify abnormal returns was based on the market model (where abnormal returns were defined earlier as $_3A_{it}$). For example, defining month 0 as the month in which the split becomes effective, month -1 as one month prior to the split, and $+1$ as one month after, FFJR calculated abnormal returns for each security over the event months -29 through $+30$. They then averaged the abnormal returns across all N securities for each event month m to obtain an average abnormal return:

$$\overline{A}_m = \frac{1}{N} \sum_{j=1}^{N} {_3A_{jm}} .$$

Next, they calculated the cumulative average abnormal return, $\overline{CA}_m$, as follows:

$$\overline{CA}_m = \sum_{k=-29}^{m} \overline{A}_k .$$

We can think of $\overline{A}_m$ as the average deviation of the returns of stocks experiencing splits (in month m) from their normal or expected relationships with the market. In the same vein, $\overline{CA}_m$ constitutes the *cumulative* deviation from month -29 through month m.

FFJR then analyzed the $\overline{CA}_m$ for all stocks experiencing splits and two subcategories comprised of firms whose percentage change in dividends for the split

---

[7]We review the FFJR paper here because it is both easy to understand and was the seminal work using the event study methodology. More recently a number of other researchers have addressed the same problem, most notably Grinblatt, Masulis, and Titman (1984).

year was greater than that of the NYSE as a whole (designated $\overline{CA}_m^+$) and those whose percentage change in dividends was smaller (designated $\overline{CA}_m^-$). Results of the study are reproduced in Figure 10.1. Note first that the abnormal returns (or "residuals," as they are called in Figure 10.1) are uniformly positive over the 29-month period prior to the split date. FFJR explained this phenomenon as a result of firms' splitting during "abnormally" good times. Further, the split announcement occurred within four months of the effective date for 90 percent of the stocks sampled. Noting that the $\overline{CA}_m$ leveled out after the split month for the combined sample of firms and observing that 71.5 percent of the split firms actually experienced larger dividend increases than the NYSE composite, FFJR hypothesized the market interprets a split announcement as a signal that the firm's earnings prospects are good and it can support a higher dividend payment. Thus, the large price increases in the months immediately preceding the split month may reflect the result of an alteration in expectations concerning the firm's future earnings. If this hypothesis is correct, the subsequent revelation of the firm's dividend payout plans should serve to confirm or refute the market's revised expectations. To test this possibility, FFJR analyzed the cumulative abnormal returns for the "dividend increase" and "dividend decrease" firms separately. The results were consistent with the revised dividend expectations hypothesis — that is, firms that experienced an increase in dividends had a modest increase in $\overline{CA}_m$, while those for which no such increase was forthcoming experienced a precipitous decline.

Earnings Announcements

One of the most widely studied sources of semistrong information is the corporate earnings announcement. Yet despite all the energy expended, the issue of whether markets fully impound the information contained in a firm's earnings report by the date of its public announcement remains unsettled. Thus, this area of efficient markets research is one in which anomalous evidence has been uncovered.

Ball and Brown (1968) were among the first to comprehensively study the adjustment of stock prices to earnings announcements. They concluded that no more than 10 to 15 percent of the information contained in the announcements had been unanticipated by the month of the preliminary announcement. May (1971) studied price reactions to interim (such as quarterly) earnings announcements.

More recently a host of researchers have documented what they consider substantial deviations from the efficient market hypothesis that are also associated with earnings announcements. All these studies evaluate the stock market's reaction to the announcement of "unexpected" earnings — that is, they first extrapolate or otherwise predict "expected" earnings. If announced earnings deviate from predicted (expected) earnings by some prespecified margin, a trade is initiated. If the deviation is positive (reflecting "unexpected" good earnings news), the stock is bought; if it is negative, the stock is sold short or purchased and held in a second portfolio whose performance is then compared with that of the "good news" portfolio. These studies unanimously report what they consider abnormally high rates of return where the unexpected earnings announcement selection strategy was followed.

Figure 10.1   FFJR Study of Stock Splits

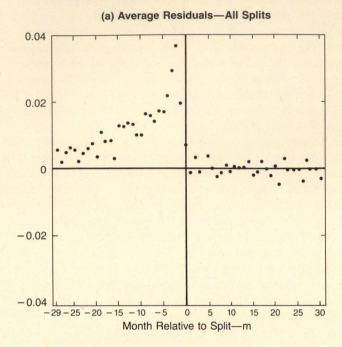

(a) Average Residuals—All Splits

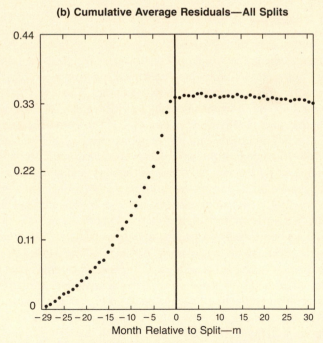

(b) Cumulative Average Residuals—All Splits

Source: E. F. Fama, L. Fisher, M. Jensen, and R. Roll, "The Adjustment of Stock Prices to New Information," *International Economic Review* (February 1969): 1–21.

A series of papers by Latané and others (1977, 1979) used a measure called *standardized unexpected earnings (SUE)* to rank order securities that were then formed into portfolios.[8] They found that portfolios of high SUE stocks outperformed the S&P 500 Stock Index. Jones and Litzenberger (1970) obtained similar results using a slightly different portfolio selection technique. In a very comprehensive study Joy, Litzenberger, and McEnally (1977) found that the market price adjustment to their estimates of unexpected earnings extended up to 26 weeks after the earnings announcement. Finally, Brown (1978) examined daily stock price behavior around the date of an estimated "unexpected" earnings announcement and found a market reaction lasting up to 45 days after that date.

The methodologies used in the "unexpected" earnings studies have varied greatly, ranging from market model abnormal returns ($_3A_{it}$) to performance evaluations with no explicit adjustment for risk. Our objective at this point is not to criticize or confirm these findings but to point out an area of semistrong-form efficient market tests in which the basic thesis has not been supported. One possible explanation for the abnormal returns observed for firms making unexpected earnings is that investors "overreact." This phenomenon has been documented in experimental psychology studies and recently observed in studies of stock market behavior. De Bondt and Thaler (1985) provide evidence that investors indeed overreact to the announcement of "unexpected" news. Specifically, they used the Center for Research in Security Prices (CRSP) monthly return file to construct portfolios of firms that had experienced very poor prior performance (loser portfolios) and portfolios of firms with very good prior performance (winner portfolios). The portfolios were formed in December of each year, contained 35 stocks each, and were held for three years thereafter. The results of this procedure were consistent with the overreaction theory: The loser portfolios outperformed the market by an average of 19.6 percent during the three-year holding period, while the winner portfolios underperformed the market by an average of 5 percent. The overreaction was thus "asymmetrical," with losers receiving a disproportionate overreaction from the market. In addition, the authors observed that most of the abnormal returns earned by the loser portfolios occurred during January (a finding consistent with the January effect discussed in a later section and in "An Institutional Note: Patterns of Stock Price Behavior"). Finally—and somewhat surprisingly—the abnormal returns for the loser portfolios were greater in years 2 and 3 of the holding period than they were in year 1.

Firm Size and Security Performance

Yet another area of research that has provided anomalous results with regard to market efficiency is that of small firms. A number of researchers have observed that small firms earn rates of return that exceed those of larger firms on a risk-ad-

---

[8]The standardized unexpected earnings metric is defined as follows:

$$SUE = (\text{Reported EPS} - \text{Estimated EPS})/(\text{Standard error of the estimate}),$$

where estimated EPS is based on a time series regression of historical earnings and the standard error of the estimate represents the standard error about this time trend.

justed basis. Of course, the fundamental question of how to appropriately risk adjust or value securities also arises here. From this body of research, we now have documentation of the following:

1. A large portion of the "size" effect occurs during the first few days of January and exists in countries other than the United States.

2. The transactions costs associated with trading in small firms are known to be higher than those attendant to trading in large firms, but this alone does not explain the size effect.

3. The magnitude of the size effect varies over time and is related to evidence concerning the "abnormal" returns earned by low P/E ratio stocks.

Banz (1981) used a Fama and MacBeth (1973) type of methodology to document a negative association between the average returns earned by stocks and their market values (on a risk-adjusted basis). Reinganum (1981) further documented the size effect and related it to the P/E effect previously identified by Basu (1977) — that is, stocks with low P/E ratios tend to have higher average risk-adjusted returns than do high P/E stocks. Basu (1983) retested the P/E effect to see if it was indeed a size phenomenon and concluded that although there was a relationship between firm size and P/E ratio, one did not completely coincide with the other. Finally, Keim (1983) analyzed the size and year-end effects and found that about half of the size effect occurs in January, with 25 percent of the total occurring during the first five days (see "An Institutional Note: Patterns of Stock Price Behavior" for further discussion of the January effect).

Two possible explanations for the importance of the year-end effect have been tested. The first is "tax-loss" selling. The argument here is that individuals are subject to income taxation and their portfolios tend to contain smaller capitalization stocks than do tax-exempt institutional investors' (due to the 5 percent ownership rule mutual funds face in order to maintain their tax-free status these funds tend not to invest in smaller firms to the extent that individual investors do). Thus, the tax-loss selling pressure at year's end is greater from small capitalization stocks. However, both Reinganum (1983) and Constantinides (1984) conclude that the January size effect cannot be completely explained by tax-loss selling. The second explanation that has been offered relates to the differential in transactions costs involved in the buying and selling of small-firm shares. Both Stoll and Whaley (1983) and Schultz (1983) studied this possibility. Stoll and Whaley utilized monthly data and concluded that a round-trip transaction in a small firm's stock every three months was sufficient to eliminate the small-firm effect. Schultz examined daily returns to New York and American Stock Exchange stocks for the period 1963 to 1979 and found average round-trip transactions costs for small firms to be 11.4 percent. However, with a one-year holding period his small-firm portfolio earned average risk-adjusted portfolio returns of 31 percent per year net of transactions costs. Thus, he concluded that transactions costs cannot explain the small-firm effect.

Barry and Brown (1984) suggest that firm size simply serves as a proxy for the availability of information on a firm's stock. They hypothesize a model in which the number of years since the security was listed on a major exchange reflects the quantity of firm information available. They conclude that there is an association between period of listing and security returns that cannot be accounted for by firm size and is unaffected by eliminating January return data from their test sample. Keown, Neustel, and Pinkerton (1986) tested the same basic hypothesis but used the number of analysts who follow a stock as the proxy for the quantity of security information available. Their results indicate the existence of both information and size effects in security returns. Thus, the size effect observed in early studies may partially reflect the availability of information, but it does not appear to be subsumed by it.

Listing on a Stock Exchange

Sanger and McConnell (1986) studied the impact on a firm's stock price of choosing to "list" its shares on the New York Stock Exchange (NYSE). They selected the period 1966 to 1977 since it spans the introduction of the National Association of Securities Dealers Automatic Quotation (NASDAQ) communications system in the over-the-counter (OTC) market. In doing so, they were able to assess the stock price behavior about the announcement date (that is, the decision to list) for a pre-NASDAQ and post-NASDAQ sample and thus test for the impact of the NASDAQ system on the market's assessment of the value of a firm's shares listed on an organized exchange. Using an event-time study, they found that significant abnormal returns did occur with the initial announcement of the listing (the abnormal returns around the actual listing date were negative); however, the pre-NASDAQ listing announcements produced significantly larger abnormal returns than did the post-NASDAQ announcements. These results suggest that the advent of NASDAQ has reduced the benefits that investors associate with listing a firm's stock on the NYSE.

Volatility in Stock Prices and Market Efficiency

Shiller (June 1981) began a series of tests for stock market efficiency by comparing the volatility of stock prices implied by the volatility of dividends to observed stock price volatility.

To understand the nature of Shiller's test, consider the following simplified stock valuation model.[9] Define stock price, $P(t)$, as the present value of future expected dividends, $E(Div_k)$; that is,

$$P(t) = \sum_{k=t+1}^{\infty} \frac{E(Div_k)}{(1 + r)^k},$$

where r is the market's required rate of return (discount rate) for the stock. Changes in $P(t)$ over time can result from variations in expected future dividends

---

[9]The description of Shiller's test offered here is greatly simplified but contains the essence of the methodology used. The interested reader is encouraged to read both Shiller (June 1981) and Marsh and Merton (1986).

and/or changes in the discount rate used in valuing them. Shiller focused his tests on the former, treating r as a constant. He then modeled the time series of historical dividends from which expected dividends could be predicted and, consequently, stock prices estimated. Next, he compared the variance in actual stock prices to the variance in the series of estimated prices. The results of his analyses are summarized in the following quotation:

Measures of stock price volatility over the past century appear to be far too high—five to thirteen times too high—to be attributed to new information about future real dividends if uncertainty about future dividends is measured by the sample standard deviation of real dividends around their long-run exponential path (p. 434)

Marsh and Merton (1986) criticize the robustness of Shiller's "variance-bound" test methodology, noting that corporate managers have been observed to "smooth" dividends via their dividend payment policies.[10] This practice lowers the variance in the observed series of dividends and *may* account for dividend movements' inadequacy in accounting for price movements. These authors conclude that while the observed volatility in stock prices does reflect variations in the shares' intrinsic value, managers, through their dividend policies, "smooth" the series of dividend payments such that their volatility does not belie the true volatility of the stock's intrinsic value.

Shiller (1986) has responded to the Marsh and Merton criticism in two ways. First, he notes that what is at issue is whether the Marsh-Merton dividend-smoothing story of corporate dividend policy is "sufficiently compelling that we think that the potential variability of dividends suggested by their model is a better measure of the true variability than is the historically observed variability around a trend" (p. 500). Second, Shiller reminds us that stock price volatility is also a function of changes in the market's discount rate, r. Neither he nor Marsh and Merton attempted to account for changes in r in their tests. Finally, Shiller suggests that "behavioral factors" should be combined with financial theory to further investigate the determinants of stock prices. This debate is sure to rage on for some time to come. Most important, however, Shiller has given us new insight into the notion of market efficiency and yet another set of empirical "tools."

Evidence: Strong-Form Tests

Strong-form tests of the efficient market hypothesis deal with information that is *not* available to the general investing public. Put another way, a strong-form information source would be one to which there is restricted or monopolistic access. Insider information concerning a firm's financial health and future prospects and knowledge about the unfilled limit orders of floor traders on securities exchanges are two examples.

The findings of strong-form tests are consistent with what would be expected. Excess profits *are* available to those possessing monopolistic access to in-

---

[10]We review the empirical studies of corporate dividend payment practices in Chapter 14.

formation. For example, Niederhoffer and Osborne (1966) found that specialists on the NYSE could use their knowledge of unfilled limit orders to generate monopoly (excess) profits. Scholes (1968) studied firms' large block trades in their own stock. He found that the market reaction took up to six days (after which corporate insiders must disclose their trading activities to the Securities and Exchange Commission). Thus, insider knowledge of block trades provides the basis for monopoly profits. Jaffe (1974) studied data on insider trading activity from the SEC's *Official Summary of Security Transactions and Holdings*. He devised a trading scheme based on insiders' actions and found that insiders indeed earned excess profits. As stated earlier, these results agree with our intuition regarding restricted or monopoly access to information. In fact, if monopoly profits could not be earned under these circumstances, one might wonder whether the capital market was responding properly to the revelation of new information.

An Institutional Note: Patterns of Stock Price Behavior

Two persistent patterns of price behavior have been identified and continue to defy adequate explanation:

▪   The *weekend effect* is the tendency for the rate of return between Friday close and Monday opening to be negative.

▪   The *January effect* is supported by empirical evidence that excess returns earned by small firms occur entirely in January and that the risk-return relationship posited by the capital asset pricing model is consistently observed only during January.

The weekend effect has been documented in a number of studies, including Cross (1973), French (1980), Gibbons and Hess (1981), Keim and Stambaugh (1984), and Jaffee and Westerfield (1985). We will review the results of the last study, since it confirms the weekend effect observed by others and also extends the analysis to the United Kingdom, Japan, Canada, and Australia.

Jaffee and Westerfield analyzed the daily returns for common stock indexes for each day of the week and obtained the average percent returns for each day of the week:

	Monday	Tuesday	Wednesday	Thursday	Friday	All Days
United States (1962–1983)	−0.126	0.017	0.107	0.028	0.082	0.023
Japan (1970–1983)*	−0.020	−0.090	0.150	0.026	0.063	0.038
Canada (1976–1983)	−0.139	0.022	0.115	0.106	0.139	0.052
United Kingdom (1950–1983)	−0.142	0.087	0.079	0.046	0.060	0.028
Australia (1973–1983)	−0.052	−0.133	0.037	0.166	0.130	0.032

*Saturday results are not reported here, although they were included in the Jaffe and Westerfield study.

The persistent negative return for Monday and positive return for Friday evidenced a similar weekend effect across all the markets tested. To test for the statistical significance of the weekend effect, the authors estimated the following regression model:

$$r_t = \alpha_1 d_{1t} + \alpha_2 d_{2t} + \ldots + \alpha_6 d_{6t} + u_t, \qquad t = 1, 2, \ldots T$$

where r_t is the daily rate of return for the stock index, $d_{1t} = 1$ if day t is a Monday and 0 otherwise, and the α_j terms represent the model coefficients where j = 1 for Monday. They then tested whether $\alpha_1 = \alpha_2 = \ldots = \alpha_6$ for the Japanese stock index and $\alpha_1 = \alpha_2 = \ldots = \alpha_5$ for all the other exchanges. In all cases they found the coefficients to differ substantially at the 1 percent level of significance. The authors concluded that foreign investors face a weekend effect in their respective stock markets that is similar to but independent of that observed in the United States.

The January effect, or seasonality in common stock returns, has been documented by a large number of researchers, beginning with Rozeff and Kinney (1976), and continues to defy explanation. These studies generally have noted that the rate of return earned during January is both positive and significantly larger than that earned in other months. This effect is particularly prominent for smaller firms, which have been found to yield higher average risk-adjusted returns than large firms. Further, Keim (1983) found that more than 50 percent of the January premium is attributable to large abnormal returns during the first week of trading in the year, particularly on the first trading day.

Representative of the January effect studies is the Tinic and West (1984) paper, which gives the following estimates of the intercept and slope coefficients of the two-parameter Fama-MacBeth (1973) model coefficients for the period January 1935 to June 1982:[a]

Averaged over	Intercept Coefficient	Slope Coefficient
January only	−0.009830	0.044509
(t-statistics)	(1.5380)	(3.3180)
Rest of year	0.005802	0.003574
(t-statistics)	(3.2629)	(1.5582)
All months	0.006138	0.005794
(t-statistics)	(3.5849)	(2.5737)

Thus, it appears that January returns differ not only from the rest of the year's but also is the only month for which there is a systematic, positive relationship between the realized returns on common stocks and their systematic risks.

Rogalski and Tinic (1985) extended the analysis of the January effect to consider seasonal variations in estimates of common stocks' systematic risk and indeed observed seasonal variations. Although this finding may account for some of the abnormal returns associated with January, it fails to explain why systematic risk varies across time in such a predictable way. The authors noted that "financial theory is silent about the causes of systematic (or on average predictable) changes in the risks of common stocks over calendar months" (p. 17).

One possible explanation for the January effect relates to tax-loss sales. The tax law makes it advantageous for individuals to realize short-term losses and long-term gains.[b] However, Constantinides (1984) concludes that tax-loss sales ex-

[a]The Fama-MacBeth estimates of the coefficients of the capital asset pricing model include an intercept term, γ_{0t} (the expected rate of return on the minimum-variance, zero-beta portfolio for period t) and a slope term, γ_{1t} (the market's risk premium).

[b]This phenomenon results from the fact that long-term gains (before the TRA of 1986) were taxed at 40 percent of the short-term gains. Thus, a short-term loss offsets short-term income, which is subject to the full tax rate, whereas long-term losses can be used to offset only long-term gains, which face a maximum tax rate of 40 percent of the investor's marginal tax rate.

plain the January effect only in cases where investors are irrational or ignorant of the price seasonality. Brown, Keim, Kleidon, and Marsh (1983) also investigated the tax-loss selling hypothesis and concluded that it could not fully explain the January effect. They noted that Australia has similar tax laws but a July through June tax year that, according to the tax-loss sale hypothesis, would predict a small-firm July return premium. They found a pronounced December–January and July–August seasonality with a premium for the portfolio of smallest firms of roughly 4 percent per month across all months. This contrasts with the United States evidence, which documents a small-firm premium concentrated in January.

Summary

We defined an efficient market as one in which prices fully reflect available information at all times. This is, of course, an idealistic notion, since information is not disclosed instantly and without cost to all market participants. Thus, for practical purposes, any study of a market's efficiency deals with the *extent* to which available information is reflected in market prices.

Fama (1970) categorized tests of the efficient market hypothesis (EMH) in a manner analogous to the notion of "degrees of efficiency." His three test categories reflect the relative availability of information to the investing public. *Weak form* tests are made to assess whether capital market prices fully reflect the information content of past market prices. *Semistrong-form* tests relate to the full reflection of the content of all publicly available information. *Strong-form* tests deal with the market's reflection of restricted-access information. The EMH literature has found no significant evidence of violation of the EMH with respect to weak-form information; however, it has found that some sources of semistrong-form information are not immediately or fully reflected in market prices. This anomalous evidence is not surprising in view of the time, and hence cost, involved in gathering and processing semistrong- and strong-form information. Thus, even in a well-functioning capital market one would not expect full revelation of information where the cost of obtaining that information exceeded its potential benefits.

Study of the EMH remains an important subset of the finance literature. It has brought financial theorists and practicing financial managers (analysts) closer together than has any other area. This is because violations of the EMH are both an opportunity for profitable arbitrage and evidence that the capital market may not be performing its resource allocation function efficiently.

Study Questions

10.1   "An efficient market is one in which prices fully reflect what is knowable." Explain this statement and briefly comment on its implications.

10.2   Compare operational and allocational efficiency with respect to a market's operations.

10.3 Discuss the following statement: "The only difference between strong-form and semistrong-form information is the calendar time in which the impact of information on security prices is analyzed."

10.4 Describe the use of a Y percent filter in testing for a capital market's weak-form efficiency.

10.5 Brown and Warner (1980) describe four basic models that have been used to assess expected or normal returns. Discuss each.

10.6 Discuss the general implication of the existence of transactions costs on market efficiency.

10.7 What are four potential sources of semistrong-form information? Strong-form information?

References[11]

S. S. Alexander, "Price Movements in Speculative Markets: Trends or Random Walks," *Industrial Management Review* (May 1961): 7–26.

————, "Price Movements in Speculative Markets: Trend or Random Walks, No. 2," in *The Random Character of Stock Market Prices,* Paul Cootner (ed.) (Cambridge, Mass.: M.I.T. Press, 1964): 338–372.

Ray Ball and Philip Brown, "An Empirical Evaluation of Accounting Income Numbers," *Journal of Accounting Research* (Autumn 1968): 160–178.

R. W. Banz, "The Relationship between Return and Market Value of Common Stocks," *Journal of Financial Economics* (March 1981): 3–18.

C. Barry and S. Brown, "Differential Information and the Small Firm Effect," *Journal of Financial Economics* (June 1984): 283–294.

S. Basu, "The Information Content of Price-Earnings Ratios," *Financial Management* (Summer 1975): 53–64.

————, "Investment Performance of Common Stocks in Relation to Their Price-Earnings Ratios: A Test of the Efficient Market Hypothesis," *Journal of Finance* (June 1977): 663–682.

————, "The Relationship between Earnings' Yield, Market Value and the Return for NYSE Common Stocks: Further Evidence," *Journal of Financial Economics* 12 (June 1983): 129–156.

M. E. Blume and R. F. Stambaugh, "Biases in Computed Returns: An Application to the Size Effect," *Journal of Financial Economics* (November 1983): 387–404.

P. Brown, D. Keim, A. Kleidon, and T. Marsh, "Stock Return Seasonalities and the Tax-Loss Selling Hypothesis," *Journal of Financial Economics* (June 1983): 105–127.

Stephen J. Brown and Jerold B. Warner, "Measuring Security Price Performance," *Journal of Financial Economics* (September 1980): 205–258.

————, "Using Daily Stock Returns in Event Studies," *Journal of Financial Economics* (March 1985): 3–31.

Stewart Brown, "Earnings Changes, Stock Prices, and Market Efficiency," *Journal of Finance* (March 1978): 17–28.

N. Chen and D. Hsieh, "An Exploratory Investigation of the Firm Size Effect," *Journal of Financial Economics* (September 1985): 451–471.

---

[11]The literature on the efficient market hypothesis is far too voluminous to fully enumerate. Therefore, only a limited bibliography of seminal works is listed.

G. M. Constantinides, "Optimal Trading with Personal Taxes: Implications for Prices and the Abnormal January Returns," *Journal of Financial Economics* (March 1984): 65–89.

Paul Cootner (ed.), *The Random Character of Stock Market Prices* (Cambridge, Mass.: M.I.T. Press, 1964).

Bradford Cornell, "Asymmetric Information and Portfolio Performance Measurement," *Journal of Financial Economics* (December 1979): 381–390.

F. Cross, "The Behavior of Stock Prices on Fridays and Mondays," *Financial Analysts Journal* (November/December 1973): 67–69.

Werner De Bondt and R. Thaler, "Does the Stock Market Overreact?" *Journal of Finance* (July 1985): 793–808.

E. F. Fama, "The Behavior of Stock Market Prices," *Journal of Business* 38 (1965): 34–105.

———, *Foundations of Finance* (New York: Basic Books, 1976).

——— and M. Blume, "Filter Rules and Stock Market Trading," *Journal of Business* (January 1966): 226–241.

———, L. Fisher, M. Jensen, and R. Roll, "The Adjustment of Stock Prices to New Information," *International Economic Review* (February 1969): 1–21.

———, "Efficient Capital Markets: A Review of Theory and Empirical Work," *Journal of Finance* (May 1970): 383–417.

——— and James D. MacBeth, "Risk, Return and Equilibrium," *Journal of Political Economics* (May/June 1973): 607–636.

D. W. French, "The Weekend Effect on the Distribution of Stock Prices: Implications for Option Pricing," *Journal of Financial Economics* (December 1984): 547–559.

K. R. French, "Stock Returns and the Weekend Effect," *Journal of Financial Economics* (March 1980): 55–69.

M. Gibbons and P. Hess, "Day of the Week Effects and Asset Returns," *Journal of Business* (October 1981): 579–596.

C. W. J. Granger and O. Morgenstern, *Predictability of Stock Market Prices* (Lexington, Mass.: Heath Lexington Books, 1970).

M. Grinblatt, R. Masulis, and S. Titman, "The Valuation Effects of Stock Splits and Stock Dividends," *Journal of Financial Economics* 13 (1984): 461–490.

J. Jaffe, "The Effect of Regulation Changes on Insider Trading," *Bell Journal of Economics and Management Science* (Spring 1974): 93–121.

J. Jaffe and R. Westerfield, "The Week-End Effect in Common Stock Returns: The International Evidence," *Journal of Finance* (June 1985): 433–454.

Michael Jensen, "The Performance of Mutual Funds in the Period 1945–64," *Journal of Finance* (May 1968): 389–416.

———, "Risk, the Pricing of Capital Assets, and the Evaluation of Investment Portfolios," *Journal of Business* (April 1969): 167–185.

C. P. Jones and R. H. Litzenberger, "Quarterly Earnings Reports and Intermediate Stock Price Trends," *Journal of Finance* (March 1970): 143–148.

Maurice Joy, Robert Litzenberger, and Richard McEnally, "The Adjustment of Stock Prices to Announcements of Unanticipated Changes in Quarterly Earnings," *Journal of Accounting Research* (Autumn 1977): 207–224.

D. B. Keim, "Dividend Yields and the January Effect," *Journal of Portfolio Management* (Winter 1986): 54–59.

———, "Dividend Yields and Stock Returns: Implications of Abnormal January Returns," *Journal of Financial Economics* 14 (1983): 473–489.

———, "Size Related Anomalies and Stock Return Seasonality: Further Empirical Evidence," *Journal of Financial Economics* 12 (June 1983): 13–32.

——— and R. Stambaugh, "A Further Investigation of the Weekend Effect in Stock Returns," *Journal of Finance* (July 1984): 819–835.

A. Keown, A. Neustel, and J. Pinkerton, "Differential Information and the Small Firm Effect" (Working paper, Virginia Polytechnic Institute and State University, 1986).

J. M. Keynes, *The General Theory of Employment, Interest and Money* (New York: Harcourt, Brace, 1936).

J. Lakonishok and M. Levi, "Weekend Effects on Stock Returns: A Note," *Journal of Finance* (June 1982): 883–889.

H. A. Latané and C. P. Jones, "Standardized Unexpected Earnings—A Progress Report," *Journal of Finance* (December 1977): 1457–1467.

———, "Standardized Unexpected Earnings—1971–1977," *Journal of Finance* (June 1979): 717–724.

Terry A. Marsh and Robert C. Merton, "Dividend Variability and Variance Bounds Tests for the Rationality of Stock Market Prices," *American Economic Review* (June 1986): 483–498.

Robert May, "The Influence of Quarterly Earnings Announcements on Investor Decisions as Reflected in Common Stock Prices," Supplement to *Journal of Accounting Research* (1971).

Victor Niederhoffer and M. F. M. Osborne, "Market Making and Reversal on the Stock Exchange," *Journal of the American Statistical Association* (December 1966): 897–917.

M. R. Reinganum, "The Anomalous Stock Market Behavior of Small Firms in January: Empirical Tests for Tax-Loss Effects," *Journal of Financial Economics* 12 (1983): 89–104.

———, "Misspecification of Capital Asset Pricing: Empirical Anomalies Based on Earnings Yields and Market Values," *Journal of Financial Economics* 9 (March 1981): 19–46.

R. J. Rendleman, Jr., C. P. Jones, and H. A. Latané, "Empirical Anomalies Based on Unexpected Earnings and the Importance of Risk Adjustments," *Journal of Financial Economics* (November 1982): 269–287.

Harry V. Roberts, "Stock Market 'Patterns' and Financial Analysis: Methodological Suggestions," *Journal of Finance* (March 1959): 1–10.

R. Rogalski and S. Tinic, "The January Size Effect: Anomaly or Risk Measurement?" (Working paper, Amos Tuck School, Dartmouth College, March 1985).

Richard Roll, *The Behavior of Interest Rates: An Application of the Efficient Market Model to U.S. Treasury Bills* (New York: Basic Books, 1970).

M. Rozeff and W. Kinney, Jr., "Capital Market Seasonality: The Case of Stock Returns," *Journal of Financial Economics* (October 1976): 379–402.

Paul A. Samuelson, "Proof that Properly Anticipated Prices Fluctuate Randomly," *Industrial Management Review* (Spring 1965): 41–49.

G. Sanger and J. McConnell, "Stock Exchange Listings, Firm Value, and Security Market Efficiency: The Impact of NASDAQ," *Journal of Financial and Quantitative Analysis* (March 1986): 1–25.

Myron Scholes, "A Test of the Competitive Market Hypothesis: the Market for New Issues and Secondary Offerings" (Unpublished Ph.D. Thesis, Graduate School of Business, University of Chicago, 1968).

P. Schultz, "Transaction Costs and the Small Firm Effects: A Comment," *Journal of Financial Economics* (June 1983): 81–88.

W. F. Sharpe, "Mutual Fund Performance," *Journal of Business* 39 (Special Supplement, January 1966): 119–138.

Robert J. Shiller, "Do Stock Prices Move Too Much to Be Justified by Subsequent Changes in Dividends?" *American Economic Review* (June 1981): 421–436.

———, "The Marsh-Merton Model of Managers' Smoothing of Dividends," *American Economic Review* (June 1986): 499–503.

———, "The Use of Volatility Measures in Assessing Market Efficiency," *Journal of Finance* (May 1981): 291–301.

H. R. Stoll and R. E. Whaley, "Transaction Costs and the Small Firm Effects," *Journal of Financial Economics* (June 1983): 57–79.

S. Tinic and R. West, "Risk and Return: January vs. the Rest of the Year," *Journal of Financial Economics* (December 1984): 561–574.

L. Ying, W. Lewellen, G. Schlarbaum, and R. Lease, "Stock Exchange Listings and Securities Returns," *Journal of Financial and Quantitative Analysis* (September 1977): 415–432.

IV

Corporate Financial Policy: Applications and Evidence

Having been exposed to the major theories of finance, we are now ready to embark on their application to corporate financial decisionmaking. A key point to be made at the outset is that the existing body of financial theory is *not* sufficiently rich to encompass every aspect of financial practice. We will frequently have to extend the implications of a theoretical result beyond its known boundaries and offer ad hoc solutions to problems for which no generally accepted theory exists. Therefore, in Part IV we focus on the real-world problems of financial management and draw on the available financial theory for their solutions. In some cases, we will be able to use well-developed and widely accepted theories; in others, we will be limited to esoteric theories for which there is little or no empirical verification.

The fundamental issues addressed in Part IV include the following: the capital budgeting decision under conditions of uncertainty (Chapter 11); the firm's financing decision (Chapters 12 and 13); the dividend policy problem (Chapter 14); option pricing theory and applications (Chapters 15 and 16); futures markets (Chapter 17); mergers and acquisitions (Chapter 18); the lease-versus-purchase problem (Chapter 19); and international finance (Chapters 20 and 21).

Chapter 11

Capital Budgeting under Uncertainty

In this chapter we discuss the problem of evaluating capital investment opportunities whose returns are not known with certainty. Although this extends our analysis of capital budgeting in Part II in an important dimension, the basic net present value and internal rate of return rules will continue to be useful.

Our discussion of the capital budgeting problem under uncertainty[1] is separated into five major topics. First, we present the theory underlying the use of the capital asset pricing model (CAPM) for analyzing the capital budgeting decision. Here we discover that the decision to acquire a new asset is, in theory, the same as the individual's decision to diversify a portfolio by incorporating that asset; thus, this theory is actually one of diversification. Next, we address the practical issues involved in using the CAPM to analyze capital budgeting proposals. Here we consider the problems associated with estimating the parameters of the CAPM, including project beta, β_1; the risk-free rate, r_F; and the market risk premium,

---

[1]Some authors (such as Knight [1937]) distinguish between the concepts of risk and uncertainty. Such a distinction involves defining decisionmaking under risk as the situation in which future outcomes are unknown but all possible outcomes and their associated probabilities of occurrence can be identified. This is the circumstance under which much of the finance literature on capital budgeting has been developed and the case that we will consider here. Uncertainty is said to exist when the future is unknown and the decisionmaker is unable to identify all possible future outcomes and/or their associated probabilities. The tools available for analyzing decisionmaking under this notion of uncertainty include the max-min rule, the min-min rule, and a host of other criteria developed in the field of decision theory (see Pratt, Raiffer, and Schlaifer [1965] for a review of this literature). In this chapter, however, we will use the terms "risk" and "uncertainty" interchangeably.

$u_M - r_F$, where u_M is the expected rate of return on the market portfolio. We then discuss the theoretical problems encountered in attempting to extend the CAPM to a multiperiod setting. Here we find that the thorny issues that arise in solving the multiperiod valuation problem provide some important restrictions on the CAPM's applicability to the evaluation of multiperiod capital expenditure opportunities. Next, we examine an alternative to the CAPM that utilizes an arbitrage type of argument to evaluate capital budgeting projects under uncertainty. Finally, we discuss the implicit risk adjustment assumption that characterizes the risk-adjusted discount rate method. Here we discover the bias that can result when using the risk-adjusted discount rate version of the net present value model to evaluate projects whose risk does *not* increase over time.

Using the CAPM to Evaluate Investment Opportunities: The Theory

This section introduces the fundamental logic underlying the use of the CAPM in analyzing capital investment opportunities. Our discussion will differ from more traditional ones in that we will analyze the decision of a firm (or individual) to expand its (his or her) portfolio of risky assets to include a new asset that, by definition, is not traded or held in anyone's portfolio. Traditional discussions presume that the new asset already exists and is valued in the market.[2] The problem with this assumption is that under conditions of market equilibrium the new asset will be appropriately valued and, as such, offer the acquiring firm a zero net present value. In our analysis, we pose the problem such that the new asset exists only in the "mind" of the firm undergoing the capital budgeting analysis. We will show that the criteria for a wealth-maximizing capital budgeting decision involves comparing the project's expected rate of return, u_I, with its risk-adjusted required rate of return, $r_F + \beta_I(u_M - r_F)$. Specifically, a project should be accepted if it satisfies the following:

$$u_I > r_F + \beta_I(u_M - r_F) . \qquad \textbf{IRR Criteria}$$

We recognize this as the uncertainty counterpart of the internal rate of return criteria discussed earlier under conditions of certainty. The only observed difference is that the "expected" rate of return is used in place of the known project rate of return and the opportunity cost of investing in the risky project is not the risk-free rate but the sum of the risk-free rate and a risk premium, $\beta_I(u_M - r_F)$, which is a function of the project's beta or systematic risk, the expected return on the market portfolio, u_M, and the risk-free rate, r_F. Alternatively, by making appropriate substitutions for the cash flow determinants of the project's expected rate of return, we can develop a net present value rule based on the CAPM—that is, accept a project where

---

[2]For example, see Rubinstein (1973).

$$\text{NPV}_I = \frac{u_Z}{1 + r_F + \beta_I(u_M - r_F)} - I > 0\,, \qquad \textbf{NPV Criteria}$$

where u_Z is the expected end-of-period cash flow generated by the project and I is the initial investment outlay. The NPV criteria can also be stated using the "certainty equivalent" formulation of the CAPM discussed in Chapter 9, that is,

$$\text{NPV}_I = \frac{u_Z - \lambda\,\text{Cov}(Z, R_M)}{1 + r_F} - I > 0\,,$$

where λ is the market price of risk, or $(u_M - r_F)/\sigma_M^2$, Z is the project's cash flow, and σ_M^2 is the variance in the market return.

We now turn to the theoretical underpinnings of both the internal rate of return and net present value models under uncertainty. We also discuss the role of financial and operating leverage in determining a project's systematic risk, which in turn determines the project's required rate of return or *hurdle rate*. (Note: The first two subsections develop the CAPM criteria for capital budgeting analyses summarized above. Those already familiar with these results can skip to the "Financial Leverage and Project NPV" section without loss of continuity.)

The Capital Budgeting Problem

Suppose that a firm is considering a capital investment project that costs I dollars now and will earn a random cash flow of Z dollars one period hence. For simplicity, assume that if the project is accepted, it will be all equity financed (later we will drop this restriction). The face value of the new stock issue needed to finance the project's undertaking is therefore I dollars. It follows that the random rate of return earned by the project is

$$R_I = \frac{Z}{I} - 1\,.$$

Note that R_I is the rate of return earned on investing in the project *based on its cost* to the firm of I dollars. Thus, this rate of return is *not* the equilibrium market rate of return that could be earned by investing in the project *after* it has been undertaken and the ownership shares appropriately valued in the market. The latter is based on the equilibrium value of the project's equity (V) such that the "equilibrium" rate of return can be defined as $(Z/V) - 1$.

The firm's decision to accept or reject the project will depend on its ability to sell the shares needed to raise the I dollars to finance it. This, in turn, will depend on investors' willingness to buy those shares. Thus, the acceptability of the proposed investment project will depend on *investors' willingness to diversify their personal investment portfolios to hold a portion of the equity in the project*. We will show that the investors' criteria for determining whether to diversify and invest in the project's equity produces the net present value decision rule.

The Individual's Portfolio Diversification Decision

As we noted earlier, the acceptability of a new investment depends solely on investors' willingness to diversify their personal portfolios to include some positive investment in the project. In CAPM equilibrium, these portfolios lie along the capital market line and consist of riskless debt (earning a rate r_F) and the (pre-project acceptance) market portfolio of all risky assets (earning a random rate of return R_M). Thus, with an initial wealth w, the investor's end-of-period income (Y), *including* the new investment (I), can be defined as follows:

(11.1) $Y = x_F w(1 + r_F) + x_M w(1 + R_M) + x_I w(1 + R_I)$,

where x_F is the proportion of the investor's wealth held in risk-free debt, x_M is the proportion invested in the market portfolio of risky assets (which does not contain the proposed investment, for it has not yet been undertaken nor have shares been issued to finance it), and x_I is the proportion invested in the proposed investment. Noting that $x_F = [1 - (x_M + x_I)]$ since $[x_F + x_M + x_I] = 1$, we can rewrite Equation 11.1 as follows:

$$Y = w(1 + r_F) + x_M w(R_M - r_F) + x_I w(R_I - r_F).$$

It bears repeating that the market portfolio of risky assets does *not* contain project I because the decision to undertake the investment has not yet been made. Now the investor's expected end-of-period income (u_Y) can be written as follows:

(11.1a) $u_Y = w(1 + r_F) + x_M w(u_M - r_F) + x_I w(u_I - r_F)$,

where $u_M = E(R_M)$ and $u_I = E(R_I)$. The variance in the investor's income is given by

(11.2) $\sigma_Y^2 = w^2(x_M^2 \sigma_{MM} + 2x_M x_I \sigma_{IM} + x_I^2 \sigma_{II})$,

where $\sigma_{II} = Var(R_I)$, $\sigma_{MM} = Var(R_M)$, and $\sigma_{IM} = Cov(R_I, R_M)$.

Our decision rule for capital budgeting is a straightforward extension of the mean-variance dominance criterion; that is, the investor will want to diversify his or her portfolio of risky assets to invest in the project — select $x_I > 0$ — if the investment will decrease the variance of portfolio income without decreasing mean portfolio income. Alternatively, the investor will select $x_I > 0$ if by doing so he or she can increase mean portfolio income without increasing the variance in that income.

We can illustrate these conditions for project acceptance (namely diversification) graphically using the concepts of the iso-mean line and iso-variance ellipse shown in Figure 11.1. The *iso-mean line* is that set of portfolios comprised of project I and the market portfolio, that is, the pairs (x_I, x_M), for which mean portfolio income is a constant. For example, if we let w = $100, $r_F = 0.05$, $u_M = 0.10$, and $u_I = 0.20$, the iso-mean line for $u_Y = \$110$ will appear as in panel a of Figure 11.1. By setting $x_I = 0.0$ and $x_M = 1.0$ and solving for u_Y using Equation 11.1a, we get

$$u_Y = \$100(1 + 0.05) + 1.0(\$100)(0.10 - 0.05)$$

$$+ 0.0(\$100)(0.20 - 0.05) = \$110.$$

**Figure 11.1   Iso-Mean and Iso-Variance Curves
and the Investor's Decision to Diversify**

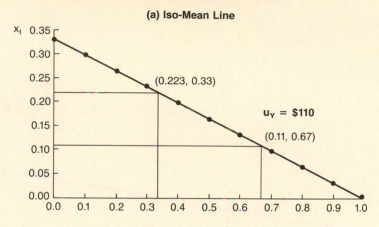

(a) Iso-Mean Line

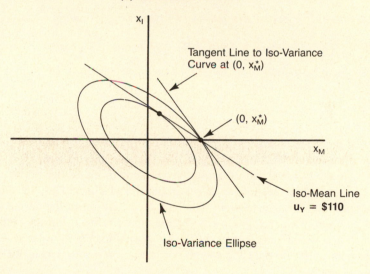

(b) Iso-Variance Curve

Further, the pairs (x_I, x_M) equal to $(0.11, 0.67)$ and $(0.223, 0.33)$ also yield an expected portfolio income equal to $110 and, consequently, lie on the same iso-mean line. Note that before any investment has been made in the project, the investor is at a position $(0, x_M^*)$ such that $x_I = 0$ and $x_M = x_M^*$ (since shares have not been issued to finance the project, the investor obviously holds none in the portfolio).

The equation for the iso-mean line is defined by setting the differential of Equation 11.1a equal to zero:

$$du_Y = \left(\frac{\partial Y}{\partial x_M}\right) dx_M + \left(\frac{\partial Y}{\partial x_I}\right) dx_I .$$

Substituting for the partial derivatives, we obtain

$$du_Y = [w(u_M - r_F)]\,dx_M + [w(u_I - r_F)]\,dx_I = 0,$$

where u_I and u_M are invariant with respect to x_I and x_M such that the slope of the iso-mean line, dx_I/dx_M, is a constant equal to

$$\frac{dx_I}{dx_M} = -\frac{u_M - r_F}{u_I - r_F}.$$

This slope expresses the rate at which the investor must exchange asset I for M to maintain the same mean portfolio income. For the example used in panel a of Figure 11.1, the slope of the iso-mean line equals $-[(0.10 - 0.05)/(0.20 - 0.05)] = -0.33$.

The *iso-variance curve* represents all the pairs (x_I, x_M) for which the variance in portfolio income equals a constant — that is, setting the differential of Equation 11.2 equal to zero,

$$d\sigma_Y^2 = \left(\frac{\partial \sigma_Y^2}{\partial x_M}\right) dx_M + \left(\frac{\partial \sigma_Y^2}{\partial x_I}\right) dx_I = 0.$$

Substituting for the partial derivatives, we obtain the following:

$$d\sigma_Y^2 = (2x_M\sigma_{MM} + 2x_I\sigma_{IM})\,dx_M + (2x_M\sigma_{IM} + 2x_I\sigma_{II})\,dx_I = 0.$$

Correspondingly, the slope of the iso-variance curve is given by

$$\frac{dx_I}{dx_M} = -\frac{x_M\sigma_{MM} + x_I\sigma_{IM}}{x_M\sigma_{IM} + x_I\sigma_{II}}.$$

Note that the slope of the iso-variance curve at the investor's initial or pre-project investment position (that is, $(x_I, x_M) = (0, x_M^*)$) is simply σ_{MM}/σ_{IM}.

Now the investor can decrease the variance in his or her portfolio income without changing its mean if, as shown in panel b of Figure 11.1, the slope of the iso-variance curve is greater than the slope of the iso-mean line at the investor's initial position of $(x_I, x_M) = (0, x_M^*)$. Stated analytically, using the slopes of the iso-mean and iso-variance curves at $(0, x_M^*)$, diversification in order to include the new project in the investor's personal portfolio is *desirable* where the following inequality holds:

(11.3) $$\frac{\sigma_{MM}}{\sigma_{IM}} > \frac{u_M - r_F}{u_I - r_F}.$$

We can restate Equation 11.3 in more familiar terms by letting $\beta_I = \sigma_{IM}/\sigma_{MM}$. Substituting the project's beta (β_I) into 11.3, we obtain a "CAPM-like" rule of project acceptance: Accept the investment if

(11.4) $$u_I > r_F + \beta_I(u_M - r_F).$$

Recall that this is the internal rate of return (IRR) rule for capital budgeting. In this instance the IRR rule can be used because the project has a *fixed* investment amount (I) such that the capital widening problem (see Chapter 5) is not an issue here. Note that project I is *not* included in the market portfolio; hence, the right-hand side of Equation 11.4 is not, strictly speaking, the CAPM.

The accept/reject region using Equation 11.4 graphically is depicted in Figure 11.2. The shaded area is the acceptance region. Thus, any project with a pair (β_I, u_I) in the shaded region will be acceptable by all investors. Hence the firm's manager will find that his or her decisions are unanimously supported by all stockholders if the following decision is used:

Accept the project if Equation 11.4 is satisfied; otherwise reject.

Recall again that the right-hand side of Equation 11.4 is *almost* the security market line or CAPM, the only difference being that the market portfolio, by design, does not include the investment project being analyzed.

Project Net Present Value

Next we relate the decision criterion in Equation 11.4 to project net present value. Recall that the random rate of return earned on the investment can be defined as

$$R_I = \left(\frac{Z}{I}\right) - 1,$$

where Z is the end-of-period cash flow the project provides and I is its initial cost. Thus, the expected rate of return on the project, u_I, equals

$$u_I = \frac{u_Z}{I} - 1,$$

where $u_Z = E[Z]$. Substituting into 11.4 yields

$$\frac{u_Z}{I} > 1 + r_F + \beta_I(u_M - r_F)$$

Figure 11.2   Accept/Reject Region

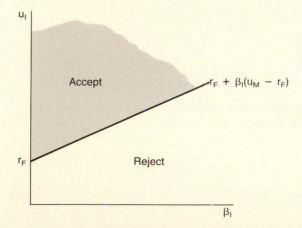

or, equivalently,

$$I < \frac{u_Z}{1 + r_F + \beta_I(u_M - r_F)}.$$

This says that if the investment expenditure is less than the present value of the project's expected earnings (when discounted at the risk-adjusted rate), the project should be accepted; that is, the project is acceptable where its net present value is positive:

(11.5) $$NPV = \frac{u_Z}{1 + r_F + \beta_I(u_M - r_F)} - I > 0.$$

To summarize, we have developed the NPV project evaluation criteria from a very simple proposition about investor behavior: An investor will want to diversify so as to include the new project in his or her portfolio only where it will reduce portfolio risk while leaving portfolio expected return unchanged. From this basic notion concerning investor portfolio preferences, we were able to develop an NPV model that utilizes a "CAPM-like" model to evaluate the proper required rate of return.

Exercise 11.1:   Evaluating a Proposed Investment

The Jetsum Manufacturing Company is currently contemplating the acquisition of a silver-plating business. A $2 million investment will be required if the project is undertaken, and the investment is expected to produce a $2.4 million cash flow in one year. Jetsum has estimated the project's beta (its asset beta) at 0.8, and the present risk-free rate is 8 percent. If the market risk premium ($u_M - r_F$) is estimated at 8.7 percent, what is the project's net present value?

Solution.   The project's required rate of return can be estimated using the right-hand side of Equation 11.4 as follows:

$$r_F + \beta_I(u_M - r_F),$$

or

$$0.08 + 0.8(0.087) = 0.1496, \text{ or } 14.96\%.$$

Using this required rate of return, we can calculate the project's NPV using Equation 11.5 as follows:

$$NPV = \frac{\$2.4M}{1.1496} - \$2M = \$88,000.$$

Since the project is expected to produce a positive NPV of $88,000, it is acceptable and should be undertaken.

Financial Leverage and Project NPV

We now turn to the use of the CAPM to evaluate the cost of capital for a project. In our initial treatment of the problem, we will assume that all debt is riskless (that is, borrowing and lending take place at the risk-free interest rate and there are no taxes. For an unlevered project the CAPM yields the cost of capital directly, as shown on the right-hand side of Equation 11.4. There the *hurdle rate*, or cost of capital, was equal to

$$r_F + \beta_I(u_M - r_F),$$

and the project's riskiness was reflected in its beta coefficient (β_I). This beta coefficient is sometimes referred to as the *asset beta*, since it reflects only the systematic risk attendant to the asset's cash flow and does not specifically reflect the use of financial leverage.

When an investment is partially financed by borrowed funds — that is, levered — we find its cost of capital in exactly the same way (namely using the right-hand side of Equation 11.4). This reflects the fact that in the context of the CAPM with no taxes, project value is not affected by the mix of debt and equity used in its financing.

In the absence of taxes, the capital budgeting criterion derived in Equation 11.4 can be reformulated in a completely equivalent form based on the required rate of return on the equity invested in the project (of course, where project is all equity financed, the two criteria are obviously the same). Recall that in order for a project to be accepted, its expected rate of return (u_I) must satisfy the following:

$$u_I > r_F + \beta_I(u_M - r_F).$$

Before we restate 11.4 in terms of the required rate of return on the project's equity financing, u_S, we must define that return as follows:

$$u_S = \frac{\overbrace{(1 + u_I)I}^{\substack{\text{Project} \\ \text{cash flow}}} - \overbrace{(1 + r_F)D}^{\substack{\text{Interest and} \\ \text{principal}}}}{S} - 1,$$

where D represents debt financing and S equity financing such that $S + D = I$. Solving for the expected rate of return on the entire project, we obtain

$$u_I = u_S\left(\frac{S}{I}\right) + r_F\left(\frac{D}{I}\right).$$

Thus, the expected rate of return earned from investing in a risky project can be thought of as a composite or *weighted average* of the expected rate of return on investing in a portfolio consisting of a proportion equal to (S/I) invested in the equity of the project earning an expected rate of return u_S and a fraction (D/I) in the risk-free asset (recall that the firm is assumed to borrow at the risk-free rate).

Further, recall that the "asset beta" for a project was defined earlier as follows:

$$\beta_I = \frac{Cov(R_I, R_M)}{\sigma_{MM}},$$

where $R_I = (Z/I) - 1$, R_M is the rate of return on the market portfolio of all risky assets, and σ_{MM} is the variance in the market return. The rate of return on the total project investment (R_I) can also be written as a weighted average of the required return on the equity invested in the project and the risk-free borrowing/lending rate; that is,

$$R_I = R_S\left(\frac{S}{I}\right) + r_F\left(\frac{D}{I}\right).$$

Substituting this definition of R_I into β_I where debt is riskless (that is, $Cov(r_F, R_M) = 0$) produces the following relationship between the project's asset beta and the beta for its equity (β_S):

$$\beta_I = \left(\frac{S}{I}\right)\beta_S,$$

where $\beta_S = Cov(R_S, R_M)/\sigma_{MM}$. Finally, substituting for both u_I and β_I in Equation 11.4 we can define the project acceptance criterion in terms of the *equity invested in the project:*

(11.6) $u_S > r_F + \beta_S(u_M - r_F).$

Note that this project acceptance criterion is completely consistent with the earlier acceptance criterion found in Equation 11.4, which was based on the total project return (u_I).[3] Note too that when we developed the criterion based on u_I, we did so for an *all-equity-financed* project. However, the use of debt financing (where there are no taxes) does not impact on the project's acceptability, as we have shown here.[4]

Operating Leverage and Systematic Risk

Operating leverage occurs when a firm incurs fixed operating expenses, in the same way that financial leverage results from a firm's use of financing sources

---

[3]To illustrate the equivalence of the "asset" and "equity" versions of the CAPM project acceptance criteria, note that the asset acceptance criterion can be written as follows:

$$u_I = u_S\left(\frac{S}{I}\right) + r_F\left(\frac{D}{I}\right) > r_F + \beta_S\left(\frac{S}{I}\right)(u_M - r_F).$$

Solving for u_S, we obtain the equity CAPM criterion found in Equation 11.4.

[4]Recall that we have assumed there are no corporate or personal taxes. When we incorporate consideration for taxes and the tax deductibility of interest expense, this "financial policy irrelevance" result will no longer hold. We return to the discussion of this issue later in the chapter when we analyze an example that requires estimating the cost of capital for a project using the CAPM and again in Chapter 12 where we discuss the cost of capital and the theory of the firm's capital structure in detail.

that require the payment of fixed finance charges. In this section we demonstrate the impact of a firm's use of operating leverage on firm value and its beta coefficient.[5] We will find that, other things equal, an increase in the use of operating leverage results in an increase in the systematic risk of the firm as a whole and the corresponding systematic risk of its equity.

Decisions that increase fixed operating expenses while reducing variable operating expenses serve to increase a firm's operating leverage, other things equal. Recall from elementary accounting or basic financial management courses that an increase in operating leverage has two important effects on the firm's operating performance. First, the increase in fixed cost will lead to an increase in the firm's breakeven level of operations. Second, the corresponding reduction in variable cost per unit of output may lead to an increase in the volatility of the firm's operating earnings.

Impact of Operating Leverage on Firm Value.   To illustrate the impact of a firm's use of operating leverage on its value and systematic risk, we will compare the firm values and beta coefficients of two alternative "cost structures." The first cost entails no fixed costs but variable costs equal to VC; the second involves the incurrence of fixed costs F* and variable costs of VC* = δVC, where δ is a positive constant less than 1. Thus, in cost structure 2 the firm utilizes operating leverage, since it incurs some fixed operating expenses (F*) in return for a reduction in its variable costs, while in cost structure 1 it has no operating leverage. Using this terminology, the firm's end-of-period rate of return for each cost structure can be summarized as follows:

<table>
<tr><td align="center">Cost Structure 1</td><td align="center">Cost Structure 2</td></tr>
</table>

$$R = \frac{Rev - VC}{V} - 1 \qquad R^* = \frac{Rev - \delta VC - F^*}{V^*} - 1$$

where R is the firm's rate of return based on its net end-of-period profit under cost structure 1, R^* is the corresponding figure for cost structure 2, V and V^* are the values of the firm under cost structures 1 and 2, respectively, and Rev is the end-of-period total revenue the firm generates under either cost structure.

The values of the firm under the two cost structures can be written as follows:[6]

$$V = \frac{E[Rev] - E[VC] - \lambda Cov(Rev - VC, R_M)}{1 + r_F}$$

and

$$V^* = \frac{E[Rev] - \delta E[VC] - F^* - \lambda Cov(Rev - \delta VC, R_M)}{1 + r_F},$$

---

where $\lambda = (E[R_M] - r_F)/\sigma_{MM}$, or the market price of risk. Comparing V with V*, we see that V* can be rewritten as a function of V as follows:

$$V^* = V + \frac{(1 - \delta)E[VC] - F^* - (1 - \delta)\lambda Cov(VC, R_M)}{1 + r_F}$$

or

$$V^* = V - \underbrace{\frac{F^*}{1 + r_F}}_{\text{Value of F}} + \underbrace{\frac{(1 - \delta)\{E[VC] - \lambda Cov(VC, R_M)\}}{1 + r_F}}_{\text{Value of reduction in VC}}.$$

Hence, in commonsense terms, the use of operating leverage will increase the firm's value (that is, $V^* > V$) only when the cash equivalent of the reduction in variable costs exceeds the present value of the added fixed costs. The impact of operating leverage on firm value can be either positive or negative depending on the reduction in variable costs (the size of δ) corresponding to the incurrence of the fixed costs (F^*).

Impact of Operating Leverage on Beta.   We can also investigate the impact of using operating leverage on the firm's systematic risk. Recall that the definition of project or firm beta can be written as follows:

$$\beta = \frac{Cov(R, R_M)}{\sigma_{MM}},$$

where σ_{MM} is the variance in the market return. Substituting the two expressions for R defined earlier (for cost structures 1 and 2) into the above equation, we obtain the following:[7]

$$\beta = \left(\frac{1}{V}\right)\left[\underbrace{\frac{Cov(Rev, R_M)}{\sigma_{MM}}}_{\text{Revenue beta}} - \underbrace{\frac{Cov(VC, R_M)}{\sigma_{MM}}}_{\text{VC beta}}\right]$$

and

$$\beta^* = \left(\frac{1}{V^*}\right)\left[\frac{Cov(Rev, R_M)}{\sigma_{MM}} - \frac{\delta Cov(VC, R_M)}{\sigma_{MM}}\right]$$

Note first that the firm's systematic risk can be decomposed into two components due, respectively, to the covariance of its revenues with the market returns (revenue beta) and to how its variable costs covary with the market (VC beta). The firm's overall beta, then, equals the sum of these beta coefficients scaled by the corresponding firm value (V or V*). In order to compare β with β^*, we must first assess the impact of using operating leverage on firm value. For example, solving

---

[7]Recall from Chapter 8 that $Cov(aX, Y) = aCov(X, Y)$ where a is a constant and X and Y are random variables.

both of the above expressions for β_{Rev} (revenue beta) and equating the results provide us with the following relationship between the firm's systematic risk under each cost structure:

$$\beta^* = \frac{V}{V*}\beta + (1 - \delta)\frac{1}{V*}\beta_{VC},$$

where β_{VC} is the beta for the variable cost component of the firm's operating earnings. Since δ is a positive constant less than 1, the relationship between β^* and β hinges on whether V* is greater or less than V (that is, whether the firm is more or less valuable as a result of using operating leverage). Assuming, for example, that V = V* and that β_{VC} is positive, the relationship is as follows:

$$\beta^* = \beta + \frac{\beta_{VC}(1 - \delta)}{V},$$

and β^* is greater than β by an amount equal to the value of the second term on the right-hand side of the above expression. Of course, this result is reversed if β_{VC} is negative, reflecting a negative covariance between the firm's operating expenses and market returns. If V* > V, the relationship between β and β^* is no longer clear.

The critical issue, however, is how V is affected by the use of operating leverage. If the use of operating leverage increases firm value, it is desirable. In effect, in such a case one of two things must have happened: (1) The use of operating leverage increased the expected firm returns by more than enough to offset any resulting increase in systematic risk, or (2) If systematic risk was decreased (β_{VC} was negative), this decline was not accompanied by a reduction in firm expected returns sufficiently large to reduce firm value.

Summary

In this section we addressed the firm's capital budgeting problem in the context of the single-period CAPM. We found that the NPV rule for project acceptance is a direct consequence of the desirability of investing in a "new" asset or project. Specifically, we derived an NPV model that uses as the project's required rate of return a "CAPM-like" risk-adjusted return—that is, at the time of the analysis, the project is *not* a part of the market portfolio, nor is it necessarily valued in accordance with CAPM equilibrium (if it were, its NPV would be zero by definition).[8]

Also, we took a preliminary look at the role of financial structure in capital budgeting.[9] We found that in the absence of taxes, financial structure does *not* impact on project value or the capital budgeting decision.

Finally, in our discussion of the impact of the firm's use of operating leverage, we decomposed a firm's systematic risk into two components related to the

---

[8]Recall from Chapter 9 that the CAPM describes the relationship between a project's expected rate of return and its risk under conditions of market equilibrium; that is, $u_i = r_F + \beta_i(u_M - r_F)$.

[9]Chapters 12 and 13 investigate the theoretical and practical issues that arise with respect to the firm's choice of capital structure.

systematic covariation between the firm's revenues and market returns and the co-variation between its variable costs and market returns. We found the impact of the firm's cost structure (that is, operating leverage) on firm value to be a function of the relative present values of the additional fixed costs associated with an increase in the use of operating leverage and the present value of the corresponding reduction in variable costs.

Estimating the Risk-Adjusted Rate of Return Using the CAPM

In evaluating a project's acceptability using the CAPM criteria in Equation 11.4, we face two basic estimation problems. The first deals with estimating the expected value of the project cash flows, u_Z. (We will not address this problem here; refer back to Chapter 6, which deals with the issues underlying the cash flows to capital budgeting projects.) The second problem deals with estimating the risk-adjusted rate of return found in the denominator of Equation 11.4, and it is this set of issues on which we will now focus. We will divide the problem of estimating a project's risk-adjusted rate of return into three subproblems: (1) evaluation of the risk-free rate; (2) estimation of the market risk premium ($u_M - r_F$); and (3) estimation of the project's systematic risk or beta coefficient. With respect to the last, note that the beta coefficient that we wish to estimate in Equation 11.4 is the *asset beta,* or unlevered beta. This creates a practical problem where we use data for "proxy" firms to estimate project betas, for these will reflect the firms' use of financial leverage.

Estimating the Risk-Free Interest Rate

The *risk-free interest rate* is, by definition, the rate that would be earned on a security having a zero probability of default. For practical purposes, the interest rates paid on securities issued by the U.S. government most closely meet this requirement. A problem arises, however, in terms of selecting the appropriate U.S. Treasury security. A wide variety of Treasury securities exist, each with a different term to maturity (for example, Treasury bills are issued with 90-, 180-, 270-, and 360-day maturities, and Treasury notes and bonds have new-issue maturities ranging up to 30 years). The theory underlying the CAPM gives us no guidance in selecting the proper term to maturity, for it assumes that there is only one period (albeit of unspecified length).[10] Thus, we are left with only an ad hoc basis for selecting the appropriate risk-free rate maturity. Simply put, one might reason that the term should match that of the project being analyzed.

One additional issue arises in selecting the appropriate risk-free interest rate: whether the rate used should be some type of estimate based on past rates or simply the current rate on the selected-maturity security. The answer is readily appar-

---

[10]We address the problems attendant to the expansion of the CAPM to a multiperiod framework in the next section.

ent when considering that we are trying to evaluate the opportunity cost of future investment. Thus, the risk-free opportunity cost of funds for a future period is, by definition, equal to the currently observed interest rate and not an average or extrapolation of past rates.

Estimating the Market Risk Premium

The *market risk premium* for the CAPM is defined as follows: $(u_M - r_F)$, where u_M is the expected rate of return on the market portfolio of risky assets.[11] Once again, we want to assess the opportunity cost of an investment over a "future" time period. Unfortunately, rates of return on equity securities are not observable and can only be estimated. This generally has led financial analysts to use historical risk premiums as the basis for estimating market risk premiums.

An important source of information on historical rates of return of both the market and interest rates was provided by Ibbotson and Sinquefield (1982), who studied the performance of four basic portfolios of securities from 1926 through 1981. The portfolios included the following:

1.   A portfolio of Treasury bills with maturities of less than one year

2.   A portfolio of long-term U.S. government bonds

3.   A portfolio of long-term corporate bonds (with annual revisions so as to maintain a constant maturity)

4.   The Standard and Poor's Composite Index of 500 common stocks

The average rates of return on each portfolio are reported in Table 11.1. Using the average of the historical risk premiums for the sample period, we observe an average market risk premium of 8.3 percent. Thus, over a very long time period the average market risk premium (as proxied by the S&P 500 Composite Index) has been around 8.3 percent over the rate of return on Treasury bills and Treasury

---

Table 11.1   Average Rates of Return Earned over the Period 1926–1981

Portfolio	Average Annual Rate of Return	Average Risk Premium (Using Treasury bills)
Common stocks	11.4%	8.3%
Corporate bonds	3.7	0.6
Government bonds	3.1	0.0
Treasury bills	3.1	0.0

Source: R. G. Ibbotson and R. A. Sinquefield, *Stocks, Bonds, Bills, and Inflation: The Past and the Future* (Charlottesville, Va.: Financial Analysts Research Foundation, 1982), Exhibit 19, p. 71.

---

[11]Morgan (1978) suggests that an equally weighted portfolio of risky securities provides the basis for predictions of security returns that are as good as those obtained using a mean-variance efficient portfolio (that is, one that plots on the ex post efficient frontier of all risky assets).

bonds. We will use this average risk premium as an estimate of the expected risk premium of investors in general.

Estimating Project Systematic Risk

In our discussion of the theoretical underpinnings of using the CAPM when analyzing capital budgeting projects, we noted that two versions of the model could be used. Specifically, we demonstrated that the capital budgeting rule could be stated in terms of an "unlevered" or project required rate of return (Equation 11.4) or a levered equity required rate of return (Equation 11.5).[12] Thus, from a theoretical perspective we are indifferent between the two criteria; however, from a practical standpoint we are not, as we now discuss.

Once again we note that we are attempting to evaluate the opportunity cost of funds for investment for a future period. However, a project's ex ante beta coefficient is not observable; thus, a project's beta must be estimated using historical data. Further complicating the estimation problem is the fact that capital investment proposals generally have no history of past returns or other data with which to estimate their betas. Even if historical returns were available, say, for a project that consisted of acquiring an investment previously undertaken by another firm, the asset would have no market-based returns since it was but one of many owned by the firm. Thus, in order to use historical market-based returns to estimate a project's systematic risk, we must turn to the use of "proxy" firms whose equity value and dividends are observable and whose betas can be estimated.[13] Note, however, that the historical market returns for proxy firms will reflect their particular financial structures. This means that the proxy beta coefficients must be appropriately adjusted for the proxy firms' use of financial leverage. Recall from our discussion on using the CAPM for evaluating projects that the relationship between the beta for a levered project and that for an unlevered project in the absence of income taxes is the following:

$$\beta_I = \beta_S\left(\frac{S}{I}\right),$$

where β_I is the *asset* or *unlevered* beta for the project, β_S is the levered equity beta for that project, I is the initial investment in the unlevered project, and S is the project's equity financing.

The relationship between the asset and equity betas can also be defined using the market values of the firm (asset), V_L, and of the firm's equity, $S_L = V_L - D$, where D represents the firm's debt financing.[14] Using market values, the

---

[12]In our earlier discussion we ignored the effect of corporate taxes and the corresponding impact of the tax deductibility of interest expense on the cost of capital and, hence, project value.

[13]Fuller and Kerr (1981) recommend the estimation of a divisional cost of capital for subcategories of projects undertaken by the firm using what they call a *pure play* technique. This simply involves identifying one or more firms that have invested all their funds in the industry or product line for which a cost of capital is to be estimated. The betas for these pure-play firms are estimated and used as the basis for estimating the beta for the project under consideration.

[14]We use D to represent the market value of the firm's debt and its face value. Hence, we assume that the debt carries a coupon interest rate equal to the market rate, which is r_F.

asset beta can be defined as the following function of its equity beta and financial leverage *in the absence of corporate income taxes:*

$$\beta_I = \beta_S\left(\frac{S_L}{S_U}\right),$$ **No Corporate Taxes**

where S_U is the value of the project's equity if the project is to be all equity financed. We will demonstrate that in the absence of corporate income taxes the firm's value is unaffected by its use of financial leverage such that $V_L = S_U$ and, consequently, with no taxes $\beta_I = \beta_S(S_L/V_L)$.[15] However, Modigliani and Miller (1963) showed that *in the presence of corporate income taxes* the following relationship between firm value and the use of financial leverage holds:[16]

$$V_L = S_U + TD,$$

where T is the firm's tax rate and TD is the value of the interest tax savings arising from the use of D dollars in debt financing. Substituting for $S_U = V_L - TD$ in the equation for β_I produces the following:

$$\beta_I = \beta_S\left[\frac{S_L}{(V_L - TD)}\right].$$ **With Corporate Taxes**

To summarize, we will estimate a project's beta through the use of proxies. Since the market rates of return observed for the proxies' equity will reflect their particular capital structures, we must adjust the equity beta estimated for them to obtain an asset beta, β_I, if we are to use Equation 11.4 to evaluate the project's required rate of return. In order to use Equation 11.6, the proxy's beta (reflecting the proxy firm's use of financial leverage) must be adjusted to reflect the project's financing mix.

A second problem arises with respect to using historical returns to estimate a proxy firm's beta. This relates to the instability of estimated beta coefficients over time (see Blume [1971] and Klemkosky and Martin [1975]). Thus, estimating a firm's beta using historical time series of firm and market returns invites a high degree of estimation error. However, this intertemporal beta instability has been found to result from random variation in the individual beta coefficients, which is largely independent across firms. Thus, combining firms into a portfolio with similar risk attributes greatly reduces this intertemporal instability.

---

[15]This relationship follows directly where we recognize that the systematic risk of a firm, β_I, is simply a weighted average of the betas for its debt, β_D, and equity, β_S:

$$\beta_I = \beta_D\left(\frac{D}{V_L}\right) + \beta_S\left(\frac{S_L}{V_L}\right).$$

Where debt is riskless, $\beta_D = 0$ and the above expression reduces to $\beta_S(S_L/V_L)$. Note that we have "switched" from book to market values here so that β_S and β_I now reflect market values, whereas in our previous discussion we used historical costs or book values to measure rates of return.

[16]We develop this valuation relationship in Chapter 12, where we discuss capital structure theory in detail.

Table 11.2 contains the mean square forecast errors found in the Klemkosky and Martin (1975) study.[17] The authors studied four different time periods and analyzed the intertemporal stability of portfolios containing one to ten securities. As shown in Table 11.2, the forecast error declined dramatically going from one to ten securities. In addition, using the beta coefficient computed from a previous period to estimate a future beta coefficient evidently provided a relatively unbiased but slightly inefficient forecast. In other words, the historical betas were not biased; the beta coefficients estimated for period t were neither persistently higher nor lower than the realized betas for the subsequent period, resulting in an unbiased forecast. Further, the predictions were somewhat inefficient — that is, beta forecasts tended to be over (under) at low (high) levels of beta and under (over) the mark for high (low) beta stocks. This inefficiency element is what Blume (1971) referred to as the tendency for beta predictions to "regress toward the mean" — that is, very high betas calculated in one period tended to be higher than those estimated for the next period, and vice versa for very low betas. However, the primary source of prediction error resulting from using last period's beta to predict next period's was "random variation" over time, which in Table 11.2 is called the random error component of the mean square error. Thus, in an effort to reduce estimation error in a firm's beta coefficient, we will use the beta coefficient for a portfolio of firms that are engaged in the same line of business.[18] We will first adjust these betas for the influence of financial leverage then average them across firms to produce the estimated "asset beta" for use in calculating the project's required rate using Equation 11.4 or 11.6.

Our discussion of the estimation of a project's beta has focused on the use of historical market rates of return for a proxy firm (or portfolio of firms). However, an alternative procedure has been suggested by Rosenberg (1985) that utilizes accounting and other data to predict a firm's beta. This procedure is particularly attractive when attempting to evaluate a project's beta, for it makes use of project specific data for use in the estimation process.

Estimating the Cost of Capital for Anheuser-Busch Brewing Company: An Example

We are now prepared to estimate the cost of capital using the CAPM. The problem will be divided into three basic steps:

1.   Estimate β_I using the proxy method, and observe the risk-free rate, r_F.

2.   Estimate the market risk premium, $u_M - r_F$.

---

[17]Mean square error is simply the average squared difference in the beta for one time period and that of the subsequent period, that is, for firms $j = 1, 2, \ldots, N$:

$$MSE = \frac{1}{N} \sum_{j=1}^{N} (\beta_{jt} - \beta_{jt-1})^2$$

The greater the intertemporal instability of the beta estimates, $\beta_{jt} - \beta_{jt-1}$, the greater is the MSE.

[18]This portfolio concept is analogous to Fuller and Kerr's (1981) notion of a "pure-play" beta.

Table 11.2   Mean Square Forecast Errors for Beta Coefficients[a]

	Portfolio Size (Number of Securities)				
	1	3	5	7	10
Period 1					
(7/47–6/52 vs. 7/52–6/57)					
Mean square error (MSE)	.17122	.07484	.05916	.04386	.04182
Portions of MSE due to:					
Bias	.00021	.00014	.00021	.00015	.00021
Inefficiency	.02422	.02178	.02363	.02192	.02320
Random error	.14678	.05291	.03531	.02179	.01839
Period 2					
(7/52–6/57 vs. 7/57–6/62)					
Mean square error (MSE)	.18387	.11008	.09196	.08754	.08544
Portions of MSE due to:					
Bias	.00084	.00084	.00095	.00095	.00095
Inefficiency	.07367	.07357	.07343	.07306	.07370
Random error	.10935	.03566	.01757	.01352	.01078
Period 3					
(7/57–6/62 vs. 7/62–6/67)					
Mean square error (MSE)	.12385	.05018	.03574	.02659	.02332
Portions of MSE due to:					
Bias	.00018	.00019	.00018	.00019	.00018
Inefficiency	.00730	.00736	.00736	.00730	.00725
Random error	.11636	.04262	.02818	.01909	.01587
Period 4					
(7/62–6/67 vs. 7/67–6/72)					
Mean square error (MSE)	.16122	.08363	.06880	.05982	.05465
Portions of MSE due to:					
Bias	.00093	.00100	.00093	.00097	.00119
Inefficiency	.03992	.03947	.03993	.03975	.03800
Random error	.12036	.04314	.02792	.01908	.01545

[a]Mean square error $= 1/N[\Sigma_j(\beta_{j,t} - \beta_{j,t-1})^2]$, where $\beta_{j,t}$ is the beta coefficient for the jth firm estimated at time t.
Source: R. C. Klemkosky and J. D. Martin, "The Adjustment of Beta Forecasts," *Journal of Finance* (September 1975): 1123–1128.

3.   Substitute the above parameters into Equation 11.4 or 11.6 to get an estimate of the risk-adjusted required rate of return.

We will use the Anheuser-Busch Brewing Company to illustrate this procedure.

Anheuser-Busch (hereafter AB) is one of the two largest brewing companies in the United States. AB and Miller (owned by Philip Morris) share approximately 55 percent of the U.S. beer market. Further, in combination with Stroh (privately held) and Heileman they account for nearly 80 percent of the total beer market. Of

the brewers who market their beer in the United States, the following are publicly
traded nationally and have sufficient data to warrant inclusion in our analysis: AB, Carling-O'Keefe, Coors, Heileman, Labatt, and Molson. We will use
these firms to form a portfolio of firms with which to estimate AB's systematic
risk. Table 11.3 contains the information needed to estimate AB's asset beta. The
resulting average β_I was 0.74, and this becomes our estimate of AB's asset beta.

Next, we observe the risk-free rate. Since the CAPM is a single-period
model, it provides no guidance for selecting a maturity for the risk-free asset.
Thus, for our purposes we will simply use the upper and lower bounds on the
term structure of U.S. government security rates. During April 1987, the shortest-
term Treasury bills yielded about 5.8 percent and long-term government bonds
8.5 percent. Although the CAPM gives us no basis for selecting among these
rates, it would seem more appropriate to use the long-term rate if we use the cost
of capital estimate as a hurdle rate for long-term capital investments. For this reason, we will use the 8.5 percent rate for our estimate of r_F.

Step 2 involves evaluating the market's risk premium (that is, $u_M - r_F$). For
this estimate we draw upon the Ibbotson and Sinquefield (1982) study of capital
market rates over the period 1926 to 1981. These authors found that $u_M - r_F$
averaged 8.3 percent over this period. Thus, we will use this figure to estimate
expectations regarding the market risk premium.

We are now ready to evaluate AB's cost of capital. Using Equation 11.4 and
the parameter estimates made above, we obtain the following:

$$r_F + \beta_I(u_M - r_F).$$

Substituting the estimates of the parameters,

$$0.085 + 0.74(0.083) = 0.1464, \text{ or approximately } 14.6\%.$$

Note that this is the firm's cost of capital and is *not* the required return on the
firm's equity. To estimate the required equity return, we must convert our asset

---

Table 11.3   Equity and Asset Betas for the Brewing Industry

Company	Equity Beta	Adjustment Factor[a]	Asset Beta[b]
Anheuser-Busch	0.80	0.94	0.75
Carling-O'Keefe	1.05	0.94	0.99
Coors (Adolph)[c]	0.75	1.00	0.75
Heileman	0.95	0.92	0.87
Labatt	0.70	0.83	0.58
Molson	0.60	0.85	0.51
		Average β_I = 0.74	

[a]Adjustment factor = $S_L/(V_L - TD)$.
[b]$\beta_I = \beta_L \times$ Adjustment factor.
[c]Coors had no debt outstanding.
Source: Data taken from *Value Line Investment Survey*, February 7, 1986, 3–14.

beta estimate of 0.74 into a levered equity beta estimate. We can do so by dividing 0.74 by the adjustment factor for AB found in Table 11.3. The resulting levered equity beta estimate is 0.79. Substituting this beta into Equation 11.6 for β_S and using the other parameters already estimated produce a required return on equity of 15.06 percent.

In closing our discussion of AB's cost of capital, we note the following points. First, we have calculated an "estimate" of AB's cost of capital, which is not only subject to estimation error but is correct only to the extent that the CAPM appropriately describes firm valuation. Second, throughout our analysis we have assumed that borrowing is riskless. If debt were risky, $(\beta_D > 0)$, the use of debt financing would, other things equal, lead to a reduction in the firm's levered or equity beta because the risky debt would share some of the systematic risk of the firm's earnings stream.[19] Finally, we have estimated the cost of capital for AB in the context of CAPM with corporate taxes, which is equivalent to the Modigliani and Miller (1963) tax-adjusted valuation model. Specifically, we gave no consideration to the existence of personal income taxes. We will return to this problem in Chapter 14 in the context of dividend policy; at this point we will simply assume that personal taxes do not impact on the firm's cost of capital.

Using the CAPM to Evaluate Multiperiod Capital Budgeting Projects

In this section we discuss the problem that arises when the project being valued using the CAPM provides cash flows that occur across multiple periods. Recall from our discussion of the CAPM that this model describes market equilibrium under a number of restrictive assumptions. The key assumption that comes into question here is the one that the investor makes only *one* portfolio composition choice (that is, there is but one time period). Note that we are discussing not the length of the time period being analyzed but the existence of an opportunity to make additional portfolio choices (revisions) prior to the end of the period during which a project is expected to provide cash flows. The ability to revise one's investment portfolio over time adds an important dimension to the valuation problem.[20] Our objective here is to discuss the conditions under which one might continue to utilize the CAPM even over a multiperiod investment horizon.

Bogue and Roll (1974), Brennan (1973), and Myers and Turnbull (1977) address the problem of using the CAPM to value multiperiod capital budgeting projects. However, Bogue and Roll (1974) contend that such use is complicated by

---

[19]Recall that the asset beta for a firm or project can be written as a weighted average of the betas of its debt and equity:

$$\beta_I = \beta_D\left(\frac{D}{V_L}\right) + \beta_S\left(\frac{S_L}{V_L}\right).$$

Thus, where $\beta_D > 0$, $\beta_S = \beta_I(V_L/S_L) - \beta_D(D/S_L)$ such that β_S for a firm that issues bonds is less than that for a similar firm that issues riskless debt.

[20]For example, see Merton (1973) and Long (1974).

the uncertainty surrounding the parameters of the CAPM as applied to future periods (that is, the risk-free rate and the covariance of the project's intermediate value prior to the end of the investment horizon with the value of the market portfolio). Thus, Bogue and Roll posit two sources of uncertainty in the multiperiod use of the CAPM that are not present in the single-period problem. Fama (1977), however, points out that neither of these sources of uncertainty are admissible if the CAPM is to be retained. He shows that the parameters of the CAPM for each future period must, in fact, be nonstochastic (known) if the CAPM is to be used in valuing multiperiod cash flow streams. His multiperiod valuation model, then, is the following:

$$V_0 = E(CF_N) \left[\frac{1}{1 + E(R_1)} \right] \left[\frac{1}{1 + E(R_2)} \right] \cdots \left[\frac{1}{1 + E(R_N)} \right],$$

where V_0 is the current market value of an asset that provides an expected cash flow, $E(CF_N)$, at the end of period N and $E(R_N)$ represents the expected rate of return on that asset for period N. In essence, Fama argues that we must know the values of the required rates of return for each future period in the planning horizon at the time the asset is being valued. This effectively eliminates the two added sources of uncertainty introduced by Bogue and Roll.

Constantinides (1980) readdressed the problems encountered in the "sequential" use of the CAPM to value multiperiod capital budgeting problems. He concluded that the CAPM can be used to value multiperiod capital budgeting problems even where its parameters are stochastic. However, he noted that application of the model becomes very complex except for the case where the effect of the nonstationarity in the model's parameters through time is of little practical consequence.

At this point we will end our brief foray into the problems of valuing multiperiod capital budgeting projects using the CAPM. Our objective here has been to identify the nature of the multiperiod valuation problem and, in so doing, inspire caution against the blind use of the single-period CAPM in evaluating capital expenditure required rates of return. In the next section, we discuss an alternative to the CAPM that is easily extended to the multiple-period case. However, as we will soon see, this method also has limitations.

Arbitrage and the Capital Budgeting Problem[21]

The method offered here for the evaluation of risky capital expenditure proposals uses the arbitrage-type argument made by Ross (1979) and others for valuing stock options. Simply stated, the proposed method involves identifying a portfolio of assets (which are traded in a market and for which market prices can be observed) that produce the same cash flow stream as the proposed investment. If, for example, the proposed investment provides cash flows that can be duplicated (spanned) by a port-

---

[21]The discussion in this section follows Gehr (1981).

folio containing 50 shares of firm A stock with a market value of $10 per share and 30 shares of firm B stock with a market value of $100 per share, the investment cash flows must have a market value of $3,500 = $10 × 50 + $100 × 30. Arbitrage enters into the solution when the asset can be acquired at a price other than $3,500, in which case there exists the opportunity to make an arbitrage profit. In this section, we will illustrate how Gehr (1981) used the assumption of no arbitrage profits to value a risky capital budgeting proposal.

A Simple Two-State, Single-Period Example

Assume there are only two states of the world that can exist at the end of the period: boom and bust. Further, there are only two traded assets: a risk-free asset that pays an 8 percent return regardless of which future state occurs and a risky asset with a current market price $s_0 = 10 that pays $s_1 = 12 if the end-of-period state is boom and $9 if it is bust. The risky capital investment entails investing $92 today in return for an end-of-period cash flow of $110 if the state is boom and $90 if it is bust. To summarize,

	Boom	Bust
s_1	$ 12	$ 9
Project cash flow	110	90

$s_0 = 10 and $r_F = 8\%$

The key to the project's valuation is to recognize that we can combine the two securities for which we can observe prices (the risk-free and traded risky securities) into a portfolio that will provide the same end-of-period cash flows as the risky project. The value of this "equivalent" cash flow portfolio can be determined using observed market prices. Note that the value of the cash flow equivalent portfolio equals the value of the risky project since the portfolio and the project, by construction, have the same cash flow regardless of which state of the world prevails at the end of the period.

To evaluate the above capital investment proposal, we utilize the following three-step procedure:

■   **Step 1:** *Determine the contents of the cash flow equivalent portfolio.* In other words, determine the number of shares of the traded risky asset, x, and the amount that must be invested in the risk-free asset, y, such that the portfolio's end-of-period cash flow will equal the risky project's cash flow; that is,

Boom: $12x + 1.08y = 110

Bust: $9x + 1.08y = $ 90$

If x and y are determined so as to satisfy the above equations, the resulting portfolio will have the same end-of-period cash flow as the risky project.

Solving the above equations simultaneously results in the following values for x and y:

$$x = 6\tfrac{2}{3} \text{ shares of the risky security}$$

$$y = \$27.78 \text{ invested in the risk-free security}$$

■ **Step 2:** *Solve for the value of the cash flow equivalent portfolio using the securities' observed market prices.* In the absence of arbitrage opportunities, the value of the cash flow equivalent portfolio will be the same as that of the risky project, since both provide the owner with exactly the same payoff regardless of the state of the world prevailing at the end of the period.

For this example, the value of the cash flow equivalent portfolio is as follows:

$$6\tfrac{2}{3}(\$10) + \$27.78 = \$94.45 .$$

■ **Step 3:** *Calculate the project's net present value.* For this example, we calculate the net present value as follows:

$$\text{NPV} = \$94.45 - \$92 = \underline{\$2.45} .$$

Hence, the project's value exceeds its initial cost by $2.45, and thus the project should be undertaken.

Note that we did not have to make any assumptions about investor preferences (that is, risk aversion) or the probability of the occurrence of the two states of nature in order to be able to value the risky project cash flow. However, we did assume that (1) investors realize there are only two possible states of the world; (2) investors know the payoffs in each state for the risky security and the proposed project; and (3) there are no arbitrage opportunities among traded assets.[22] This last assumption led us to conclude that once the risky project is undertaken and its securities become traded in the capital market, it must have a value equal to that of its cash flow equivalent portfolio.[23]

An alternative solution procedure for valuing the project's cash flow can be used. Note that the valuation scheme we have described thus far is based on the simple proposition that the values of two assets (the risky project and the risky security) must be equal if they provide the same end-of-period cash flows in all states of the world. Thus, we made no assumption as to the decisionmaker's risk aversion. The arbitrage valuation principle must hold for all investors regardless of their individual preferences with regard to risk. Thus, let us assume for the moment that investors are risk neutral such that they would value the risky capital investment project by discounting its expected end-of-period cash flow back to the present using the risk-free rate. Note, however, that we do not know the probabilities associated with each state of the world. Since there are only two states (boom

---

[22]Implicit here are the assumptions that there are no transactions costs and the capital market (where risky and risk-free securities are traded) is competitive.

[23]The risky project is said to be "spanned" by securities available in the capital market, since its cash flows can be duplicated by a portfolio comprised of existing securities.

and bust), we can estimate these probabilities using the equation for the value of the risky security:

$$\overbrace{\text{Expected cash flow}}$$

(11.7)
$$s_0 = \frac{s_1(\text{boom})\Psi + s_1(\text{bust})(1 - \Psi)}{1 + r_F}$$

$$\$10 = \frac{\$12\Psi + \$9(1 - \Psi)}{1.08},$$

where Ψ is the probability that the boom state will occur and $(1 - \Psi)$ the probability of bust. Solving for the probabilities that satisfy the above expression, we find that the probability corresponding to boom is 0.6 and the probability of bust is 0.4. If we apply these probabilities to the valuation of the risky project (once again assuming risk neutrality), we obtain the following:

$$\text{Project value} = \frac{\$110 \times 0.6 + \$90 \times (1 - 0.6)}{1.08} = \$94.45,$$

which is the same result we obtained earlier using the arbitrage argument.[24]

Note that while the risk neutrality assumption was unnecessary, its use simplified the analysis. This was because under risk neutrality, the value of a risky stream is simply the present value of the expected cash flow discounted at the risk-free interest rate.

A More Complex Multiperiod Example

In our previous example we had only one future period and, consequently, a single risk-free rate of return. We now consider an example where there are two future periods and, hence, two single-period risk-free interest rates. In addition, the traded risky security will have payoffs in the second period that are contingent on the state of the world that arises in the first period.

Our example is summarized in Table 11.4. The multiperiod project involves investing $140 in year 0 with the cash flow consequences depicted in the table. Note that the risk-free interest rate need not be the same for each future period; however, it is assumed to be known, as are the stock prices and cash flows for each possible state of the world in each period. We solve for the value of the multiperiod project using the risk-neutral valuation procedure outlined for the single-period example. Specifically, we value the project at the end of one year by evaluating the probabilities implicit in a risk-neutral valuation of the second-year cash flows and apply these probabilities to the project cash flows in states D and E

---

[24]This approach was suggested in the context of option pricing theory by Cox and Ross (1976).

Table 11.4   Multiperiod Capital Budgeting Problem

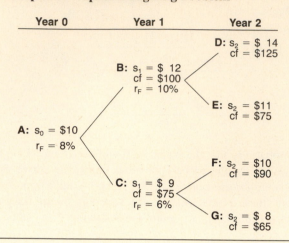

| Year 0 | Year 1 | Year 2 |

A: $s_0 = \$10$
$r_F = 8\%$

B: $s_1 = \$\ 12$
cf $= \$100$
$r_F = 10\%$

C: $s_1 = \$\ 9$
cf $= \$75$
$r_F = 6\%$

D: $s_2 = \$\ 14$
cf $= \$125$

E: $s_2 = \$11$
cf $= \$75$

F: $s_2 = \$10$
cf $= \$90$

G: $s_2 = \$\ 8$
cf $= \$65$

s_t = share price of traded risky security in year t
r_F = risk-free interest rate
cf = end-of-period cash flow from investing in risky project

and separately to the cash flows for states F and G. We then use these year 1 project values to value the project at time 0.[25]

We begin solving the multiperiod problem posed in Table 11.4 by evaluating project value at the end of year 1 if state B has occurred. The first step involves assessing the probabilities associated with states D and E assuming a risk-neutral investor. We follow the alternative procedure presented in Equation 11.7 for solving the single-period problem:

$$\$12 = \frac{\$14\Psi + (1 - \Psi)\$11}{1.10}.$$

Solving for Ψ, we get 0.733; consequently, the probability attached to state E is $1 - 0.733 = 0.267$. Using these probabilities we can now calculate the value of the project at the end of year 1 if state B has occurred:

$$\text{Project value} = \frac{\$125(0.733) + \$75(0.267)}{1.10} = \$101.50.$$

Performing a similar analysis assuming that state C has occurred produces a project value of $83.73. We now use these two project values for states B and C to evaluate the current market value of the project; that is, the two-period project has been reduced to the single-period problem shown in Table 11.5.

---

[25]The solution procedure is similar to dynamic programming, whereby we evaluate the most distant branches of the probability tree first and work our way backward to the present.

Table 11.5   Stage 2: The Single-Period Problem

Year 0	Year 1
	B: $s_1 = \$12$ Project value $= \$101.50 + \$100$
$s_0 = \$10$	**C:** $s_1 = \$9$ Project value $= \$83.73 + \$75$

Note that project value at the end of year 1 if state B occurs equals the value of the year 2 cash flow ($101.50) plus the year 1 cash flow for state B. Assessing the risk-neutral valuation probabilities implicit in the state B and C stock prices, we obtain the following:

$$\$10 = \frac{\$12\Psi + \$9(1 - \Psi)}{1.08}$$

such that the implied probability of state B occurring (Ψ) is 0.60 and that of state C thus is 0.40. We then find the value of the risky project by using these probabilities as if we were risk neutral:

$$\text{Project value} = \frac{\$201.50 \times 0.6 + \$158.73 \times 0.4}{1.08} = \$170.73.$$

Thus, given the cost of $140 the project offers a positive net present value of $30.73.

The analysis easily could be extended to any number of periods. However, we should note the basic limitations of the proposed methodology. In general, the problem is one of data availability. A quick review of Table 11.4 reveals that the data requirements of the proposed method are not trivial. Specifically, we must identify the possible states of the world as well as the corresponding state prices for the risky asset, s, and corresponding cash flows for the project, cf. In addition, we assume that the single-period interest rates for each period of the project's life are known. Perhaps most important, however, is the need to identify a traded security whose value is known in each state in which the project provides a cash flow. As restrictive as these requirements appear, the arbitrage method does provide useful insight into the valuation of risky project cash flow streams. The fundamental insight of the proposed methodology is that it bases the value of a nontraded asset (the capital budgeting project) on the value of a portfolio of traded securities that can be combined into a portfolio with equivalent cash flows to the project. Later we will use the same basic insight to value call options on common stock.[26]

---

[26]In Chapter 15, we will develop the binomial option pricing model using a "hedge" portfolio comprised of the underlying common stock and a risk-free bond that provides the same cash flow return as the call option.

Time and Risk Adjustments for Risky Cash Flows

Thus far, the primary tool used for incorporating risk into the evaluation of a project's net present value has involved using the CAPM to evaluate a risk-adjusted required rate of return. The project's future cash flow(s) was(were) then discounted back to the present for comparison with the investment cost and, consequently, serve(d) as the basis for the accept/reject decision. This procedure combines two types of analyses in such a way that errors can easily arise for certain types of projects. Specifically, the use of the "risk-adjusted discount rate" methodology combines consideration for project riskiness and the time value of money; that is, the time adjustment of future cash flows is combined with the assessment of their riskiness via the use of a single discount rate that takes both these factors into account. It has been argued that this type of "combined" analysis can seriously bias management against long-term projects in which the riskiness of the cash flows does not increase continuously over time.[27] To illustrate this attribute of the risk-adjusted discount method, we define the certain equivalent risk adjustment model as follows:

(11.8)
$$PV = \frac{\alpha_t NCF_t}{(1 + r_F)^t},$$

where PV is the present value of the net cash flow received in year t, NCF_t (which has been adjusted to equal its "certain equivalent" by multiplying it by the certain equivalent factor for year t equal to α_t). Note that since the cash flow being discounted is the equivalent of a certain cash flow, it is discounted using the risk-free rate, r_F. Equation 11.8 is an alternative to the risk-adjusted discount rate model in that the risk adjustment is brought about by adjusting the risky cash flow to equal its certain equivalent. Thus, α_t is the risk adjustment factor.

To see the inherent relationship between time and a particular risk-adjusted discount rate, consider the following example. Table 11.6 contains the estimates of the risky cash flows for a four-year project whose initial cost is $4,000. The risk-free interest rate is 6 percent and the risk-adjusted interest rate 10 percent; hence, the "risk premium" is 4 percent over the risk-free rate. The certain equivalent factors calculated in the last column are determined so as to produce the same present value as the risk-adjusted present value found in the third column.[28] We can make two observations with respect to these certain equivalent factors. First, they decrease over time, implying an increase in risk over time where the risk-adjusted discount rate procedure is used. Second, looking at the changes in the certain equivalent factors over time, we see that they decrease over time—that is, the difference in the year 1 certain equivalent factor of 0.964 and the year 2 factor

---

[27]Robichek and Myers (1966) first noted this problem, while Hodder and Riggs (1985) utilized the same argument as a rejoinder to Hayes and Garvin (1982) and other critics of discounted cash flow techniques who claim that such tools are inherently biased against long-term investments. Hodder and Riggs contend that it is the incorrect use of discounted cash flow techniques that is at fault, not the methods themselves.

[28]The footnote to Table 11.6 describes how the certain equivalent factors were calculated.

Table 11.6   Time and Adjustment for Risk Inherent in Risk-Adjusted Discount Rate Methodology

Year	Risky Cash Flow	Present Value (10%)	Certain Equivalent Adjustment Factor (α_t)[a]
0	−$4,000	−$4,000	1.000
1	2,000	1,818	0.964
2	2,000	1,653	0.929
3	2,000	1,503	0.895
4	2,000	1,366	0.862

[a]The calculation of the certain equivalent factor involves finding the value that will give the same certain equivalent present value that the risk-adjusted discount rate method does, that is,

$$PV = \underbrace{\frac{NCF_t}{(1 + k)^t}}_{\substack{\text{Risk-adjusted} \\ \text{present value}}} = \underbrace{\frac{\alpha_t NCF_t}{(1 + r_F)^t}}_{\substack{\text{Certain equivalent} \\ \text{present value}}},$$

where k is the risk-adjusted discount rate. Solving for α_t, we obtain the following relationship:

$$\alpha_t = \frac{(1 + r_F)^t}{(1 + k)^t}.$$

of 0.929 is 0.035 — slightly larger than the corresponding decrease in the certain equivalent factor occurring between years 2 and 3, years 3 and 4, and so forth. Hence, the use of the risk-adjusted discount rate methodology implicitly presumes that risk increases with time, albeit at a decreasing rate.

The point here is that when the risk-adjusted discount model is used to discount cash flows for a multiperiod risky investment, an implicit assumption is being made with respect to how risk changes over time. If the assumption of increasing risk with time is inappropriate, the model must be changed to reflect this. Two options are available: (1) We can revert to a certain equivalent NPV model, in which case we must evaluate different certain equivalent factors for each year in which the project provides a cash flow, or (2) we can use a risk-adjusted discount rate model by periodically adjusting the discount rate to account for the project's changing risk characteristics. Neither alternative is easy; however, if we are to properly account for project risk over time, one or the other method of adjustment will be necessary for projects whose risk does not increase proportionately with time.

The Relationship between the Certainty Equivalent and Risk-Adjusted Discount Rate Methods for Risk Adjusting Project Cash Flows: A Mathematical Overview

Two methods are generally used to risk adjust a project's future cash flows: the risk-adjusted discount rate (RADR) method and the certainty equivalent (CE) method. In the former, the rate used to discount a project's future cash flows is adjusted upward to reflect higher risk. For example, we can think of the RADR as being the sum of the risk-free rate of interest and a risk premium reflecting the added riskiness of the cash flow being discounted. Thus, for a $1 risky cash flow to be received t years hence we calculate its present value as follows:

(i)
$$\frac{\$1}{(1 + k)^t},$$

where k is the RADR reflecting the sum of the risk-free rate (r_F) and a risk premium.

The certainty equivalent method requires that the project's risky cash flow be adjusted to its certainty equivalent and then discounted using the risk-free interest rate. Thus, where we define α_t to be the certainty equivalent factor corresponding to a $1 risky cash flow to be received in year t, the present value of the cash flow can be stated as follows:

(ii)
$$\frac{\$1\alpha_t}{(1 + r_F)^t}$$

Note that the certainty equivalent factor can be interpreted as a certain cash flow (which is equivalent to the risky cash flow in the opinion of the analyst) divided by the risky cash flow. Therefore, a certainty equivalent factor of 0.8 means that the analyst would be just as happy with a $0.80 certain cash flow in period t as with a $1 risky cash flow. The certainty equivalent factor then provides a direct measure of the specific risk adjustment attached to a particular cash flow. We will now make use of this observation to evaluate the nature of the risk adjustment over time that is inherent in the RADR method.

If we set Equation i equal to Equation ii and solve for α_t, we can evaluate the nature of the risk adjustment inherent in a particular risk premium.

$$\alpha_t = \left(\frac{1 + r_F}{1 + k}\right)^t$$

Recall that the risk premium is simply the difference in the risk-free rate, r_F, and the RADR, k.

To evaluate the impact of increasing the risk premium on the risk adjustment through time, consider the following example: Assume that the risk-free rate is 8 percent and consider RADRs of 10 percent, 12 percent, 14 percent, 20 percent, and 40 percent for a stream of $1 cash flows to be received annually over the next

8 years. For example, for the year 1 cash flow, where the RADR is 20 percent, the α_t is calculated as follows:

$$\alpha_1 = \left(\frac{1 + 0.08}{1 + 0.2}\right)^1 = 0.9.$$

The various values of α_t for the examples considered here are plotted in the following figure.

CEs for Alternative RADRs and an 8 Percent Risk-Free Rate

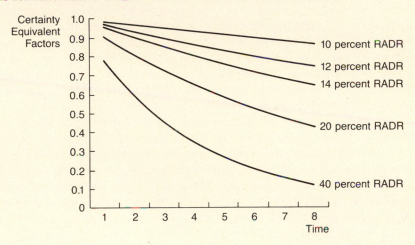

Note first that the CEs decline with the increase in time, t. Thus, by using the RADR method where a single risk premium is added to the discount rate used for all future years, we are implicitly assuming that the riskiness of the more distant cash flows increases with time and in the manner reflected in the figure. Actually, the risk premium is the same for all future periods; however, since the premium is compounded for more distant future periods, the "risk adjustment" increases with time. The assumption of an increasing risk adjustment over time may be intuitively appealing; however, the RADR method reflects a risk-adjustment increase in a particular manner, which may or may not be appropriate for a given project.

Summary

There is both good and bad news with respect to the analysis of the capital budgeting problem under uncertainty. The good news is that the same net present value and internal rate of return rules that were used to analyze the capital budgeting problem under certainty can be used in an uncertain world. The bad news is that in this case they are far more difficult to apply. In this chapter, we first demonstrated

the theoretical underpinnings of the use of the capital asset pricing model to analyze capital budgeting projects. Here we discovered that using the CAPM easily
can be derived as a "diversification" condition for an individual investor; that is,
the conditions under which an individual investor will want to diversify his or her
portfolio to include investment in the new asset provide the basis for deriving the
CAPM capital budgeting criterion.

Application of the CAPM rule to the analysis of capital budgeting raises a
number of practical problems, the most troublesome of which is its use in a multiperiod setting when the theory is couched in a single-period setting. Here we
found that using the model in a multiperiod setting where the resulting risk-
adjusted discount rate is assumed to be the same for all future periods is theoretically feasible, although difficult in practice. Further, we found that evaluating the
parameters of the CAPM even in a single-period setting involves some complex
estimates. Of particular significance was the need to estimate a project's systematic risk. Here we found it necessary to use proxy firms—firms whose line of
business is similar to that of the project—to estimate equity betas, which we then
adjusted to reflect the project's leverage.

We also considered an arbitrage model of the capital budgeting problem.
Here the key element is the assumption that the project's cash flows are "spanned"
by a combination of existing assets whose market values are known. We then
found the value of the project by valuing the portfolio of existing assets whose
cash flows "replicated" the project's. This model is also useful in both a multiperiod and single-period context. Like the CAPM, its primary shortcoming lies in
its application. In this case we must identify project cash flows in all possible
states of the world and in all future periods of the investment's life as well as existing assets that have payoffs in the same states. Once we have accomplished
this, we can solve for the project's value by valuing a portfolio of securities having payoffs in the same states.

Finally, we noted a conceptual problem that arises in blindly using the risk-
adjusted discount rate method to evaluate multiperiod investment proposals,
namely the model's implicit assumption that risk increases with time and, further,
proportionately with time. In some types of projects, this may not be a bad approximation; in those where the future is less risky than earlier time period cash
flows, using this model can seriously bias the analysis against project acceptance.

Study Questions

11.1   "The capital budgeting problem under uncertainty can be likened to the
individual's portfolio decision." Explain.

11.2   "The CAPM capital budgeting criterion can be stated in terms of project
cash flows or equity cash flows; in either case the same accept/reject decisions will be made." Explain.

11.3   What is the relationship between an asset's beta and the beta for a levered
project?

11.4   The CAPM can be extended to the situation where there are multiple time
periods under some restricted conditions. Discuss these conditions.

11.5   Explain the use of the concepts of bias, inefficiency, and random error with respect to the analysis of forecast errors in general and the prediction of beta in particular.

11.6   Describe the "arbitrage" approach to capital budgeting proposed by Gehr (1981).

Study Problems

11.1   Abercrombe and Winston Sailmakers, Inc. (AWSI) is attempting to estimate its cost of capital for use in analyzing a proposed expansion of its production facilities. It would like to use the capital asset pricing model as the basis for making a "benchmark estimate" and has collected the following information for that purpose:

Company	Equity Beta (β_s)	Firm Value (V_L)	Equity Value (S_L)
AWSI	1.20	$ 60M	$48M
Seemore Sail	1.60	100M	60M
Fullblown Sheets	1.00	20M	18M

AWSI estimates the market risk premium at approximately 9 percent and will use an 8 percent risk-free rate.

a. Estimate AWSI's cost of capital for its proposed expansion in a world of no taxes.

b. If AWSI faces a 40 percent marginal tax rate on its corporate income, what will its cost of capital be?

c. If AWSI decides to maintain a 20 percent debt-to-value ratio in its capital structure, what will be its cost of equity capital? (The firm faces a 40 percent marginal tax rate.)

11.2   Campbell-Newhouse Company (CNC) is primarily engaged in two businesses: (1) producing and marketing fresh fruits, vegetables, fruit by-products, and desserts and (2) leasing railroad cars and other shipping containers through its Central State Leasing Division. In addition, CNC has extensive real estate holdings in Texas and Hawaii. These properties were acquired many years ago as agricultural land; however, over time they have experienced tremendous growth in value. Of particular interest is the company's ownership of one of the smaller Hawaiian islands. The firm has used this land to grow native fruits for many years but recently has begun to consider the opportunity cost to its shareholders of not developing the property as a resort or at least selling it to another firm that would. In its deliberations CNC has come up with what its management feels is the most viable option with respect to the proposed development. The plan calls for the investment of $100 million over the next three years to develop a 200-room hotel, two golf courses, and related facilities. The proposed investment would be financed with a $70 million long-term note that could be placed privately with the aid of the firm's investment banker.

The note would call for an interest rate of 11 percent and would be due in full in 15 years with interest payable semiannually. The remaining $30 million would be provided by CNC from its own earnings.

A serious problem has arisen, however, with respect to valuing the proposed investment. Specifically, the firm would like to use the CAPM to obtain a ballpark estimate of the required investment return but cannot decide on the appropriate way to assess the project's systematic risk. It is debating two lines of thought. The first suggests that the firm's total intrinsic value (based on its management's and investment banker's judgment) is composed of 60 percent real estate value and 40 percent other business. Therefore, the firm's equity returns should be used to estimate the investment's systematic risk. The firm's analysts estimate its beta coefficient at approximately 1.15; this reflects a total firm market value of $312 million ($72 million in bonds and $240 million in common equity) and the firm's 40 percent income tax rate. Although the new project will involve investing in resort property, the firm's current market value is based largely on the investment community's assessment of the real estate value of the firm's land holdings, which generally are located in resort areas. The second line of reasoning suggests that the riskiness of the resort investment is potentially quite different from that of the firm's other investments and that a set of proxy firms should be identified and used as the basis for determining the proposal's systematic risk. In fact, a group of four such firms whose equities are traded and for which betas have been estimated have been identified. The relevant data on each proxy are as follows:

Proxy Firm	Equity Beta	Debt/ Equity Ratio
1	1.6	0.70
2	1.7	0.75
3	2.1	0.90
4	1.4	0.60

Each proxy firm has a total market value of about $200 million and a tax status similar to CNC's.

a. Evaluate the project and equity betas for the proposed resort investment using both of the above methods. Be sure to note any assumptions you must make in arriving at your estimates.

b. If the long-term government bond rate is approximately 10 percent and the average market risk premium is 8.3 percent, what is your estimate of the required rate of return for the proposed investment?

11.3   The R&M Company manufactures solar collectors used to convert ordinary sunlight into electric power. The technology was developed by Cliff Richardson and Melanie Moss while they were faculty members in the department of electrical engineering at the University of Texas at Austin. The conversion process was initially developed as a part of the U.S. space program under funding from NASA. Richardson and Moss (R&M) discovered and patented a means of producing the conversion panels at a cost that is economically viable for large office buildings and apartment complexes. However, except for several successful experiments, the technology has yet to have a commercial application.

In the spring of 1987, R&M were approached by a large commercial developer, Al Niece Construction Co., who proposed that they furnish electric power to one of their large office buildings, under construction in Dallas. Niece suggested that the project first be undertaken with the idea that it would provide 90 percent of the building's electrical power for two years. To entice the young company to undertake the project, Niece offered to loan the company $3 million at a below market rate of 8 percent, which compares favorably with the current market rate on a similar loan of 10 percent. The loan would be taken down immediately, with interest paid annually and the principal amount due at the end of two years.

If R&M undertake the project, they estimate that gross revenues will be $6 million per year for each of the next two years, at which time the project will be terminated. (Actually, the project will be reevaluated in two years. For purposes of the project analysis, however, a two-year horizon should be used.) Operating expenses are estimated to equal half the estimated revenues, and the entire project is expected to cost R&M $4 million. R&M plan to depreciate the cost of the project over two years using straight-line depreciation. The firm faces a 34 percent tax rate.

R&M's equity was offered to the public for the first time in 1983 and has been relatively volatile over its short history. In fact, the company's chief financial officer, Jessica Hagan, recently noted in a published investment advisory service that the firm's beta factor (a measure of systematic risk based on the covariation of the company's stock price changes with the market for all stocks) was 2.90. This number was among the highest for all reported stocks and reflected the highly volatile nature of the firm's prior research contract work. When Jessica sat down to evaluate the required rate of return for the solar project she was very uncomfortable with the company's beta as the basis for her analysis for the following reasons: (1) the proposed project involves the construction and operation of an electrical power source, whereas the firm's prior business had been exclusively contract research and (2) three-fourths of the proposed investment will be financed by borrowing, whereas the firm had previously relied on about 40 percent debt financing. Both of these factors led Jessica to reevaluate the project's systematic risk. The first step in this analysis involved collecting the following data on three utility companies that Jessica considered to be roughly comparable in their "riskiness" to the proposed project.

Firm	Debt/Equity Ratio	Equity Beta
A	0.9	1.5
B	1.0	2.0
C	1.8	3.5

In addition, Jessica plans to use a risk-free borrowing rate of 10 percent and a market risk premium of 6 to 8 percent. (The market risk premium is the difference between the expected rate of return for the market portfolio and the risk-free rate of interest. The range of estimates used here reflects the results of a major study of historical returns.)

a. Estimate the beta for the investment project (the asset beta).

b. What is the required rate of return for the project based on the capital asset pricing model?

c. What is the required "equity" rate of return based again on the use of the capital asset pricing model and the proposed financing mix?

d. What is the project's NPV using no debt financing? Using the proposed financing mix?

e. Should the project be undertaken? Discuss.

11.4   The Sampson P. Mallory Electric Company is evaluating the possibility of expanding its operations into the manufacture and sale of electric fuel pumps used in compact cars. The pumps are used in conjunction with a fuel injection system that has rapidly become standard in both foreign and domestic compact cars. Mallory has decided to evaluate the project over a two-year horizon with the assumption that at the end of the second year the project cash flow will reflect the sale value of the new division (that is, the new division will be analyzed "as if" it were to be sold at the end of two years, although it could well be maintained). Mallory has estimated interest rates for the next two years and has decided to restrict its attention to only two possible states of the world (boom and recession). Further, with the help of the firm's investment banker, it has obtained forecasts for the market index in each future state of nature for years 1 and 2. The project estimates are as follows:

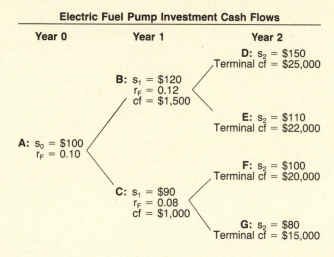

Electric Fuel Pump Investment Cash Flows

Year 0	Year 1	Year 2
A: $s_0 = \$100$ $r_F = 0.10$	**B:** $s_1 = \$120$ $r_F = 0.12$ cf $= \$1,500$	**D:** $s_2 = \$150$ Terminal cf $= \$25,000$
		E: $s_2 = \$110$ Terminal cf $= \$22,000$
	C: $s_1 = \$90$ $r_F = 0.08$ cf $= \$1,000$	**F:** $s_2 = \$100$ Terminal cf $= \$20,000$
		G: $s_2 = \$80$ Terminal cf $= \$15,000$

a. What is the maximum investment that Mallory should make in the fuel pump project?

b. What are the minimum end-of-year-1 abandonment values for states B and C that would lead Mallory to abandon the project after one year's operation?

11.5   The Ellis Company is presently evaluating the possible offering of a new and innovative line of soap products, which may or may not catch on with the consuming public. For this reason, Ellis has used a higher risk premium in discounting the project's future cash flows. In fact, the company used a 25 percent rate of return, whereas it normally utilizes 15 percent for its investments in existing product lines. In reviewing the project, the chairman of the board asked what assumptions were being incorporated in the analysis to account for the fact that the more distant future cash flows would surely be even more risky than the near-term ones. Janice Watson, a newly hired financial analyst, was assigned responsibility for responding to the chairman's query. What should Watson's response be to this problem?

11.6   Randy Battson Enterprises is involved in the analysis of two capital budgeting projects. The company wants to use the capital asset pricing model to evaluate the investor's required rate of return on each and has commissioned an outside consulting firm (Blose and Associates) to perform the analysis. Unfortunately, the consultant's report has been misplaced and Jim Alderson (chief financial analyst for Battson) must present his analysis to the board of directors of the firm in 15 minutes. Following a series of hasty phone calls, which were unsuccessful in locating the necessary information, Alderson has decided to reconstruct the lost estimates of project betas from the following notes, which he was able to locate.

Project	Covariance with the Market
A	0.0400
B	−0.0065

The variance in the market portfolio was estimated at 0.015. Further, he plans to use the current rate of interest on Treasury bills (90 day) of 7 percent for the risk-free rate and will consider two estimates of the market risk premium (6 and 8 percent). What required rates of return should Alderson take to the board, based on this information?

References

Bruce F. Baird, *Introduction to Decision Analysis* (North Scituate, Mass.: Duxbury Press, 1978).

M. Blume, "On the Assessment of Risk," *Journal of Finance* (March 1971): 1–10.

Z. Bodie and R. Taggart, "Future Investment Opportunities and the Value of the Call Provision on a Bond," *Journal of Finance* (September 1978): 1187–1200.

M. C. Bogue and R. R. Roll, "Capital Budgeting of Risky Projects with 'Imperfect' Markets for Physical Capital," *Journal of Finance* (May 1974): 601–613.

M. Brennan, "An Approach to the Valuation of Uncertain Income Streams," *Journal of Finance* (June 1973): 661–674.

G. Constantinides, "Admissible Uncertainty in the Intertemporal Asset Pricing Model," *Journal of Financial Economics* (March 1980): 71–86.

J. C. Cox and S. A. Ross, "The Valuation of Options for Alternative Stochastic Process" (Working paper no. 2–75, University of Pennsylvania, April 1975).

———, and M. Rubinstein, "Option Pricing: A Simplified Approach," *Journal of Financial Economics* (September 1979): 229–263.

———, "The Valuation of Options for Alternative Stochastic Processes," *Journal of Financial Economics* (January/March 1976): 145–166.

E. Fama, "Risk Adjusted Discount Rates and Capital Budgeting under Uncertainty," *Journal of Financial Economics* (June 1977): 3–24.

R. J. Fuller and H. S. Kerr, "Estimating the Divisional Cost of Capital: An Analysis of the Pure-Play Technique," *Journal of Finance* (December 1981): 997–1009.

A. Gehr, Jr., "Risk Adjusted Capital Budgeting Using Arbitrage," *Financial Management* (Winter 1981): 14–19.

R. S. Hamada, "The Effect of the Firm's Capital Structure on the Systematic Risk of Common Stock," *Journal of Finance* (May 1972): 435–452.

———, "Portfolio Analysis, Market Equilibrium, and Corporation Finance," *Journal of Finance* (March 1969): 13–21.

D. Harrington, "Whose Beta Is Best?" *Financial Analysts Journal* (July/August 1983): 67–73.

R. H. Hayes and D. A. Garvin, "Managing as If Tomorrow Mattered," *Harvard Business Review* (May/June 1982): 70–79.

J. E. Hodder and H. E. Riggs, "Pitfalls in Evaluating Risky Projects," *Harvard Business Review* (January/February 1985): 128–135.

R. G. Ibbotson and R. A. Sinquefield, *Stocks, Bonds, Bills, and Inflation: The Past and the Future* (Charlottesville, Va.: Financial Analysts Research Foundation, 1982).

H. Kim, "A Mean-Variance Theory of Optimal Capital Structure and Corporate Debt Capacity," *Journal of Finance* (March 1978): 45–64.

R. C. Klemkosky and J. D. Martin, "The Adjustment of Beta Forecasts," *Journal of Finance* (September 1975): 1123–1128.

F. H. Knight, *Risk, Uncertainty, and Profit* (New York: A. M. Kelley, 1937).

J. B. Long, "Stock Prices, Inflation and the Term Structure of Interest Rates," *Journal of Financial Economics* (July 1974): 131–170.

R. D. Luce and H. Raiffa, *Games and Decisions* (New York: Wiley, 1958).

R. C. Merton, "An Intertemporal Capital Asset Pricing Model," *Econometrica* (September 1973): 867–887.

F. Modigliani and M. Miller, "Taxes and the Cost of Capital: A Correction," *American Economic Review* (June 1963): 433–443.

I. G. Morgan, "Market Proxies and the Conditional Prediction of Returns," *Journal of Financial Economics* (December 1978): 385–398.

S. C. Myers, "Interactions of Corporate Financing and Investment Decisions—Implications for Capital Budgeting," *Journal of Finance* (March 1974): 1–25.

——— and S. M. Turnbull, "Capital Budgeting and the Capital Asset Pricing Model: Good News and Bad News," *Journal of Finance* (May 1977): 321–332.

J. Pratt, H. Raiffer, and R. Schlaifer, *Introduction to Statistical Decision Theory* (New York: McGraw-Hill, 1965).

A. A. Robichek and S. C. Myers, "Conceptual Problems in the Use of Risk-Adjusted Discount Rates," *Journal of Finance* (December 1966): 727–730.

B. Rosenberg, "Prediction of Common Stock Betas," *Journal of Portfolio Management* (Winter 1985): 5–14.

——— and A. Rudd, "The Corporate Uses of Beta," *Harvard Business Review* (1985): 42–52.

S. A. Ross, "A Simple Approach to the Valuation of Risky Streams," *Journal of Business* (July 1979): 254–286.

M. E. Rubinstein, "A Mean-Variance Synthesis of Corporate Financial Theory," *Journal of Finance* (March 1973): 167–181.

Appendix 11A

Capital Widening and the Optimal Scale of Production

In this appendix we generalize our discussion of the capital budgeting problem under uncertainty to include consideration for the optimal scale of investment (the capital widening issue as it was defined in Chapter 5) where project returns decline with the scale of investment. This discussion parallels our earlier treatment of the capital widening problem under certainty and produces results that can be interpreted in a similar manner.

The capital widening problem discussed in Chapter 5 was one of *how much to invest in a productive asset*. In order to address the same fundamental issue under uncertainty, we consider it in what economists refer to as a "short-run" situation; that is, the initial or immediate level of investment in plant and equipment (fixed assets) is assumed to be fixed, while the level of output and, consequently, variable costs of production and revenues result from the firm's output or production decision. The specific form of the capital widening problem addressed here reduces to that of determining the value-maximizing level of productive output where the firm faces increasing marginal costs of production. These rising marginal costs result from the increased intensity with which the fixed investment in plant and/or equipment is used to produce product. Specifically, the rate of return earned from the project, $R_I = (Z/I) - 1$, diminishes as the level of productive activity increases.

Diminishing returns to scale can result from one or both of two basic factors: (1) a declining product (output) price in response to increased firm output and (2) an increasing production cost resulting from the diminishing marginal productivity of the variable inputs used in conjunction with fixed factors of production. We will analyze only the latter source of diminishing returns to scale here. Note that the declining output price assumption is tantamount to assuming an "imperfectly competitive product market." Thus, this particular characterization of the optimal scale problem is one in which the firm exhibits enough market power to enable its production decisions to impact on the market price(s) of the product(s) it produces and sells. We will not address this particular setting for the scale problem.

Diminishing returns to scale are introduced here via the relationship between the project's random cash flow, Z, and the investment outlay, I. To develop this relationship, we will assume the following:

1. The price per unit of output from the proposed investment, P, is a random variable that is not a function of output quantity, Q.

2. The investment outlay for the project consists of a fixed component, I, which is deterministic and not a function of output quantity. In addition, this fixed expenditure occurs at the beginning of the period, and the initial cost of the project is simply I dollars.

The random, end-of-period net cash flow from investing in the project can be defined as follows:

$$Z = P \cdot Q - V(Q),$$

where $V(Q)$ is a function that represents the total variable cost of producing Q units of output. Further, for simplicity we will assume that $V(Q)$ increases with Q at an increasing rate (that is, $V'(Q) > 0$ and $V''(Q) > 0$).

The optimal scale of productive activity is found by maximizing project NPV with respect to output quantity, Q (the scale variable). In other words, using the certainty equivalent form of the CAPM, the objective can be stated as follows:

maximize

$$NPV = \frac{u_Z - \left(\dfrac{u_M - r_F}{\sigma_{MM}}\right) \text{Cov}[P \cdot Q - V(Q), R_M]}{1 + r_F} - I,$$

where u_Z is the expected value of Z. Note too that $u_Z = u_p Q - V(Q)$. Setting the derivative of the objective function equal to zero provides a first-order condition for a maximum NPV;[1] that is,

$$NPV' = [u_p - V'(Q)] - \frac{\text{Cov}[P \cdot Q - V(Q), R_M]}{Q\sigma_{MM}}(u_M - r_F) = 0,$$

where u_p is the expected product price per unit. This expression then reduces to the following:

---

[1] Differentiating NPV with respect to Q, we obtain the following:
$$NPV' = [u_p - V'(Q)] - \text{Cov}(P, R_M)(u_M - r_F)/\sigma_{MM}.$$
Next, we multiply the second term on the right-hand side by Q/Q and, noting that $\text{Cov}(V(Q), R_M) = 0$ since $V(Q)$ is a constant for any value of Q, we can now write NPV' in the form used in the text.

Figure 11A.1   Optimal Scale of Production Decision

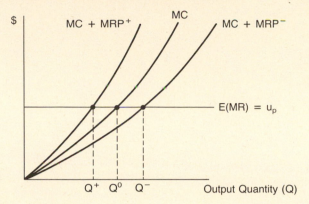

Q^+ = optimal output where $\beta_I > 0$
Q^0 = optimal output where $\beta_I = 0$
Q^- = optimal output where $\beta_I < 0$

$$u_p = V'(Q) + \beta_I\left(\frac{1}{Q}\right)(u_M - r_F).$$

We can interpret this equation as follows: The optimal scale of productive activity (optimal level of output) occurs where the expected marginal revenue from producing the last unit of output, u_p, just equals the marginal cost of that unit, $V'(Q)$, plus a marginal risk premium (the last term on the right-hand side of the above first-order condition).

The impact of the marginal risk premium on the solution to the optimal scale decision is depicted graphically in Figure 11A.1. Note that the optimal investment level (output quantity) decreases for projects with positive beta coefficients (β_I) when compared to the certainty case and increases for negative β_I projects; this is because the marginal risk premium is positive for $\beta_I > 0$, since MC > AVC for all Q (as we have assumed here).[2] Thus, we observe that the presence of uncertainty *does* affect the optimal scale of investment, but that impact can be either positive or negative depending on the sign of the systematic risk of the project in question.

---

[2]Where MC is marginal cost and AVC is average variable cost.

Chapter 12

Capital Structure Theory

Perhaps no area of financial management has commanded as much attention as the capital structure problem. Simply put, a firm's capital structure represents the mix of securities that it has sold in order to finance its asset acquisitions. The *capital structure problem*, then, deals with the firm's choices of the types of securities to issue. Capital structure theories seek to explain how the financing mix is determined.

A variety of capital structure theories have appeared in the finance literature. For our purposes, we will categorize these theories into two basic groups:[1] (1) *frictionless market theories*, which share the assumption that individuals and firms can buy and sell securities without incurring transactions costs and (2) *costly transaction theories*. Included in the first category are the original capital structure theories of Modigliani and Miller (1958, 1963), Miller (1977), and DeAngelo and Masulis (1980). The second contains a range of theories that capture the various effects of costly capital market transactions. Here we find the pure transactions cost or "pecking-order" theory attributed to Donaldson (1961);[2] the debt capacity

---

[1]This is but one possible basis for categorizing the various capital structure theories. Myers (1984) dichotomized these theories into either "static trade-off" or "pecking-order" theories. Alternatively, Taggart (1985) discusses three categories, including "perfect market," "debt capacity," and "financing hierarchy" theories.

[2]In his presidential address to the American Finance Association in 1983, Myers referred to Donaldson's description of corporate capital structure practice as supporting a "pecking-order" theory of corporate financing decisions.

theories, which rely on bankruptcy to limit a firm's use of debt financing (for example, Robichek and Myers [1966], Kraus and Litzenberger [1973], Scott [1976], and Kim [1976]); the agency models (such as Jensen and Meckling [1976], Myers [1977], and Smith and Warner [1979]); and the signaling model proposed by Ross (1977).

This chapter is organized as follows. First, we overview the frictionless market theories of the firm's capital structure. Specifically, we synthesize the original Modigliani and Miller (1958, 1963) papers in the context of the bond market equilibrium model posed by Miller (1977) and extend this synthesis to encompass the DeAngelo and Masulis (1980) results (in Appendix 12A), which include the legal restrictions on a firm's ability to take full advantage of its tax credits (such as investment tax credits). For simplicity, we conduct this discussion in a "certainty" environment; extension to an uncertain world would complicate the exposition and add little to the results.[3] In the next section, we review the various capital structure theories involving costly transactions. One of the first types of transactions costs considered in this set of theories was that of firm failure or bankruptcy. A number of authors have "appended" the notion of bankruptcy costs to the Modigliani and Miller (1963) tax-corrected valuation model, thereby limiting a firm's ability to use debt financing to enhance shareholder wealth. In addition, we also discover that in a world where information is costly, managers can make decisions that may be inconsistent with shareholder wealth maximization and hence introduces an "agency cost" explanation for the firm's capital structure choices. Finally, it has been suggested that in a world where management has information on the firm's future prospects that differs from (is superior to) that available to outside investors and where it is costly for shareholders and investors to monitor managers' behavior, management can use its capital structure decisions to "signal" information to investors regarding the firm's financial outlook. In this context, we examine the signaling theory of the firm's capital structure decisions proposed by Ross (1977).

Capital Structure Theories under Conditions of Frictionless Markets

Before introducing the general model that we will use to synthesize the body of capital structure theory, we must explain what we mean by frictionless markets. Specifically, the following attributes characterize a *frictionless market:*
There are no costs incurred in making transactions in any market. In particular, there are no information costs, brokerage fees, or other costs associated with the purchase or sale of securities or other assets.
Note that we assume not only that securities can be bought and sold costlessly but that the firm's real assets can also be purchased or sold with no transactions costs. The inclusion of the market for real productive assets is important because in the event of a firm's failure, its assets can be sold without penalty in the secondary

---

[3]Of the papers discussed in this section, only the DeAngelo and Masulis study was explicitly developed in an uncertain environment. Modigliani and Miller used the notion of "risk classes" to abstract from the necessity of incorporating uncertainty into their results, while Miller simply developed his analysis in a certainty framework.

market. In the next section, we will drop this assumption and see that where a failed firm's assets can be resold only by incurring the costs associated with transacting in the secondary market (a distress sale), the firm will be less willing to utilize debt financing because of the increased probability of financial distress.

Our discussion of capital structure theories with frictionless capital markets follows the general model posed by Miller (1977) in his presidential address to the American Finance Association. Basically this involves an analysis of the corporate bond market, including the supply of savings that individuals provide to the bond market, the demand for those funds by firms, and the consequent equilibrium. We begin our discussion by briefly reviewing the individual's consumption/savings decision (see Chapter 2) and then evaluate the situation where neither individuals nor firms pay income taxes. This no-tax case provides the basis for developing the original Modigliani and Miller (1958) no-tax valuation model. Next, we introduce the existence of corporate taxes (but no personal taxes) and develop the Modigliani and Miller (1963) tax-corrected valuation model (with a twist, as we will see). We then consider both personal and corporate taxes and develop Miller's (1977) capital structure propositions. Finally, we introduce constraints on the firm's ability to utilize its tax credits (such as investment tax credits) and derive the DeAngelo and Masulis (1980) theory of the capital structure. Throughout the analysis we will evaluate the demand for and supply of funds to the corporate bond market and, in so doing, synthesize an important portion of the capital structure theory literature into a common framework.

The Market for Corporate Bonds and the Individual's Savings Allocation Decision between Equity and Bonds

In this section, we develop a model for the corporate bond market that consists of a supply of funds provided by individual savers and the demand for those funds by corporations. Our model reflects a number of simplifying assumptions. Specifically, we consider a competitive market for bonds and stocks in which both types of securities are assumed to pay a certain return in one period; that is, a \$1 investment in bonds yields a return of $(1 + r_B)$, while a \$1 investment in stock (equity) provides an end-of-period return of $(1 + r_E)$. We further assume that individuals maximize the returns on their investments in the financial markets and that corporations maximize their market values.

To develop a model of bond market equilibrium, we proceed as follows. First we investigate the individual's investment choice between placing savings in bonds or in stocks and from there develop the supply of funds to the bond market. Then we analyze the corporation's choice between the use of debt and equity financing, which in turn enables us to analyze the demand for funds in the bond market.

The Individual Investor's Savings Decision and the Supply of Funds to the Bond Market.   Suppose there are many investors (indexed by i) who make a savings decision in the current period equal to s_i.[4] The savings decision reflects the

---

[4] We will be using the two-period Fisher model developed in Chapter 2 as the basis for our analysis of the individual's consumption/savings decision.

individual's current and future period income (m_{i0}, m_{i1}) and preferences for intertemporal consumption. If we let c_{i0} and c_{i1} represent the individual's consumption for the two periods, we can define savings with the following relationship:

$$c_{i0} = m_{i0} - s_i .$$

The individual must now determine how to allocate the s_i dollars between bond (b_i) and stock (e_i) investments. This choice is made by maximizing the utility of the consumption stream, which implies maximizing the end-of-period wealth, w_{i1} for a given savings decision:

maximize

$$w_{i1} = (1 + r_B)b_i + (1 + r_E)e_i ,$$

with the following constraints:

1.   Savings must be allocated between bonds and equities; that is,

$$s_i = b_i + e_i \quad \text{or} \quad e_i = s_i - b_i .$$

2.   Equity cannot be sold short;[5] that is,

$$e_i > 0 .$$

3.   If bonds are issued (sold short), they cannot exceed the present value of the individual's wealth; that is,

$$-b_i \geq - \left[m_{i0} + \frac{m_{i1}}{1 + r_B} \right] = -w_{i0} .$$

Note that constraints 2 and 3 eliminate the possibility of a "money machine" whereby the individual could issue the low-return security (sell short) and purchase the higher-return security without limit.

We can now define next period's consumption as follows:

$$c_{i1} = m_{i1} + (1 + r_B)b_i + (1 + r_E)e_i .$$

Note that if $r_B > r_E$ the individual will save by buying only bonds, while if $r_E > r_B$ the individual will invest only in equity. We can represent this straightforward result using the Fisher two-period consumption diagram shown in Figure 12.1.[6] Here the rate of return earned on bonds exceeds that earned on equity; thus, the

---

[5]Some authors would argue — perhaps justifiably — that restrictions such as that on short sales constitute a "market friction." However, as noted earlier, we have chosen to define market frictions to include the costs of trading, such as those of information gathering and processing. For those who prefer to include short-sale restrictions under the general rubric of market frictions, this section could be retitled "Capital Structure Theories with No 'Transactions Costs'."

[6]Note that in a world of complete certainty the individual's behavior can be described as "plunging" in that all of his or her savings will be placed in either bonds or equities depending on which offers the higher yield. Of course, in a world of uncertainty the relevant comparison would reflect an appropriate risk premium for the equity securities, but the result would be the same.

Figure 12.1 Individual's Savings Allocation Choice between Bonds and Equities

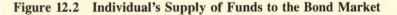

Future Consumption c_{i1}

Trading Line Given Investment in Equity Only

m_{i1}

Trading Line Given Investment in Bonds Only

m_{i0} c_{i0}

Current Consumption

optimal savings allocation is $s_i = b_i$. Correspondingly, if $r_E > r_B$, the saver will (given borrowing constraint 3) borrow the maximum possible amount and invest the entire proceeds in equity securities.

We can now evaluate the individual's supply of funds to the bond market. We will assume that the individual saves more as the interest rate rises. Further, we let s_i^* denote the individual's saving when $r_B = r_E$. Then we obtain the supply function, S_i, for funds to the bond market as depicted in Figure 12.2. The supply of funds to the bond market is perfectly elastic over the range $(-[m_{i0} + m_{i1}/(1 + r_E)], s_i^*)$, since $r_B = r_E$. When $r_B > r_E$, the individual increases his or her savings and *all* those funds are channeled into the bond market. The supply of sav-

Figure 12.2 Individual's Supply of Funds to the Bond Market

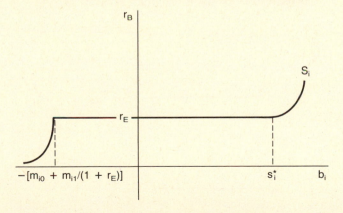

r_B

r_E

S_i

$-[m_{i0} + m_{i1}/(1 + r_E)]$ s_i^* b_i

ings to the bond market as a whole will look the same as the individual's supply function except that it will begin increasing at $s^* = \Sigma\ s_i^*$, where s^* is obtained by summing over all individuals.

The Corporate Financing Decision and the Demand for Funds in the Bond Market.   The demand for funds in the bond market is assumed to come exclusively from corporations that seek to maximize the value of their debt and equity claims — that is, corporations will select the mix of financial contracts that will maximize their values. Let $V_j^L = B_j + E_j$ denote the market value of the securities issued by (levered) corporation j, where B_j is the value of the firm's debt and E_j the value of its equity. Also, let X_j represent the corporation's earnings for the period. The value of the firm's equity can then be written as follows:

$$E_j = \frac{X_j - (1 + r_B)B_j}{1 + r_E}$$

Thus, the value of the levered firm can be expressed as follows:

(12.1) $$V_j = \frac{X_j - (1 + r_B)B_j}{(1 + r_E)} + B_j = \frac{X_j}{(1 + r_E)} + \left[1 - \frac{1 + r_B}{1 + r_E}\right]B_j.$$

In this very simple setting, the corporation's demand for funds via the sale of bonds is perfectly elastic so long as the required rate of return on bonds equals the required rate of return on equity (see Figure 12.3). Recall again that we have assumed a world of complete certainty such that the required rates of return on all securities will be the same in equilibrium. Under conditions of uncertainty, the demand for bond funds would be horizontal where the required rate of return on bonds equaled that on equity *minus* a risk premium.

Equilibrium in the Bond Market (Modigliani/Miller [1958]).   We are now in a position to consider bond market equilibrium. Recall that in our discussion of both

Figure 12.3   Corporation's Demand for Bond Funds

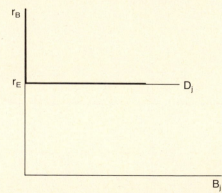

the supply of funds to the bond market by individuals and the demand for those
funds by corporations there were no taxes; that is, individuals paid no personal
taxes on their income from bonds or stocks and corporations got no tax deductions
for interest expenses they incurred. Thus, the equilibrium in the bond market that
we analyze first is the *no-tax case* considered by Modigliani and Miller (1958).

Figure 12.4 contains the market supply of and demand for bond funds
derived earlier. Note that there is but one equilibrium interest rate, $r_B^* = r_E$; however, there is a whole spectrum of debt levels for which equilibrium exists (that is,
the equilibrium amount of bond financing ranges from no bonds to s* or [0, s*]).
Hence, there is no optimal level of bond funds in the bond market but a continuum
ranging from zero to s*.

Note what happens to the valuation expression for the firm found in Equation 12.1 when we substitute the equilibrium bond rate, $r_B^* = r_E$ for r_B:

$$V_j = \frac{X_j}{1 + r_E} = V_j^U.$$

Thus, under conditions of bond market equilibrium the value of the levered firm,
V_j, equals that of the unlevered firm, V_j^U. Hence, the use of financial leverage
does not impact on the firm's value. This was the basic conclusion reached by
Modigliani and Miller in their 1958 classic capital structure paper.

The Modigliani/Miller capital structure irrelevance result can also be stated
in terms of a firm's *cost of capital*. Note that we can define the weighted average
cost of capital for the firm as follows:

(12.2)
$$r_A = \left(\frac{B}{V}\right)r_B + \left(\frac{E}{V}\right)r_E,$$

where $V = V^L = V^U$ and r_A is the weighted average cost of capital. However,
under conditions of bond market equilibrium (where $r_B^* = r_E$), the firm's cost of
capital reduces to the following:

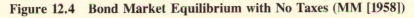

Figure 12.4   Bond Market Equilibrium with No Taxes (MM [1958])

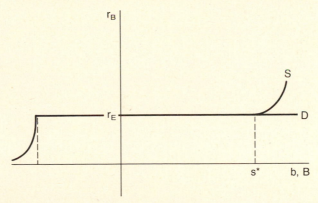

$$r_A = \left(\frac{B + E}{V}\right)r_E = r_E.$$

The weighted average cost of capital under conditions of market equilibrium, then, is the same for all debt/equity mixes. This should come as no surprise, for under conditions of bond market equilibrium there is no cost advantage to the firm of using either debt or equity financing. Thus, to summarize, where there are no taxes paid by either individuals or corporations, (1) there is no advantage to the corporation's use of financial leverage and (2) as already noted, there is no optimal level of bond financing for the market as a whole.

An Institutional Note: The U.S. Income Tax Code

Under the 1986 revision of the U.S. tax code, corporations face a maximum income tax of 34 percent and individuals a maximum of 28 percent. To gain some perspective on the income tax system currently in place, we must go back in history. The following dates and events mark the evolution of the U.S. income tax code:

- 1862 The first income tax on individual incomes was instituted, with a maximum rate of 10 percent. The tax was in effect for only 10 years.

- 1895 The Supreme Court ruled that an attempt to resurrect the personal income tax was unconstitutional.

- 1909 The first tax on corporate profits was enacted, with a 1 percent rate.

- 1913 The Sixteenth Amendment was ratified, granting Congress the power to levy and collect income taxes. A 1 percent income tax was enacted for most taxpayers, with a 7 percent maximum. Capital gains (appreciation in the value of capital assets) were fully taxed.

- 1918 The tax rate on corporate profits rose to 12 percent, and the maximum tax rate on individual income skyrocketed to 77 percent (from only 15 percent in 1916).

- 1921 Long-term capital gains received preferential (reduced) tax treatment for the first time.

- 1929 The maximum tax rate on individual income dropped to 24 percent (down from a postwar high of 46 percent in 1924).

- 1941–1945 The maximum tax rate on individual income was increased to 94 percent; corporate profits greater than $50,000 became taxed at 40 percent.

- 1952 Corporate tax rates rose to 30 percent for the first $50,000 of taxable income and 52 percent for the remainder.

- 1954 Accelerated depreciation rules providing for more rapid writeoff of corporate asset expenses were instituted.

- 1962 A 7 percent investment tax credit for new-asset purchases was instituted.

- 1964 The maximum tax rate on individual income was lowered to 77 percent.

- 1969 The top tax rate for individual income was further reduced to 50 percent.

- 1975 The investment tax credit on new-asset purchases was raised to 10 percent.

- 1978 The top tax rate on capital gains was reduced to 28 percent from a high of 49 percent. The maximum corporate tax rate was cut to 46 percent beginning in 1979.

- 1981   Tax brackets for individual income were indexed to inflation. The accelerated cost recovery system (ACRS) was instituted to replace the existing depreciation system. (This allows for liberalization of the cost recovery from major asset acquisitions.) The maximum capital gains tax rate for individuals was decreased to 20 percent.

- 1986   The maximum tax rate for corporate income dropped from 46 percent to 34 percent and that for individual income from 50 percent to 28 percent. Interest on consumer credit was phased out, and capital gains income became taxable as ordinary income.

A cursory review of the "checkered" history of the U.S. tax code suggests the difficulty that theorists encounter in attributing corporate financial policies to taxes alone. Certainly firms and individuals consider their tax rates when making their choices; however, if taxes were the single most important factor in firms' and individuals' financing decisions, the wide variation in tax rates over the post–Civil War period would suggest equally wide variation in financing patterns. In Chapter 13 we review corporate financing patterns and find that they have been amazingly stable.

Source: "Tax Reform—At Last," *Business Week,* September 1, 1986, 54–57.

Corporate Taxes and the Modigliani/Miller (1963) Tax-Corrected Model

In 1963, Franco Modigliani and Merton Miller published a correction to their 1958 seminal paper on capital structure. In this paper they reevaluated the impact of financial structure on firm value in the presence of corporate income taxes. The key feature of their analysis was the differential tax treatment of dividends to common shareholders and interest paid to bondholders at the corporate level. Interest expense is deductible from corporate income while dividends are not, thus offering the corporation a "tax subsidy" where bond financing is used. We will now investigate the role of corporate taxes in the context of our bond market equilibrium model. To do so we need modify only the demand function for funds in the bond market, for the introduction of corporate taxes affects the firm's choice of bond versus equity financing.

The Demand for Corporate Bond Funds with Corporate Income Taxes. Now consider the situation where corporations pay income taxes at a rate t_c and interest on the bonds they have issued is tax deductible. The corporation's taxable income then becomes $(X_j - r_B B_j)$ to produce the following value of the firm's equity:

$$E_j = \frac{X_j - (1 + r_B)B_j - (X_j - r_B B_j)t_c}{1 + r_E}.$$

The value of the levered firm, which is simply $V_j = B_j + E_j$, can be rewritten in a manner analogous to Equation 12.1:

$$(12.3) \qquad V_j = \left[\frac{X_j(1 - t_c)}{1 + r_E} \right] + \left[1 - \frac{1 + r_B(1 - t_c)}{1 + r_E} \right] B_j .$$

Note that when we substitute $r_B = r_E$ into the above expression, it reduces to the following familiar form:

$$(12.4) \qquad V_j = \underbrace{\left[\frac{X_j(1 - t_c)}{1 + r_E} \right]}_{\substack{\text{Value of} \\ \text{unlevered firm}}} + \underbrace{\frac{r_B t_c B_j}{1 + r_B}}_{\substack{\text{Value of interest} \\ \text{tax savings}}} .$$

The above valuation model is the single-period version of the Modigliani/Miller (1963) tax-corrected model that is widely used throughout the finance literature to describe how using financial leverage adds to firm value via the present value of the interest tax savings on debt financing. In this model, the firm realizes an increase in its interest tax savings for every dollar of debt financing it uses without limit. Thus, the optimal capital structure under this circumstance would involve 99 percent debt. However, we will later demonstrate that an anomaly arises when we consider the equilibrium interest rate in the bond market. There we find that this rate is not $r_B = r_E$ but $r_B = r_E/(1 - t_c)$ or $r_E = r_B(1 - t_c)$ such that the after-tax cost of bonds equals the after-tax cost of equity financing.

  To derive the firm's demand for funds from the bond market, we note that in Equation 12.3 V_j^L is increasing with the use of bond financing so long as $r_E > r_B(1 - t_c)$ and decreasing in B_j, where the inequality is reversed. The resulting corporate demand for bond financing is reflected in Figure 12.5. The market demand is found by aggregating across the demands of all firms. Note that the firm's

Figure 12.5   Demand for Bond Funds with Corporate Taxes

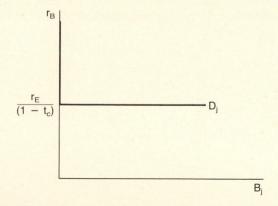

demand for bond financing in Figure 12.5 differs from its no-corporate-tax counterpart in Figure 12.3 only with respect to the bond rate at which the demand
function becomes horizontal (perfectly elastic). In the no-tax case depicted in
Figure 12.3 this occurs where $r_B = r_E$, and in the presence of corporate taxes depicted in Figure 12.5 it occurs where $r_B(1 - t_c) = r_E$.

Bond Market Equilibrium with Corporate Taxes (Modigliani/Miller [1963]).
Since we have not changed the tax treatment of individual income, the supply of
funds to the bond market is unchanged from Figure 12.2; however, the demand for
bond financing is now represented by the function in Figure 12.5. Combining the
demand for and supply of funds in the bond market, we determine the equilibrium
conditions therein with corporate taxes. Figure 12.6 contains a graphical representation of market equilibrium.

The resulting equilibrium interest rate calls for $r_B^* = r_E/(1 - t_c)$, as we
noted when discussing the Modigliani/Miller (1963) tax-corrected valuation model
for the levered firm. In this scenario there does exist an optimal level of bond
financing equal to B* and, consequently, an optimal financial mix consisting
of bonds and equity for the economy as a whole. Note too that under this set of
conditions the values of the levered and unlevered firm are again equal:

(12.3) $$V_j^L = \frac{X_j(1 - t_c)}{1 + r_E} + \left[1 - \frac{1 + r_B(1 - t_c)}{1 + r_E}\right] B_j.$$

That is, substituting for $r_B = r_B^* = r_E/(1 - t_c)$ in Equation 12.3, we get

$$V_j^L = \frac{X_j(1 - t_c)}{1 + r_E} = V_j^U.$$

Thus, under conditions of market equilibrium the tax savings advantage of debt
financing that we observed in Equation 12.4 (in the MM [1963] tax-corrected
model) is driven down to zero. This rather paradoxical result is a direct consequence of our having considered equilibrium conditions in the corporate bond

---

Figure 12.6   Bond Market Equilibrium with Corporate Taxes (MM [1963])

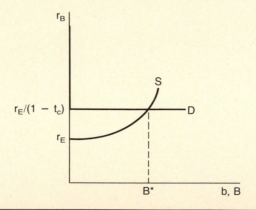

market and is not surprising when we stop to think about what market equilibrium means: that under conditions of market equilibrium there is no incentive for investors or firms to change their holdings/positions in the bond market. Thus, the tax savings advantage of debt financing noted in Equation 12.4 must be reduced to zero if bond market equilibrium is to be achieved. Note too that under conditions of market equilibrium there exists an optimal quantity of bond financing for the market as a whole, as we observed in Figure 12.6.

Personal Taxes and the Miller (1977) Model

We now introduce personal income taxes where bond interest income is taxed at a rate of t_p and equity income is not taxed (as Miller assumed). Thus, a \$1 investment in bonds will yield to the investor an after-tax return of $r_B(1 - t_p)$ at the end of the period. Similarly, a \$1 investment in stocks will yield a return of r_E. Investors' bond tax rates range from 0 to T, where $T > t_c$ depending on the investors' levels of taxable income. (The TRA of 1986 lowered the maximum personal tax rate, T, below the maximum corporate rate, t_c. However, in 1977 t_c was less than T.) Thus, investors supply funds to the bond market if $r_B(1 - t_p) > r_E$ or, equivalently, $r_B > r_E/(1 - t_p)$. The market supply of funds to the bond market, then, is the maximum amount of funds investors supply at each bond rate, which depends partly on the distribution of investors across tax brackets. Note that the supply of funds to the bond market increases with r_B because as r_B rises, investors in higher tax brackets are drawn into the market; this occurs in addition to the increased saving by investors already in the bond market. Figure 12.7 graphically depicts the market supply of funds to the bond market.

Since the corporate demand for bond funds is the same as that already derived for the corporate tax case (see Figure 12.5), we can now consider the nature of bond market equilibrium under both personal and corporate taxes. The equilibrium interest rate is $r_B^* = r_E/(1 - t_c)$ or $r_B^*(1 - t_c) = r_E$. Hence, the marginal investor has a tax rate on bond income of $t_p = t_c$, and all investors with

---

Figure 12.7   Bond Market Equilibrium with Personal and Corporate Taxes (Miller [1977])

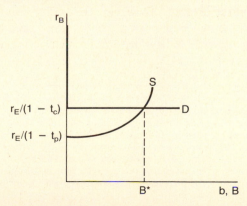

$t_p < t_c$ will invest their savings in bonds while those with $t_p > t_c$ will invest in equities. (The basic results of the 1977 Miller model continue to hold under the TRA of 1986 if all personal tax rates are less than the maximum corporate tax rate.) Note too that there is an equilibrium bond level, B^*, for the market as a whole. However, the interest rate on bonds is bid up to the point at which the value of the tax shelter is zero. Once again we utilize Equation 12.3 and the equilibrium interest rate in the bond market r_B^*, that is,

$$V_j^L = \underbrace{\frac{X_j(1 - t_c)}{1 + r_E}}_{V_j^U} + \underbrace{\left[1 - \frac{1 + r_B^*(1 - t_c)}{1 + r_E}\right]B_j}_{\text{Gain from leverage}}.$$

However, where we substitute the equilibrium bond rate, $r_B^* = r_E/(1 - t_p)$ and the gain from leverage disappears such that

$$V_j^L = V_j^U.$$

Thus, market equilibrium conditions in the bond market (even in the presence of personal and corporate taxes) produce conditions under which the firm's capital structure choice is a matter of indifference to its owners. However, unlike in the cases considered thus far, there *is* an optimal debt-to-equity ratio in the market as a whole. This optimal *aggregate* capital structure will, in turn, reflect the distribution of aggregate savings across the spectrum of personal tax brackets. In Figure 12.7, the optimal level of debt financing for the market as a whole equals B^*.

Limitations on Corporate Tax Credits and the DeAngelo/Masulis (1980) Model

DeAngelo and Masulis (1980) utilized the legal limit imposed on a firm's ability to use tax credits to offset taxable income to define a limit on the firm's willingness to use debt financing. Simply stated, if a firm benefits from using debt financing from the interest tax savings it provides, it will find the use of debt advantageous only so long as it can take advantage of the tax deductibility of interest. DeAngelo and Masulis noted that the firm's ability to utilize its investment and other tax credits was limited by the availability of taxable income; thus the firm could not use bond interest to offset all its taxable income without losing its tax credits.[7] The limitation placed on the level of "allowable" tax credits varies with the whim of Congress; however, the important point is that the firm's ability to utilize its interest expense as a tax-deductible item depends on the fraction of allowable deduc-

---

[7]Tax credits reduce a firm's tax liability dollar for dollar. For example, if a firm purchases a machine for $100,000 and that machine qualifies for a 10 percent investment tax credit, the firm will be able to offset its tax liability for the year in which the purchase is made by $10,000. Correspondingly, if the firm were in a 40 percent tax bracket and incurred $10,000 in interest expense, it could reduce its "taxable income" by $10,000, which in turn would save it only $4,000 in taxes. Thus, $1 in tax credits offsets $1 in taxes, while $1 in tax-deductible expenses reduces taxes by a fraction of $1 equal to the marginal tax rate (40 percent). The investment tax credit has been an "on again, off again" fact of life in this country in recent years. The TRA of 1986 made it "off again" for the present.

tions, the level of the firm's taxable income, and the amount of tax-deductible expenses and credits it accrues from its operations (such as depreciation on fixed assets and investment tax credits).[8]

Details on the development of the DeAngelo/Masulis model are included in Appendix 12A. Basically, the key result of this analysis was that the presence of a limit on a firm's ability to take advantage of its tax credits will produce an optimal capital structure for each individual firm and for the economy as a whole. The firm's optimal capital structure will entail using that level of debt financing at which its total tax credits (including the impact of interest expense on taxable income) sum to the maximum allowable amount within the guidelines of the tax code.

Summary

Our objective in this section has been to synthesize the subset of the capital structure literature pertaining to frictionless markets. These theories are unique because they use tax considerations to explain the marginal benefits and, in some cases, the marginal costs associated with using debt financing. The Modigliani/Miller 1958 and 1963 papers are the original works in this subset of the capital structure literature. These studies were "partial equilibrium" in nature in that they did not consider the implications of all firms' and investors' combined activities on equilibrium in the corporate bond market. The Miller (1977) presidential address to the American Finance Association extended the original Modigliani/Miller papers in two important ways. First, it incorporated consideration for differential personal taxation on bond versus stock income; second, it utilized the more general "bond market equilibrium" type of analysis that we used here. We used this basic model as the basis for synthesizing the earlier Modigliani/Miller papers with the Miller model and also extended it to incorporate the primary tenets of the DeAngelo/ Masulis (1980) model (discussed in detail in Appendix 12A). In the latter case, we considered the legal limitations on a firm's ability to utilize its tax credits.

At this point, it is time to assess the ability of capital structure theory to explain observed financing practice. On the positive side, we note that both the Miller (1977) and DeAngelo/Masulis (1980) models provide the basis for determining an optimal capital structure (that is, debt and equity mix) for the economy as a whole. In addition, DeAngelo and Masulis lay the groundwork for determining an optimal debt/equity mix for individual firms that will reflect each one's taxpaying status. In Chapter 13, we will review the empirical evidence on capital structure. A quick preview of that material reveals that firms do engage in active capital structure management, as the cross-sectional differences in capital structures across firms (and industries) manifest. Further, firms seem to differ signifi-

---

[8]Of course, there are "other" ways of accruing tax savings via the sale of those benefits. For example, during the period 1981 to 1982 under the "safe harbor" provision of the Economic Recovery and Tax Act of 1981, firms could sell their unused tax credits via "paper lease transactions." The TEFRA tax act of 1982 substantially eliminated (or at least made more difficult) such tax credit sales via financial lease agreements.

cantly in the maturity structure of their debt and use complex financial contracts involving call provisions, convertibility features, sinking funds, and warrants. At this time we will simply observe that the phenomena explained by capital structure theory are very involved and that the body of theory we have reviewed thus far, although helpful, does not even hint at many of the practical considerations that the firm encounters in making financing choices. In an effort to enhance the explanatory power of our capital structure models, in the next section we expand the underlying set of assumptions to include the roles of costly market transactions and uncertainty. In addition, we examine the dynamic nature of the firm's financing choices.

Uncertainty, the Fisher Model, and the Modigliani/Miller Theorem: A Mathematical Overview

Here we consider the same complete financial markets model treated in "Fisher's Separation Theorem: A Mathematical Overview," except we also allow for debt instruments. As expected, the 1958 Modigliani/Miller theorem holds in this setting because investors can costlessly augment or counteract any corporate leverage decisions. This result holds, also as expected, regardless of whether the corporation's debt is risky or safe. We will proceed in simple stages, first showing the result for safe debt and then for risky debt.

As before, let $s = 1, 2, \ldots, S$ denote the set of states of nature and let p_s denote the price of an asset that pays \$1 in state s and nothing otherwise. Now let p_f and N_f denote the share price and number of shares issued by corporation f. Similarly, let q_f and B_f denote the share price of the bond contract and number of shares issued by corporation f. Suppose the manager issues enough shares of debt and equity to finance an investment expenditure of I_f dollars now. Also suppose the payoff on the investments is $(\Pi_{f1}, \ldots, \Pi_{fS})$ so that the payoff depends on the state s.[a] Let D_f and E_f^L denote the market values of the corporation's debt and equity issues, respectively. Let V_f^L denote the value of the levered corporation, where $V_f^L = D_f + E_f^L$. Then the Modigliani/Miller result says that the value of the levered corporation equals the value of the unlevered corporation; that is, $V_f^L = V_f^U$, where V_f^U denotes the value of the unlevered (all equity) firm.

Now consider an unconstrained version of the investor's maximization problem. To do this, define consumption now and then in terms of the financial assets. Let x_s be the number of shares of asset s purchased and let x_f be the number of shares of firm f purchased by the investor. Similarly, let y_f be the number of bonds purchased by the investor. Define a safe debt contract as a promise to pay \$1 in each state of nature. The investor's consumption now and then may be represented as

(i)
$$c_0 = m_0 - \sum_{s=1}^{S} p_s x_s - p_f x_f - q_f y_f$$

[a]The investment of I_f dollars is assumed to be fixed in this analysis.

and

(ii) $$c_{1s} = m_{1s} + x_s + x_f \frac{\Pi_{fs}}{N_f} + y_f, \qquad s = 1, 2, \ldots, S.$$

The investor makes the saving and portfolio choices to maximize expected utility, where expected utility is

$$\sum_{s=1}^{S} u(c_0, c_{1s})\Psi_s$$

and, as before, the consumption pairs are defined by (i) and (ii). Maximizing expected utility with respect to x_s, x_f, and y_f, respectively, yields the following first-order conditions:

(iii) $$-p_s\left[\sum_{s=1}^{S} D_1 u \Psi_s\right] + D_2 u \Psi_s = 0$$

(iv) $$\sum_{s=1}^{S}\left[-p_f D_1 u + D_2 u\left(\frac{\Pi_{fs} - B_f}{N_f}\right)\right]\Psi_s = 0$$

(v) $$\sum_{s=1}^{S}\{-q_f D_1 u + D_2 u\}\Psi_s = 0$$

Using (iii), we may note that

(vi) $$p_s = \frac{D_2 u \Psi_s}{\sum_{s=1}^{S} D_1 u \Psi_s}$$

as previously. Then, using (iv) and (vi), we note that the firm's share price is

(vii) $$p_f = \sum_{s=1}^{S} p_s\left(\frac{\Pi_{fs} - B_f}{N_f}\right).$$

It follows that the stock market value of the levered corporation f is

(viii) $$E_f^L = p_f N_f = \sum_{s=1}^{S} p_s(\Pi_{fs} - B_f).$$

Similarly, using (v) and (vi), we obtain

$$q_f = \sum_{s=1}^{S} p_s.$$

This is the expected result, because the riskless debt contract is equivalent to purchasing one share of stock of each type s. Any other result would yield an arbitrage opportunity. It follows that the market value of the corporate debt is

(ix) $$D_f = q_f B_f = \sum_{s=1}^{S} p_s B_f.$$

Using (viii), observe that the market value of the unlevered firm is $V_f^U = E_f^U$, where

$$V_f^U = \sum_{s=1}^{S} p_s \Pi_{fs}.$$

Finally, note that by (viii) and (ix), the value of the levered corporation is

$$V_f^L = D_f + E_f^L = \sum_{s=1}^{S} p_s \Pi_{fs} = V_f^U.$$

Hence we have the 1958 Modigliani/Miller theorem in its simplest form under uncertainty.

Next we want to introduce risky debt instruments. Suppose firm f has issued bonds for which it promises to repay B_f dollars at the end of the period if the firm's earnings are sufficient; then the return to all bondholders in state s is $\min\{B_f, \Pi_{fs}\}$. The return per share is $\min\{B_f, \Pi_{fs}\}/B_f = \min\{1, \Pi_{fs}/B_f\}$, and letting q_f denote the share price of the corporation risky debt, we obtain consumption now and then as

(x) $$c_0 = m_0 - \sum_{s=1}^{S} p_s x_s - p_f x_f - q_f y_f$$

and

(xi) $\quad c_{1s} = m_{1s} + x_s + x_f \left(\dfrac{\Pi_{fs} - B_f}{N_f} \right) + y_f \min\{1, \Pi_{fs}/B_f\}, \qquad s = 1, 2, \ldots, S.$

Now the first-order condition for debt purchase becomes

$$\sum_{s=1}^{S} \{-q_f D_1 u + \min\{1, \Pi_{fs}/B_f\} D_2 u\} \Psi_s = 0.$$

If we let $\min\{1, \Pi_{fs}/B_f\} = 1$ for all states of nature in the event $\mathbf{S} = \{s \,|\, \Pi_{fs} \geq B_f\}$ and $\min\{1, \Pi_{fs}/B_f\} = \Pi_{fs}/B_f$ for all states of nature in the bankruptcy event $\mathbf{B} = \{s \,|\, \Pi_{fs} < B_f\}$, the first-order condition may be rewritten as

$$q_f = \sum_{\mathbf{S}} p_s + \sum_{\mathbf{B}} p_s \Pi_{fs}/B_f.$$

Note that the total market value of the firm's risky debt is $D_f = q_f B_f$ and

$$D_f = \sum_{\mathbf{S}} p_s B_f + \sum_{\mathbf{B}} p_s \Pi_{fs} = \sum_{\mathbf{SUB}} p_s \min\{B_f, \Pi_{fs}\}.$$

This result is also intuitively appealing because in this case one bond is equivalent to a portfolio of stock with a \$1 payoff for all s in $\mathbf{S}$ and with a fraction Π_{fs}/B_f of a dollar payoff for all s in $\mathbf{B}$.

Next consider the value of the corporation with risky debt in its capital structure. If we let E_f^L denote the value of equity,

$$E_f^L = \sum_{\mathbf{SUB}} p_s \max\{0, \Pi_{fs} - B_f\} = \sum_{\mathbf{S}} p_s [\Pi_{fs} - B_f]$$

and the total value of the corporation is $V_f^L = E_f^L + D_f$, or

$$V_f^L = \sum_{s=1}^{s} p_s \Pi_{fs} = V_f^U .$$

Note that this is the 1958 Modigliani/Miller capital structure irrelevance result with risky debt.

Capital Structure Theories with Costly Transactions

In his 1961 study of the financing practices of U.S. corporations, Donaldson made the following observation:

Management strongly favored internal generation as a source of new funds even to the exclusion of external funds except for occasional unavoidable "bulges" in the need for funds. (p. 67)

He further noted that the occasional "bulges-in-funds" requirements were seldom met by reducing the firm's dividend payout. Further, when external financing was required, firms rarely resorted to the sale of common stock:

Though few companies would go so far as to rule out a sale of common stock under any circumstances, the large majority had not had such a sale in the past 20 years and did not anticipate one in the foreseeable future. This was particularly remarkable in view of the very high Price-Earnings ratios of recent years. Several financial officers showed that they were well aware that this had been a good time to sell common, but the reluctance still persisted. (pp. 57–58)

Myers (1984) characterized this view of the firm's financing decision in what he termed a *pecking-order* theory. Specifically, he noted the following pecking order for financing decisions:[9]

1.   Firms prefer internal sources of funds.

2.   Firms adapt their dividend payout policies to reflect their anticipated investment opportunities, although dividends are sticky and target payout ratios are only gradually adjusted to shifts in the extent of valuable investment opportunities. (We return to a more complete discussion of dividend policy in Chapter 14.)

3.   Sticky dividend policies, plus unpredictable fluctuations in profitability and investment opportunities, mean that internally generated cash flow may be more or less than investment outlays. If it is less, the firm first draws down its cash balance or marketable securities portfolio. If it is more, the firm first pays off debt or invests in cash or marketable securities. If the surplus persists, the firm may gradually increase its target payout ratio.

4.   If external financing is required, firms issue the safest security first: They start with debt, then possibly hybrid securities such as convertible bonds, then possibly equity as a last resort.

---

[9]The following paraphrases Myers' pecking-order theory.

Note the following important attributes of the Myers pecking-order theory:

1.   There is no target debt/equity mix.

2.   There are two types of equity, internal and external, one being the first priority for new financing and the other the last.

3.   Consequently, each firm's debt/equity financing mix reflects its cumulative requirements for external financing.

In essence, the firm's observed financing mix, according to the pecking-order theory, is a historical artifact reflecting its profitability, dividend policy, and investment opportunities.[10] Note too that while the pecking-order theory may "describe" corporate financing practice accurately,[11] it does not explain why such policy is optimal or even desirable. In this regard, two types of capital structure theory have been offered: *managerial capitalism* and *transactions costs*. We discuss each of these in turn.

Managerial Capitalism

The managerial capitalism explanation for the pecking-order theory is built on the notion that corporations are run by professional managers who act as agents for the firms' owners (stockholders).[12] According to this theory, managers avoid using external financing sources because doing so would subject them to the discipline of the marketplace.[13] Thus, this rationale for the pecking-order theory is based on a divergence of management decisionmaking from the goal of maximizing shareholder wealth.[14] This notion garnered little support in the financial literature until the appearance of the seminal work of Jensen and Meckling (1976), which introduced the concept of agency costs. In brief, *agency costs* arise where contracts involving one or more persons (principals) are used to engage another person (agent) to perform some service on their behalf, which involves delegating some decisionmaking authority (discretion) to the agent. If the agent seeks to maximize his or

---

[10]Miller (1977) refers to a neutral mutation hypothesis, summarized by Myers (1984) as follows:
Firms fall into certain financing patterns which have no material impact on firm value. The habits may make the managers feel better, and since they do no harm, no one cares to stop or change them. In this setting the identification of these financing patterns and their consequent use to predict financing behavior would not be explaining anything of any importance. (p. 576)

[11]Myers (1984, p. 582) notes that during the period 1973 to 1982, nonfinancial corporations (in the aggregate) financed 62 percent of their investments (including inventory and other current assets) with internally generated funds. The remaining funds came from external sources, with common stock making up only 6 percent. Thus, in the aggregate the pecking-order theory provides a very plausible description of corporate financing practice.

[12]See, for example, Berle (1954) and Berle and Means (1932).

[13]In Chapter 18, we discuss the mergers and acquisitions market as a means of forcing the discipline of the capital market on the managements of the modern corporation. In this context, it appears that separation of ownership and control, which forms the basis for the managerial capitalism theory of the firm, can operate only within the bounds of the market for corporate control, which in turn reflects legal restrictions on the ability of a firm or group of investors to take control of another firm and the transactions costs incurred in such an acquisition.

[14]Berle and Means (1932) note that "The separation of ownership from control produced a condition where the interests of owner and of ultimate manager may, and often do, diverge, and where many of the checks which formerly operated to limit the use of power disappear." (p. 7)

her personal utility and there are costs in monitoring agent behavior, these costs constitute the costs of agency.[15] Since agency costs represent a type of "transactions" cost associated with the corporate form of organization, we will discuss them further in the next section.

Transactions Costs, Agency Costs, Asymmetric Information, and the Firm's Capital Structure Decision

The second rationale for the pecking-order theory is consistent with the notion of maximizing shareholder wealth. In its simplest form it is based on the differences in flotation or issue costs associated with the retention of earnings and issuance of debt versus equity securities. Superficially, it can be observed that the retention of earnings does not require the incurrence of the flotation costs associated with the sale of a primary issue of securities (either debt or equity). The distinction between bonds' flotation costs and stocks' lies in the subtleties of the transactions costs associated with debt and equity. One rationale that purports to explain differences in issue costs for equity and debt relates to the costs attendant to the problem of *moral hazard* that arises where the information set available to the firm's management is superior to that available to outside investors.[16] This situation is commonly called one of *asymmetric information*. Although the implications of information asymmetry for the firm's financing decisions has not been fully explored, it has provided the basis for a growing body of financial literature that offers some very useful insights on this topic.[17]

Leland and Pyle (1977) noted that the firm's management (the insiders) has access to information about the firm's financial prospects that is superior to outsiders'. Thus, if management acts in the best interests of the firm's owners, it will offer to sell new-equity shares only when it feels their market price is "favorable" to the present owners. This simply means that management will issue common stock only when it feels that the shares' value based on its knowledge of the firm's financial worth is less than or equal to their actual current market value. On the other hand, if management feels the firm's shares are undervalued, it will not issue new stock. Now consider investors' reaction to the announced issue of common shares. If they feel that the firm's management is maximizing owner wealth, they will view the new stock issue as a "signal" that the firm's shares are overvalued in the marketplace. Next, consider the "signal" provided by the firm's decision to issue bonds. In this scenario, management's decision to issue debt could be interpreted as a sign that, based on its inside information, it believes the shares are underval-

---

[15]Jensen and Meckling (1976, p. 308) define these agency costs to include (1) the principal's monitoring expenditures (for observing and controlling the agent's behavior), (2) the agent's bonding expenditures, and (3) the residual loss suffered from imperfect monitoring (incomplete fulfillment of the contracted task).

[16]The moral hazard problem is perhaps best explained in the context of the dilemma faced by an insurance company when it sells insurance. The problem arises because the individual purchasing the insurance knows more about the risks he or she faces than does the insurer. As a result, the purchaser has an incentive to understate, or even withhold, the true nature of the risk being insured.

[17]Leland and Pyle's study was a first attempt at applying the notions of moral hazard and asymmetric information to the firm's financing choice between debt and equity. Myers and Majluf (1983) offer yet another attempt to develop the implications of asymmetric information for corporate financing decisions. We discuss both these papers in the following pages.

ued. In fact, Ross (1977) constructed a theory of capital structure choice based on this description of the manager/firm financing decision.[18] Note that the preference for internal equity financing is also consistent with the asymmetric information hypothesis in that managers, in seeking to maximize the owners' wealth, will retain earnings only when doing so will further that goal. The important point here is that the presence of asymmetric information, combined with a shareholder-wealth-maximizing management team, establishes a preference for debt over equity financing, which completes the pecking-order story—that is, internal equity financing is preferred over external equity or debt and debt is preferred to equity when external financing is utilized.

Myers and Majluf (1983) suggest yet another cost of relying on external financing that is consistent with the pecking-order theory. They argue that asymmetric information creates the possibility that the firm will choose not to issue debt or equity and therefore pass up a positive net present value project. For example, if an investment opportunity would cost $10 million and provides future cash flows with a present value of $11.5 million, its net present value is $1.5 million. However, if the firm must issue new equity in order to finance the investment and, due to the problem of asymmetric information, must sell $12 million of common stock to raise the necessary $10 million, it will choose not to finance the project.[19] Thus, a positive net present value project will be passed up because the underpricing needed to get it financed via a public security offering will outweigh its positive net present value. Note that the opportunity loss of the positive NPV project is avoided where internally generated funds are used. Further, Myers and Majluf argue that where the project's NPV is sufficiently positive to induce the firm to issue outside securities, the firm will issue the "safest" security it has available, namely debt. The rationale here is that this security is the one whose market value will change the least (that is, will require the smallest price concession in order to induce investors to buy it). Thus, Myers and Majluf offer yet another rationale for the preference for debt over equity securities that is consistent with the pecking-order theory.[20]

Further support for the preference for internal over external investment financing was provided by Jensen and Meckling (1976).[21] These theorists used the

---

[18]Note that for the "signal" to be believed (that is, valid), Ross tied management's compensation to the final outcome for the firm. Without some connection of management's compensation to the firm's true financial prospects, the signal would not be believable and consequently would not be a valid signal.

[19]Note that the firm raises only $10 million when it sells the $12 million equity issue (due to the underpricing required to stimulate the sale); however, once the project is undertaken and investors become aware of its true worth, the shares will be worth $12 million. The reason for the difference in value relates to the moral hazard problem discussed above where management has information superior to the investment community's and cannot convince new stockholders of the project's true worth because of their desire to maximize the wealth of their existing, pre-project-financing shareholders. One might logically ask why management cannot reveal information about the new project sufficient to convince investors of its true worth. One possible answer relates to the value of the proprietary information concerning the project. If the project is announced in all its detail, the firm's competitive advantage may be lost. (See Chapter 6 for a discussion of the source of positive net present value projects.)

[20]Myers and Majluf's argument is built on the rationale suggested by Akerlof (1970) for the collapse of certain types of markets due to asymmetric information and the accompanying moral hazard problem.

[21]An excellent synthesis of the role of agency costs in capital structure theory is found in Barnea, Haugen, and Senbet (1981). These authors identify three sources of agency problems that impact on financing decisions:

agency costs incurred in the corporate form of organization to argue for an optimal mix of internal (retained earnings) and external (debt or equity) financing. Consider the situation where the firm's owner is also the manager. Here the owner bears the full costs and benefits associated with his or her actions; thus, the decision to engage in on-the-job consumption of "perks" would be completely consistent with owner utility maximization. However, note what happens when the firm utilizes external financing via either debt or equity. Suppose the firm is financed 50 percent by the owner/manager and 50 percent by a combination of debt and equity capital raised from outside investors. In this instance, the owner/manager can consume perks and realize 100 percent of the benefits but need bear only 50 percent of their cost. Of course, owners will attempt to monitor agents' behavior, but since monitoring is both costly and imperfect, some perk consumption is inevitable. The point here is that the higher the proportion of external financing, the greater will be the manager's incentive to engage in perk consumption. Thus, based on this line of reasoning one can argue that there will exist a trade-off between the benefits of utilizing external financing (such as the ability to take advantage of positive net present value investment opportunities that outstrip the firm's ability to finance them through internal profits) and the added costs of agency attendant to the increased reliance on such sources.

Limiting the Use of Debt Financing

So far we have provided arguments that support the preference for internal over external financing as well as for debt over new-equity issues. Why, then, do firms, at least occasionally, issue equity? In this section we will discuss the various "debt capacity" theories offered in the finance literature. Myers and Pogue (1974) summarize these theories as follows:

1.   Management "chickens out first."

2.   The owners "chicken out first."

3.   The creditors "chicken out first."

The first of these "poultry" theories can be rationalized using the managerial capitalism idea discussed earlier. The basic idea is that management may stand to lose more than shareholders in the event of firm failure. For example, managers will suffer the costs of searching for new jobs and, if there is any stigma associated with managing a failed firm, will see the value of their human capital (managerial

---

1.   Market imperfections can lead to management's (the agent's) inability to reveal the exact nature of the firm to debt and equity financiers (the principals) costlessly (the problem of informational asymmetry noted above and discussed in Haugen and Senbet [1979], Leland and Pyle [1977], and Ross [1977]).

2.   The existence of debt financing under limited liability incites stockholders to accept suboptimal and high-risk projects that transfer wealth from bondholders to stockholders and to forgo new, profitable investment opportunities when previously issued debt is supported by existing assets and the option to undertake these investments (see Bodie and Taggart [1978] and Myers [1977]) and generates bankruptcy costs associated with resolving stockholder-bondholder disputes if insolvency occurs (see, for example, Kim [1978], Kraus and Litzenberger [1973], and Lee and Barker [1977]).

3.   Partial ownership of the firm by the owner-manager can motivate him or her to seek an excessive number of perks (see Jensen and Meckling [1976]).

talent) decline. To the extent that the firm's owners are unable (or unwilling, due
to monitoring costs) to force their financial structure preferences on management
policies, management may choose to use less financial leverage than the owners
would desire and/or creditors supply.

The arguments supporting limited use of debt financing that are based on the
"owners-chicken-out-first" theory have been built primarily on the existence of
costs of financial distress. Simply put, if debt financing increases the risk of financial distress and there are significant costs associated with financial distress and
failure, the limited use of debt financing can be justified. Consider the simple diagram in Figure 12.8. Here the value of the levered firm is assumed to be maximized where the optimal level of debt financing equals B*. This optimum reflects
the interplay of the benefits of using financial leverage[22] and the increasing
prospect of financial failure and the accompanying costs of more borrowing.[23]

A number of theorists have considered the role of financial distress costs on
the firm's optimal financial structure.[24] The fundamental format for each of those
models can be summarized as follows:

$$V_j^L = V_j^U + \text{VITS} - \text{VEBC},$$

Figure 12.8   Firm Value, Financial Leverage, and the Costs of Bankruptcy

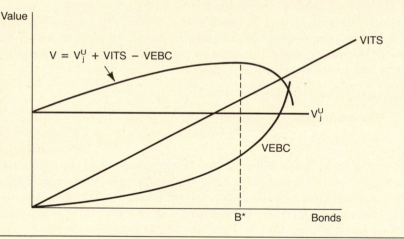

[22]These benefits might include the present value of interest tax savings as well as the net present value
of investment projects financed via debt that could not be financed internally due to limited profits or
via a new-equity sale because of the asymmetric information problem analyzed by Myers and Majluf
(1983).

[23]In Chapter 13, we will consider the costs of financial distress in more detail. In addition, we will survey some of the empirical evidence regarding their magnitude.

[24]For example, see Kim (1976), Lee and Barker (1977), Scott (1976), Kraus and Litzenberger (1973),
and Haugen and Senbet (1978).

where V_j^L is the value of levered firm j, V_j^U the value of the unlevered firm, VITS the value of the interest tax savings,[25] and VEBC the value of the expected costs of bankruptcy/financial distress. To clarify the last two terms, let us specify the probability of financial distress as the probability that the firm's cash flow is not sufficient to meet its financial obligation, that is, $\Psi[X \leq f(D)]$, where X is the firm's random cash flow and f(D) is its financial obligation. The firm's financial obligation is a function f of its use of debt financing.[26] Given the firm's probability distribution of cash flows, X, the increased use of financial leverage will, other things equal, increase the probability of financial distress. The optimal financial structure, then, will result where the firm's value is maximized or where the following condition holds:

$$\frac{\partial V}{\partial D} = \frac{\partial \text{VITS}}{\partial D} - \frac{\partial \text{VEBC}}{\partial D} = 0$$

or

$$\underbrace{\frac{\partial \text{VITS}}{\partial D}}_{\substack{\text{Marginal} \\ \text{benefit of} \\ \text{debt}}} = \underbrace{\frac{\partial \text{VEBC}}{\partial D}}_{\substack{\text{Marginal} \\ \text{cost of} \\ \text{debt}}}.$$

We have purposely left this discussion vague so that we may pose the basic argument without the complexities that would result from a more complete specification. The analysis reduces to a trade-off between the rising expected cost of financial distress and the increasing benefits accruing from the use of financial leverage.

The third "poultry" theory of debt capacity (the creditors chicken out first) has not led to any elaborate notions of corporate debt capacity. However, one might argue that at times this is the most binding constraint on a firm's ability to borrow additional funds. For example, creditors might limit a firm's borrowing to force the owners to maintain a significant stake in its operations and thereby align their own incentives with the owners'. In other words, if the owners are the residual claimants of the firm's earnings but have little of their own funds invested,

---

[25]We will not specify this term in any greater detail at this time; however, recall that the form of the interest tax savings term will differ depending on whether personal taxes are assumed to exist and whether the tax treatment of stock dividends differs from that of interest on bonds.

[26]Kim (1976) identifies three major components of bankruptcy costs: (1) Depending on whether bankruptcy takes the form of liquidation or reorganization, there may be either a "shortfall" (the losses associated with the distress sale of assets in imperfect secondary markets) or "indirect" costs, respectively; (2) the "deadweight" administrative expenses that arise in bankruptcy proceedings that must be paid to third parties (lawyers and others who become involved in the firm's operations only in the event of bankruptcy); and (3) lost tax credits resulting from the discontinuance of the firm's operations.

they will be motivated to make very risky investments with the creditors' funds.[27] Thus, the creditors have good reason to limit the company's use of debt funds. The issue here is whether the creditors' wish to limit debt use arises before that of the owners or managers; it is this question on which current theory offers little insight.

Summary

The role of the financing decision in determining the value of the business firm is central to the study of finance and constitutes a significant portion of the finance literature. In this chapter, we surveyed some of the seminal developments in the theory of the firm's capital structure decisions. We used the Modigliani/Miller (1958) paper as a starting point for our discussion of modern developments in capital structure theory. We discussed three capital structure theories directly descended from this study: the Modigliani/Miller (1963) tax-corrected model, the Miller (1977) personal tax model, and the DeAngelo/Masulis (1980) tax credit limitation model. In addition, we noted the body of capital structure theories that attempt to use bankruptcy or failure costs to rationalize the limits of a firm's willingness to use debt funds. These papers also follow the general "static trade-off" format of the original Modigliani/Miller work.

We reviewed a set of capital structure theories based on the existence of costly transactions and uncertainty. Many of these originate from the work of Donaldson (1961) and begin with the basic observation that a firm's capital structure choices are made in a dynamic fashion over time. Its decisions reflect a "pecking order" for the various sources of financing whereby internally generated earnings are used first to finance new investments, followed by debt, and finally by the sale of new-equity shares. Until recently, however, the finance profession has not incorporated Donaldson's empirical observations on corporate financing practice into the mainstream of financial theory. The seminal work of Jensen and Meckling (1976) introduced agency cost considerations (which hinge on the existence of costly transactions and uncertainty) into financial theory, which in turn provided a theoretical rationale for many of Donaldson's observations. This body of theory continues to grow and today is probably the dominant area of capital structure research.

Study Questions

12.1   Discuss the individual's savings allocation decision between debt and equity securities where there are no taxes on personal or corporate income. How is this decision affected by the presence of personal taxes on bond and stock income?

---

[27]We will return to this problem in Chapter 16, where we apply option pricing theory to the firm's financial management. In essence, the firm's common stock is characterized as a call option on the cash flow produced by its real assets. The firm's owners then can increase the value of their shares (call options) by increasing the riskiness (variability) of the asset cash flow stream. This incentive to increase asset return variability comes at the expense of the creditors, whose fixed return claims are reduced in value by the increased risk in the firm's asset investments.

12.2 How does a restraint on a firm's ability to utilize its tax credits affect its decision to use financial leverage?

12.3 What are the principal elements of the "pecking-order" theory of corporate financing decisions? Is this a static or a dynamic theory of the firm's capital structure decision?

12.4 If the "neutral mutation" hypothesis appropriately describes corporate financing decisions, what are its implications for the study and practice of corporate finance?

12.5 What is the "managerial capitalism" theory of a firm's financing decisions? Why would you suppose that this theory has gained little following in the finance literature?

12.6 What is the "incentive problem" underlying the Myers/Majluf (1983) discussion of the impact of asymmetric information on the firm's investment/financing decisions? Illustrate your answer with an example.

12.7 Assuming a world in which corporations pay taxes at a rate t_c and individuals pay personal taxes on bond income at a rate t_i and no tax on equity income, analyze the impact on bond market equilibrium of an increase in the individual income tax rate on equity income to a rate t_j.

12.8 In a world in which only corporate income is taxed (interest expense is tax deductible), what would be the impact of an increase in the corporate tax rate on a firm's demand for bond financing? What would be the effect on its cost of capital?

12.9 Bankruptcy or default costs are sometimes thought to be an important deterrent to the use of debt financing. Discuss this point from the perspective of the firm's owners, its management, and its creditors.

Study Problems

12.1 Companies A and B differ only with respect to their capital structures. Company A is financed 30 percent with debt and 70 percent with equity, while company B has only 10 percent debt and 90 percent equity financing. For simplicity, assume that both firms issue risk-free bonds.
   a. Investor 1 owns 1 percent of firm A's common stock. Can the investor create the same return by investing in company B? If so, how? (Hint: Assume that the investor can borrow and lend on the same terms as the two firms.)
   b. Investor 2 owns 2 percent of company B's common stock. Can this investor create a set of cash flows identical to the investment using company A's stock? If so, how?
   c. Show that investor 1 would not select the alternative investment strategy if the value of company B were greater than that of company A.

12.2 Suppose there are only three groups of investors with the following personal tax rates:

Group	Tax Rate
A	55%
B	30
C	0

Each group has $500 million to invest and can choose from perpetual bonds and common stock. Interest from corporate bonds requires the payment of personal tax but is deductible from corporate taxes (the corporate tax rate is 50 percent). All cash flows are known with certainty, and the rate of return on common stock is $r_s = 10$ percent.

a. Derive the aggregate supply function for loanable funds.

b. Suppose the maximum aggregate demand for loanable funds is $1.5 billion. Derive the aggregate demand function for loanable funds.

c. What is the market equilibrium "aggregate" capital structure? In equilibrium, which investors will hold bonds? Which will hold stock? What will be the equilibrium interest rate on bonds?

d. If the aggregate cash flows to firms (before interest and taxes) are $300 million, what is the total market value of all firms in the economy? (Assume level perpetuities.)

e. Show that in equilibrium an unlevered firm has no incentive to issue debt and retire equity. Similarly, demonstrate that a levered firm will have no incentive to reduce its use of financial leverage.

12.3   Bumyang International, Inc. and Doragy Electric Company are virtually identical in all respects other than their capital structures. Bumyang has total assets of $100 million and is all equity financed, while Doragy's $100 million in assets is partly financed by $40 million in bonds on which it pays 10 percent interest annually. During 1986, both firms earned $50 million before interest and taxes, and each faced a 46 percent marginal tax rate on corporate income.

a. Calculate the rate of return earned on the two firms' common equity.

b. If the required rate of return on Bumyang's unlevered equity is 15 percent, what is the value of its shares? (Hint: Assume that the firm's earnings are a level perpetuity.)

c. Doragy's equity has a current market value of $150 million. If individuals can borrow and lend at the 10 percent corporate borrowing rate, is this an equilibrium value for Doragy's stock?

12.4   Consider the following two firms:

	Company A	Company B
Total assets	$50 million	$50 million
Bonds (8%)	$20 million	$40 million
Corporate tax rate	30%	30%
Earnings before interest and taxes	$10 million	$10 million
Shares outstanding	300,000	100,000

a. If the frictionless capital market assumptions are met and the value of company A's stock is $83.33 per share, what should be the value of company B's shares? (Hint: Assume that individual investors can borrow and lend at the 8 percent corporate borrowing rate.)

b. What is the required rate of return for an unlevered firm under the above conditions?

12.5   The Ridley Manufacturing Company is presently all equity financed and is contemplating the simultaneous issuance of (perpetual) bonds and retirement of common stock. The firm currently has a total market value of $45 million and pays corporate taxes at a rate of 40 percent. If the firm can borrow at a rate of 8 percent and if the Modigliani/Miller (1963) assumptions characterize the economy, what would be the impact of the following changes in the firm's capital structure on its market value?
a. 25 percent debt financing
b. 75 percent debt financing

12.6   Under conditions of market equilibrium as described by Miller (1977), the market rate of interest on bonds is 8 percent. If firms pay corporate taxes at a rate of 40 percent, what would be the impact of an increase in the personal tax rate on bond interest to 45 percent? (Assume there is no tax on equity income.)

12.7   Construct a graph depicting the impact of a shift in the personal tax rate on bond income in the context of the Miller (1977) model of bond market equilibrium.

References

G. A. Akerlof, "The Market for 'Lemons': Quality and the Market Mechanism," *Quarterly Journal of Economics* (August 1970): 488–500.

A. Barnea, R. A. Haugen, and L. W. Senbet, *Agency Problems and Financial Contracting* (Englewood Cliffs, N.J.: Prentice Hall, 1985).

———, "Market Imperfections, Agency Problems, and Capital Structure: A Review," *Financial Management* (Summer 1981): 7–22.

A. A. Berle, *The 20th Century Capitalist Revolution* (New York: Harcourt, Brace and World, 1954).

——— and G. C. Means, *The Modern Corporation and Private Property* (New York: Harcourt, Brace and World, 1968, original edition, 1932).

Z. Bodie and R. Taggart, "Future Investment Opportunities and the Value of the Call Provision on a Bond," *Journal of Finance* (September 1978): 1187–1200.

R. Dammon, "A Security Market and Capital Structure Equilibrium under Uncertainty with Progressive Taxes" (Working paper, Carnegie-Mellon University, August 1985).

——— and R. Green, "Tax Arbitrage and the Existence of Equilibrium Prices for Financial Assets" (Working paper, Carnegie-Mellon University, February 1986).

——— and L. W. Senbet, "The Effect of Taxes on the Interaction between Production and Finance" (Working paper, University of Wisconsin–Madison, May 1986).

H. DeAngelo and R. Masulis, "Optimal Capital Structure under Corporate and Personal Taxation," *Journal of Financial Economics* 8 (March 1980): 3–29.

G. Donaldson, *Corporate Debt Capacity: A Study of Corporate Debt Policy and the Determination of Corporate Debt Capacity* (Boston: Division of Research, Harvard Graduate School of Business Administration, 1961).

———, *Strategy for Financial Mobility* (Boston: Division of Research, Harvard Graduate School of Business Administration, 1969).

E. Fama, "Agency Problems and the Theory of the Firm," *Journal of Political Economy* (April 1980): 288–307.

R. Haugen and L. W. Senbet, "The Insignificance of Bankruptcy Costs to the Theory of the Optimal Capital Structure," *Journal of Finance* (May 1978): 383–394.

——— , "New Perspectives on Informational Asymmetry and Agency Relationships," *Financial Management* (November 1979): 671–694.

——— , "Corporate Finance and Taxes: A Review," *Financial Management* (Autumn 1986): 5–21.

——— , and E. Talmor, "Debt, Dividends, and Taxes: Equilibrium Conditions for Simultaneous Tax Neutrality of Debt and Dividend Policies," in *Research in Finance* (D.C. Heath Research Volume, 1986).

M. Jensen and W. H. Meckling, "Theory of the Firm: Managerial Behavior, Agency Costs and Ownership Structure," *Journal of Financial Economics* (October 1976): 305–360.

E. H. Kim, "A Mean-Variance Theory of Optimal Capital Structure and Corporate Debt Capacity," *Journal of Finance* (March 1978): 45–63.

A. Kraus and R. H. Litzenberger, "A State-Preference Model of Optimal Financial Leverage," *Journal of Finance* (September 1973): 911–922.

W. Y. Lee and H. H. Barker, "Bankruptcy Costs and the Firm's Optimal Debt Capacity," *Southern Economics Journal* (January 1977): 1453–1465.

H. Leland and D. Pyle, "Informational Asymmetries, Financial Structure, and Financial Intermediation," *Journal of Finance* (May 1977): 371–387.

R. L. McDonald, "Government Debt and Private Leverage: An Extension of the Miller Theorem," *Journal of Public Economics* 22 (December 1983): 303–325.

M. H. Miller, "Debt and Taxes," *Journal of Finance* (May 1977): 261–275.

F. Modigliani and M. Miller, "Corporate Income Taxes and the Cost of Capital: A Correction," *American Economic Review* 53 (June 1963): 433–443.

——— , "The Cost of Capital, Corporation Finance and the Theory of Investment," *American Economic Review* 48 (June 1958): 261–297.

S. Myers, "The Capital Structure Puzzle," *Journal of Finance* 39 (July 1984): 575–592.

——— , "Determinants of Corporate Borrowing," *Journal of Financial Economics* (November 1977): 147–175.

——— and N. S. Majluf, "Corporate Financing and Investment Decisions When Firms Have Information That Investors Do Not Have" (Working paper, Sloan School of Management, M.I.T., March 1983).

——— and G. A. Pogue, "A Programming Approach to Corporate Financial Management," *Journal of Finance* (May 1974): 579–599.

A. A. Robichek and S. C. Myers, "Problems in the Theory of Optimal Capital Structure," *Journal of Financial and Quantitative Analysis* (June 1966): 1–35.

S. A. Ross, "Debt and Taxes and Uncertainty," *Journal of Finance* (July 1985): 637–658.

——— , "The Determination of Financial Structure: The Incentive Signalling Approach," *Bell Journal of Economics* (Spring 1977): 23–40.

J. H. Scott, "The Theory of Optimal Capital Structure," *Bell Journal of Economics* (Spring 1976): 33–59.

C. W. Smith and J. B. Warner, "On Financial Contracting: An Analysis of Bond Covenants," *Journal of Financial Economics* (June 1979): 117–161.

J. Stieglitz, "Taxation, Corporate Financial Policy and the Cost of Capital," *Journal of Public Economics* (February 1973): 1–34.

R. A. Taggart, Jr., "Taxes and Corporate Capital Structure in an Incomplete Market," *Journal of Finance* 35 (June 1980): 645–659.

——— , "Effects of Regulation on Utility Financing: Theory and Evidence," *Journal of Industrial Economics* (March 1985): 257–276.

S. Titman, "The Effect of Capital Structure on a Firm's Liquidation Decision," *Journal of Financial Economics* (March 1984): 137–151.

Appendix 12A

The DeAngelo/Masulis Model: A Mathematical Overview

Consider the case in which the firm has Δ_j dollars in tax deductions resulting from non-cash charges such as accounting depreciation and Γ_j dollars in tax credits (investment tax credits derived from the purchase of new plant and equipment). Thus, the firm's taxable income is $X_j - \Delta_j - r_B B_j$, and its gross tax is $T_j = t_c(X_j - \Delta_j - r_B B_j)$. The value of *utilized* tax credits, then, is the following:

$$\min[\gamma t_c(X_j - \Delta_j - r_B B_j), \Gamma_j]$$

This result is due to the statutory ceiling, which limits usable tax credits to a fraction, γ, of the gross tax liability.

Now consider the debt value such that the firm fully utilizes all of its tax credits; that is, let B_j^* be the amount such that

$$\gamma t_c(X_j - \Delta_j - r_B B_j^*) = \Gamma_j$$

or, equivalently,

$$B_j^* = \frac{X_j - \Delta_j - \left(\dfrac{\Gamma_j}{\gamma t_c}\right)}{r_B}.$$

Note that all tax credits are fully utilized for all $B_j \leq B_j^*$. For $B_j > B_j^*$, the corporate tax credits are only partially utilized. Thus, the value of the firm if $B_j \leq B_j^*$ is

$$V_j = B_j + \frac{X_j - (1 + r_B)B_j - t_c(X_j - \Delta_j - r_B B_j) + \Gamma_j}{1 + r_E}$$

and, if $B_j > B_j^*$,

$$V_j = B_j + \frac{X_j - (1 + r_B)B_j - (1 - \gamma)t_c(X_j - \Delta_j - r_B B_j)}{1 + r_E}.$$

Since we suppose that the firm selects B_j to maximize its value, observe that if $B_j \le B_j^*$,

(12A.1a) $$\frac{dV_j}{dB_j} = 1 - \frac{1 + r_B(1 - t_c)}{1 + r_E}$$

and, if $B_j > B_j^*$,

(12A.1b) $$\frac{dV_j}{dB_j} = 1 - \frac{1 + r_B[1 - (1 - \gamma)t_c]}{1 + r_E}.$$

In order to derive the firm's demand for bond funds, we must find the value-maximizing debt level for each r_B. In that regard, we will consider the following three cases and derive that value for each:

-   **Case 1:** $r_B = \dfrac{r_E}{1 - t_c}$

-   **Case 2:** $\dfrac{r_E}{1 - t_c} > r_B > \dfrac{r_E}{1 - (1 - \gamma)t_c}$

-   **Case 3:** $r_B = \dfrac{r_E}{1 - (1 - \gamma)t_c}$

Firm Valuation and the Demand for Bond Funds Where $r_B = r_E/(1 - t_c)$

In this case, the derivative is zero for all $B_j \le B_j^*$ and negative for $B_j > B_j^*$. We obtain the value function shown in Figure 12A.1. Note that in this case all debt levels between zero and B_j^* are optimal and the tax credits are fully utilized.

Firm Valuation and the Demand for Bond Funds Where $r_E/(1 - t_c) > r_B > r_E/[1 - (1 - \gamma)t_c]$

In this case, the derivative in Equation 12A.1 is positive for $B_j \le B_j^*$ and negative for $B_j > B_j^*$. Hence, B_j^* is the optimal debt level and the firm just utilizes all its tax credits, as Figure 12A.2 illustrates. Since

(12A.2) $$B_j^* = \frac{X_j - \Delta_j - \dfrac{\Gamma_j}{\gamma t_c}}{r_B},$$

it follows that this debt level (B_j^*) increases as r_B decreases in this range.

**Figure 12A.1   Firm Valuation and the Use of Debt Financing
Where $r_B = r_E/(1 - t_c)$**

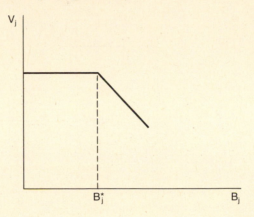

**Figure 12A.2   Firm Valuation and the Use of Debt Financing
Where $r_E/(1 - t_c) > r_B > r_E/[1 - (1 - \gamma)t_c]$**

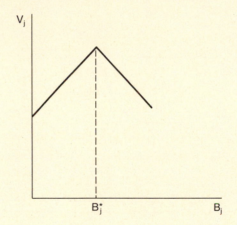

Firm Valuation and the Demand for Bond Funds
Where $r_B = r_E/[1 - (1 - \gamma)t_c]$

In this case, the derivative in Equation 12A.1 is positive for $B_j \leq B_j^*$ and zero thereafter, as shown in Figure 12A.3. Note that debt levels greater than B_j^* are optimal.

Equilibrium in the Bond Market

Using the results of the three cases illustrated in Figures 12A.1, 12A.2, and 12A.3, we obtain the corporate demand for bond funds shown in Figure 12A.4.

Figure 12A.3   Firm Valuation and the Use of Debt Financing
Where $r_B = r_E/[1 - (1 - \gamma)t_c]$

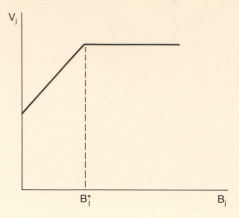

Figure 12A.4   Bond Market Equilibrium in the DeAngelo/Masulis Model

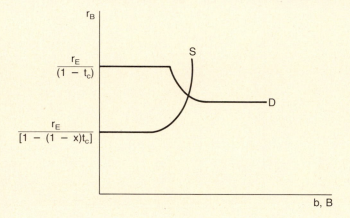

Note that the downward-sloping segment of the demand for bond funds is described by Equation 12A.2. The equilibrium shown in Figure 12A.4 (where the
intersection of supply and demand occurs in the case 2 region of the demand function) will determine an optimal debt level for each firm, and firms will fully utilize
their tax credits. Thus, as DeAngelo and Masulis (1980) have demonstrated, in a
world in which a firm's tax credits are limited, there will exist an optimal capital
structure for the market as a whole, but there will also be an optimal capital structure for each firm. The latter entails use of that level of debt financing for which
the firm's total tax credits (including interest expense) sum to the maximum allowable under the tax code. Note that should the equilibrium bond rate occur in the
perfectly elastic segment of the demand for bond funds where $r_B = r_E/(1 - t_c)$,

we get the Miller (1977) result — that is, there will exist an optimal capital structure for the market as a whole but *no* such level for the individual firm.[1]

References

H. DeAngelo and R. Masulis, "Optimal Capital Structure under Corporate and Personal Taxation," *Journal of Financial Economics* 8 (March 1980): 3–29.

M. H. Miller, "Debt and Taxes," *Journal of Finance* (May 1977): 261–275.

---

[1]DeAngelo and Masulis (1980) establish the existence of an interior optimal capital structure under certainty in footnote 13 of their paper.

Chapter 13

Capital Structure: Evidence and Applications

In Chapter 12, we discussed a number of theories that attempt to explain how a firm's financing decisions impact its value. In this chapter, we review some of the empirical evidence on these theories and discuss the role of financing decisions in capital budgeting analyses. Our objective here is twofold. First, we review the empirical evidence regarding how firms finance their assets and tests of the various capital structure theories. Second, we discuss some of the practical issues involved in incorporating financing decisions into the analysis of project net present value. In this regard, we review several formulations of the NPV model, including the traditional one that utilizes the weighted average cost of capital as a discount rate.

Corporate Financial Structure and the Cost of Capital: The Evidence

Overview

The basic question of whether a firm's financing decisions impact on its value remains unresolved; in fact, Myers titled his presidential address to the 1983 meeting of the American Finance Association "The Capital Structure Puzzle." However, a great deal of work on this question has been done. We will summarize this research in terms of three categories. The first deals with the descriptive research on U.S. corporate financing patterns. These studies were designed not to test particular theories but to simply describe how firms historically have chosen to finance their assets. The second area encompasses all the studies that have attempted to explain the cross-sectional characteristics of individual firms' capital structures. This research includes analyses of industrial classification as an explanatory variable as well as of the fundamental factors suggested by various capital structure theories. The third area includes the studies that have attempted to directly verify the valuation implications of firms' capital structure decisions. Some of the more recent studies in this area have employed the "event study" methodology discussed in Chapter 10. It is impossible to survey all the research in this chapter; however, we provide a condensed but representative overview.

Aggregate Financing Patterns[1]

In this section, we review the empirical evidence on the question of how corporations finance their assets. This is a critically important issue, for if all corporations were found to utilize the same basic financial structure over time, capital structure design would become a far less challenging area of study. Later we will review studies that have sought to "explain" individual firm financial structure design using variables derived from corporate practice and financial theory.

Taggart (1984) extensively analyzed the financing patterns of U.S. corporations over the period 1901 to 1979. Using a variety of ratio measures of financial structure, he arrived at the following conclusions:

1. The use of debt financing by U.S. corporations increased dramatically over the post–World War II period and particularly during the 1960s and 1970s. However, the present level of debt financing does *not* appear to be unusually high relative to the prewar period.

2. The use of short-term liabilities has become increasingly important over time. In fact, the overall increase in debt financing in the past two decades appears to be traceable to the increased use of short-term debt, while the use of long-term debt has remained relatively stable.

3. There has been a decline in the number of new issues of both common and preferred stock. In addition, the level of internally generated equity funds appears to be low relative to previous years. Whether this represents a cyclical swing or a trend effect is not clear. However, if one takes a long-term perspective to include the pre–World War II period, the current low level of internally generated funds is understandable.

Table 13.1 summarizes corporate financing patterns for the period 1901 to 1984. These sources of funds data clearly indicate the nature of actual corporate financing practice and further confirm Taggart's observations from financial ratio data.

---

[1]This section relies heavily on the work of Taggart (1984).

Table 13.1 Financing Patterns of U.S. Corporations, 1901–1984

Period	Total Debt	Long-Term Debt[a]	Total Short-Term Liabilities	Short-Term Credit Market Debt[b]	New Stock Issues	Gross Internal Funds
1901–1912	0.31	0.23	0.08		0.14	0.55
1913–1922	0.29	0.12	0.17		0.11	0.60
1923–1929	0.26	0.22	0.04		0.19	0.55
1930–1939	−0.33	−0.05	−0.29		0.19	1.14
1940–1945	0.15	−0.05	0.20		0.05	0.80
1946–1949	0.30	0.18	0.12	0.05	0.05	0.65
1950–1954	0.31	0.14	0.17	0.05	0.06	0.63
1955–1959	0.31	0.14	0.17	0.06	0.04	0.65
1960–1964	0.30	0.13	0.16	0.07	0.02	0.69
1965–1969	0.40	0.15	0.25	0.12	0.01	0.59
1970–1974	0.47	0.18	0.29	0.14	0.05	0.48
1975–1979	0.38	0.12	0.27	0.12	0.01	0.60
1980–1984	0.36	0.10	0.26	0.15	−0.02	0.66

[a]Bonds and mortgages.

[b]Bank loans, commercial paper, acceptances, finance company loans, and U.S. government loans.

Sources: Data from Board of Governors of the Federal Reserve System, *Flow of Funds Accounts* (various years) and R. W. Goldsmith, *Financial Intermediaries in the American Economy Since 1900* (Princeton, N.J.: Princeton University Press, 1958). Reproduced with permission from Robert A. Taggart, "Corporate Financing: Too Much Debt," *Financial Analysts Journal* (May/June 1986): 38.

Studies of Firm Financial Structures

A number of studies have attempted to explain the financing choices of individual firms. The earlier ones frequently were based on very loosely reasoned causal factors but were able to explain a significant proportion of the observed variation in corporate financial structures. More recent research has employed variables suggested by capital structure theories, such as those discussed in Chapter 12. However, the results of those studies, as we will see, have not been significantly better than the earlier ones in terms of their explanatory power.

For simplicity we will classify these studies into one of two broad groups: those that attempted to assess the importance of industry classification as a predictor of corporate financial practice and those that analyzed the roles of more fundamental factors in explaining corporate financial structure. Table 13.2 enumerates some of these studies.

Industry Influence on Financial Structure.   Schwartz and Aronson (1967) presented the first of a series of papers investigating the usefulness of industry classification as a predictor of financial structure. Except for the Remmers et al. (1974) paper, these studies consistently found a significant link between financial structure and industry class. Three points should be made regarding their findings. First, while statistically significant, the explanatory power of these models generally has been 50 percent or lower, leaving half the variation in financial structure unexplained by whatever variable(s) are being "proxied" by industry class. Second, pairwise comparisons of industry financial ratios frequently have yielded insignificant differences; that is, only some industry financial ratios differ. Third, studies by Martin et al. (1979) and Friend and Hasbrouck (1986) found that industry classification actually serves as a proxy for a number of fundamental factors related to the firm's size, earnings volatility, bankruptcy costs, and asset growth. We will review more research directed toward these fundamental variables in the next section.

Fundamental Determinants of Financial Structure.   Beginning with Hurdle (1974), a number of researchers have sought to utilize variables that are hypothesized to proxy the fundamental forces guiding the design of a firm's capital struc-

---

Table 13.2   Determinants of Corporate Financial Structure

Author/Date	Leverage Metric[a]	Predictor Variable(s)[b]
A. Industry Influence on Financial Structure		
Schwartz and Aronson (1967)	CE/TA	
Scott (1972)	CE/TA	
Remmers et al. (1974)	TD/TA	Industry class
Scott and Martin (1985)	CE/TA	
	TIE	

(continued)

Table 13.2   *(continued)*

B. Fundamental Determinants of Financial Structure

Hurdle (1974)	TD/TA	Market share
		Growth in sales
		Profitability
		Firm size
		Earnings volatility
		Asset turnover
Sullivan (1974)	TD/TIC	Barriers to entry
		Industry concentration
Toy et al. (1974)	TD/TA	Asset growth
		Profitability
		Earnings volatility
Lee and Barker (1977)	I/TA	Profitability
		Earnings volatility
		Bankruptcy costs
		Asset growth
		Firm/market cash flow correlation
Kerr (1979)	LTD/TIC	Growth in sales
		Earnings volatility
		Profitability
		Management risk aversion
Martin et al. (1979)	FC/TA	Bankruptcy cost
	CE/TA	Profitability
		Growth potential
		Capital intensity
		Dividend policy
Ferri and Jones (1979)	TD/TA	Industry class
		Firm size
		Business risk
		Operating leverage
Titman and Wessels (1986)	LTD/BVE	Asset structure
	STD/BVE	Non-debt tax shields
	CD/BVE	Asset uniqueness
	LTD/MVE	Industry class
	STD/MVE	Size
	CD/MVE	Earnings volatility
		Profitability
Friend and Hasbrouck (1986)	LTD/TA	Asset composition
		Size
		Profitability
		Insider holdings

---

[a]CE/TA = Common equity/total assets   FC/TA = Finance charges/total assets
TD/TA = Total debt/total assets   LTD/BVE = Long-term debt/book value equity
TIE = Times interest earned   STD/BVE = Short-term debt/book value equity
TD/TIC = Total debt/total invested capital   CD/BVE = Convertible debt/book value equity
I/TA = Interest expense/total assets   MVE = Market value of equity
LTD/TIC = Long-term debt/total invested capital

[b]Many of the predictor variables have been abbreviated to conserve space.

Table 13.3   Fundamental Factors Influencing Capital Structure Design

Factor	Hypothesized Sign[a]	Observed Sign
Growth[b]	+	+
Profitability[c]	±	−
Firm size	+	+
Earnings volatility (operating leverage)[d]	−	±
Bankruptcy cost	−	−
Market power[e]	+	−

[a]The dependent variable assumed here for summary purposes is the debt/total assets ratio, although a number of different metrics have been used.

[b]Growth is sometimes measured using sales and at other times assets or profits.

[c]Operating profits before interest. Lee and Barker (1975) hypothesized that the net operating income/total assets ratio is directly associated with a firm's use of financial leverage. However, other researchers have both hypothesized and observed an inverse relationship.

[d]Toy et al. (1974) found a positive relationship and the remaining studies an inverse relationship.

[e]Both Hurdle (1974) and Sullivan (1974) looked at industry concentration, barriers to entry, and, in general, market power as influences on firm financing patterns. Although they hypothesized a positive relationship, they observed a negative correlation. Spence (1984) also documented the role of product market competition in explaining a firm's financing decisions.

ture. Table 13.3 summarizes these variables, including the hypothesized and actual (observed) sign of each. The table reveals that higher levels of financial leverage have unambiguously accompanied higher growth and larger firm size. On the other hand, lower levels of financial leverage have generally been associated with firms having higher profitability and larger expected costs of bankruptcy and those possessing significant market (monopoly) power.

By and large, the above studies were not based on a rigorously defined theory of financial structure decisions. DeAngelo and Masulis (1980), however, offered a model of the corporate use of financial leverage and interpreted its empirical implications using the results of previous research (including some of those noted here). This model predicts that financial structures will be sensitive to changes in (1) leverage costs (bankruptcy, reorganization, or other agency cost of debt), (2) the corporate tax rate, and (3) the investment tax shield. Because of the numerous changes in the tax code over the past 50 years (income tax rates for corporations and individuals and the investment tax credit), we would expect to see a similar pattern of volatility in corporate financing practice. (See "An Institutional Note: The U.S. Income Tax Code" in Chapter 12.) As we noted in discussing the Taggart (1984) study, corporate financing practice has been inconsistent throughout the twentieth century. However, beyond noting the instability of the time series of financial ratio metrics, little has been done to establish any causality between fluctuations in the above-mentioned factors over time and variations in financial structures.

Regarding industry cross-sectional predictions, DeAngelo and Masulis' model predicts that differential investment tax shields and/or marginal costs of leverage will induce differential optimal capital structures for firms. The authors note the ample evidence of differences in investment tax shields across industries (see also Vanik [1978]; Muskie [1976]; Siegfried [1974]; and Rosenberg [1969]). Thus, given these differences in available tax credits across industries, they predict different levels of financial leverage as well. This, of course, generally has been borne out by the studies of the industry influence on capital structure reviewed earlier. There is, however, a fly in the ointment with respect to these results. The DeAngelo/Masulis theory predicts an *inverse* relationship between capital structure and investment tax shields, but studies by Bradley et al. (1984), Boquist and Moore (1984), and Dammon and Senbet (1986) contradict this. Thus, although it does appear that tax shields and capital structures differ across industries, the hypothesized negative relationship has not been observed.

Titman and Wessels (1986) made yet another attempt to identify the factors underlying the firm's capital structure choices. Their study is unique in several respects. First, they examined a broad set of theoretical arguments on the determinants of the firm's capital structure choice, including traditional Modigliani/Miller-based theories, agency theory, and Ross's signaling theory (see Chapter 12 for a discussion of these). Second, they used three types of capital structure metrics based on long-term, short-term, and convertible debt. Finally, they used a factor analysis technique to identify the independent variables used in their tests; this helped control for the problems of measurement encountered when using proxy variables for the determinants of a firm's capital structure. Their results, although inconclusive (by the authors' own admission), generally were consistent with existing theory. Specifically, they observed that debt levels were negatively related to the "uniqueness" of a firm's line of business. This observation was consistent with the implications of Titman's (1984) study, which posited that firms that can impose high costs on their customers, workers, and suppliers in the event of liquidation have lower debt ratios. They also found that transactions costs may well be a critical factor in determining a firm's capital structure. This observation was supported by the finding that short-term debt ratios were inversely related to firm size, which could possibly reflect the high transactions costs that small firms face when issuing long-term financial instruments. In addition, they found support for an effect on debt ratios arising from non-debt tax shields, earnings volatility, collateral value, and future growth. However, they concluded their analysis by stating that "it remains an open question whether our measurement model does indeed capture the relevant aspects of the attributes suggested by these theories" (p. 32).

Friend and Hasbrouck (1986) provide yet another test of the fundamental determinants of a firm's financial structure, but with a new twist. They included variables related to the proportion of the firm's stock that insiders hold. The rationale for including this variable relates to an agency-type argument wherein the owners/managers utilize less debt than outside owners would desire since they face a greater risk of loss in the event of firm failure. The insiders, it is argued, have a larger "stake" in the firm than outside investors due to both their large (relative to their total wealth) holdings of the firm's marketable securities and their investment of their human capital in the firm. If as a result of these factors the insiders are generally less well diversified than the outsiders, they will find it in their best interest to try to reduce the firm's exposure to financial risk. Thus, this

agency argument appeals to "managerialism," or the notion that managers make
financing decisions that reflect their own interests rather than those of the firm's
shareholders. The authors found a significant negative correlation between the size
of insider holdings and the firm's debt ratio. Thus, they concluded that insider
ownership (a proxy for the strength of management's incentive to deviate from
owner-wealth-maximizing debt levels) exerts a negative influence on corporate financing decisions. In summing up their work, however, they lament the relatively
low explanatory power of their model, which, like other studies in this area, was
less than 50 percent. Thus, the present consensus on this issue in the finance literature appears to indicate that the determinants of a firm's capital structure are still
subject to debate and require further empirical investigation.

Valuation and Corporate Financial Structure

The majority of the research related to valuation and a firm's financial structure
design has followed from the pioneering work of Modigliani and Miller (1958,
1963) and Miller (1977). Its objective has been to assess whether there exists an
optimal capital structure that minimizes the firm's cost of capital. More recently,
Masulis (1980, 1983) has had some success with "event study" methodology in
identifying the market's reaction to (and hence the valuation effect of) changes in
a firm's capital structure.

Testing for the Existence of an Optimal Capital Structure.   Modigliani and
Miller (1958) tested for the relationship between firm value and capital structure
using a cross-sectional regression of the "estimated" cost of capital on the debt/to-
tal assets ratio for a sample of 42 oil companies and 43 electric utilities. They
found no significant relationship between these variables (the correlation coefficients were 0.12 for the utilities and 0.04 for the oil companies). In a subsequent
study by Weston (1963) that incorporated the impact of earnings growth and firm
size into the cross-sectional regression, the correlation between cost of capital
and capital structure rose to 0.53. The Weston regression equation appeared as
follows:

$$K_{wacc} = 5.91 - 0.0265d + 0.00A - 0.0822E,$$

where K_{wacc} is the weighted average cost of capital for the firm measured by the
ratio of after-tax "total earnings" divided by the market value of all its securities, d
is the ratio of the market value of senior securities divided by the market value of
all securities, A is total assets measured by their book value, and E is the annual
compound growth rate in earnings per share measured over the period 1949 to
1959. Both the leverage (d) and earnings growth variables (E) were found to be
significantly negatively correlated with the cost of capital. Weston suggested that
Modigliani and Miller's finding of no significant relationship between leverage
and the cost of capital resulted from the negative correlation between earnings
growth and leverage. Hence, when earnings growth was included in the model,
the net effect of leverage surfaced. The inverse relationship observed here suggests that higher levels of financial leverage would decrease a firm's cost of capital. Note, however, that Weston made no attempt to include a proxy variable

for bankruptcy or agency costs, which would serve to limit a firm's use of debt financing.

Miller and Modigliani (1966) provided further empirical evidence regarding the impact of capital structure on firm value for firms in the electric utility industry. Specifically, they decomposed the value of the firm into four components: the capitalized value of the firm's existing assets, growth potential, size, and the tax subsidy on debt. They then performed cross-sectional tests for the years 1954, 1956, and 1957. They found that existing assets accounted for 68 to 75 percent of firm value, growth potential for 22 to 24 percent, firm size, which was inversely correlated with firm value, for 1 to 2 percent, and the interest tax subsidy for 2 to 10 percent. These results are frequently cited as empirical support for the interest tax subsidy value created by debt financing.

Corporate Exchange Offers, Capital Structure, and Valuation.   Masulis (1983) cited the valuation impact of corporate financing decisions via the use of an event study methodology (discussed in Chapter 10) to study the impact of corporate exchange offers on equity value. Exchange offers provide an opportunity to examine the impact of "pure" financing decisions on security prices. Here a firm simply offers to exchange one security for another security or group of securities. Since these arrangements involve little or no additional cash flow into or out of the firm, they are a useful vehicle for studying the impact of capital structure on security valuation. Note, however, that the source of the valuation impact is not unambiguous, for the exchange offer may serve as a "signal" of new information to market participants; allow for the removal of a particularly onerous set of covenants attached to the security issue being eliminated; reflect the impact of the restructuring on the interest tax subsidy; or reflect some wealth redistribution effects among the different groups of securityholders. However, by studying the value of the firm's securities around the time of an exchange offer, we can assess the "net" impact of all of the above sources and, in some cases, actually differentiate among them.

Masulis studied the valuation impact of 133 exchange offers that occurred in the United States during the period 1963 to 1978. His findings can be summarized as follows:

1.   Increases in leverage led to increases in equity value.

2.   The value of nonconvertible senior securities was inversely related to changes in financial leverage.

3.   The magnitude of the change in value of the nonconvertible senior securities was both significant and substantially greater where the new issue was of equal or greater seniority.

4.   Firm value varied directly with the use of financial leverage.

5.   Estimates of the lower bound of the impact of a $1 change in the level of debt on firm value were between $0.23 and $0.45.

In summary, Masulis' evidence is consistent with the notions that taxes provide an incentive to use debt financing, of the existence of a positive debt level information effect, and of the presence of a leverage-induced wealth transfer across security classes.

Bankruptcy Costs as a Restraint on the Use of Debt

A number of authors have utilized bankruptcy costs to restrain a firm's use of debt financing (see Scott [1976], Lee and Barker [1977], and Kim [1978]). Recall from Chapter 12 that in these models firm value is characterized as follows:

$$V_L = V_U + VITS - VEBC,$$

where V_L is the value of a levered firm, V_U is the value of the same firm if unlevered, VITS is the value of the interest tax savings accruing to the firm from its use of debt financing,[2] and VEBC is the value of the expected costs of bankruptcy. The optimal capital structure, then, is found where the marginal benefits of using more debt (that is, the increment to the value of the interest tax savings) just equals the marginal cost of adding more debt (the increment to the value of the expected cost of bankruptcy).

Before reviewing the empirical evidence that bankruptcy costs are a deterrent to the use of debt financing, we should note that some authors minimize their importance on theoretical grounds. Haugen and Senbet (1978), for example, argue that where there are significant costs attendant to bankruptcy there will exist an incentive for voluntary reorganization in order to avoid them; that is, the owners, creditors, or an independent investor group will observe the potential gains from avoiding a costly bankruptcy and proceed to reorganize the firm accordingly. We will return to this argument shortly.

Due to the difficulty of observing bankruptcy costs, only a very limited number of studies have sought to measure their magnitude. Warner (1977) studied the explicit costs of bankruptcy for a sample of 11 bankrupt railroads. These costs included only the legal and administrative costs of bankruptcy and omitted the associated indirect costs (such as the opportunity cost of management's time and energy invested in staving off the impending bankruptcy). He found that the average bankruptcy costs were $2 million per firm and were spread out over an average of 13 years, during which time the railroad was reorganized and ultimately released from the bankruptcy court. These costs averaged 5.3 percent of the value of the railroad's combined debt and equity securities just before bankruptcy. Where the firm's value had been estimated five years prior to bankruptcy, these costs were only 1.4 percent. Thus, if the probability of bankruptcy is as high as 0.25, the expected cost of bankruptcy will be only $0.25 \times 0.014 = 0.0035$, or 0.35 percent of the firm's value. Further, if the expected bankruptcy is anticipated five years hence and the discount rate is 10 percent, $VEBC = 0.0035V_L/(1.10)^5 = 0.002173V_L$. Hence, Warner's results suggest that the direct costs of bankruptcy are trivial and therefore do not significantly limit the use of debt financing.

---

[2]Recall from Chapter 12 that the size of these tax savings depends on the corporate tax rate and the relative personal tax rates on bond and equity income.

Recall that Warner did not consider the indirect costs associated with corporate bankruptcy. These costs consist largely of "opportunities forgone" when a firm's management turns its energies away from seeking profitable investment opportunities and directs them toward avoiding the impending financial crisis. Obviously, the indirect costs of financial distress are not easy to observe or measure. Further, in a world of incomplete information where management is privy to superior knowledge of the firm's true financial condition (that is, asymmetric information), the advent of a default on one of the firm's financial obligations "forces" management to reveal the true state of the firm's financial affairs. Thus, default on a debt obligation may not lead to a formal bankruptcy proceeding or an informal reorganization (as suggested by Haugen and Senbet [1978]), but it may provide a "signal" to investors that will lead them to devalue the firm's shares. Therefore, the use of financial leverage in a world of asymmetric information can have a cost associated with the increased likelihood that management will be forced to reveal "unpleasant" information that otherwise would go unrecognized by investors.

Still another argument can be made for the relevance of bankruptcy costs. This relates to the losses suffered by the firm's managers in the event the firm fails while under their guidance, that is, a devaluation of their human capital. Management therefore will seek to avoid this circumstance even though the costs to the firm's shareholders may be insignificant. The loss in firm value resulting from management's attempt to avoid the risk of failure by underutilizing financial leverage thus can be thought of as an agency cost that the firm's owners bear.

Summary

As with the theories discussed in Chapter 12, the empirical evidence on the existence of an optimal capital structure, although mixed, permits a number of observations. First, firms within broad industry groups tend to have similar capital structures. This indicates that there may be some factors coincident with industry class that impact on the firm's capital structure design. In addition, certain "fundamental" firm attributes have been found to be consistently related to a firm's capital structure. For example, growth in sales, earnings, and firm size have been found to be positively correlated with a firm's tendency to use debt financing, while expected bankruptcy costs have been found to be inversely related. Second, the historical time series of corporate financing decisions indicates significant swings between the debt and equity financing. At this juncture, financial theory fails to explain the variation in financing patterns over time. Finally, although a number of authors have suggested that market (monopoly) power should increase the firm's use of debt financing, the evidence consistently has been to the contrary: It seems that increased market power leads a firm to use less, not more, financial leverage.

All of this implies that firms have different financing patterns that are at least partially explainable by certain observable firm characteristics. This suggests that there may well be an optimal capital structure for broad groups of firms (such as crudely defined industries) if not for individual firms. Thus, a financial manager is well advised to note how other firms have designed their capital structures (they may know something he or she does not). In addition, since bond rating agencies such as Standard and Poor's and Moody are sensitive to capital structure ratios in relation to industry norms, it may pay to conform to those standards in the absence of a better guide to capital structure management.

Corporate Financial Structure and the Cost of Capital: Applications

In this section, we discuss a number of net present value models that have been posed in the finance literature. Each model either explicitly or implicitly incorporates the impact of the firm's financing decision. Our objective here is to show how each model does so and, in so doing, illustrate the models' basic similarities.

Alternative Specifications for Net Present Value[3]

The net present value (NPV) model used in most finance texts is defined as follows:

$$NPV = \sum_{t=1}^{N} \frac{NCF_t}{(1 + K_{wacc})^t} - I,$$

where NCF_t = net cash flow to the project in period t, I = initial investment in the project, and K_{wacc} = weighted average cost of capital corresponding to the project's financing. In this section we will discuss the origin of this model as well as a number of other, equally valid NPV expressions. In so doing, we will discover both the strengths and limitations of the traditional NPV model.

In Chapter 5, we developed the general equation for project net present value: NPV equals the value of the project's incremental cash flows (ΔV) less its initial cost (I), that is,

(13.1) $NPV = \Delta V - I.$

In this section we will derive five alternative and equivalent specifications for project NPV based on three different but completely equivalent specifications for ΔV.

The basic procedure for defining alternative specifications of project NPV is as follows:

- **Step 1:** Derive an expression for ΔV.

- **Step 2:** Substitute the expression for ΔV into Equation 13.1.

Each of our first three definitions of ΔV comes from the same basic model, and each is totally consistent with the others. As a result, all three definitions of project NPV are equivalent and produce identical estimates of the impact of a project's acceptance on shareholder wealth (that is, NPV) when properly used. The final two definitions rely on additional assumptions that, if upheld, make all five definitions equivalent.

---

[3]The material in this section relies on Martin (1987).

Simplifying Assumptions. In order to facilitate our discussion of the valuation expressions, we will make a number of simplifying assumptions:

1. All cash flows are level perpetuities. This includes the stream of operating earnings accruing to the firm (project being valued) as well as interest on debt.

2. Debt is perpetual, and interest rates are constant. The firm issues perpetual debt with a fixed coupon rate equal to the market interest rate.

3. All after-tax earnings are paid out to the common shareholders in dividends.

4. The tax rate on firm income is constant.

5. The firm's assets have perpetual lives.

Assumptions 1 through 5 simply mean that the firm and its securities can be valued as level perpetuities. This will simplify the expressions we will use in deriving ΔV.

Firm Valuation and Project NPV. Given the above assumptions, the value of a firm or capital investment project can be defined as follows:

(13.2)
$$\Delta V \equiv \Delta S + \Delta D,$$

where ΔS = value of stockholders' equity in the project
$$= \frac{(\Delta X - r\Delta B)(1 - T)}{K_e}$$

ΔD = value of debt used to finance the project
$$= r\Delta B/r$$

ΔX = annual operating earnings (before interest and taxes) expected from the project

ΔB = face value of debt used to finance the project (also market value, as per Assumption 2)

K_e = market's required rate of return for equity invested in the project

r = coupon rate and market rate of interest on firm's debt

Substituting the above definition for ΔS into Equation 13.2, we obtain

(13.2a)
$$\Delta V \equiv \frac{(\Delta X - r\Delta B)(1 - T)}{K_e} + \Delta D.$$

This constitutes our first definition for the project's value. Substituting for ΔV in the NPV expression in Equation 13.1, we define our first expression for NPV:

$$NPV \equiv \frac{(\Delta X - r\Delta B)(1 - T)}{K_e} + \Delta D - I.$$

By Assumption 2, we know that $\Delta D = \Delta B$, where ΔB is the amount of debt used to finance the project such that the equity financing for the investment, ΔS^*, equals $I - \Delta D$. Project NPV, then, can be written as follows:

(13.1a)
$$NPV_1 = \frac{(\Delta X - r\Delta B)(1 - T)}{K_e} - \Delta S^*.$$

In other words, NPV_1 is the present value of the equity cash flows less the amount of equity invested in the project. This particular formulation was proposed by Solomon (1955) and has been called the *flow through to equity* definition of NPV since it focuses directly on equity cash flow and invested equity.[4]

Before proceeding to our second NPV model, we should note that in an uncertain environment K_e is a function of both the operating risks associated with the project (that is, uncertainty associated with ΔX) and that derived from the financing mix ($\Delta D/\Delta V$) used. Both the Modigliani/Miller (1963) tax-adjusted valuation model and the Miller (1977) personal tax model provide possible specifications for the relationship between K_e and $\Delta D/\Delta V$. We will discuss each later.

The second definition for NPV relies on an algebraic reformulation of ΔV as found in Equation 13.2a. Specifically, solving 13.2a for $\Delta X(1 - T)$ produces the following:

$$\Delta X(1 - T) = K_e \Delta V - K_e \Delta D + r \Delta B(1 - T).$$

Noting that $\Delta V - \Delta D = \Delta S$ and dividing through both sides of the above expression by ΔV produces

$$\frac{\Delta X(1 - T)}{\Delta V} = K_e \left(\frac{\Delta S}{\Delta V}\right) + r(1 - T)\left(\frac{\Delta B}{\Delta V}\right).$$

Substituting ΔD for ΔB and solving for ΔV on the left-hand side of the above expression, we obtain our second definition for ΔV:

(13.2b)
$$\Delta V = \frac{\Delta X(1 - T)}{K_e \left(\dfrac{\Delta S}{\Delta V}\right) + r(1 - T)\left(\dfrac{\Delta D}{\Delta V}\right)}.$$

Note that Equation 13.2b necessarily equals 13.2a, since one is derived from the other.

Substituting 13.2b into 13.1 produces the second definition for NPV:

(13.1b)
$$NPV_2 = \frac{\Delta X(1 - T)}{K_e \left(\dfrac{\Delta S}{\Delta V}\right) + r(1 - T)\left(\dfrac{\Delta D}{\Delta V}\right)} - I.$$

This definition generally is referred to as the *weighted average cost of capital (WACC)* formulation in that the present value of the after-tax operating cash flow, $\Delta X(1 - T)$, is found by discounting at the weighted average cost of capital. Note that the weighted average cost of capital is defined using as weights the "market values" of debt and equity relative to that of the project (that is, the weight attached to the cost of equity is $\Delta S/\Delta V$, and the corresponding weight for debt is $\Delta D/\Delta V$).

---

[4]This term was coined by Taggart (1977), who provides a similar discussion of NPV models.

The third definition for NPV uses yet another version of ΔV derived from Equation 13.2a. This time we solve 13.2a for $\Delta X(1 - T) + r\Delta BT$. The result is

$$\Delta X(1 - T) + r\Delta BT = K_e\Delta V - K_e\Delta D + r\Delta B.$$

Again, recognizing that $\Delta V - \Delta D \equiv \Delta S$ and dividing through by ΔV produces

$$\frac{\Delta X(1 - T) + r\Delta BT}{\Delta V} = K_e\left(\frac{\Delta S}{\Delta V}\right) + r\left(\frac{\Delta B}{\Delta V}\right).$$

Solving for ΔV on the left-hand side of this expression and substituting for $\Delta D = \Delta B$ produces

(13.2c)
$$\Delta V = \frac{\Delta X(1 - T) + r\Delta DT}{K_e\left(\dfrac{\Delta S}{\Delta V}\right) + r\left(\dfrac{\Delta D}{\Delta V}\right)}.$$

This expression for ΔV was used by Arditti and Levy (1977) to define NPV as follows:

(13.1c)
$$NPV_3 = \frac{\Delta X(1 - T) + r\Delta DT}{K_e\left(\dfrac{\Delta S}{\Delta V}\right) + r\left(\dfrac{\Delta D}{\Delta V}\right)} - I.$$

Note that the interest tax shelter $(r\Delta DT)$ is part of the cash flows in this expression and the weighted average cost of capital uses the "before-tax" cost of debt. Once again, however, since Equation 13.2c came from a reformulation of 13.2a, NPV_3 is the same as NPV_1 and NPV_2.

Net present value models 1 through 3 have all been based on the identity found in Equation 13.2 and do not reflect any theoretical explanation for the impact of financing mix on project value. The fourth and fifth NPV expressions are based on the Modigliani/Miller (1963) tax-adjusted valuation model. Thus, these expressions are based on the following valuation model for a levered investment project:

(13.3)
$$\Delta V = \Delta V_U + PV(ITS),$$

where ΔV_U = value of after-tax operating earnings of the project if financed totally by equity
$$= \frac{\Delta X(1 - T)}{K_U}$$

K_U = required rate of return for an all-equity-financed project

$PV(ITS)$ = present value of interest tax shelter on debt used to finance the project
$$= \frac{r\Delta DT}{r} = \Delta DT$$

ΔD = market value of debt used to finance the project

Recall from our discussion of capital structure theory in Chapter 12 that this valuation model relies on a number of assumptions, including (1) competitive and frictionless capital markets, (2) the existence of corporate (firm) income taxes but no personal taxes, (3) tax-deductible interest expense, and (4) investors who maximize the expected utility of their wealth.[5]

Substituting Equation 13.3 into 13.1 for ΔV produces the fourth expression for NPV:

(13.1d)
$$NPV_4 = \frac{\Delta X(1 - T)}{K_U} + T\Delta D - I.$$

Note that Equation 13.1d is equivalent to 13.1a, 13.1b, and 13.1c *only* where the

---

[5]We can easily demonstrate the consistency of the Modigliani and Miller (1958) capital structure irrelevance proposition and the CAPM. Consider the value of an unlevered firm V_U, defined as follows:

(i)
$$V_U = \frac{E[X_1] - \lambda Cov(X_1, R_M)}{1 + r_F},$$

where X_1 is the end-of-period risky cash flow produced by the firm's investments, R_M is the market return, λ is the market price of risk, and r_F is the risk-free interest rate. Now let the firm issue D, debt that requires a return equal to the risk-free rate, r_F. The proceeds of the debt issue are used to retire a portion of the firm's equity. The value of the levered firm's equity, S, can now be defined as follows:

(ii)
$$S = \frac{E[X_1] - (1 + r_F)D - \lambda Cov[X_1 - (1 + r_F)D, R_M]}{1 + r_F}.$$

However, since the debt is risk free, $Cov(r_F D, R_M) = 0$ and the value of the levered firm's equity reduces to the following:

$$S = \frac{E[X_1] - \lambda Cov(X_1, R_M)}{(1 + r_F)} - D.$$

Noting that $V_L = S + D$, we observe the following:

(iii)
$$V_L = \frac{E[X_1] - \lambda Cov(X_1, R_M)}{1 + r_F} = V_U.$$

We can also illustrate the consistency between the Modigliani and Miller (1963) tax correction model of firm value and the CAPM. Consider first the impact of a corporate income tax, t_c, on the value of the unlevered firm found in (i) above:

(iv)
$$V_U = \frac{E[X_1](1 - t_c) - \lambda Cov(1 - t_c)(X_1, R_M)}{1 + r_F}.$$

Now allow the firm to borrow D dollars requiring interest payable at the risk-free rate. It uses the proceeds to repurchase some of its own equity. The resulting equity value would be the following:

$$S = \frac{E[X_1] - (1 + r_F)D - (E[x_1] - r_F D)t_c - \lambda(1 - t_c)Cov(x_1, R_M)}{1 + r_F},$$

which can also be rewritten as follows:

(v)
$$S = \frac{E[X_1](1 - t_c) + r_F D t_c - \lambda(1 - t_c)Cov(X_1, R_M)}{(1 + r_F)} - D,$$

such that

(vi)
$$V_L = V_U + r_F D t_c/(1 + r_F),$$

which is the single-period version of the Modigliani and Miller (1963) proposition.

additional assumptions underlying 13.3 are fulfilled. Note too that 13.1d is also Myers' (1974) adjusted present value (APV).[6]

The fifth definition of NPV involves solving Equation 13.3 for a weighted average cost of capital based on K_U. This entails solving for $\Delta X(1 - T)$ using 13.3 as follows:

$$K_U(\Delta V - T\Delta D) = \Delta X(1 - T).$$

Dividing through by ΔV, we obtain

$$K_U\left[1 - \left(\frac{\Delta D}{\Delta V}\right)T\right] = \frac{\Delta X(1 - T)}{\Delta V}.$$

Finally, solving for ΔV on the right-hand side of the above expression yields

(13.3a)
$$\Delta V = \frac{\Delta X(1 - T)}{K_U\left[1 - \left(\frac{\Delta D}{\Delta V}\right)T\right]}.$$

Substituting 13.3a for ΔV in 13.1 produces

(13.1e)
$$NPV_5 = \frac{\Delta X(1 - T)}{K_U\left[1 - T\left(\frac{\Delta D}{\Delta V}\right)\right]} - I,$$

which is a simple reformulation of Equation 13.1d. Again the equivalence of 13.1d and 13.1e with 13.1a through 13.1c requires the Modigliani/Miller assumptions underlying 13.3 in addition to Assumptions 1 through 5.

A Numerical Example

The equivalence of the five NPV models found in Equations 13.1a through 13.1e can be demonstrated using a simple numerical example. Consider the following investment proposal:

ΔX = \$120 (annual [perpetual] net cash flow)
  T = 0.5 (corporate income tax rate)
  K_e = 0.2 (required rate of return of common shareholders, which reflects both the operating and financing risk inherent in the project and its financing)
K_U = 0.1714 (required rate of return on the project if all equity financed)[7]

---

[6]Technically, NPV_4 presumes a fixed and known level of debt financing throughout the project's perpetual life. We address the significance of this assumption later in conjunction with the maintenance of a constant debt-to-value ratio throughout the project's life (an assumption underlying the traditional WACC version of NPV or NPV_2).

[7]For our present analysis, it is sufficient to recognize that in the context of the MM (1963) tax-adjusted valuation model,

$$K_e = K_U + (K_U - r)(1 - T)(\Delta D/\Delta S)$$

such that

$$K_U = [K_e + r(1 - T)(\Delta D/\Delta S)]/[1 + (1 - T)(\Delta D/\Delta S)]$$

and, using the example inputs,

$$K_U = 0.1714.$$

r = 0.1 (interest rate on firm's debt, which also equals creditors' required rate
of return)

I = \$400 (initial project outlay or cost)

ΔB = \$200 (amount of debt used to aid in project's financing; since coupon rate
equals creditors' required rate of return [by Assumption 2], ΔB = ΔD
[book value equals market value of debt])

Note that Assumptions 1 through 5 are assumed to hold in addition to those underlying the Modigliani/Miller valuation model in Equation 13.3. Using 13.1a, NPV_1
is calculated as follows:

$$NPV_1 = \frac{(\$120 - \$20)(1 - 0.5)}{0.2} + \$200 - \$400$$

$$= \$250 + \$200 - \$400 = \underline{\$50}.$$

Now, using the traditional weighted average cost of capital formulation in Equation 13.1b,

$$NPV_2 = \frac{\$120(1 - 0.5)}{0.2\left(\frac{\$250}{\$450}\right) + 0.1(1 - 0.5)\left(\frac{\$200}{\$450}\right)} - \$400$$

$$= \$450 - \$400 = \underline{\$50}.$$

Note that technically we cannot solve for NPV using 13.1b without knowing the
value of the project cash flows (ΔV = \$450), since we must know ΔV in order to
be able to estimate the weighted average cost of capital. Note too that the weights
appropriate for use in calculating the weighted average cost of capital are based on
market values. We will return to this point in a moment; for now, simply assume
that ΔS/ΔV and ΔD/ΔV are known.

Using the Arditti/Levy (1977) formulation in Equation 13.1c, we calculate

$$NPV_3 = \frac{\$120(1 - 0.5) + 0.1(\$200)0.5}{0.2\left(\frac{\$250}{\$450}\right) + 0.1\left(\frac{\$200}{\$450}\right)} - \$400$$

$$= \$450 - \$400 = \underline{\$50}.$$

Note that once again it is necessary to know ΔV (so that we can estimate the
"before-tax" weighted average cost of capital) *before* NPV_3 can be calculated.

Calculating project NPV using the two Modigliani/Miller-based models involves substituting into Equations 13.1d and 13.1e, respectively:

$$NPV_4 = \frac{\$120(1 - 0.5)}{0.1714} + \frac{(\$200)(0.1)(0.5)}{0.1} - \$400$$

$$= \$350 + \$100 - \$400 = \underline{\$50}$$

and

$$NPV_5 = \frac{\$120(1 - 0.5)}{0.1714\left[1 - \left(\dfrac{\$200}{\$450}\right)0.5\right]} - \$400$$

$$= \frac{\$60}{0.1333} - \$400 = \underline{\$50}.$$

The same NPV is found under both formulations and also agrees with the previous calculations. Again we need to know ΔV before calculating NPV_5.

Two points can be made in summarizing the results of our calculations. First, all five models produced identical results, since they are equivalent under the requisite set of assumptions used in their derivation. Second, models 13.1b, 13.1c, and 13.1e share the requirement that ΔV be known before the weighted average cost of capital can be evaluated. However, ΔV, which equals NPV + I, is the object of the analysis — in other words, with either 13.1b, 13.1c, or 13.1e, we cannot estimate the appropriate weighted average cost of capital until we have valued project cash flows (that is, ΔV and, consequently, NPV are known), but we cannot estimate ΔV until we know the weighted average cost of capital. There is no totally satisfactory way to circumvent this problem; it is simply a result of how we arrived at a weighted average cost of capital formulation for NPV.

The popular rationale for using weighted average cost of capital NPV formulas like 13.1b, 13.1c, and 13.1e is as follows: The firm applies its "target" financing mix in evaluating $\Delta S/\Delta V$ and $\Delta D/\Delta V$; thus, these estimates are obtained "independently" of the project's NPV evaluation. Of course, this does not solve the technical dilemma, but it does provide a way of *operationalizing* the above three weighted average cost of capital formulations.

Finally, note that Equation 13.1a embeds the impact of project financing in the cost of equity capital, K_e; that is, K_e reflects the project's financial and operating risk characteristics. However, as we noted earlier, Equation 13.1a is simply a reformulation of the definitional identity found in 13.2 and does not reflect a theoretical explanation for this relationship between K_e and the project's financing mix. Thus, although 13.1a does not suffer from the "chicken-egg" problem that characterizes the weighted average cost of capital formulations of NPV (13.1b, 13.1c, and 13.1e), it has yet another shortcoming. Thus, only Equation 13.1d, the adjusted present value method, provides an NPV model that (1) does not suffer from the circularity encountered in the weighted average cost of capital models *and* (2) provides an "explicit" basis (that is, a theory) for evaluating the impact of debt financing on project value. This does not mean that the APV methodology is "correct" for, as noted, it depends on the assumptions underlying the Modigliani/ Miller tax-adjusted valuation model. However, the APV model at least *attempts* to deal with the impact of project financing mix on NPV.

Project Financing Mix and NPV

The basic issue in this section is the age-old question of how financing mix impacts on project valuation. As we noted at the close of the previous section, of the five NPV models considered here only the APV models (13.1d and 13.1e) incorporate such a theory. This theory was proposed by Modigliani and Miller in their now classic 1963 paper. The MM model utilized corporate taxes in a "partial-partial equilibrium" setting (that is, viewing only one side of the market) in which individuals allocate their savings between bonds and stocks in a world where only corporate income is taxed. The original Modigliani/Miller theories were based on partial equilibrium analysis in that the savings level was assumed to be given. Thus, the Modigliani/Miller 1958 and 1963 results were derived in a framework wherein individuals may not adjust their savings decisions to reflect changes in firms' supplies of bonds and, consequently, adjustments in the market interest rate.[8]

Miller (1977) incorporated personal taxes into the analysis. Specifically, the present value of the interest tax shelter is modified to reflect the personal tax consequences of bond versus stock income. Thus, in a world in which individuals pay tax on stock income at a rate t_s and must pay a tax rate t_b on bond income, the present value of the interest tax shelter resulting from the corporation's use of debt financing becomes

(13.4)
$$PV(ITS) = \left[1 - \frac{(1 - T)(1 - t_s)}{1 - t_b} \right] \Delta D .$$

Thus, with different personal tax rates on bond and stock income, the marginal tax shelter on each dollar of debt *changes* from the corporate tax rate, T (with only corporate taxes), to the term in brackets in Equation 13.4. Note that where $t_s = t_b$ the marginal tax shelter per dollar of debt financing reduces to T and the original Modigliani/Miller corporate tax–adjusted valuation model continues to hold. With the passage of the Tax Reform Act of 1986, this is precisely the case — $t_s = t_b$. (Actually, the act provided for a transition period. During 1987, the maximum tax rate on capital gains was 28 percent, and for 1988 and after it is $t_s = t_b$.) However, prior to this revision in the tax code, due to the lower capital gains tax rate applicable to stock income, t_s was less than t_b and the present value interest tax shelter in 13.4 was less than its counterpart in 13.3. Note that this inequality holds for all $T < 1$.[9]

One final aspect of the impact of the debt/equity mix on project NPV deserves attention because of the confusion it has produced in the academic literature. This concerns the fact that we have *assumed* a constant debt/equity mix (in market value terms) throughout the perpetual lives of the projects analyzed here; that is, we have assumed perpetual cash flows and perpetual debt such that the financing mix indeed remains constant throughout the project's life. However, if a project is partially financed by installment financing (wherein debt is retired over

---

[8]Recall that we used the Miller (1977) model as the basis for our synthesis of the Modigliani and Miller (1958, 1963) papers. In the Miller setup, we allowed savings to be an increasing function of the interest rate.

[9]The maximum tax rate on corporate income was 46 percent under the 1985 tax law and has not exceeded 52 percent in recent years. With the Tax Reform Act of 1986 the maximum corporate tax rate was reduced to 34 percent and $t_s = t_b$ such that Equation 13.4 reduces to $T\Delta D$, which is the Modigliani and Miller (1963) result.

its life), the costs of debt and equity technically could vary over the project's life to reflect the changing financing mix. Some authors, including Arditti and Levy (1977) and M. Ben-Horim (1979), have contended that NPV models 13.1b and 13.1c will give different NPV estimates except in special circumstances (for example, the perpetuity case used here). However, Boudreaux and Long (1979) demonstrated that the two models are indeed identical if used "properly." *Proper use requires that the market value ratio of debt to total project value be held constant over the project's life.* On this same point, Myers (1974) has shown that APV and the traditional weighted average cost of capital models generally will *not* yield the same levered valuations of a project's cash flows. Chambers, Harris, and Pringle (1982) and Ezzell and Miles (1983) evaluated the practical significance and theoretical explanation for this difference, respectively. Miles and Ezzell (1980) offered an adjusted version of the MM weighted average cost of capital formula that provides for a constant debt-to-value ratio throughout the project's life (as opposed to a constant-dollar level of debt). Further, this respecification accounts for the fact that future debt levels will follow the random pattern of project cash flows and, consequently, project value. The time pattern of project interest tax savings, then, is a random variable that Miles and Ezzell suggest should be discounted using the project's unlevered cost of equity. Thus, to reflect the maintenance of a constant debt-to-value ratio throughout the project's life and the random nature of future tax savings on the use of debt financing, the denominator of Equation 13.1e must be adjusted as follows:

$$K_U - \left(\frac{\Delta D}{\Delta V}\right) r T \left(\frac{1 + K_U}{1 + r}\right).$$

This "adjusted MM" weighted average cost of capital formula is entirely consistent with the traditional weighted average cost of capital, which, it will be recalled, assumes that the project's debt-to-value ratio remains constant throughout its life.

We conclude this discussion by noting that no NPV model that presumes a constant financing mix will provide an appropriate basis for project valuation where the financing mix varies over the project's investment life. Thus, regardless of the NPV model used, an appropriate analysis involves giving proper consideration to the actual financing mix that characterizes the project over its life. In addition, although the equivalence of all the NPV models discussed here is easy to demonstrate where all cash flows are level perpetuities, the key element in this similarity lies not in the project life or the time pattern of project cash flows but in the retention of the same set of assumptions or restrictions for all models and using that set which is *most* restrictive. In the cases analyzed here, the traditional NPV or WACC model's assumptions were found to be most restrictive. These included a constant cost of equity and debt over the project's life, a constant tax rate, *and* a constant ratio of debt-to-realized-value financing mix. The standard version of the MM or APV models assumes a constant level of debt financing and a *known* stream of interest tax savings as opposed to a constant ratio of debt to value, which implies an *unknown* stream of future interest tax savings (where project cash flows are risky and, consequently, realized project value varies randomly over time).

The basic issue that arises in choosing between the traditional WACC version of NPV and one of the MM-based (unadjusted) models lies in the debt transaction plan for the project. In other words, maintenance of a constant debt-to-value ratio implies continual readjustment in the project's financing mix to reflect (random) changes in its value over its life. On the other hand, the unadjusted MM-based versions of project NPV presume that a constant or fixed level of debt financing with known interest tax savings will be outstanding over the project's life. Since most textbook presentations of the traditional WACC model of NPV do not specify the need to maintain a constant debt-to-value ratio over the project's life, this restriction of the model frequently goes unrecognized.

Summary

In this chapter, we surveyed the evidence on how firms finance their assets as well as a number of models that have been used to explain those decisions. There appear to be discernible differences in firms' financing patterns both over time and across industries. To date, financial researchers' efforts to explain these variations have met with only partial success; only about half the variation in firm financial structures has been "explained" by a firm's industry class and/or the fundamental characteristics that are thought to influence financing choices.

In addition, we reviewed several net present value models and the impact of financing decisions on each. We found these models to be structurally different but functionally identical if the same set of restrictions was placed on each. In particular, we found that the traditional weighted average cost of capital model of project NPV requires that the debt-to-value ratio (in market value terms) be constant in each year of the project's life. More important, we investigated the technical "chicken-egg" problem that arises when using any weighted average cost of capital NPV model.

Much remains unresolved in the capital structure literature. Although there are a number of theories on how firm value is affected by a firm's capital structure design, none are universally heralded as "the" model. There appears to be room for even more dissertations on the capital structure problem.

Study Questions

13.1 The traditional weighted average cost of capital NPV model makes a very restrictive assumption about the firm's debt policy throughout the life of a capital budgeting project. What is that assumption, and how does it compare with the assumption underlying the "original" version of the MM (1963) tax-adjusted valuation model?

13.2 If firms rather than industries make capital structure decisions, why do we care whether firms within industries have similar capital structures?

13.3 The Modigliani and Miller (1958) study of corporate capital structures found no significant relationship between a firm's cost of capital and its mix of debt and equity financing. However, repeating the study later, Weston

(1963) found a highly significant relationship between these variables. How can this be?

13.4   Warner (1977) argues that the costs of bankruptcy are so low that they are an insignificant impediment to a firm's use of financial leverage. Discuss.

13.5   What is the "chicken-egg" problem encountered when attempting to use a weighted average cost of capital in analyzing capital investments?

Study Problems

13.1   The Barnhill Publishing Company is considering the acquisition of a new laser technology typesetter. The typesetter is expected to produce annual net cash flows (before interest and taxes) of $1,700 per year forever. Barnhill can purchase the typesetter for $6,000 and has arranged to borrow $2,000 at a rate of 10 percent per annum. Internal discussions of the appropriate cost of capital for the project have yielded an estimated cost of equity capital of 20 percent given the planned use of debt financing. In addition, Barnhill uses a 34 percent tax rate in its evaluation of capital expenditures.
   a. What is the traditional weighted average cost of capital for the project?
   b. Calculate the project's net present value in terms of the second definition of NPV in Equation 13.1b.
   c. Calculate the Arditti/Levy (1977) cost of capital for the project and its corresponding net present value.
   d. What is the difference between the traditional weighted average cost of capital and the Arditti/Levy cost of capital? Explain.
   e. Assuming that all cash flows (including interest on debt) are level perpetuities, calculate the project's adjusted present value (see Equation 13.1d).
   f. What is the MM (1963) weighted average cost of capital for the project?

13.2   If Problem 13.1 involved a 10-year project life, how would your analysis be affected? (No computations required — just discuss.) Be sure to include consideration for debt repayment and asset depreciation.

13.3   Babel Enterprises estimates its cost of equity, K_e, at 20 percent. The market rate of interest on Babel's debt is 12 percent, making its total market value 80 percent of the market value of its equity. If Babel's marginal tax bracket is 34 percent, what is the firm's unlevered cost of equity financing, K_U? (Hint: Assume that there are no personal taxes.)

13.4   One day in June 1987, Meagan Bishop was in her boss's office awaiting the weekly meeting of Xavier Manufacturing Company's financial analysis staff. These meetings usually lasted from one to two hours and involved a review of the past week's work and a brief outline of the work for the upcoming week. However, the current meeting was different, as was immediately apparent to Bishop as she entered the company conference rooms, because the company's financial vice-president, Bill Wheelis, was in attendance.

The problem was one of basic operating procedure used in evaluating capital expenditure proposals. Xavier considered itself quite progressive among its competitors in that it had relied on discounted cash flow techniques for almost 15 years while they still depended heavily on payback and average rate of return. However, Wheelis had just attended a two-week financial planning program at Big State University, where he had learned the virtues of the adjusted present value method. What appealed to him most about APV was its direct consideration of the impact of project financing in the form of the interest tax savings term. The reason for Wheelis' visit was to "suggest" that Xavier's financial analysis staff consider utilizing APV in place of the weighted average cost of capital NPV model it currently employed.

a. If you were Bishop, how would you explain to Wheelis how the firm's present methodology incorporated consideration for its financing mix?

b. Should personal taxes be considered in evaluating APV? If so, how?

13.5   At the close of Xavier's weekly staff meeting (see Problem 13.4) Meagan Bishop suggested that she would "run the numbers" on a sample capital budgeting project to demonstrate the equivalence of the present weighted average cost of capital model and the adjusted present value model espoused by Bill Wheelis. She gathered the following information for her illustrative problem:

- Project cash flows were assumed to be level perpetuities equal to $500 per year (before taxes), and the asset would *not* depreciate.

- The firm's marginal tax rate was 34 percent.

- The firm's cost of equity was estimated as 20 percent based on current capital market conditions and the firm's present debt/equity ratio of 80 percent.

- The firm's borrowing rate was 10 percent (debt was assumed to be perpetual).

- The project would require an investment of $2,000.

a. Calculate the weighted average cost of capital for the project needed to maintain the 80 percent debt/equity ratio.

b. What is the project's net present value using the weighted average cost of capital from part a?

c. What is the project's APV? (Ignore personal taxes.)

d. Answer parts b and c where the project provides cash flows only over the next 20 years.

References

F. D. Arditti and H. Levy, "The Weighted Average Cost of Capital as a Cutoff Rate: A Critical Analysis of the Classical Textbook Weighted Average Cost of Capital," *Financial Management* (Fall 1977): 24–34.

A. J. Auerbach, "Real Determinants of Corporate Leverage," in *Corporate Capital Structures in the United States,* ed. B. M. Friedman (Chicago: University of Chicago Press, 1984), 301–324.

A. Barnea, R. A. Haugen, and L. W. Senbet, "Market Imperfections, Agency Problems and Capital Structure: A Review," *Financial Management* (Summer 1981): 7–22.

M. Ben-Horim, "Comment on 'The Weighted Average Cost of Capital as a Cutoff Rate,'" *Financial Management* (Summer 1979): 18–21.

J. A. Boquist and W. T. Moore, "Inter-industry Leverage Differences and the DeAngelo-Masulis Tax Hypothesis," *Financial Management* (Spring 1984): 5–9.

K. J. Boudreaux and H. W. Long, "The Weighted Average Cost of Capital as a Cutoff Rate: A Further Analysis," *Financial Management* (Summer 1979): 7–15.

M. Bradley, G. A. Jarrell, and E. H. Kim, "On the Existence of an Optimal Structure: Theory and Evidence," *Journal of Finance* (July 1984): 857–878.

D. R. Chambers, R. S. Harris, and J. J. Pringle, "Treatment of Financing Mix in Analyzing Investment Opportunities," *Financial Management* (Summer 1982): 24–41.

J. C. Ciccolo, Jr., "Changing Balance Sheet Relationships in the U.S. Manufacturing Sector, 1926–77," in *The Changing Roles of Debt and Equity in Financing U.S. Capital Formation,* ed. B. M. Friedman (Chicago: University of Chicago Press, 1984).

R. M. Dammon and L. Senbet, "The Effect of Taxes on the Interaction between Production and Finance" (Working paper, University of Wisconsin, May 1986).

H. DeAngelo and R. Masulis, "Optimal Capital Structure under Corporate and Personal Taxation," *Journal of Financial Economics* (March 1980): 3–29.

J. R. Ezzell and R. B. Porter, "Correct Specification of the Cost of Capital and Net Present Value," *Financial Management* (Summer 1979): 13–17.

J. R. Ezzell and J. A. Miles, "Capital Project Analysis and the Debt Transaction Plan," *Journal of Financial Research* (Spring 1983): 25–31.

M. Ferri and W. Jones, "Determinants of Financial Structure: A New Methodological Approach," *Journal of Finance* (June 1979): 631–644.

B. M. Friedman, *Corporate Capital Structures in the United States* (Chicago: University of Chicago Press, 1984).

J. Friend and J. Hasbrouck, "Determinants of Capital Structure" (Working paper no. 7, Rodey L. White Center for Financial Research, University of Pennsylvania, 1986).

J. M. Gahlon and R. D. Stover, "Debt Capacity and the Capital Budgeting Decision," *Financial Management* (Winter 1979): 55–59.

R. W. Goldsmith, *Financial Intermediaries in the American Economy Since 1900* (Princeton, N.J.: Princeton University Press, 1958).

———, *A Study of Saving in the United States,* 3 vols. (Princeton, N.J.: Princeton University Press, 1956).

———, R. E. Lipsey, and M. Mendelson, *Studies in the National Balance Sheet of the United States,* 2 vols. (Princeton, N.J.: Princeton University Press, 1963).

S. E. Greenbaum and C. F. Haywood, "Secular Change in the Financial Services Industry," *Journal of Money, Credit and Banking* 3 (1971): 571–589.

R. S. Hamada, "The Effect of the Firm's Capital Structure on the Systematic Risk of Common Stock," *Journal of Finance* (May 1972): 435–452.

———, "Portfolio Analysis, Market Equilibrium, and Corporation Finance," *Journal of Finance* (March 1969): 13–21.

R. Haugen and L. Senbet, "The Insignificance of Bankruptcy Costs to the Theory of the Optimal Capital Structure," *Journal of Finance* (May 1978): 383–394.

G. V. Henderson, Jr., "In Defense of the Weighted Average Cost of Capital," *Financial Management* (Autumn 1979): 57–61.

D. M. Holland and S. C. Myers, "Trends in Corporate Profitability and Capital Costs," in *The Nation's Capital Needs: Three Studies,* ed. R. Lindsay (New York: Committee for Economic Development, 1979).

Hai Hong, "Inflation and Market Value of the Firm: Theory and Tests," *Journal of Finance* (September 1977): 1031–1048.

G. J. Hurdle, "Leverage, Risk, Market Structure and Profitability," *Review of Economics and Statistics* (November 1974): 478–485.

R. G. Ibbotson and R. A. Sinquefield, "Stocks, Bonds, Bills, and Inflation: The Past and the Future," (Charlottesville, Va.: Financial Analyst's Research Federation, 1982).

M. Jensen and W. Meckling, "Theory of the Firm: Managerial Behavior, Agency Cost and Capital Structure," *Journal of Financial Economics* (October 1976): 305–360.

H. S. Kerr, "The Determinants of Intra-Industry Capital Structure" (Paper presented at the Annual Meeting of the Western Finance Association, San Francisco, June 1979).

H. Kim, "A Mean-Variance Theory of Optimal Capital Structure and Corporate Debt Capacity," *Journal of Finance* (March 1978): 45–64.

——— , W. G. Lewellen, and J. J. McConnell, "Financial Leverage Clienteles: Theory and Evidence," *Journal of Financial Economics* 7 (1979): 83–109.

R. K. Klemkosky and J. D. Martin, "The Adjustment of Beta Forecasts," *Journal of Finance* (September 1975): 1123–1128.

S. Kuznets, *Capital in the American Economy: Its Formation and Financing* (Princeton, N.J.: Princeton University Press, 1961).

W. Y. Lee and H. Barker, "Bankruptcy Costs and the Firm's Optimal Debt Capacity: A Positive Theory of Capital Structure," *Southern Economics Journal* (January 1977): 1453–1465.

W. G. Lewellen, "A Pure Financial Rationale for the Conglomerate Merger," *Journal of Finance* (May 1971): 521–537.

J. Lintner, "The Financing of Corporations," in *The Corporation in Modern Society*, ed. E. S. Mason (Cambridge, Mass.: Harvard University Press, 1960).

J. D. Martin, "Alternative NPV Models," *Advances in Financial Planning* (Greenwich, Conn.: JAI Press, 1987).

——— , J. W. Petty, and D. F. Scott, Jr., "An Empirical Assessment of the Determinants of Corporate Financial Policy" (Paper presented at the Annual Meeting of the Financial Management Association, Boston, 1979).

——— and D. F. Scott, Jr., "A Multivariate Analysis of the Impact of Industry Class on Capital Structure" (Working paper no. 84/85-2-34, University of Texas at Austin, July 1985).

R. Masulis, "The Effects of Capital Structure Change on Security Prices: A Study of Exchange Offers," *Journal of Financial Economics* (June 1980): 139–178.

——— , "The Impact of Capital Structure Change on Firm Value: Some Estimates," *Journal of Finance* (March 1983): 107–126.

J. Miles and J. R. Ezzell, "The Weighted Average Cost of Capital, Perfect Capital Markets, and Project Life: A Clarification," *Journal of Financial and Quantitative Analysis* (September 1980): 719–730.

M. M. Miller, "Debt and Taxes," *Journal of Finance* (May 1977): 261–275.

——— and F. Modigliani, "Some Estimates of the Cost of Capital to the Electric Utility Industry, 1954–57," *American Economic Review* (June 1966): 333–391.

F. Modigliani and M. M. Miller, "The Cost of Capital, Corporation Finance and the Theory of Investment," *American Economic Review* (June 1958): 261–297.

——— , "Taxes and the Cost of Capital: A Correction," *American Economic Review* (June 1963): 433–443.

E. Muskie, "Tax Expenditures: Compendium of Background Material on Industrial Provisions" (Committee on the Budget, U.S. Senate 94th Cong. 2d sess., 1976).

S. C. Myers, "The Capital Structure Puzzle," *Journal of Finance* (July 1984): 575–592.

——— , "Interactions of Corporate Financing Decisions — Implications for Capital Budgeting," *Journal of Finance* (March 1974): 1–25.

——— , "Procedures for Capital Budgeting under Uncertainty," *Industrial Management Review* (Spring 1968).

T. J. Nantell and C. R. Carlson, "The Cost of Capital as a Weighted Average," *Journal of Finance* (December 1975): 1343–1355.

L. Remmers, A. Stonehill, R. Wright, and T. Beekhuisen, "Industry and Size as Debt Ratio Determinants in Manufacturing Internationally," *Financial Management* (Summer 1974): 24–32.

L. Rosenberg, "Taxation of Income from Capital by Industry Group," in *Taxation of Income from Capital,* ed. A. C. Harberger and M. J. Bailey (Washington, D.C.: Brookings Institution, 1969): 123–184.

M. E. Rubinstein, "A Mean-Variance Synthesis of Corporate Financial Theory," *Journal of Finance* (March 1973): 167–181.

A. W. Sametz, "Trends in the Volume and Composition of Equity Finance," *Journal of Finance* (1964): 450–469.

L. D. Schall, "Asset Valuation, Firm Investment, and Firm Diversification," *Journal of Business* (January 1972): 11–28.

————, G. L. Sundem, and W. R. Geijsbeek, Jr., "Survey and Analysis of Capital Budgeting Methods," *Journal of Finance* (March 1978): 281–287.

E. Schwartz and J. R. Aronson, "Some Surrogate Evidence in Support of the Concept of Optimal Financial Structure," *Journal of Finance* (March 1967): 10–18.

D. F. Scott, Jr., "Evidence on the Importance of Financial Structure," *Financial Management* (Summer 1972): 45–50.

————, and J. D. Martin, "Industry Influence on Financial Structure," *Financial Management* (Spring 1975): 67–73.

————, "A Multivariate Analysis of the Impact of Industry Class on Capital Structure" (Working paper no. 84/85-2-34, University of Texas at Austin, 1985).

J. Scott, "A Theory of Optimal Capital Structure," *Bell Journal of Economics and Management Science* (Spring 1976): 33–54.

A. C. Shapiro, "In Defense of the Traditional Weighted Average Cost of Capital as a Cutoff Rate," *Financial Management* (Summer 1979): 22–23.

J. Siegfried, "Effective Average U.S. Corporation Income Tax Rates," *National Tax Journal* 27 (1974): 245–259.

C. Smith and R. L. Watts, "The Investment Opportunity Set and Corporate Policy Choices" (Working paper, University of Rochester, 1986).

E. Solomon, "Measuring a Company's Cost of Capital," *Journal of Business* (October 1955): 240–252.

A. M. Spence, "Capital Structure and the Firm's Product Market Environment," in *Corporate Capital Structures in the United States,* ed. B. M. Friedman (Chicago: University of Chicago Press, 1984).

T. G. Sullivan, "Market Power, Profitability and Financial Leverage," *Journal of Finance* (December 1974): 1407–1415.

R. A. Taggart, Jr., "Capital Budgeting and the Financing Decision," *Financial Management* (Summer 1977): 59–64.

————, "Secular Patterns in the Financing of U.S. Corporations," in *Corporate Capital Structures in the United States,* ed. B. M. Friedman (Chicago: University of Chicago Press, 1984).

A. J. Taub, "Determinants of the Firm's Capital Structure," *Review of Economics and Statistics* (November 1975): 410–416.

S. Titman, "The Effect of Capital Structure on a Firm's Liquidation Decision," *Journal of Financial Economics* (March 1984): 137–151.

———— and R. Wessels, "The Determinants of Capital Structure Choice" (Working paper, UCLA, January 1986).

N. Toy, A. Stonehill, L. Remmers, R. Wright, and T. Beekhuisen, "A Comparative International Study of Growth, Profitability, and Risk as Determinants of Corporate Debt Ratios in the Manufacturing Sector," *Journal of Financial and Quantitative Analysis* (November 1974): 875–886.

C. Vanik, "Annual Corporate Tax Study, Tax Year 1976," *Congressional Record* (95th Cong., 2d sess., 1978), E168–E176.

G. M. von Furstenberg, "Corporate Investment: Does Market Valuation Matter in the Aggregate?" *Brookings Papers on Economic Activity* 2 (1977): 347–397.

J. B. Warner, "Bankruptcy Costs: Some Evidence," *Journal of Finance* (May 1977): 337–347.

J. F. Weston, "A Test of Cost of Capital Propositions," *Southern Economic Journal* (October 1963): 105–112.

Chapter 14

Dividend Policy:
Theory and Evidence

Corporate dividend policy deals with the firm's decision about how much of its earnings to pay out to its common stockholders in cash dividends. Since earnings paid out to common shareholders are not available for financing new investments, the corporate dividend policy decision is intertwined with corporate financial policy (discussed in Chapters 12 and 13). The fundamental theoretical question is, "Why does a firm's dividend policy affect (or not affect) the wealth of the firm's common shareholders?" If, for example, dividend policy affects the corporation's stock market value — and particularly if an increase in dividends increases that value — the owners will prefer that earnings be paid to them in dividends and that new investments be financed through the sale of new securities (debt and/or equity). When financial theorists have held the firm's investment policy constant (so as to isolate the impact of its dividend policy), they generally have found that its dividend policy does *not* impact on share value. However, some theorists have argued that the firm's dividend policy decision affects the firm's willingness to undertake its investment opportunities (for example, where there exists a differential "cost" of retaining earnings versus paying dividends and raising equity funds via the sale of new common shares). Under this circumstance dividend policy will impact on firm value, albeit indirectly.[1]

---

[1]Recall from Chapter 12 that the "pecking-order" theory of corporate financial policy suggests that internal (retained earnings) financing is the most preferred form of project financing (followed, respectively, by the issuance of debt and new common shares). This preference is at least partially based on the lower costs of retention versus new security sales. The costs of a new security issue were related to their transactions costs in the form of investment banker fees and the underpricing of the new issue because of the asymmetric information/moral hazard problem that accompanies the sale of securities.

In addition to the theory of dividend policy, we discuss the empirical evidence on the dividend payment practices of U.S. corporations and their impact on common stock prices. Specifically, we review Lintner's (1956) classic study of corporate dividend policy. Then we survey the literature that tests for the impact of corporate dividend policy on the firm's stock market value. Finally, we discuss the evidence on the impact of common stock repurchases on equity value. Although a number of motives can be used to explain a firm's decision to repurchase its shares, share repurchase is relevant here because it offers an alternative to the payment of a cash dividend.

Theories of Corporate Dividend Policy

Theories of corporate dividend policy can be categorized into two broad groups. The first contains theories that attempt to exploit the role of the corporate and personal tax code in determining an optimal dividend policy. Here capital markets are assumed to be frictionless in the sense used in Chapter 12;[2] that is, investors and firms can buy and sell securities without incurring any transactions costs. The second category expands the analysis to include transactions costs.[3] These costs include brokerage fees incurred by both firms and investors when they trade in the capital market and the implications of asymmetric information for securities prices (discussed in Chapter 12).

Frictionless Capital Markets and Tax-Based Dividend Policy Theories

We will use the concept of a *frictionless capital market* here in the same context as that used in our discussion of capital structure theory in Chapter 12: A frictionless capital market is one in which there are no transactions costs involved in buying and selling securities. This means, for example, that firms can sell new security issues without incurring brokerage or investment banker fees and without suffering any losses due to the need to discount the selling price to entice investors to purchase the issues. Further, investors can buy and sell any quantity of securities they wish without incurring broker fees or affecting the market price of the securities being traded. The frictionless market assumption is obviously unrealistic; however, it gives us a starting point for our analysis from which we can later expand to include more realistic conditions.

No Personal Taxes: Miller and Modigliani (1961).   In general, the value of a firm's common stock, e, can be thought of as the present value of its expected fu-

---

[2]We will review two seminal papers here, including Miller and Modigliani (1961) and Miller and Scholes (1978).

[3]Contributions to this literature include Jensen and Meckling (1976), Ross (1977), Bhattacharya (1979), Rozeff (1982), and Hakansson (1982).

ture dividends, Div_t, discounted at the required rate of return assessed by the capital market, K_e:

(14.1)
$$e = \frac{Div_1}{(1 + K_e)^1} + \frac{Div_2}{(1 + K_e)^2} + \cdots.$$

To illustrate the impact of dividend policy on stock market value, we will first consider the case where there are no personal taxes on dividend income or capital gains income from common stock. In addition, we will hold the firm's investment policy constant by assuming that the firm will undertake the optimal level of investment regardless of the dividend policy it selects. Further, we will assume that to finance its new investments, the firm will use either internally generated profits (retained earnings) or the sale of new common stock. Thus, to hold constant any possible effect of the firm's debt/equity financing decision on equity value, we will assume that the firm is all equity financed.

Now consider the impact of dividend policy on equity value by analyzing the disposition of the firm's cash flows in any period t. Specifically, note that the following "cash-in-equals-cash-out" identity must hold for any period t:

(14.2)
$$\underbrace{X_t + NF_t}_{\text{Cash in}} = \underbrace{Div_t + I_t + (1 + K_e)NF_{t-1}}_{\text{Cash out}},$$

where X_t represents the net cash flow the firm earns in period t due to its investments in place at the beginning of the period;[4] NF_t is the amount of new funds needed to finance investments in the current period; $(1 + K_e)NF_{t-1}$ is the required return to the suppliers of NF_{t-1} dollars in funds in period $t - 1$;[5] Div_t represents the period t dividend payment; and I_t is the optimal (value-maximizing) dollar level of investment to be made in period t. For simplicity, we will assume that all cash flows occur at the end of the period. Finally, note that for t = 0 Equation 14.2 reduces to $Div_0 = I_0 - NF_0 = 0$.

Solving Equation (14.2) for Div_t produces the following:

$$Div_t = (X_t - I_t) + NF_t - (1 + K_e)NF_{t-1}.$$

Substituting this expression for the dividend term in the equity valuation model in Equation 14.1 produces the following:

(14.1a)
$$e = \frac{(X_1 - I_1)}{(1 + K_e)^1} + \frac{(X_2 - I_2)}{(1 + K_e)^2} + \cdots$$
$$+ \frac{[NF_1 - (1 + K_e)NF_0]}{(1 + K_e)^1} + \frac{[NF_2 - (1 + K_e)NF_1]}{(1 + K_e)^2} + \cdots.$$

---

[4] If corporate income is taxed, X_t represents the firm's after-tax net income.

[5] This includes both the "return on" and "return of" the funds raised in the previous period (that is, $K_e NF_{t-1}$ and NF_{t-1}).

Note that the summation of the second set of terms involving NF_t reduces to $-NF_0$.[6] Therefore, the value of the firm's equity reduces to

(14.1b)
$$e = \frac{X_1 - I_1}{(1 + K_e)^1} + \frac{(X_2 - I_2)}{(1 + K_e)^2} + \cdots -NF_0 \,.$$

In this form, the value of the firm's equity is simply the net present value of its investments where the firm's shareholders make an initial investment equal to NF_0 along with periodic investments of I_t, which produce a stream of future cash flows equal to X_t. More important, note that the value of the firm's equity, e, is independent of the choice of dividend policy in that it depends *only* on the firm's investment outlays, I_t, and corresponding future cash flows from those investments, X_t. This is the essence of the Miller/Modigliani (1961) dividend policy irrelevance theorem.

Personal Taxes: Miller and Scholes (1978).   If personal taxes exist and dividend income is taxed at a higher rate than price appreciation (capital gains), at first glance there will appear to be an investor bias against the payment of dividends.[7] In other words, if dividend income is taxed at the full marginal tax rate, t_p, while the price appreciation that would have resulted from the retention of those earnings is taxed at a rate πt_p, where $\pi < 1$, then, other things equal, taxes paid will be minimized and investor income maximized where no dividends are paid.

Miller and Scholes (1978) argued, however, that dividend income can be "laundered" or converted into nontaxed income such that the effective tax rate on dividends would be zero. In brief, the tax-laundering scheme works as follows. Assume that you receive \$1,000 in dividend income from the XYZ Company. If you simply take the dividend income and do nothing else, you will pay taxes on the full \$1,000 at the ordinary income tax rate.[8] Miller and Scholes noted, however, that the tax liability created by the dividend income can be eliminated by borrowing an amount such that the interest expense will equal the dividend income of \$1,000 and investing the proceeds in an investment that will produce a tax-free

---

[6]Rewriting the two NF_t terms in Equation (14.1a), we get the following:

$$\frac{NF_1}{(1 + K_e)^1} - NF_0 + \frac{NF_2}{(1 + K_e)^2} - \frac{NF_1}{(1 + K_e)^1},$$

which reduces to

$$-NF_0 + \frac{NF_2}{(1 + K_e)^2}.$$

By successive substitutions, the second set of terms eventually reduces to $-NF_0$.

[7]In 1985 the first \$100 (\$200 if filing jointly) of an individual's dividend income was not taxed, but the excess over this amount was taxed as ordinary income just like wages and salaries. On the other hand, long-term capital gains resulting from the sale of stock held for at least one year if purchased prior to June 22, 1984, or six months if purchased after June 22, 1984, were taxed at 40 percent of the personal tax rate. Thus, if an individual's marginal tax rate was 30 percent, long-term capital gains were taxed at a rate of $0.4 \times 0.3 = 0.12$, or 12 percent. However, the Tax Reform Act of 1986 eliminated the capital gains tax advantage by subjecting dividends and price appreciation to the same personal tax rate.

[8]Assuming that your \$100 exclusion (\$200 if filing jointly) has been utilized.

return equal to the $1,000 in interest expense. For example, if the individual's borrowing rate is 10 percent you must borrow $10,000 in order to create the necessary interest expense of $1,000. Now assume that you take the $10,000 and invest it in a pension plan whose earnings proceeds are tax deferred. If the pension plan invests the $10,000 to earn a 10 percent return, you will realize a $1,000 increase in the value of your holdings that is not taxed.[9] The net result is that the tax liability created by the dividend income will have been eliminated, and you will realize an "untaxed" return equal to the dividend income. Thus, this "laundering" scheme involves simply substituting one form of income that is taxed—dividends—for one that is not—pension income. Note that this scheme works perfectly where the individual has available investment alternatives earning untaxed returns equal to the rate at which funds can be borrowed. Even if the scheme works imperfectly, it provides a means of reducing the effective tax rate on dividend income. The key point here is that if dividend income is not needed to support current consumption it can be converted, via the Miller/Scholes tax-laundering scheme, into income that will be taxed at a later date and at a lower rate (which may be zero in the limit). Appendix 14A summarizes this argument in the context of the Fisher intertemporal consumption model under conditions of uncertainty.

Note that the effectiveness of the Miller/Scholes tax-laundering scheme is limited. Specifically, under Section 163(d) of the tax code, individuals can deduct a maximum of $10,000 in interest expense related to investments in addition to investment income when determining their personal tax liability.[10] This means that there is a limit on the amount of dividend income that can be sheltered via this scheme.[11] Note too that the Miller/Scholes study is inconsistent with Miller (1977), discussed in Chapter 12—that is, their dividend tax avoidance scheme must work for interest income as well (see footnote 10). If this is so, the supply curve of

---

[9]Note that the riskiness of the individual's portfolio is unaffected by the tax-laundering scheme so long as the riskiness of the tax-free investment (pension plan, individual retirement account, Keogh, and so on) is the same as the loan's. The simplest case is the one in which the individual borrows at the risk-free rate and makes a risk-free (tax-deferred) investment, such as a certificate of deposit issued by a commercial bank whose deposits are insured by the Federal Deposit Insurance Corporation.

[10]Since 1976, investment income has been defined to include dividend income, interest received, and rent/royalty income. Prior to 1976, it also included realized capital gains; thus, the dividend tax-laundering scheme posed by Miller and Scholes could also be used to shelter capital gains. Feenberg (1981, p. 267) notes that the inclusion of capital gains in the investment income limitation on tax-deductible interest expense means that capital gains can be deferred indefinitely; thus, the tax code was irrelevant to the dividend payout question prior to 1976.

[11]The $10,000 limit came into existence through the Tax Reform Act of 1975. During the period 1969 through 1975, the limit was 150 percent of the sum $25,000, plus investment income, and prior to 1969 there was no limit. Thus, one might wonder why *any* personal taxes were paid prior to 1969 when the Miller/Scholes tax-laundering scheme was unconstrained by the tax authorities. There are limitations to an individual's ability to shelter labor income. However, Miller and Scholes extended their analysis to argue that "the 'income' tax is dead" (1978, p. 361) and that the U.S. tax code effectively provides for a "consumption" tax in that income not consumed can be sheltered from income tax. Perhaps the major tax revision of 1986 can be viewed as a partial agreement with this position.

Finally, note that we have discussed the Miller/Scholes dividend tax avoidance idea in terms of frictionless markets, where market frictions were related to the presence or absence of transactions costs. It could be argued that restrictions on an individual's ability to carry out this scheme constitute a market friction. We have simply defined market friction to include only transactions costs involved in buying and selling securities.

loanable funds to the bond market will be unaffected by personal taxes and, consequently, will be flat, thus restoring the tax advantage of debt financing.[12]

Transactions Costs, Asymmetric Information, Agency Costs, and Dividend Policy

The presence of transactions costs in the purchase and sale of securities in the capital market acts to reduce the effectiveness of the various arbitrage schemes discussed in the previous section to eliminate the importance of dividend policy
under differential personal tax treatments of dividend and capital gains income. In
addition, where a firm's management is privy to information concerning the company's financial prospects that is superior to the investing public's, the firm's dividend policy may be an effective vehicle for "signaling" those prospects to
investors. Finally, it has been argued that the payment of dividends tends to reduce the agency costs attendant to the separation of ownership and control. Thus,
three basic arguments can be made for the importance of corporate dividend policy. The first involves a breakdown of tax arbitrage (laundering) schemes, because
these schemes are costly to implement; the second relates to the "information content" of the firm's dividend announcements; and the third concerns the agency
costs associated with the retention of firm earnings.

Transactions Costs and Tax Arbitrage Schemes.   Consider first the case where
there are no personal taxes. Earlier we demonstrated that where there are no transactions costs, the value of the firm's equity is not affected by its dividend policy
but is solely a function of the firm's investment opportunities (holding financing
policy constant). In fact, in the absence of transactions costs and personal taxes,
two firms with the same investment prospects must have the same market value
(in a competitive capital market) even though they might have different dividend
payment policies. This is because individuals can create "homemade" dividends
by selling off portions of the stock of the non-dividend-paying firm or reinvesting
the dividends paid by the dividend-paying firm. In this way, investors can costlessly "undo" any dividend policy that a firm might select, which in turn means
that they will not pay a premium for the stock of a firm that happens to follow a
dividend policy that matches their intertemporal cash flow preferences. Note what
happens, however, when investors incur transactions costs in purchasing or selling
shares of stock required to "undo" the firm's dividend policy. Other things equal,
investors will now seek out the firm whose dividend payment policy most closely
matches their preferences for current and future cash flow so as to minimize the
costs incurred in the manufacture of homemade dividends.[13] Thus, the presence of
transactions costs in the purchase and sale of securities in the capital market will
serve to reduce investors' willingness to utilize the tax arbitrage schemes described earlier to eliminate the tax consequences of corporate dividend payments.

---

[12]See Dammon (1985) for a comprehensive discussion of this issue.

[13]Under this scenario, the firm would develop "investor clienteles" whose preferences for dividend income closely matched its dividend payment policies.

Exercise 14.1:   Arbitrage and Corporate Dividend Policy

Consider the following two firms, which are identical in every respect except for their dividend payment policies. Firm A plans to pay its present shareholders a dividend of $5 per share in the current period, whereas firm B plans to pay only $2 per share. Assume that the two firms will operate for two full years and then liquidate their assets to the shareholders. It is now December 31, 1987, and the two firms share the following information for 1988:

	Firm A	Firm B
Estimated earnings (after taxes)	$800,000	$800,000
Dividends for 1988	500,000	200,000
Retained earnings	$300,000	$600,000
Planned investment for 1988	600,000	600,000
Equity issue for 1988 (sold for approximately $22 per share)	300,000	0

Both firms anticipate 1989 after-tax total earnings of $920,000 and will liquidate their assets for an after-tax total of $2 million. There are no taxes on personal income from common stock, and purchases and sales of either firm's common stock entail no transactions costs.

1. Calculate the dividends in total and per share to be paid to the "original" shareholders of each firm at the end of 1989.

Solution.   First, calculate the number of shares of stock for each firm:

> *Firm A:*
> Outstanding shares $500,000/$5 = 100,000 shares
> New shares $300,000/$22 = 13,636 shares
> Total   100,000 + 13,636 = 113,636 shares
> *Firm B:*
> Outstanding shares $200,000/$2 = 100,000 shares

The dividend per share to be paid to the firm A shareholders at the end of 1989 is calculated as follows:

$$(\$2,000,000 + \$920,000)/113,636 \approx \$25.68 \text{ per share.}$$

Similarly, for firm B,

$$(\$2,000,000 + \$920,000)/100,000 = \$29.20 \text{ per share.}$$

2. If investors require a return of 20 percent on both firms' shares, what are their values per share at the present time?

Solution.

Firm A:

$$V_A = \$5/1.2 + \$25.68/(1.2)^2 \approx \$22$$

Firm B:

$$V_B = \$2/1.2 + \$29.20/(1.2)^2 \approx \$22$$

3. If firm A were selling for $2 more per share than your estimated value for firm B from question 2, what would be the reaction of investors?

Solution.   In this case, arbitrage would be possible by selling firm A shares and buying firm B shares until firm A was selling for the same price as firm B.

4. Assume now that investors want no dividend income until 1989. How can investors create their own dividend policy (that is, undo the dividend payment policies of the two firms)?

Solution.   For both firms, investors can simply reinvest the dividends paid.

Information Content of Dividend Announcements.   The notion that dividends convey information to investors is not new. However, formal attempts to incorporate this idea into the theory of dividend policy are of relatively recent origin and are a part of a subset of the information economics literature commonly referred to as *signaling* models. Before discussing some of these theories, we will first briefly review the circumstances under which a signaling model can be used. Miller (1986) notes that a potential for signaling arises any time the sellers of a commodity know more about its quality than do the buyers.[14] If buyers are unable to determine the quality of the products in the market because they cannot distinguish their relative quality, they will offer prices that reflect their perception of the "average" quality.[15] Sellers who know that the quality of their products are at the upper end of the spectrum will have an incentive to signal this fact to buyers so as to command above-average prices. If they successfully signal their products' superior quality to buyers, they will command higher prices and, consequently, no longer have to compete with other products in the market. In this way, the higher-quality products leave and the quality of the remaining products must decline. This leads still more sellers of products exhibiting above-average quality (that is, above the new, lower average for the market) to attempt to signal their products' superiority to buyers. If this process is carried to an extreme, the quality of every

---

[14]The introduction to the economic circumstance that leads to a firm's need to signal follows the discussion found in Miller (1986).

[15]In the signaling literature, an equilibrium characterized by buyers offering sellers prices that reflect average quality is referred to as a "pooling" equilibrium.

seller's product will be signaled to buyers, product quality will have been fully revealed, and the product will be priced accordingly.[16]

In Chapter 12, we noted that a firm's choice of debt/equity financing mix may unambiguously "signal" to the investing public information on the firm's financial condition (that is, the prospects for future cash flows). Ross (1977) made a similar argument with respect to the firm's choice of dividend policy. If a firm raises its dividends, Ross argues, the capital market will interpret this as a signal that its management (based on its superior knowledge of the firm's future cash flow prospects) is convinced that the firm's future cash flows will be sufficient to meet its debt obligations plus the higher dividends without jeopardizing its financial integrity (that is, without increasing the risk of failure and its attendant costs).[17] Note that the signaling argument relates to the use of dividend policy changes to transfer information to the investing public. Thus, the higher the firm's dividend payout (as a proportion of its earnings), other things equal, the better its financial prospects and, consequently, the higher its stock market value.

What, if anything, keeps managers from using changes in dividend policy to "falsely" signal an increase in the firm's financial prospects?[18] The answer offered here relates to the transactions costs incurred by firms whose earnings prospects are insufficient to support the higher level of dividend payments. In other words, if the firm's earnings cannot support the higher dividend payments announced by a change in dividend payout, the firm will periodically find itself suffering the transactions costs associated with entering the capital market to raise the funds needed to maintain the higher dividend payout.[19]

Bhattacharya (1979) used Ross's signaling theory to develop an argument for the payment of dividends even where the Miller/Scholes (1978) tax-laundering scheme does not effectively eliminate the personal tax consequences of dividends.[20] Bhattacharya argued that even where dividends create a personal tax liability for the firm's shareholders, management will pay cash dividends to signal the firm's future investment prospects to the capital markets. The crux of this argument is the cost effectiveness of dividend policy compared with alternative means of signaling the firm's future financial prospects to the investing public. Thus, an optimal dividend policy results from trading off the information benefits

---

[16]If this occurs, the resulting equilibrium is referred to in the signaling literature as a "separating" equilibrium.

[17]Here we define the costs of financial failure or bankruptcy as the "transactions costs" attendant to the firm's liquidation or sale to another firm in the event of its failure.

[18]The notion here is that in order for a signal to be "believable," it must be costly. Miller (1986) summarizes this idea very simply by noting the folk wisdom that "talk is cheap."

[19]Note that the firm would suffer the impact of a negative signal if it decreased its dividend payout (perhaps even greater in magnitude than the original increase resulting from the initial increase in dividend payout) and, consequently, would attempt to maintain the higher payout.

[20]John and Williams (1985) provide another signaling model of corporate dividend policy wherein the cost associated with the payment of corporate dividends takes the form of the personal tax penalty accompanying dividend income to individuals. However, Miller (1986) argues that the personal tax penalty argument is not particularly convincing because corporations paid dividends persistently even before the personal tax penalty on dividend income existed and do so in countries having very different systems of taxation.

associated with paying higher dividends for the higher personal taxes that the firm's stockholders must pay on dividend versus capital gains income.[21]

Agency Cost Considerations and Corporate Dividend Policy.   Rozeff (1982) and Easterbrook (1984) have argued that increased dividend payments reduce the volume of funds over which management has discretionary control and thus reduces the costs of agency. In other words, when the firm retains earnings it does not subject its investment decisions to the discipline of the capital market; thus, there exists an agency cost with respect to management's discretion over the use of retained earnings that is not incurred when the firm must go to the capital markets to raise investment funds.

---

[21]The research in this area is quite voluminous, including that of Talmor (1981) and Bar-Yosef and Huffman (1986). The latter paper develops an incentive-signaling theory that offers a reasonable explanation for observed corporate dividend policies. In particular, this model suggests that the size of the declared dividend is an increasing function of the firm's expected cash flow and that the higher the uncertainty in this cash flow, the lower will be the dividend payout ratio.

The Tax Reform Act of 1986 effectively eliminated the "tax rate" differential between dividend income and capital gains. However, capital gains are not taxed until realized, such that the tax deferral benefit associated with unrealized capital gains is still available.

Exercise 14.2:   *Laundering Corporate Dividends*

Amelia Barnes is considering investing $10,000 that she just inherited from her grandparents. She is 28 years old and earns a six-digit income, so she does not need any additional taxable income. In addition, she has fully utilized her $100 dividend exemption; thus, any additional dividend income received from investing her inheritance would be subject to the full 40 percent marginal tax rate that she currently pays.

1. Devise a "dividend-laundering" scheme for Barnes whereby any dividend income received from her investment might be converted to tax-free income. Assume that she can borrow at a 10 percent rate and that she is self-employed and thus can set up a Keogh retirement account, in which risk-free investments earning a return of 10 percent can be made.

Solution.   Assume Barnes receives $1,000 in dividend income by investing her $10,000 inheritance in a high-dividend-yield stock. In order to neutralize the tax consequences of her dividend income, she can borrow $10,000 at 10 percent and invest the proceeds in a Keogh retirement account that earns a 10 percent risk-free rate.

Dividends received	$1,000
Less interest paid	1,000
Taxable income	0
Nontaxable income (Keogh investment)	$1,000

Thus, Barnes has invested her $10,000 inheritance to earn a $1,000 per year dividend that, through the use of a "tax-laundering" scheme, is essentially untaxed.

2. What practical limitations do you see in Barnes' ability to launder dividend income? Discuss.

Solution.   The scheme works perfectly where the individual has available investment alternatives earning untaxed returns equal to the rate at which funds can be borrowed. In this instance, Barnes is able to invest the proceeds of a loan requiring an interest rate of 10 percent in an untaxed Keogh account that earns a safe 10 percent return. Also, see footnote 11 related to the limitation on the deductibility of investment interest expense.

Jensen (1986) and Kensinger and Martin (1986) have argued that in some cases agency costs with respect to retained earnings can be large enough to create capital market pressures to "restructure" the firm in an effort to remove control over these earnings from its management.[22] The restructuring may take many forms, including a corporate takeover by another firm or group of investors, a leveraged buyout (LBO),[23] or reorganization of a part of the firm's assets into a royalty trust or limited partnership.[24] The basic result of all these arrangements is the same: Managerial discretion over the use of corporate earnings is reduced. In the case of a takeover, control over the acquired firm's discretionary cash flow

---

[22]Jensen suggests that the changes in the U.S. oil industry in the mid-1980s provide an excellent set of examples of corporate restructuring motivated by attempts to reduce the agency costs associated with management's discretionary control over earnings. Examples of the "misguided" efforts of these firms to diversify out of the oil industry (using funds generated by the high profits of the post-1973 energy embargo) abound; these include Exxon's acquisition of Reliance Electric, Mobil's acquisition of Montgomery Ward, and Sohio's purchase of Kennecott Copper.

[23]Leveraged buyouts are discussed in greater detail in Chapter 18, where we cover mergers and acquisitions, specifically in an "Institutional Note" on this topic.

[24]Mesa Petroleum formed a royalty trust for its oil-producing properties wherein its stockholders became the direct beneficiaries of the income produced by these holdings. Sun Oil and Apache Petroleum have utilized master limited partnerships to perform essentially the same function. Note that by removing these "cash flow–producing assets" from the corporation, these firms' managements made the companies look far less attractive to potential takeover bidders. The reason, however, was that the potential benefits of takeover related to elimination of the agency cost associated with managing the cash flows from the oil properties and the formation of the master limited partnership or royalty trust effectively eliminated this agency problem.

(earnings) may simply be shifted from one management team to another[25] or, if the acquisition is financed by bonds or other new security issues, its mode of financing may effectively "use up" what Jensen (1986) refers to as the "free cash flows" of the acquired firm and, consequently, return their control to the capital market.

The leveraged buyout is an example of a firm being acquired by a small group of investors and removed from public trading (that is, taken private). In this case, the acquiring group uses a large amount of debt financing to make the purchase. The resulting increased debt service requirements then soak up the acquired firm's free cash flow and, consequently, reduce the amount of earnings over which the management team has discretionary control.

The royalty trust and master limited partnership forms of organization represent yet another means of restructuring a corporation (or a portion of its assets) so as to remove the managers' discretionary control over the firm's earnings.[26] Both of these organizational forms have been successfully used in the oil industry. Here the corporation's oil-producing properties are "spun off" or placed in another organization whose ownership is transferred to the firm's shareholders in accordance with their ownership interest in the corporation. There are two primary effects of the formation of the royalty trust and master limited partnership. First, the tax consequences of ownership in these organizational forms are transferred directly to the owners, since there is no "separate" corporate entity that is itself subject to taxation. Second — and more important with respect to the arguments being made here — the management of the new organization is charged with the efficient operation of the firm's existing properties but may be granted little or no authority (discretion) with respect to the income produced by those assets; that is, management is granted only very limited control over the retention/reinvestment of earnings. The organization's revenues and expenses are credited directly to the owners' accounts according to a fixed contractual formula. Once these accounting allocations have been made, the individual partners receive their pro rata shares of the cash produced by the organization's assets and make their own reinvestment decisions. In effect, these organizational forms grant the capital market control over the earnings retention/dividend policy decision.

Dividend Policy: The Evidence

The empirical research on dividend policy can be categorized under three broad headings. The first deals with "descriptions" of corporate practice. Examples of this research include Lintner (1956), Brittain (1966), and Fama and Babiak (1968), who provided a series of studies on the dividend payment practices of U.S. corpo-

---

[25]In Chapter 18, we discuss the mergers and acquisitions literature in the context of this notion of different management teams competing in the capital market for control over the acquired firm's cash flows. Jensen and Ruback (1983) refer to this literature under the rubric of "Market for Corporate Control."

[26]Since the Tax Reform Act of 1984, new royalty trusts have not enjoyed the same desirable tax advantages as their predecessors and have been replaced by master limited partnerships. See Chapter 3, "An Institutional Note: Master Limited Partnerships As an Alternative to the Corporation."

rations. The second category of empirical research involves the impact of dividend policy on the value of the firm and its equity. This topic has been the focus of much of the recent research. We will review the papers of Brennan (1970), Black and Scholes (1974), Litzenberger and Ramaswamy (1979, 1982), Stone and Bartter (1979), Miller and Scholes (1982), and Morgan (1982) in an effort to establish the current state of research on the impact of dividends on stock value. The third area of empirical research deals with a "peripheral" issue: the impact of share repurchases on a stock's market value. Stock repurchases are undertaken for a number of reasons, which we will discuss in detail. One important purpose is their use as substitutes for cash dividends. For this reason we will review a selection of papers on the market's reaction to stock repurchases, including Norgaard and Norgaard (1974), Stewart (1976), Masulis (1980), Dann (1981), and Vermaelen (1981).

Our objective in this section is not to review in detail all of the above studies but to present the underlying rationale for a selected subset of the empirical literature on dividend policy and note the principal conclusions of each. In this way we hope to describe the "flavor" of this research without getting bogged down in details. The References section at the end of the chapter provides a much more complete listing of the research in this important area of corporate finance.

Corporate Practice

In his classic study of the dividend payment practices of a sample of 28 U.S. corporations, Lintner (1956) established the empirical basis for his *stable dividend hypothesis*.[27] Lintner began his study by interviewing the top managements of 28 firms in an effort to discover the determinants of corporate dividend payment practice. From those interviews he noted two key attributes of corporate dividend policy: Corporate managements tended to (1) establish target dividend payouts as a proportion of earnings and (2) set their dividend payments to adjust "slowly" over time toward the desired fraction of earnings. From these two observations, Lintner hypothesized the following relationship between dividends and earnings:

(14.3)
$$D_t^* = rE_t,$$

where D_t^* is the "target" dividend payment per share for year t; r is the payout ratio (dividends divided by earnings); and E_t is firm earnings per share in year t. Lintner then hypothesized (based on the second observation above) that firms seek to maintain stable dividend payouts by changing or adapting them each year by only a fraction of the change indicated by earnings in conjunction with the target payout ratios. In other words, the change in a firm's dividend from year t − 1 to t is characterized as follows:

(14.4)
$$D_t - D_{t-1} = a + c(D_t^* - D_{t-1}),$$

---

[27]We will discuss this idea in detail later; for now, note that corporations generally have sought to maintain a stable or uninterrupted stream of cash dividend payments to their shareholders.

where a is a constant such that even where $D_t^* = D_{t-1}$ there is some positive expected increment to dividends and c is a constant "speed of adjustment" factor. Substituting Equation 14.3 into 14.4, we obtain the "partial adjustment model" Lintner used to "explain" the corporate dividend payment practices of U.S. corporations; that is,

(14.5) $D_t = a + b_1 E_t + b_2 D_{t-1} + E_t,$

where $b_1 = cr$, $b_2 = (1 - c)$, and E_t is an error term. Using the period 1915 to 1951, Lintner estimated Equation 14.5 for the entire period as well as a number of subperiods. The results were quite impressive, explaining over 95 percent of the variation in D_t.

Both Lintner and Brittain (1966) used Equation 14.5 to explain corporate dividend policy but utilized "aggregate" data in most of their tests. Fama and Babiak (1968), in contrast, used firm data, as well as a more extensive set of tests. They found that the two variables in the Lintner partial adjustment model performed well compared to the many other models tested. Hence, Lintner's results and, consequently, the stable dividend hypothesis appear to be very robust.

Dividends and Stock Market Value

The empirical studies reviewed in this section share one attribute: All seek to determine whether there is a variable omitted in the capital asset pricing model (CAPM) related to dividend yield. Brennan (1970) developed an "after-tax" version of the CAPM and performed a cross-sectional test[28] for the impact of dividend yield (Y_p) on stock returns using the following model:

(14.6) $R_p = a_0 + a_1 \beta_p + a_2 Y_p + E_p,$

where R_p is the holding period return on a portfolio of securities formed by ranking stocks according to their dividend yield; β_p is the portfolio beta; and E_p is an error term. Brennan found that the coefficient on the dividend yield term (a_2) was both positive and statistically significant. This indicated that investors require a higher risk-adjusted return on dividends as opposed to capital gains; that is, the higher a firm's dividend yield, the higher its required rate of return (and, hence, the lower its market value), other things equal.

Black and Scholes (1974) criticized Brennan's research method for including a "cross-sectional bias." The source of the bias was the significant correlation observed between dividend yield and beta. To avoid the problems inherent in Brennan's cross-sectional research design, they devised a time series test utilizing the following model:

(14.7) $R_j = \delta_0 + \beta_j (R_M - \delta_0) + \dfrac{\delta_1 (Y_j - Y_M)}{Y_M},$

---

[28]We use the term *cross-sectional test* here to refer to the method employed to select the sample data used in the test. Specifically, a cross-sectional test involves using data for many different firms sampled on a given date. This methodology contrasts with a *time series test*, in which the sample comes from the same firm but is observed, or "sampled," over many time periods.

where R_j, β_j, and Y_j retain their previous definitions but refer to security j; R_M is the holding period return on the market portfolio; Y_M is the dividend yield on the market portfolio; and both δ_0 and δ_1 are parameters of the model. Note that δ_1 is the measure of the yield effect and the other coefficient the zero-beta return estimate.[29]

The time series approach utilized by Black and Scholes offered the potential for avoiding the multicollinearity observed between dividend yield and beta and thus the source of bias in Brennan's tests.[30] To do so they had to obtain an intermediate set of portfolios by first ranking the stocks into ex ante yield quintiles and then ranking ex ante beta estimates to form five subgroups within each quintile. Next, they selected weights for these intermediate portfolios so as to produce a composite zero-beta portfolio with an ex ante dividend yield equal to the ex ante market yield. Finally, they estimated the value of δ_1 from the time series of security returns on the zero-beta portfolios. They concluded that there was no significant relationship between stock returns and dividend yield or dividend payout.

Stone and Bartter (1979) provided yet another refinement for the Brennan methodology that was also designed to eliminate the multicollinearity arising between dividend yield and beta. These authors utilized a linear program to construct "iso-beta" portfolios. Such portfolios have constant ("iso") betas equal to the market beta and further exemplify the constraints that (1) the yield range across the portfolios be maximized (to increase the test's power) and (2) the yield increment among the portfolios be uniform. By holding the beta for each portfolio constant, the yield-beta correlation is rendered unimportant. Using both ordinary least squares and generalized least squares fits, Stone and Bartter found the yield variable to be statistically significant in explaining the returns of their iso-beta portfolios.

Litzenberger and Ramaswamy (1979) noted — and attempted to correct for — a potential "information" bias found in prior studies of the impact of the dividend yield factor on stock market value. This problem had arisen in measuring the dividend yield variable; specifically, prior studies had simply used the ratio of dividends paid over the holding period under study divided by the end-of-period stock price. The problem here relates to the potential "information impact" of a dividend announcement. For example, if the announced dividend is larger than expected (signaling an increase in future earnings and dividends), the stock price (ex-dividend) may actually rise such that, other things equal, the dividend yield will decline. Of course, the opposite could also occur. Thus, measurement of the dividend yield is complicated and fraught with potential error. Litzenberger and Ramaswamy attempted to avoid any information impact in the measurement of dividend yield as follows. If a firm declared its dividend prior to month t and went ex dividend in month t, the expected dividend yield was computed using the actual

---

[29]The *zero-beta return* refers to Black's (1972) notion of a zero-beta asset whose returns are uncorrelated with those of the market portfolio. Refer to Chapter 9 for a discussion of the zero-beta CAPM.

[30]*Multicollinearity* refers to the presence of correlation between the independent variables in a multiple-variable model. The problem multicollinearity creates is that we can no longer "ferret out" what each variable in the model contributes to its explanatory power. In this case, this means that the importance of β_j and Y_M in Equation 14.7 is "muddled."

dividend paid in period t divided by the price at the end of period t − 1. If the firm both declared and went ex dividend in the same period t, the dividend yield was computed using the last previous regular dividend (going back up to one year). If no regular dividend was found during this period, the yield variable was set equal to zero. The results indicated a strong positive relationship between dividend yield and the expected returns of NYSE stocks.

In a subsequent study, Litzenberger and Ramaswamy (1982) provided yet another examination of the dividend yield effect on stock returns by using the expected as opposed to the observed dividend yield for each stock in the month of the dividend's payment. They estimated the expected dividend yield with information available prior to the dividend payment so that the dividend yield variable would be completely free of any information impact of the dividend announcement. The results of this study indicated a significant positive and nonlinear relationship between common stock expected returns and dividend yield. It should be noted that the results of this second test were weaker (that is, the dividend yield term was smaller) than the earlier ones, indicating the potential "information effect" of measuring dividend yield concurrently with the dividend payment.

Miller and Scholes (1982) likewise investigated the announcement effect associated with dividend policy. They utilized a number of possible specifications for the dividend yield variable and found their results to be highly sensitive to these. They concluded that the yield effect found in previous studies had actually been a "dividend announcement" effect rather than a personal-tax-induced dividend yield effect. Specifically, to assess the presence of any potential information effects, they analyzed the impact of dividend yield first including and then excluding firms that declared their dividends in the month used to evaluate dividend yield. Where those securities whose dividends were declared in advance of the announcement month were used to assess the impact of dividend yield on stock value, the yield variable was found to be statistically insignificant. Thus, if yield-related effects did exist, they could not be attributed to differences in the dividend yields of the firms actually paying dividends in the month under study.

Morgan (1982) used portfolios of securities with dividend yields that could be reasonably well predicted by sophisticated time series models fitted to past data. He then related abnormal returns for these portfolios to forecasted dividend yields using pooled cross-sectional and time series estimates. The results of these tests were mixed, some supporting the existence of a significant dividend yield effect on expected returns and others not. Specifically, Morgan found common stock returns to be positively related to dividend yield (realized or forecast), as the after-tax version of the CAPM suggests; however, the observed relationship was inconsistent with the simple linear relationship implied by the model. Thus, on this latter point the Litzenberger and Ramaswamy (1979, 1982) papers both presented evidence of a nonlinear relationship between stock returns and dividend yield.

Table 14.1 summarizes (in chronological order) the empirical tests for a dividend-tax effect in security returns, including those studies discussed here. As the table shows, the importance of dividend yield to stock value remains a controversial issue. Although most of the evidence points to the existence of a dividend yield factor being priced in the capital market, it would be premature at this point to call it conclusive. Miller and Scholes (1982) argued that this factor is an

Table 14.1   Tests for a Dividend Yield Factor in Common Stock Expected Returns

Study	Study Period	Data	Yield Coefficient[a]	t-Statistic
Brennan (1970)	1946–1965	Monthly	0.34	2.83
	1965–1968			
Black and Scholes (1974)	1936–1966	Monthly	0.0009	0.94
Stone and Bartter (1979)	1947–1970	Monthly	0.56	2.01
Litzenberger and Ramaswamy (1979)	1936–1977	Monthly	0.24	8.62
Rosenberg and Marthe (1979)	1931–1966	Monthly	0.40	1.88
Blume (1980)	1936–1976	Quarterly	0.52	2.07
Gordon and Bradford (1980)	1926–1978	Monthly	0.18	8.51
Litzenberger and Ramaswamy (1982)	1940–1980	Monthly	0.14–0.23	4.38–8.79
Miller and Scholes (1982)	1940–1978	Monthly	0.04	1.3
Morgan (1982)	1936–1977	Monthly	0.21	11.00

[a]This coefficient corresponds to the dividend yield variable and can be interpreted as an "implied" personal tax rate on dividend income.

"information or announcement" effect that is confounded with the measurement of dividend yield rather than a personal-tax-induced dividend effect per se. However, subsequent research by Litzenberger and Ramaswamy and Morgan suggests that this is not the case.

Still another body of research has attempted to resolve the controversy surrounding the dividend tax effect by examining the ex-dividend–day price adjustment of securities. These studies have also provided controversial results. For example, Campbell and Beranek (1955), Durand and May (1960), and Elton and Gruber (1970) observed that the securities of dividend-paying firms decline less than the amount of the dividend on the ex-dividend day. Elton and Gruber attributed this to differential taxation on dividends and capital gains. However, Miller and Scholes (1982) argued that the pricing anomaly cannot be attributed to dividend taxes because there is no tax differential on short-term capital gains. Thus, any differences arising from taxes would be arbitraged away by short-term traders. Kalay (1982), after adjusting for biases in the Elton and Gruber study, found that the ex-dividend–day price adjustment was not significantly different from the dividend. Eades, Hess, and Kim (1984) found a pricing anomaly in the price of *nontaxable* distributions, indicating that the effect is not tax related. Finally, Barone-Adesi and Whaley (1985) used an entirely different procedure to examine implied ex-dividend prices and did not detect a tax effect. Thus, the jury appears to still be out about whether taxes on dividends affect equity returns.

Share Repurchase

If a corporation decides to engage in the repurchase of its outstanding common shares, the result is to (1) reduce the number of shares outstanding and (2) transfer cash from the corporate coffers to those shareholders who tender their shares. In the latter respect, a share repurchase is similar to the payment of a cash dividend.

A corporation can repurchase its shares in one of three ways: open market purchases, privately negotiated transactions, or a tender offer. *Open market repurchases* simply involve the firm's acquisition of shares by placing an order with a broker just like any individual investor. *Privately negotiated repurchases* involve acquiring a block of shares from an individual or group of investors desiring to sell. This type of repurchase is frequently associated with a firm's attempts to fend off an unfriendly takeover attempt.[31] With the cash *tender offer,* the firm advertises its willingness to purchase a given quantity of its shares for a set price within a specified time limit. The empirical research reviewed here primarily concerns the last form of repurchase, for it is the predominant mode of repurchase activity.

A wide variety of reasons why firms engage in stock repurchase activity have been offered. Rather than enumerating them here, however, we will discuss them as they are proposed in the research that we summarize.

The Norgaard and Norgaard (1974) paper is unique among the studies discussed here in that it did not attempt to assess the market's reaction to the initiation of a tender offer repurchase. Instead, it sought to determine whether the financial attributes of repurchasing firms differed significantly from those of nonrepurchasing firms. Using a variety of measures of financial condition, including the ratio of book value to market value per share, payout ratios, and return on net worth, these authors successfully distinguished between repurchasing and nonrepurchasing firms. Using multiple discriminant analysis, the Norgaards concluded that repurchasing firms had below-normal expectations for profits caused by either industry circumstances, poor management, or both.[32] They further concluded that firms engaged in repurchases in order to hide their otherwise lackluster performance. Based on the study's concluding remarks, one might anticipate a negative reaction to the repurchase of a firm's shares in an efficient market. However, as we review the studies of the market reaction to repurchase activity, we will find that the opposite is true.

Stewart (1976) provided one of the early studies of market reaction to repurchase activity. Segmenting a sample of repurchasing firms by the percentage of shares being acquired (less than 1.25, 1.25 to 2.24, 2.25 to 3.24, 3.25 to 4.24, 4.25 to 5.24, and 5.25 percent or more), Stewart observed the following. First,

---

[31]In Chapter 18 we discuss corporate takeovers and the repurchase of blocks of shares as a means of settling a takeover dispute. Such repurchases are viewed by some as a payoff to the unfriendly suitor and are sometimes referred to as "greenmail."

[32]*Multiple discriminant analysis (MDA)* is a statistical method similar to multiple regression. One can think of an MDA model as a multiple regression equation in which the dependent variable being predicted is discrete, for example, 0 if the firm repurchases its stock and 1 if it does not. The dependent variable can have two or more discrete values. For example, Altman (1968) used an MDA model to predict bankrupt and nonbankrupt firms, while Pinches and Mingo (1973) analyzed corporate bond ratings using four categories of ratings as the dependent variable.

the stock market performance of repurchasing firms was generally superior to that of nonrepurchasing firms, although in some cases this did not materialize for several years (for example, for the largest repurchase group the superior performance was first noted after almost five years). Second, the intermediate share repurchase group (3.25 to 4.24 percent) experienced the greatest increase in market value. Stewart's study was unique in two major respects. First, Stewart looked at the long-term effects of repurchase, spanning several years, whereas subsequent studies examined very-short-term announcement effects within a few days of the announced repurchase. Second, he used no "risk adjustment" for equity returns, while subsequent studies used various methods for removing the influence of general market influences on stock returns.

Masulis (1980) provided the first of three major studies of the announcement impact of a tender offer repurchase. He examined the price reactions of common stock, preferred stock, and various categories of nonconvertible securities surrounding an announced repurchase in an effort to identify their source. Masulis proposed four possible reasons for a market reaction to a tender offer repurchase:

1.   Personal tax savings resulting from the differential tax treatment of dividends versus capital gains

2.   Corporate tax shield increases resulting from the use of debt financing to finance the repurchase

3.   Wealth transfers across security classes due to changes in the firm's use of financial leverage

4.   Wealth transfers between tendering and nontendering stockholders.

The first reason relates to the fact that the gains to investors who tender their shares due to share repurchases are taxed as capital gains (where the shares tendered are held for the requisite one-year holding period), while cash dividends are taxed as ordinary income. Thus, Masulis hypothesized, the repurchase of a firm's shares should result in a temporary positive price impact reflecting the opportunity to realize capital gains income via the sale of the shares. Recall that this argument contradicts the Miller and Scholes (1978) tax arbitrage hypothesis reviewed earlier in the chapter. Those authors argued that the personal tax differential on dividend and capital gains income is inconsequential where individuals can engage in tax arbitrage by exchanging taxable for nontaxed income. At this point, simply note that in order for there to be a market reaction to share repurchase due to personal tax considerations, the Miller/Scholes tax arbitrage scheme must not be functioning as they propose.

The second reason for a market reaction to repurchase noted above is that the firm's use of debt to finance a repurchase will create greater interest tax savings (according to the Modigliani and Miller [1963] tax-adjusted valuation model)[33] and hence lead to an increase in equity value. Thus, Masulis hypothe-

---

[33]See Chapter 12 for a discussion of capital structure theory.

sized that the market's reaction to repurchase is actually a reaction to the firm's re-structuring of its capital structure to include more financial leverage.

Masulis' third explanation suggests that the distribution of cash via share re-purchase allows the common shareholders as a group to benefit at the expense of the firm's creditors. This is an imperfect "me-first" argument that goes as follows. Other things equal, the reduction in the amount of equity capital via a share repur-chase makes the firm's debt more risky. Given no change in the value of the repur-chasing corporation's productive assets, the loss in value of its risky debt becomes a gain to the wealth of the nontendering stockholders. Thus, the repurchase of a firm's shares can permit the firm's shareholders to transfer wealth from the credi-tors to themselves.

The fourth explanation relates to tender offer premiums and the existence of differential costs of tendering shares among different groups of shareholders. Since the right to tender shares is nontransferable, shareholders who tender capture the entire premium paid at the expense of the nontendering shareholders. If the cost of tendering shares is higher for some groups of shareholders than for others, the wealth impact of the premiums for tendered shares will not be shared equally by all.

Masulis employed a standard event study methodology to the daily returns of 199 repurchasing firms.[34] He found a positive 17 percent abnormal (that is, un-related to firm- or market-based factors) return over the two-day period consisting of the announcement day and the day preceding for a tender offer repurchase. In addition, he identified evidence of some anticipatory market reaction to the repur-chase that indicated possible insider trading. Unfortunately, Masulis was unable to pinpoint the source of the market reaction beyond noting that it was probably due to a combination of the above factors.

Dann (1981) proposed that in addition to the factors mentioned by Masulis, the market may react to a share repurchase as a "signal" of new information re-garding the firm's future investment and earnings prospects. According to this hy-pothesis, the act of repurchase could signal either good or bad news — that is, that management, using its superior inside information, believes the shares are under-valued in the marketplace or that the firm has limited investment prospects. Fur-ther, the repurchase might signal management's anticipation of a takeover attempt, which has been shown to produce substantial gains to the acquired firm's share-holders,[35] or, conversely, management's conviction that it cannot profitably rein-vest the shareholders' funds at acceptable rates of return, which would, in turn, be viewed as bad news. Dann reasons that since management must initiate a repur-chase, it will not do so except to signal good news; thus, the repurchase signal is more likely to be positive than negative.

Using an event study methodology very similar to Masulis', Dann formed portfolios in event time (that is, with returns aligned relative to a repurchase event

---

[34]We discuss the "event study" methodology in Chapter 10.

[35]We review the mergers and acquisitions literature in Chapter 18. Jensen and Ruback (1983) noted that the average gain (in excess of general market movements) accruing to the shareholders of acquired firms ranges from 20 to 30 percent.

date) comprised of repurchasing firms' common stock, straight debt, straight preferred stock, and convertible preferred stock, respectively. In this way Dann was able to assess whether any wealth transfers accompanied share repurchases.[36] For the common stock portfolio, the announcement-day portfolio return was 8.95 percent and the day-after return 6.93 percent. Note that these were *not* risk-adjusted returns but "raw" daily holding period returns. The average daily return over the 50-day comparison period ending 11 days prior to the announcement was -0.09 percent, confirming the significance of the market impact of the announced repurchase. The portfolio returns for the announcement day observed for the convertible debt, straight preferred, and convertible preferred securities were all positive, while the return for the straight debt portfolio was negative but very small. Hence, the magnitude of these returns was insufficient to explain the very large and significant common stock returns. Dann thus found no evidence to support the hypothesis of wealth transfer among debt, preferred, and common stock holders. This contrasted with Masulis' result, which suggested that such a wealth transfer could partly explain the positive market reaction of common shareholders to an announced repurchase.

Further, Dann found no evidence to support the personal tax savings hypothesis. Stock prices were observed to increase permanently subsequent to the repurchase announcement, whereas they should have increased only temporarily if the benefits of repurchase involved a one-time reduction in personal taxes (that is, a transfer of fully taxed dividends for lower-taxed capital gains). Because of the above findings, Dann concluded that the signaling hypothesis was the only plausible explanation for the observed positive market reaction to share repurchase.

In a very comprehensive study of share repurchase, Vermaelen (1981) examined the market's reaction to purchases via tender offer as well as open market transactions. In addition, Vermaelen devised a framework for analyzing the market's pricing of common stock in relation to tender offer repurchases. His main objective was to determine whether increased legislation was needed to regulate the repurchase phenomenon, since some believed that insiders could manipulate stock prices through repurchase activity at the expense of the firm's other security holders.

Vermaelen's tender offer sample consisted of 131 offers by 111 firms over the period 1962 to 1977. Utilizing an event study methodology, he observed significant returns on event days -4, -2, -1, 0, and $+1$. Although statistically significant, the event day $+1$ return of 1.08 percent was deemed practically insignificant. Thus, Vermaelen concluded that the market reaction to repurchase is even quicker than that reported by previous researchers and, further, that the information or signaling argument was the most plausible explanation for the market's reaction to tender offer share repurchases.

In summary, studies of share repurchase activity have found a positive market value reaction for the affected firm's common stock that results from neither personal tax nor wealth transfer sources. It would appear that share repurchase is

---

[36] A wealth transfer results when the value of one class of securities (such as common stock) rises and another (such as bonds) falls as a result of the share repurchase.

viewed as a signal of positive information to the market regarding its future earnings prospects. Why this particular communication vehicle is used to make such announcements is an unresolved issue.

Summary

Corporate dividend policy deals with the fundamental question of how much of its earnings a firm should pay out to its shareholders in common stock dividends. Alternatively, since earnings not paid in dividends are retained and reinvested in the firm, we can think of dividends as the "residual" earnings that are not reinvested. Although these points of view are opposite sides of the same coin, the approach that one takes in addressing the dividend policy question is not inconsequential. If we seek to determine the firm's value-maximizing dividend payout policy, we are "assuming" that this practice does affect its equity value; that is, we presume that investors care about the fraction of the firm's earnings that they receive in dividends rather than that retained and reinvested. The view that dividend policy is determined by first evaluating how much of a firm's earnings to retain and reinvest focuses on the firm's available internal uses for the funds and excludes investors' preferences for cash dividends. Thus, the key issue in corporate dividend policy is whether a firm's dividend payment policy impacts on its equity value. If the answer is affirmative, the selection of an optimal dividend policy is a valid management concern. In this chapter, we reviewed the principal themes underlying the theoretical research on the dividend policy question. Specifically, this work has focused on either tax-related issues or the information content of a firm's dividend policy.

We found that tax considerations played a prominent role in the early theories of corporate dividend policy. For example, Miller and Modigliani (1961) demonstrated the irrelevance of corporate dividend policy in the absence of taxes and transactions costs. The initial results incorporating the differential tax treatment for capital gains and dividend income suggested that dividends indeed matter and that their payment adversely affects firm value. However, Miller and Scholes (1978) argued that where tax arbitrage schemes are available to individuals, the presence of differential personal tax treatment of dividend and capital gains income does not lead to a preference for the nonpayment of dividends. Thus, the tax-based theories of dividend policy have been unable to explain the motivation underlying the payment of corporate dividends. In Appendix 14A, we utilize the Fisher intertemporal consumption model (introduced in Chapter 2 but modified here to reflect uncertainty) to formally review and synthesize this body of theory.

The second line of theoretical research related to dividend policy is based on relaxing the "frictionless market" assumption used in developing the tax-based dividend policy theories. Specifically, these theories consider the effects of costly market transactions, asymmetric information, and agency costs in deriving explanations of why firms pay dividends. Costly market transactions restrict individual investors' ability to "undo" the corporation's dividend policy and create "homemade dividends," as Miller and Modigliani (1961) suggest, or to utilize the tax arbitrage schemes suggested by Miller and Scholes (1978) to "dispel" the personal tax bias against dividend income. With costly information gathering and processing, the firm's management will find itself privy to outside investors. Ross (1977) and others have suggested that the firm's dividend policy in this circumstance serves as a cost-effective way to "signal" the firm's prospects to outsiders. Finally, Rozeff (1982), Easterbrook (1984), and Jensen (1986) have suggested that the payment of dividends helps reduce management's control over the firm's pool of earnings. Jensen (1986) even suggests that in some instances the agency costs associated with discretionary managerial control over earnings have become great enough to inspire corporate takeover attempts.

We also reviewed three categories of empirical research on dividend policy. The first "describes" corporate dividend payment practices of U.S. corporations. Here we found that firms tend to pay stable cash dividends that change with a lag to reflect permanent changes in their earnings. The second addresses the impact of dividend payment practices on share value. This research directly confronts the primary theoretical issue in dividend policy, and its results have been mixed and controversial. Brennan (1970) found a positive risk premium for the returns of stocks that paid dividends. Black and Scholes (1974) reexamined the same question with a new research methodology designed to eliminate what they felt was an important "cross-sectional bias" in Brennan's tests; their findings failed to identify a significant dividend yield factor in security returns. Stone and Bartter (1979) added yet another refinement to the Brennan methodology and found evidence of a significant dividend yield factor, as did Litzenberger and Ramaswamy (1979, 1982) and Morgan (1982). However, Miller and Scholes (1982) provided evidence of no dividend yield component in equilibrium security returns, suggesting that others' findings in this regard reflected a dividend "announcement" effect. Thus, the impact of dividend policy on share value is still an unsettled issue.

The final category of empirical research on dividend policy relates to the impact of repurchases on equity value. When a firm repurchases its own shares, it provides a surrogate for a cash dividend. Thus, studies of the impact of share repurchase on share value offer evidence of the importance of dividend policy. In brief, they note that share repurchase generally has been followed by a positive change in share value. However, this reaction does not appear to result from either personal tax or wealth transfer sources, indicating that it may well reflect new, positive information revealed by the firm's decision to repurchase.

Study Questions

14.1   In words, explain why investors will be indifferent to the payment of cash dividends in a world where dividend income is not taxed and the firm incurs no transactions costs in the sale of new common stock.

14.2   How does the presence of transactions costs impact on the dividend irrelevance arguments of Miller and Modigliani (1961) and Miller and Scholes (1978)? Explain.

14.3   What is the agency cost problem associated with the firm's dividend retention/payment policy? Discuss.

14.4   Why might the announcement of the firm's intention to pay cash dividends affect its share value? Explain.

14.5   How can a leveraged buyout be used to resolve the agency problem attendant to a firm's decision to retain and reinvest earnings?

14.6   "Although dividend incomes are taxed at a higher rate than capital gains (prior to the Tax Reform Act of 1986) firms persistently paid them." Explain this "puzzle."

Study Problems

14.1   The Harwell Manufacturing Company earned $2 per share last year and paid an $0.80 dividend. The company estimates that it can earn 15 percent on its investments into the indefinite future and plans to maintain its current dividend payment practice.
  a. What is the value of Harwell's stock if the required rate of return for its shares in the market is 20 percent?
  b. Estimate the value of Harwell's stock where the rate of return on reinvestment is 15 percent for each of the next three years and then levels off to 10 percent thereafter.
  c. What would happen to the value of Harwell's stock (using the assumptions in part a) if the company changed its dividend payout ratio to 0 percent? To 100 percent?
  d. What is the optimal dividend policy for Harwell to follow under the conditions stated in part a? Discuss.

14.2   H. B. Carver, Inc. earns $90,000 annually on its existing assets and has a debt/equity ratio of 45 percent, which it plans to maintain into the indefinite future. The firm pays out 40 percent of its earnings in dividends and does not plan to issue any new shares of stock. If investors require a 15 percent return on their investments in the firm's stock and the company expects to require a 20 percent return on reinvested funds, what is the present value of its shares?

14.3   Demonstrate the irrelevance of corporate dividend policy in the absence of personal and corporate taxes.

14.4   Mario LaMacho invested $50,000 in the common stock of L. E. Young, Inc. and expects to receive dividends of $1,000 at year's end. Mario presently is paying taxes on his personal income at the 35 percent rate and already has fully utilized his dividend exemption. Devise a "dividend-laundering" scheme for Mario that will eliminate his personal tax liability for next year's dividends. Be careful to note all necessary assumptions.

14.5   The following model can be used to describe the value of a firm's common stock:

$$V = \frac{(1 - b)E}{1 + K} + \frac{(1 - b)E(1 + br)}{(1 + K)^2} + \frac{(1 - b)E(1 + br)^2}{(1 + K)^3} + \cdots$$

or

$$V = \frac{(1 - b)E}{K - br},$$

where   E = current earnings per share
       b = fraction of earnings retained
    (1 − b)E = d = dividends per share
       r = rate of return the firm earns by reinvesting its earnings
       K = market's required rate of return for stock

Using the above model, determine the firm's optimal dividend payout ratio and, consequently, its optimal retention ratio.

14.6   The ABC Company pays a dividend of $3 per share. Its present dividend yield and price earning ratio are 0.2 and 3, respectively. The company can earn 25 percent on its investments into the indefinite future and plans to maintain its current dividend payment.

a. What are ABC's current earnings?

b. What is the value of ABC's stock if the required rate of return for its shares in the market is 15 percent?

References

E. Altman, "Financial Ratios, Discriminant Analysis and the Prediction of Corporate Bankruptcy," *Journal of Finance* (September 1968): 589–609.

P. Asquith and D. W. Mullins, Jr., "The Impact of Initiating Dividend Payments on Shareholders' Wealth," *Journal of Business* 56 (1983): 640–659.

A. J. Auerbach, "Stockholder Tax Rates and Firm Attributes," *Journal of Public Economics* 21 (1983): 107–127.

H. K. Baker, G. E. Farrelly, and R. B. Edelman, "A Survey of Management Views on Dividend Policy," *Financial Management* 14 (Autumn 1985): 78–84.

G. Barone-Adesi and R. E. Whaley, "The Valuation of American Call Options and the Expected Ex-Dividend Stock Price Decline," *Journal of Financial Economics* 17 (1986): 91–111.

S. Bar-Yosef and L. D. Brown, "A Reexamination of Stock Splits Using Moving Betas," *Journal of Finance* 32 (September 1977): 1069–1080.

S. Bar-Yosef and R. Kolodny, "Dividend Policy and Capital Market Theory," *Review of Economics and Statistics* 58 (May 1976): 181–190.

S. Bar-Yosef and L. Huffman, "The Information Content of Dividends: A Signalling Approach," *Journal of Financial and Quantitative Analysis* (March 1986): 47–58.

S. Bar-Yosef and B. Lev, "Historical Earnings versus Inflation-Adjusted Earnings in the Dividend Decision," *Financial Analysts Journal* 39 (March/April 1983): 41–50.

S. Bar-Yosef, "Dividend Policy and Signalling" (School of Business Administration, The Hebrew University of Jerusalem, 1983, Mimeographed).

W. H. Beaver, P. Kettler, and M. Scholes, "The Association between Market Determined and Accounting Determined Risk Measures," *Accounting Review* 45 (October 1970): 654–682.

S. Bhattacharya, "Imperfect Information, Dividend Policy, and the 'Bird in the Hand' Fallacy," *Bell Journal of Economics* 10 (Spring 1979): 259–270.

———, "Nondissipative Signalling Structures and Dividend Policy," *Quarterly Journal of Economics* 95 (August 1980): 1–24.

F. Black, "Capital Market Equilibrium with Restricted Borrowing," *Journal of Business* (July 1972): 444–455.

———— , "The Dividend Puzzle," *Journal of Portfolio Management* (Winter 1976): 5–8.

———— and M. Scholes, "The Effects of Dividend Yield and Dividend Policy on Common Stock Prices and Returns," *Journal of Financial Economics* (May 1974): 1–22.

———— , "The Pricing of Options and Corporate Liabilities," *Journal of Political Economy* 81 (May/ June 1973): 637–659.

L. Blose and J. Martin, "The Effect of Personal Taxes on Common Stock Prices: An Empirical Investigation Based upon the 1981 Revision in the U.S. Tax Code" (Working paper, University of Texas, March 1987).

M. E. Blume, "Stock Returns and Dividend Yields: Some More Evidence," *Review of Economics and Statistics* (November 1980): 567–577.

L. D. Booth and D. J. Johnston, "The Ex-Dividend Day Behavior of Canadian Stock Prices: Tax Changes and Clientele Effects, *Journal of Finance* 39 (June 1984): 457–475.

D. F. Bradford and R. H. Gordon, "Taxation and the Stock Market Valuation of Capital Gains and Dividends," *Journal of Public Economics* 14 (1980) 109–136.

M. Brennan, "Taxes, Market Valuation and Corporate Financial Policy," *National Tax Journal* (December 1970): 417–427.

J. A. Brittain, *Corporate Dividend Policy* (Washington, D.C.: The Brookings Institution, 1966).

J. A. Campbell and W. Beranek, "Stock Price Behavior on Ex-Dividend Dates," *Journal of Finance* 10 (December 1955): 425–429.

R. Dammon, "A Security Market and Capital Structure Equilibrium under Uncertainty with Progressive Personal Taxes" (Working paper, Carnegie-Mellon University, August 1985).

———— and R. Green, "Tax Arbitrage and the Existence of Equilibrium Prices for Financial Assets" (Working paper, Carnegie-Mellon University, February 1986).

———— and L. Senbet, "The Effect of Taxes on the Interaction between Production and Finance" (Working paper, University of Wisconsin–Madison, May 1986).

L. Dann, "Common Stock Repurchases: An Analysis of Returns to Bondholders and Stockholders," *Journal of Financial Economics* (June 1981): 113–138.

P. G. Darling, "The Influence of Expectations and Liquidity on Dividend Policy," *Journal of Political Economy* 65 (June 1957): 209–224.

H. DeAngelo and R. W. Masulis, "Leverage and Dividend Irrelevancy under Corporate and Personal Taxation," *Journal of Finance* (May 1980): 453–464.

D. A. Dubofsky and L. Bierman, "The Effect of Discount Dividend Reinvestment Plan Announcements on Equity Value" (Working paper, Texas A&M University, December 1985).

D. Durand and A. May, "The Ex-Dividend Behavior of American Telephone and Telegraph Stock," *Journal of Finance* 15 (March 1960): 19–31.

L. Eades, P. J. Hess, and E. H. Kim, "On Interpreting Security Returns during the Ex-Dividend Period," *Journal of Financial Economics* 13 (1984): 3–34.

F. H. Easterbrook, "Two Agency-Cost Explanations of Dividends," *American Economic Review* 74 (1984): 650–659.

E. J. Elton and M. J. Gruber, "Marginal Stockholder Tax Rates and the Clientele Effect," *Review of Economics and Statistics* (February 1970): 68–74.

———— and J. Rentzler, "The Ex-Dividend Day Behavior of Stock Prices: A Re-examination of the Clientele Effect: A Comment," *Journal of Finance* 39 (June 1984): 551–556.

D. Emmanuel, "Debt and Taxes, Dividends and Taxes, and Taxes" (Working paper, University of Texas at Dallas, February 1983).

E. Fama and H. Babiak, "Dividend Policy: An Empirical Analysis," *Journal of the American Statistical Association* (December 1968): 1132–1161.

———— , L. Fisher, M. C. Jensen, and R. Roll, "The Adjustment of Stock Prices to New Information," *International Economic Review* 10 (February 1969): 1–21.

D. Feenberg, "Does the Investment Interest Limitation Explain the Existence of Dividends?" *Journal of Financial Economics* (September 1981): 265–270.

M. Fieldstein and J. Green, "Why Do Companies Pay Dividends?" *American Economic Review* 73 (March 1983): 17–30.

I. Friend and M. Puckett, "Dividends and Stock Prices," *American Economic Review* 54 (September 1964): 656–682.

R. Geske, "The Value of Corporate Liabilities as Compound Options," *Journal of Financial and Quantitative Analysis* 12 (November 1977): 541–552.

M. J. Gordon, "Dividends, Earnings and Stock Prices," *Review of Economics and Statistics* 41 (May 1959): 99–105.

R. Gordon and D. Bradford, "Taxation and the Stock Market Valuation of Capital Gains and Dividends," *Journal of Public Economics* 14 (1980): 109–136.

———, *The Investment, Financing, and Valuation of the Corporation* (Homewood, Ill.: Irwin, 1962).

———, "The Savings Investment and Valuation of a Corporation," *Review of Financial Economics and Statistics* 44 (February 1962): 37–51.

N. Hakansson, "To Pay or Not to Pay Dividends," *Journal of Finance* (May 1982): 415–428.

R. S. Hanson, J. M. Pinkerton, and A. J. Keown, "On Dividend Reinvestment Plans: The Adoption Decision and Stockholder Wealth Effects," *Review of Business and Economic Research* 20 (Spring 1985): 1–10.

R. A. Haugen and L. W. Senbet, "New Perspective on Informational Asymmetry and Agency Relationships," *Journal of Financial and Quantitative Analysis* 14 (November 1979): 671–694.

P. J. Hess, "The Ex-Dividend Behavior of Stock Returns: Further Evidence on Tax Effects," *Journal of Finance* 37 (May 1982): 445–456.

———, "The Dividend Debate: 20 Years of Discussion," in *The Revolution in Corporate Finance*, J. Stern and D. Chew, Jr., eds. (New York: Basil Blackwell, Inc., 1986).

M. C. Jensen, "Agency Costs of Free Cash Flow, Corporate Finance and Takeovers," *American Economic Review* (May 1986): 323–329.

——— and W. Meckling, "Theory of the Firm: Managerial Behavior, Agency Costs and Ownership Structure," *Journal of Financial Economics* (October 1976): 305–360.

——— and R. S. Ruback, "The Market for Corporate Control," *Journal of Financial Economics* (April 1983): 5–50.

A. Kalay, "Comment: Haugen and Senbet Paper," *Journal of Financial and Quantitative Analysis* 14 (November 1979): 711–714.

———, "Signalling, Information Content, and the Reluctance to Cut Dividends," *Journal of Financial and Quantitative Analysis* 15 (November 1980): 855–869.

———, "Stockholder-Bondholder Conflict and Dividend Constraints," *Journal of Financial Economics* 10 (1982): 211–233.

———, "The Ex-Dividend Day Behavior of Stock Prices: A Re-examination of the Clientele Effect: A Reply," *Journal of Finance* 34 (June 1984): 557–561.

D. B. Keim, "Dividend Yields and the January Effect," *Journal of Portfolio Management* (Winter 1986): 54–60.

———, "Dividend Yields and Stock Returns: Implications of Abnormal January Returns," *Journal of Financial Economics* 14 (1985): 473–489.

A. J. Keown, S. Perumpral, and J. Pinkerton, "Market Reaction to the Formulation of Automatic Dividend Reinvestment Plans: An Empirical Investigation" (Working paper, Virginia Polytechnic Institute and State University, October 1983).

John Kose and Joseph Williams, "Dividends, Dilution and Taxes: A Signalling Equilibrium," *Journal of Finance* (September 1985): 1053–1070.

J. W. Kensinger and J. D. Martin, "Royalty Trusts, Master Partnerships, and Other Organizational Means for 'Unfirming' the Firm," *Midland Corporate Finance Journal* 4 (Summer 1986): 72–80.

H. Leland and D. H. Pyle, "Informational Asymmetries, Financial Structure, and Financial Intermediaries," *Journal of Finance* 32 (May 1977): 371–388.

J. Lintner, "Distribution of Income of Corporations among Dividends, Retained Earnings, and Taxes," *American Economic Review* 46 (May 1956): 97–113.

———, "Dividends, Earnings, Leverage, Stock Price and the Supply of Capital to Corporations," *Review of Economics and Statistics* 44 (August 1962): 243–269.

———, "Dividend Policy and Market Valuation: A Reply," *Journal of Business* 36 (January 1963): 116–119.

———, "Optimal Dividends and Corporate Growth under Uncertainty," *Quarterly Journal of Economics* 88 (February 1964): 49–95.

R. Litzenberger and K. Ramaswamy, "Dividends, Short Selling Restrictions, Tax-Induced Investor Clienteles and Market Equilibrium," *Journal of Finance* (May 1980): 469–482.

———, "The Effects of Dividends on Common Stock Prices: Tax Effects or Information Effects?" *Journal of Finance* (May 1982): 429–443.

———, "The Effects of Personal Taxes and Dividends on Capital Asset Prices: Theory and Empirical Evidence," *Journal of Financial Economics* (June 1979): 163–196.

R. Litzenberger and J. C. Van Horne, "Elimination of the Double Taxation of Dividends and Corporate Financial Policy," *Journal of Finance* 33 (June 1978): 737–757.

J. B. Long, Jr., "The Market Valuation of Cash Dividends: A Case to Consider," *Journal of Financial Economics* 6 (1978): 235–264.

S. L. Lummer, "The Uncertain Dividend Clientele Effect" (Working paper, Texas A&M University, rev. January 1986).

J. S. McCallum, "The Impact of the Capital Gains Tax on Bond Yields," *National Tax Journal* 26 (December 1973): 575–583.

T. A. Marsh and R. C. Merton, "Dividend Behavior for the Aggregate Stock Market," *Journal of Business* 60, no. 1 (1987): 1–40.

R. Masulis, "Stock Repurchase by Tender Offer: An Analysis of the Causes of Common Stock Price Changes," *Journal of Finance* (May 1980): 305–318.

M. H. Miller, "Debt and Taxes," *Journal of Finance* (May 1977): 261–275.

——— and F. Modigliani, "Dividend Policy, Growth and the Valuation of Shares," *Journal of Business* 34 (October 1961): 411–433.

——— and M. Scholes, "Dividends and Taxes," *Journal of Financial Economics* (December 1978): 333–364.

———, "Dividends and Taxes: Some Empirical Evidence," *Journal of Political Economy* 90 (1982): 1118–1141.

M. H. Miller, "The Informational Content of Dividends," forthcoming in *Macroeconomics: Essays in Honor of Franco Modigliani,* ed. John Bossons, Rudiger Dornbusch, and Stanley Fischer (Cambridge, Mass.: M.I.T. Press, 1986).

F. Modigliani and M. Miller, "Taxes and Cost of Capital: A Correction," *American Economic Review* (June 1963): 433–443.

I. G. Morgan, "Dividends and Capital Asset Prices," *Journal of Finance* (September 1982): 1071–1086.

R. Norgaard and C. Norgaard, "A Critical Examination of Share Repurchase," *Financial Management* (Spring 1974): 44–50.

H. Pastoriza, "Valuing Utility Earnings, Distributed and Retained," *Analysts Journal* 1 (July 1945): 14–18.

P. P. Peterson, D. R. Peterson, and N. H. Moore, "The Adoption of New-Issue Dividend Reinvestment Plans and Shareholder Wealth" (Working paper, Florida State University, November 1985).

R. R. Petit and R. Westerfield, "A Model of Capital Asset Risk," *Journal of Financial and Quantitative Analysis* 7 (March 1972): 1649–1668.

R. R. Petit, "Taxes, Transactions Costs and the Clientele Effect of Dividends," *Journal of Financial Economics* 5 (1977): 419–436.

R. H. Pettway and R. P. Malone, "Automatic Dividend Reinvestment Plans of Nonfinancial Corporations," *Financial Management* (Winter 1973): 11–18.

G. Pinches and K. A. Mingo, "A Multivariate Analysis of Industrial Bond Rates," *Journal of Finance* (March 1973): 1–18.

J. M. Poterba and L. H. Summers, "New Evidence That Taxes Affect the Valuation of Dividends," *Journal of Finance* (December 1984): 1397–1415.

R. R. Reilly and T. I. Nantell, "Dividend Reinvestment," *Journal of Midwest Finance Association* (1981).

B. Rosenberg and V. Marathe, "Test of Capital Asset Pricing Hypothesis," *Research in Finance* (1979): 115–223.

S. A. Ross, "The Determination of Financial Structure: The Incentive-Signalling Approach," *Bell Journal of Economics* 8 (Spring 1977): 23–40.

M. Rozeff, "Growth, Beta and Agency Costs as Determinants of Dividend Payout Ratios," *Journal of Financial Research* 5 (1982): 249–259.

M. Rubinstein, "The Valuation of Uncertain Income Streams and the Pricing of Options," *Bell Journal of Economics* 7 (Autumn 1976): 407–425.

C. W. Smith, "Option Pricing: A Review," *Journal of Financial Economics* 3 (January/March 1976): 3–51.

———, "Investment Banking and the Capital Acquisition Process," *Journal of Financial Economics* 15 (1986): 3–29.

M. A. Spence, "Competitive and Optimal Responses to Signals: An Analysis of Efficiency and Distribution," *Journal of Economic Theory* 8 (March 1974): 296–332.

———, "Job Market Signalling," *Quarterly Journal of Economics* (August 1973): 355–379.

S. Stewart, "Should a Corporation Repurchase Its Own Stock?" *Journal of Finance* (June 1976): 911–921.

B. K. Stone and B. J. Bartter, "The Effect of Dividend Yield on Stock Returns: Empirical Evidence on the Relevance of Dividends" (W.P.E. 76-78, Georgia Institute of Technology, Atlanta, 1979).

———, "Systematic Interest-Rate Risk in a Two-Index Model of Returns," *Journal of Financial and Quantitative Analysis* (November 1974): 709–721.

E. Talmor, "Asymmetric Information, Signalling and Optimal Corporate Financial Decisions," *Journal of Financial and Quantitative Analysis* 14 (November 1981): 413–438.

L. Vanthienen and T. Vermaelen, "The Effect of Personal Taxes on Common Stock Prices: The Case of a Belgian Tax Reform" (Working paper, Catholic University of Leuven and the University of Chicago, rev. November 1986).

T. Vermaelen, "Common Stock Repurchases and Market Signalling: An Empirical Study," *Journal of Financial Economics* (June 1981): 139–183.

J. R. Woolridge, "Dividend Changes and Security Prices," *Journal of Finance* (December 1983): 1607–1615.

Appendix 14A

A Synthesis of Dividend Policy and Taxes under Uncertainty Using the Fisher Intertemporal Consumption Model

Our objective in this appendix is to provide a formal synthesis of the portion of the dividend policy theoretical literature that relies on corporate and personal tax considerations to explain the motivation for the payment (or nonpayment) of dividends. In Chapter 14, we referred to this body of research as the *frictionless market theories* of corporate dividend policy. In particular, we discussed the seminal papers of Miller and Modigliani (1961) and Miller and Scholes (1978). The model we use here to synthesize this literature is the *Fisher intertemporal consumption model* modified to consider uncertain future consumption.[1]

To review briefly, corporate dividend policy deals with the question of how much of its earnings a firm should pay out to its shareholders in common stock dividends. Dividend policy is only one component of the corporation's financial policy, but it does affect the source of the funds the company uses to finance its investment projects. If it has no effect on the corporation's stock value, it does not matter whether the company uses retained earnings or another source of funds. Alternatively, if dividend policy does affect the stock market value and particularly if an increase in dividends increases that value, the firm will prefer outside funds to retained earnings for a particular project. In addition, if the dividend has an impact on stock value, project selection may be affected as well.

---

[1]We introduced the Fisher model under conditions of certainty about future outcomes in Chapter 2 as the basis for analyzing the individual's single- and multiple-period intertemporal consumption problem. Here we will utilize a single-period model where end-of-period outcomes are random.

In order to concentrate on the dividend policy issue, we will hold the corporate investment decision fixed. Then the dividend policy question may be viewed as one of whether the corporation should raise funds internally or externally. We show that in a competitive market system with no taxes the 1958 Modigliani/Miller result on the irrelevance of the firm's capital structure may be combined with the 1961 Miller/Modigliani result on the irrelevance of dividend policy to show that the *source* and *type* of funds used to finance an investment project has no effect on the corporation's value. We show that in a competitive market system with personal taxes, the relevance of dividend policy depends on consumers' ability to launder their tax obligations using tax arbitrage schemes.

In this appendix, we review the theory of dividend policy using the Fisher intertemporal consumption model, in which the individual selects a consumption pair, that is, a known dollar consumption level in the first period and a random dollar consumption level in the second. The consumer's dollar consumption in the second period depends on how much he or she saves and on how that saving is allocated among the safe and risky assets available. This model allows us to demonstrate the Miller and Modigliani (1961) and Miller and Scholes (1978) results. We also demonstrate that in the absence of the tax arbitrage schemes suggested by Miller and Scholes, the presence of a tax on dividend income is sufficient to make nonpayment of dividends optimal for the corporation.

The Miller/Modigliani (1961) Theorem

In this section, we demonstrate the 1961 Miller/Modigliani theorem on the irrelevance of dividend policy in the context of the Fisher model. We modify the model to incorporate a risky stock market. The stock market allows investors to trade claims to uncertain returns in the second period; equivalently, the stock market allows risk sharing, but only incompletely. Let (c_{i1}, C_{i2}) be the consumption pair for individual i where c_{i1} is the dollar expenditure on consumption in the first period and C_{i2} is a random variable denoting consumption in the second period; C_{i2} depends on the individual's savings decision and portfolio choice. Let (y_{i1}, y_{i2}) denote the individual's income in the two periods. Given certainty and a competitive capital market, we would have a certain dollar expenditure on consumption in period 2: $C_{i2} = y_{i2} + (1 + r)S_i$, where r is the certain rate of return on all financial instruments and $S_i = y_{i1} - c_{i1}$ is the dollar amount of savings. Given uncertainty and competitive bond and stock markets,

(14A.1) $$C_{i2} = y_{i2} + [(1 + r)x_{i0} + \Sigma_j x_{ij}(1 + R_j)]S_i,$$

where, as above, S_i is the amount saved; r is the interest rate on a safe asset; R_j is the random rate of return on risky stock $j = 1, \ldots, N$; x_{ij} is the proportion of saving allocated by individual i to risky stock j; and x_{i0} is the proportion of S_i allocated to the safe asset. Then $x_i = (x_{i0}, x_{i1}, \ldots, x_{iN})$ is the portfolio choice and S_i the savings decision of individual i. The pair (S_i, x_i) determines the random variable C_{i2} as shown in Equation 14A.1. Of course, the portfolio choice must be made by the individual such that

$$x_{i0} + x_{i1} + \ldots + x_{iN} = 1$$

or, equivalently,

$$S_i[x_{i0} + x_{i1} + \ldots + x_{ij}] = S_i \,,$$

where $S_i x_{ij}$ is the dollar investment in asset j by individual i. Alternatively, let $b_i = S_i x_{i0}$ denote the dollar amount saved and invested in bonds and $e_{ij} = S_i x_{ij}$ denote the dollar amount saved and invested in risky stock j. Then

$$S_i = b_i + \Sigma_j e_{ij} \,,$$

and Equation 14A.1 may be rewritten as

(14A.2) $$C_{i2} = y_{i2} + b_i(1 + r) + \Sigma_j e_{ij}(1 + R_j) \,.$$

Next, we introduce a dividend. Let D_{j1} denote the total number of dollars in dividends for firm j paid now to holders of record in firm j in proportion to their ownership. Since we want to consider predividend values, suppose that the sequence of events is as follows: Firms announce their dividend policies, D_{j1}, and trading occurs in the bond and stock markets; then dividends are paid, and first-period consumption takes place. The portfolio and savings decisions affect current consumption. To see this, let E_j denote the stock market value of firm j. Then the proportion of the firm owned by investor i is e_{ij}/E_j; thus, this investor receives a dividend payment now in the amount $(e_{ij}/E_j)D_{j1}$. It follows that consumption now may be expressed as

(14A.3) $$c_{i1} = y_{i1} - S_i + \Sigma_j \left(\frac{e_{ij}}{E_j}\right) D_{j1}$$

$$= y_{i1} - b_i - \Sigma_j e_{ij} + \Sigma_j \left(\frac{e_{ij}}{E_j}\right) D_{j1} \,.$$

The investor's problem is to select a savings and investment plan that will maximize expected utility. Let u_i be the investor's increasing concave utility function. Then the individual selects (e_i, b_i) where $e_i = (e_{i1}, \ldots, e_{iN})$ to

$$\text{maximize } H_i(e_i, b_i) = \int u_i(c_{i1}, C_{i2})dP_i \,,$$

where (c_{i1}, C_{i2}) are as defined in Equations 14A.2 and 14A.3.

Now consider the firm's problem. Let the pair (z_{j1}, Z_{j2}) denote the firm's earnings in periods 1 and 2, respectively, where z_{j1} is known and Z_{j2} is a random variable. Assume that the firm's investment decision is fixed such that its random gross earnings next period will not be affected by the dividend policy choice. Further, for simplicity suppose that z_{j1} is sufficient to cover the investment expenditure if it is retained; if it is not, the firm must issue equity or debt to cover its fixed investment expenditure that will yield the random gross earnings Z_{j2}. If the firm selects $D_{j1} > 0$ and issues debt $B_j = D_{j1}$ to finance its investment,

(14A.4) $$1 + R_j = \frac{Z_{j2} - (1 + r)D_{j1}}{E_j} \,.$$

Note that due to the 1958 Modigliani/Miller theorem on the irrelevance of the firm's capital structure decision, we need not consider alternative financing decisions.

Now consider the consumption choices available to the individual given alternative dividend policy choices. Using Equation 14A.4, 14A.3 may be rewritten as

(14A.5)
$$C_{i2} = y_{i2} + b_i(1 + r) + \Sigma_j \left(\frac{e_{ij}}{E_j}\right)[Z_{j2} - (1 + r)D_{j1}]$$

$$= y_{i2} + b_i(1 + r) + \Sigma_j \left(\frac{e_{ij}}{E_j}\right)Z_{j2} - \Sigma_j \left(\frac{e_{ij}}{E_j}\right)D_{j1}(1 + r).$$

Note that if firm j increases its dividend from zero to $D_{j1} > 0$, the initial effect on the consumer will be to increase current consumption by the amount $(e_{ij}/E_j)D_{j1}$. However, by investing $(e_{ij}/E_j)D_{j1}$ in bonds, the consumer may maintain the same consumption now. Also note that this same transaction will yield the same random variable, C_{i2}. Hence, any dividend decision can be reversed by a savings decision, which implies that the firm's dividend policy will have no effect on its stock market value.

To determine the firm's stock market value given alternative dividend policy choices, consider the first-order conditions for the consumer's problem:

(14A.6)
$$D_j H_i = \int D_1 u_i \left[-1 + \left(\frac{D_{j1}}{E_j}\right)\right] dP_i$$

$$+ \int \left[\frac{D_2 u_i[Z_{j2} - (1 + r)D_{j1}]}{E_j}\right] dP_i = 0$$

for $j = 1, \ldots, N$;

(14A.7)
$$D_{N+1} H_i = \int [-D_1 u_i + (1 + r)D_2 u_i] dP_i = 0.$$

Note that Equation 14A.7 may be equivalently expressed as

$$\frac{\int D_1 u_i dP_i}{\int D_2 u_i dP_i} = 1 + r,$$

which simply says that the temporal marginal rate of substitution must equal one plus the rate of return on bonds. Using Equations 14A.6 and 14A.7, it is apparent that if $D_{j1} = 0$,

$$(1 + r)\int D_2 u_i dP_i = \left(\frac{1}{E_j}\right)\int D_2 u_i Z_{j2} dP_i$$

or, equivalently,

$$E_j = \frac{\int D_2 u_i Z_{j2} dP_i}{(1 + r) \int D_2 u_i dP_i}.$$

Next, consider the case in which $D_{j1} > 0$. The Miller/Modigliani (1961) dividend irrelevance result is that the stock market value (including the dividend) will be unchanged. Again using Equations 14A.6 and 14A.7, we obtain

$$\frac{1}{E_j} \int D_2 u_i [Z_{j2} - (1 + r) D_{j1}] dP_i = (1 + r) \int D_2 u_i \left(1 - \frac{D_{j1}}{E_j}\right) dP_i$$

or

$$E_j = \frac{\int D_2 u_i Z_{j2} dP_i}{(1 + r) \int D_2 u_i dP_i},$$

which establishes the Miller/Modigliani theorem in the context of the Fisher model. Note too that the firm's dividend policy can be the pair (D_{j1}, D_{j2}), where D_{j2} is the dividend paid to stockholders in period 2; however, this will not change the dividend irrelevance result, since the cash flow to stockholders in period 2 is $[Z_{j2} - (1 + r) D_{j1} - D_{j2}] + D_{j2} = Z_{j2} - (1 + r) D_{j1}$. The form of the Miller/Modigliani result demonstrated here is slightly more robust than is a similar result for the case $(0, D_{j2})$, because it allows consumers to alter their savings/portfolio decisions in response to the firm's dividend policy announcement.

Differential Personal Taxes on Bond and Stock Income

We now turn our attention to the case in which the consumer pays a tax on bond and dividend income. In the last section, we noted that the Miller/Modigliani dividend result is trivially true if the firm's dividend policy takes the form $D_j = (0, D_{j2})$. However, now consumer i has a tax rate t_i and thus pays a tax $t_i(e_{ij}/E_j)D_{j2}$ on dividend income in period 2. Because of this observation, it is often claimed that consumers will prefer firms that do not pay dividends. In fact, it is also claimed that if firms j and k are in the same industry such that $Z_{j2} = Z_{k2}$ and $D_{j2} > 0$ while $D_{k2} = 0$, the stock market value of firm k will exceed that of firm j; that is, $E_k > E_j$.

To consider this claim, suppose that all consumers have a positive tax rate t_i on bond, dividend, and wage income. Consumer i then has a consumption pair (c_{i1}, C_{i2}) where

$$c_{i1} = y_{i1}(1 - t_i) - b_i - \Sigma_j e_{ij}$$

and

$$C_{i2} = y_{i2}(1 - t_i) + b_i[1 + r(1 - t_i)] + \Sigma_j \left(\frac{e_{ij}}{E_j}\right)[Z_{j2} - D_{j2} + D_{j2}(1 - t_i)]$$

$$= y_{i2}(1 - t_i) + b_i[1 + r(1 - t_i)] + \Sigma_j \left(\frac{e_{ij}}{E_j}\right)Z_{j2} - t_i\Sigma_j\left(\frac{e_{ij}}{E_j}\right)D_{j2}$$

$$= y_{i2}(1 - t_i) + b_i(1 + r) + \Sigma_j\left(\frac{e_{ij}}{E_j}\right)Z_{j2} - t_i\left[rb_i + \Sigma_j\left(\frac{e_{ij}}{E_j}\right)D_{j2}\right].$$

The expression for consumption in period 2 implicitly assumes that the consumer pays a nonnegative tax on bond and dividend income; equivalently, it assumes that $b_i > 0$ and $e_{ij} > 0$. Since we want to allow the consumer to borrow — $b_i < 0$ — or sell stocks short — $e_{ij} < 0$ — we will let T_{i2} denote the consumer's tax in period 2. Then

$$T_{i2} = t_iy_{i2} + t_i \max\left\{0, rb_i + \Sigma_j\left(\frac{e_{ij}}{E_j}\right)D_{j2}\right\}.$$

The individual's consumption in period 2 may be rewritten as

$$C_{i2} = y_{i2} + b_i(1 + r) + \Sigma_j\left(\frac{e_{ij}}{E_j}\right)Z_{j2} - T_{i2}.$$

Note that $T_{i2} \geq t_iy_{i2}$ and is strictly greater when some tax is paid on bond or dividend income. Note too that the consumer can always eliminate the tax on dividend income by appropriately levering his or her personal portfolio; however, of course, it may not always be optimal to do so to the point where the tax on dividend income is eliminated. In the case we have constructed ($Z_{j2} = Z_{k2}$, $D_{j2} > 0$, and $D_{k2} = 0$), it is not necessary for the investor to lever the portfolio to eliminate the tax on dividend income; rather, the investor may simply shift the investment from firm j to firm k. Because of the tax on dividend income, we claim that investors will prefer firm k to firm j and, hence, $E_k > E_j$. To establish this claim, suppose $E_j \geq E_k$. In equilibrium, it must not be true that the investor can costlessly increase expected utility by altering the portfolio. If this is the case, then the investor has an arbitrage opportunity. To see this, suppose the investor decreases his or her holding of stock j and increases that of stock k by the same amount, that is, adjusts the portfolio by moving in the direction $v = (0, \ldots, -1, \ldots, 1, \ldots, 0)$, where -1 is the jth and 1 the kth element of the vector $v\varepsilon\mathbf{R}^{N+1}$. Let D_vH_i denote the derivative of H_i in the direction v. Then

$$D_v H_i(e_i, b_i) = -D_j H_i(e_i, b_i) + D_k H_i(e_i, b_i)$$

$$= -\int \left[-D_1 u_i + D_2 u_i \left(\frac{1}{E_j}\right)(Z_{j2} - t_i D_{j2}) \right] dP_i$$

$$+ \int \left[-D_1 u_i + D_2 u_i \left(\frac{1}{E_k}\right) Z_{k2} \right] dP_i$$

$$= \left[\left(\frac{1}{E_k}\right) - \left(\frac{1}{E_j}\right) \right] \int D_2 u_i Z_{j2} dP_i$$

$$+ t_i \left(\frac{D_{j2}}{E_j}\right) \int D_2 u_i dP_i$$

$$= \left(\frac{E_j - E_k}{E_j E_k}\right) \int D_2 u_i Z_{j2} dP_i$$

$$+ t_i \left(\frac{D_{j2}}{E_j}\right) \int D_2 u_i dP_i \,.$$

Hence, it is easily observed that $D_v H_i > 0$ if $E_j \geq E_k$, which is a contradiction. Therefore, given $D_{j2} > 0$ and $D_{k2} = 0$, it follows that $E_k > E_j$. More important, note that the value-maximizing firm can costlessly increase its value by eliminating its dividend. In this case, firm j will find that $D_{j2} = 0$ is optimal, in which case $E_j = E_k$.

The Miller/Scholes Theorems

We next consider the Miller/Scholes argument that investors are indifferent to the firm's dividend policy despite the tax differential in favor of capital gains. We will show that the Miller/Scholes result holds due to a tax arbitrage arrangement. As before, we assume that t_i is the investor's tax rate on bond and dividend income. Like Miller and Scholes, suppose that in addition to stocks and bonds the investor may hold insurance policies that are riskless investments yielding a return of $1 + r$ at the end of the period. Further, suppose that insurance companies hold only riskless bonds in their own portfolios. Now let $b_i = (b_{i1}, b_{i2})$ where b_{i1} is the dollar investment in bonds and b_{i2} the dollar investment in insurance. By going short in bonds — that is, borrowing — the investor creates a tax shield for dividend income. Thus, the investor's consumption pair is (c_{i1}, C_{i2}) where

$$c_{i1} = y_{i1}(1 - t_i) - b_{i1} - b_{i2} - \Sigma_j e_{ij} \,,$$

and

$$C_{i2} = y_{i2} + (b_{i1} + b_{i2})(1 + r) + \Sigma_j \left(\frac{e_{ij}}{E_j}\right) Z_{j2} - T_{j2}$$

where

$$T_{j2} = t_i \max\left\{0, y_{i2} + rb_i + \Sigma_j \frac{e_{ij}}{E_j} D_{j2}\right\}.$$

Note that if the investor sets

$$b_{i1} = -\left(\frac{1}{r}\right)\Sigma_j\left(\frac{e_{ij}}{E_j}\right)D_{j2},$$

all dividend income will be sheltered from taxation and $T_{i2} = t_i y_{i2}$. To demonstrate the Miller/Scholes dividend irrelevance result, we need to show that all taxes on dividend income may be eliminated. It suffices to show that there is an arbitrage direction v. Let $v = (0, \ldots, 0, -1, 1)$ be a vector in $\mathbf{R}^{N+2}$ and, as before, let $H_i(e_i, b_i)$ denote the expected utility function; now, however, b_i is the vector (b_{i1}, b_{i2}). Then

$$D_v H_i = -\int \{-D_1 u_i + D_2 u_i[1 + r(1 - t_i)]\}dP_i$$

$$+ \int [-D_1 u_i + D_2 u_i(1 + r)]dP_i$$

$$= rt_i \int D_2 u_i dP_i$$

$$> 0.$$

Since $D_v H_i > 0$ it follows that all taxes on dividend income may be eliminated; it should also be noted that all taxes on ordinary income may be eliminated as well. This result is easily seen by noting that by selling bonds short and buying insurance, the investor shields more dividend income from taxation and thus increases his or her portfolio income without changing the riskiness of the income distribution.

Alternatively, still assuming that $D_j = (0, D_{j2})$, it is possible to construct a tax arbitrage scheme using a pension plan. Let r_i denote the consumer's investment in the retirement plan. Since the consumer pays tax on income net of the investment in the retirement program, we obtain consumption now and later as

$$c_{i1} = (y_{i1} - r_i)(1 - t_i) - b_i - \Sigma_j e_{ij}$$

and

$$C_{i2} = y_{i2}(1 - t_i) + b_i[1 + r(1 - t_i)] + r_i(1 + r)(1 - t_i)$$

$$+ \Sigma_j\left(\frac{e_{ij}}{E_j}\right)Z_{j2} - t_i\Sigma_j\left(\frac{e_{ij}}{E_j}\right)D_{j2}.$$

Note that if we let $b_i = -r_i(1 - t_i)$ and

$$r_i = \left[\frac{1}{r}(1 - t_i)\right]\Sigma_j\left(\frac{e_{ij}}{E_j}\right)D_{j2} = \left[\frac{1}{r}(1 - t_i)\right]D_i,$$

the consumer may maintain current consumption c_{i1} constant and eliminate the tax on dividend income in the next period. This suggests that if the investor borrows $1 - t_i$ dollars and places 1 dollar in the pension plan, there will be an arbitrage profit. To see this, let

$$H_i(e_i, r_i, b_i) = \int u_i(c_{i1}, C_{i2}) dP_i$$

and let $v = [0, 1, -(1 - t_i)]$, where 0 is a vector of zeros in $\mathbf{R}^N$. Then

$$D_v H_i = \int D_1 u_i [-(1 - t_i) + (1 - t_i)] dP_i$$

$$+ \int D_2 u_i \{-[1 - t_i][1 + r(1 - t_i)] + [1 + r][1 - t_i]\} dP_i$$

$$= (1 - t_i) rt_i \int D_2 u_i dP_i$$

$$> 0.$$

It follows that all taxes on dividends will be eliminated with this arbitrage scheme. As Miller and Scholes argued, the pension plan and insurance policy are equivalent instruments in the sense that either allows the consumer to launder dividend income. However, note that when the investor has laundered all dividend income, there is still an arbitrage opportunity with either scheme to continue to eliminate taxes. To see this with the pension plan scheme, let

$$b_i = -(r_i^0 + r_i^1)(1 - t_i)$$

and

$$r_i = r_i^0 + r_i^1,$$

where

$$r_i^0 = \left[\frac{1}{r}(1 - t_i)\right] D_i.$$

Then

$$C_{i2} = y_{i2}(1 - t_i) + b_i[1 + r(1 - t_i)] + r_i(1 + r)(1 - t_i) + \Sigma_j \left(\frac{e_{ij}}{E_j}\right) Z_{j2} - t_i D_i$$

$$= y_{i2}(1 - t_i) - (r_i^0 + r_i^1)[1 + r(1 - t_i)] + (r_i^0 + r_i^1)(1 + r)(1 - t_i)$$

$$+ \Sigma_j \left(\frac{e_{ij}}{E_j}\right) Z_{j2} - t_i D_i$$

$$= y_{i2}(1 - .t_i) - (1 - t_i) D_i \left[\frac{1 + r(1 - t_i)}{r(1 - t_i)}\right] - r_i^1(1 - t_i)(1 + r)(1 - t_i)$$

$$+ \frac{(1 + r)(1 - t_i)D_i}{r(1 - t_i)} + r_i^1(1 + r)(1 - t_i) + \Sigma_j\left(\frac{e_{ij}}{E_j}\right)Z_{j2} - t_iD_i$$

$$= y_{i2}(1 - t_i) + \Sigma_j\left(\frac{e_{ij}}{E_j}\right)Z_{j2} + r_i^1(1 - t_i)rt_i.$$

Hence, the consumer may continue beyond the point at which all dividend income is sheltered; by doing so, he or she is able to shelter more of the retirement income. Note that saving in this case is

$$S_i = r_i(1 - t_i) + b_i + \Sigma_je_{ij}$$

and thus for $v = [0, 1, -(1 - t_i)]$, $D_vS_i = 0$. Hence, the saving constraint does not limit the arbitrage opportunity. Only an additional constraint of the form $r_i \le \Theta y_{i1}$, which limits the investment in the pension plan to no more than a fraction, Θ, of current income, will stop the consumer's movement. Of course, as long as $\Theta y_{i1} \ge r_i^0$, all dividend income will be sheltered and the Miller/Scholes result will follow.

Finally, assume that dividends take the form $D_j = (D_{j1}, 0)$. Of course, a dividend now means tax now and, in the context of this model, the investor cannot create a tax shield now. However, there are a number of ways in which the investor can defer dividend income and its corresponding tax. A Miller/Scholes type of argument in this context would involve deferring dividend income one period and eliminating the tax on dividend income in the process. In this case, consumption now and later takes the form

$$c_{i1} = (y_{i1} - r_i)(1 - t_i) - b_i - \Sigma_je_{ij} + (1 - t_i)D_i,$$

where

$$D_i = \Sigma_j\left(\frac{e_{ij}}{E_j}\right)D_{j1}$$

and

$$C_{i2} = r_i(1 + r)(1 - t_i) + b_i[1 + r(1 - t_i)] + \Sigma_j\left(\frac{e_{ij}}{E_j}\right)Z_{j2} - (1 + r)D_i.$$

Note that current dividend income may be eliminated by investing an appropriate amount in the pension plan. For example, by letting $r_i = D_i$, the dividend income may be transferred from now to later; however, in this case a tax must be paid in the next period on the principal and interest from the pension plan. To compensate for the increased tax obligation, let $r_i = r_i^0 + r_i^1$, where $r_i^0 = D_i$, and $r_i^1 = (1 + r)D_i/r(1 - t_i)$, and let $b_i = -r_i^1(1 - t_i)$. By making this portfolio adjustment, the consumer may transfer the dividend forward, eliminate the tax on dividend income (that is, including the tax on the interest income he or she incurs by transferring the dividend income forward one period), and otherwise maintain a constant current consumption level. Alternatively, the consumer can set $r_i^0 = t_iD_i/(1 - t_i)$ to eliminate just the tax on current dividends. Then, by moving away from the portfolio (e_i, r_i^0, b_i) in the direction $v = [0, 1, -(1 - t_i)]$, the consumer may maintain current consumption constant and eliminate the tax on dividend income that has been transferred to the next period via the pension plan. As before, an institutional constraint such as $r_i \leq \Theta y_{i1}$ must exist in order to limit the use of this arbitrage opportunity. In either case, if the constraint $r_i \leq q y_{i1}$ is not binding until all tax on dividend income is sheltered, the Miller/Scholes type of argument holds in this Fisher model under uncertainty.

References

R. Brealey and S. Myers, *Principles of Corporate Finance* (New York: McGraw-Hill, 1984).

M. H. Miller and F. Modigliani, "Dividend Policy, Growth, and the Valuation of Shares," *Journal of Business* 34 (October 1961): 411–433.

M. H. Miller and M. S. Scholes, "Dividends and Taxes," *Journal of Financial Economics* 6 (December 1978): 333–364.

F. Modigliani and M. H. Miller, "Corporation Income Taxes and the Cost of Capital: A Correction," *American Economic Review* (June 1963): 433–443.

——— , "The Cost of Capital, Corporate Finance, and the Theory of Investment," *American Economic Review* (June 1958): 261–297.

Chapter 15

Option Pricing Theory

An *option* is a contract between two people that conveys the right to buy or sell specified property at a given price for a designated time period. The person who creates and offers the contract for sale is called the writer or seller; the other party is called the owner or buyer. When the contract is made, the buyer pays cash to the writer for the right to buy or sell at a known price, which removes some risk in a future transaction. The owner of the option contract has the right to buy or sell the underlying asset but has no obligation to do so. The latter is the distinguishing characteristic of an option contract as opposed to *forward* and *futures* contracts, for which there *is* an obligation to execute or, using options terminology, exercise the contract.

Option contracts come in two forms: calls and puts. A *call option* is a contract that permits the holder to buy an asset during a specified time interval for a designated price and requires the seller to sell.[1] At the time the contract is written, both parties agree to both the purchase price and the time period within which the option can be exercised. A *put option* differs from a call option in that it allows the holder to sell rather than purchase the asset.

Option contracts are also described by the type of restriction placed on the exercise period. A *European option* contract can be exercised only upon its termination — that is, on its expiration date — whereas an *American option* can be

---

[1]As noted above, the seller is sometimes called the *writer*, and selling an option is called *writing an option*. *Writer* is probably the more accurate term, however, because the only thing sold is the contract.

exercised at any time up to and including the exercise date. The American option contract obviously offers the holder greater flexibility, which apparently makes its valuation more difficult. For this reason we will focus our initial discussion on the European option.

Various forms of options have been in use for a long time; however, it is only recently that stock options have been traded on an "organized exchange." The Chicago Board Options Exchange (CBOE) was organized in April 1973 and initially allowed trading of call options on only 16 widely traded common stocks. Since that time, three additional exchanges have begun to offer option trading. Today stock options are actively traded on over 400 stocks and more than 10,000 contracts.

Financial theorists have found that a number of financial contracts other than stock options can be viewed as options. For example, a firm's common stock can be considered a call option on its real (that is, productive) assets, with the exercise price equal to its debt obligations. To see this, let V be the value of the firm — the sum of its real assets — and D be the value of its debt, for which the real assets are security. The stockholders could sell the firm for V, provided V exceeds D, and obtain V − D. If V is less than D, the stockholders can walk away with no obligation, giving the lenders the real assets in satisfaction of the debt. Thus, in effect the stockholders have a call option on the value of the firm, V, with exercise price D.

Certain types of investments that a firm makes can also be considered call options. For example, a firm's research and development expenditures can be viewed as call options on the values of the productive ideas they create, with the exercise price equal to the investment outlay required to put these ideas into operation.

An Institutional Note: Options Jargon

Long: The buyer of the option contract is said to have a long position, or to hold the contract long.

Short: The seller or writer of the option contract is said to be in a short position, or to have sold the option short.

In the money: An option is in the money if exercising it would produce a positive gain for the investor. For example, a call contract with striking price K is in the money at time t if the market price, $P(t)$, is greater than K.

Out of the money: An option is out of the money if exercising it would produce a loss.

Naked position: An investor holds a naked position if he or she holds only one of the following: the underlying asset, a single call option, or a single put option.

Hedged position: A hedge is any combination of the underlying asset and the options written on it.

Straddle: A straddle is a hedge consisting of the same position on a call option and a put option on the same asset and having the same exercise dates and same

In the R & D example, the exercise price and the contract's duration are both random, a situation to which our analysis does not apply. In this chapter we will focus our attention on stock options, for these have been the center of research activity. However, these valuation procedures apply to other option contracts, with appropriate modifications.

This chapter is organized as follows. First, we describe option contracts, define their terminology, and translate it into a tractable model. We use this model to value a call option and illustrate it with option price data from the financial press. Then we discuss the valuation of European call options using a simple two-state, binomial option pricing model. This particular model is a very useful pedagogical vehicle. Moreover, it is more general than many other models used to value call options, since it permits values to be obtained by taking appropriate limits; the Black/Scholes (1973) continuous time option pricing formula, for example, can be obtained in this way, and these results also apply to European put option contracts. However, we eventually establish a relation between the values of European put and call options, called the *put-call parity relation,* which makes separate derivation of European put values unnecessary. Finally, we show when American call options have the same value as corresponding European call options.

Options Terminology

In this section, we define the components of options contracts and explain how to read option price information in the financial press. Our description is somewhat simplified, but it contains the five important elements of a stock option contract, as follows:

---

striking prices. Writing both the call and the put creates a written or short straddle; buying both produces a long straddle. Values of these hedges at maturity are shown in Figures 15.1 and 15.2.

Bullish: An investor's position is bullish if an increase in the value of the underlying asset is in the investor's favor.

Bearish: An investor's position is bearish if a decrease in the value of the underlying asset is in the investor's favor.

Spread: A spread is a hedge consisting of different positions on the same type of option on the same asset and having the same exercise dates but different striking prices. It is also called a "money spread" to distinguish it from a time spread in which the striking prices are the same but the exercise dates differ. Taking the long position with a call having striking price K_1 and going short with a call having striking price $K_2 > K_1$, both maturing at time T, create a spread in which the investor's value at time T increases with P(T). Spreads of this type are called *bullish* spreads, since an increase in the price, P(T), between K_1 and K_2 increases their value. A *bearish* spread is obtained by reversing positions. Figures 15.3 and 15.4 illustrate bullish and bearish spreads, respectively.

**Figure 15.1   Long Straddle Obtained by Buying a Call and a Put,
Both with Striking Price K**

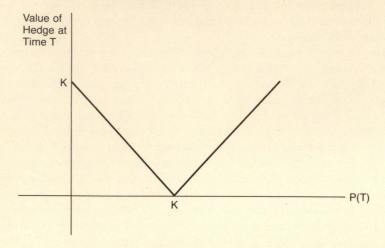

**Figure 15.2   Short Straddle Obtained by Selling a Call and a Put,
Both with Striking Price K**

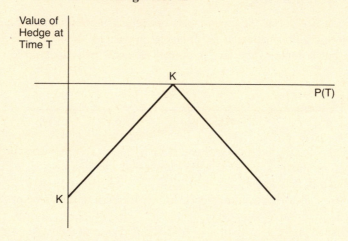

1.   The type of option — put or call

2.   The underlying asset on which the option is written — the particular common stock, land tract, and so on that the contract owner buys or sells if the contract is exercised

3.   The expiration date

4.   The exercise (striking) price

5.   The exercise terms — American or European

Figure 15.3   Bullish Spread Obtained by Buying a Call with Striking Price K_1 and Selling a Call with Striking Price $K_2 > K_1$

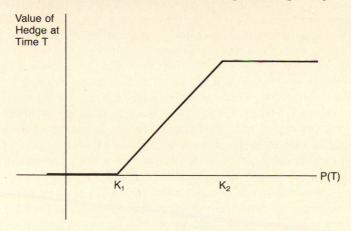

Figure 15.4   Bearish Spread Obtained by Selling a Call with Striking Price K_1 and Buying a Call with Striking Price $K_2 > K_1$

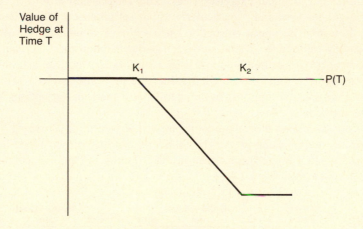

Let P(t) represent the price at time t of the stock on which the option contract is written (the underlying asset could be a bond, real estate, or some other asset rather than a stock). Next, let t = 0 be the current time (usually measured in days or years, whichever is more convenient). At the current time, P(0) is known but P(t) is a random variable for $0 < t \le T$, where T is the term of the contract. Note, however, that we *do* assume individuals have probability beliefs regarding each P(t) such that the joint probability distributions of the P(t), t > 0, are known at t = 0 to all.

When the holder of a call option buys the asset on which it is written, the option is said to have been *exercised*. The price paid for the underlying asset upon exercise is called the *exercise* or *striking price,* which we designate K. Let T represent the maturity date of the option. At time t, the term of the option is T − t. Hence, at the current time, t = 0, the term is T − 0 = T years. At the maturity date, the term is T − T = 0. In an American stock option contract, the holder of a call option pays a price, Call(T), for the contract at t = 0 and receives the right to buy 100 shares of common stock for an exercise price K on any date t ≤ T. (When it is important to display the parameters that determine the option's value, we will write Call(P(t), T − t, K) for the value of an American call option with term T − t, and having a striking price of K and current price of P(t) and the value of the corresponding European option with a lowercase c but otherwise using the same symbols.) Certainly Call(T) > 0 as long as there is a positive probability that P(t) > K for some t ≤ T. This is true because the holder of the call option has the right to purchase the stock for a price K when its market price is P(t), thus providing a profit equal to P(t) − K. The writer or issuer of the call receives a payment equal to Call(T) at t = 0 and assumes the risk of having to sell the specified number of shares of common stock for a price K when P(t) > K.

The holder of an American put option pays a price Put(T) at t = 0 for the right to sell a specified number of shares of stock for an exercise price K on dates t ≤ T. The put option has value if there is a positive probability that P(t) < K over the option's term. Later we will demonstrate a relationship that must exist between the values of a European call and European put option written on the same stock and having identical exercise prices. This relationship is referred to as the *put-call parity theorem* and is particularly important because it allows us to calculate the value of a European put option once we have computed the value of the corresponding call option. There is no such parity theorem for American options. However, under our assumptions, investors always hold American call options until the last moment; thus, their market values are the same as those of the corresponding European call options. In order to value American put options, we must use other methods.

Before discussing the valuation of options, we will first consider how option data appear in the financial press. The following example presents data for a fictitious option, ABC, in the format used in the "Trading in Options" column of the October 5, 198X, *New York Times:*

Option	Strike Price	Calls — Last			Puts — Last		
		Oct	Jan	Apr	Oct	Jan	Apr
ABC							
33-1/8	30	3	3-3/4	r	1/8	5/8	1-1/4
33-1/8	35	1/8	1	1-1/4	1-7/8	3	r
33-1/8	40	r	r	1/2	r	r	r

The first column simply identifies the data as ABC's and gives its New York Stock Exchange closing price of $33.125 per share for October 4, 198X. In the matrix formed by the remaining columns, each row gives the striking price and market prices of three American call options and three American put options. The striking price is the same for all six options in any given row (for example, all six options in the first row have a striking or exercise price of $30 per share). The "Oct Jan Apr" headings give the expiration dates for the options in the respective columns. In addition, options expire on the third Friday of each respective month (and in the current year). For example, if neither 198X nor 198X + 1 is a leap year, and if January 1, 198X is a Tuesday, then the expiration dates for the options listed in the above table are October 19, 198X, January 18, 198X + 1, and April 19, 198X + 1. Consequently, the terms of the three options (as of October 5, 198X) are 14, 105, and 195 days, respectively. The "r" symbol simply indicates that no options have been traded for that position in the matrix and thus the price was not observable on October 4, 198X. The call options with an exercise price of $30 were traded at $3 and $3.75 per share for the October and January maturities, respectively. Finally, the options' prices are quoted on a per share basis but actually trade in contracts for 100 shares. Thus, the October call option with a striking price of $30 actually traded for $300 per contract.

Using the Black/Scholes (1973) Option Pricing Model

At this point we illustrate the most important result of option pricing theory: the *Black/Scholes option pricing formula*. Later we will derive it by first deriving a binomial option pricing formula and then applying a limit argument. The Black/Scholes option pricing formula is

$$\text{call}(S, T, K) = SN(y) - Kv^{T}N(y - \sigma\sqrt{T}),$$

where $\quad y = \left(\dfrac{1}{\sigma\sqrt{T}}\right) \ln\left(\dfrac{S}{v^{T}K}\right) + \dfrac{\sigma\sqrt{T}}{2}$

$\quad v = 1/(1 + r)$, r being the riskless interest rate

$\quad S =$ current price of the stock on which the option is written

$\quad K =$ striking price

$\quad T =$ maturity of option

$\quad \sigma\sqrt{T} =$ standard deviation of the log/price ratio $\ln(P(T)/S)$, or, equivalently,

$\qquad \sigma^{2}T =$ the variance of the log/price ratio

$\quad N(z) =$ standardized normal cumulative distribution function; that is, $N(z) = \Pr(Z \le z)$, where Z has a normal distribution with mean 0 and variance 1.

In order to use this formula to calculate the value of ABC's options, we must first determine the risk-free interest rate. We use the yield to maturity of a U.S. Treasury bill maturing at about the same time as the option, which we will assume is 12 percent per annum. We can obtain a reasonable estimate of $\sigma^{2}T$ from a sample of historical stock prices. Since the sample may involve price changes over periods of more or less than T years, the variance per year, σ^{2}, is usually estimated based on a sample and then multiplied by T. The variance per year of $\ln(P(T)/S)$, which is commonly denoted σ^{2}, is called the stock's *price volatility*. The expected value per year of $\ln(P(T)/S)$ is denoted μ. It does not appear in the Black/Scholes formula. Estimating σ^{2} involves

1. Taking a sample of prices $P_{0}, \ldots, P_{n}$, corresponding to times $t_{0} < t_{1}, \ldots,$ $< t_{n}$ and durations $d_{i} = t_{i} - t_{i-1}$ for $i = 1, \ldots, n$

2. Calculating the values $(1/d_{i})[\ln(P_{i}/P_{i-1})]$, $i = 1, \ldots, n$ and then calculating the sample mean, m, and sample variance, s^{2}, using the following formulas:

Sample mean: $m = \left(\dfrac{1}{n}\right) \sum\limits_{i=1}^{n} \left(\dfrac{1}{d_i}\right) \left[\ln\left(\dfrac{P_i}{P_{i-1}}\right)\right]$

Sample variance: $s^2 = \left(\dfrac{1}{n}\right) \sum\limits_{i=1}^{n} \left[\left(\dfrac{1}{d_i}\right)\ln\left(\dfrac{P_i}{P_{i-1}}\right) - m\right]^2$

When the prices are equally spaced over time, the d_i are all equal. Letting d denote this value, the formulas become

$$m = \left(\dfrac{1}{dn}\right) \sum\limits_{i=1}^{n} \left[\ln\left(\dfrac{P_i}{P_{i-1}}\right)\right]$$

$$s^2 = \left(\dfrac{1}{dn}\right) \sum\limits_{i=1}^{n} \left[\ln\left(\dfrac{P_i}{P_{i-1}}\right) - m\right]^2.$$

In order to estimate $T\mu$ and $T\sigma^2$, we would divide m and s^2 by d and multiply by T. For example, if we observe weekly data, then $d = \frac{1}{52}$ years; thus, we first calculate a sample variance for weekly data and multiply by 52 to obtain an estimate of the volatility. If we subsequently need to calculate the value of an option maturing in 90 days, we multiply the volatility by $T = \frac{90}{365}$ to obtain an estimate of the variance of $\ln(P(T)/S)$. It is worth noting that the formulas give only estimates of μ and σ^2; the true values remain unknown. To be precise, we should use different symbols (m and s^2) to distinguish the estimates derived in the above formulas from the true values, which are denoted μ and σ^2. Different methods of estimating these parameters could yield different values, although they should be close if based on samples taken at about the same time. (Symbols such as $\hat{\mu}$ and $\hat{\sigma}^2$ rather than m and s^2 are sometimes used to denote estimates of μ and σ^2.)

We collected ABC common stock prices for 14 consecutive weeks from July 2, 198X, through October 1, 198X. The prices and calculations of the sample mean and variance are shown in Table 15.1. The sample mean is not used explicitly in the Black/Scholes option pricing formula, a curious fact that we discuss later; it is used in the formula for $\sigma^2 T$ for convenience only. The sample variance of 0.0027 for our weekly data must be divided by $d = \frac{1}{52}$ to obtain the volatility σ^2. This leads to an estimate of

$$\sigma^2 = (52)(0.0027) = 0.1404$$

and

$$\sigma = 0.3747.$$

As of October 5, the Black/Scholes formula for the price of a call option on one share of ABC with a striking price of K = 30, expiring October 19, would be estimated as follows:

$$S = 33.125$$

$$K = 30$$

$$T = \tfrac{14}{365} = 0.0384$$

$$v = 1/(1.12)$$

Table 15.1   ABC Stock Prices, 198X

Week (1)	Date (2)	High (3)	Low (4)	Average (5)	ln(Price Ratio) (6)
0	7/02	29.375	28.750	29.063	0.033830
1	7/09	30.250	29.875	30.063	−0.068844
2	7/16	28.375	27.750	28.063	−0.020248
3	7/23	27.750	27.250	27.500	0.097374
4	7/30	30.500	30.125	30.313	0.103710
5	8/06	34.000	33.250	33.625	−0.003724
6	8/13	33.750	33.250	33.500	0.038431
7	8/20	35.250	34.375	34.813	0.040463
8	8/27	36.625	35.875	36.250	−0.049480
9	9/04	34.750	34.250	34.500	0.000000
10	9/10	36.750	34.250	34.500	0.042560
11	9/17	36.500	35.500	36.000	−0.049832
12	9/24	34.625	33.875	34.250	−0.018417
13	10/01	33.750	33.500	33.625	

$d = \frac{1}{52}$ $m = 0.572$
$dm = 0.011$ $s^2 = 0.1404$
$ds^2 = 0.0027$ $s = 0.3747$

$$v^T K = 30/(1.12)^{14/365} = 29.87$$

$$y = \left(\frac{1}{\sigma\sqrt{T}}\right) \ln\left(\frac{S}{v^T K}\right) + \frac{\sigma\sqrt{T}}{2}$$

$$= \left(\frac{1}{(0.3747)(0.0384)^{1/2}}\right) \ln\left(\frac{33.125}{29.87}\right) + \frac{(0.3747)(0.0384)^{1/2}}{2}$$

$$= \left(\frac{1}{0.0734}\right)(0.1034) + \frac{0.0734}{2}$$

$$= 1.44$$

$$y - \sigma\sqrt{T} = 1.37$$

$$\text{call}(S, T, K) = SN(y) - Kv^T N(y - \sigma\sqrt{T})$$

$$1.44 = 33.125N(1.44) - 29.87N(1.37).$$

The values $N(1.44)$ and $N(1.37)$ are obtained from Table 15.2:

$$N(1.44) = 0.9251 \text{ and } N(1.37) = 0.9147.$$

Hence, the Black/Scholes option pricing formula yields

$$\text{call}(T) = 33.125(0.9251) - 29.87(0.9147)$$

$$= \$3.32 \text{ per share.}$$

This is slightly higher than the price of $3 per share at which the option actually traded. We discuss the empirical evidence regarding the "fit" of the Black/Scholes model to observed option prices in Chapter 16.

Table 15.2 Cumulative Standard Unit Normal Distribution

z	.00	.01	.02	.03	.04	.05	.06	.07	.08	.09
.0	.5000	.5040	.5080	.5120	.5160	.5199	.5239	.5279	.5319	.5359
.1	.5398	.5438	.5478	.5517	.5557	.5596	.5636	.5675	.5714	.5753
.2	.5793	.5832	.5871	.5910	.5948	.5987	.6026	.6064	.6103	.6141
.3	.6179	.6217	.6255	.6293	.6331	.6368	.6406	.6443	.6480	.6517
.4	.6554	.6591	.6628	.6664	.6700	.6736	.6772	.6808	.6844	.6879
.5	.6915	.6950	.6985	.7019	.7054	.7088	.7123	.7157	.7190	.7224
.6	.7257	.7291	.7324	.7357	.7389	.7422	.7454	.7486	.7517	.7549
.7	.7580	.7611	.7642	.7673	.7704	.7734	.7764	.7794	.7823	.7852
.8	.7881	.7910	.7939	.7967	.7995	.8023	.8051	.8078	.8106	.8133
.9	.8159	.8186	.8212	.8238	.8264	.8289	.8315	.8340	.8365	.8389
1.0	.8413	.8438	.8461	.8485	.8508	.8531	.8554	.8577	.8599	.8621
1.1	.8643	.8665	.8686	.8708	.8729	.8749	.8770	.8790	.8810	.8830
1.2	.8849	.8869	.8888	.8907	.8925	.8944	.8962	.8980	.8997	.9015
1.3	.9032	.9049	.9066	.9082	.9099	.9115	.9131	.9147	.9162	.9177
1.4	.9192	.9207	.9222	.9236	.9251	.9265	.9279	.9292	.9306	.9319
1.5	.9332	.9345	.9357	.9370	.9382	.9394	.9406	.9418	.9429	.9441
1.6	.9452	.9463	.9474	.9484	.9495	.9505	.9515	.9525	.9535	.9545
1.7	.9554	.9564	.9573	.9582	.9591	.9599	.9608	.9616	.9625	.9633
1.8	.9641	.9649	.9656	.9664	.9671	.9678	.9686	.9693	.9699	.9706
1.9	.9713	.9719	.9726	.9732	.9738	.9744	.9750	.9756	.9761	.9767
2.0	.9772	.9778	.9783	.9788	.9793	.9798	.9803	.9808	.9812	.9817
2.1	.9821	.9826	.9830	.9834	.9838	.9842	.9846	.9850	.9854	.9857
2.2	.9861	.9864	.9868	.9871	.9875	.9878	.9881	.9884	.9887	.9890
2.3	.9893	.9896	.9898	.9901	.9904	.9906	.9909	.9911	.9913	.9916
2.4	.9918	.9920	.9922	.9925	.9927	.9929	.9931	.9932	.9934	.9936
2.5	.9938	.9940	.9941	.9943	.9945	.9946	.9948	.9949	.9951	.9952
2.6	.9953	.9955	.9956	.9957	.9959	.9960	.9961	.9962	.9963	.9964
2.7	.9965	.9966	.9967	.9968	.9969	.9970	.9971	.9972	.9973	.9974
2.8	.9974	.9975	.9976	.9977	.9977	.9978	.9979	.9979	.9980	.9981
2.9	.9981	.9982	.9982	.9983	.9984	.9984	.9985	.9985	.9986	.9986
3.0	.9987	.9987	.9987	.9988	.9988	.9989	.9989	.9989	.9990	.9990
3.1	.9990	.9991	.9991	.9991	.9992	.9992	.9992	.9992	.9993	.9993
3.2	.9993	.9993	.9994	.9994	.9994	.9994	.9994	.9995	.9995	.9995
3.3	.9995	.9995	.9995	.9996	.9996	.9996	.9996	.9996	.9996	.9997
3.4	.9997	.9997	.9997	.9997	.9997	.9997	.9997	.9997	.9997	.9998

Values of N(z) corresponding to z for the normal curve.

Source: Paul E. Green, *Analyzing Multivariate Data* (Hinsdale, Ill.: Dryden Press, 1978).

A Mathematical Review of Option Calculations Using a Personal Computer

A personal computer equipped with a spreadsheet program, such as an IBM PC with LOTUS 1-2-3 or an Apple Macintosh with Excel, makes calculating Black/Scholes call options fairly easy to do. The only difficulty for readers familiar with such a program might be calculating the cumulative normal density function $N(z)$ for the two values $z = y$ and $z = y - \sigma\sqrt{T}$. The problem is that $N(z)$ is not in the library of mathematical functions provided in spreadsheet programs. This can be overcome by using one of the Hastings approximations to $N(z)$ (Hastings, 1955; Abramovitz, 1965).

We illustrate here a method of calculating Black/Scholes call option values using the simplest of the Hastings approximations. It gives values of $N(z)$ accurate to at least four decimal places. The more complex formulas are even more accurate, but four places is sufficient for our purposes.

Our goal is to give formulas for calculating $call(S, T, K)$ given the values of S, T, K, σ, and r as described in the Black/Scholes equation. We have implemented this set of formulas on a personal computer with a spreadsheet program and believe that readers familiar with these programs will be able to do likewise.

Step 1.   Store the variables S, T, K, σ, and r in a range of cells.

Step 2.   Calculate

$$y = \frac{\ln(S/v^T K)}{\sigma\sqrt{T}} + \frac{\sigma\sqrt{T}}{2}.$$

The natural logarithm is available in the program library.

Step 3.   Store the following constants to be used in the Hastings approximation:
$p = 0.33267$
$a_1 = 0.4361836$
$a_2 = -0.1201676$
$a_3 = 0.9372980$

Step 4.   Calculate $Z(y)$ also to be used in the Hastings approximation.

$$Z(y) = \frac{1}{\sqrt{2\pi}\exp(y^2/2)}$$

The constant π and the exponential function are both in the program library.

Step 5.   If y is positive, let $t = 1/(1 + py)$, otherwise let $t = 1/(1 - py)$. Now calculate $N(y)$ using the Hastings formula

$$N(y) = 1 - Z(y)[a_1t + a_2t^2 + a_3t^3] \quad \text{for } y > 0$$

$$= Z(y)[a_1t + a_2t^2 + a_3t^3] \quad \text{for } y \leq 0.$$

Step 6. Repeat Steps 2 through 5 with y replaced by $y - \sigma\sqrt{T}$. This can be done by copying the corresponding range of cells to a new range and changing the formula in the y cell.

Step 7. Calculate $\text{call}(S, T, K) = SN(y) - K(1 + r)^{-T}N(y - \sigma\sqrt{T})$.

The program we have described has obvious practical uses. It can be made even more useful, for example, by calculating T given only the current date and the month of expiration. The spreadsheet date functions can be used to calculate the date of the third Friday of the expiration month. See the program written by Richard Reich, "New Uses for Excel," *MacUser* (December 1985): 41–44, for example. The program also has pedagogical value. It can be used to work many of the exercises at the end of this chapter. Graphs of $\text{call}(S, T, K)$ as functions of one of the values S, T, K, σ, or r with the others fixed could be easily produced on the computer screen. This makes it easy to determine how $\text{call}(S, T, K)$ changes as σ increases while the other variables are fixed.

Valuation of European Options

In this section, we develop a valuation model for European options. As we noted earlier, a European option can be exercised only at maturity, while an American option can be exercised at any time up to and including the maturity date. Thus, the European option is easier to value because we need consider only one possible exercise date. Consider a European option on a stock whose price at time t is denoted P(t) for $0 \leq t \leq T$. The option matures at time T. Our goal is to derive a formula for the value of the option at the current time, 0, in terms of quantities obtainable at that time: $S = P(0)$, r the risk-free interest rate, and parameters of the distribution of the random variables P(T) that we would estimate from observations of previous price movements. To further simplify the development of our option valuation formula, we assume that the stock pays *no* cash dividends within the interval $(0, T)$ and that P(T) has the following (binomial) probability distribution (which is assumed to be known at $t = 0$):

$$P(T) = P_u \text{ with probability } \pi \text{ (where } 0 < \pi < 1)$$

and

$$P(T) = P_d \text{ with probability } (1 - \pi).$$

The u and d subscripts represent "up" and "down," respectively. Later we will relax some of these assumptions.

Assumptions

To simplify the analysis, we will make the following assumptions:

1. All parties can invest or borrow at a riskless rate r per year, and r is assumed to be constant over the term of the option contract. Note, however, that interest rates are specified in terms of years even if converted more frequently, and $1 invested at the riskless rate r accumulates to $(1 + r)^T$ in T years.

2. There are no costs associated with exercising the option.

3. There are no riskless arbitrage opportunities (that is, there is no way to combine option contracts and the underlying stock into a portfolio that will produce a riskless profit).

4. The holder will exercise the option if it is profitable to do so.

5. There is no possibility of default on the contract.

6. It is possible to purchase and sell "fractions" of a security or asset.

7. The stock pays no dividends during the option's life.

Some of these assumptions, especially 1, 2, 6, and 7, obviously are unrealistic. Certainly interest rates *do* change over the term of an option contract, there *are* brokerage fees that must be paid when an option is purchased and when it is exercised, and securities and assets *cannot* be bought and sold in fractional amounts. Further, we are interested in options written on stocks with dividends due during the options' lives. Nevertheless, at this stage all of the above assumptions are necessary for simplifying the derivation of the option valuation equation. Once we have derived the model, we can evaluate the significance of these assumptions.

Binomial Option Pricing Model[2]

The value of a European call option, call(T), depends on r, K, T, P_u, P_d, S, and, apparently, π. Note too that it must be true that $(1 + r)^T S < P_u$; otherwise, there would be an opportunity for a riskless arbitrage. In other words, if the preceding inequality were turned around, investors could sell the stock for S and invest the proceeds to earn the riskless rate r and receive greater end-of-period wealth than they could by investing in the risky stock (that is, $(1 + r)^T S - P(T) > 0$ with probability 1 at time T). On the other hand, if $(1 + r)^T S < P_d$, the stock would outperform a riskless investment with probability 1. Again this would allow a riskless arbitrage profit, as follows: Borrow S dollars and buy the stock at t = 0, yielding a return $P(T) - (1 + r)^T S > 0$ at time T. Thus, the absence of riskless arbitrage requires that the following condition hold for S, P_u, P_d, and r:

$$P_d < (1 + r)^T S < P_u.$$

---

[2]The following development follows Cox, Ross, and Rubinstein (1979).

If this condition is satisfied, there will be *no* riskless arbitrage opportunities involving borrowing and lending at r and buying and selling the stock.

We begin our discussion of the derivation of a valuation formula for the call option by considering its value at maturity, call(S, 0, K). At time T, the option will have a nonzero value *only* where $P(T) > K$, that is, where the stock's price exceeds the option's exercise price. If $P(T)$ exceeds K, the option holder can buy a share of stock from the option writer for K dollars and then sell it in the market for $P(T) > K$ dollars. In practice, the option writer simply pays the holder the difference, $P(T) - K$, to settle the contract. Therefore, at time T the value of the call option can be expressed as follows:

(15.1) $$\text{call}(P(T), 0, K) = \max(0, P(T) - K),$$

where $\max(a, b)$ is a function that takes on the value of the larger of the two arguments a and b. For the option to have value (in the context of our two-state example), K must be less than P_u. In addition, although it is not necessary, we will assume that $K > P_d$. Thus, call(S, T, K) is the value of a contract that at time T has value $(P_u - K)$ with probability π and value 0 with probability $(1 - \pi)$.

A Mathematical Review of max(x, y) and min(x, y) Operators

In describing the payoffs of put and call options, we utilize maximum and minimum operators. The operator $\max(x, y)$ denotes the larger of the values x or y, and $\min(x, y)$ denotes the smaller of x or y. In evaluating option values we will need to perform some elementary algebraic operations on expressions involving $\max(x, y)$ and $\min(x, y)$. Here we discuss two such operations, (1) adding or subtracting a constant from the arguments of the operators and (2) converting a max to a min or vice versa. In symbols, the two operations are as follows:

(i)
$$\max(x, y) - z = \max(x - z, y - z)$$
$$\min(x, y) - z = \min(x - z, y - z)$$

and

(ii)
$$\min(x, y) = -\max(-x, -y).$$

These relations are established by evaluating each side of the equations for each of the cases $x \leq y$ and $x > y$ and verifying that both sides are equal in each case. For example, if $x \leq y$, the left side of the first equation in (i) is

$$\max(x, y) - z = y - z.$$

To evaluate the right side when $x \leq y$, we note that $x - z \leq y - z$ and hence,

$$\max(x - y, y - z) = y - z.$$

Thus the two are equal if $x \leq y$. A similar analysis applies to the case $x > y$. This establishes the first equation above. The others are established similarly.

Now suppose that at time 0 an investor buys one share of stock and sells call options on x shares. The value of this portfolio at time 0, then, is

$$S - x \, \text{call}(T).$$

At time T, the value of the portfolio will be the following:

$$P_u - x(P_u - K) \text{ with probability } \pi \text{ if } P(T) = P_u$$

or

$$P_d \text{ with probability } 1 - \pi \text{ if } P(T) = P_d$$

Now suppose that x, the number of shares on which call options are sold or written, is chosen such that the investment has a time T value equal to P_d even if the price of the stock is P_u at time T; that is, x is selected such that the portfolio's payoff is the same whether the stock price at time T is P_u or P_d and, therefore, the portfolio is riskless. The reason for forming this riskless portfolio is that we can easily value its payoff by discounting it back to the present using the riskless interest rate. Given that we determine x so as to produce a certain or riskless payoff equal to P_d, that payoff must equal the following:

$$P_d = (1 + r)^T[S - x\,call(T)].$$

In addition, we know that in order for the payoff to equal P_d even where $P(T) = P_u$, the following expression must also hold:

$$P_d = P_u - x(P_u - K).$$

Solving this expression for the value of x produces the following:

$$x = \frac{P_u - P_d}{P_u - K}.$$

Therefore, by buying the stock for a price S and writing call options on x shares (defined above), the investor produces a "certain" or riskless return equal to P_d. Hence, investing $S - x\,call(T)$ in this "portfolio" produces a riskless end-of-period return of P_d and, consequently,

$$P_d = (1 + r)^T[S - x\,call(T)].$$

Solving this expression for call(T) and substituting the appropriate value of x (which produces the riskless portfolio return) produce the following option valuation model:

(15.2) $$call(S, T, K) = \left[S - \frac{P_d}{(1 + r)^T}\right]\left[\frac{P_u - K}{P_u - P_d}\right].$$

All the variables on the right-hand side of Equation 15.2 are known at $t = 0$. Thus, this formula is an effective means of calculating call(T). Exercise 15.1 illustrates its use.

Exercise 15.1:   Using the Binomial Option Pricing Formula (A)

Suppose that a stock selling for a current price of $S = \$33$ has an equal probability of selling for $32 or $38 at time T (which is 105 days, or $\frac{105}{365}$ years, hence). If the striking price on a European call option maturing at time T is $35 and the riskless interest rate is 10 percent, what is the value of the option today?

Solution.   Using the binomial option pricing formula (Equation 15.2), we can solve for call(T) as follows:

$$\text{call}(S, T, K) = \left(33 - \frac{32}{1.0278}\right)\left(\frac{38 - 35}{38 - 32}\right)$$

$$= \$0.9327 \text{ per share.}$$

Note that the riskless interest rate for the 105-day term of the option contract equals $(1 + 0.10)^{105/365} = 1.0278$. Thus, in the option valuation formula $(1 + r)^T = 1.0278$. An option contract on 100 shares of common stock would be worth $\$0.9327 \times 100$ shares $= \$93.27$.

Deriving a More General Option Valuation Model

In the preceding section, we derived the binomial option valuation model found in Equation 15.2:

(15.2) $$\text{call}(S, T, K) = \left[S - \frac{P_d}{(1 + r)^T}\right]\left[\frac{P_u - K}{P_u - P_d}\right].$$

For convenience, we assumed that the exercise price was greater than P_d. If it is not, the value of the call option maturing at time T (that is, the payoffs at t = T) is the following:

$$\text{call}(S, 0, K) = \begin{cases} P_u - K \text{ with probability } \pi \\ P_d - K \text{ with probability } 1 - \pi. \end{cases}$$

Correspondingly, buying the stock and selling x call options produces a portfolio with values at time T of

$$P_u - x(P_u - K) \text{ with probability } \pi$$

or

$$P_d - x(P_d - K) \text{ with probability } 1 - \pi.$$

Choosing x such that the portfolio values (payoffs) are equal makes the portfolio riskless. The riskless payoff from such a portfolio must equal $(1 + r)^T[S - \text{call}(S, 0, K)]$. Solving

$$P_u - x(P_u - K) = P_d - x(P_d - K)$$

for x, we see that x must equal 1 and the portfolio value must equal the exercise price, K, regardless of whether P(T) equals P_u or P_d. Hence, $K = (1 + r)^T [S - \text{call}(T)]$, and

(15.3) $$\text{call}(T) = S - \frac{K}{(1 + r)^T}.$$

We can combine both option valuation equations, 15.2 and 15.3, into one by using the function f defined for each real number z as $f(z) = \max(0, z - K)$. A portfolio constructed by buying one share of stock and selling x shares of the call option has one of the following values at time T:

$$P_u - xf(P_u) \text{ with probability } \pi$$

or

$$P_d - xf(P_d) \text{ with probability } 1 - \pi.$$

Since we have chosen x such that these two payoffs are equal, we can set them equal to each other and solve for the appropriate value of x as follows:

$$x = \frac{P_u - P_d}{f(P_u) - f(P_d)}.$$

The corresponding value of the portfolio, then, is the following:

$$\frac{P_d f(P_u) - P_u f(P_d)}{f(P_u) - f(P_d)}.$$

Since the portfolio was constructed to have a riskless return, the above return must also (by the no riskless arbitrage axiom) equal $(1 + r)^T[S - x\,\text{call}(T)]$. Equating these values and substituting for x provide us with the following general option valuation model:

$$(1 + r)^T[S - x\,\text{call}(T)] = \frac{P_d f(P_u) - P_u f(P_d)}{f(P_u) - f(P_d)}.$$

Solving for call(T), we get

$$\text{call}(T) = \frac{1}{x}\left[S - \frac{P_d f(P_u) - P_u f(P_d)}{(1 + r)^T(f(P_u) - f(P_d))}\right].$$

Letting $v = 1/(1 + r)$ and simplifying terms give

$$\text{call}(T) = \frac{[f(P_u) - f(P_d)]S - v^T[P_d f(P_u) - P_u f(P_d)]}{P_u - P_d}$$

or

$$\text{call}(T) = \frac{v^T\{[f(P_u) - f(P_d)]S(1 + r)^T - [P_d f(P_u) - P_u f(P_d)]\}}{P_u - P_d},$$

which can also be written as follows:

$$\text{call}(T) = \frac{v^T\{f(P_u)[S(1 + r)^T - P_d] + f(P_d)[P_u - S(1 + r)^T]\}}{P_u - P_d}.$$

Portfolios constructed in the above manner are called *hedges* or *hedge portfolios*. By construction, the payoff to such a hedge portfolio is riskless; thus, we were able to value the portfolio as a riskless asset.

Now we let $q_1 = [S(1 + r)^T - P_d]/(P_u - P_d)$. Earlier we observed that no riskless arbitrage implied that $P_d < (1 + r)^T S < P_u$ and, hence, $0 < q_1 < 1$. This allows us to interpret the valuation formula for the call option at time 0 as the expected discounted value of the option at time T. The expectation is calculated relative to the distribution determined by q_1 rather than π; that is, if the investor assumes $P(T)$ has the distribution

$$P(T) = \begin{cases} P_u \text{ with probability } q_1 \\ P_d \text{ with probability } 1 - q_1, \end{cases}$$

the value of the call option is simply

$$\text{call}(T) = v^T[f(P_u)q_1 + f(P_d)(1 - q_1)].$$

Substituting

$$E[f(P(T))] = f(P_u)q_1 + f(P_d)(1 - q_1),$$

we derive our general option pricing model:

(15.4)
$$\text{call}(S, T, K) = \frac{E[f(P(T))]}{(1 + r)^T}$$

$$= v^T E[f(P(T))]$$

$$= v^T[f(P_u)q_1 + f(P_d)(1 - q_1)],$$

where, $q_1 = [S(1 + r)^T - P_d]/(P_u - P_d)$, $v = 1/(1 + r)$, and $f(P(T)) = \max(0, P(T) - K)$. Note that the value of the call option simply equals its expected payoff when discounted at the riskless rate, r. In the option pricing literature, this type of valuation model is referred to as a *risk-neutral valuation relationship* — that is, the value of a risky call option is found by discounting its expected payoff back to the present using the riskless interest rate. Hence, the option is valued "as if" it were risk neutral. We are able to do this because we have set up a "riskless" hedge portfolio, determined its value, and, based on that value (which is the present value of the riskless payoff discounted to the present at the riskless rate), derived the option's value.

We can view the risk-neutral valuation of an option in yet another way. Consider the interpretation of the parameter q_1. Imagine that investors are concerned only with expected discounted future values calculated at time 0; specifically, they are *indifferent* toward variance from expected values (that is, they are risk neutral). Since there are no riskless arbitrage opportunities, all investments of the same initial amount must have the same discounted expected values. In other words, if all investors are risk neutral, all investments will be valued based on the present values of their expected end-of-period payoffs. Further, where there are no opportunities for riskless arbitrage, all risky assets with the same current value will also have the same expected payoffs. Supposing that investors continue to use a one-price-change model with parameter π for $P(T)$, we find that $S = v^T[\pi P_u + (1 - \pi)P_d]$ because all investors view buying one share of stock as being the same as investing the price of a share of stock in bonds having the same expected payoff.

Solving this equation for π gives $\pi = q_1$; thus, q_1 is the parameter of the distribution that investors would use if they were all indifferent to risk (to variance of return on investment).

Valuing a European Put and the Distribution of P(T)

In this section we demonstrate that the value of a European put or call option, under the conditions stated above, does *not* depend *explicitly* on the distribution that investors choose for modeling the value of the underlying asset. Recall that $f(P(T)) = \max(0, P(T) - K)$ equals $P(T) - K$ if $K < P_d$. Thus, $E[f(P(T))] = E[P(T) - K] = E[P(T)] - K = q_1 P_u + (1 - q_1)P_d - K = (1 + r)^T S - K$, and the formula reduces to $\text{call}(S, T, K) = S - Kv^T$. In the case of $P_d < K < P_u$, it reduces to $\text{call}(S, T, K) = q_1(P_u - K)v^T$. Of course, the value is zero if K exceeds P_u.

  The above argument is quite general in that we could replace $f(z) = \max(0, z - K)$ by any real function $g(z)$ for which $g(P_d) \neq g(P_u)$ and for which there is a market value W at time 0 for the asset whose return at time T is $g[P(T)]$. In such circumstances, we must have

$$W = v^T E[g(P(T))]$$

$$= v^T[q_1 g(P_u) + (1 - q_1)g(P_d)],$$

where $q_1 = [S(1 + r)^T - P_d]/(P_u - P_d)$. Note that the hedge distribution does not depend on the function $g(z)$. Taking $g(z) = \max(0, K - P(T))$, for example, we see that $g[P(T)]$ is the value of a European put that expires at time T. Hence, the value of a European put at time 0 is

(15.5) $$\text{put}(S, T, K) = v^T E[\max(0, K - P(T))],$$

where the expectation is calculated using the distribution of risk-neutral investors. Equivalently, but using other symbols,

$$\text{put}(S, T, K) = v^T\{\max(0, K - P_u)q_1 + \max(0, K - P_d)(1 - q_1)\}$$

or,

$$\text{put}(S, T, K) = \begin{cases} v^T K - S & \text{if } K > P_u \\ v^T(K - P_d)(1 - q_1) & \text{if } P_d \leq K \leq P_u \\ 0 & \text{if } K < P_d. \end{cases}$$

Exercise 15.2:   Using the Binomial Option Pricing Formula (B)

We will use our general formulas to find the values of the call and put options corresponding to the data in Exercise 15.1 as follows:

$P_u = 38$

$P_d = 32$

$S = 33$, $S(1 + r)^T = 33(1.10)^{105/365} = 33.9173$

$q_1 = (33.9173 - 32)/(38 - 32) = 0.3196$

$K = 35$

$$E[\max[P(T) - K, 0]] = (38 - 35)q_1 + 0(1 - q_1) = 0.95865.$$

$$\text{call}(T) = v^T E[\max[P(T) - K, 0]] = 0.9328, \quad \text{or} \quad \$93.28 \text{ per } 100 \text{ shares.}$$

$$E[\max[K - P(T), 0]] = 0(q_1) + (35 - 32)(1 - q_1) = 2.04135.$$

$$\text{put}(T) = v^T E[\max[K - P(T), 0]] = 1.9861, \quad \text{or} \quad \$198.61 \text{ per } 100 \text{ shares.}$$

Multiple Price Changes and Option Valuation

So far we have considered only one price change for the random price $P(T)$ of the underlying asset; that is, we have supposed that only two prices are possible at time T. In probabilistic terms, we could say that $P(T)$ had a binomial distribution with parameters $n = 1$ and q_1, namely, one trial with the probability of success (price increase) being q_1. Now we will allow more price changes. In order to do this but remain tractable, we will suppose that $P(T)$ results from $n = 2$ trials or price changes. On each trial, the probability of a price increase is q_2 and that of a price decrease is $1 - q_2$; the subscript 2 refers to the two price changes. Soon we will consider stocks that change n times in the interval $(0, T)$. The rates of change in prices are not annual but effective for T/n years. In order to be compatible and to simplify notation, we will let a_n be the riskless accumulation factor effective for T/n years, which is equivalent to r per annum—that is, $a_n = (1 + r)^{T/n}$. When there are two price changes $(n = 2)$, we will let u_2 and d_2 denote the price increase and decrease factors for the periods $(0, T/2)$ and $(T/2, T)$, respectively. At time T, two price changes will have occurred and the possible asset prices — values of $P(T)$ — will be

$u_2 d_2 S$ if one increase and one decrease occur

$d_2^2 S$ if two decreases occur

$u_2^2 S$ if two increases occur.

Note that the no-arbitrage axiom implies $d_2 < a_2 < u_2$, just as $P_d < (1 + r)^T S < P_u$ in the one-price-change case. We hope to determine the value $\text{call}(S, T, K)$ of a call option at time 0 by an argument analogous to the one-price-change model. In order to do this, we will assume that an investor can costlessly construct a hedge portfolio at times 0 and $T/2$ (just after observing the market price of the stock at each time) in order to maintain a riskless position by buying the stock and selling shares of the call option. We will assume that the first price occurs in the period $(0, T/2)$ and the second in $(T/2, T)$. At time T, the price $P(T)$ will change to $P(T) = u_2 P(T/2)$ or $P(T) = d_2 P(T/2)$. Therefore, given the price $P(T/2)$ at time $T/2$, the investor will be able to form hedge portfolios as in the model discussed earlier, since one price change occurs in the interval $(T/2, T)$. Using Equation 15.4, the value of the call option at time $T/2$ will be

$$\text{call}\left(P\left(\frac{T}{2}\right), \frac{T}{2}, K\right) = a_2^{-1}\left\{f\left(u_2 P\left(\frac{T}{2}\right)\right)q_2 + f\left(d_2 P\left(\frac{T}{2}\right)\right)(1 - q_2)\right\}$$

or

$$\text{call}\left(P\left(\frac{T}{2}\right), \frac{T}{2}, K\right) = v^{T/2} E\left\{f(P(T)) \,\bigg|\, P\left(\frac{T}{2}\right)\right\},$$

where we recall that

$v = 1/(1 + r)$
$r = $ effective interest rate per annum
$f(z) = \max(0, z - K)$
$q_2 = [a_2 P(T/2) - d_2 P(T/2)]/[u_2 P(T/2) - d_2 P(T/2)]$
$\quad = (a_2 - d_2)/(u_2 - d_2)$
$P(T/2) = $ stock price at time $T/2$

Note that q_2 is between 0 and 1 and can be interpreted as a probability just as we did for q_1 in the $n = 1$ case.

The value of the call option at time $T/2$ [call$(P(T/2), T/2, K)$] is one of two values depending on that of the underlying asset at that time, $P(T/2)$. Then call$(u_2 S, T/2, K)$ denotes the value given that $P(T/2) = u_2 S$ and call$(d_2 S, T/2, K)$ denotes the value given that $P(T/2) = d_2 S$. Now let us consider the formation of a riskless hedge portfolio comprised of the stock and call options. At time 0, the investor buys one share of the stock and issues x call options. The net investment at time 0, then, is $S - x\,\text{call}(S, T, K)$. At time $T/2$, the hedge portfolio is worth

$$P\left(\frac{T}{2}\right) - x\,\text{call}\left(P\left(\frac{T}{2}\right), \frac{T}{2}, K\right),$$

which in turn has one of two values:

$$u_2 S - x\,\text{call}\left(u_2 S, \frac{T}{2}, K\right)$$

or

$$d_2 S - x\,\text{call}\left(d_2 S, \frac{T}{2}, K\right).$$

Equating these values and solving for x give the investment in the call option such that the portfolio value at time $T/2$ is the same no matter what the stock price does (in other words, such that it will be riskless):

$$x = \frac{(u_2 - d_2)S}{\text{call}\left(u_2 S, \frac{T}{2}, K\right) - \text{call}\left(d_2 S, \frac{T}{2}, K\right)}.$$

Substituting x into either expression for the end-of-period payoffs gives their common value in terms of mid-period values:

$$u_2 S - x\,\text{call}\left(u_2 S, \frac{T}{2}, K\right) = u_2 S - \frac{(u_2 - d_2)S\,\text{call}\left(u_2 S, \frac{T}{2}, K\right)}{\text{call}\left(u_2 S, \frac{T}{2}, K\right) - \text{call}\left(d_2 S, \frac{T}{2}, K\right)}$$

$$= \frac{\left[d_2\text{call}\left(u_2 S, \frac{T}{2}, K\right) - u_2\text{call}\left(d_2 S, \frac{T}{2}, K\right)\right]S}{\text{call}\left(u_2 S, \frac{T}{2}, K\right) - \text{call}\left(d_2 S, \frac{T}{2}, K\right)}.$$

This value is obtained with certainty at time $T/2$ and thus must have the same time $T/2$ value as would result from investing $S - \text{call}(S, T, K)$ to earn the riskless rate. Hence, the present value of the riskless hedge portfolio also equals

$$a_2[S - x\,\text{call}(S, T, K)].$$

Setting the above value of the hedge portfolio equal to the value of the hedge portfolio's riskless period $T/2$ payoff and solving for $\text{call}(S, T, K)$ give the call valuation formula:

$$u_2 S - x\,\text{call}\left(u_2 S, \frac{T}{2}, K\right) = a_2[S - x\,\text{call}(S, T, K)]$$

and, hence,

$$x\left[a_2\text{call}(S, T, K) - \text{call}\left(u_2 S, \frac{T}{2}, K\right)\right] = (a_2 - u_2)S.$$

From this we see that

$$a_2\text{call}(S, T, K) = \text{call}\left(u_2 S, \frac{T}{2}, K\right) + x^{-1}(u_2 - a_2)S$$

$$= \text{call}\left(u_2 S, \frac{T}{2}, K\right) + \left[\text{call}\left(u_2 S, \frac{T}{2}, K\right)\right.$$

$$\left. - \text{call}\left(d_2 S, \frac{T}{2}, K\right)\right](1 - q_2)$$

$$= \text{call}\left(u_2 S, \frac{T}{2}, K\right)q_2 + \text{call}\left(d_2 S, \frac{T}{2}, K\right)(1 - q_2)$$

$$\text{call}(S, T, K) = v^{T/2}E\left[\text{call}\left(P\left(\frac{T}{2}\right), \frac{T}{2}, K\right)\right].$$

Substituting

$$\mathrm{call}\left(P\left(\frac{T}{2}\right), \frac{T}{2}, K\right) = v^{T/2}E\left[f(P(T)) \mid P\left(\frac{T}{2}\right)\right],$$

we find that

$$\mathrm{call}(S, T, K) = v^{T/2}E\left[\mathrm{call}\left(P\left(\frac{T}{2}\right), \frac{T}{2}, K\right)\right]$$

$$= v^{T/2}E\left[v^{T/2}E\left[f(P(T)) \mid P\left(\frac{T}{2}\right)\right]\right]$$

$$= v^T E\left[E\left[f[P(T)] \mid P\left(\frac{T}{2}\right)\right]\right]$$

or

(15.6) $$\mathrm{call}(S, T, K) = v^T E[f[P(T)]].$$

Thus, even in the case where there are two periods in which the price may change, the call option valuation equation, 15.4, continues to hold but with a different probability, q_2. Investors calculate the expected value of $f[P(T)]$ as if it were binomial with parameters $n = 2$ and $\pi = q_2 = [(1 + r)^{T/2} - d_2]/(u_2 - d_2)$ and discount the option's expected payoff using the riskless rate over the term of the option contract, T.

In the general case of n price changes during the period $[0, T]$, the price moves either up by a factor of u_n or down by a factor of d_n in each of n periods $[0, T/n], [T/n, 2T/n], [2T/n, 3T/n], \ldots, [(n - 1)T/n, T]$. The price at time T given that k increases and $n - k$ decreases occurred, is

$$P(T) = u_n^k d_n^{n-k} S,$$

where $P(0) = S$ is the price at time 0. The probability that $P(T)$ takes this value is $C_{n,k}\pi^k(1 - \pi)^{n-k}$, where $C_{n,k}$ denotes the binomial coefficient $n!/[(n - k)!\,k!]$ and $\pi = q_n = (a_n - d_n)/(u_n - d_n)$. We can think of an upward price movement as a "success" and a "trial" as a single price movement in one of the time intervals within T where the trials are statistically independent. This leads to a general binomial option price formula in the same way that we just discussed for $n = 1$ or 2. It is easier to write if we let $b(k; \pi, n)$ denote the probability that exactly k successes occur in n independent trials, with the probability of a success on one trial being π. Investors use the formula with $\pi = q_n$ where

$$q_n = \frac{a_n - d_n}{u_n - d_n}.$$

The formula for the valuation of a call option with multiple periods ($n \geq 1$) is

(15.6) $$\mathrm{call}(S, T, K) = v^T E[f[P(T)]],$$

which can be rewritten using the binomial probability distribution notation as follows:

$$\text{call}(S, T, K) = v^T \sum_{k=0}^{n} b(k; q_n, n) f(u_n^k d_n^{n-k} S)$$

or

(15.7) $$\text{call}(S, T, K) = v^T \sum_{k=0}^{n} b(k; q_n, n) \max(0, u_n^k d_n^{n-k} S - K).$$

This formula is particularly useful, for it can be rewritten in a form that is analogous to the Black/Scholes option pricing formula. Let $B(k; \pi, n)$ denote the binomial cumulative probability distribution with parameters π and n:

$$B(k; \pi, n) = \text{Prob}(k \text{ or fewer successes in n trials})$$

$$B(k; \pi, n) = \sum_{j=0}^{k} \text{Prob}(j \text{ successes})$$

$$B(k; \pi, n) = \sum_{j=0}^{k} b(j; \pi, n).$$

Writing all of the possible values of $P(T)$ in increasing order,

$$d_n^n S < d_n^{n-1} u_n S < d_n^{n-2} u_n^2 S < \dots,$$

would allow us to find the smallest value of j for which the option has positive value, that is, for which $d_n^{n-j} u_n^j S$ exceeds K. Letting z denote this integer,

$$\max(0, d_n^{n-j} u_n^j S - K) = 0 \quad \text{for } j < z$$

and

$$\max(0, d_n^{n-j} u_n^j S - K) = d_n^{n-j} u_n^j S - K \quad \text{for } j \geq z.$$

Substituting into the formula for $\text{call}(S, T, K)$, we get

$$\text{call}(S, T, K) = v^T \sum_{j=z}^{n} b(j; q_n, n) (d_n^{n-j} u_n^j S - K).$$

This breaks down into two summations:

$$\text{call}(S, T, K) = v^T \sum_{j=z}^{n} b(j; q_n, n) d_n^{n-j} u_n^j S - v^T \sum_{j=z}^{n} b(j; q_n, n) K$$

and the second summation reduces to

$$K v^T [1 - B(z - 1; q_n, n)],$$

$B(z - 1; q_n, n)$ being the probability that the stock price will fail to reach the striking price, K, at time T. The first summation can also be written as a binomial probability but with a parameter q_n' in place of q_n. The new parameter is obtained by moving $v^T = 1/a_n^n$ inside the summation and examining a term:

$$v^T b(k; q_n, n) u_n^k d_n^{n-k} = \left(\frac{1}{a_n^n}\right) C_{n,k} q_n^k (1 - q_n)^{n-k} u_n^k d_n^{n-k}$$

$$= C_{n,k} \left(\frac{q_n u_n}{a_n}\right)^k \left[\frac{(1 - q_n) d_n}{a_n}\right]^{n-k}.$$

Now let $q_n' = q_n u_n / a_n$. It can be shown that $1 - q_n' = (1 - q_n) d_n / a_n$ and that each term can be written as follows:

$$v^T b(k; q_n, n) u_n^k d_n^{n-k} = C_{n,k} (q_n')^k (1 - q_n')^{n-k} = b(k; q_n', n).$$

Hence, the first summation can be written as $S[1 - B(z - 1; q_n', n)]$. The general form of the binomial option pricing formula then becomes

(15.8) $\text{call}(S, T, K) = S[1 - B(z - 1; q_n', n)] - Kv^T[1 - B(z - 1; q_n, n)]$

$$= S\text{Prob}[P(T) \geq K | n \text{ and } q_n']$$

$$- Kv^T \text{Prob}[P(T) \geq K | n \text{ and } q_n],$$

where S = stock price at time 0
K = striking price at maturity
v = $1/(1 + r)$, r being the riskless annual interest rate
T = option's term
n = number of price changes
$q_n' = q_n u_n / a_n$
$q_n = (a_n - d_n)/(u_n - d_n)$, the probability of a price increase during T/n years as assessed by risk-neutral investors

Exercise 15.3 illustrates the $n = 1$ and $n = 2$ models.

Exercise 15.3:   Using the Binomial Option Pricing Formula with $n = 1$ and $n = 2$

The $n = 1$ Case

Suppose that a stock selling for a current price of $S = \$33$ will sell for $32 or $38 at time T (which is 105 days, or $\frac{105}{365}$ years, hence). If the striking price on a European call option maturing at time T is $K = \$35$ and the riskless interest rate is 10 percent, what is the value of the option today?

Solution.   Note that, as before, the riskless rate of interest for the 105-day term of the option contract equals 10 percent; thus, $a_1 = (1 + 0.10)^{105/365} = 1.0278$. In the option valuation formula, then, $v^T = 1/1.0278 = 0.973$. The possible values of $P(T)$ are 38 and 32; hence, $z = 1$ and $z - 1 = 0$. Now we must determine q_1 and q_1' so that we can find $B(0; q_1, n)$ and $B(0; q_1', n)$. Since $u_1 S = P_u$, $u_1 33 = 38$

and, hence, $u_1 = 38/33 = 1.1515$. Similarly, $d_1 S = P_d$ implies that $d_1 = 32/33 = 0.9697$. Now we obtain $q_1 = (1.0278 - 0.9697)/(1.1515 - 0.9697) = 0.3196$ and $q_1' = (0.3196)(1.1515)/(1.0278) = 0.3580$.

k	$b(k; q_1, 1)$	$B(k; q_1, 1)$	$b(k; q_1', 1)$	$B(k; q_1', 1)$
0	0.6804	0.6804	0.6420	0.6420
1	0.3196	1.0000	0.3580	1.0000

The general formula in this case gives

$$\text{call}(S, T, K) = S[1 - B(z - 1; q_1', n)] - Kv^T[1 - B(z - 1; q_1, n)]$$

$$= 33[1 - B(0; q_1', 1)] - 35(0.973)[1 - B(0; q_1, n)]$$

$$= 33[0.3580] - 35(0.973)(0.3196)$$

$$= 0.9300 .$$

This agrees, within round-off error, with the first calculation.

The n = 2 Case

Here we wish to determine the price of a European call option on a stock selling for a current price of $S = \$33$, expiring at time T (which is 105 days, or $\frac{105}{365}$ years, hence). The striking price is $K = \$35$, and the riskless interest rate is 10 percent per annum. Suppose that there are $n = 2$ stock price changes before the option expires. If the price increases, it does so at a T-year rate, semiannually, of 16 percent; if it decreases, the rate of decrease is 4 percent.

Solution.   Note that the riskless interest rate for the 105-day term of the option contract equals $(1 + 0.10)^{105/365} = 1.0278$. Thus, $v^T = 1/1.0278 = 0.9730$, and the effective rate per T/2 years, r_2, satisfies $1 + r_2 = a_2 = (1.0278)^{1/2} = 1.0138$. Using the binomial option pricing model developed in Equation 15.8, we solve for $\text{call}(S, T, K)$ as follows:

$$\text{call}(S, T, K) = S[1 - B(z - 1; q_2', 2)] - Kv^T[1 - B(z - 1; q_2, 2)]$$

$$= 33[1 - B(z - 1; q_2', 2)] - 35(0.973)[1 - B(z - 1; q_2, 2)] .$$

We still need z, q_2, and q_2'. Since $u_2^2 = (1 + 0.16/2)^2$, $u_2 = 1.08$ and, similarly, $d_2 = 0.98$. Hence, $q_2 = (1.0138 - 0.98)/(1.08 - 0.98) = 0.338$, and $q_2' = q_2(1.08)/(1.0138) = 0.360$. In order to determine z, we need to examine the possible values of P(T), which are

$$33d_2^2 = 33(0.98)^2 = 31.69$$

$$33d_2 u_2 = 33(0.98)(1.08) = 34.93$$

$$33u_2^2 = 33(1.08)^2 = 38.49 .$$

Therefore, the option has a positive value if there are $z = 2$ price increases, since P(T) exceeds $K = 35$ only for the value corresponding to 2 increases. To apply the formula, we need $B(z - 1; q'_2, 2)$ and $B(z - 1; q_2, 2)$. These values are as follows:

k	$b(k; q_2, 2)$	$B(k; q_2, 2)$	$b(k; q'_2, 2)$	$B(k; q'_2, 2)$
0	0.438	0.438	0.410	0.410
1	0.448	0.886	0.460	0.870
2	0.114	1.000	0.130	1.000

The price is

$$\text{call}(S, T, K) = S[1 - B(z - 1; q'_n, n)] - Kv^T[1 - B(z - 1; q_n, n)]$$

$$= 33[1 - B(1; q'_2, 2)] - 35(0.973)[1 - B(1; q_2, 2)]$$

$$= 33(1 - 0.870) - 35(0.973)(1 - 0.886)$$

$$= 33(0.130) - 35(0.973)(0.114)$$

$$= \$0.4077 \text{ per share, or } \$40.77 \text{ per contract of } 100 \text{ shares.}$$

Derivation of the Black/Scholes Option Pricing Model

Appendix 15A provides a rigorous derivation of the Black/Scholes formula. Its result is such that as an appropriate limit is taken with price changes becoming more frequent and smaller in magnitude, the binomial option pricing formula becomes

(15.9) $$\text{call}(S, T, K) = SN(y) - Kv^T N(y - \sigma\sqrt{T})$$

where $y = \left(\dfrac{1}{\sigma\sqrt{T}}\right)\ln\left(\dfrac{S}{v^T K}\right) + \dfrac{\sigma\sqrt{T}}{2}$

$v = 1/(1 + r)$, r being the riskless interest rate
S = current price of stock
K = striking price
T = term of option
$\sigma^2 T$ = variance in log/price ratio $\ln[P(T)/S]$

and $N(z)$ denotes the standard normal distribution function:

$$N(z) = (2\pi)^{-1/2} \int_{-\infty}^{z} \exp\left(\frac{-u^2}{2}\right) du \, .$$

The limit of the binomial probabilities in the binomial option pricing formula,

$$\text{call}(S, T, K) = S[1 - B(z - 1; q'_n, n)] - Kv^T[1 - B(z - 1; q_n, n)]$$

$$= S\text{Prob}[P(T) \geq K | n \text{ and } q'_n] - Kv^T \text{Prob}[P(T) \geq K | n \text{ and } q_n],$$

are the normal probabilities $N(y)$ and $N(y - \sigma\sqrt{T})$. According to the derivation in Appendix 15A, the parameters of the Black/Scholes and binomial models are related as follows:

$$u_n = \exp\left[\sigma\left(\frac{T}{n}\right)^{1/2}\right]$$

$$d_n = \exp\left[-\sigma\left(\frac{T}{n}\right)^{1/2}\right]$$

$$q_n = \frac{(1 + r)^{T/n} - d_n}{u_n - d_n},$$

and, letting

$$y^2 = \frac{T}{n} \quad \text{and} \quad \rho = \ln(1 + r),$$

we obtain

$$(1 + r)^{T/n} = \exp(\rho y^2)$$

$$q_n = \frac{\exp(\rho y^2) - \exp(-\sigma y)}{\exp(\sigma y) - \exp(-\sigma y)}$$

$$q_n' = \frac{\exp(\sigma y)q_n}{a_n} = \frac{\exp(\sigma y)q_n}{\exp(\rho y^2)}$$

$$= \frac{\exp(\sigma y) - \exp(-\rho y^2)}{\exp(\sigma y) - \exp(-\sigma y)}.$$

It can be shown using L'Hospital's rule, or the power series expansion,

$$\exp(h) = 1 + h + \frac{h^2}{2} + \ldots$$

that q_n tends to $\frac{1}{2}$ as n tends to infinity. Therefore, when we use the Black/Scholes model as an approximation to the binomial model, we accept the consequence that over a small time interval the price is as likely to go up as down. Similarly, it can be shown that the expected values of the binomial distributions tend to $T[\ln(1 + r) - \sigma^2/2]$ and the variances tend to $\sigma^2 T$ as n tends to infinity. That the mean, μT, of $\ln[P(T)/S]$ may not equal $T[\ln(1 + r) - \sigma^2/2]$ is curious but does not affect the calculation of the option value because it depends only on σ^2.

There is another way to look at this. Once we defined u_n and d_n, we determined the hedge probability, q_n:

$$q_n = \frac{(1 + r)^{T/n} - \exp\left[-\sigma\left(\frac{T}{n}\right)^{1/2}\right]}{\exp\left[\sigma\left(\frac{T}{n}\right)^{1/2}\right] - \exp\left[-\sigma\left(\frac{T}{n}\right)^{1/2}\right]}.$$

Since the binomial probability distributions are completely specified by the parameters n and q_n, so are the limiting distributions. We chose

$$u_n = \exp\left[\sigma\left(\frac{T}{n}\right)^{1/2}\right]$$

and

$$d_n = \exp\left[-\sigma\left(\frac{T}{n}\right)^{1/2}\right]$$

to ensure that the binomial variances would tend to $\sigma^2 T$. These specifications are in themselves sufficient to ensure convergence of the binomial means, but to $T[\ln(1 + r) - \sigma^2/2]$ rather than $T\mu$.

The Derivation of the Jump Process Option Pricing Model: A Mathematical Overview

Now we show how a different limit might occur as the price change intervals become increasingly smaller. Suppose that the probability of a price increase q_n in the interval of T/n years tends to 0 rather than $\frac{1}{2}$ as in the preceding section but in such a way that the expected number of increases is λT rather than infinity. We will assume that λ is estimated from observations of price movements. In this case (large n and small q), the binomial distribution tends to the Poisson distribution in the sense that the binomial probability $b(k; n, q_n)$ of k successes in n trials tends to the Poisson probability $p(k, \lambda T)$ of k successes in T years where

$$p(k, \lambda T) = \frac{e^{-\lambda T}(\lambda T)^k}{k!}$$

and $nq_n \to \lambda T$ as $n \to \infty$ (Feller [1968]).

We still must choose u_n and d_n and will make a choice that will ensure that the binomial variances converge to the Poisson distribution. One way is to require that for all n,

$$u_n = u \quad \text{and} \quad d_n = e^{-\xi T/n},$$

where ξ and u are to be determined subject to $\xi > 0$ and $u > 1$. We estimate the parameter u from observing price changes. Then, using $\ln(1 + r) = \rho$, $\delta_n = \ln(u)$, and $\epsilon_n = \xi T/n$, we see that

$$q_n = \frac{(1 + r)^{T/n} - d_n}{u_n - d_n}$$

$$= \frac{e^{\rho T/n} - e^{-\xi T/n}}{u - e^{-\xi T/n}},$$

which tends to zero as n tends to infinity (as we wish). In order to get a Poisson limit, we also require that $nq_n \to \lambda T$ as $n \to \infty$. It can be shown by L'Hospital's rule or by using the series expansions that

$$nq_n = \frac{e^{\rho T/n} - e^{-\xi T/n}}{\dfrac{u - e^{-\xi T/n}}{n}}$$

$$= \frac{T[\exp(\rho h) - \exp(-\xi h)]}{h[u - \exp(-\xi h)]}$$

(where $h = T/n$) tends to $T(\rho + \xi)/(u - 1)$. Thus, ξ is determined implicitly as a function of u and λ by

$$\lambda T = T\left(\frac{\rho + \xi}{u - 1}\right)$$

$$\lambda = \frac{\rho + \xi}{u - 1}$$

$$\xi = \lambda(u - 1) - \ln(1 + r).$$

Now $\Pr[\Sigma X_i(n) \geq x] = \Pr[u^J d_n^{n-J} \geq K/S] = \Pr[J \geq z_n]$, where J is the number of price increases in T years and

$$z_n = \frac{x + \xi T}{\ln(u) + \dfrac{\xi T}{n}}.$$

The z_n tends to $(x + \xi T)/\ln(u)$; thus, $\Pr[\Sigma X_i(n) \geq x]$ tends to $\Phi(z, \lambda T) = \Sigma p(j, \lambda T)$, where the sum is over those integers j greater than or equal to $z = (x + \xi T)/\ln(u)$ and $p(j, \lambda T) = e^{-\lambda T}(\lambda T)^j/j!$.

Since $q'_n = q_n u/(1 + r)^{T/n}$, then $nq'_n \to \lambda T u$. Thus, the limiting distribution of $\Pr[\Sigma X'_i(n) \geq x]$ is Poisson with parameter $\lambda' T = \lambda T u$. We therefore obtain the *jump process option pricing model* as the limiting approximation to the binomial formula:

$$\text{call}(S, T, K) = S\Pr[\Sigma X'_i(n) \geq x] - Kv^T \Pr[\Sigma X_i(n) \geq x]$$

(15.10) $$\text{call}(S, T, K) = S\Phi(z, \lambda T u) - Kv^T \Phi(z, \lambda T),$$

where λ = expected number of price changes per unit of time
          u = factor price increase
          $\xi = \lambda(u - 1)^2 - u \ln(1 + r)$

$$z = \frac{\ln\left(\dfrac{K}{S}\right) + \xi T}{\ln(u)}$$

$$\Phi(z, \lambda T) = \Sigma_{j \geq z} \frac{e^{-\lambda T}(\lambda T)^j}{j!}$$

          v = 1/(1 + r), r being the risk-free interest rate
          S = current price of stock
          K = striking price
          T = term of option

Put-Call Parity of European Options

Regardless of the nature of the probability distribution of the end-of-period price, $P(T)$, of the underlying asset, there is a relationship between the values of otherwise identical European call and put options. This relationship is referred to as *put-call parity*, because it permits the calculation of one value given the other. Let K be the common striking price of European put and call options to be exercised at time T. At time T, the value of the call option to its owner is

$$P(T) - K \quad \text{if } P(T) > K$$

$$0 \qquad\qquad \text{if } P(T) \leq K.$$

On the other hand, the value of the put to its owner is

$$0 \qquad\qquad \text{if } P(T) > K$$

$$K - P(T) \quad \text{if } P(T) \leq K.$$

These long positions are shown in Figures 15.5 and 15.6.

The value of the put to the other party, that is, of its short position, is

$$0 \qquad\qquad \text{if } P(T) > K$$

$$P(T) - K \quad \text{if } P(T) \leq K.$$

An investor holding a long position in the call and a short position in the put has the sum of their values. Hence, at time T such a holding has a value of

$$P(T) - K + 0 \quad \text{if } P(T) > K$$

$$0 + P(T) - K \quad \text{if } P(T) \leq K.$$

This shows that the total value of being long on a call and short on a put is always $P(T) - K$ regardless of the price distribution of the underlying asset at time T. A mathematical statement of this fact is

---

Figure 15.5   Call Option Value

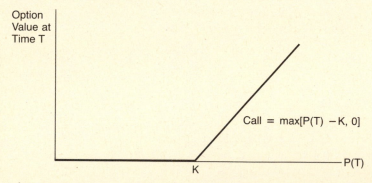

Figure 15.6   Put Option Value

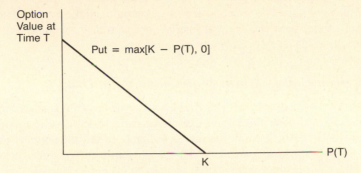

$$P(T) - K = \max[P(T) - K, 0] - \max[K - P(T), 0].$$

Rearrange this to obtain

$$P(T) - \max(P(T) - K, 0) = K - \max(K - P(T), 0).$$

The left side is the value at time T of a portfolio obtained at time 0 by selling one call option and buying one share of stock, for a total expenditure of $-S +$ call(S, T, K). The right side is the value at time T of a portfolio obtained by investing Kv^T at the riskless rate and selling one put option, for a total expenditure of $-Kv^T +$ put(S, T, K). Since the two portfolios have the same values at time T, regardless of how $P(T)$ turns out, by the no-riskless-arbitrage axiom, they must have the same values at time 0, giving $-S +$ call$(S, T, K) = -v^T K +$ put(S, T, K). Therefore, we must have

$$\text{put}(S, T, K) + S = \text{call}(S, T, K) + v^T K,$$

which gives a means of calculating values of European puts in terms of European calls. For European options, it suffices to value call options and use this put-call parity relation to determine put option values.

Valuation of American Options

Overview

From a practical standpoint, American options are far more important than European options because virtually all traded options — even those traded in Europe, Japan, Hong Kong, and so forth — are of the American type. However, analyzing American options is more complex because of the possibility that they will be exercised before the last possible exercise date. Of course, if all investors believe that a particular option's value exceeds the amount obtainable by exercising it early, they will all agree that it should be held up to the last possible moment. In this case, the market price will be the same as that given by the European option price formulas developed earlier. We will see that under the same assumptions, all investors will conclude that *call* options should be held up to the last possible moment and, consequently, have the same market value as otherwise identical European call options. The situation for *put* options is markedly different, as we will explain. First, however, we will justify our claim that American call options have the same value as their European counterparts.

An American Call Is Worth More Alive Than Dead[3]

In this section, we will see that the market value of an American call option is greater than the value obtained from exercising it (in which case it is "dead"). If the owner wanted cash, it would be more profitable to sell the contract (letting it continue to "live") than to exercise it. This is obviously the case for a call option that is slightly out of the money — that is, has an exercise value of zero because the current price, $P(t)$, is smaller than K, the striking price — since there is a positive probability that it will be in the money before it expires. However, this is true of all call options.

For a total investment of $call(P(t), T - t, K) + K(1 + r)^{-(T-t)}$ at time t, $0 < t < T$, an investor obtains

$$P(T) \quad \text{if } P(T) > K$$

$$K \quad \text{if } P(T) \leq K$$

at time T. In other words, buying a European option at time t to be exercised at time T and investing the discounted value of the striking price in a risk-free savings account yield an outcome that is always greater than the value of the underlying asset. By the no-arbitrage axiom, the current market value of the combination must be greater than that of the stock. Therefore,

$$call(P(t), T - t, K) + K(1 + r)^{-(T-t)} \geq P(t).$$

Of course, $K > K(1 + r)^{-(T-t)}$; thus,

$$call(P(t), T - t, K) + K > P(t).$$

As we noted earlier, the value of the American option, $Call(P(t), T - t, K)$, is not less than that of the corresponding European option, $call(P(t), T - t, K)$. Hence, for all values of $P(t)$,

$$Call(P(t), T - t, K) + K > P(t).$$

However, a sharper inequality holds if $K > P(t)$, because $Call(P(t), T - t, K)$ is nonnegative. Therefore, $Call(P(t), T - t, K) > P(t) - K$ if $P(t) > K$, and $Call(P(t), T - t, K) \geq 0$ even if $P(t) \leq K$. But the right-hand sides of these inequalities are the precise values of exercising the American option at time t: It will produce $P(t) - K$ for the holder if $P(t) > K$ and nothing otherwise. Therefore, the market value of an American call option is greater than or equal to the value obtained

---

[3]Much of the discussion in this section is based on Merton (1973).

from exercising it. No American call option holder will exercise the option to buy the underlying asset until the last possible moment. If the holder wants the cash $P(t) - K$ that exercising the option would provide, he or she will do better to sell it. It follows that American options are always held to maturity as if they were European options. This establishes our claim that the formulas for valuing European call options can be applied to American call options.

American Put Options

In this section, we develop a valuation model for American put options. As we noted earlier, investors will exercise European put and call options and American call options only at maturity. However, an American put option may be exercised at any time up to and including the maturity date, which makes it harder to value. We will return to the binomial option pricing model to develop a valuation technique for American puts. The technique presented here, which we have adapted from Parkinson (1977), is realistic. However, it requires a computer program for practical applications, because

1.   Real options are exercised only at discrete times rather than any time before maturity.

2.   The binomial option pricing model applies to options that can be exercised at a number of discrete times.

Exercise 15.4 illustrates the problem of valuing "semi-American" puts. The example suggests a general method for valuing American put options: For each n, calculate the price $Put_n(S, T, K)$ of a "semi-American" put, which can be exercised only at times $T/n, 2T/n, \ldots, T$. The value $Put(S, T, K)$ of the American put is the limit of the values $Put_n(S, T, K)$ of the otherwise identical semi-American puts as n approaches infinity. To calculate $Put_n(S, T, K)$, we proceed as in Exercise 15.4 — that is, we work backward from the end of the period to the beginning (a process called *backward induction*). The put will be alive at time $t_{n-1} = (n - 1)T/n$ provided that

$$Put_n\left(P\left(\frac{jT}{n}\right), T - \frac{jT}{n}, K\right) > \max\left[P\left(\frac{jT}{n}\right) - K, 0\right] \quad \text{for } j = 1, \ldots, n - 2$$

where $t_j = jT/n$. Therefore, its value, given that it is alive, will be

$$Put_n\left[P\left(\frac{(n - 1)T}{n}\right), \frac{T}{n}, K\right] = \max(P(t_{n-1}) - K, v^{T/n}E\{\max[K - P(T), 0]\}).$$

At time t_{n-2}, given that the put is alive, its value will be

$$Put_n\left[P\left(\frac{(n - 2)T}{n}\right), \frac{2T}{n}, K\right] = \max\left\{P(t_{n-2}) - K, v^{T/n}E\left[Put_n\left(\frac{(n - 1)T}{n}, \frac{T}{n}, K\right)\right]\right\}.$$

This follows from the general form of the one-period binomial option pricing formula. Continuing in this way, we obtain a finite sequence of recursive formulas that eventually will produce a value for $Put_n(S, T, K)$. For a large value of n, this will give a good approximation to $Put(S, T, K)$.

Exercise 15.4:   Using the Binomial Option Pricing Model for Puts

Consider the following stock data:

S = current price of stock = $33

T = maturity of option = $\frac{105}{365}$ years

K = striking price = $32

r = risk-free interest rate per annum = 10%

n = number of stock price changes before option expires = 2

$u_2 = 1.5$

$d_2 = 0.5$

$a_2 = (1.0278)^{1/2} = 1.0138$

$q_2 = (1.0138 - 0.5)/(1.5 - 0.5) = 0.5138$

Determine the value of a "semi-American" put, that is, a put option that can be exercised only at times 0, T/2, or T.

Solution.   At time $T/2$, the stock price will be either $33(1.5) = 49.50$ or $33(0.5) = 16.50$. If the option is not exercised at time $T/2$, it will become a contract that will be held to maturity; hence, the one-period general formula under the binomial option pricing model applies. Given $P(T/2) = 49.50$, we find that the value of holding the put for another period rather than exercising it is

$$v^{T/2}E[\max[K - P(T), 0] \mid P^{(T/2)} = 49.50]$$

$$= (0.9864)[(0.5138)(0) + (0.4862)(7.25)]$$

$$= 3.48 .$$

This exceeds the value (0) of exercising the option at time $T/2$ given that $P(T/2) = 49.50$. Hence, given that the price is 49.50 at $T/2$, the value of the put is

$$\text{put}\left(49.5, \frac{T}{2}, K\right) = \max(3.48, 0) = 3.48 .$$

If the stock decreases to 16.50 at time $T/2$, the value of waiting until time T to exercise it is

$$v^{T/2}E\left\{\max[K-P(T),0]\,|\,P\!\left(\frac{T}{2}\right)=16.50\right\}$$

$$= (0.9864)\,[(0.5138)\,(7.25)+(0.4862)\,(23.75)]$$

$$= 15.06\,.$$

Alternatively, the put contract can be exercised at time T/2, with the holder of the long position winning $32 - 16.50 = 15.50$ per share. Because this exceeds the value of waiting another period, it is the value of the put given that $P(T/2) = 16.50$. In other words,

$$\mathrm{put}\!\left(16.5,\frac{T}{2},K\right)=\max(15.06,15.50)=15.50\,.$$

The value of waiting a period at time 0 is

$$v^{T/2}E[\max[K-P(T/2),0]] = (0.\,9864)\,[(0.5138)\,(3.48)+(0.4862)\,(15.50)]$$

$$= 9.20\,.$$

This exceeds the value (0) of exercising the put immediately, Therefore,

$$\mathrm{put}(33,T,K)=\max(9.20,0)=9.20\,.$$

Figure 15.7 illustrates what is happening.

Figure 15.7   Possible Stock Prices and Their Probabilities[a]

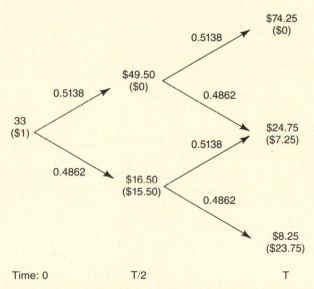

Time: 0   T/2   T

[a]The value when exercising a put with a striking price of 32 is shown in parentheses.

In order to apply this, we would have to program a computer to do the calculations. For a 90-day stock option, there would be 90 formulas to evaluate. In contrast, with call options we could use the Black/Scholes approximation and value them with one formula. There are alternative approaches. Geske and Johnson (1984) have established a formula for valuing American puts like the Black/Scholes formula. It requires a mathematical tool, stochastic calculus, which we have avoided. Their method, based on compound options, still requires a computer program for solutions, but such a program would be computationally more efficient than one based on backward programming. If stochastic calculus is used in developing the Black/Scholes formula, rather than the limit argument we presented, then the Geske/Johnson formula has a pedagogical advantage in that it follows from the same framework.

A third computational approach for valuing American puts based on approximating solutions to a second-order partial differential equation was developed by MacMillan (1986) for stocks that do not pay dividends. This approach, called quadratic approximation, still requires stochastic calculus for its development. Barone-Adesi and Whaley (1986) have shown that this technique can be used to approximate values of American put options on other assets or futures. The development of this approach to option valuation, including options on futures, is unified by Stoll and Whaley (1986). The quadratic approximation method is not as pleasing theoretically as the backward programming technique or the compound option (Geske/Johnson) approach, because, at least in theory, it produces only an approximate solution. However, in practical applications, the approximations are quite good, and the quadratic approximation computer programs are said to be one hundred times more efficient than programs based on the compound option method (Barone-Adesi/Whaley, 1986). We briefly describe this method in Appendix 15C.

Summary

In this chapter, we developed valuation formulas for European call and put options and American call options. Each formula is a discounted expected value. Both the discount rate and the probability distribution over which the expectation is made reflect risk neutrality; this is possible because under our assumptions about the market, investors can create hedge portfolios. We did not value options on stocks that might pay dividends during their lives; extensions of the formulas presented here can be used to calculate prices of such options.

The formulas for options on stocks with known dividend payment rates are a straightforward generalization of those we have presented. The Whaley/Stoll treatment includes this generalization. The valuation of options on stocks with random dividend payments is considered in Geske (1978).

Empirical studies have attempted to verify the various option pricing formulas. Although there are systematic biases in some—for example, the Black/Scholes call option formula—apparently these are not great. Options are so important in finance and these formulas are so easy to use that they have been widely accepted despite their flaws. Following is a summary of the option pricing formulas studied in this chapter.

Black/Scholes Formula for American or European Call Options

(15.9) $$\text{call}(S, T, K) = SN(y) - Kv^T N(y - \sigma\sqrt{T}),$$

where $y = \left(\dfrac{1}{\sigma\sqrt{T}}\right) \ln\left(\dfrac{S}{v^T K}\right) + \dfrac{\sigma\sqrt{T}}{2}$

$v = 1/(1 + r)$, r being the risk-free interest rate
S = current price of stock
K = striking price
T = term of option
$\sigma^2 T$ = variance in price at maturity
$N(z) = \Pr(Z \leq z)$, Z being a normal random variable with mean 0 and variance 1

Put-Call Parity

$$\text{put}(S, T, K) = v^T K - S + \text{call}(S, T, K)$$

Black/Scholes Formula for European Put Options

$$\text{put}(S, T, K) = Kv^T N(-y + \sigma\sqrt{T}) - SN(-y),$$

where the terms are defined in the same way as for call options.

Study Problems

15.1   A portfolio consists of two long call options, one with a striking price of $35 per share and the other with a striking price of $45 per share; both are written on the same stock. Each contract allows the owner to buy 100 shares. What is the exercise value of the portfolio if the stock price is
a. $30 per share?
b. $37 per share?
c. $48 per share?

15.2   A certain stock currently sells for $25 per share. At time T, it will sell for either $25.50 or $26.00 per share. Call options to hedge 100 shares with various striking prices are available. How many options should be purchased in order to create a perfect hedge (that is, a riskless portfolio) with a call option whose striking price is
a. $25.75?
b. $25?

15.3   The owner of 100 shares of a stock currently selling for $33 per share can sell for $100 a 90-day call option with a striking price of $35 per share. Cash can be invested at the risk-free rate of 7 percent per annum. What will be the value of the owner's portfolio at the end of the 90-day period (1) without selling the option and (2) selling the option if the stock price at the end of the period is

        a. $30 per share?
        b. $34 per share?
        c. $38 per share?
        d. $42 per share?

15.4   Consider the case of a buyer using the same data as in 15.3. What will be the value of the owner's portfolio at the end of the 90-day period (1) without buying the option and (2) buying the call option (instead of selling it) if the stock price at the end of the period is
        a. $30 per share?
        b. $34 per share?
        c. $38 per share?
        d. $42 per share?

15.5   For the one-period binomial options, we have $\text{call}(S, T, K) = v^T E[\max(0, P(T) - K)]$ and $\text{put}(S, T, K) = v^T E[\max(0, K - P(T)]$. Then show that put-call parity holds.

15.6   Use the Black/Scholes formula to calculate values of call options for $S = \$50$ per share, $T = 0.1667$ years, $r = 6\%$ per year, $\sigma = 0.3$ per year, and $K = \$45$, $\$50$, and $\$60$ per share. Sketch the graph of $\text{call}(50, 0.1667, K)$ as a function of K.

15.7   a. Use the Black/Scholes formula to calculate values of call options for $S = \$50$ per share, $T = 0.1667$ years, $r = 6\%$ per year, $K = \$25$ per share, and $\sigma = 0.25$, 0.5, and 0.75 per year. Sketch the graph of this option as a function of the volatility σ.
        b. Calculate part a after changing K to $50 per share.
        c. Calculate part a after changing K to $100 per share.

15.8   Calculate Problem 15.6 for put options instead of call options.

15.9   Calculate Problem 15.7 for put options instead of call options.

15.10   Investigate the behavior of the values given by the Black/Scholes formula for call options as the volatility changes but the other variables are fixed. Establish the following facts:
        a. If $S > v^T K$, then $\text{call}(S, T, K)$ approaches $S - v^T K$ as σ approaches 0.
        b. If $S \le v^T K$, then $\text{call}(S, T, K)$ approaches 0 as σ approaches 0.
        c. $\text{call}(S, T, K)$ approaches S as σ approaches $+\infty$.

15.11   Calculate Problem 15.10 for put options.

15.12   Investigate the behavior of the values given by the Black/Scholes formula for call options as the stock price S changes but the other variables are fixed. Establish the following facts:
        a. $\text{call}(S, T, K)$ tends to $+\infty$ as S tends to $+\infty$.
        b. $\text{call}(S, T, K)$ tends to 0 as S tends to 0.

15.13   Investigate the behavior of the values given by the Black/Scholes formula for call options as the exercise price K changes but the other variables are fixed. Establish the following facts:

      a. call(S, T, K) tends to S as K tends to 0.

      b. call(S, T, K) tends to 0 as K tends to $+\infty$. (Hint: See the L'Hospital's rule examples in the Mathematical Compendium.)

15.14 Calculate Problem 15.13 for put options.

15.15 Investigate the behavior of the values given by the Black/Scholes formula for call options as the risk-free interest rate r changes but the other variables are fixed. Establish the following facts:

      a. call(S, T, K) is an increasing function of r.

      b. call(S, T, K) approaches S as r approaches $+\infty$.

15.16 Calculate Problem 15.15 for put options.

15.17 Investigate the behavior of the values given by the Black/Scholes formula for call options as the term of the option T changes but the other variables are fixed. Establish the following facts:

      a. call(S, T, K) tends to S as T tends to $+\infty$.

      b. call(S, T, K) tends to max(0, S − K) as T tends to 0.

15.18 Calculate Problem 15.17 for put options.

References

M. Abramovitz and I. A. Stegun, *Handbook of Mathematical Functions* (Mineola, N.Y.: Dover, 1965).

G. Barone-Adesi and R. E. Whaley, "Efficient Analytic Approximation of American Option Values" (Working paper no. 15, Institute for Financial Research, University of Alberta. Forthcoming in *Journal of Finance*, June 1987).

F. Black and M. Scholes, "The Pricing of Options and Corporate Liabilities," *Journal of Political Economy* 81 (1973): 637–659.

J. Cox and S. Ross, "The Valuation of Options for Alternative Stochastic Processes," *Journal of Financial Economics* (January/March 1976): 145–166.

———— and M. Rubinstein, "Option Pricing: A Simplified Approach," *Journal of Financial Economics* (September 1979): 229–263.

W. Feller, *An Introduction to Probability Theory and Its Applications I* (New York: Wiley, 1968).

R. Geske, "The Pricing of Options with Stochastic Dividend Yield," *Journal of Finance* (May 1978): 617–625.

R. Geske and H. E. Johnson, "The American Put Option Valued Analytically," *Journal of Finance* 34 (December 1984): 1511–1524.

C. Hastings, Jr., *Approximations for Digital Computers* (Princeton, N.J.: Princeton University Press, 1955).

L. G. MacMillan, "Analytic Approximation for the American Put Option," *Advances in Futures and Options Research* (1986).

R. Merton, "Theory of Rational Option Pricing," *Bell Journal of Economics and Management Science* (Spring 1973): 141–183.

M. Parkinson, "Option Pricing: The American Put," *Journal of Business* (January 1977): 21–36.

R. Reich, "New Uses for Excel," *Mac User* (December 1985): 41–44.

H. R. Stoll and R. E. Whaley, "New Option Installments: Arbitrage Linkages and Valuations," *Advances in Futures and Options Research* (1986), 25–62.

Appendix 15A

Derivation of the Black/Scholes Option Pricing Model

According to the binomial option pricing model, the end-of-period price, $P(T)$, is given by $P(T) = Su_n^J d_n^{n-J}$, where J is the number of increases of the n possible price changes. J is a binomial random variable with parameters n and π. Let $\delta_n = \ln(u_n)$ and $\varepsilon_n = -\ln(d_n)$. Then

$$P(T) = S\exp[X_1(n) + X_2(n) + \ldots + X_n(n)],$$

where the $X_i(n)$'s are independent and distributed identically as

$$X(n) = \delta_n \qquad \text{with probability } \pi$$

$$X(n) = -\varepsilon_n \qquad \text{with probability } 1 - \pi.$$

Note that

$$E[X(n)] = \pi\delta_n - (1 - \pi)\varepsilon_n = \pi(\delta_n + \varepsilon_n) - \varepsilon_n$$

and

$$\text{Var}[X(n)] = \pi(1 - \pi)(\delta_n + \varepsilon_n)^2.$$

The binomial option pricing formula now can be rewritten in the following form:

$$\text{call}(S, T, K) = S\text{Pr}[P(T) \geq K \mid n, q_n'] - Kv^T\text{Pr}[P(T) \geq K \mid n, q_n]$$

$$= S\text{Pr}[\Sigma X_i'(n) \geq x] - Kv^T\text{Pr}[\Sigma X_i(n) \geq x],$$

where $x = \ln(K/S)$ and $X(n)$ and $X'(n)$ are determined by letting the binomial random variable have a probability of success, π, equal to q_n and q'_n, respectively. If the sums $\Sigma X_i(n)$ and $\Sigma X'_i(n)$ ($n = 1, 2, \ldots$) converge to limits Y and Y' in the sense that

$$\Pr[\Sigma X_i(n) \geq x] \to \Pr(Y \geq x)$$

and

$$\Pr[\Sigma X'_i(n) \geq x] \to \Pr(Y' \geq x) \quad \text{as } n \to \infty,$$

then, as an approximation for options on stocks whose prices change daily ($T/n = \frac{1}{365}$ years), we can use

$$\text{call}(S, T, K) = S\Pr(Y' \geq x) - Kv^T\Pr(Y \geq x).$$

Such a formula requires less work provided we can determine the limiting distributions and therefore is worth our consideration. We will first consider what Y is so that we may find Y'. In order to determine Y, we will examine how prices change.

There are in fact only two possible limits, Y, for the sequence of sums $\Sigma X_i(n)$. The first is the normal distribution and, in this case, the binomial option pricing formula tends toward the Black/Scholes option pricing formula. The second is the Poisson distribution, and the corresponding limit is called the jump process option pricing formula developed by Cox and Ross (1976). In the first model, the prices change frequently but by very small amounts, with the result that they are a continuous function of time. In the second model, the prices change relatively infrequently but by large amounts, resulting in prices that usually remain constant over time but occasionally jump to new levels (this is probably how the second formula got its name). However, this model is rarely used; almost all practical work is based on the Black/Scholes model.

Suppose that — perhaps based on our observations of prior price movements or our feelings about future ones — we can determine estimates of the mean and variance of the stock price $P(T)$ at time T. In principle, we could just as well estimate means and variances of logarithms of prices, which are more convenient to use. Thus, we assume that estimates of the mean and variance of $\ln(P(T))$ have been determined. The mean is traditionally written as the initial value plus the expected growth rate over the period:

$$E[\ln[P(T)]] = \ln(S) + \mu T.$$

The left-hand side might be estimated from sample observations of $\ln(P(T))$, for example. Since $\ln(S)$ is known, we can obtain an estimate of μ:

$$\mu = \left(\frac{1}{T}\right)(E[\ln(P(T))] - \ln(S)).$$

The variance is usually written as

$$\text{Var}[\ln(P(T))] = \sigma^2 T.$$

As before, we estimate the left-hand side from sample observations of $\ln(P(T))$ and determine σ^2 by dividing by T. If there are n opportunities for the price to change and the probability of a price change is $\pi = q_n$, then $\ln(P(T)) = \ln(S) + \Sigma X_i(n)$ and

$$E[\ln(P(T)) \mid \pi = q_n \text{ and n price changes}] = \ln(S) + E[\Sigma X_i(n)]$$
$$= \ln(S) + nE[X(n)].$$

Since

$$E[X(n)] = \pi\delta_n - (1 - \pi)\varepsilon_n = \pi(\delta_n + \varepsilon_n) - \varepsilon_n,$$

then

$$E[\ln(P(T)) \mid \pi = q_n \text{ and n price changes}] = \ln(S) + n[\pi(\delta_n + \varepsilon_n) - \varepsilon_n].$$

As n approaches infinity, this should converge.

We will see that once we have specified the limit of the variances, we can calculate the limit of the means. For the moment, we denote it by ν. In other words, as $n \to \infty$,

$$n[\pi(\delta_n + \varepsilon_n) - \varepsilon_n] \to \nu.$$

For the variance of the log of the price, we have

$$\text{Var}[\ln(P(T)) \mid \pi = q_n \text{ and n price changes}] = \text{Var}[\Sigma X_i(n)]$$
$$= n\text{Var}[X(n)].$$

We will specify that the limit be $\sigma^2 T$ as $n \to \infty$. Since

$$\text{Var}[X(n)] = q_n(1 - q_n)(\delta_n + \varepsilon_n)^2,$$

we must have

$$n[q_n(1 - q_n)(\delta_n + \varepsilon_n)^2] \to \sigma^2 T \text{ as } n \to \infty.$$

Now we introduce a possible choice for

$$\delta_n = \ln(u_n) \quad \text{and} \quad \varepsilon_n = -\ln(d_n),$$

which yields the Black/Scholes formula. Suppose that price changes occur such that each of the following holds:

1. $\delta_n = \varepsilon_n$ for all n.

2. $\delta_n = \sigma(T/n)^{1/2}$ for all n.

The first condition means that the logarithm of the rates of increase or decrease are equal — that is, the logarithms of the prices follow a "random walk." Note that the hedge probability, q_n, is determined once δ_n and ε_n are given, thus, the binomial distributions (and their limits) are too. We have completely specified the parameters even though we have not yet determined the mean of the limit. The above two conditions certainly lead to the limit variance $\sigma^2 T$, but not to a mean of μT. It turns out that the most we can require is that the variances tend toward $\sigma^2 T$ and that the means converge to something, which we denoted by ν. With the choice of δ_n and ε_n described above, the limit requirement for the means becomes

$$n\delta_n(2q_n - 1) \text{ converges to } \nu \text{ as } n \to \infty.$$

As a result, the means converge to $\nu = T[\ln(1 + r) - \sigma^2/2]$, not necessarily μT.

We can show this as follows. Each binomial random variable $X_i(n)$ has mean $\delta_n(2q_n - 1)$, and $n\delta_n(2q_n - 1)$ tends to ν. On the other hand, recalling that

$$\delta_n = \ln(u_n) \quad \text{and} \quad \varepsilon_n = -\ln(d_n)$$

and

$$q_n = \frac{(1 + r)^{T/n} - d_n}{u_n - d_n},$$

and letting

$$y^2 = \frac{T}{n} \quad \text{and} \quad \rho = \ln(1 + r),$$

we obtain

$$(1 + r)^{T/n} = \exp(\rho y^2)$$

$$u_n = \exp(\delta_n) = \exp\left(\sigma\left(\frac{T}{n}\right)^{1/2}\right) = \exp(\sigma y)$$

$$d_n = \exp(-\varepsilon_n) = \exp(-\delta_n) = \exp(-\sigma y)$$

and

$$n\delta_n(2q_n - 1) = \frac{T}{y^2}(\sigma y)\left[\frac{2[\exp(\rho y^2) - \exp(-\sigma y)]}{[\exp(\sigma y) - \exp(-\sigma y)]} - 1\right].$$

Thus,

$$n\delta_n(2q_n - 1) = \left(\frac{T\sigma}{y}\right)\left[\frac{2\exp(\rho y^2) - \exp(-\sigma y) - \exp(\sigma y)}{\exp(\sigma y) - \exp(-\sigma y)}\right].$$

Of course, as n tends toward infinity, $y = (T/n)^{1/2}$ approaches zero. By using L'Hospital's rule, or the series expansion

$$e^h = 1 + h + \frac{h^2}{2} + \dots,$$

it can be shown that as $y \to 0$, the expression on the right-hand side tends to $T(2\rho - \sigma^2)/2$. Hence, we must have

$$\nu = \frac{T[2 \ln(1 + r) - \sigma^2]}{2}.$$

Now the choice of δ_n equal to $\sigma(T/n)^{1/2}$ is derived by examining the limit requirements for the variances

$$n[q_n(1 - q_n)(\delta_n + \varepsilon_n)^2] \to \sigma^2 T \quad \text{as } n \to \infty.$$

For each n,

$$n[q_n(1 - q_n)(\delta_n + \varepsilon_n)^2] = 4nq_n(1 - q_n)\delta_n^2$$

because $\delta_n = \varepsilon_n$. Then, for large n, $2n\delta_n q_n$ is approximately $n\delta_n + \nu$ and $2\delta_n q_n$ is approximately $\delta_n + \nu/n$, because $n\delta_n(2q_n - 1)$ is approximately ν. Hence,

$$4nq_n(1 - q_n)\delta_n^2 = (2n\delta_n q_n)(2\delta_n - 2\delta_n q_n)$$

is approximately

$$2(n\delta_n + \nu)\left(2\delta_n - \delta_n - \frac{\nu}{n}\right),$$

which equals

$$n\delta_n^2 - \frac{\nu^2}{n},$$

and this must approach $\sigma^2 T$ as $n \to \infty$. Since $\nu^2/n \to 0$ as $n \to \infty$, we must have $n\delta_n^2 \to \sigma^2 T$ as $n \to \infty$. This makes $\delta_n = \sigma(T/n)^{1/2}$ a reasonable choice regardless of what the means converge to.

Now

$$\Pr[\Sigma X_i(n) \ge x] = \Pr[S_n \ge x_n],$$

where S_n is the sum of the standardized variables

$$\frac{X_i(n) - E[X(n)]}{\{Var[X(n)]\}^{1/2}}$$

and

$$x_n = \frac{x - n\delta_n(2q_n - 1)}{[q_n(1 - q_n)4\delta_n^2]^{1/2}}.$$

Note that

$$\frac{x_n}{\sqrt{n}} = \frac{x - n\delta_n(2q_n - 1)}{[nq_n(1 - q_n)4\delta_n^2]^{1/2}},$$

which tends toward $(x - \nu)/(\sigma^2 T)^{1/2}$ as n approaches infinity by the limit requirements for means and variances. Thus, $\Pr[S_n \ge x_n]$ tends toward $\Pr[S_n/\sqrt{n} \ge (x - \nu)/(\sigma\sqrt{T})]$ as $n \to \infty$. However, by the central limit theorem, $S_n/\sqrt{n}$ tends toward the standardized normal distribution as n approaches infinity (Feller [1968, p. 244]). Therefore, in the formula

$$call(S, T, K) = SPr[\Sigma X_i'(n) \ge x] - Kv^T Pr[\Sigma X_i(n) \ge x],$$

we can approximate $\Pr[\Sigma X_i(n) \geq x]$ by its limit. This leads to replacing $\Pr[\Sigma X_i(n) \geq x]$ with

$$\Pr[Z \geq z] = 1 - N(z),$$

where

$$z = \frac{x - \nu}{\sigma \sqrt{T}}$$

and $N(z)$ denotes the distribution function of Z, a standard normal random variable. Thus,

$$N(z) = (2\pi)^{-1/2} \int_{-\infty}^{z} \exp\left(\frac{-u^2}{2}\right) du .$$

We use the relation $\nu = T \ln(1 + r) - T\sigma^2/2$ to eliminate ν:

$$z = \frac{x - \nu}{\sigma \sqrt{T}}$$

$$= \frac{\ln\left(\dfrac{K}{S}\right) - T \ln(1 + r) + \dfrac{T\sigma^2}{2}}{\sigma \sqrt{T}}$$

$$= \frac{\ln\left(\dfrac{K}{S}\right) + \ln v^T}{\sigma \sqrt{T}} + \frac{\sigma \sqrt{T}}{2}$$

$$= \frac{\ln\left(\dfrac{Kv^T}{S}\right)}{\sigma \sqrt{T}} + \frac{\sigma \sqrt{T}}{2} .$$

The same argument applies to the limit of $\Pr[\Sigma X_i'(n) \geq x]$ as n tends toward infinity. We need only calculate the limit of

$$\frac{X_n'}{\sqrt{n}} = \frac{x - nE[X'(n)]}{\{nVar[X'(n)]\}^{1/2}} \quad \text{as } n \to \infty .$$

Since

$$nE[X'(n)] = n\delta_n(2q_n' - 1) = n\delta_n(2q_n - 1) + 2n\delta_n(q_n' - q_n)$$

and the first term tends toward ν, it suffices to evaluate the limit of $2n\delta_n(q_n' - q_n)$ as n approaches infinity. Using

$$q_n' = q_n \exp\left(\frac{\beta T}{n} - \sigma \sqrt{\frac{T}{n}}\right)$$

or

$$q_n' = q_n \exp(\beta y^2 - \sigma y)$$

where, as before, $y^2 = T/n$, and L'Hospital's rule, or the series expansion

$$e^h = 1 + h + \frac{h^2}{2} + \ldots,$$

it can be shown that $2n\delta_n(q_n' - q_n)$ tends toward $\sigma^2 T$ as n approaches infinity. Similarly, it can be shown that $n\text{Var}[X'(n)]$ tends toward $\sigma^2 T$. Hence, $x_n'/\sqrt{n}$ tends toward

$$\frac{x - \nu - \sigma^2 T}{\sigma\sqrt{T}} = \frac{x - \nu}{\sigma\sqrt{T}} - \sigma\sqrt{T}$$

$$= z - \sigma\sqrt{T}.$$

Thus, $\Pr[\Sigma X_i'(n) \geq x]$ tends toward $1 - N(z - \sigma\sqrt{T})$. Therefore, one limiting case of the binomial option pricing formula is

$$\text{call}(S, T, K) = S\Pr[\Sigma X_i'(n) \geq x] - Kv^T\Pr[\Sigma X_i(n) \geq x]$$

$$= S[1 - N(z - \sigma\sqrt{T})] - Kv^T[1 - N(z)].$$

We can obtain an equivalent form by using the fact that normal distribution is symmetric such that $1 - N(\zeta) = N(-\zeta)$ for all ζ. Thus, we finally obtain the Black/Scholes option pricing formula:

$$\text{call}(S, T, K) = SN(-z + \sigma\sqrt{T}) - Kv^T N(-z)$$

(15A.1) $$= SN(y) - Kv^T N(y - \sigma\sqrt{T}),$$

where $y = -z + \sigma\sqrt{T}$

$$= \left[\frac{\ln(S/Kv^T)}{\sigma\sqrt{T}} + \frac{\sigma\sqrt{T}}{2}\right]$$

$v = 1/(1 + r)$, r being the risk-free interest rate
S = current price of stock
K = striking price
T = maturity of option
$\sigma^2 T$ = current estimate of the variance in price at maturity

We repeat that it is unnecessary to estimate the mean, μT, of $\ln[P(T)/S]$, only its variance, $\sigma^2 T$, is required. It is also unnecessary to estimate the factors u_n and d_n, although we must assume that the stock price changes are small and very frequent.

References

F. Black and M. Scholes, "The Pricing of Options and Corporate Liabilities," *Journal of Political Economy* 81 (1973): 637–659.

J. Cox and S. Ross, "The Valuation of Options for Alternative Stochastic Processes," *Journal of Financial Economics* (January/March 1976): 45–166.

W. Feller, *An Introduction to Probability Theory and Its Applications I* (New York: Wiley, 1968).

Appendix 15B

Derivation of the Jump Process Option Pricing Model

Suppose that the probability of a price increase q_n in an interval of T/n years tends toward 0 rather than $\frac{1}{2}$ as in Appendix 15A but in such a way that the expected number of increases is λT rather than infinity. In this case (large n and small q), the binomial distribution tends toward the Poisson distribution in the sense that the binomial probability $b(k; n, q_n)$ of k successes in n trials tends toward the Poisson probability $p(k, \lambda T)$ of k successes in T years where

$$p(k, \lambda T) = \frac{e^{-\lambda T}(\lambda T)^k}{k!}$$

and $nq_n \to \lambda T$ as $n \to \infty$ (Feller [1966, p. 156]).

Since the limiting distribution is Poisson, its mean and variance are equal. Their common value is λT. In analogy with the development in Appendix 15A, we will choose values of u_n and d_n, which will allow $n \times q_n$ to tend to λT as n tends to infinity.

The following choice is similar to that suggested by Cox, Ross, and Rubinstein (1979):

$u_n = u$, where u is a constant greater than 1

$d_n = \exp(-\xi T/n)$, where ξ is a positive constant.

With these choices, we have

$$q_n = \frac{(1 + r)^{T/n} - d_n}{u_n - d_n}$$

$$= \frac{(1 + r)^{T/n} - \exp\left(-\dfrac{\xi T}{n}\right)}{u - \exp\left(-\dfrac{\xi T}{n}\right)}$$

$$= \frac{\exp(\rho y) - \exp(-\xi y)}{u - \exp(-\xi y)},$$

where $\rho = \ln(1 + r)$ and $y = T/n$ and, as required, q_n tends toward zero as n approaches infinity (equivalently, y tends toward zero from the right). This can be established using L'Hospital's rule, or the series expansion for exp(h). The requirement that $nq_n \rightarrow \lambda T$ as n tends toward infinity implies that

$$\frac{T[\exp(\rho y) - \exp(-\xi y)]}{y[u - \exp(-\xi y)]} \rightarrow \lambda T \quad \text{as } y \rightarrow 0^+.$$

However, calculating this limit, again using L'Hospital's rule, or the series expansion for exp(h), yields

$$\frac{T[\exp(\rho y) - \exp(-\xi y)]}{y[u - \exp(-\xi y)]} \rightarrow \frac{T(\rho + \xi)}{u - 1} \quad \text{as } y \rightarrow 0^+.$$

By the uniqueness of the limit, we know that

$$\lambda T = \frac{T(\rho + \xi)}{u - 1}$$

or

$$\lambda = \frac{\rho + \xi}{u - 1}.$$

Factors c and u might be estimated from observed price changes, and then λ would be determined by the above equations. Another approach would be to estimate λ (the frequency of price changes) and u (the rate of increase, given that a price increase occurs), then ξ would be determined by

$$\xi = \lambda(u - 1) - \rho.$$

Assuming the factors ξ and u have somehow been estimated, we obtained the limiting distribution as a function of the estimates.

Note that

$$Pr[\Sigma X_i(n) \geq x] = Pr[u^J d_n^{n-J} \geq x] = Pr[J \geq z_n],$$

where J is the number of price increases in T years and

$$z_n = [x + \xi T(1 - J/n)]/\ln(u).$$

The z_n tend toward $(x + \xi T)/\ln(u)$. Thus,

$$Pr[\Sigma X_i(n) \geq x] \text{ tends toward } \Phi(z, \lambda T) = \Sigma p(j, \lambda T),$$

where the sum is over those integers j greater than or equal to

$$z = (x + \xi T)/\ln(u).$$

Since

$$q'_n = q_n u/(1 + r)^{T/n},$$

then $nq'_n \to \lambda Tu$. Thus, the limiting distribution of $Pr[\Sigma X'_i(n) \geq x]$ is Poisson with parameter $\lambda' T = \lambda Tu$. Hence, we obtain the jump process option pricing model:

$$call(T) = SPr[\Sigma X'_i(n) \geq x] - Kv^T Pr[\Sigma X_i(n) \geq x]$$

or

(15B.1) $$call(T) = S\Phi(z, \lambda Tu) - Kv^T \Phi(z, \lambda T),$$

where

$$S = \text{current price of stock}$$

$$K = \text{striking price}$$

$$T = \text{maturity of option}$$

$$v = 1/(1 + r), \text{ r being the risk-free interest rate}$$

$$\lambda = \text{frequency of price changes}$$

$$u = \text{rate of price increase, given that a price change occurs}$$

$$\xi = \lambda(u - 1) - \ln(1 + r)$$

$$z = [\ln(S/K) + \xi T]/\ln(u)$$

$$\Phi(z, \lambda T) = \Sigma e^{-\lambda T}(\lambda T)^j/\text{all } j \geq z$$

References

J. Cox, S. Ross, and M. Rubinstein, "Option Pricing: A Simplified Approach," *Journal of Financial Economics* (September 1979): 229–263.

W. Feller, *An Introduction to Probability Theory and Its Applications I* (New York: Wiley, 1968).

Appendix 15C

Alternative Derivations of Option Values

A standard framework using stochastic calculus to derive option values has developed in the options literature. It was used by Merton (1973) and Black and Scholes (1973) for deriving call option prices, such as the Black/Scholes formula. Recently, Stoll and Whaley (1986) and Barone-Adesi and Whaley (1987) have used it to derive put option and futures option values. Hundreds of other papers on options use the same structure, sometimes implicitly.

Here, briefly, is the framework we are considering. (See the Mathematics Compendium for a review of stochastic calculus.)

1. The stock price S is described by a diffusion process. Its stochastic differential equation is given by

$$dS = \alpha S dt + \sigma S dz,$$

where α and σ are known constants and $z(t)$ is a standard Brownian motion.

2. We assume the risk-free interest rate per year, r, is constant. (The original model developed by Merton allows for a varying, indeed stochastic, default-free interest rate.) Let $B(t)$ denote the value of $1 invested at the risk-free rate for t years. Then $B(t) = (1 + r)^t$ also satisfies a differential equation:

$$dB = \ln(1 + r)(1 + r)^t dt$$
$$= \rho B(t) dt,$$

where we let $\rho = \ln(1 + r)$.

3.   The option that we are considering, but not specifying at this point, could be
a call or put, either European or American. However, its value must be determined by the market. By this we mean that there is a function $H(S, B, t)$
of three variables: the current price of the stock S, the bond price B, and the
current time t. Thus, if we want to value American puts we would assume

$$H(S, B, t) = Put(S, T - t, K)$$

for an option with term $T - t$ at time t, exercise price K, and current price S.

4.   There are no transactions costs, taxes, or dividends. Borrowing and short
sales are allowed at every instant of time.

The functional dependence of the option value on S, B, and t implies by
Itô's lemma that H also satisfies a stochastic differential equation:

$$dH = \frac{\partial H}{\partial S} dS + \frac{\partial H}{\partial B} dB + \frac{\partial H}{\partial t} dt + \frac{1}{2} \frac{\partial^2 H}{\partial S^2} (dS)^2$$

$$= \left(\frac{\partial H}{\partial S} \alpha S + \frac{\partial H}{\partial B} \mu B + \frac{\partial H}{\partial t} + \frac{1}{2} \sigma^2 S^2 \frac{\partial^2 H}{\partial S^2} \right) dt + \sigma S \frac{\partial H}{\partial S} dz.$$

Now we consider an arbitrage portfolio, that is, a portfolio having no initial investment, which is sustained entirely by trading (borrowing and short-selling to invest long). Let

w_1 = number of dollars invested in the stock,
w_2 = number of dollars invested in the option,
w_3 = number of dollars invested in the riskless asset.

Since this is an arbitrage portfolio, at every instant of time, $w_1 + w_2 + w_3 = 0$.
The investments w_1, w_2, and w_3 change continuously, and, hence, are stochastic
processes also. The value of the portfolio is

$$0 = w_1 + w_2 + w_3.$$

The number of shares of each asset is denoted $N_1 = w_1/S$, $N_2 = w_2/H$, and
$N_3 = w_3/B$. With this notation we have

$$0 = N_1 S + N_2 H + N_3 B.$$

Now we obtain the differential:

$$0 = N_1 dS + N_2 dH + N_3 dB + S dN_1 + H dN_2 + B dN_3$$

$$+ dN_1 dS + dN_2 dH + dN_3 dB.$$

The last six terms represent the net cash flow from non-capital-gains sources. The
usual approach is to add the assumption that they net to 0, although it is rarely
stated explicitly. This gives the differential for the portfolio's value as

$$0 = N_1 dS + N_2 dH + N_3 dB$$

$$= \frac{w_1}{S} dS + \frac{w_2}{H} dH + \frac{w_3}{B} dB.$$

Substituting in the differentials dS, dB, and dH gives

$$0 = \frac{w_1}{S}(\alpha Sdt + \sigma Sdz) + \frac{w_2}{H}(\mathscr{L}Hdt + \gamma Hdz) + \frac{w_3}{B}\rho Bdt,$$

where

$$\mathscr{L}H = \frac{1}{2}\sigma^2 S\frac{\partial^2 H}{\partial S^2} + \rho B\frac{\partial H}{\partial B} + \frac{\partial H}{\partial t} + \alpha S\frac{\partial H}{\partial S}$$

and

$$\gamma H = \sigma S\frac{\partial H}{\partial S}.$$

Rearranging terms gives

$$0 = (w_1\alpha + w_2\mathscr{L} + w_3\rho)dt + (w_1\sigma + w_2\gamma)dz.$$

The next step is to require that the trading be done so as to maintain a riskless portfolio. This means the diffusion coefficient should be 0. We now have two equations for w_1, w_2, and w_3:

$$w_1 + w_2 + w_3 = 0$$

$$w_1\sigma + w_2\gamma = 0.$$

Assume that w_1, w_2, and w_3 satisfy these two equations. Then Y is a risk-free arbitrage portfolio, hence its expected return is 0. This gives a third equation:

$$w_1\alpha + w_2\mathscr{L} + w_3\rho = 0.$$

The three equations

$$w_1 + w_2 + w_3 = 0,$$

$$\sigma w_1 + \gamma w_2 = 0,$$

and

$$\alpha w_1 + \mathscr{L}w_2 + \rho w_3 = 0$$

can be replaced by two equations in w_1 and w_2 by substituting $w_3 = -(w_1 + w_2)$:

$$\sigma w_1 + \gamma w_2 = 0$$

$$(\alpha - \rho)w_1 + (\mathscr{L} - \rho)w_2 = 0.$$

In order for this to have a non-zero solution, we must require that the determinant of this system be 0. Hence,

$$(\mathscr{L} - \rho)\sigma = (\alpha - \rho)\gamma.$$

Now, recalling that

$$\mathscr{L}H = \frac{1}{2}\sigma^2 S^2 \frac{\partial^2 H}{\partial S^2} + \rho B \frac{\partial H}{\partial B} + \frac{\partial H}{\partial t} + \alpha S \frac{\partial H}{\partial S}$$

and

$$H\gamma = \sigma S \frac{\partial H}{\partial S},$$

we find that

$$(\mathscr{L} - \rho)H\sigma = (\alpha - \rho)H\gamma$$

$$\mathscr{L}H - \rho H = (\alpha - \rho)\left(\frac{1}{\sigma}H\gamma\right)$$

$$= (\alpha - \rho)S\frac{\partial H}{\partial S}$$

$$\frac{1}{2}\sigma^2 S^2 \frac{\partial^2 H}{\partial S^2} + \rho B \frac{\partial H}{\partial B} + \frac{\partial H}{\partial t} + \alpha S \frac{\partial H}{\partial S} - \rho H - (\alpha - \rho)S\frac{\partial H}{\partial S} = 0$$

$$\frac{1}{2}\sigma^2 S^2 \frac{\partial^2 H}{\partial S^2} + \rho B \frac{\partial H}{\partial B} + \rho S \frac{\partial H}{\partial S} + \frac{\partial H}{\partial t} - \rho H = 0.$$

This is the differential equation for any of the option values: calls and puts, American or European, all satisfy it. The model developed in the text uses no functional dependence of H on B, that is, $\partial H/\partial B = 0$. This is also commonly assumed to be the case. This gives what has come to be known as the Black/Scholes equation for the option:

$$\frac{1}{2}\sigma^2 S^2 \frac{\partial^2 H}{\partial S^2} + \rho S \frac{\partial H}{\partial S} + \frac{\partial H}{\partial t} - \rho H = 0.$$

(Sometimes t is used to denote $T - t$, in which case $\partial H/\partial t$ would be replaced by $-\partial H/\partial t$.) The distinct solutions to the Black/Scholes equation are obtained by applying different boundary conditions. They are summarized in the following table.

Option Type	H	Boundary Condition
European Call	$H(S, t) = \text{call}(S, T - t, K)$	At $t = T$, $H(S, T) = \max(0, S - K)$ for all S.
American Call	$H(S, t) = \text{Call}(S, T - t, K)$	$H(S, t) = \max(H^*(S, t), S - K)$, where $H^*(S, t)$ denotes the value of the call option if it is not exercised and $H(S, T) = \max(0, S - K)$.
European Put	$H(S, t) = \text{put}(S, T - t, K)$	At $t = T$, $H(S, T) = \max(0, K - S)$.
American Put	$H(S, t) = \text{Put}(S, T - t, K)$	$H(S, t) = \max(H^*(S, t), K - S)$, where $H^*(S, t)$ denotes the value of the put option if it is not exercised and $H(S, T) = \max(0, K - S)$.

Technically, two boundary conditions are needed to solve the Black/Scholes differential equation. Only one is noted above, with the second being $H(0, T) = 0$ for calls. Intuitively, this second condition requires that if the stock has zero value (at any time T), the call option also has a value of zero. The condition for puts is analogous.

The Black/Scholes equation subject to the European call option boundary conditions can be solved by techniques developed to solve the heat equation of thermodynamics. See Merton (1973) for the details. The result, of course, is the Black/Scholes formula for European call options. This technique could also be used for European put options, but the put-call parity relation gives the European put in terms of the European call. There is no such relation for American options. Hence, even in the case where American call options have the same value as European call options, one still has to solve the Black/Scholes equation subject to the American put boundary conditions in order to value American put options. This has been done by Geske and Johnson (1984) and MacMillan (1986), using two quite different methods (called, respectively, compound option approximation and quadratic approximation). Barone-Adesi and Whaley (1987) used methods similar to MacMillan to value American futures options.

Here we briefly describe the quadratic approximation method. The details are in both of the last two papers cited; we are following the latter very closely. Begin by defining the exercise premium of the American put:

$$E(S, t) = Put(S, t^* - t, X) - put(S, t^* - t, X),$$

whose current price is S, term is $t^* - t$, and exercise price is X. Both put options satisfy the Black/Scholes equation, so $E(S, t)$ does as well:

$$\frac{1}{2}\sigma^2 S^2 \frac{\partial^2 E}{\partial S^2} - \rho E + \rho S \frac{\partial E}{\partial S} + \frac{\partial E}{\partial t} = 0.$$

Now we change time variables by setting $T = t^* - t$, so that $\partial E/\partial t = -\partial E/\partial T$. Also, we define $N = 2\rho/\sigma^2$. The Black/Scholes equation for E becomes

$$S^2 \frac{\partial^2 E}{\partial S^2} - NE + NS \frac{\partial E}{\partial S} - \frac{N}{\rho} \frac{\partial E}{\partial T} = 0.$$

The next step is to define

$$K = 1 - e^{-\rho T}$$

and

$$f(S, K) = \frac{E(S, T)}{K(T)}.$$

Then, since $E = Kf$, we find that

$$\frac{\partial^2 E}{\partial S^2} = K \frac{\partial^2 f}{\partial S^2},$$

$$\frac{\partial E}{\partial T} = f \frac{\partial K}{\partial T} + K \frac{\partial f}{\partial K} \frac{\partial K}{\partial T},$$

and, substituting into the Black/Scholes equation,

$$S^2 \frac{\partial^2 f}{\partial S^2} + NS \frac{\partial f}{\partial S} - \frac{N}{K} f - (1 - K)N \frac{\partial f}{\partial K} = 0.$$

The term $(1 - K)N(\partial f/\partial K)$ approaches 0 as T tends to 0 or $+\infty$. Hence, the approximate solution obtained by setting $(1 - K)N(\partial f/\partial K) = 0$ and solving

$$S^2\frac{\partial^2 f}{\partial S^2} + NS\frac{\partial f}{\partial S} - \frac{N}{K}f = 0$$

should be close to the true value for options with very long or very short terms to expiration. This is an ordinary differential equation, whose solution is well understood. This approximation is what Barone-Adesi and Whaley call the quadratic approximation. The result is the following solution. Here, very briefly, are the details.

Set $f = aS^q$ and substitute into the last equation.

$$S^2[aq(q - 1)S^{q-2}] + NS(aqS^{q-1}) - \frac{N}{K}aS^q = 0$$

$$aS^q\left[q(q - 1) + Nq - \frac{N}{K}\right] = 0$$

$$q^2 + (N - 1)q - \frac{N}{K} = 0.$$

The quadratic formula gives two values for q:

$$q_1 = \frac{-(N - 1) - \sqrt{(N - 1)^2 + 4(N/K)}}{2}$$

$$q_2 = \frac{-(N - 1) + \sqrt{(N - 1)^2 + 4(N/K)}}{2}.$$

The general solution is

$$f = a_1 S^{q_1} + a_2 S^{q_2},$$

where a_1 and a_2 are yet to be determined. Note too that $q_1 < 0$ and $q_2 > 0$. Our approximate solution for the American put is obtained as follows.

$$E(S, T) = Kf$$

$$Put(S, T, X) - put(S, T, X) = Kf$$

$$Put(S, T, X) = put(S, T, X) + K(a_1 S^{q_1} + a_2 S^{q_2}).$$

Since $Put(S, T, X) - put(S, T, X)$ approaches 0 as S tends to $+\infty$, we must set $a_2 = 0$. Thus, only a_1 and q_1 are of interest. We drop the subscript from the approximation to obtain

$$Put(S, T, X) = put(S, T, X) + KaS^q.$$

The approximation on the right-hand side will not work for small values of S since $q < 0$ and we must have $a > 0$. However, for large values it should work well. To determine the cut-off value of S, we set the right-hand side equal to the exercise value $X - S$ and solve for S. We denote the solution by S^*. Thus the two curves $X - S$ and $\text{put}(S, T, X) + KaS^q$ will intersect at $S = S^*$. The value of a will be determined so that the curves join smoothly at the point of intersection. Thus a and S^* will satisfy

$$\frac{\partial}{\partial S}(X - S) = \frac{\partial}{\partial S}[\text{put}(S, T, X) + KaS^q]$$

$$-1 = -e^{-\rho T}N(d_1 S^*) + Kaq(S^*)^{q-1}$$

$$a = \frac{-[1 - e^{-\rho T}N(d_1 S^*)]}{Kq(S^*)^{q-1}}$$

and

$$X - S^* = \text{put}(S^*, T, X) + Ka(S^*)^q.$$

The result is the following approximation.

Quadratic Approximation to the American Put Option Value

$$\text{Put}(S, T, X) = \text{put}(S, T, X) + A\left(\frac{S}{S^*}\right)^q \quad \text{if } S > S^*$$

$$\text{Put}(S, T, X) = X - S \qquad\qquad\qquad \text{if } S \le S^*,$$

where S $=$ current stock price
   T $=$ term to expiration
   X $=$ exercise price
   $q = -\dfrac{(N - 1) - \sqrt{(N - 1)^2 + 4(N/K)}}{2}$
   $K = 1 - e^{-\rho T}$
   $N = 2\rho/\sigma$
   $\rho = \ln(1 + r)$ where r is the riskless interest rate
   $A = -\left(\dfrac{S^*}{q}\right)[1 - e^{-\rho T}N(-d)]$
   $d = \dfrac{1}{\sigma\sqrt{T}}\ln(S^*(1 + r)^T/x) + \dfrac{\sigma\sqrt{T}}{2}$

and S^* is determined by solving the following equation iteratively:

$$X - S^* = \text{put}(S^*, T, X) - \frac{[1 - e^{-\rho T}N(-d_1)]S^*}{q}.$$

References

G. Barone-Adesi and R. E. Whaley, "Efficient Analytic Approximation of American Futures Option Values," *Journal of Finance* (Forthcoming, June 1987).

R. Geske and H. E. Johnson, "The American Put Valued Analytically," *Journal of Finance* 39 (December 1984): 1511–1524.

L. W. MacMillan, "Analytic Approximation for the American Put Option," *Advances in Futures and Options Research* 1 (September 1986).

R. C. Merton, "The Theory of Rational Option Pricing," *Bell Journal of Economics and Management Science* 4 (Spring 1973): 141–183.

H. R. Stoll and R. E. Whaley, "New Option Instruments: Arbitrage Linkages and Valuation," *Advances in Futures and Options Research* 1 (Part A): 25–62.

Chapter 16

Option Pricing:
Evidence and Applications to
Corporate Financial Policy

In Chapter 15, we discussed the theory underlying the pricing of options on stocks. In this chapter, we survey the empirical tests of option pricing models as well as the application of option pricing theory to the evaluation of corporate securities and capital investments. With respect to the former, we find that the Black/ Scholes (1973) model fits observed option price data surprisingly well, although it tends to misprice at- or in-the-money options.[1] In addition, we demonstrate the applicability of option pricing theory to both bond and stock valuation. The literature generally refers to this particular application as *contingent claims analysis*.[2] Finally, we note the usefulness of contingent claims analysis in the characterization and evaluation of capital budgeting projects. This topic has gained increasing importance in the corporate finance literature, where it is now recognized that many capital investment opportunities contain option components (such as the option to abandon a project if it proves to be less profitable than anticipated or a purchase option on a leased asset).

This chapter is organized as follows. First, we present the empirical evidence on the predictive capabilities of extant option pricing models. With a few exceptions, this literature involves tests of the original Black/Scholes (1973)

---

[1]A call option is "in the money" when its exercise value is positive. For a discussion of option terminology, see "An Institutional Note: Options Jargon" in Chapter 15.

[2]A contingent claim is simply a security whose payoff depends on the value of one or more other securities.

497

model. Next, we discuss the use of contingent claims analysis for a wide range of corporate finance problems. This type of analysis is of relatively recent origin and is primarily of a conceptual rather than analytical nature.

Review of Empirical Tests of Option Pricing Theories

A number of attempts have been made to verify the predictive power of the various option pricing models that have appeared in the finance literature. In this section we review some of those papers, recognizing that their number far exceeds the scope of this text. The majority of the empirical tests have focused on the original Black/Scholes model, although the more recent ones have compared it with its present-day counterparts.

The Black and Scholes Tests (1972)

Black and Scholes (1972) used price data on over-the-counter option prices to test their model's usefulness in predicting call option prices. The data spanned contracts written on a total of 545 securities during the period 1966 through 1969. Black and Scholes used their option pricing model to estimate the options' theoretical values and compared these with the observed market prices of the option contracts to identify overvalued and undervalued options. They then combined the options with shares of the underlying stocks so as to produce a risk-free hedge portfolio. They then revised the individual stock/option hedge portfolios daily in order to maintain the risk-free hedge. In brief, they found that option buyers paid prices that were consistently higher than the formula price, while option writers received prices that were roughly equal to the predicted price. In addition, they found that the difference between the price paid by option buyers and the formula price was greatest for options on low-risk stocks. However, after considering transactions costs, they concluded that abnormal profits were not available to market speculators.

The Galai (1977) and Bhattacharya (1980) Studies

Galai (1977) tested the efficiency of the CBOE using option price data for the period April 26, 1973, through November 30, 1973. Data were available for 152 trading days, with 245 options written on 32 underlying stocks, and the entire sample contained a total of 16,327 option prices. Galai recognized the fact that testing for the efficiency of the CBOE involves joint hypotheses, that is, testing for both the efficiency of the market and the appropriateness of the option pricing formula being used to generate "efficient market option prices." Galai *assumed* that the Black/Scholes (1973) model was the appropriate one and proceeded to test for the efficiency of the CBOE. He found that "after considering transactions costs, significant 'excess' profits could not be earned by trading on the CBOE." Specifically, Galai found that non–CBOE members could not expect consistent above-normal profits. In addition, he found that market maker excess returns were statistically insignificant, although they did demonstrate a strong tendency to be positive.

Bhattacharya (1980) performed a set of tests on the Black/Scholes model in an attempt to control for the joint hypothesis problem encountered when testing for option market efficiency. Further, he observed that in addition to option market efficiency and the appropriateness of the particular pricing formula being used, market efficiency tests involve estimating the parameters of the pricing formula. Therefore, a test of option market efficiency involves testing three hypotheses jointly:

1.   The structural form of the option pricing formula

2.   The measurement of the inputs of the model

3.   The efficiency of the option market.

Bhattacharya proposed a test methodology that controlled for hypotheses 2 and 3 to permit testing of the structural form of the Black/Scholes model under ideal conditions. In his tests he observed that the model exhibited a systematic bias in the pricing of call options. However, except for at-the-money options with only one day to maturity, the magnitude of the bias was "operationally" insignificant. Operational significance was defined as a return of 70 cents per contract per day, which was the estimated transactions cost (see Rendleman and Carabini [1979]).

The MacBeth and Merville (1979) and Beckers (1980) Studies

MacBeth and Merville (1979) and Beckers (1980) compared the Black/Scholes model with the Cox and Ross (1976) constant elasticity of variance diffusion process model. The practical difference in these two option pricing models is that the Black/Scholes model assumes the variance in the returns of the underlying stock is a constant while the Cox/Ross model allows the variance to "vary" with the stock price level.

The MacBeth and Merville study utilized data on all options traded on the CBOE for six companies (AT&T, Avon, Eastman Kodak, Exxon, IBM, and Xerox) during the period December 31, 1975, through December 31, 1976. They concluded that stock prices indeed appear to be generated by a constant elasticity of variance diffusion process[3] and that the Cox/Ross model fits the market prices of options better than does the Black/Scholes model.

Beckers (1980) tested whether the variance of stock returns was constant using over 1,200 daily stock prices observed for the period September 18, 1972, through September 7, 1977. This test resulted in a rejection of the hypothesis of a constant variance and indicated that the variance was an inverse function of stock price for the majority of the stocks used. An analysis of the constant elasticity of variance model revealed that its prices were higher than the Black/Scholes prices

---

[3]The constant elasticity of variance model represents one assumption about how the variance in price changes might vary with the level of the underlying stock's price. In particular, it assumes that the instantaneous variance in the stock's rate of return at time t, $\sigma(P, t)$ equals σP^r, where σ is a constant and the superscript r is a constant less than 1. This class of stochastic processes has the property that the elasticity of the variance is a constant, r, that is, $(d\sigma/dP)(P/\sigma) = r$. The square root process is a special case of the constant elasticity of variance model where $r = \frac{1}{2}$. Also, the Black/Scholes model is built on the assumption that $r = 1$ such that the variance in dP/P is equal to a constant, σ.

for in-the-money and at-the-money options. Since other researchers have found similar deviations, Beckers suggested that the constant elasticity of variance model may provide a reasonable alternative to the Black/Scholes model.

The Ball and Torous (1985) Test of the Merton (1976) Jump Process Model

A number of studies have documented the systematic biases of the Black/Scholes model. The Merton (1976) option pricing model specifically admits the existence of "jumps" or discontinuities in the returns of the stocks underlying options and offers the potential for eliminating the biases of the Black/Scholes model.

Ball and Torous (1985) examined the daily common stock returns of 30 NYSE firms and confirmed the existence of statistically significant jumps in the majority. However, when they estimated the prices of the call options on these same stocks, they found no statistically significant difference in the option prices! Thus, it appears that stock returns are characterized by a jump diffusion process; however, the relatively high frequency and low intensity of the jumps observed by Ball and Torous suggest that the Black/Scholes model fits the data about as well as does the Merton jump process model. The authors did point out, however, that the returns of other securities on which options are written may be more appropriately described by large and infrequent jumps and, consequently, their option prices more accurately described by the Merton model.

The Klemkosky and Resnick (1979) Test of Put-Call Parity

Klemkosky and Resnick (1979) investigated the efficiency of the CBOE with regard to the relative pricing of put and call options on the same securities. Specifically, they exploited the theoretical relationship that must hold in an efficient market between the prices of puts and calls on the same stock and with the same maturity and exercise price (we review the basic put-call parity theorem in the next section). The authors constructed a set of tests based on long and short hedges, utilizing puts and calls on 15 companies whose options were listed on the CBOE, the AMEX, and the Philadelphia Stock Exchange. The period of study spanned July 1977 through July 1978, and a total of 606 long and short hedges were constructed, with the total number of observations per company varying from 16 to 68.

An analysis of the "profitability" of the hedge portfolios revealed that approximately 57 percent of the long hedges appeared unprofitable and 43 percent profitable and of the short hedges, 55 percent appeared profitable. Klemkosky and Resnick conjectured that the difference in the proportion of profitable long versus short hedges reflects the converter's burden of risk in undertaking a short rather than long conversion. They concluded that the small degree of inefficiency detected in their tests was a result of overpriced call options.

Rubinstein's (1985) Nonparametric Tests of Alternative Option Pricing Models

Rubinstein utilized a large sample of option price data comprised of virtually all reported trades and quotes on the CBOE for the period August 23, 1976, through

August 31, 1978. With these data he was able to test seven competing option pricing models based on the following six option pricing theories: (1) the original Black/Scholes (1973) model, (2) the Cox/Ross (1975) pure jump model, (3) the Merton (1976) mixed diffusion–jump model, (4) the Cox/Ross (1976) constant elasticity of variance diffusion model, (5) the Geske (1979) compound option diffusion model, and (6) the Rubinstein (1983) displaced diffusion model.[4]

The important results of his tests included the following:

1. Short maturity out-of-the-money options were priced significantly higher relative to other options than the Black/Scholes model would have predicted.

2. Striking price biases relative to the Black/Scholes model were also statistically significant but reversed themselves after long time periods.[5]

3. None of the option pricing models tested were able to explain the reversal in the striking price biases.

Rubinstein concluded that none of the models tested were able to explain all the observations over time. He suggested a need for an explanation of structural changes in the ability of a particular model to explain option prices using macroeconomic variables such as the level of stock prices in general or interest rates. Obviously much work remains in developing a reliable predictor of call option prices.

Applications of Option Pricing Theory to Corporate Finance

Option pricing theory constitutes one of the primary theoretical paradigms in finance. Since the publication of the Black/Scholes model in 1973, the use of option pricing formulas by practitioners and financial theorists has spread dramatically. Option pricing theory has become an increasingly important framework in which to address corporate finance problems, specifically those related to the valuation of corporate assets and liabilities. In fact, Black and Scholes noted in their 1973 work that corporate securities may be viewed as options (or "contingent claims") on the value of the firm, as the title of their paper suggests.

Contingent Claims Analysis

In general, a contingent claim is a security whose payoffs depend on the prices of one or more other securities. Thus, a stock option is a contingent claim whose value depends on the price of the stock on which it is written. *Contingent claims*

---

[4]Models 2 and 3 modify the Black/Scholes model to allow for jumps or discontinuities in the stochastic process used to describe stock price changes over time. The last three models relax the constant variance assumption of the Black/Scholes model.

[5]The striking price bias phenomenon relates to the observed relationship between an option's striking or exercise price and its implied volatility. The implied variance is computed by substituting the current market price of an option in an option pricing model and then solving for the implicit variance in stock returns.

analysis, then, is the general term for the techniques used to value options and other securities whose payoffs depend on the values of other assets or securities.

We will consider two types of applications of contingent claims analysis to corporate finance: (1) the pricing of corporate securities (including debt and equity) and (2) the evaluation of capital investment opportunities. Throughout our discussion we will eschew the presentation of proofs and/or option pricing formulas (Chapter 15 formally discusses the theoretical underpinnings of these formulas). This will permit us to focus on the "intuition" behind the use of contingent claims analyses in addressing corporate finance problems.

Review of the Basic Concepts of Option Pricing

Before discussing the application of contingent claims analysis to financial management, we will review the basic characteristics of call and put option contracts. First, an American call option provides its owner with the right to purchase one share of stock with current price $P(0)$, at an exercise price K, on or before the contract's expiration date T periods hence. We refer to the value of such an option with the notation $Call(P(0), T, K)$. This has been explained in Chapter 15. For example, $Call(P(T), 0, K)$ represents the value of an American call option on a stock whose current price is $P(T)$ dollars and that matures today (that is, $t = T$ such that there are 0 days until the expiration date) with an exercise price of K. Further, recall that the value of a call option at maturity equals its payoff, which can be expressed as

$$Call(P(T), 0, K) = max(0, P(T) - K),$$

where $max(a, b)$ refers to the maximum value of either a or b as discussed in Chapter 15. In this case, the value of the call option at expiration equals the maximum of the difference in the price of the underlying stock on that date and the exercise price and zero. If $P(T) < K$ the option has no value, and if the inequality is reversed the option's value equals $P(T) - K$. Note too that the values of the American and European call options are the same on date T. Recall that we refer to a European call option using a lowercase c; that is, where $t = T$,

$$\underbrace{Call(P(T), 0, K)}_{\substack{\text{American} \\ \text{call}}} = \underbrace{call(P(T), 0, K)}_{\substack{\text{European} \\ \text{call}}}.$$

(Merton [1973] demonstrated that for non-dividend-paying stocks the values of American and European call options are equal at earlier times as well.)

An American put option gives the owner the right to sell one share of stock for an exercise price K at or before the contract's maturity date T periods hence. We will use $Put(P(0), T, K)$ to refer to such an option contract. Thus, at maturity, $t = T$, the value of the put contract is

$$Put(P(T), 0, K) = max(0, K - P(T)).$$

Hence, the put option contract "pays off" when things go poorly for the stock, that is, when $P(T) < K$. In this sense, a put option is like insurance. Note too that the values of the American put and its European counterpart (denoted "Put" and "put," respectively) are the same at expiration: $Put(P(T), 0, K) = put(P(T), 0, K)$.

We need review only one additional concept before proceeding to apply contingent claims analysis to corporate finance: put-call parity. *Put-call parity* is simply the relationship that exists between the values of European put and call options written on the same stock and having identical expiration dates and exercise prices. To see this relationship, suppose that we create a portfolio consisting of one share of stock and one put option on that share and sell (short) a call option. The portfolio "payoff" at expiration, then, will appear as follows:

$$\underbrace{P(T)}_{1} + \underbrace{\max(0, K - P(T))}_{2} - \underbrace{\max(0, P(T) - K)}_{3},$$

where term 1 is the price of stock when the option is exercised, term 2 is the payoff on the put option, and term 3 is the payoff on the call option. Note that both options have the same expiration date and exercise price.

We now demonstrate that this portfolio's combined expiration date payoff equals the exercise price, K, regardless of the value of the underlying stock on that date (that is, the portfolio's payoff is riskless). If we evaluate the portfolio payoff where $P(T) < K$, we find that

$$P(T) + K - P(T) - 0 = K.$$

Further, in the remaining case, where $P(T) \geq K$, the portfolio's payoff also equals K:

$$P(T) + 0 - P(T) + K = K.$$

Thus, no matter what the state of the world when the option expires $(t = T)$, the portfolio's payoff will be the same and, consequently, risk free. Using discrete compounding and a risk-free rate r, the value of the portfolio today can be defined as follows:

$$P(0) + put(P(0), T, K) - call(P(0), T, K) = Kv^{T}.$$

Note that each term on the left-hand side of the above equation is the current or present market value of the payoff from the portfolio at time $t = T$; that is, the first term represents the current market price of the share of stock, the second the current market value of the put, and the third the current market value of the call. Note also that $Kv^{T} = K/(1 + r)^{T}$ where r is the risk-free rate of interest. Solving for the current value of the call option produces the following:

$$call(P(0), T, K) = P(0) + put(P(0), T, K) - Kv^{T}.$$

Alternatively, the difference in the value of a call and put option can be calculated based on observable values:

(16.1) $$call(P(0), T, K) - put(P(0), T, K) = P(0) - Kv^{T}.$$

This relationship between the values of put and call options is the put-call parity theorem for European options. It will prove very helpful when we consider the use of option pricing theory in evaluating corporate securities.

Valuation of Discount Bonds: A Mathematical Overview

The value of a discount bond (that is, one which pays no interest until maturity) can be stated in terms of a portfolio of options using the $\max(x, y)$ and $\min(x, y)$ operators. Recall the following two relationships, which were discussed in "A Mathematical Review of $\max(x, y)$ and $\min(x, y)$ Operators" in Chapter 15:

(i) $$-\min(x, y) = \max(-x, -y)$$
(ii) $$\min(x, y) - y = \min(x - y, 0).$$

Using these two simple rules for manipulating max and min operators, we can "rearrange" the payoffs from complex corporate securities so as to be able to recognize the options or contingent claims that make up those securities' payoffs. For example, the payoff at maturity of a firm's zero coupon (discount) bonds, $D(T)$, is

(iii) $$D(T) = \min[B(T), V(T)],$$

where $B(T)$ is the face value of the bonds at time T, when they are due, and $V(T)$ is the time T value of the firm's assets. The intuition behind this expression for the value of the firm's discount bonds is straightforward. If the value of the firm's assets equals or exceeds the face value of its debt obligations — that is, $V(T) \geq B(T)$ — the bondholders will receive full repayment. If the value of the firm's assets is less than its debt obligations, the bondholders will receive $V(T)$. We can rearrange this payoff structure by first adding and subtracting $B(T)$ to the bond payoff on the right-hand side of (iii):

$$D(T) = B(T) + \min[0, V(T) - B(T)].$$

Further, if we convert the min expression to its max equivalent, we get the following:

(iv) $$D(T) = B(T) - \max[B(T) - V(T), 0].$$

We recognize the first term on the right-hand side of (iv) as the payoff on the firm's debt if it were risk free. The second term represents a put option on the value of the firm's assets with an exercise price equal to the face value of its debt, $B(T)$. In other words, if at time T the value of the firm's assets, $V(T)$, is less than the face value of its debt, $B(T)$, the put option will pay the holder the difference, $B(T) - V(T)$. Thus, the payoff on the firm's risky debt, $D(T)$, can be thought of as a combination of the payoff on its debt if it were risk free less the payoff on a put option on the value of the firm's assets with an exercise price equal to its debt obligation. The current value of the firm's risky debt, then, can be thought of as the value of a risk-free bond with face value $B(T)$ minus the value of the put with payoff equal to $\max[B(T) - V(T), 0]$.

Pricing of Corporate Securities

Traditional discussions of security valuation treat the valuation of the firm's individual securities as independent problems; that is, the valuation of a firm's bonds would be discussed in terms of the present value of the principal and interest payments to the bondholders, while the same firm's equity would be valued in terms of the present value of expected dividends. The contingent claims approach to security valuation differs in that it approaches the valuation of *all* of the firm's classes of securities simultaneously. Specifically, bonds, stocks, and hybrid combinations of the two (such as convertibles) are all valued in terms of the value placed on the assets of the firm as a whole. The key point here is that the values of the firm's securities are all "contingent" on the value of its assets or investments. Hence, with contingent claims analysis all of the firm's securities are valued simultaneously.[6]

Common Stock as a Contingent Claim.   Consider a firm that issues discount bonds that mature in T periods and require a cash payment of B(T) dollars. If the value of the firm's assets at time T equals V(T), the value of its equity in year T is

$$P(T) = \max[V(T) - B(T), 0].$$

We recognize this as a payoff of a call option on the value of the firm's assets having an exercise price equal to the face value of the firm's discount bonds, B(T), and an expiration date T periods hence. Thus, in the simple example used here (where the firm issues zero coupon bonds), the current value of the firm's equity, P(0), can be represented by a European call option as follows:

(16.2) $$P(0) = call(V(0), T, B(T)).$$

In keeping with the objective of this chapter, we will not seek an explicit valuation relationship for the options we identify. We will seek only to explain the many ways in which contingent claims analysis can be used to enhance our understanding of corporate finance problems.

Valuing Discount (Zero Coupon) Bonds.   In the above example, we assumed that the firm has issued pure discount or zero coupon bonds requiring a period T payment of K dollars. To value these bonds, we use the put-call parity relationship found in Equation 16.1. Specifically, using 16.1 to evaluate options written on the value of the firm's assets, we can write the following expression for firm value:

$$V(0) = call(V(0), T, B(T)) + B(T)v^T - put(V(0), T, B(T)).$$

---

[6]It should be recognized that option valuation theory historically has been based on a partial equilibrium type of analysis — that is, an option is valued "given" the value of the underlying asset. Thus, the option is technically a *redundant asset* in the sense that its payoff can be constructed from a portfolio comprised of *existing* assets. What this means for our discussion is that we can use contingent claims pricing theory to value a firm's securities simultaneously (its stock and bonds) *given* that we know the value of its assets. However, we do *not* value the underlying assets simultaneously; their value is assumed to be known.

Further, since the value of the firm, V(0), equals the sum of the equity plus debt values — that is, $V(0) = P(0) + D(0)$ — we can substitute Equation 16.2 for P(0) and define the value of the firm's risky bonds as follows:

(16.3) $$D(0) = B(T)v^T - put(V(0), T, B(T)).$$

The value of the firm's risky debt therefore equals the value of its debt if risk free (the first term on the right-hand side of Equation 16.3) less the value of a put option written on the value of the firm's assets and with an exercise price equal to the face value of its bonds, B(T). Note that the put option represents the value of a loan guarantee for the firm's risky debt."[7] In other words, if the firm's bonds were risk free, their current market value would simply equal the first term on the right-hand side of 16.3. Since the firm's bonds are risky, their value is less than that of riskless bonds by an amount equal to the value of the loan guarantee.

Valuing Coupon Bonds.   With coupon bonds the valuation of the firm's stock and bonds is more complicated, but the basic principle remains the same. The source of the added complexity is the fact that the firm's equity now represents a "series" of call options on its assets with an exercise price equal to the sum of the periodic coupon interest requirements of its bonds plus any sinking fund payments. Actually, for all but the last coupon and sinking fund payment, the firm's equity is represented by an option on an option, or a *compound option;* that is, when the equityholders make a payment of principal and interest to the bondholders, they acquire an option to continue to make those payments until the time at which the bonds have been successfully retired. Geske (1977) evaluated the problem of valuing compound options.

For securities with very complex payoff structures, such as callable coupon bonds, analytical solutions to the bond valuation problem do not exist. However, where "no-arbitrage" partial equilibrium conditions can be defined, numerical procedures can be used to derive the option's value. Geske and Shastri (1985) provide a very useful review of several of these procedures.

Valuing Convertible Bonds.   Ingersoll (1977) and Mikkelson (1978) developed a contingent claims valuation model for convertible discount bonds. The bonds are convertible into shares of stock equal to a proportion, α, of the value of the firm at maturity $(t = T)$. Alternatively, the bondholder can choose to receive the face value of the bonds, B(T). Thus, the maturity value of the bonds can be described as follows:

(16.4) $$D_c(T) = \min\{V(T), \max[B(T), \alpha V(T)]\},$$

where the subscript c refers to the bonds' convertibility.

---

[7]The mathematical review of max and min operators provides a derivation of the loan guarantee (put option).

We can rewrite Equation 16.4 as follows:

$$D_c(T) = B(T) - \max[B(T) - V(T), 0] + \max[\alpha V(T) - B(T), 0],$$

which we recognize as the cash payoff on a risky bond (terms 1 and 2 on the right-hand side of the above equation) and a call option on a fraction, α, of the firm's end-of-period value. Using option terminology, the current value of convertible bonds can be expressed as follows:

(16.5) $$D_c(0) = D(0) + \text{call}(\alpha V(0), T, B(T)),$$

where $D_c(0)$ is the value of the firm's risky (nonconvertible) debt and call($\alpha V(0)$, T, B(T)) is the value of the conversion feature.

Exercise 16.1:   Valuing Convertible Bonds

The Purilee Manufacturing Company has the following financial structure: 10,000 shares of common stock and 1,000 convertible bonds. Each convertible bond has a par value of $1,000 and can be converted into 10 shares of common stock at maturity (only). If the bonds are converted, the firm must issue $10 \times 1,000 = 10,000$ new shares of common stock to the bondholders in exchange.

1. What is the minimum V(T) for which the bondholders will want to convert their bonds?

Solution.   If conversion takes place, the bondholders will receive the following ownership share in the firm:

$$\frac{1,000 \text{ bonds} \times 10 \text{ shares}}{10,000 \text{ old shares} + 10 \times 1,000 \text{ new shares}}$$

or

$$\frac{10,000}{20,000} = 0.5, \quad \text{or 50\% of the firm.}$$

Thus, the bondholders will find it advantageous to convert where

$$0.5V(T) > \$1,000 \times 1,000 \text{ (par value of bonds)}.$$

Solving for the critical value of V(T), we get $2 million. Thus, if the value of the firm's assets at time T exceeds $2 million, the bondholders will find it advantageous to convert their bonds to common stock rather than take the par or maturity value of the bonds in payment.

2. Calculate the values of the firm's stock and bonds on date T where V(T) is less than \$1 million; greater than \$1 million but less than \$2 million; and greater than \$2 million.

Solution

V(T) < \$1 Million		\$1 Million < V(T) < \$2 Million	V(T) > \$2 Million
Bonds	V(T)	\$1 million	0.5 V(T)
Stock	0	V(T) − \$1 million	0.5 V(T)

Valuing Subordinated Debt. Firms generally issue several classes of bonds where the "priority" of claim on the firms' earnings varies among classes. Black and Cox (1976) analyzed the case where a firm issues two classes of bonds. Both bonds are discount bonds and mature T periods hence. Let K_1 represent the face value of the senior bond issue at maturity and K_2 the same quantity for the subordinated bond issue. The value of the firm's equity in period T, then, can be described as follows:

$$P(T) = max\{V(T) - [K_1 + K_2], 0\}.$$

Thus, the stockholders receive a positive cash flow only if the value of the firm's assets is sufficient to satisfy all bond claims. The cash flow received by the senior bondholders can be described as follows:

$$D_1(T) = min[V(T), K_1] = K_1 - max[K_1 - V(T), 0],$$

which we recognize as the terminal cash flow for risky bonds developed in Equation 16.4. The cash flow to the subordinated bondholders is somewhat more complex:

$$D_2(T) = max\{min[V(T) - K_1, K_2], 0\},$$

which can also be written as

$$D_2(T) = max\{[V(T) - K_1 - max(V(T) - (K_1 + K_2), 0)], 0\},$$

which we recognize as the payoff on an option on an option, or a compound option, which can also be written:

$$D_2(T) = max(\{V(T) - K_1 - max[P(T), 0]\}, 0).$$

Therefore, the terminal value of the subordinated bonds, $D_2(T)$, equals the payoff on a call option written on the value of the firm's assets less the face value of the senior debt and with an exercise price equal to $max[V(T), 0]$. In option pricing terminology,

(16.6)　　　　　　　　$D_2(0) = call\{V - K_1, T, max[P(T), 0]\}.$

Again we recognize the fact that the firm's subordinated debt represents a compound option since its value depends on the value of the firm's equity, which is itself an option on the value of the firm's assets.

Using Contingent Claims Analysis in Evaluating Capital Budgeting Decisions

Traditional capital budgeting analyses involve calculating and evaluating project net present value. In Chapter 6, we discussed some of the difficult issues that arise in this type of analysis with respect to estimating project cash flows. In particular, we noted that consideration should be given to the "options" that accompany a capital investment opportunity, for example, the option to abandon a project at various periods during its useful life. The abandonment option may take the form of a guaranteed trade-in value for the asset. Thus, the abandonment option can be thought of as a put option with an exercise price equal to the guaranteed trade-in value.[8]

Conceptualizing Capital Budgeting Proposals in a Contingent Claims Framework.   Contingent claims analysis provides a standpoint from which to analyze the value of the "flexibility" or "opportunities" attendant to any investment decision. For example, a firm in the microcomputer industry may be acquired for a substantial premium over its preacquisition market value. On the surface, the acquisition may look like a negative net present value investment. However, it may represent a "strategic decision" to enter into a new industry and, as such, carry with it valuable "opportunities" for future investment. These opportunities are, perhaps, unspecified options to make future investments in the microcomputer industry. In a sense, this type of option is "strategic" in that it involves investment outside the firm's current line of business activity.

Using the Option Pricing Model to Value Investment Proposals Directly.   So far we have discussed the use of contingent claims analysis in conceptualizing the flexibility attendant to many capital investment proposals. However, Banz and Miller (1978) have suggested a procedure for using the Black/Scholes (1973) model to value state contingent claims,[9] which in turn are used to value project cash flows involved in capital budgeting analyses.

---

[8]Some very difficult issues arise in valuing such an option, however. First, the asset on which the put is written frequently is not actively traded, making construction of the risk-free hedge portfolio needed to assess the option's value infeasible. In addition, the asset's value at expiration is partially a function of the type of use it receives—that is, its terminal value may be driven to zero through abusive usage. Note that this poses the same type of problem for valuing the put option as does the payment of cash dividends. Finally, the option may offer the holder the opportunity to exercise at any time up to the expiration date (it may be an American put option). We noted the added complexities attendant to the valuation of this type of option in Chapter 15. These problems have been addressed in some detail by Myers and Majd (1983) and Lee, Martin, and Senchack (1982).

[9]A state contingent claim is one that provides the holder with a cash payoff only if a particular state of nature occurs.

The proposed methodology involves two steps: (1) setting up the problem in a time state preference framework (see Appendix 7A) and (2) calculating the prices of the state contingent claims (identified in step 1) using the Black/Scholes option pricing model. To illustrate the procedure, we will consider a single-period capital investment proposal that requires an initial cash outlay of I_0 dollars and provides a risky cash flow return at the end of one year. In general terms, the net present value of the project can be defined as follows:

$$NPV = \text{Present value of project cash flows} - I_0.$$

Using the time state preference model, we can define the present value of the end-of-year project net cash flow and, consequently, project NPV as follows:

(16.7) $$NPV = \Sigma_s v(s)NCF(s) - I_0,$$

where $v(s)$ is the current price of a state s security that pays off $1 at the end of the current period if state s occurs and $NCF(s)$ is the net cash flow for the project if state s occurs. Thus, the product of $v(s)$ and $NCF(s)$ is the current or present value of the project's next-period cash flow if state s materializes. The sum of these products across all possible states, then, is the value of the project's future cash flow. Note that $v(s)$ includes consideration for both the time value of money and consumer preferences for income in state s.

Two attributes of this formulation of project net present value have hindered its further development and use:

1.   It is difficult to decide how to define "states of the world."

2.   Even if we can identify states of the world, we are still left with the task of defining the state prices, $v(s)$.

Banz and Miller argued that states of the world could be defined based on "ranges of rates of return on the market portfolio." For example, they suggested three states of the world: recession, normal, and boom. Using historical rates of return for the market portfolio of risky assets, they suggested that recession corresponded to market returns ranging from −87.47 to 0.06 percent; normal corresponded to returns between 0.06 and 20.42 percent; and boom meant returns ranging from 20.42 to 171.83 percent. One can easily imagine expanding the number of states to accommodate whatever the analyst feels is appropriate.

Banz and Miller then calculated the values of the state contingent claims, $v(s)$, using the Black/Scholes model as follows:

$$v(s) = \exp(-r)\{N[d_2(r_m, s)] - N[d_2(r_m, s + 1)]\},$$

where r = risk-free interest rate
                 $N(z)$ = normal cumulative density function evaluated at z
                 (r_m, s) = minimum rate of return for state s

$$d_2(r_m, s) = \frac{-\ln[1 + (r_m, s)] + \left[r - \frac{\sigma_m^2}{2}\right]}{\sigma_m}$$

$$d_2(r_m, s + 1) = \frac{-\ln[1 + (r_m, s + 1)] + \left[r - \frac{\sigma_m^2}{2}\right]}{\sigma_m}$$

σ_m = standard deviation in market returns

We can now calculate the value of each state contingent claim, v(s). To do so, we must estimate σ_m and then evaluate each remaining term in the Black/Scholes model. Of course, there will be as many values of v(s) to estimate as there are states of the world.

The preceding discussion has been couched in terms of a single-period example; however, the analysis can be readily extended to consider multiple future periods. The resulting NPV model becomes

$$NPV = \Sigma_t \Sigma_s v(s, t) NCF(s, t) - I_0,$$

where the additional argument "t" simply identifies the time period in which the cash flow is received. The present value of the project cash flows is now the sum of the present values of the state contingent payoffs of the project over all future periods. The multiperiod problem is further complicated because of the dependencies that can arise among the states of the world over time. We will not delve further into the problem here but refer the interested reader to the Banz and Miller (1978) paper.

Limitations of Contingent Claims Analysis in Evaluating Capital Budgeting Proposals.   As useful as contingent claims analysis may be in "characterizing" complex investment opportunities, it has its shortcomings. Most notable is the absence of a secondary market for the underlying (real) asset. This means that the arbitrage-type derivations of option pricing formulas are no longer appropriate for the valuation of these assets. Thus, when it comes to actually calculating the value of real asset investment options, the state of the art in option pricing theory is severely limited.

The Banz/Miller approach is a promising alternative use of option pricing technology in the evaluation of capital budgeting projects. However, this method simply provides a basis for valuing the state contingent payoffs of a capital investment proposal and does not model the project itself as an option or portfolio of options. Nevertheless, the very act of identifying and characterizing the options associated with a capital budgeting proposal cannot help improving the final evaluation.

Summary

Option pricing theory has been a major theoretical paradigm in the finance literature since 1973. Since the publication of the seminal work by Black and Scholes, the options literature has taken three different but related paths. The first consists of developing additional valuation models that generalize the results of the Black/Scholes (1973) model. Examples include the pure jump model of Cox and Ross (1976) and the jump diffusion model of Merton (1976). The second is comprised of tests of these models' predictive power. We reviewed some of this literature and found that the original Black/Scholes model continues to hold up well against its more recent competitors. The third strain of option pricing literature describes the applications of option pricing analysis or contingent claims analysis to a wide variety of corporate finance problems. In discussing a subset of this literature, we saw that all the corporation's securities can be viewed as contingent claims or options whose values depend on the values of the firm's assets. This recognition has led a number of researchers to delve into the pricing of complex securities, such as convertible and callable bonds, using contingent claims analysis. Yet another subset of this third strain of literature relates to the developing research on the use of contingent claims analysis to evaluate "real" asset investment opportunities. Such analysis generally involves "conceptualizing" the determinants of the value of an investment opportunity in a productive asset utilizing a portfolio of options. The most obvious example from the capital budgeting literature is probably the abandonment problem. The option to abandon an investment prior to its physical demise has value and has long been recognized as important in the correct evaluation of a capital budgeting proposal. However, the application of option pricing technology to problem analysis offers the hope for recognition of the true worth of this important facet of investment analysis.

Study Problems

16.1   The maturity value of a risky discount bond can be described as

$$\min[V(T), B(T)],$$

where V(T) is the value of the firm's assets at time T and B(T) the face value of the firm's bonds.

a. Describe the intuition behind this characterization of a risky bond.

b. Demonstrate the consistency of the above expression with the following alternative characterization of a risky discount bond's maturity value:

$$B(T) - put(V, 0, B).$$

c. Discuss the nature of the complications that are added to the valuation of bonds using a contingent claims approach where the bonds require both coupon interest payments and sinking fund installments.

16.2   Assume the following information:

$$P(0) = \$45$$

$$K = \$40$$

$$r = 0.12$$

$$put(P, T, K) = \$2.$$

Use the put-call parity relationship to solve for the value of a European call option where T = 30, 60, and 90 days.

16.3   Financial lease contracts frequently incorporate purchase options on the leased asset. Prior to the tax act of 1981, these options had to carry an exercise price equal to the fair market value of the leased asset upon expiration of the lease contract. However, under the current law, purchase options for the residual value of leased assets can be written to include a fixed exercise price. Discuss the characterization of such an option in a contingent claims framework. What problems do you foresee in its valuation?

16.4   In March 1988 Shemling, Inc. issued 1,500 convertible bonds with $1,000 par value. These bonds are convertible into 100 shares of Shemling common stock on the maturity date, March 31, 1989. Shemling currently has 1 million shares of common stock outstanding.

   a. If at maturity the bondholders will receive $1,000 in principal plus $150 in interest if they do not convert, under what circumstances would they find it advantageous to convert?

   b. If the value of the firm's assets is $4,500,000 on March 31, 1989, what will be the value of its bonds, options, and common stock?

   c. Answer part b where the value of the firm's assets is only $1,350,000.

16.5   The quarterly dividend payment on an adjustable-rate preferred stock (ARPS) issue is adjusted to reflect the maximum interest rate paid on 90-day Treasury bills, 10-year Treasury notes, and 20-year Treasury bonds at the close of the previous quarter. The dividend rate is also constrained by a maximum (ceiling) and a minimum (floor) that are set at the time the issue is sold. Further, the dividend rate is set equal to the maximum of the above three rates plus a "reset" or "refloat" adjustment, which is also set at the time of issue. Using this information, characterize the dividend for quarter t for an ARPS issue as a portfolio of options. (Hint: To simplify your analysis, let the unconstrained dividend rate for quarter t, $d_t = \max[r_{TB}, r_{TN}, r_B] + \text{Reset}$; also let r_c = rate ceiling and r_f = rate floor.)

16.6   The Carrington Express Company has two classes of pure discount bonds outstanding. Both issues mature at the same time, and the firm pays no common stock dividends. They consist of a senior bond issue and a subordinated issue. Write out general expressions for the payoffs to each of the three classes of security holders on the debt's maturity date.

16.7   Manning Enterprises is evaluating two production technologies for its newly developed personal computer modem. The modem involves using a newly developed microchip that allows the user to utilize transmission rates for graphics data over standard phone lines at rates as high as 12,000 baud as compared with standard devices on the market that allow transmission rates of 300 or 1,200 baud. The two production technologies are quite different. The first is a "flexible" automated production facility that can be "reprogrammed" to produce a wide variety of products, including the new modem. The second is a limited-purpose facility that would allow only minimal alterations in the modem's design without necessitating expensive modifications. After carefully analyzing the expected cash flows from the investment in each facility, Manning has concluded that the second alternative offers the higher net present value. Manning's board of directors has received the report and raised the flexibility issue, requesting that the two NPVs be reassessed to specifically reflect this attribute. Outline a procedure that the analyst might follow to accomplish this task.

References

C. Ball and W. Torous, "On Jumps in Common Stock Prices and Their Impact on Call Option Pricing," *Journal of Finance* 40 (March 1985): 155–173.

R. Banz and M. Miller, "Prices for State Contingent Claims: Some Estimates and Applications," *Journal of Business* 51 (1978): 653–672.

S. Beckers, "The Constant Elasticity of Variance Model and Its Implications for Option Pricing," *Journal of Finance* 35 (June 1980): 661–673.

M. Bhattacharya, "Empirical Properties of the Black-Scholes Formula under Ideal Conditions," *Journal of Financial and Quantitative Analysis* 15 (1980): 1081–1105.

F. Black and J. C. Cox, "Valuing Corporate Securities: Some Effects of Bond Indenture Provisions," *Journal of Finance* 31 (1976): 351–367.

F. Black and M. Scholes, "The Pricing of Options and Corporate Liabilities," *Journal of Political Economy* 81 (1973): 637–659.

———, "The Valuation of Option Contracts and a Test of Market Efficiency," *Journal of Finance* 27 (1972): 399–417.

M. Brennan and E. Schwartz, "Convertible Bonds: Valuation and Optimal Strategies for Call and Conversion," *Journal of Finance* 32 (1977): 1699–1715.

J. C. Cox and S. F. Ross, "The Pricing of Options for Jump Processes" (Working paper no. 2-75, Rodney L. White Center for Financial Research, University of Pennsylvania, April 1975).

———, "The Valuation of Options for Alternative Stochastic Processes," *Journal of Financial Economics* 3 (1976): 145–166.

D. Galai, "Characterization of Options," *Journal of Banking and Finance* 1 (December 1977): 373–385.

——— and R. W. Masulis, "The Option Pricing Model and the Risk Factor of the Stock," *Journal of Financial Economics* 3 (1976): 53–81.

R. Geske, "The Valuation of Compound Options," *Journal of Financial Economics* 7 (March 1979): 63–81.

———, "The Valuation of Corporate Liabilities as Compound Options," *Journal of Financial and Quantitative Analysis* 12 (1977): 541–552.

——— and K. Shastri, "Valuation by Approximation: A Comparison of Alternative Option Valuation Techniques," *Journal of Financial and Quantitative Analysis* 20 (March 1985): 45–71.

J. E. Ingersoll, "A Contingent-Claims Valuation of Convertible Securities," *Journal of Financial Economics* (May 1977): 289–322.

J. W. Kensinger, "Budgeting for R&D: An Application of Option Pricing" (Working paper 80–104, Southern Methodist University, 1980).

———, "Project Abandonment As a Put Option: Dealing with the Capital Investment Decision and Operating Risk Using Option Pricing Theory" (Working paper 80–121, Southern Methodist University, 1980).

R. Klemkosky and B. Resnick, "Put-Call Parity and Market Efficiency," *Journal of Finance* (December 1979): 1141–1155.

W. Y. Lee, J. D. Martin, and A. J. Senchack, "The Case for Using Options to Evaluate Salvage Values in Financial Leases," *Financial Management* 11 (1982): 33–41.

J. MacBeth and L. Merville, "An Empirical Examination of the Black-Scholes Call Option Pricing Model," *Journal of Finance* (December 1979): 1173–1186.

S. Majd and S. C. Myers, "Valuing the Government's Tax Claim on Risky Assets" (Unpublished manuscript, Sloan School of Management, M.I.T., 1983).

S. P. Mason and R. C. Merton, "The Role of Contingent Claims Analysis in Corporate Finance," in *Recent Advances in Corporate Finance,* ed. E. I. Altman and M. G. Subrahmanyam (Homewood, Ill.: Irwin, 1985): 7–54.

R. Merton, "Option Pricing When Underlying Stock Returns Are Discontinuous," *Journal of Financial Economics* 3 (January/March 1976): 1173–1186.

————, "The Theory of Rational Optional Pricing," *Bell Journal of Economics and Management Science* (Spring 1973): 141–183.

W. Mikkleson, "An Examination of the Agency Cost of Debt Rationale for Convertible Bonds and Warrants" (Unpublished manuscript, University of Rochester, 1978).

S. C. Myers and S. Majd, "Calculating Abandonment Value Using Option Pricing Theory" (Working paper, Sloan School of Management, M.I.T., 1983).

R. Rao and J. D. Martin, "Another Look at the Use of Options Pricing Theory to Evaluate Real Asset Investment Opportunities," *Journal of Business Finance and Accounting* 8 (1981): 421–429.

R. Rendleman and C. Carabini, "A Re-Examination of the Efficient Markets Hypothesis: A Review of Recent Empirical Work" (Unpublished manuscript, 1979).

M. Rubinstein, "Displaced Diffusion Option Pricing," *Journal of Finance* 38 (March 1983): 213–217.

————, "Nonparametric Tests of Alternative Option Pricing Models Using All Reported Trades and Quotes on the 30 Most Active CBOE Option Classes from August 23, 1976 through August 31, 1978," *Journal of Finance* 35 (June 1985): 455–480.

C. W. Smith, "Alternative Methods for Raising Capital: Rights versus Underwritten Offerings," *Journal of Financial Economics* 5 (1977): 273–307.

————, "Applications of Option Pricing Analysis," in *The Modern Theory of Corporate Finance*, ed. M. C. Jensen and C. W. Smith, Jr. (New York: McGraw-Hill, 1984): 288–330.

R. Stultz, "Options on the Minimum or Maximum of Two Risky Assets: Analysis and Applications," *Journal of Finance* 10 (1982): 161–185.

Chapter 17

Futures Markets: Theory and Practice[1]

In this chapter we introduce futures contracts, particularly financial futures. First, let us define some terminology. A *forward contract* is a contract calling for delivery of a standardized quantity and quality of an asset on a future date for a price agreed upon today (when the contract is written). A *long position* in a forward contract is a commitment to buy; a *short position* is a commitment to sell. On the transaction date, the seller delivers the asset, and the buyer pays the price set by the contract.

A futures contract is like a forward contract except that the gain or loss that the buyer or seller takes due to the difference in the contract price and the market price on the settlement date is realized daily. Forward contracts are simpler in operation since they require only one cash transaction, while futures contracts require a cash transaction each day. Forward contracts are usually custom tailored to the needs of the parties, and actual delivery of the asset is much more common than in the case of futures contracts. Residential real estate transactions are usually arranged with forward contracts: The buyer and seller agree on a price, the buyer offers and the seller accepts an initial deposit. At closing, which may be months later, the transaction is completed at the agreed price.

Futures contracts on commodities (butter, corn, or pork bellies) and financial assets (stocks and bonds and related indices) are standardized and arranged

---

[1]Cheng-kun Kuo, the University of Wisconsin at Parkside, collaborated with us on this chapter.

through clearinghouses. The buyer and seller rarely meet and the asset is not as likely to be delivered. Instead, the difference in prices is settled in cash. The daily cash resettlement is called *marking to the market*.[2] Because of this, the clearinghouses require futures traders to maintain a margin account with a certain minimum balance. This is another important difference between futures and forward contracts. The following example will help clarify this important difference.

Example 1.   On March 1 the buyer opens a contract requiring delivery on March 11 of a $1 million 90-day U.S. Treasury bill at a price of $980,000. If this were a forward contract, the buyer would pay $980,000 on March 11 and receive the $1 million 90-day bill. The market prices on March 2 through March 10 would not matter. However, as a futures contract, the cash positions of the buyer and seller adjust each day to reflect changes in the futures price. On March 2 the market's opinion of bills delivered on March 11 has changed; the futures price is now $981,250. The buyer's March 11 position has improved, because if the trade takes place at this price the buyer gains $1,250. Because it is a futures contract, this gain is credited to the buyer's account (and debited to the seller's account) on March 2. This will draw down the the seller's required margin. If the margin gets too low, the clearinghouse will require additional cash to reestablish the minimum margin. On March 3, the futures price changes again, and again the parties settle up. Table 17.1 shows futures prices and cash transactions. (The prices are for

---

Table 17.1   Futures Prices and Related Cash Transactions

Date	Futures Price for 3/11 Delivery	Effect on the Account Of	
		Buyer	Seller
3/1	$980,000	—	—
3/2	981,250	$ 1,250	$(1,250)
3/3	982,500	1,250	(1,250)
3/4	983,750	1,250	(1,250)
3/5	983,750	0	0
3/6	No Trading		
3/7	No Trading		
3/8	981,250	(2,500)	2,500
3/9	980,000	(1,250)	1,250
3/10	979,375	(625)	625
3/11	978,750	(625)	625
	Total	(1,250)	1,250

On March 11, forward contract buyers and futures contract buyers each wind up losing. Sellers gain. The difference is in the timing and magnitude of the cash flows required to mark to the market.

---

[2]Even with financial futures, delivery can be less than straightforward. For example, futures on long-term U.S. bonds allow the seller to deliver any bond that satisfies certain parameters of the contract. But on the delivery date, many bonds having different market values will have the right parameters. Obviously, the seller will attempt to deliver the cheapest one. The buyer must take this into account when making the initial investment. We are ignoring this problem.

illustrative purposes. It is not likely that prices would vary this much in such a short time.)

A futures contract is similar to an option contract (discussed in Chapters 15 and 16) in that it provides an opportunity to buy or sell something in the future. However, there are important differences between them. First, in a futures contract the contracted futures price is market determined, whereas in an option contract the striking price is simply given and agreed upon by all option traders.

Further, the market competitively determines the option's value, that is, the value of the right to buy or sell the underlying asset at the agreed-upon striking price. Second, execution of an option contract takes place at the contract owner's discretion, whereas a futures contract holder must fulfill the contract obligations if the contract is held to maturity. Third, options offer the potential for limited loss but unlimited profit. In futures trading, on the other hand, losses are not limited to the investor's initial investment (this risk will be discussed later). However, it should be noted that options investors do not get something for nothing; they pay a premium for the options' relative safety.[3]

Futures contracts on commodities such as grain, meat (for example, pork bellies), or gold have existed for many years. However, financial futures contracts are much more recent in origin. The first such contract was introduced on October 20, 1975, by the Chicago Board of Trade (CBOT); it was written on GNMA CDRs (Government National Mortgage Association Collateralized Depository Receipts, or "Ginnie Mae" CDRs). Since their introduction, the market for financial futures has grown at a staggering pace. Financial futures contracts currently are traded on a number of exchanges;[4] in fact, by 1985 the volume of trading in financial futures overshadowed that of traditional commodity futures. This growth may well be a result of the volatility of interest and foreign exchange rates during that period, which led to a demand for futures contracts as a means of reducing a firm's exposure to the attendant risks. It should be noted that there are a number of ways to protect a firm's asset values against adverse interest rate fluctuations; however, the use of financial futures is the least expensive. Financial futures also provide traders with opportunities for arbitrage or speculative investments. Thus, two basic reasons for the rapid growth of the financial futures market have been offered: hedging (that is, risk reduction) and speculation. We will investigate each of these motives in turn.

This chapter is organized as follows. First, we review some definitions and other institutional considerations peculiar to the financial futures market. Next, we develop the arguments used to explain the need for futures markets. We then address the problem of valuing a futures contract and an option on a future. Here we dis-

---

[3]An option on a futures contract gives the option owner the right to acquire a futures contract with a futures price equal to the exercise price of the option. The futures option gives investors the volatility of futures plus the limited liability associated with options in general. Ramaswamy and Sundaresan (1985) and Barone-Adesi and Whaley (1987) have developed valuation models of options on futures. Later we will briefly review the Barone-Adesi and Whaley model.

[4]Exchanges that trade in financial futures are: Amex Commodities Exchange (ACE), Chicago Board of Trade (CBOT), Commodity Exchange, New York (COMEX), International Monetary Market of the Chicago Mercantile Exchange (IMM), New York Futures Exchange of the New York Exchange (NYFE), Kansas City Board of Trade (KCBT), and Index and Options Market (IOM).

cuss the role of the "spot" term structure of interest rates in such valuations and demonstrate how futures prices of various maturities can be used to derive a "futures" term structure of interest rates. Next, we examine the transactions costs that explain the observed differences in the spot and futures term structures. We discuss the well-known Cox, Ingersoll, and Ross (CIR) (1981) proposition of equilibrium futures pricing and, in light of our discussion of the transactions costs and observed market participants' behavior, conclude that the CIR proposition leaves much to be desired. Then we review various strategies for hedging with futures contracts. Finally, we briefly consider some issues raised by futures trading, particularly the forecasting ability of futures prices and the information role of futures markets.

Institutional Considerations

Financial Futures Price Quotations

Table 17.2 contains the price quotes for financial futures calling for the delivery of 90-day Treasury bills for selected future months as of June 11, 1986. The first column lists the different contracts as distinguished by their maturities.[5] The next four columns represent prices per $100 of face[6] of the opening, the highest, the

Table 17.2 Price Quotes on Treasury Bill Futures

TREASURY BILLS (IMM) — $1 mil.; pts. of 100%

	Open	High	Low	Settle	Chg	Discount Settle	Chg	Open Interest
Mr87	93.43	93.49	93.37	93.53	+.03	6.47	−.03	946
June	93.14	93.24	93.12	93.27	+.04	6.73	−.04	769
Sept	92.88	92.96	92.83	93.00	+.05	7.00	−.05	413
Dec	. . .	. . .	. . .	92.73	+.05	7.27	−.05	138

Est vol 9,000; vol Tues 8,000; open int 34,000, −434.

---

[5]In the maturity month, trading on the maturing contract terminates on the second business day following the Federal Reserve three-month T-bill auction of the third week of the month. The auction is usually held on a Monday.

[6]The corresponding futures contract value (the invoice price of a trade at this price) is

$$\text{Invoice price} = \$1,000,000 - \frac{(\text{Days to maturity})}{360} \times \text{Settle} \times \$1,000,000$$

where Settle = 100 − Price per $100. Therefore, a price of 95 per $100 corresponds to an invoice price of $987,500.

lowest, and the final trade of the day. The sixth column ("chg") measures the difference between the June 11 settlement quotation (the "Settle" column) and that of the previous trading day; for example, the "Mr87 +.03" measures the change of settlement quotation from June 10 to June 11. The two columns under "Discount" represent the discount yield and the yield change from the previous day, where the discount yield has been obtained by subtracting the settlement quotation from 100. For example, the Discount–Settle for the March 1987 contract is $100 - 93.53 = 6.47$, or a Discount–Chg of -0.03 from June 10. The last column, "Open Interest," describes the total number of outstanding contracts for each maturity. For example, there were 946 contracts outstanding for March 1987 Treasury bills on June 11, 1986. Finally, the bottom line summarizes the estimated trading volume for the day and its comparison with the previous day's volume, as well as the total open interest for all maturities and its one-day change.

Forward versus Futures Markets[7]

In contrast to the forward markets, where contract terms are negotiable and the contract typically is nontransferable, futures markets are well organized and deal with standardized futures contracts. Trading takes place on the floor of exchanges at "pits," as they are commonly called. The clearinghouse,[8] by acting as "a buyer to every seller and a seller to every buyer," substitutes its trustworthiness for that of individual traders. Thus, a trader who has entered a futures contract finds that the other party (the one obliged to honor the contract) is the clearinghouse. In other words, a futures trader need not be concerned about the credit status of the other party because the clearinghouse guarantees contract performance. From an individual trader's point of view, this guarantee ensures convenience and liquidity, which are desirable because:

1. There usually are a limited number of delivery periods per year; for example, T-bill futures contracts expire only in March, June, September, and December.

2. The trader's planned trading period may change. For example, a speculator who has determined that a previously anticipated market movement will not materialize may be prompted to change his or her portfolio.

Today, most financial futures contracts can be divided into three major categories according to the financial instruments specified for delivery:[9]

1. *Interest rate futures (debt futures):* T-bills, T-notes, T-bonds, GNMA (CDRs), GNMA(CFTs), certificates of deposit, and Eurodollars

---

[7]Readers who are interested in the difference between equilibrium forward and futures prices are referred to Cox, Ingersoll, and Ross (1981).

[8]Every exchange has a clearinghouse that transfers funds from losers to winners on a daily basis. The clearinghouse deals only with its authorized clearing members; nonclearing members clear all positions through a clearing member's account.

[9]For a detailed description of each contract and its trading rules, see a "professional" reference book such as Sarnoff (1985). Also, the publications of the various exchanges list their own specific requirements.

2.   *Foreign currency futures:* pounds sterling, Canadian dollars, Deutschmarks, Dutch guilders, French francs, Japanese yen, Mexican pesos, and Swiss francs

3.   *Stock index futures:* NYSE Composite Index, Standard & Poor's 500, Value Line Index, and Major Market Index.

The third category deserves further explanation. These futures do not call for delivery of real or financial assets. At delivery, stock index futures are settled in cash, marked to the market[10] at the closing value of the respective underlying spot stock market index on the last trading day. All three of the above types of stock index futures contracts are "sized" at 500 times the respective underlying index's value. For example, if the index value is 109.85, the contract value will be $500 \times 109.85 = \$54,925$.

Trading in these futures began in 1982 and since then they have become increasingly important. Table 17.3 shows, for example, that the S&P 500 alone ranks among the top contracts available for futures trading. The value represented by the combined trading of these contracts often rivals that of spot trading.[11]

Table 17.3   Relative Popularities of Selective Contracts

	Total Outstanding Contracts
Interest rate futures:	
T-bill (IMM)	34,439
T-note (IMM)	76,590
T-bond (IMM)	218,358
GNMA (CBT)	1,741
Bank CD (IMM)	112
Eurodollar (IMM)	180,033
Foreign currency futures:	
Pound sterling (IMM)	35,611
Canadian dollar (IMM)	13,345
Deutschmark (IMM)	48,271
Japanese yen (IMM)	41,394
Swiss franc (IMM)	29,574
Stock index futures:	
NYSE Composite Index	15,071
Standard & Poor's 500 (CME)	98,602
Value Line Index (KCBT)	14,375

Source: *The Wall Street Journal,* June 12, 1986.

---

[10]"Marking to the market" will be discussed in detail in a later section. Briefly, the effect of marking to the market is to reset the value of a futures contract to zero.

[11]Other, related index futures exist. S&P 100 and Mini Value Line are worth $200 and $100 times that index, respectively. Interested readers are referred to Weiner (1984) or Smith (1985) for a comprehensive discussion of this category of futures contract. Figlewski (1985) and Junkus and Lee (1985) describe how to use these futures for hedging purposes.

Under certain conditions, forward and futures prices will be the same. As we will see, these conditions are so strong that they are rarely satisfied. However, the framework in which they are the same is frequently used in theoretical studies. The framework requires the usual assumptions — no transactions costs and no riskless arbitrage. If we also have

1.   Investors with sufficient resources or credit to meet the mark-to-the-market conditions

2.   An organized market for forward and futures contracts

3.   A known, constant risk-free interest rate during the contract period

the market will not distinguish between forward and futures contracts. For example, the price in January for May pork bellies will be the same for both forward and futures contracts.[12]

To see that the prices must be the same under the above conditions, we let f denote the forward price and F the futures price of a share of stock to be traded T years hence. Consider two portfolios. The first portfolio consists of a forward contract — an amount A invested at the riskless rate r, which will accumulate to f in T years. Thus $A = fv^T$, where $v = 1/(1 + r)$. The second portfolio consists of a "rollover" futures scheme on the same stock, also to be traded T years hence, and an investment of $B = Fv^T$, which accumulates to F in T years. The futures contracts can be held to maturity, under our assumptions, with the gains and losses due to marking to the market accrued to the trading date. A "rollover" scheme is a set of contracts, one opened each day, but for differing sizes. The initial contract is to buy v^{T-d} shares after T years (d = 1/365 is the duration of a day measured in years). Let F_1 be the futures price at the end of the first day that the long position has a gain (or loss) of $(F_1 - F)v^{T-d}$. Its accumulated value when the contract matures T − d years later is $(F_1 - F)v^{T-d}(1 + r)^{T-d} = F_1 - F$. The second day another contract is opened so that the total long position is v^{T-2d}. At the end of the day resettlement takes place with a gain (or loss) to the long position of $(F_2 - F_1)v^{T-2d}$, which accumulates to $(F_2 - F_1)$ when the contract matures after T − 2d years. The process continues. Each day the rollover long position is increased by a factor of $(1 + n)^d$ so that at maturity it is exactly one contract. The gains (or losses) will accumulate with interest to $(F_1 - F) + (F_2 - F_1) + \cdots + (S - F_{N-1}) = S - F$ where S is the stock price at maturity. The following table shows how the rollover futures position works:

Day	Long Position	Gain (or Loss)	Value at Maturity
1	v^{T-d}	$(F_1 - F)v^{T-d}$	$F_1 - F$
2	v^{T-2d}	$(F_2 - F_1)v^{T-2d}$	$F_2 - F_1$
3	v^{T-3d}	$(F_3 - F_2)v^{T-3d}$	$F_3 - F_2$
.	.		
.	.		
.	.		
N − 1	v^d	$(F_{N-1} - F_{N-2})v^d$	$F_{N-1} - F_{N-2}$
N	1	$S - F_{N-1}$	$S - F_{N-1}$
		Total at Maturity:	$S - F$

---

[12]This section follows Whaley (1986).

Now we can display the values of the two portfolios:

Position	Portfolio A		Portfolio B	
	Initial Value	Maturity Value	Initial Value	Maturity Value
Long Risk-Free	fv^T	f	Fv^T	F
Long Forward	0	$S - f$		
Long Rollover			0	$S - F$
Net Position	fv^T	S	Fv^T	S

We see that the two portfolios have the same maturity values regardless of how the stock price moves. Since there are no riskless arbitrage opportunities, the port-folios must have the same initial values as well. Hence $f = F$.

Why Futures Markets?

Hedging against Unanticipated Price Changes

An important purpose served by futures markets is that of facilitating the hedging of price and interest rate risk.[13] Commodity futures have long been used to protect against price risk, while financial futures provide effective ways to hedge against interest rate fluctuations.

Investors undertake hedging with the expectation that losses incurred in dealing with the spot position will be at least partially offset by corresponding gains in the futures position. Spot position (or cash position) refers to the holding or "opportunity" of holding actual commodities or financial assets. For example, a farmer expects a crop six months after planting time. In anticipation of a price decline, the farmer may enter a futures contract to sell the crop. (Of course, if the futures position is maintained it would also offset a gain due to a price increase.) Although the farmer does not actually hold the crop during the six-month period, there is an opportunity of holding it. Opportunity holding of assets is an important notion and, as we will see, plays an important role in most hedging activities. Practical financial hedging activities are described in Examples 2 and 3.

Example 2:   Using Futures to Adjust Portfolio Mix.   Some portfolio man-agers believe in market timing. They hope to profit from shifting investments in anticipation of market moves. This example shows how a manager could use futures instead of trading stocks and bonds and make a profit to the extent he or she can anticipate market movements. Transactions costs for buying and selling securities are much higher than futures costs. Another advantage of using futures is that it makes it easier to verify the manager's claim to be able to anticipate the market, because there are no compounding variables involved.

---

[13]With futures markets, it is easier and less expensive for investors to control the amount of risk expo-sure in their investments.

Suppose that the current market value of the portfolio is $15,000,000 with $10,000,000 in stocks and $5,000,000 in bonds. The manager predicts a stock market decline and wants to sell $5,000,000 of stocks and buy $5,000,000 of bonds. We will compare this to selling one-year futures on a stock market index and buying one-year futures on a bond index. Suppose the current one-year futures value of the stock index is 100. Each contract is for $500 times 100 = $50,000. Shorting the market $5,000,000 requires selling 100 contracts.

Similarly, suppose the one-year futures value of the bond index is 100. The manager establishes a one-year long bond position by purchasing 100 bond contracts.

Now suppose that the stock market declines 10 percent, and the bond market improves by 10 percent. If the manager trades the assets, the market value of the portfolio one year hence would be as follows:

Bonds	$10,000,000 × 1.10	= $11,000,000
Stocks	$5,000,000 × 1/1.10	= $4,545,454
Total Market Value		$15,545,454

The stock index having declined makes each short stock contract worth $50,000 − $45,454 = $4,546. Similarly, each long bond contract is worth $55,000 − $50,000 = $5,000. If the manager uses futures, the market value after one year will be as follows:

Bonds	$5,000,000 × 1.10	= $5,500,000
Stocks	$10,000,000 × 1/1.10	= $9,090,909
Stock Futures	$4,546 × 100	= $454,600
Bond Futures	$5,000 × 100	= $500,000
Total Market Value		$15,545,509

The results differ due to rounding. The same result is achieved without trading assets, at a substantial savings in transactions costs.

The past decade has witnessed erratic swings in interest rates.[14] Whenever interest rates change, the values of all portfolios change to reflect the current yield available in the marketplace. These uncertain changes in portfolio value resulting from interest rate fluctuations are referred to as *interest rate risk*. This type of risk is an important consideration for any firm that invests in financial assets. For example, banks and savings and loan associations hold short-term, easily marketable U.S. Treasury bills to maintain a liquid reserve; wide swings in the values of such portfolios obviously reduce their usefulness as a liquidity reserve. The possibility of reducing or eliminating interest rate risk by hedging requires that a firm concentrate its energy in fields of its true comparative advantage or specialization rather than on potentially disastrous price or interest rate volatilities. Therefore,

---

[14]In the 60-month period from the beginning of 1977 through the end of 1982, rates changed direction 14 times in the case of 91-day T-bills and 22 times for 182-day T-bills.

hedging via financial futures transactions has become an integral part of financial managers' working day.

Example 3.[15]   An insurance company has issued a policy that pays medical benefits to the employees of a large corporation. The policy pays stipulated benefits for four years in exchange for a single initial premium of $10,000,000. The insurance company actuary arrived at the $10,000,000 premium by calculating the present value of expenses (commissions, profit, etc.) to be $3,000,000 and the present value of future benefits to be $7,000,000. The actuarial assumptions on which the calculation was based included an inflation rate of 5 percent per year and an interest rate of 8 percent (along with other assumptions about mortality, morbidity, unemployment, etc.). Of the actuary's assumptions, the inflation rate is the most uncertain. The actuary's report explains that the benefits actually paid will depend on actual inflation.

Summary of Actuary's Calculations

Year	Expected Benefits (Inflation at 5%)	Present Value (Discounted at 8%)
1	$1,970,598	$1,824,628
2	2,069,128	1,773,944
3	2,172,585	1,724,668
4	2,281,214	1,676,760
	Total Expected Present Value:	$7,000,000

In effect, the insurance company has borrowed $7,000,000. The amount it must repay is random—whatever the stipulated benefits amount to. But, based on the actuarial assumptions, the company has the above expectations. The company invests the $7,000,000 in zero-coupon risk-free bonds, matching the expected benefits (which for ease of presentation we suppose are paid at the end of each year). Thus the company is practicing asset and liability matching. The expected benefit payments are equal to the bond maturities. However, the bond maturities will not change with inflation, but the benefits will.

Expected Cash Flow for the Insurer

Year	Expected Benefits (Inflation at 5%)	Bond Maturities (Zero Coupon 8% Bonds)
1	$1,970,598	$1,970,598
2	2,069,128	2,069,128
3	2,172,585	2,172,585
4	2,281,214	2,281,214

---

[15]Adapted from Nye and Kolb (1986).

The management of the insurance company asks its actuary to determine the effect of an unexpected increase in the inflation rate of 2 percent, in conjunction with a 2 percent increase in interest rates. The actuary bases the calculation on the assumptions that the changes are effective just after the policy is issued, the premium collected, and the 8 percent bonds purchased. The changes are assumed to remain in effect for the entire four years. The bond portfolio is not changed.

Actuary's Revision of Expected Cash Flows

Year	Expected Benefits (Inflation at 7%)	Bond Maturities (Zero Coupon 8% Bonds)	Net Loss
1	$2,008,133	$1,970,598	$ 37,535
2	2,148,703	2,069,128	79,575
3	2,299,112	2,172,585	126,527
4	2,460,050	2,281,214	178,836
			$422,473

The effect of an unanticipated 2 percent shift in interest rates is shown in the net loss column. In order to hedge against such a change the insurance company sells futures on bonds. Determining the optimal amount of risk to hedge will be done later in this chapter. For now, suppose the insurance company wants to hedge most of the inflation risk. Suppose too that futures contracts are available for 1, 2, 3, and 4 year periods, each calling for delivery of 90-day risk-free bonds. If V_1 denotes the benefits paid at the end of the first year, B_1 the value of the 8 percent bond maturity, and FP_1 the value of the futures contract, the company's net position at the end of the first year is $V_1 - B_1 - NFP_1$, where N is the number of one-year futures it should sell. We consider determining N so that $V_1 - B_1 - NFP_1$ is minimized with respect to interest rate changes. This leads to

$$\frac{dV_1}{dr} - \frac{dB_1}{dr} - \frac{NdFP_1}{dr} = 0,$$

where the derivatives are with respect to r, the risk-free interest rate. Of course B_1 is fixed, so $dB_1/dr = 0$. Recall from Chapter 4 that the change in the present value of a cash flow relative to a change in interest rates is related to the Macaulay duration of the cash flow. In general, we have

$$D = \frac{-\dfrac{dV}{V}}{\dfrac{dr}{R}},$$

where D is the duration, V is the present value of the cash flow, and $R = 1 + r$. This equation applies to both assets and liabilities, so after rearranging terms, we find that

$$dV_1 = -D(V_1)\left(\frac{V_1}{R}\right)dr$$

and

$$dFP_1 = -D(FP_1)\left(\frac{FP_1}{R}\right)dr,$$

where D( ) denotes duration of the indicated cash flow. Now substitution in the equation involving N eventually leads to

$$N = \left[\frac{D(V_1)}{D(FP_1)}\right]\left[\frac{V_1}{FP_1}\right].$$

The duration $D(FP_1)$ is equal to the duration of the deliverable assets (this is left as an exercise), which is a 90-day zero coupon bond. In Chapter 4, we showed that the duration of a zero coupon bond is equal to its maturity. Hence $D(FP_1) = 90/360 = 0.25$ years. The first-year benefits payments are all paid at the end of the year, so like a zero coupon bond, duration $D(V_1) = 1$ year. Hence, we arrive at the value of N:

$$N = \frac{4V_1}{FP_1}.$$

The futures price of a 90-day, $1,000,000 zero coupon bond calculated at 8 percent is $980,969. This yields N = 8. The calculations are similar for years 2, 3, and 4 and are left as exercises. The following table gives the results.

Year	1	2	3	4
N	8	16.8	26.5	37

If a 2 percent increase does occur, and the insurance company does not change its holdings of bonds and futures, this is how its position would develop. The future contracts are initiated when interest is 8 percent so the initial futures price for a $1,000,000 contract is $980,969 (= $1,000,000/1.08^{0.25}$). After a shift to 10 percent (= 8 percent + 2 percent inflation), the futures price is $976,467 (= $1,000,000/1.10^{0.25}$). Thus each contract will yield $4,502 to the seller.

Year	Expected Benefits (Inflation at 7%)	Bond Maturities (Zero Coupon 8% Bonds)	Futures Proceeds	Net Loss
1	$2,008,133	$1,970,598	$ 36,016	$ 1,519
2	2,148,703	2,069,128	72,932	6,643
3	2,299,112	2,172,585	119,303	7,224
4	2,460,050	2,281,214	166,574	12,262
				$27,648

The futures hedge reduced the impact of an increase in inflation of 2 percent from a loss of $422,473 to a loss of $27,648 over the four-year period. The values of N for all four years were determined in the first year in order to minimize the net loss due to changes in inflation. The outcome depends on actual inflation. Determining the effect of a decrease in inflation rates (with the same futures holding) is a similar calculation, which we leave to the reader.

Futures market participants can be categorized as hedgers or speculators. A *hedger* typically is stuck with a spot position that cannot be effectively traded within a reasonable time period. This is a "nontradable asset" case; for example, the farmer discussed earlier is stuck with the "opportunity" holding of the spot asset for the six-month period to the crop's maturity.[16] The hedger then tries to protect the value of this spot position by shifting the risk of unanticipated price changes to a speculator. A *speculator* is an investor who is willing to assume the risk of an adverse price change in the affected commodity and expects to be compensated for doing so. In contrast to hedgers, speculators may have an entirely flexible position in terms of trading assets; that is, they are free to open or close out any spot or futures position in response to market movements.

It is generally conceded that interest rates fluctuate randomly over time;[17] in fact, anyone who can sensibly predict the next interest rate movement could be a millionaire in no time. For example, the expectation that interest rates on bonds will go down implies that bond prices will rise. Thus, by simply purchasing the bond in the spot market or taking a long position in the futures market, the speculator can reap profits from the anticipated interest rate movement. It has been argued that investors respond so quickly to released new information that the possibility of sustained successful speculation would be quite slim.[18] This argument supports the assertion that hedging—the risk-shifting motive—is the predominant reason for the enormous growth of the financial futures markets. However, speculators' contributions are not limited to absorbing unwanted hedging risks. Later in the chapter, we will see how speculators' expertise and arbitrage activities contribute to the efficiency of spot markets.

Hedging with Financial Futures

Hedging with futures contracts can provide an inexpensive way to reduce or eliminate interest rate risk. Hedging interest rate risk traditionally has involved the use of one of a variety of *immunization* strategies. An immunization strategy is a procedure designed to protect asset or portfolio value from unanticipated fluctuations due to price or interest rate changes. Most commonly used immunization strategies are "duration based."[19] *Duration,* as Macaulay proposed, can be expressed as[20]

(17.1)
$$D = \frac{-(dS/S)}{(dR/R)},$$

---

[16]Of course, the farmer can sell the crop in the forward market at any time during the production period if such a market exists and the forward price is desirable.

[17]Interested readers are referred to the booklet by Roll (1970).

[18]We discussed the speed with which information becomes reflected in market prices in Chapter 10.

[19]For a discussion of this type of immunization strategy, see Grove (1974).

[20]The original Macaulay definition of duration was

$$D = \sum_{t=1}^{m} \frac{tC_t}{R^t} \Big/ \sum_{t=1}^{m} \frac{C_t}{R^t},$$

where C_t is the cash flow from the asset at time t and m is the asset's maturity. This expression is mathematically equivalent to Equation 17.1 for infinitesimal changes in the asset's yield. For a review of duration, see Chapter 4.

where S is the instrument's spot price and R equals 1 plus the asset's yield (for example, yield to maturity). Equation 17.1 measures the response of price to a proportional change in the interest rate.

To illustrate the notion of immunization, suppose that a company's asset portfolio has a maturity structure that is different from its liability portfolio's — that is, the duration of its assets differs from the duration of its liabilities. By setting the duration of the asset and liability portfolios equal, any change in interest rates will affect both sides equally; thus, the company will have been immunized against interest rate changes. However, as time passes and interest rates change, the company must adjust its asset and/or liability portfolio so as to continually equate their durations.[21] Needless to say, this constant readjustment is costly, especially during periods of extremely volatile interest rates. Hedging through futures market transactions can be much more cost effective than adjusting the firm's asset and/or liability portfolio.[22] Example 2 illustrates this.

Valuing Futures Contracts

Term Structure of Interest Rates

Bonds with different maturity dates offer different interest rates.[23] At any point in time it is possible to derive a term structure of interest rates from a representative financial instrument such as the yields on risk-free zero coupon U.S. Treasury issues. On a 90-day pure discount bond, the annualized yield at time 0 is

$$\frac{\text{Face value} - S}{S} \times \frac{360}{90},$$

where S represents the instrument's current market price and face value the payment promised by the issuer at maturity. The annualized yield on a 180-day pure discount bond can be calculated by the same formula, substituting 180 for 90.

The collection of these yields at time 0 represents the *spot term structure*.[24] Futures contracts written on these Treasury issues will generate a *futures term structure*. For example, the futures rate on a 1-year loan 5 years hence can be calculated as follows:

$$\frac{F_1(0, 5) - \text{Face value}}{F_1(0, 5)},$$

---

[21]This point can be easily seen from the original definition of duration in footnote 20. Readers interested in comparing strategies involving futures contracts and duration are referred to Kolb (1984).

[22]For a "round" — that is, the initiation and closing out of a futures contract — a trader could pay as little as $8.

[23]For an extensive discussion on the term structure of interest rates, see Van Horne (1984).

[24]We can calculate forward rates from spot rates. For example, the implied forward rate on a 1-year loan 5 years hence would be $(_5R_1 - 1)$, where

$$_5R_1 = \frac{(1 + {_0r_6})^6}{(1 + {_0r_5})^5}$$

and $_0r_6$ is the current (period 0) spot rate for a 6-year loan.

where $F_1(0, 5)$ represents the futures price at time 0 of a futures contract maturing 5 years later that calls for the delivery of a financial instrument maturing at the end of year 6 provided the contract still exists at that time. The forward rate implicit in the futures term structure can be calculated in the same way as the forward rate implicit in the spot term structure (see footnote 24).

The two term structures will not be perfectly parallel because trading in spot versus futures contracts involves different transactions costs. Of course, if there were no transactions costs, arbitrageurs would force them to converge.[25]

Transactions Costs Incurred in Trading Financial Futures

Except for brokerage fees and other costs of conducting arbitrage, futures trading involves *marking to the market* or *daily resettlement*. As soon as a transaction is made in a futures market, both parties are requested to deposit an *initial margin* in the form of cash or marketable securities. The purpose of these deposits is to guarantee performance under the contract terms. Such a guarantee is important in futures market trading because traders agree to buy or sell a commodity at a specified price only on the contract maturity date rather than on the date the contract is written. Later, as futures prices change, the clearinghouse requires daily cash resettlements for all contracts traded. Each day the losing party — either a buyer or a seller of futures contracts — must pay the full amount of the change in the futures price that occurred on that day. Brokers must pay additional sums to the clearinghouse to cover losses sustained by their customers. The customers, in turn, must deposit additional funds with their brokers in order to maintain the value of their accounts at the required *maintenance margin*. These immediate settlements of accounts constitute marking to the market.

The required minimum margin deposit is usually based on the daily price change limit set by the exchange.[26] With all traders prepared for price changes on the next trading day, contract performance is thus guaranteed. If a losing trader finds it difficult to put up the necessary funds to replenish the margin account after daily resettlement, he or she may quit at that point without creating any default.

Thus, the margin requirement (the initial margin plus all later margin variations) serves to insure the healthy functioning of the futures markets. By making the margin payments, the purchaser and seller acquire the right to benefit from price changes. In the interest rate futures markets, the initial margin requirement may be satisfied by depositing an interest-earning government security with the broker. The trader still earns interest on the instrument deposited; therefore, the initial margin requirement is no trouble for traders who already hold government

---

[25]If interest rates on futures contracts differ significantly from forward rates, the markets are said to be inefficient and there exists an opportunity for arbitrage. For a summary of the empirical evidence on market efficiency related to the spot versus futures markets, see Van Horne (1984), Chapter 10. This book also discusses conditions under expectations and backwardation, the factors in the term structure of interest rates that most often influence forward and futures prices. We briefly discuss backwardation in a later section.

[26]Organized exchanges usually stipulate minimum and maximum price changes. For example, for any bid or ask the minimum price change set by the IMM is 1 basis point (0.01 percent), or $25. The daily maximum price change is 50 basis points, which is equivalent to $1,250.

bonds or bills. However, daily resettlements from margin variations must be paid in cash, which may create a liquidity problem for traders when the market has persistently moved against their positions. Note that it is because of uncertain future interest rates that investors are motivated to use futures contracts for hedging. However, the requirement of daily resettlement may impose some interest rate risk on both buyer and seller.

The liquidity problem is further augmented by the high leverage present in futures contract trading. The initial margin usually is less than 10 percent and, for some commodities, may be less than 1 percent of the futures price. For example, for the IMM (International Monetary Market of the Chicago Mercantile Exchange) $1 million 90-day T-bill futures contract, the initial margin is only $1,500. Thus the trader's leverage is extremely high and, hence, so is risk. A slight change in the contracted price of the same futures may imply a substantial change in the amount of money in a trader's account. For example, a 0.1 percent change in a futures contract price of $1 million equals a $1,000 change in margin. The $1,000 change in the $1,500 initial margin represents a 67 percent change in the trader's equity. It is this leverage factor that makes naked futures contracts high-risk investments.

Therefore, an investor who intends to hold futures contracts (for any reason) must consider the liquidity problem implied by the requirement of daily resettlement. Although exchanges impose daily price change limits, such market intervention may not substitute for the basic economic changes. That is why at certain times, when the market has consistently been moving in the same direction, the IMM may allow for expanded daily price limits of 75 basis points or even no limits. This suggests that the daily price change limit may delay the liquidity strain for only a time.

Equilibrium Pricing of Futures Contracts

Although most futures traders do not hold the contract until maturity, those who do are guaranteed delivery on the maturity date. The delivery ensures convergence of the futures price with the commodity's cash price. Let us denote the futures price at time t of a contract maturing at time d as $F(t, d)$; then, at maturity the futures price is exactly the spot price, $S(d)$:

(17.2) $$F(d, d) = S(d).$$

If this convergence fails to occur, an opportunity for an arbitrage profit will exist. For example, if the futures price is greater than the spot price, an arbitrageur can purchase in the spot market, sell the futures contract, and deliver the instrument at the higher futures market price. Therefore, convergence must occur and thus provide a basis for futures contract pricing.

Earlier discussions noted that the value of financial assets is equivalent to price. However, this is *not* the case with futures contracts. Entering a futures contract costs nothing; further, except for marking to the market, no cash flow takes place until the contract's maturity. Therefore, at the time of contracting futures contracts have no value. A futures price is roughly the price that market participants expect will prevail at maturity. After the futures price has been fixed by contracting, the futures contract may have (positive or negative) value as a result of price fluctuation. Consequently, the futures price does not equal the value of the futures contract. Note too that the requirement of daily resettlement essentially resets the contract's value to zero every day.

A well-known proposition by Cox, Ingersoll, and Ross (CIR) (1981) concerning futures prices states that *the futures price, F(t, d), is the value at time t of a contract that pays at time d the following amount:*

(17.3) $S(d)R_t R_{t+1} \ldots R_{d-1},$

where d is the maturity of the futures contract; $S(d)$ is the price at time d of the financial instrument on which the contract is written; and R_t is 1 plus the spot interest rate prevailing from time t to time $t + 1$, for $t = 1, 2, \ldots, d - 1$.

We have stated the CIR result in its original generality. However, we have been working in a more restrictive setting, with constant risk-free interest rates, for example. In our setting this result is quite easy to establish, indeed it follows from the equivalence of forward and futures values. It is not surprising then that the CIR argument (presented in Appendix 17A) uses the same rollover futures technique used to show the equivalence of futures and forward values.

In the notation used earlier, r is the continuously compounded annual risk-free interest rate. In this setting the proposition is that the futures price $F(t, d)$ is the value of a contract promising a single cash flow of $S(d)(1 + r)^T$ at time $d = t + T$. To see this, consider a portfolio consisting of the amount $F(t, d)$ invested at time t at the risk-free rate and $(1 + r)^T$ long forward contracts (or equivalently, rollover futures arrangements) calling for delivery at time d. The value of the portfolio at time t is $F(t, d)$, the futures price. At time d, the value is

$$F(t, d)(1 + r)^T + (1 + r)^T[F(d, d) - F(t, d)] = S(d)(1 + r)^T.$$

Daily Resettlement and the Risk of Ruin

A question raised by Kuo (1986) originates from observations of futures traders' practice — namely, not all traders in the futures markets close out their positions daily. A "typical" trader (with limited net worth) who does not close out his or her futures position for some time will, due to the randomness of futures prices and the requirement of daily resettlement, face the risk of "ruin" in the form of liquidity exhaustion. To forestall this problem and avoid being forced to quit futures contract holdings, traders are advised to set aside a certain amount of "working capital" with which to meet brokers' "margin calls."[27] Note that *especially for hedgers,*[28] maintaining the desired futures position is the key to an effective hedge. If a hedger is forced to close out the position early (due to excessive margin calls), the hedge will become ineffective. Only when the hedger has no additional source of financing with which to make up the deteriorated maintenance margin account is the futures position liquidated.

---

[27]Cox and Kuo (1986) suggest a way to derive "optimal working capital" for sustaining futures contracts holding.

[28]Recall that the most important purpose served by futures markets is hedging.

Strategies Involving Futures Contracts

Short Hedge

A *short hedge* involves the sale of a futures contract. This type of hedge usually arises when the hedger has a commitment to sell some spot assets in the future. For convenience we limit the discussion to bond futures, but similar remarks apply to other futures contracts. Because of the risk of a decline in value in response to a rise in interest rates, the hedger sells a futures contract that calls for delivery of the same or a similar instrument whose price will move closely with those of the spot assets.[29] Note that a commitment to buy forward in the spot market at a fixed price can also be hedged by this strategy;[30] then, if the spot price really declines, the loss in the spot position can be offset by the gain in the futures, since the selling price in the futures position is fixed by the futures contract. There are many potential users of short hedges. For example, mortgage bankers and savings and loan institutions that acquire pools of mortgages are susceptible to losses if interest rates rise before they resell the mortgages.[31]

Using the mean-variance, two-period framework, suppose that a short hedger pays $S(0)$ for a spot position (for example, GNMA certificates) and simultaneously sells a futures contract maturing at time d at an agreed-upon price of $F(0, d)$. Suppose that at time t the hedger sells the GNMA at the current price of $S(t)$ and also closes the futures position by buying a futures contract priced at $F(t, d)$. With payments $S(0)$ and $F(t)$ and receipts $F(0)$ and $S(t)$, the total return is

(17.4) $[F(0, d) + S(t)] - [S(0) + F(t, d)] = [F(0, d) - S(0)] - [F(t, d) - S(t)]$.

Therefore, the expected return of the hedged portfolio, E_{sh}, is

(17.5) $E_{sh} = [F(0, d) - S(0)] - E[F(t, d) - S(t)]$

and the variance, σ_{sh}^2, is $\mathrm{Var}[F(t, d) - S(t)]$; that is,

(17.6) $\sigma_{sh}^2 = \sigma_F^2 + \sigma_S^2 - 2\mathrm{Cov}(F, S)$.

In "The Optimal Hedge: A Mathematical Overview," we incorporate this mean and variance information.

Long Hedge

A *long hedge* involves the purchase of a futures contract and provides some protection against an interest rate decrease. For example, a firm with a commitment to sell a mortgage at a fixed price will incur an opportunity loss if interest rates decline. It may hedge against the loss by buying GNMA futures. If interest rates do

---

[29]This is sometimes called a *cash hedge.*

[30]This is an *anticipatory hedge.* Some argue that the anticipatory hedge is more pertinent in financial futures markets (see Franckle and Senchack [1982]).

[31]A mortgage can be viewed as a commitment to buy an asset at a fixed price.

decline, there will be a gain from the futures position that will offset the opportunity loss in the spot position resulting from the fixed GNMA contract price.

The long hedger's return is the opposite of the short hedger's. Suppose the future fixed price to sell on the spot market is $S(0)$, the purchase price of the GNMA futures is $F(0, d)$, and at time t the hedger sells the contract at $F(t)$. The total return at time t is $[F(t, d) - F(0, d)] + S(0)$. The hedger wants to compare this hedged return with the true spot market price, $S(t)$. The true return is

(17.7) $[F(t, d) - F(0, d)] + [S(0) - S(t)] = [F(t, d) - S(t)] - [F(0, d) - S(0)]$.

Thus, the expected return for the hedged portfolio is

(17.8) $E_{1h} = E[F(t, d) - S(t)] - [F(0, d) - S(0)]$.

The variance of the return for this long hedger is the same as that for the short hedger, since the random variables, $F(t, d)$ and $S(t)$, are the same.

The Optimal Hedge: A Mathematical Overview

An optimal hedging position can be derived by applying Markowitz's mean-variance portfolio approach. In the case of a short hedge, the expected return of the hedged position, denoted by E_{sh}, is given by Equation 17.5; the corresponding expected return without hedging, E_{uh}, is simply

(17.9) $E_{uh} = E[S(t)] - S(0)$.

If a risk-free asset exists, a portfolio P, composed of that asset and the hedged and unhedged positions, has an expected rate of return of E_p:

$$E_p = X_{sh}E_{sh} + X_{uh}E_{uh} + (1 - X_{sh} - X_{uh})r$$

(17.10) $= r + X_{sh}(E_{sh} - r) + X_{uh}(E_{uh} - r)$,

where r is the risk-free rate of return, X_{sh} is the proportion invested in the hedged position, and X_{uh} is the proportion invested in the unhedged position.

Portfolio variance can be expressed as follows:

(17.11) $\sigma_p^2 = X_{sh}^2\sigma_{sh}^2 + X_{uh}^2\sigma_{uh}^2 + 2X_{sh}X_{uh} \, \text{Cov}(sh, uh)$,

where σ_{uh}^2 is the variance of the unhedged position, which is simply the variance of the spot asset price, σ_S^2. Further, $\text{Cov}(sh, uh)$ denotes the covariance between the returns of the hedged and unhedged positions. Therefore, we can formulate the hedger's problem by the *quadratic programming* method — namely, the hedger selects a portfolio with the minimum standard deviation for a given expected return:

$$\min \sigma_p = [X_{sh}^2\sigma_{sh}^2 + X_{uh}^2\sigma_{uh}^2 + 2X_{sh}X_{uh} \, \text{Cov}(sh, uh)]^{1/2}$$

subject to

(17.12) $E_p^* = r + X_{sh}(E_{sh} - r) + X_{uh}(E_{uh} - r)$,

where E_p^* represents a given return. The Lagrangian function, then, is

(17.13) $L = \sigma_p - \lambda\{E_p^* - [r + X_{sh}(E_{sh} - r) + X_{uh}(E_{uh} - r)]\}$.

At the optimal proportion, X_{sh}^*, the following conditions hold:

(17.14) $\frac{1}{2}[2X_{sh}\sigma_{sh}^2 + 2X_{uh}\,\mathrm{Cov}(sh, uh)]\sigma_p^{-1} = \lambda(E_{sh} - r)$.

(17.15) $\frac{1}{2}[2X_{uh}\sigma_{uh}^2 + 2X_{sh}\,\mathrm{Cov}(sh, uh)]\sigma_p^{-1} = \lambda(E_{uh} - r)$.

Dividing Equation 17.14 by Equation 17.15 and denoting $k = X_{sh}/X_{uh}$ as the proportion of the spot assets that are hedged, we obtain

(17.16) $\dfrac{E_{sh} - r}{E_{uh} - r} = \dfrac{k\sigma_{sh}^2 + \mathrm{Cov}(sh, uh)}{\sigma_{uh}^2 + k\,\mathrm{Cov}(sh, uh)}$.

Therefore, after simplifying, we obtain the optimal hedge ratio:

(17.17) $k^* = \dfrac{\mathrm{Cov}(sh, uh)\,(E_{uh} - r) - \sigma_{uh}^2(E_{sh} - r)}{\mathrm{Cov}(sh, uh)\,(E_{sh} - r) - \sigma_{sh}^2(E_{uh} - r)}$.

This optimal hedge ratio gives the proportion of spot assets that should be hedged given the current information about spot and futures prices.

The Cross Hedge and Basis Risk

The difference between the futures and spot price at any point in time is called the *basis*. Let us denote the basis at time t as $b(t)$; thus, $b(t) = S(t) - F(t)$. We expect that when the hedge is perfectly effective, one position's gain will be totally offset by the other position's loss; that is, the perfect hedge will be obtained when Equation 17.4 or 17.7 is zero. Based on this notion, the traditional theory of hedging features the *direct hedge,* which means taking equal and opposite positions in a futures contract involving the same cash good. However, in practice it is often difficult to find a futures contract written on an identical commodity (or perfect substitute) with the desired covariance between spot and futures prices. Especially in the interest rate futures markets, traders usually hold several instruments and hedge them with groups of different instruments. The hedged and hedging instruments may differ with respect to (1) risk level, (2) coupon, (3) maturity, (4) time span covered by the instrument being hedged, and (5) instrument deliverable against the futures contract. Therefore, a cross hedge obviously is more common than a direct hedge.

    In a *cross hedge,* one type of instrument is hedged with another. However, with a cross hedge different commodities underlying the futures and cash positions will have different price sensitivities to economic shocks. Cootner (1967, p. 66) commented, "In normal hedging practice, price changes are not expected to be offsetting and while risks will be reduced, they will not be eliminated." Therefore, we expect that the total return, such as in Equation 17.4 or 17.7, will rarely be zero. This is the *basis risk* of hedging, since the total return is the difference between the basis of the initiation and that of the closing out of a futures contract. In other words, basis risk exists in most hedging transactions and cannot be completely eliminated except in the rare case of a perfect hedge.

Portfolio Approach to Hedging

Anderson and Danthine (1981) argued that the existence of basis risk means that a hedge with only a single futures contract may be less desirable than one involving a portfolio of futures. By holding a well-diversified portfolio of futures contracts, the chief uncertainty associated with futures price fluctuations becomes the portfolio's systematic *market risk*. In this case, the most effective hedging occurs where diversifiable risk is eliminated. Anderson and Danthine applied mean-variance analysis to a two-period framework (periods 0 and 1) to derive the optimal hedging portfolio. In particular, supposing that n different futures contracts are available for hedging m spot assets, a typical agent's period 1 net revenue, π, is given by

(17.18) $\pi = [S(1) - S(0)]^T X(S) - [F(1, d) - F(0, d)]^T X(F)$,

where X(F) is a column vector representing the amount of the futures sold at time t = 0 and X(S) is a column vector representing the spot positions to be sold at t = 1. (The superscript T denotes the transposed matrix.) The hedger's optimal hedging problem, then, can be formulated as the ordinary mean-variance portfolio approach with $E(\pi)$ and $Var(\pi)$.

Note that this formulation of the problem differs from Equation 17.12 (see "The Optimal Hedge: A Mathematical Overview") in that it does not distinguish between hedged and unhedged positions; all spot and futures positions can be changed in response to market conditions. The basis risk involved in Equation 17.18 is the major concern here.[32] Note too that this portfolio approach obscures the distinction between hedgers and speculators. A hedger becomes a speculator whenever all spot holdings can be freely disposed of at any point in time. In fact, some researchers have argued that all futures traders should be viewed simply as profit maximizers.

Hedging Corporate Bond Holdings with U.S. T-Bond Futures[33]

Changes in the market values of a wide variety of debt instruments are dominated by changes in a common term structure. This implies that the hedging potential of particular interest rate futures is not limited to the respective underlying instruments. We now present an example of how T-bond futures can be used to hedge the price risk of corporate bond holdings. In particular, this example shows

---

[32]Kuo (1986) extended this mean-variance, two-period portfolio approach to a dynamic optimal hedging model that explicitly takes into account the cost/revenue of working capital financing and the total budget constraint for daily resettlement.

[33]This section is adapted from Kuberek and Pefley (1983). Refer to this paper for a practical example.

that under certain assumptions, the optimal hedge ratio can be estimated directly from applying simple regression to the time series of past prices. This approach certainly has merit, since computer software for performing simple regression is readily available.

Bond investors who wish to avoid the interest rate risk inherent in these investments can do so by selling the appropriate financial futures contract. The optimal hedge ratio is derived by assuming that the hedger seeks to minimize the variance of the "unexpected" return, $U(1)$, on his or her combined spot/futures position, as defined by the following:

(17.19) $$U(1) = S(0)r_S(1) - X(F)[F(1, d) - F(0, d)],$$

where $S(0)$ is the dollar value of the spot position at time 0 and $r_S(1)$ the unexpected rate of return on the spot position from time 0 to time 1. Therefore,

(17.20) $$\frac{U(1)}{S(0)} = r_S(1) - \frac{X(F)}{S(0)}[F(1, d) - F(0, d)]$$

$$= r_S(1) - \frac{X(F)F(0, d)}{S(0)}\left[\frac{F(1, d)}{F(0, d)} - 1\right]$$

$$= r_S(1) - xr_F(1),$$

where x represents the hedge ratio, $X(F)F(0)/S(0)$, and $r_F(1)$ the rate of return from futures trading; $F(1, d)/F(0, d) - 1$. Thus, the variance of $U(1)/S(0)$, the unexpected rate of return on a hedged portfolio, is

$$Var[r_S(1)] + x^2 Var[r_F(1)] - 2x Cov[r_S(1), r_F(1)].$$

Minimizing this variance with respect to x, we obtain the optimal hedge ratio:

(17.21) $$x^* = \frac{Cov[r_S(1), r_F(1)]}{Var[r_F(1)]}.$$

Therefore, the optimal number of futures, $X(F)^*$, is

(17.22) $$X(F)^* = \frac{x^*S(0)}{F(0, d)}.$$

By assuming that $r_S(1)$ and $r_F(1)$ are stationary, normal processes, we can express their relationship by

(17.23) $$r_S(1) = \alpha + \beta r_F(1) + u(1)$$

and, provided that the error term is serially uncorrelated,[34] the ordinary least square estimator, β_{OLS}, is

---

[34]These are standard assumptions for ordinary least square estimators.

$$\beta_{\text{OLS}} = \frac{\text{Cov}[r_S(1), r_F(1)]}{\text{Var}[r_F(1)]},$$

since $\text{Cov}[r_F(1), u(1)] = 0$ and $u(1) \sim N(0, \sigma^2)$. Therefore, by Equation 17.23, β_{OLS} will be a best linear unbiased estimator for the optimal hedge ratio. Thus, we can use past data to estimate the optimal hedge ratio by the simple regression model, Equation 17.23. In this case, we need not estimate individual parameters as we did for the optimal hedge ratio in Equation 17.17.

Note that in order to apply the model to daily futures prices, opening prices are preferred to settlement prices, since the former represent actual opening transactions on a given day while the latter are set by agreement and do not necessarily reflect an actual transaction.

An Institutional Note: Interest Rate Swaps

An *interest rate swap* generally involves two firms that "exchange" their interest payment obligations.[a] The motivation for such a transaction arises where one firm owns a set of assets that provide predominantly fixed returns but has incurred liabilities whose interest rates fluctuate with market rates (for example, a large savings and loan association whose assets consist primarily of fixed-rate mortgages but whose liabilities are made up of deposits in accounts whose rates fluctuate with market rates). On the other side of the transaction is a firm whose asset portfolio provides rates of return that fluctuate with the market interest rate and whose liabilities are largely fixed-rate securities (such as a large, international bank that has issued long-term fixed-rate bonds but invests in short-term loans whose rates of return mirror current market rates). By exchanging interest payment obligations, the two firms more closely match them with their earnings and thus reduce their exposure to interest rate risk. Note that the two firms do not actually "swap" liabilities or lend money to each other (each remains responsible for its own liabilities) but simply agree to make interest payments to each other for the duration of the swap contract. Further, swaps do not appear on either firm's balance sheet; they merely alter the two parties' exposure to interest rate risk.

The use of interest rate swaps originated in the Eurobond market in late 1981. The first U.S. transaction took place in 1982 between the Student Loan Marketing Association (Sallie Mae) and the ITT Financial Corporation, with Sallie Mae making floating-rate payments to ITT. Since then, the market for swaps has

---

[a]Interest rate swaps are only one type of swap agreement. Other types that have gained widespread use in recent years include currency swaps, commodity swaps, and basis rate swaps. For a discussion of these, see Smith, Smithson, and Wakeman (1986).

grown rapidly. Although there are no reporting requirements for swaps, their total dollar value was "conservatively" estimated at over $80 billion during 1984.[b]

A financial intermediary, such as an investment banker or commercial bank, usually arranges and services the swap transaction. The intermediary's functions include origination of the deal (arranging the swap) and servicing the contract once it has been concluded. In the latter instance, the intermediary serves as a settlement agent by collecting the interest payments from the two parties and paying the net difference to each. It can also act as a clearinghouse or dealer, in which case each party has an agreement only with the intermediary and does not know who the other swap party is. In this way, the intermediary builds up an inventory of swap agreements by completing one side of the contract at a time.

The actual swap agreement can be extremely complex; however, a typical agreement involves $25 million to $75 million and has a 3- to 10-year maturity on one side and a floating-rate loan on the other. A number of rate indices have been used for the floating-rate component. The London Interbank Offered Rate (LIBOR) was the index most often used in the early agreements; more recent swaps have been based on the U.S. prime rate, the Treasury bill rate, and other short-term costs of borrowing.

It is frequently argued that interest rate swaps arise because they permit firms to borrow in markets in which they lack a comparative advantage.[c] The basic idea here is that a firm, via a swap arrangement, can "refinance" using funds obtained from a market to which it ordinarily would not have access and at terms it could not achieve on its own. This brings up the question of market efficiency in the pricing of the swap terms that the firm receives. The voluminous literature on market efficiency (see Chapter 10) has fostered a healthy suspicion of claims that firms can achieve below-market financing rates via interest rate swaps. However, it may well be true that a firm can "refinance" its liabilities via a swap arrangement at a lower cost than it could obtain by entering into a refunding arrangement for its existing liabilities. To the extent that such transactions costs economies can be achieved, the interest rate swap would be preferred to refunding.

In essence, interest rate swaps provide a vehicle for "hedging" a firm's exposure to interest rate risk. In this chapter, we learned that futures markets provide yet another means for hedging interest rate risk exposure. It has been argued that interest rate swap agreements can be tailored to the parties' specific needs more closely and at a lower cost than can interest rate futures contracts. In other words, interest rate futures are "standardized" contracts that are traded on an organized market. Standardization of contracts and contract terms facilitates their exchange in an organized market, but it also makes them much more difficult to tailor to the parties' specific needs. Also, swaps can be arranged to cover a longer period than futures contracts and swaps have no margin requirements.

[b]This estimate was provided by Salomon Brothers, *The Economist*, March 16, 1985, Table 16, p. 30.

[c]Here comparative advantage in borrowing is reflected in lower borrowing rates and/or transactions costs.

Source: Jan G. Loeys, "Interest Rate Swaps: A New Tool for Managing Risk," *Federal Reserve Bank of Philadelphia Business Review* (May/June 1985), 17–25.

Options on Financial Futures

Options on futures contracts, also called *futures options,* require the delivery of the underlying futures contract if the option is exercised. Futures options are relatively new but have been accepted quite readily. They are written on commodity as well as financial futures. They are traded around the world, and all of the traded contracts are of the American type. Wolf (1982) describes futures options on commodities given valuation formulas for European futures options. More recently several papers on American futures option valuation have appeared — Ramaswamy and Sundaresan (1986), Stoll and Whaley (1986), and Barone-Adesi and Whaley (1987). Stoll and Whaley treat both financial and commodity futures options. The following development follows Stoll and Whaley and the work of others on which Stoll and Whaley relied — MacMillan (1986), Barone-Adesi and Whaley (1987), and Whaley (1986). We continue to concentrate on financial futures; only financial futures options are considered here.

Consider a long futures contract initiated at time t when the futures price is $F = F(t, d)$, expiring at time $d = t + T$ and requiring delivery of one share of the spot asset. An option could be written on the futures contract any time between t and d, the option expiring on or before time d. For simplicity, suppose that the option, like the futures, is written at time t and expires at time d. Let K be the exercise price. When the price $F(s, d)$, $t < s \le d$, is greater than K, the owner of a call option can obtain the futures by exercising the option and gain $F(s, d) - K$. There are no mark-to-the-market requirements until the option is exercised. However, after exercising the option, the option owner would have to mark to the market or close out the futures position. Thus the futures option is similar to a futures contract, but without the risk of adverse price movements until the option is exercised.

Of course, the futures option owner pays for this reduction in risk. The price paid is given by a formula analogous to the Black-Scholes formula for stock options. The European futures option pricing formula is due to Black (1976). Of course, our aim is to value American futures options. The method we prefer is the quadratic approximation technique (originally due to MacMillan), which relies on the European formula value plus an early exercise adjustment. We discussed this method briefly in Chapter 15. We will show here how it applies to futures options. First we consider Black's formula for European futures options, interesting because of the role they play in valuing American futures options.

Consider a long futures contract maturing at time $d = t + T$, requiring delivery of an asset having price $S(d)$ at time d. The futures price at time t is denoted $F = F(t, d)$ as before. A European call option on the futures contract initiated at time t, maturing at d, and having a striking price of K, gives the owner the right to take possession of the futures contract at time d for a price of K. At the end of the trading day the futures contract is marked to the market, in effect setting $F(d, d) = S(d)$. Thus the contract is of value to the option owner when $S(d) > K$. We denote the value by call(F, T, K). Black's formula is

$$\text{call}(F, T, K) = v^T[FN(y) - N(y - \sigma\sqrt{T})]$$

where $y = \left(\dfrac{1}{\sigma\sqrt{T}}\right) \ln(F/K) + \sigma\sqrt{T}/2$

$v = 1/(1 + r)$, r is the annual risk-free interest rate

$F = F(t, d)$, the futures price at time t

K = the exercise price

T = the time to expiration of the option and the futures contract

$\sigma^2 T$ = the variance of the log–price ratio, that is, σ is the futures price volatility

and $N(z)$ denotes the standardized normal cumulative distribution function evaluated at $z = y$ and $z = y - \sigma\sqrt{T}$. Note the similarity to the Black-Scholes call option stock formula of Chapter 15. The difference is in the first term, which is $SN(y)$ in the stock option formula where $S = S(t)$, but $v^T FN(y)$ here. This is explained by the relation $F = (1 + r)^T S$, which follows from this no-riskless-arbitrage argument: From the CIR proposition discussed in Appendix 17A we know that $F = F(t, d)$ is the value of a contract that pays $S(d) (1 + r)^T$ at time $d = t + T$. Another way to achieve the same result is to buy $(1 + r)^T$ shares of the asset at time t. The price of the asset purchase is $S(1 + r)^T$, and its value at time T is $S(d) (1 + r)^T$. The no-riskless-arbitrage axiom implies that the two portfolios have the same initial value, thus $F = S(1 + r)^T$. This explains the relation of the Black European futures option formula to the Black-Scholes stock option pricing formula.

The European and American values differ substantially for options that are deep in the money. The two values of $N(z)$ in Black's formula are approximately 1 for the large values of $z = y$ and $z = y - \sigma\sqrt{T}$, which occur for deep-in-the-money options. (This is because the ratio F/K and its natural logarithm are huge for deep-in-the-money contracts, so y and $y - \sigma\sqrt{T}$ are also very large values.) Hence the European formula gives approximately $v^T(F - K)$ as the option's value. However, an American option can be exercised immediately for $F - K$, so clearly the value of an American futures call is not the same as the corresponding European futures call.

Put-Call Parity for European Futures Options

There is a parity relation for European futures options similar to the parity relation for European stock options. Consider a portfolio consisting of a short futures contract and a long call option; that is, the owner has an obligation to sell at F and an option to buy at K. Here are the possible results at time $d = t + T$:

Position	Value If $S(d) > K$	Value If $S(d) \leq K$
Portfolio 1		
Short Futures	$F - S(d)$	$F - S(d)$
Long Call	$S(d) - K$	0
Total	$F - K$	$F - S(d)$

The initial value of the above portfolio is call(F, T, K). A second portfolio consists of an investment of $(F - K)v^T$ at the risk-free interest rate and a long put; that is, the owner has $F - K$ at maturity in addition to the right to sell at K. The results at time d are as follows:

Position	Value If $S(d) > K$	Value If $S(d) \leq K$
Portfolio 2		
Long Risk-Free	$F - K$	$F - K$
Long Put	0	$K - S(d)$
Total	$F - K$	$F - S(d)$

The initial value of this portfolio is $(F - K)v^T + \text{put}(F, T, K)$. The two portfolios have the same values at time d, regardless of how the prices move. Therefore, by the no-riskless-arbitrage principle, the initial values are the same:

$$\text{call}(F, T, K) = \text{put}(F, T, K) + (F - K)v^T.$$

The importance of the relation is that Black's formula for European call options on futures contracts, combined with the parity relation, gives a formula for European put options on futures contracts. And the European put value plus the early exercise premium yields the American value.

There are no parity equations for American futures options. However, the following inequalities give relations that American futures options must satisfy.

$$Fv^T - K \leq \text{Call}(F, T, K) - \text{Put}(F, T, K) \leq F - Kv^T.$$

The left-hand inequality follows from considering a portfolio consisting of a long call option, a short put option, a short futures contract, and a risk-free borrowing rate of $Fv^T - K$. (Note that this is analogous to the argument for European options.)

Initial Value	Intermediate Value at s $t < s < t + T$	Terminal Value	
		$S(d) > K$	$S(d) \leq K$
$-\text{Call}(F, T, K)$	$\text{Call}[F(s, d), T - s, K]$	$S(d) - K$	0
$\text{Put}(F, T, K)$	$-\text{Put}[F(s, d), T - s, K]$	0	$S(d) - K$
0	$[F - F(s, d)]v^{T-s}$	$F - S(d)$	$F - S(d)$
$Fv^T - K$	$K(1 + r)^s - Fv^{T-s}$	$K(1 + r)^T - F$	$K(1 + r)^T - F$

The total at maturity is $K(1 + r)^T - K$, which is positive. At any intermediate time s, the total if the put is exercised against the portfolio is

$$\text{Call}[F(s, d), T - s, K] - [K - F(s, d)] + [F - F(s, d)]v^{T-s}$$

$$+ K(1 + r)^s - Fv^{T-s}$$

$$= \text{Call}[F(s, d), T - s, K] + K(1 + r)^s - K + F(s, d)(1 - v^{T-s}).$$

Since K, $F(s, d)$, and the factors multiplying these values are positive, the call option price is positive at the intermediate time s even if the put is exercised. Hence, the initial value of the portfolio must be negative. (This is another application of the no-arbitrage principle.) Hence the left-hand side of the inequality is established. The right-hand side is similar, and is left as an exercise.

Valuing American Futures Options

The valuation method presented here is MacMillan's quadratic approximation, presented in Chapter 15 where it was applied to value American put options. Whaley and Barone-Adesi (1987) adapted his method to futures options. Its application to futures is discussed by Stoll and Whaley (1986) also. We follow this last reference closely.

Consider an American call option on a futures contract. An argument similar to that given in Chapter 15 for American puts establishes the following formula:

$$\text{Call}(F, T, K) = \text{call}(F, T, K) + B\left(\frac{F}{F^*}\right)^q \quad \text{when } F < F^*$$

$$= F - K \qquad\qquad\qquad \text{when } F \geq F^*$$

where F^* is the critical futures price defined below. The European option is calculated using Black's formula. The parameters B, F^*, q, and k are determined as follows:

$$B = \left(\frac{F^*}{q}\right)[1 - v^T N(d)]$$

$$d = \frac{1}{\sigma\sqrt{T}}\left[\ln\left(\frac{F^*}{K}\right)\right] + \frac{\sigma\sqrt{T}}{2}$$

$$q = \frac{[1 + \sqrt{(1 + 4k)}]}{2}$$

$$k = \frac{2\ln(1 + r)}{\sigma^2(1 - v^T)}$$

The critical futures price F^* is determined by solving iteratively the following equation:

$$F^* - K = \text{call}(F^*, T, K) + \frac{[1 - v^T N(d)]F^*}{q}.$$

Note that d must be recalculated at each iteration, since it depends on F^*. F^* is the critical futures price. Above this value, the American call on a future should be exercised immediately, yielding the owner $F - K$. For $F < F^*$, the American call option value exceeds the European option value by the early exercise premium, which is approximately $B(F/F^*)^q$.

For an American put option on a futures contract, the analogous formula is as follows:

$$\text{Put}(F, T, K) = \text{put}(F, T, K) + A\left(\frac{F}{F^*}\right)^p \quad \text{when } F > F^{**}$$

$$= K - F \qquad\qquad\qquad \text{when } F \leq F^{**}$$

The European option is calculated using Black's formula. The parameters F^{**}, p, and k are determined as follows:

$$A = -\left(\frac{F^{**}}{p}\right)[1 - v^T N(-d)]$$

$$d = \frac{1}{\sigma\sqrt{T}}\left[\ln\left(\frac{F^*}{K}\right)\right] + \frac{\sigma\sqrt{T}}{2}$$

$$p = \frac{[1 - \sqrt{(1 + 4k)}]}{2}$$

$$k = \frac{2\ln(1 + r)}{\sigma^2(1 - v^T)}$$

The critical futures price F* is determined by solving iteratively the following equation:

$$F^{**} - K = \text{put}(F^{**}, T, K) + \frac{[1 - v^T N(-d)]F^*}{p}.$$

Note that d must be recalculated at each iteration, since it depends on F*. F* is the critical futures price below which an American put on a future should be exercised immediately.

Issues in Futures Trading

Forecasting Ability of Futures Prices

Since futures prices are the prices agreed upon for delivery on a forward date, an interesting question arises as to whether they are unbiased predictors of expected futures spot prices. Generally they are not. Both logic and empirical evidence indicate that biases can be introduced into the relationship by the uncertainty associated with instantaneous spot interest rates, inflation exposure, or the marginal utility of future consumption of risk-averse traders.

   One bias was introduced by Keynes. He argued that since hedgers are net short,[35] they should pay risk premiums to induce speculators to cover their necessarily long positions. Such a risk premium would be subtracted from the expected spot price to yield the futures price:

   Futures price = Expected future spot price − Risk premium.

In other words, if supply and demand conditions for the spot asset remain the same between now and the maturity of the futures contract, the futures price should be lower than the current spot price because of the risk premium. Keynes termed this phenomenon *normal backwardation*. If this is correct, we may witness futures prices that are below expected spot prices. However, with factors such as the above introducing biases from all directions, risk aversion, although necessary for

---

[35]Hedgers usually have spot assets for sale on a forward date. According to our discussion of hedging strategies, this is the case of a short hedge. Keynes argued that in aggregation, such hedgers are net short.

a risk premium, is neither necessary nor sufficient for normal backwardation—that is, futures prices may be above expected spot prices because of the biases introduced into the former.[36] Consequently, many empirical tests have failed to verify normal backwardation. However, the issue is far from settled; for example, more sophisticated econometric methods may be developed for isolating the risk premium from real-world complexity such that the existence of normal backwardation can be verified.

In general, we conclude that futures prices are not unbiased predictors of expected future spot prices.

Information Role of Future Markets

Another important question with respect to futures trading is whether speculators will be so aggressive as to destabilize spot market prices. This question has far-reaching implications. For example, did the wild interest rate fluctuations of 1975 through 1980 result from the rapid growth of futures markets? In 1958, a similar issue prompted Congress to enact a law prohibiting futures trading in onions. Supporters of the law argue that futures markets are intrinsically more volatile than spot markets and futures market traders are more highly levered and speculative than spot investors. These factors have resulted in spot market destabilization because of the relentless arbitrage activities of futures traders.

However, empirical evidence to date does not support the destabilization hypothesis. Studies have shown that—contrary to claims by onion growers—futures trading has a stabilizing influence on spot prices; in other words, the random fluctuations in spot prices could be significantly reduced because of the existence of futures trading on spot assets. Cox (1976) suggested that futures trading increases market information and thereby increases the efficiency of spot prices. By "efficiency," he meant that spot prices provide more accurate signals for resource allocation when the given commodity has a futures market. This increase in information efficiency occurs because futures markets attract an additional set of traders (speculators) to the commodity's market. It is argued that a sufficient number of speculators who are willing to assume risk in inventory ownership and who possess forecasting skills actually moderates cash or spot price fluctuations. A recent study by Bortz (1984) concluded that there is no evidence that supports the assertion that the futures market in T-bonds has destabilized the underlying spot market.

Summary

In this chapter, we examined the nature of futures contracts, their importance in the economy, and the valuation theory and trading strategies relevant for futures

---

[36]According to expectations theory, speculators, being risk seekers, will squeeze out any risk premium. Therefore, on average the risk premium will be around zero. See Van Horne (1984) for a discussion of these theories.

markets. The current literature on futures markets is far from complete. As pointed out, the liquidity problem encountered by futures traders has been largely neglected by academicians. This issue eventually may prove to have extensive theoretical and empirical implications. For example, if those traders against whose positions the market has consistently moved try to liquidate their positions, will such action affect the demand for or supply of futures contracts? We hope the abundant market data generated by the rapid growth in these markets will provide the answers to questions such as this.

The futures markets are not without their problems. For example, when the number of futures contracts outstanding exceeds the total number of outstanding securities deliverable against them, a substantially short or long futures position is likely to affect the securities in question. In this case, the possibility of (spot) prices being seriously affected by either sheer demand or manipulation is an interesting topic of research.[37]

Study Problems

17.1   In September a pension fund manager is told to anticipate a year-end contribution of $1,000,000 from the pension plan sponsor. The manager decides that when the cash is received, in late December or early January, it will be invested in 90-day U.S. Treasury bills until a privately placed bond deal can be arranged. Describe how the manager can hedge the interest rate in September that the bills will yield by opening a futures position. Describe how the long-term bond interest rate that the private placement will yield can be hedged now by opening a futures position.

17.2   On September 1, the IMM index of 90-day U.S. Treasury bills for contracts calling for December (same-year) delivery is 92.54. On October 1, the index is 90.35. What is the dollar amount of the opportunity lost to the pension fund in Problem 17.1 if the manager does not hedge in the futures market?

17.3   Describe the three factors that may cause a liquidity problem for futures traders.

17.4   Explain the differences between a futures contract and an option on the same stock or index.

17.5   In January Joe and Nancy expect to finalize the purchase of a new home, which they will move in to in June. They will borrow $100,000 in January on a 15-year note to pay for part of the house. The rest of the purchase price, which has been fixed in a forward contract, and their share of transaction expenses amount to $20,000, which they will pay in cash. Current 15-year mortgage rates are 8.5 percent per year. Describe how Joe and Nancy can hedge the risk of a mortgage rate increase in the futures market. Of U.S. short-term bonds, U.S. long-term bonds, and a

---

[37] This problem has already occurred in the options markets.

stock market index, which is likely to provide the best hedge? What size position (and which way — long or short) should they take? What risk do they take by opening such a futures contract? Answer the same questions for a hedge based on an option to open a futures contract.

17.6   On September 1, the volatility of U.S. Treasury futures is 0.01. The risk-free rate r is 10 percent. The futures price (per $100 of face value) for December (same-year) delivery is 97.50. What does Black's formula give for the value of a call option to open a futures contract on December 1 with an exercise price of 90? (Hint: Convert price indices to corresponding invoice prices.)

17.7   Use the quadratic approximation to estimate the value of the early exercise privilege of an American option analogous to the one described in Problem 17.6. (The value of F*, the critical futures price, is $1,072,660.)

References

R. W. Anderson and J. P. Danthine, "Cross Hedging," *Journal of Political Economy* 89 (1981): 1182–1196.

———, "Hedging and Joint Production: Theory and Illustrations," *Journal of Finance* 35 (May 1980): 487–501.

M. R. Asay, "Implied Margin Requirements on Options and Stocks," *Journal of Portfolio Management* (Spring 1981): 55–59.

G. Barone-Adesi and R. E. Whaley, "Efficient Analytic Approximation of American Option Values," *Journal of Finance* (June 1987).

F. Black, "The Pricing of Commodity Contracts," *Journal of Financial Economics* 3 (January–March 1976): 167–179.

G. A. Bortz, "Does the Treasury Bond Futures Market Destabilize the Treasury Bond Cash Market?" *Journal of Futures Markets* 4 (Spring 1984): 25–38.

M. J. Brennen, "The Supply of Storage," *American Economic Review* 48 (1958): 50–72.

———, G. Courtadon, and M. Subrahmanyam, "Options on the Spot and Options on Futures," *Journal of Finance* 40 (December 1985): 1303–1317.

B. Brown and C. R. Geisst, *Financial Futures Markets* (New York: St. Martin's Press), 1983.

D. R. Cappoza and B. Cornell, "Treasury Bill Pricing in the Spot and Futures Markets," *Review of Economics and Statistics* 71 (1979): 513–520.

P. H. Cootner, "Speculation and Hedging," *Food Research Institute Studies* 7 (1967): Supp. 65–106.

J. C. Cox, "Futures Trading and Market Information," *Journal of Political Economy* 84 (1976): 1215–1237.

———, J. E. Ingersoll, Jr., and S. A. Ross, "The Relation between Forward Prices and Futures Prices," *Journal of Financial Economics* 9 (December 1981): 321–346.

S. H. Cox, Jr., and C. K. Kuo, "Underwriting Traders of Financial Futures," *Proceedings of the Symposia in Statistics and Festschrift in Honor of V. M. Joshi* (Boston: D. Reidel, 1986).

L. H. Ederington, "The Hedging Performance of the New Futures Markets," *Journal of Finance* 34 (March 1979): 157–170.

S. Figlewski, "Hedging with Stock Index Futures: Theory and Application in a New Market," *Journal of Futures Markets* 5 (Summer 1985): 183–199.

C. T. Franckle, "The Hedging Performance of the New Futures Markets: Comment," *Journal of Finance* 35 (December 1980): 1273–1279.

——— and A. J. Senchack, "Economic Considerations in the Use of Interest Rate Futures," *Journal of Futures Markets* 2 (1982): 107–118.

K. P. French, "A Comparison of Futures and Forward Prices," *Journal of Financial Economics* 12 (1983): 311–342.

G. Gordon and A. L. Rebell, *Financial Futures and Investment Strategy* (Homewood, Ill.: Dow Jones-Irwin, 1984).

F. L. Grauer and R. H. Litzenberger, "The Pricing of Commodity Futures Contracts, Nominal Bonds and Other Risky Assets under Commodity Price Uncertainty," *Journal of Finance* 34 (1979): 69–83.

M. A. Grove, "On Duration and the Optimal Maturity Structure of the Balance Sheet," *Bell Journal of Economics and Management Science* 5 (Autumn 1974): 696–709.

T. Ho, "Intertemporal Commodity Futures Hedging and the Production Decision," *Journal of Finance* 39 (1984): 351–376.

R. A. Jarrow and G. S. Oldfield, "Forward Contracts and Futures Contracts," *Journal of Financial Economics* 9 (December 1981): 373–382.

L. L. Johnson, "The Theory of Hedging and Speculation in Commodity Futures," *Review of Economic Studies* 27 (1960): 139–151.

J. C. Junkus and C. F. Lee, "Use of Three Stock Index Futures in Hedging Decisions," *Journal of Futures Markets* 5 (Summer 1985): 201–222.

A. Kamara, "Issues in Futures Markets: A Survey," *Journal of Futures Markets* 2 (1982): 261–294.

R. W. Kolb, *Interest Rate Futures: A Comprehensive Introduction* (Reston, Va.: Reston, 1984).

———, G. Gay, and W. Hunter, "Liquidity Requirements for Financial Futures Investments," *Financial Analysts Journal* (May/June 1985): 60–68.

R. C. Kuberek and N. G. Pefley, "Hedging Corporate Debt with U.S. Treasury Bond Futures," *Journal of Futures Markets* 3 (1983): 345–353.

C. K. Kuo, "The Risk of Ruin in Futures Market Trading" (Ph.D. diss., University of Texas at Austin, 1986).

R. Lang and R. Rasche, "A Comparison of Yields on Futures Contracts and Implied Forward Rate," *Federal Reserve Bank of St. Louis Review* (December 1978): 21–30.

L. G. MacMillan, "Analytic Approximation for the American Put Option," *Advances in Futures and Options Research* 1 (1986).

H. M. Markowitz, *Portfolio Selection: Efficient Diversification of Investments* (New York: Wiley, 1959).

R. Merton, "Optimal Consumption and Portfolio Rules in a Continuous-Time Model," *Journal of Economic Theory* 3 (1971): 373–413.

M. A. Monroe, "On the Estimation of Supply and Demand Functions: The Case of Interest Rate Futures Markets," *Research in Finance,* vol. 4 (New York: JAI Press, 1983), 91–122.

G. E. Morgan, "Forward and Futures Pricing of Treasury Bills," *Journal of Banking and Finance* 5 (December 1981): 483–496.

D. J. Nye and R. W. Kolb, "Inflation, Interest Rates, and Property–Liability Insurance Risk," *Journal of Risk and Insurance* (March 1986): 144–154.

W. Poole, "Using T-Bill Futures to Gauge Interest-Rate Expectations," *Federal Reserve Bank of San Francisco Economic Review* (1978): 7–19.

M. Powers and D. Vogel, *Inside the Financial Futures Markets,* 2d ed. (New York: Wiley, 1984).

K. Ramaswamy and S. M. Sundaresan, "The Valuation of Options on Futures Contracts," *Journal of Finance* 40 (December 1985): 1319–1340.

R. Reich, "New Uses for Excel," *MacUser* (December 1985): 141–146.

R. J. Rendleman and C. E. Carabini, "The Efficiency of the Treasury Bill Futures Market," *Journal of Finance* 34 (1979): 895–914.

R. F. Richard and M. Sundaresan, "A Continuous Time Equilibrium Model of Commodity Prices in a Multigood Economy," *Journal of Financial Economics* 9 (1981): 347–372.

R. Roll, *The Behavior of Interest Rates: An Application of the Efficient Market Model to U.S. Treasury Bills* (New York: Basic Books, 1970).

R. L. Rosa, "Financial Consequences of Trading Commodity Futures Contracts," *Illinois Agricultural Economics* (1975): 27–31.

D. J. S. Rutledge, "Trading Volume and Price Variability: New Evidence on the Price Effects of Speculation," in *International Futures Trading Seminar,* vol. 5 (Chicago: Chicago Board of Trade, 1978), 160–186.

P. Sarnoff, *Trading in Financial Futures* (New York: Universe Books, 1985).

C. D. Smith, *How to Make Money in Stock Index Futures* (New York: McGraw-Hill, 1985).

C. W. Smith, Jr., C. W. Smithson, and L. M. Wakeman, "The Evolving Market for Swaps," *Midland Corporate Finance Journal* (Spring 1986): 20–32.

J. L. Stein, "The Simultaneous Determination of Spot and Futures Prices," *American Economic Review* (December 1961): 223–235.

B. Stewart, "An Analysis of Speculative Trading in Grain Futures," *USDA Technical Bulletin*, no. 1001, 1949.

H. R. Stoll and R. E. Whaley, "New Option Instruments: Arbitrage Linkages and Valuation," *Advances in Futures and Options Research* 1 (1986): 25, 62.

L. G. Telser and H. N. Higinbotham, "Organized Futures Markets: Costs and Benefits," *Journal of Political Economy* 85 (1977): 969–1000.

J. C. Van Horne, *Financial Market Rates and Flows* (Englewood Cliffs, N.J.: Prentice-Hall, 1984).

N. S. Weiner, *Stock Index Futures: A Guide for Traders, Investors, and Analysts* (New York: Wiley, 1984).

R. E. Whaley, "On Valuing American Futures Options," *Financial Analysts Journal* 42 (May–June 1986): 49–59.

H. Working, *Selected Writings of Holbrook Working* (Chicago: Chicago Board of Trade, 1977).

A. Wolf, "Fundamentals of Commodity Options on Futures," *Journal of Futures Markets* 2 (1982): 391–408.

Appendix 17A

Proof of the Cox, Ingersoll, and Ross (CIR) Proposition

A well-known proposition by Cox, Ingersoll, and Ross (1981) concerning futures prices states that the futures price, $F(t, d)$, is the value at time t of a contract that pays at time d the following amount:

$$(17A.1) \qquad \qquad S(d)R_tR_{t+1} \ldots R_{d-1},$$

where d is the maturity of the futures contract; $S(d)$ is the price at time d of the financial instrument on which the contract is written; and R_k is 1 plus the spot interest rate prevailing from time k to time $k + 1$, for $k = 1, 2, \ldots, d - 1$.

   Equation 17A.1 can be derived by evaluating the results of the following strategy:

1. At time t, take an amount $F(t)$ and invest it in one-period bonds. Then continually reinvest in these bonds the principal and the accumulated interest at $t + 1, t + 2, \ldots$, until time $d - 1$. The current outlay for this investment is $F(t)$, while the payoff at time d is

$$F(t, d)R_tR_{t+1} \ldots R_{d-1}.$$

2. At each time j, $j = t, t + 1, \ldots, d - 1$, take a long position in N_j futures contracts, where $N_j = R_tR_{t+1} + \cdots + R_j$. Liquidate each contract after one period, and continually reinvest the (possibly negative) proceeds $[F(j + 1, d) - F(j, d)]$ and all accumulated interest in one-period bonds until time d. The current outlay is zero, while the payoff at time d is

$$\sum_{j=1}^{d-1} \{N_j[F(j + 1, d) - F(j, d)]\}R_{j+1}R_{j+2} \ldots R_{d-1}.$$

Combining steps 1 and 2, we obtain:

$$F(t, d)R_tR_{t+2} \ldots R_{d-1} + [F(d, d) - F(t, d)]R_tR_{t+2} \ldots R_{d-1}$$

$$= F(d, d)R_tR_{t+2} \ldots R_{d-1}$$

$$= S(d)R_tR_{t+1} \ldots R_{d-1},$$

that is, Equation 17A.1.

As already stated, the daily resettlements essentially reset the value of the futures contract to zero. Except for a small "round cost" charged by the broker, this "zero-bound" value is equivalent to liquidating the old contract and establishing a new one. This is exactly the strategy adopted in the CIR proposition to prove Equation 17A.1.

Chapter 18

Mergers and Acquisitions: Theory and Evidence

Firms can grow in one of two fundamental ways: internally via the acquisition of productive assets that are then placed into service or externally through the acquisition of another "ongoing" firm. Although both avenues to firm growth are obviously related, the analysis of the second type creates some special problems. For this reason, the subject of mergers and acquisitions has spawned its own specialized literature, which provides the basis for this chapter.

Merger and acquisition activity historically has been very volatile. For example, during 1974 there were only 926 merger completions involving the acquisition of interests of $1 million or more, while in 1986 there were 4,024 such transactions involving over $149,901 million.[1] Until the merger wave of the eighties, the industrial giants had been impervious to takeover attempts. However, the worldwide depression in the oil industry, combined with a more relaxed stance toward mergers by the Federal Trade Commission, has produced the largest mergers in history. In July 1981, Du Pont acquired control of Conoco for a record $7.3 billion following attempted takeovers by both Seagram Company of Canada and Mobil Oil Corporation. This merger created the seventh largest industrial company in the nation, with sales of over $32 billion. However, its status was eclipsed by the acquisition of Gulf Oil Company by Standard Oil of California for $13.2 billion in March 1984. This merger followed a lengthy takeover struggle between Gulf's

---

[1] See *Mergers and Acquisitions Almanac and Index* (May/June 1987).

management and a group of investors led by T. Boone Pickins of Mesa Petroleum. The Pickins group may have lost the war, but their $760 million gain on an investment of $1 billion certainly took some of the sting out of the defeat.

Table 18.1 lists the five biggest "deals" of 1985. Included are mergers that were announced during the year but which were not completed in 1985, as well as the advisers to the parties involved and the fees paid to them (where known).

Mergers and acquisitions can be classified according to the relationship between the business activities of the acquiring and acquired firm. A *horizontal* merger involves the merging of two firms that are involved in the same type of business activity; the combination of two retail department store chains would be an example. A *vertical* merger involves two firms in different stages of related production activities, such as a publishing house and a book binding company. Finally, a *conglomerate* merger involves two firms that produce and market products or services that are completely unrelated; an example would be the combination of a steel fabricating company, which produces and sells oil field drilling equipment, and a retail grocery chain. The various explanations for mergers differ with the type of combination involved. Heretofore the conglomerate type of merger has been the most difficult to explain. However, there do exist some "pure" financial theories of conglomerate mergers, which we will review later.

The term *takeover* is the one most frequently used to describe the subject matter of this chapter. Thus, we refer to the market for takeovers as one that encompasses all cases where one operating firm acquires control of, or otherwise combines with, another. The combination may be effected by the two entities "merging" or by the purchase of the target firm's stock by the acquiring firm via a *tender offer*. In mergers or tender offers, the acquiring firm offers to buy the target's common stock at a price above its current market value. In the case of a merger, the acquiring and target firms' managements negotiate the terms of the merger and then seek the approval of the target's shareholders. In a tender offer, the acquiring firm makes its purchase offer directly to the shareholders. The shareholders then must decide whether or not to tender their shares to the acquirer.

In a merger or successful tender offer, the acquired firm generally ceases to exist, and its operations are subsumed by the acquirer. Some mergers have resulted in the creation of an entirely new entity; that is, the two previously independent firms "consolidate" to form a new firm. However, the usual result is the former, wherein the acquirer becomes the merged firm.

Jensen and Ruback (1983) have suggested that at the heart of the merger and acquisition problem is the question of which management team has control over the new corporation's assets. They define *corporate control* as consisting of the package of rights necessary for overseeing the management of the corporation's resources—that is, the rights to hire, fire, and set the compensation of top-level managers (see Fama and Jensen [1983a, 1983b] for a detailed discussion of this concept of corporate control). In this context, we can think of the market for takeovers as the "market for corporate control," where management teams (from different firms) vie for control over the target firm's assets. This approach to the merger and acquisition literature is unique. The traditional assumption has been that financiers and activist stockholders are the parties who buy control of a company and exercise corporate control in the above sense. Jensen and Ruback, how-

Table 18.1 Five Largest Mergers of 1985

Acquirer	Adviser (Fee)	Acquired	Adviser (Fee)	Amount (Billions)
General Electric	Goldman (NA)	RCA Corporation	Lazard F. (NA)	$6.28
Kohlberg, Kravis, Roberts & Company	Kidder-Peabody (NA)	Beatrice	Solomon (NA) Lazard F. (NA)	$6.2
Philip Morris	F. Boston ($10.1 M)	General Foods	Goldman ($7.1 M) Shearson ($7.1 M)	$5.75
General Motors	Solomon ($8 M)	Hughes Aircraft Co.	F. Boston (NA) M. Stanley (NA)	$5.3
Allied Corporation	F. Boston ($10 M)	Signal Companies	Lazard F. ($10 M)	$5.0

Source: *Institutional Investor* 20 (January 1986): 264–265.

ever, see management teams as the primary activist parties; here shareholders play a relatively passive role until their votes are required to ratify management's actions. This "managerial control" notion of the market for corporate takeovers is certainly more pragmatically appealing than the traditional shareholder model.

The fundamental issues addressed in the literature on mergers and acquisitions can be summarized as follows:

1. *How large are the gains (losses) to the shareholders of the bidding and target firms?* At issue here is whether engaging in the takeover of another firm is in the best interests of the shareholders of each firm.

2. *Does the opposition to takeover attempts by target firms' managers have a net favorable or unfavorable impact on their shareholders' wealth?* Certainly some resistance to takeover attempts serves to drive up the acquiring firm's bid. However, the issue here is whether the target firm's management resists only to the extent necessary to maximize the wealth of their shareholders or goes beyond this limit in an effort to preserve its control over the corporation's assets.

3. *Is the market for corporate control competitive?* The concern here is whether or not all those firms that would expect to experience a positive net present value from an acquisition become engaged in, and actively bid for, its control.

In addition to the above, a number of studies have attempted to assess the effectiveness of antitrust activity with regard to corporate takeovers. Although this issue is important, we will not attempt to review it here.

This chapter is organized as follows. First, we consider the theory of mergers in light of the existing empirical evidence regarding merger activity. Then we consider the present state of research on mergers and acquisitions.

Mergers and Acquisitions: Theory

Shareholder Wealth and Corporate Takeovers: A Simple Example

The acquisition of one firm by another has long been a source of research interest in finance as well as in industrial organizations. The primary issue here has been: Do mergers and acquisitions enhance the wealth of acquiring firms' stockholders? If so, why? We will use this fundamental issue to introduce the basic valuation question that has arisen in the corporate takeover literature. Later we will present a more formal analysis. For our purposes now, consider the following simplified example.

Firms A and B are all equity financed, and each produces and markets the same product—doorknobs. Following are financial data for the two firms:

	A	B	A + B
Sales	$ 500,000	$ 500,000	$1,000,000
Expenses	400,000	400,000	800,000
Net income	100,000	100,000	200,000
Firm value[a]	$1,000,000	$1,000,000	$2,000,000

[a]Assuming no taxes, level perpetuities, a 100 percent dividend payout, and a 10 percent required rate of return on equity.

Note that by combining the two firms (column 4) we simply "add" their sales, expenses, incomes, and, finally, market values. This analysis is appropriate where there are no "synergistic" effects associated with the merger, that is, where the combined firm simply realizes the sales, expenses, income, and required rate of return of the two individual firms. In this instance, an investor could purchase the shares of each firm and "create" or duplicate the earnings stream that he or she would realize from the merged firm. It is obvious, then, that in the absence of synergy, mergers do not create wealth for the shareholders of the acquired or acquiring firm. This does not mean that diversification is undesirable; it simply implies that where individual investors can realize the benefits of diversification within their personal portfolios and there are no sources of synergy, diversification at the firm level will be redundant.

Mergers and Acquisitions with the CAPM

In a world characterized by the capital asset pricing model, we can easily demonstrate that in the absence of synergy, mergers and acquisitions do not increase the wealth of the takeover firm's shareholders. Consider firms A and B with the following market values (in the context of the CAPM):[2]

$$V_A = \frac{E(X_A) - \lambda Cov(X_A, R_M)}{1 + r_f}$$

$$V_B = \frac{E(X_B) - \lambda Cov(X_B, R_M)}{1 + r_f},$$

where X represents the firms' operating earnings, $\lambda = [E(R_M) - r_f]/\sigma_M^2$ (that is, the market price of risk), R_M is the rate of return on the market portfolio, and r_f is the risk-free interest rate. To simplify the example used here, we assume that both firms are entirely equity financed. If firm A decides to acquire control of firm B where there is no source of synergy in the merger such that $E(X_{A+B}) = E(X_A) + E(X_B)$, then, in accordance with the CAPM, the value of the combined firm will be

$$V_{A+B} = \frac{E(X_A + X_B) - \lambda Cov[(X_A + X_B), R_M]}{1 + r_f}.$$

---

[2]This is the certain equivalent form of the CAPM discussed in Chapter 9.

However, noting that[3]

$$E(X_A + X_B) = E(X_A) + E(X_B)$$

and

$$Cov[(X_A + X_B), R_M] = Cov(X_A, R_M) + Cov(X_B, R_M),$$

we see that:

$$V_{A+B} = V_A + V_B.$$

Therefore, in the absence of synergy there are no gains to the merging of two previously separate operating firms.

Theoretically we can think of synergy as creating an increment to the cash flows of the two firms being combined through merger, Δ, such that the value of the merged firm becomes

$$V_{A+B} = V_A + V_B + V_\Delta,$$

where $V_\Delta = [E(\Delta) - \lambda Cov(\Delta, R_M)]/(1 + r_f)$. Note that in order for the synergy to be due to the merger, it must be obtainable *only* where one firm acquires *control* over the other (that is, the benefits of synergy are *not* available to individual investors through diversifying their personal portfolios). Thus, so long as firm A does not have to pay a premium in excess of V_Δ (more than $V_B + V_\Delta$) for firm B, the acquisition will enhance the wealth of firm A's stockholders. Note too that firm B's shareholders gain the excess over V_B that they receive for their shares.

In the next section, we discuss the various sources of synergy gains from takeovers that create the theoretical basis for Δ. These sources of synergy, then, are the starting point for a "theory" of why mergers and acquisitions take place.

Potential Sources of Takeover Gains

We use *synergy* as a catchall term to describe the gains from mergers. A number of potential sources of synergy have been suggested in the merger and acquisition literature. Some of the more frequently mentioned ones are discussed in the following paragraphs.

Tax Considerations.   There are three instances in which taxes can play a significant role in explaining the occurrence of a merger or acquisition. The first relates to *underutilized tax credits*. In this case, a firm is in a position where its past losses (which can be carried forward to offset future tax liabilities) make it attractive for acquisition by a firm with a large current tax liability. The importance of this factor varies with the availability of alternative methods for taking advantage of unused tax credits. For example, the Economic Recovery Tax Act of 1981 (ERTA) created a provision for the direct sale of tax losses via the use of *safe har-*

---

[3]We discussed the properties of the expectations operator in Chapter 8.

bor leases.[4] However, the Tax Equity and Fiscal Responsibility Act of 1982 largely eliminated this provision, consequently making it more difficult for firms to use financial leases as a vehicle for selling unused tax credits.

A second way in which taxes influence the decision to acquire control of another firm relates to the *differential taxes paid on ordinary earned income and capital gains*. The lower taxes on capital gains are an incentive for firms with available cash to acquire companies with high growth potential. Since such a company will use all or most of its earnings to support its needs for asset acquisition, there will be little or no ordinary income created by the transaction (that is, the growth company pays few or no cash dividends during the time its stock is being held). At the time the firm is sold, the acquirer recognizes the increase in the growth firm's value as a capital gain, which in turn is taxed at a much lower rate than is ordinary income from operations.

Still another tax inducement to mergers and acquisitions arises where the owners of the acquired firm "exchange" their common stock for either common or preferred stock of the acquiring firm. In this instance, the acquired firm's stockholders effectively relinquish control of the acquired firm and reap whatever gains in value they have created without facing any tax liability at the time of the exchange. This occurs because "technically" they are still owners (albeit of the acquiring firm). These shareholders will incur a tax liability on the exchange only at the time they sell their shares in the acquiring firm.

Taxes play a particularly important role in mergers in which the acquired firm is a small or closely held company. In these circumstances, the controlling factor may be the personal tax implications for one or a limited number of major stockholders.

Avoiding the Costs of Bankruptcy and Increased Debt Capacity.[5]

Levy and Sarnat (1970) and Lewellen (1971) have suggested that mergers can create "financial synergy." The source of this synergy takes the form of a reduction in the expected costs of bankruptcy resulting from the merger of two firms whose earnings are less than perfectly positively correlated. Simply put, the diversification effect of the merger on the firm's earnings stream reduces the probability of bankruptcy, which, in combination with costly bankruptcy, leads to reduced expected costs of bankruptcy for the merged firm.

---

[4]Safe harbor or paper leases were intended to allow firms to effectively sell the tax benefits accompanying the purchase of plant and equipment to companies in higher corporate tax brackets. ERTA required the IRS to ignore its "true lease" requirements when evaluating such leases; thus, the leases could be structured strictly as a tax benefit sale without the risk of the IRS disallowing them. The Tax Equity and Fiscal Responsibility Act (TEFRA) of 1982 effectively terminated this provision of the 1981 tax law.

The Tax Reform Act of 1986 has eliminated the tax rate differential between ordinary income and capital gains income. However, capital gains are still not taxed until they are realized (the asset or firm is sold), thus there remains a tax "preference" for capital gains over ordinary income.

[5]We use the term *debt capacity* here to refer to the amount of borrowing a firm can carry in light of its ability to service the required principal and interest on that debt. We leave unspecified how this capacity is determined and refer the reader to Chapter 12 for a discussion of the possibilities.

Higgins and Schall (1975), Galai and Masulis (1976), and Scott (1977) have since pointed out that the financial synergy argument is not as clear-cut as it appears. First, in the absence of nonfinancial sources of synergy, the combination of two firms, other things equal, should not increase the market value of the combination above the sum of their individual premerger values. However, the market value of the combined firm's debt will rise with the merger, for it will then be protected by the equity of *both* the previously independent firms. Consequently, with the rise in debt value and a constant firm value, the value of the combined firm's equity must fall. This effect can be reversed, however. To do so, the management of the merged firm must increase the use of financial leverage such that the risk of insolvency will rise back to its premerger level for the independent firms. Thus, where there are tax subsidy advantages to using debt financing (as in the Modigliani and Miller [1963] tax-adjusted valuation model), the value of the merged firm and, consequently, its equity will rise due to the present value of the tax savings on the added debt of the merged firm.

Still another case for mergers can be made that rests on the reduced likelihood of bankruptcy. However, this argument is based on the desire of the firm's incumbent management to retain control of the firm (sometimes referred to as "managerialism"). Here the merging firm's management may not push the merged firm's risk of insolvency up to the premerger level, thus taking less than full advantage of the additional debt capacity created by the merger and, consequently, the potential increase in shareholder wealth. Thus, we see that mergers may be in the best interests of both the incumbent managerial team and the acquiring firm's stockholders. However, managerialism may lead management to take less than full advantage of the potential wealth created by the merger; in this instance, the merger may not benefit the shareholders.

Reduced Agency Costs.   The separation of ownership and control in the modern corporate enterprise gives rise to a classic principal-agent problem. In addition, as a result of the transactions costs incurred in exercising corporate control via proxy fights, corporations' security holders (bondholders and stockholders) effectively charge a "malfeasance" or "agency cost premium" when supplying funds to the corporation. The conglomerate form of organization offers the potential for an "organizational" solution to (or reduction in the magnitude of) the owner-agent problem; that is, the corporate level or holding company management can effectively monitor the managements of the individual firms within the conglomerate. Recognizing this potential "economy of scope" in monitoring, investors offer funds to the conglomerate at a reduced agency cost premium. Hence, the conglomerate's value rises above the sum of the premerger firms' values.

A question naturally arises as to the source of these purported economies of scope in monitoring. One possible answer lies in the need for maintaining proprietary information within the firm. Due to the loss in value of proprietary information if made public (announcement of the firm's clientele, new product plans and strategies, and so on), the firm's management is obliged not to reveal fully all the information needed to evaluate its past operating decisions and future plans (the information needed to effectively monitor management's behavior). However, this need for secrecy does not exist between the holding company management and the operating divisions. Thus, the owners of the holding company stock can rely on the holding company's management to perform in-depth analyses of the operating performances of divisional managers and thus bypass the agency problem inherent at that level of organization. Of course, the owners still must monitor the activities of the holding company's management. However, if economies of scope in monitoring exist, the holding company or conglomerate form of organization should constitute a source of value in mergers.

To summarize, in a world of costly and incomplete information with separate ownership and management, the monitoring of financial contracts becomes necessary.[6] If one organizational form economizes on the costs of such monitoring activity, the firm's cost of financing will be lowered and, *ceteris paribus*, its value increased, by moving toward that type of organization. It has been argued that the costs of monitoring a firm's compliance with financial contracts are reduced by the formation of a conglomerate firm. To the extent that this is true, an agency theory of conglomerate merger exists.

---

[6]In essence, these are the conditions under which there exists a principal-agent problem in the corporate form of organization.

An Institutional Note: Leveraged Buyouts

A leveraged buyout (LBO) is a method of corporate acquisition whereby a firm is "taken private" by a group of investors—that is, the company is purchased from its shareholders by a small group of investors and the stock is not traded in the open market. The financing of the acquisition involves borrowing against the assets of the acquired firm (leverage).

The motivation behind LBOs is twofold. Frequently the target company is an unproductive division of a larger corporation. Thus, the seller "spins off" this division to a group of investors via an LBO. The investors, on the other hand, purchase the firm with the hope of making it more profitable and then selling out via a public stock offering in five to seven years. If it works, the investors can realize spectacular rewards. For example, Gibson Greeting Cards was acquired from RCA in 1982 for $80 million (only $1 million of which was cash). One-and-a-half years later, the company's initial public stock offering placed the firm's value at $290 million. (See Table 18.2.)

Table 18.2 Sample of Recent Leveraged Buyouts

Company	Date	Status	Purchaser
American Brass	12/10/85	Division	Other
California Home Brands	5/15/85	Company	Other
Conair	6/21/85	Company	Management
Denny's	1/25/85	Company	Management
First National Supermarkets	9/13/85	Company	Management
Formica	5/31/85	Division	Management
GNB	4/23/85	Division	Other
Guardian Industries	2/20/85	Company	Management
Jupiter Industries	10/7/85	Company	Management
Kaiser Agriculture	3/7/85	Division	Management
SFN	2/4/85	Company	Management
Levi-Strauss	9/3/85	Company	Management

Source: A list of the 400 largest private companies published in *Forbes*; other data taken from announcements in *The Wall Street Journal*.

There is, however, a downside to LBOs. These deals are so levered that their success or failure depends on the target firm's earnings. Specifically, those earnings must be sufficient to service the large amount of debt used in the acquisition. One example of an LBO that soured is Thatcher Glass Corporation, which was bought from Dart and Kraft in 1981 for $140 million. Thatcher ended up in Chapter 11 bankruptcy proceedings in 1984. The LBO lenders were owed $77 million, and the majority of the firm's assets were sold for only $40 million.

Source: Gary Weill, "ABCs of LBOs: What Makes Leveraged Buyouts Popular," *Barron's*, August 19, 1985, 42.

Elimination of Inefficient Management.   A number of authors have argued that the market for mergers and acquisitions (corporate takeovers) (1) forces managements to operate efficiently and (2) are in the best interests of firms' stockholders. The idea behind this argument is that an inefficient management cannot remain in power where there exist arbitrageurs who will seek to acquire the shares of inefficiently managed firms, replace managements, and reap the benefits resulting from increased firm efficiency.

The first aspect of managerial efficiency relates to the operating policies and performance of the firm's management. Here we refer to a well-meaning but ineffective management. This phenomenon is frequently observed in small, closely held corporations in which either managerial expertise is unaffordable or the owners fail to see the value of obtaining it. Firms started by R&D staffs often fall victim to the attitude that the product is all that matters in making a successful firm and eschew the pursuit of capable operating managers.

The second aspect of management efficiency relates to managers' goals and objectives. With separation of a firm's ownership and control, managers may pursue objectives that are consistent with their own best interests and in conflict with the owners'. This principal-agent problem is the basis for the "managerial" theory of mergers, or "managerialism," discussed earlier. However, as already noted, an active market for corporate control will limit management's ability to follow goals that deviate from owner wealth maximization.

Acquisition of Market Power.   If the acquired firm is a direct competitor of the acquiring firm, some degree of market power will be created by their combination. However, Section 7 of the Clayton Act makes illegal any merger that may substantially reduce competition or create a monopoly. In addition, the Celler-Kefauver amendment of 1950 extended the scope of the Clayton Act. Since their enactment, both the Department of Justice and the Federal Trade Commission have brought several hundred Section 7 cases to court in an effort to block mergers that might enhance acquiring firms' market power.

An Institutional Note: Measurement of Industry Concentration

In analyzing the potential impact of a merger or acquisition on competition, a key concern is the change in industry concentration — that is, will a limited number of firms dominate the industry? Any merger of two firms in the same industry will necessarily reduce the number of separate firms operating in that industry, other things equal. However, the issue is whether there will result a significant increase in the proportion of industry sales controlled by a small number of firms (that is, their market share). The degree of industry concentration traditionally has been assessed using one of two measures: the industry concentration ratio and the Herfindahl index.

An *industry concentration ratio* is simply the proportion of the market held by the largest number of firms. For example, in 1977 the 4 largest tire manufacturers (out of 121 firms) produced 70 percent of the industry's output, while the 4 largest sawmills (out of 6,966 firms) controlled only 17 percent of industry production. For these same industries, the top 20 firms controlled 97 percent and 36 percent of industry production, respectively. Concentration ratios are also calculated based on firm sales. However, regardless of the basis for the analysis, the concentration ratio is at best only a proxy for the level of competition a firm in a particular industry faces. For example, the calculation generally does not include the impact of foreign producers or of the availability (or lack) of ready substitutes.

The *Herfindahl index* is calculated as the sum of the squared market shares of all the firms in the industry (that is, $\sum_{j=1}^{N} S_j^2$ firms in the industry, where S_j is the market share of the jth firm). The index can range from a high of 1, where one firm has 100 percent of the market, to a low of $1/N$, where each of the N firms in the industry has an equal market share. Consider the case where there are five firms in an industry with market shares of 0.50, 0.40, 0.05, 0.03, and 0.02. The Herfindahl index for this industry would equal $0.50^2 + 0.40^2 + 0.05^2 + 0.03^2 + 0.02^2 = 0.4138$. Where the two smallest firms merge, the index becomes 0.415, which represents an increase of only 0.28 percent. Now consider another five-firm industry in which all five firms initially have 20 percent of the market, resulting in a Herfindahl index of 0.20. If two of these firms merged, the index would become 0.28, that is, an increase of 40 percent.

Industry concentration ratios have been used in research on the determinants of a firm's financial structure. Recall from Chapter 13 that both Hurdle (1974) and Sullivan (1974) hypothesized that firms operating in highly concentrated industries tend to use more financial leverage than firms operating in less concentrated industries. However, recall that empirical evidence has not supported this hypothesis but has indicated an inverse relationship between the average use of financial leverage in an industry and that industry's concentration ratio.

Source: *Statistical Abstract of the United States, 1981* (Washington, D.C.: U.S. Government Printing Office, 1981), Table 1427.

Reductions in Production and/or Distribution Costs.   Economies of scale in the use of production and distribution assets as well as economies of scope in managerial assets are the basis for this merger benefit. Economies of scale arise from the increased intensity with which an asset is utilized in producing a product or service. We generally associate such economies with the physical production of a product such as sheet steel or electric power. If a firm with excess capacity is able to acquire another firm that utilizes the same productive facilities but lacks capacity, the merged entity can reap economies of scale by combining production facilities to meet its overall sales opportunities.

Economies of scope arise from applying an asset or skill (such as managerial planning and control talent) across a greater array of operations. For example, planning for financing needs requires the same basic set of skills regardless of the product or service being produced. Therefore, if a firm has excess capacity in managerial planning and budgeting capabilities, it may effectively reap economies of scope by entering into a merger with another firm even if the two firms' products and services are completely unrelated (in a vertical or horizontal sense). Williamson (1981) coined the term *M-form organization* to describe the holding company type of enterprise used by several diverse types of firms. In this organizational form, low-frequency types of activities, such as planning, budgeting, and treasury functions, are delegated to the holding company level and high-frequency types—those related to the firm's day-to-day operations—are assigned to the operating divisions. This type of organization might be explained as an attempt to take advantage of the economies of scope available from managerial activities such as planning, budgeting, and raising funds. Recall that the agency cost theory of conglomerate mergers was founded on the economies of scope in monitoring compliance with the covenants of financial contracts that could be achieved by a merger.

Mergers and Acquisitions: Evidence[7]

Overview

Empirical tests of the various theories of corporate takeovers found in the finance literature utilize the event study methodology (discussed in Chapter 10) almost exclusively. The primary question they address is that of who benefits from corporate takeovers and by how much. In this section, we will review the empirical evidence on this issue as well as the two issues discussed at the beginning of the chapter. That is, we will also examine the literature that tests for the impact of managerial resistance to corporate takeovers on shareholder wealth. Finally, we will review a paper that poses a novel test of the competitiveness of the corporate takeover market.

Review of Event Study Methodology

An *event study* entails analyzing holding period returns on the shares of common stock of a firm that is *hypothesized* to have been affected by a particular informa-

---

[7]This section draws on Jensen and Ruback (1983).

An Institutional Note: The Language of Corporate Takeover Bids

Saturday night special: A hostile tender offer that gives target shareholders an unreasonably short time period in which to decide whether to tender their shares. The objective of this type of tender offer is to "stampede" these shareholders into making a decision *before* the target firm's management can mount an effective campaign to oppose the bid for control. In 1979, however, the SEC revised its Regulation 14D and adopted Regulation 14E, which established a minimum "hold open" time of 20 days for tender offers.

Front-end loaded tender offers: In this "two-step" takeover procedure, an initial offer is made for 51 percent of the firm's shares. Once those shares have been tendered, the firm offers to merge with the target firm by exchanging its shares for the target's. The merger terms frequently are less attractive than the initial tender offer, thus providing an incentive to tender early.

Bootstrap or toehold bids: In this strategy, a firm too small to acquire control of a larger firm makes an initial tender offer for a noncontrolling block of the target firm's shares. Once this tender offer is successfully completed, the acquiring firm tries to use the percentage of the target firm's shares acquired as the basis for obtaining credit in an amount sufficient to finance the acquisition of a controlling interest in the target firm.

Source: Robert A. Prentice, "Target Board Abuse of Defensive Tactics: Can Federal Law be Mobilized to Overcome the Business Judgment Rule?" *Journal of Corporation Law* (Winter 1983): 337–360.

---

tion event. Thus, in assessing the wealth effects of a takeover, the "information event" is the announcement of the merger or tender offer.

The event study methodology involves (1) identifying the date on which the information event occurred (for example, the date on which the firm announced its intention to acquire control of another firm); (2) observing the holding period returns on the firm's common stock for the pre-announcement through post-announcement period under study; (3) assessing the expected or "normal" rates of return for the affected firm over the test period; and (4) calculating the excess or "abnormal" returns for the firm as the difference in the realized or actual returns and the expected returns.[8] These abnormal returns are then averaged across all the

---

[8]Several methods have been used to identify expected or "normal" returns. Brown and Warner (1980, 1985) performed simulation studies on the monthly and daily data in event studies and offered recommendations about which methods were more effective in identifying "abnormal" return behavior.

firms in the test sample in "event time," that is, in relation to the proximity to the announcement rather than calendar date. For example, we might calculate the average abnormal return for the announcement date as well as for each day included in the period 10 days before the announcement and 10 days after. Since the announcements occur at different points in calendar time, we would average the calendar days to obtain each of the average abnormal returns for the hypothetical 21-day test period. We would observe a significant "wealth effect" where the abnormal returns on the announcement date (or over the announcement period) were found to be statistically different from zero.

Wealth Impact of Takeover Activities

Overview.   By far the most popular research topic in the mergers and acquisitions literature has been the question of who benefits from corporate takeover activity. Jensen and Ruback (1983) summarized this literature and noted the following.[9] First, the average abnormal return to the shareholders of target firms in successful merger attempts was 30 percent where a tender offer was used to acquire control, and the average benefit derived from merger was 20 percent. For the bidding firm, the story is quite different: Shareholders received an average benefit of only 4 percent where a tender offer was used and zero where a merger was involved. These results point to the significant gains to the shareholders of acquired or target firms but raise the issue of why bidding firms engage in takeovers given the absence of any abnormal returns to their shareholders. Table 18.3 summarizes a number of the more recent studies' findings on this issue.[10]

When the wealth impact of "unsuccessful" takeover attempts is analyzed, the results are quite different. The average abnormal return to target firm shareholders from unsuccessful tender offer and merger attempts was −3 percent, and the returns to the bidding firm's shareholders were also negative.

Gains to Bidding Firms.   The absence of any real benefits to takeover activity for the acquiring firm's shareholders brings into question the rationale for engaging in such activity. However, Asquith, Bruner, and Mullins (1983) — hereafter ABM — demonstrated the existence of positive gains to acquiring firms that prior studies had not (methodologically) observed. Specifically, ABM hypothesized the following.

First, merger activity frequently reflects the adoption of a strategic plan for obtaining control over the assets of a number of companies. As such, they suggested that some of the positive impact of a firm's merger activity may be reflected in the announcement of its "intention" to engage in a strategy involving the acquisition of other operating companies. By simply assessing the market reaction to an individual merger announcement, previous studies may have missed part of the market's capitalization of the firm's decision to enter into the merger, thus introducing a potentially important sample selection bias. Specifically, previous

---

[9]See Jensen and Ruback (1983), Tables 1 and 2.

[10]Table 18.3 was compiled by Jensen and Ruback (1983) and is reprinted here with permission.

Table 18.3 A Survey of Abnormal Returns for Mergers and Tender Offers (Sample size and t-statistic[a] are given in parentheses.)

Study	Sample Period	Event Period	Bidding Firms		Target Firms	
			Successful (%)	Unsuccessful (%)	Successful (%)	Unsuccessful (%)
A. Tender Offers: Announcement Effects						
Dodd and Ruback (1977)	1958–1978	Offer announcement month	+2.83 (124, 2.16)	+0.58 (48, 1.19)	+20.58 (133, 25.81)	+18.96 (36, 12.41)
		Month of and month following offer announcement	+3.12 (124, 2.24)	−1.71 (48, −0.76)	+21.15 (133, 15.75)	+16.31 (36, 6.32)
Kummer and Hoffmeister (1978)	1956–1974	Offer announcement month	+5.20 (17, 1.96)	NA	+16.85 (50, 10.88)	+21.09 (38, 11.87)
Bradley[b] (1980)	1962–1977	20 days before through 20 days after announcement	+4.36 (88, 2.67)	−2.96 (46, −1.31)	+32.18 (161, 26.68)	+47.26 (97, 30.42)
Jarrell and Bradley (1980)	1962–1977	40 days before through 20 days after offer announcement	+6.66 (88, 3.35)	NA	+34.06[c] (147, 25.48)	NA
Bradley, Desai, and Kim (1983)	1963–1980	10 days before through 10 days after offer announcement	NA	−0.27 (94, 0.24)	NA	+35.55[d] (112, 36.61)
Bradley, Desai, and Kim (1982)	1962–1980	10 days before through 10 days after offer announcement	+2.35 (161, 3.02)	NA	+31.80 (162, 36.52)	NA
Ruback (April 1983)	1962–1981	5 days before through offer announcement	NA	−0.38 (48, −0.63)	NA	NA
Weighted average abnormal return.[e,h]			+3.81 (478, NA)	−1.11 (236, NA)	+29.09 (653, NA)	+35.17 (283, NA)

B1. Mergers: Two-Day Announcement Effects

Study	Years	Interval				
Dodd (1980)	1970–1977	Day before and day of offer announcement	−1.09 (60, −2.98)	−1.24 (66, −2.63)	+13.41 (71, 23.80)	+12.73 (80, 19.08)
Asquith (1983)	1962–1976	Day before and day of offer announcement	+0.20 (196, 0.78)	+0.50 (89, 1.92)	+6.20 (211, 23.07)	+7.00 (91, 12.83)
Eckbo (1983)	1963–1978	Day before through day after offer announcement	+0.07[f] (102, −0.12)	+1.20[g] (57, 2.98)	+6.24[f] (57, 9.97)	+10.20[g] (29, 15.22)
Weighted average abnormal return.[h]			−0.05 (358, NA)	+0.15 (212, NA)	+7.72 (339, NA)	+9.76 (200, NA)

B2. Mergers: One-Month Announcement Effects

Study	Years	Interval				
Dodd (1980)	1970–1977	20 days before through first public announcement	+0.80 (60, 0.67)	+3.13 (66, 2.05)	+21.78 (71, 11.93)	+22.45 (80, 10.38)
Asquith (1983)	1962–1976	19 days before through first public announcement day	+0.20 (196, 0.25)	+1.20 (87, 1.49)	+13.30 (211, 15.65)	+11.70 (91, 6.71)
Eckbo (1983)	1963–1978	20 days before through 10 days after public announcement	+1.58[f] (102, 1.48)	+4.85[g] (57, 3.43)	+14.08[f] (57, 6.97)	+25.03[g] (29, 12.61)
Asquith, Bruner, and Mullins (1983)	1963–1979	20 days before announcement day through announcement day	+3.48 (170, 5.30)	+0.70 (41, 0.41)	+20.5 (35, 9.54)	+10.0 (19, 3.45)
Malatesta (1983)	1969–1974	Public announcement month	+0.90 (256, 1.53)	NA	+16.8 (83, 17.57)	NA
Weighted average abnormal return.[h]			+1.37 (784, NA)	+2.45 (251, NA)	+15.90 (457, NA)	+17.24 (219, NA)

continued

Table 18.3 *continued*

B3. Mergers: Total Abnormal Returns from Offer Announcement through Outcome

Study	Years	10 days before offer announcement through 10 days after outcome date	Day before offer announcement through outcome date	10 days before offer announcement through 10 days after cancellation date	
Dodd (1980)	1970–1977	+33.96 (71, 7.66)	−7.22 (60, −2.50)	−5.50 (66, −2.05)	+3.68 (80, 0.96)
Asquith (1983)	1962–1976	+15.50 (211, 6.01)	−0.10 (196, −0.05)	−5.90 (89, −3.15)	−7.50 (91, −1.54)
Wier[j] (1983)	1962–1979	NA	NA	+3.99 (16, 0.89)	−9.02 (17, −1.82)
Weighted average abnormal return.[h]		+20.15 (282, NA)	−1.77 (256, NA)	−4.82 (171, NA)	−2.88 (188, NA)

[a]NA = not available.

The non-italicized t-statistics were obtained directly from the cited study or calculated using standard errors reported in the study. In the absence of this information, we have approximated the t-statistics. The italicized t-statistics in panel A are calculated as: $t = \bar{X}\sqrt{N}/S\sqrt{\bar{T}}$, where $\bar{X}$ is the reported abnormal return, N is the number of observations in the sample, T is the number of days over which the abnormal returns are cumulated, and S is the per day per observation standard deviation. $S = 2.39$ percent and is calculated as the average of the implied per day observation standard deviation in all of the studies. The italicized t-statistics in panel B3 were calculated as: $t = \bar{X}\sqrt{N}/S\sqrt{\bar{T}}$, where $\bar{T}$ is the average number of days in the average cumulative return, and the standard deviation is from the original study.

[b]These data are plotted in Bradley (1980). Bradley provided the numerical values in private correspondence.

[c]The abnormal return for successful targets is measured over the period 40 days before through 5 days after the offer announcement.

[d]The abnormal return for unsuccessful targets in the announcement month.

[e]The weighted average excludes the announcement month results of Dodd and Ruback (1977) and includes their results for the month of and month following the announcement.

[f]Includes mergers not challenged by antitrust authorities.

[g]Sample consists of mergers that were challenged by antitrust authorities. Eckbo (1983) reports that most of these acquisitions were not completed.

[h]The abnormal returns are weighted by samples in calculating the weighted average. Overlapping sample problems are ignored.

[i]Asquith, Bruner, and Mullins (1983) provided the data for successful and unsuccessful target firms in private correspondence.

[j]Sample includes only mergers that are canceled after antitrust complaints under Section 7 of the Clayton Act.

Source: Reprinted with permission from Michael C. Jensen and Richard S. Ruback, "The Market for Corporate Control: The Evidence," *Journal of Financial Economics* (April 1983): 5–50.

studies have begun their sample selection process by identifying "targets" of take-over attempts. This procedure fails to identify bidding firms that may be engaged in a series of takeover attempts (some successful and others unsuccessful). To the extent that engaging in a program of takeover attempts is valuable to the share-holders of such a firm, it is important to determine whether a particular takeover attempt is its first, second, or tenth. The information content of its undertaking the acquisition program may be fully reflected in the initial stages of the process.

Second, ABM hypothesized that a fundamental structural shift occurred in the market for corporate takeovers with the passage of the Williams Act in 1968.[11] This act essentially made it more difficult for a firm to acquire control over an-other, thereby transferring a larger share of the takeover gains to the target firm's shareholders.

Third, ABM noted the importance of the relative sizes of the bidding and target firms. By analyzing abnormal rates of return, it may be impossible to detect the expected return impact of any given takeover because the target firm is so small relative to the bidding firm that it will have an insignificant or unobservable effect on its market returns.

Finally, ABM reassessed the importance of a successful takeover attempt on a bidding firm's shareholder wealth where all of the above factors have been con-trolled for in the experiment.

The results of the ABM study were enlightening. First, they found that the average gain to the bidder was 4.1 percent in cases where the size of the target was 10 percent or more of the bidder's equity, compared to an average abnormal return of only 1.7 percent when the target firm was less than 10 percent. This re-sult confirms the commonsense notion that the size of the abnormal rate of return corresponding to a particular takeover should reflect the size of the target relative to the bidding firm. Second, ABM found that the pre-1969 abnormal returns to bidders averaged 4.4 percent and the post-1969 returns only 1.7 percent. This finding confirms the purported impact of the Williams Act noted earlier. However, the study was unable to provide any conclusive evidence of a "merger program" announcement effect. Thus, it would appear that any capitalization of the benefits of a merger program is spread over the period of the acquisition activity rather than being impounded in the abnormal returns surrounding the first of a series of takeover attempts. Third, the study confirmed the widespread observation that the success or failure of a takeover attempt has a very important impact on the benefits to the bidder's shareholders. More important, however, it demonstrated that with a more carefully designed study the benefits to the bidder's shareholders are indeed positive, albeit much lower than those realized by the target firm's shareholders.

Dennis and McConnell (1986) performed a very comprehensive study of the gains to the bidding firm's security holders. Specifically, they looked at all of the firm's senior securities, including convertible and nonconvertible preferred stock and bonds as well as common stock. In so doing, these authors were able to detect

---

[11]See Smiley (1975) for a review of the Williams Act and its impact on the "costs" of takeover activity.

gains in mergers that were captured by classes of security holders other than the common stockholders. With respect to the latter, Dennis and McConnell concluded: "There is no evidence that acquiring companies' common stockholders lose and there is statistically reliable evidence that they gain" (p. 43). They also found that on average, acquired companies' nonconvertible bondholders and acquiring companies' convertible bondholders, nonconvertible preferred stockholders, and nonconvertible bondholders neither gain nor lose statistically significant amounts in mergers. Dennis and McConnell conjectured that by looking at the gains (losses) to all classes of senior security holders of acquiring and acquired firms, they were able to detect those that typically do not accrue to the common stockholders alone. From this they concluded that "mergers, on average, are wealth creating activities for combined firms and for both the acquired and acquiring companies individually" (p. 43).

Managerial Resistance to Takeovers

Takeovers and Managerialism.   It has been argued that takeovers serve as an external control mechanism that limits the ability of an incumbent management to follow policies that deviate from shareholder wealth maximization. Given the costs of engaging in a takeover attempt, it is unlikely that the threat of takeover entirely eliminates management actions that conflict with shareholder wealth maximization. In addition, it is extremely difficult to assess the wealth impact of such activities. However, we can get some evidence on the prevalence of managerial resistance to takeover attempts by observing the "defensive" tactics that can be used to thwart an attempted takeover. Further, there have been some indirect tests of the impact of these defensive tactics on shareholder wealth, which we review in the following paragraphs.

Managerial Actions to Reduce the Risk of Takeover.   A number of actions can be taken by an incumbent management to resist a takeover attempt.

Change in the State of Incorporation.   The rules governing the control of a firm, including the conditions under which a merger is to be ratified (such as the proportion of the firm's stockholders who must approve the merger before it can be effected) are included in the firm's corporate charter. Since each state has its own set of laws regarding corporate charters, the state in which the firm chooses to incorporate is important. For example, when Mesa Petroleum was actively seeking the control of Gulf Oil Corporation, one of the defensive actions Gulf's management took was to seek the approval of its stockholders to move its state of incorporation to Delaware, whose corporate charter laws would allow the firm greater flexibility in resisting takeover.

   Dodd and Leftwich (1980) studied 140 firms that had changed their state of incorporation over the period 1927 to 1977 and found that 126 firms had moved to Delaware and only 6 firms had left that state. However, they found that positive rather than negative returns to the shareholders resulted from the change of state of incorporation. Thus, these findings fail to support the "managerialism" notion that a change in state of incorporation is motivated by an attempt to foil a takeover attempt that would be beneficial to the firm's shareholders. This is indirect evidence of managerialism, for a number of wealth-enhancing reasons for changing the state of incorporation surely exist.

An Institutional Note: The Language of Managerial Defensive Tactics against "Unfriendly" Takeover Attempts

Creation of an antitrust problem: Here the target firm acquires one of the tender offerer's competitors.

Acquisition of a Canadian subsidiary: Once this has been accomplished, the acquiring firm will have to obtain the consent of the Canadian government under the Foreign Investment Act of Canada. This, of course, can add substantially to the time required for accomplishing the takeover.

Acquisition of a "safe harbor": A safe harbor is a "heavily regulated" firm, such as a television station or trucking firm. This action, then, requires approval of a government agency of the acquisition, which also slows down the process and consequently makes the target firm less attractive.

Cyanide capsule: Here the target firm (prior to the takeover attempt) builds into its financial contracts clauses that will be "triggered" if a takeover becomes effective. For example, the firm might have a loan agreement that accelerates payment in the event the firm's control changes hands.

Golden parachutes: This type of agreement provides financial security for the top management of the target company if the firm falls victim to an unfriendly takeover. Such agreements are triggered with the takeover and provide management with "bonuses." Some would argue — perhaps rightfully — that this tactic actually promotes consistency of management and shareholder interests with regard to corporate control. In any case, management is "protected" from the personal costs associated with a loss of control of the firm via a successful corporate takeover attempt.

"Lock-up" option: Here the target firm makes an agreement with a "preferred" takeover candidate (sometimes referred to as a *white knight*) granting that firm an advantage in acquiring the takeover target.

"Pac Man" defense: This involves the target firm attempting to turn the tables by making a tender offer for the control of the original tender offerer.

Sale of the "crown jewel": This tactic is sometimes used as part of a *scorched earth* or *poisoned well* approach to making takeover less desirable. The target firm simply "sells" whatever asset(s) make it a particularly attractive takeover target. In conjunction with the *lock-up* tactic noted above, the target firm may simply "agree" to sell its crown jewel in the event of a successful takeover and not actually sell it.

Corporate suicide: Here the target firm decides to liquidate its assets in the face of a hostile takeover attempt.

Compiling a "black book" or "Pearl Harbor file": Here the target firm prepares for the possibility of a takeover by formulating a set of defensive tactics in response.

Porcupine provisions: Here the firm modifies its corporate charter to include provisions that make the acquisition of corporate control more difficult. Examples include adding *super majority* requirements for shareholder approval of mergers in the corporation's articles of incorporation, issuing *treasury stock* to "friendly" parties, and moving the firm's state of incorporation to a state with stronger *shark repellent*, or antitakeover laws.

Source: Robert A. Prentice, "Target Board Abuse of Defensive Tactics: Can Federal Law be Mobilized to Overcome the Business Judgment Rule?" *Journal of Corporation Law* (Winter 1983): 337–360.

Managerial Opposition.   Management can also engage in publicity campaigns to state its opposition to a particular takeover attempt. It can elicit the bids of other firms in an attempt to drive up the tender price sufficiently to frighten off the bidder. One might liken this type of defense mechanism to that used by some animals, that is, to puff themselves up so as to look too large for a predator to swallow.

Two studies have tried to grasp the impact of antitakeover amendments on shareholder wealth. DeAngelo and Rice (1983) studied 100 firms that had adopted super-majority, lock-up, and other provisions during the period 1974 to 1978.[12] Their results indicated that antitakeover amendments had had little impact on shareholder wealth. However, it is not clear whether the announcement of these amendments was a clear signal of "bad news to the shareholders." In fact, such an announcement may have been interpreted by the shareholders as an increased likelihood of a takeover attempt, which would have been "good news." Linn and McConnell (1983) studied the stock market behavior of a sample of 388 firms that had adopted antitakeover amendments over the period 1960 to 1980. Using a number of tests in an effort to more precisely identify the dates of the actual information releases, they found no evidence to support a negative reaction to the passage of these amendments. In fact, a sample of firms that had *removed* antitakeover amendments showed some slight evidence of such a reaction.

Kummer and Hoffmeister (1978) studied the abnormal returns surrounding announcements of tender offers that were opposed by incumbent managements

[12]See "An Institutional Note: The Language of Managerial Defense Tactics" for definitions of corporate takeover jargon.

and of those to which managements were unopposed. Their findings indicated that the opposed tender offers yielded the highest abnormal returns to the target's shareholders. Here the average abnormal return for the announcement month was 19.8 percent versus 16.45 percent in cases where the offer was unopposed and the takeover eventually was successful. In the 15 cases where the tender offer takeover was opposed and eventually failed, the target shareholders suffered an abnormal loss of 11.7 percent over the 10 months following announcement.

Dodd (1980) found evidence indicating that managerial opposition to tender offers harms the target firm's shareholders. The average abnormal return to shareholders on the day before and day of a termination announcement was -5.57 percent in cases where the target firm canceled the offer and -9.75 percent in those involving cancellation by the bidder. If the target firm canceled the merger due to a more beneficial bid, the cancellation probably would have had a positive impact on target firm share value. Thus, the negative returns Dodd observed are consistent with the notion that the target firm's management is not acting in its shareholders' best interests.

Thus, in the studies reported here there is mixed evidence supporting the notion that managerial resistance to takeovers via antitakeover amendments is detrimental to shareholder wealth. Of course, as we noted at the beginning of this section, some resistance to takeover certainly *is* in the shareholders' best interests. In effect, where no detrimental effect was observed, we may be observing a basic inability of a firm's management to deter takeover attempts (through incorporation of antitakeover amendments in the corporate charter) to an extent that would be detrimental to shareholders' interests.

Share Repurchases.   Frequently a firm will repurchase a portion of its own stock. This type of activity is aimed at clearing the "floating stock" from the market — that is, it is commonly believed that at any given time there are a group of shareholders at the margin who would readily tender their shares for a modest premium. Fearing a takeover attempt, management might engage in a repurchase of its own shares so as to clear the market of them. Another, related activity involves the repurchase of large blocks of shares from targeted major shareholders who are considered potential sellers in the event of a takeover attempt. In some cases, the targeted repurchase may be at a substantial premium and involve the purchase of the holdings of an individual or group who has been engaged in a takeover attempt.

Standstill Agreements.   Sometimes a target firm can reach an agreement with a firm that has been purchasing its shares to cease doing so. This is known as a *standstill agreement*. Dann and DeAngelo (1983) studied 30 firms that had successfully negotiated standstill agreements. The average abnormal returns to the target firm's stockholders was a significant -4.52 percent on the day before and day of the announcement. In addition, Bradley and Wakeman (1983) presented evidence that the negotiation of a standstill agreement has the same impact on a target firm's shareholder wealth as a termination of the merger negotiation process. Both these studies support the hypothesis that managerial actions with respect to standstill agreements have a detrimental effect on the wealth of the target firm's shareholders.

Going Private.   One extreme tactic for avoiding takeover involves a firm's *going private* — that is, by repurchasing its shares, a firm can reduce the number of shareholders such that its stock will no longer be publicly traded. This might involve a leveraged buyout of the firm by the incumbent management, in which case the firm belongs to the management. If this tactic is used, managers will become the owners and the conflict of interest between management and shareholders will cease to exist.

DeAngelo, DeAngelo, and Rice (1982) studied the impact of 72 firms' having gone private over the period 1973 to 1980. They found that the public shareholders (those who sold their shares) realized an average abnormal return of 30.4 percent during the 40 days before through the date of announcement. Certainly this evidence does not indicate that the selling shareholders are harmed by the firm's going private.

Summary.   The empirical evidence on the impact of managerial resistance to takeover attempts is mixed. This is not surprising, because a certain amount of resistance serves to bid up the takeover offers for the target firm's shares. In addition, if there is any information "signaled" to the target firm's shareholders by management's actions to reduce the risk of takeover, it is that there is a reason to be concerned about a possible takeover. This is, of course, a desirable valuation signal given the positive wealth impact observed for the shareholders of target firms from takeover attempts. The jury still appears to be out on this issue, primarily because of the difficulty of designing an unambiguous test.

Competition in the Market for Corporate Control

The Importance of Competition.   Ruback (April 1983) notes that the competitiveness of the market for corporate acquisitions is of concern for three basic reasons:

1.   A competitive acquisitions market serves to reduce (if not eliminate) the principal-agent problem arising when corporate ownership and control are separate (see Fama [1978] and Smiley [1975]). The idea here is quite simple: In such a market, firms that do not follow the shareholder wealth maximization objective are acquired by firms that do.

2.   A competitive acquisitions market ensures an efficient allocation of corporate resources. This point follows directly from the first in that resources not allocated in accordance with owner wealth maximization are eliminated by takeovers of the inefficient firms.

3.   A competitive acquisitions market reduces the need for legislation such as the Williams Act as well as state tender offer laws aimed at "protecting" shareholders of target firms from takeovers for tender offers below the targets' "fair market value." In such a market, takeover attempts serve to bid the values of target firms' equity up to their highest level under the most efficient use of the firms' resources.

Ruback defines a *competitive acquisitions market* as one in which bidders take advantage of all profitable takeover opportunities. Thus, in such a market all positive net present value takeover bids will be offered; conversely, a firm that drops out of the bidding does so because the net present value of the takeover at higher bid prices is negative. There are a number of reasons why a bidder might withdraw even where the net present value of the acquisition at the (as yet un-known) successful offer price might be positive. These include collusion among the bidders, irrational (non–wealth maximizing) behavior, entry restrictions (such as legal barriers to firms' entry into a particular industry or sector of the econ-omy), and bidders' use of strategic behavior (that is, even though the net present value of acquisition is positive for a higher bid, the bidder feels that a competitor has an even higher net present value for it).

Testing for Competition in the Takeover Market.   Ruback designed and im-plemented a novel approach to testing the competitiveness of the corporate take-over market based on the following attribute of a competitive acquisitions market: If the market for corporate acquisitions is competitive, the net present value of a successful takeover by a firm that discontinues bidding should be negative. In other words, a firm that discontinues bidding in such a market should do so be-cause its estimated net present value of the acquisition, based on its evaluation of the expected successful bid price, is negative. To implement such a test, Ruback analyzed the net present values of 48 unsuccessful tender offers. The net present value of the unsuccessful bidder's final bid, $G_u(P_u)$, was estimated as follows:

$$G_u(P_u) = CPE_{t-5, t} E_{t-6},$$

where P_u is the total money bid made by the unsuccessful bidder for the equity of the target firm; $CPE_{t-5, t}$ is the cumulative prediction error (abnormal return) for the period beginning five days before the announcement of the bidder's final bid and ending with the date of the bid; and E_{t-6} is the total equity value of the bidder six days prior to the announcement of the final bid.

The rationale behind the above measure is as follows. Bradley (1980) found that information concerning the announcement of an acquisition bid leaks out dur-ing the five days prior to the announcement. Thus, assuming that the market capi-talizes what it feels to be the net wealth impact on the bidder resulting from the acquisition over these five days, the net present value (that is, net change in bidder shareholder wealth) equals the product of the cumulative abnormal return during this five-day period and the market value of the bidder's equity six days prior to the bid announcement. One caveat is that the change in bidder equity value noted above reflects both the anticipated net present value of the acquisition and the probability of success. Hence, the above gain from the acquisition is its full net present value *only* where the probability of success is unity.

The test statistic used is not the net present value of the acquisition based on the last bid, for it is assumed that with rational bidding this is positive. Instead, the criterion used to assess the competitiveness of the acquisitions market is the net present value of the bid *if* the bidder had offered the *successful* offer price, P_s. Thus, the appropriate net present value for analyzing market competition is

$$G_u(P_s) = \frac{E_{t-6} CPE_{t-5, t}}{\pi} - (P_s - P_u),$$

which measures the net present value to the unsuccessful bidder had it made the successful bid, P_s. The numerator of the first term on the right-hand side of the above equation is simply $G_u(P_u)$, which is divided by the probability of success (π) reflected in the market's assessment of the announced bid of P_u. In his tests, Ruback assumed that π was unity or that the market capitalized the merger net present value as if the probability of success were 100 percent. Later he relaxed this assumption and performed a sensitivity analysis on the test results using different values for π.

Ruback found that out of the 48 unsuccessful bids analyzed, 29 exhibited negative net present values at the eventually successful bid price — that is, $G_u(P_s) < 0$ — regardless of the level of π. In 12 cases, the net present value of the acquisition depended on the level of π assumed to be reflected in the market's assessment of the announced bid. In 7 cases, the results clearly conflicted with the competitive market hypothesis. There the net present value of the acquisition at the higher successful bid was positive regardless of the assumption made about π. Thus, the findings of this study generally support the competitiveness of the acquisitions market.

Ruback performed a sensitivity analysis on the 12 cases where the net present value of the acquisition at the successful bid depended on π. He found that in 4 cases the net present values became positive where the probability of success impounded in the market's reaction to the unsuccessful bid was between 0.25 and 0.5. For the remaining 8 cases to exhibit positive net present values, the market's assessment of the chances of success of the unsuccessful bid had to be less than 0.25. Unfortunately, there is no basis for assessing the market's π for an unsuccessful bid. However, in order for Ruback's test findings to constitute evidence of a noncompetitive market for acquisitions, the π impounded in the market's evaluation of the unsuccessful bid would have to be very low (less than 0.5).

Summary

The study of mergers and acquisitions entails considering the special problems that arise when one firm acquires control over another. Merger theories have attempted to explain why firms engage in the acquisition of productive resources by acquiring other operating firms. These theories revolve around (1) tax considerations, (2) avoidance of the costs of insolvency and bankruptcy, (3) the benefits derived from increased debt capacity, (4) replacement of inefficient managements, (5) acquisition of market power, and (6) economies of scale and scope resulting in reduced costs of production and/or distribution of the merged firm's product or service.

In reviewing the empirical evidence on mergers and acquisitions, we found three fundamental areas of concern:

1. How large are the gains (losses) to the shareholders of the acquiring and acquired firms?

2. What is the impact of managerial opposition to takeover attempts on the wealth of the target firm's shareholders?

3. How competitive is the market for corporate takeovers?

The evidence indicated the following. First, with regard to wealth effects of mergers and acquisitions, we found that bidding or acquiring firms characteristically pay significant premiums over the pre-acquisition market values of acquired firms' equity. However, the bidding firms' shareholders realize much smaller (positive) gains. An examination of managerial attempts to resist takeover attempts indicated that these efforts (change of state of incorporation, antitakeover amendments, share repurchases, standstill agreements, and so on) have either a zero or negative effect on the wealth of the target firm's shareholders. However, the impact of these activities is small relative to the gains to target firm shareholders from a successful acquisition. We also saw that the evidence regarding the competitiveness of the takeover market clearly supports a high level of bidder competition. This was reflected in the fact that the net present value of takeover by unsuccessful bidders (had they raised their bids to the eventually successful bid level) was consistently negative. This indicated that firms that dropped out of the bidding for a given acquisition did so because they anticipated a negative net present value for a higher (successful) bid.

Even with the wealth of empirical research devoted to the problems surrounding mergers and acquisitions, some very fundamental questions remain unanswered. For example, although we can theorize as to the sources of gain from acquisition activity, we have difficulty identifying the particular source of gain to any given acquisition. In addition, debate continues as to the efficacy of existing and proposed legislation designed to inhibit acquisition activity. Although it is simple to justify the restriction of "competition-reducing" acquisition activity, it is difficult to rationalize legislation aimed at restricting tender offer activity where no loss of competition in the affected product markets is anticipated. Finally, it has been hypothesized that a well-functioning market for corporate takeovers serves to reduce the problem of agency arising from the separation of ownership and control of the modern corporation. However, there is no hard evidence as to the effectiveness of the takeover market in this regard.

Study Questions

18.1   Distinguish between takeovers initiated via a merger and by a tender offer.

18.2   It has been suggested that mergers and acquisitions be viewed in terms of a market for corporate control. Explain this concept and contrast it with the traditional view of the market in which takeovers take place.

18.3   Discuss briefly the potential sources of synergy in corporate takeovers.

18.4   With the separation of ownership and control in the corporate enterprise, there arises the basis for a principal-agent conflict. Discuss the role of a competitive market for takeovers in eliminating this conflict.

18.5   Some researchers have suggested that the positive wealth impact on target firm shareholders accompanying a takeover attempt may result from one of two basic sources. The first is "synergy," wherein the acquiring firm (due to some specialized resource, such as superior management) is able to initiate a value-increasing operating strategy in the event of a successful takeover. The second is that the acquiring firm's management is able to identify "undervalued firms" and, by initiating its takeover attempt, signal that information to the market (hence the "revaluation" of the target firm). Devise an event type of study for differentiating between these two hypotheses.

References

K. J. Arrow, "Vertical Integration and Communication," *Bell Journal of Economics* (Spring 1975): 173–183.

Paul Asquith, "Merger Bids, Uncertainty, and Stockholder Returns," *Journal of Financial Economics* (April 1983): 51–84.

———, Robert F. Bruner, and David W. Mullins, Jr., "The Gains to Bidding Firms from Merger," *Journal of Financial Economics* (April 1983): 121–139.

——— and E. Han Kim, "The Impact of Merger Bids on the Participating Firms' Security Holders," *Journal of Finance* 37 (1982): 1209–1228.

Michael Bradley, "Interfirm Tender Offers and the Market for Corporate Control," *Journal of Business* 53 (1980): 345–376.

———, Anand Desai, and E. Han Kim, "The Rationale behind Interfirm Tender Offers: Information or Synergy?" *Journal of Financial Economics* (April 1983): 183–206.

——— and L. MacDonald Wakeman, "The Wealth Effects of Targeted Share Repurchases," *Journal of Financial Economics* (April 1983): 301–328.

Stephen J. Brown and Jerold B. Warner, "Measuring Security Price Performance," *Journal of Financial Economics* 8 (1980): 205–258.

———, "Using Daily Stock Returns in Event Studies," *Journal of Financial Economics* 14 (March 1985): 3–31.

Celler Committee Staff Report, *Investigation of Conglomerate Corporations* (Washington, D.C.: U.S. Government Printing Office, 1971).

E. Celler, *Investigation of Conglomerate Corporations Hearings before the Antitrust Subcommittee of the Committee on the Judiciary,* House of Representatives, 1969–1970, Parts 1–7 (Washington, D.C.: U.S. Government Printing Office, 1971).

Larry Y. Dann, "Common Stock Repurchase: An Analysis of Returns to Bondholders and Stockholders," *Journal of Financial Economics* 9 (1981): 113–138.

——— and Harry DeAngelo, "Standstill Agreements, Privately Negotiated Stock Repurchases, and the Market for Corporate Control," *Journal of Financial Economics* 11 (1983): 274–300.

Harry DeAngelo, Linda DeAngelo, and Edward M. Rice, "Going Private: Minority Freezeouts and Stockholder Wealth" (Working chapter no. MERC82-18, Managerial Economics Research Center, Graduate School of Management, University of Rochester, 1982).

Harry DeAngelo and Edward M. Rice, "Antitakeover Charter Amendments and Stockholder Wealth," *Journal of Financial Economics* 11 (1983): 329–359.

D. K. Dennis and J. J. McConnell, "Corporate Mergers and Security Returns," *Journal of Financial Economics* 16 (June 1986): 143–187.

Peter Dodd, "Merger Proposals, Management Discretion and Stockholder Wealth," *Journal of Financial Economics* 8 (1980): 105–138.

——— and Richard Leftwich, "The Market for Corporate Charters: 'Unhealthy Competition' versus Federal Regulation," *Journal of Business* 53 (1980): 259–283.

Peter Dodd and Richard Ruback, "Tender Offers and Stockholder Returns: An Empirical Analysis," *Journal of Financial Economics* 5 (1977): 351–374.

Peter Dodd and Jerold B. Warner, "On Corporate Governance: A Study of Proxy Contests," *Journal of Financial Economics* 11 (1983): 401–438.

Frank H. Easterbrook and Daniel R. Fischel, "Auctions and Sunk Costs in Tender Offers," *Stanford Law Review* 35 (1982): 1–21.

———, "Corporate Control Transactions," *Yale Law Journal* 91 (1982): 698–737.

————, "The Proper Role of a Target's Management in Responding to a Tender Offer," *Harvard Law Review* 94 (1981): 1161–1203.

————, "Takeover Bids, Defensive Tactics, and Shareholders' Welfare," *The Business Lawyer* 36 (1981): 1733–1750.

————, "Voting in Corporate Law," *Journal of Law and Economics* 26 (1983): 395–427.

B. Espen Eckbo, "Horizontal Mergers, Collusion, and Stockholder Wealth," *Journal of Financial Economics* 11 (1983): 241–273.

J. C. Elbert, "Mergers, Antitrust Law Enforcement and Stockholder Returns," *Journal of Finance* 31 (1976): 715–732.

E. Fama, "Agency Problems and the Theory of the Firm," *Journal of Political Economy* 88 (1980): 288–307.

————, "The Effects of a Firm's Investment and Financing Decisions on the Welfare of Its Security Holders," *American Economic Review* 68 (1978): 272–284.

———— and Michael C. Jensen, "Agency Problems and Residual Claims," *Journal of Law and Economics* 26 (June 1983): 327–349.

————, "Separation of Ownership and Control," *Journal of Law and Economics* 26 (1983): 301–325.

D. Galai and R. W. Masulis, "The Option Pricing Model and the Risk Factor of Stock," *Journal of Financial Economics* (January/March 1976): 53–82.

Ronald J. Gilson, "The Case against Shark Repellent Amendments: Structural Limitations on the Enabling Concept," *Stanford Law Review* 34 (1982): 775–836.

————, "Seeking Competitive Bids versus Pure Passivity in Tender Offer Defense," *Stanford Law Review* 35 (1982): 51–67.

————, "A Structural Approach to Corporations: The Case against Defensive Tactics in Tender Offers," *Stanford Law Review* 33 (1981): 819–891.

S. Grossman and O. Hart, "Takeover Bids, the Free-Rider Problem, and the Theory of the Corporation," *Bell Journal of Economics* (Spring 1980): 42–64.

R. C. Higgins, "Discussion," *Journal of Finance* (May 1971): 543–545.

———— and L. D. Schall, "Corporate Bankruptcy and Conglomerate Merger," *Journal of Finance* (March 1975): 93–113.

G. J. Hurdle, "Leverage, Risk, Market Structure, and Profitability," *Review of Economics and Statistics* (November 1974): 478–485.

Michael C. Jensen, "Organization Theory and Methodology," *Accounting Review* 58 (1983): 319–339.

Michael C. Jensen and William H. Meckling, "Rights and Production Functions: An Application to Labor-Managed Firms and Codetermination," *Journal of Business* 52 (1979): 469–506.

————, "Theory of the Firm: Managerial Behavior Agency Costs and Ownership Structure," *Journal of Financial Economics* 3 (1976): 305–360.

Michael C. Jensen and Richard S. Ruback, "The Market for Corporate Control: The Evidence," *Journal of Financial Economics* (April 1983): 5–50.

Arthur J. Keown and John M. Pinkerton, "Merger Announcements and Insider Trading Activity: An Empirical Investigation," *Journal of Finance* 36 (1981): 855–869.

H. Kim and J. McConnell, "Corporate Mergers and Co-Insurance of Corporate Debt," *Journal of Finance* 32 (1977): 349–363.

Benjamin Klein, Robert Crawford, and Armen A. Alchian, "Vertical Integration, Appropriable Rents, and the Competitive Contracting Process," *Journal of Law and Economics* 21 (1978): 297–326.

D. Kummer and R. Hoffmeister, "Valuation Consequences of Cash Tender Offers," *Journal of Finance* 33 (1978): 505–516.

T. Langetieg, "An Application of a Three-Factor Performance Index to Measure Stockholders' Gains from Merger," *Journal of Financial Economics* 6 (1978): 365–384.

Ronald C. Lease, John J. McConnell, and Wayne H. Mikkelson, "The Market Value of Control in Publicly-Traded Corporations," *Journal of Financial Economics* 11 (April 1983): 439–472.

H. Levy and M. Sarnat, "Diversification, Portfolio Analysis and the Uneasy Case for Conglomerate Mergers," *Journal of Finance* (September 1970): 795–802.

W. G. Lewellen, "A Pure Financial Rationale for the Conglomerate Merger," *Journal of Finance* (May 1971): 521–545.

——— and B. Huntsman, "Managerial Pay and Corporate Performance," *American Economic Review* (September 1970): 710–720.

Scott C. Linn and John J. McConnell, "An Empirical Investigation of the Impact of 'Antitakeover' Amendments on Common Stock Prices," *Journal of Financial Economics* 11 (April 1983): 361–400.

J. Lintner, "Conglomerate and Vertical Responses to Market Imperfection: Expectations, Mergers and Equilibrium in Purely Competitive Markets," *American Economic Review* (May 1971): 101–111.

Paul H. Malatesta, "The Wealth Effect of Merger Activity and the Objective Functions of Merging Firms," *Journal of Financial Economics* 11 (April 1983): 155–182.

Gershon Mandelker, "Risk and Return: The Case of Merging Firms," *Journal of Financial Economics* 1 (1974): 303–335.

Henry G. Manne, "Mergers and the Market for Corporate Control," *Journal of Political Economy* 73 (1965): 110–120.

Ronald W. Masulis, "The Effects of Capital Structure Change on Security Prices: A Study of Exchange Offers," *Journal of Financial Economics* 8 (1980): 139–178.

———, "Stock Repurchase by Tender Offer: An Analysis of the Causes of Common Stock Price Changes," *Journal of Finance* 35 (1980): 305–319.

Wayne H. Mikkelson, "Convertible Calls and Security Returns," *Journal of Financial Economics* 9 (1981): 237–264.

F. Modigliani and M. Miller, "Corporate Income Taxes and the Cost of Capital: A Correction," *American Economic Review* 53 (June 1963): 433–443.

S. C. Myers, "Procedures for Capital Budgeting under Uncertainty," *Industrial Management Review* (Spring 1968): 1–19.

Richard S. Ruback, "Assessing Competition in the Market for Corporate Acquisitions," *Journal of Financial Economics* 11 (April 1983): 141–154.

———, "The Cities Service Takeover: A Case Study," *Journal of Finance* (May 1983): 319–330.

———, "The Conoco Takeover and Stockholder Returns," *Sloan Management Review* 23 (1982): 13–33.

L. D. Schall, "Asset Valuation, Firm Investment, and Firm Diversification," *Journal of Business* (January 1972): 11–28.

J. H. Scott, Jr., "On the Theory of Conglomerate Mergers," *Journal of Finance* (September 1977): 1235–1250.

Robert Smiley, "The Effect of the Williams Amendment and Other Factors on Transactions Costs in Tender Offers," *Industrial Organization Review* 3 (1975): 138–145.

R. C. Stapleton, "Mergers, Debt Capacity and the Valuation of Corporate Loans," in *Mergers and Acquisitions,* ed. M. Keenan and L. J. White (Lexington, Mass.: D. C. Heath, 1982), Chapter 2.

Robert Stillman, "Examining Antitrust Policy toward Horizontal Mergers," *Journal of Financial Economics* 11 (April 1983): 225–240.

T. G. Sullivan, "Market Power, Profitability and Financial Leverage," *Journal of Finance* (December 1974): 1407–1415.

T. Vermaelen, "Common Stock Repurchases and Market Signalling: An Empirical Study," *Journal of Financial Economics* 9 (1981): 139–183.

R. Westerfield, "A Note on the Measurement of Conglomerate Diversification," *Journal of Finance* (September 1970): 909–914.

Peggy G. Wier, "The Costs of Antimerger Lawsuits: Evidence from the Stock Market," *Journal of Financial Economics* 11 (April 1983): 207–224.

O. E. Williamson, *Corporate Control and Business Behavior* (Englewood Cliffs, N.J.: Prentice-Hall, 1970).

———, *Markets and Hierarchies: Analysis and Antitrust Implications* (New York: Free Press, 1975).

———, "The Modern Corporation: Origins, Evolution, Attributes," *Journal of Economic Literature* 19 (1981): 1537–1568.

———, "The Vertical Integration of Production: Market Failure Considerations," *American Economic Review* (May 1971): 112–123.

Chapter 19

Lease Financing

Lease financing has become an increasingly important source of financing for U.S. industry since World War II. The total dollar value of all equipment leases in the United States is estimated at between $200 and $250 billion. New equipment leases written in 1984 alone were estimated to be $74.4 billion, a $13.2 billion increase from the previous year.[1] Financial leases clearly are of concern to financial theorist and manager alike.

Leasing is an alternative to purchasing an asset in order to acquire the services of that asset. By leasing an asset, the lessee essentially acquires its use value from the lessor, who actually purchased and owns (retains title to) the asset. Simply stated, ownership of a productive asset conveys two types of "property rights" to the owner: (1) to use the asset throughout its productive life and (2) to sell or dispose of it for its salvage value. In this context, the lessee acquires all or a portion of the "use value" of the asset in return for making a set of rental payments to the lessor. The lessor retains title to the asset and, hence, the right to sell or dispose of it for its salvage value. Thus, leasing distributes the rights of ownership by separating the asset's use value from its salvage value. In this chapter, we investi-

---

[1] From a speech by John Giddings at the 1984 annual meeting of the American Association of Equipment Lessors.

gate why this separation may be a valuable service and, consequently, provide a rationale for using lease financing.[2]

    This chapter is organized as follows. First, we discuss some institutional considerations in lease financing, including definitions of some key terms encountered in the financial leasing industry, the accounting treatment of leases, and a brief survey of the tax treatment of leases. Next, we investigate the net present value advantage of lease financing, or lease versus purchase analysis. We begin by demonstrating the conditions under which lease financing does not affect the wealth of the shareholders of the lessee firm; we then relax these assumptions in order to discover the possible reasons for using lease financing. Finally, we examine a lease purchase model that can be used to evaluate the economic consequences of leasing versus purchasing an asset.

Institutional Considerations

The leasing industry has developed its own set of terminology and institutions that often complicates the study of financial leases. In this section, we establish a set of definitions that will allow us to look beyond the jargon to the economic significance of the issues discussed in the leasing literature. In addition, financial leases have long been utilized as a means of transferring the tax advantages of an asset's legal ownership from the user of the asset to another party that more highly values those benefits. Thus, the Internal Revenue Service has set forth specific guidelines for considering the "legality" of financial lease agreements with respect to their tax consequences.

The Language of Leasing

The leasing industry has developed its own jargon, which can pose a major obstacle to grasping the issues in the study of lease financing. We begin our discussion of the leasing terminology by dividing lease contracts into two broad categories: financial leases and operating leases. A *financial lease* is a noncancelable contractual commitment to acquire the use value of an asset. Its key feature is that it essentially

---

[2]In Chapter 1 we noted that the finance literature contains both positive (what is) and normative (what should be) theory. We also saw that normative theory frequently arises in one of two ways: as an extension of the predictions of a positive theory or as a guide to rational action where no positive theory has been verified (that is, provided predictions that are widely accepted as verified or observed in the world to which it applies). The theory presented in this chapter combines positive and normative theories in that it deals with the investment decision, for which the value maximization theory is generally thought to provide acceptable guidance, and considers the impact for the financing decision. In the latter case, as we saw in Chapters 12 and 13, positive theories of financial structure have been less successful in garnering empirical verification. Thus, in this area we must resort to normative theories to explain how the financing decision "should" be made. Specifically, when we analyze the lease versus purchase decision, we will find that we must somehow evaluate the relative impact on firm value of a dollar of lease financing versus a dollar of debt financing. Because no widely accepted positive theory is available to aid our judgment here, we pose a normative conjecture that their impact is exactly the same.

transfers the lessee the entire use value of the asset to the lessee. The accounting profession has set forth a set of requirements that a lease must satisfy in order to be considered a financial lease. An *operating lease* differs from a financial lease in that it is cancelable at any time after giving the lessor proper notice. In other words, an operating lease is a more flexible agreement wherein the lessee acquires only a portion of the asset's use value. An example of an operating lease is the renting of a crane by a construction company for use in constructing an office building. After the building is completed, the construction company returns the crane to the lessor and will not rent it again unless needed. With a financial lease, on the other hand, the construction company essentially would own the services of the crane whether or not it was being used. Thus, a financial lease is very similar to asset ownership in that the lessee acquires the asset's services for an extended period.

The financial lease contract has been an important subject in the finance literature, for its use constitutes a long-term commitment by the firm. With a financial lease, a firm acquires all or most of the asset's use value and, consequently, makes a capital investment decision to acquire a fixed asset using the lease to finance the acquisition. Throughout this chapter, we will confine our discussion to financial rather than operating leases.

Financial leases can be categorized as direct leases or sale-and-leaseback agreements depending on how the lease contract originated. With a *direct lease,* the lessee acquires the services of an asset that it did not previously own. In a *sale-and-leaseback agreement,* the firm essentially converts an ownership position to a lease by selling an asset it had previously acquired (owns) to another entity (the lessor) and then leases it back. Here the firm essentially "refinances" the asset — changes its means of acquiring the asset's *use services* — from purchase to lease, and sells the asset's salvage value to the lessor. In the next section, we discuss the possible motivations for entering into each type of arrangement.

Financial leases can also differ with respect to the risks and burdens of ownership that the lessee is expected to assume over the lease's term. With a *net lease,* the lessee assumes the duties of providing for the maintenance of the leased asset, acquiring insurance on it, and paying any taxes involved. Thus, in a net lease the lessee assumes all of the duties that it would perform if it were the owner of the asset while under lease. In a *net-net lease* the lessee must, in addition to the duties assumed under a net lease, return the asset to the lessor at the end of the lease with a preestablished value.

Finally, the *leveraged lease* is a lease agreement wherein the lessor engages in borrowing (financial leverage) to finance the purchase of the leased asset. Thus, when we discuss leveraged leasing we simply recognize that there are three parties involved in a financial lease agreement: lessee, lessor, and lender. Most financial leases are leveraged lease agreements, and our analysis of the benefits of lease financing will incorporate this fact. It should be noted that in a leveraged lease the lessee rather than the lessor guarantees payment of the loans used to finance the asset's acquisition. In addition, lease or rental payments frequently are sent to the financial institution that loaned the funds to the lessor so that the loan principal and interest payments can be deducted from them before the lessor receives any payment.

Accounting Treatment of Leases

The key issue that arises in the accounting treatment of leases is whether or not the lease must be included in the firm's balance sheet. Prior to January 1977, most financial lease contracts were not included in the body of the lessee's balance sheet; instead, the lessee's lease payment liabilities were documented in footnotes to the balance sheet and current lease payments recorded as expenses in the firm's current-period income statement. With the adoption of *Statement of Financial Accounting Standards No. 13,* the accounting profession changed its position on the inclusion of financial lease obligations in the balance sheet.[3] In so doing, it adopted the standard that the economic effect of the lease transaction should govern its accounting treatment. Thus, when a lease "essentially" transfers the benefits and risks attendant to ownership to the lessee, the lessee should account for the leased asset in a manner similar to that for a purchased asset. Likewise, the financial obligation incurred through the lease should be accounted for as a liability in the firm's balance sheet. SFAS 13 distinguished between *capital leases,* which must be included in the balance sheet, and operating leases, which need not be.

A financial (capital) lease is one that meets one or more of the following criteria:

1. The lease transfers ownership of the property to the lessee by the end of the lease term.

2. The lease contains a bargain repurchase option.

3. The lease term is equal to 75 percent or more of the estimated economic life of the leased property.

4. The present value of the minimum lease payments equals or exceeds 90 percent of the excess of the fair value of the property over any related investment tax credit retained by the lessor.[4]

Table 19.1 illustrates the capitalization of a financial lease. Note that the lease appears both as an asset (leased property) and a liability (capitalized lease obligations). The dollar amounts in the statement represent the present value of the lease

Table 19.1   Capitalization of a Financial Lease

Assets		Liabilities and Stockholders' Equity	
Current assets	$100	Current liabilities	$ 75
Plant and equipment	250	Long-term debt	75
Leased assets	150	Capital lease obligations	150
		Stockholders' equity	200
Total	$500	Total	$500

[3]Financial Accounting Standards Board, *Statement of Financial Accounting Standards No. 13,* "Accounting for Leases" (Stamford, Conn.: FASB, November 1976).

[4]Ibid., 9–10.

obligation over the term of the lease contract. The discount rate used is the lower of (1) the lessee's incremental borrowing rate and (2) the lessor's implicit interest rate (where that rate can be determined). Operating leases are not included in the body of the balance sheet but are recorded in footnotes.

Tax Treatment of Leases

Lease payments made by the lessee are fully deductible from its income for tax purposes but are taxable income for the lessor. In addition, the depreciation expense associated with the asset is tax deductible for the lessor just as any other expenses associated with ownership of the asset. If the asset qualifies for an investment tax credit, the lessor is entitled to take that credit. In essence, the lessor is the owner of the asset and, as such, is entitled to all the tax benefits and costs associated with ownership.

The problem that arises with respect to taxes concerns whether the lease "qualifies" as a lease for tax purposes. The Internal Revenue Service applies a set of true lease requirements to lease contracts to determine whether they are truly leases or de facto installment sales. If a lease is disallowed, the lessor cannot claim the investment tax credit, deduct the depreciation expense associated with the asset from its taxable income, or in any way treat the asset as if it really owned it. The lessee, then, must treat the asset as if it owned it. Needless to say, the issue here relates to the fact that leases can be used to "sell" the tax benefits attendant to asset ownership to a firm that places a higher value on those benefits (that is, is in a higher tax bracket). Thus, the IRS true lease requirements are designed to determine whether the lease is a lease in name only and actually constitutes a sale of the asset. The true lease requirements deal with the term of the lease (30 years or less) and the reasonableness of the return to the lessor (for example, 7 to 12 percent on the lessor's investment, the presence of an option to renew the lease, and the existence of an option to purchase the leased asset upon the lease's expiration), among other factors. There are no hard and fast rules for the IRS assessment of a lease, but these are the areas that it gives close scrutiny.[5]

The Tax Equity and Fiscal Responsibility Act of 1982 (TEFRA) created a new category of leases, called *finance leases,* which effectively liberalized the true lease requirements. A finance lease is one that would be classified as a lease for federal tax purposes (under the true lease requirements) except that the lessee has an option to purchase the asset at the end of the lease for an exercise price of at least 10 percent of the original asset's purchase price and the lease covers "limited use" property (property of use only to the lessee, such as a nuclear power plant).[6]

---

[5]The Economic Recovery Tax Act of 1981 created the "safe harbor" or "paper" lease, which essentially lifted the IRS true lease requirements. The objective of the safe harbor provision was to allow companies with insufficient tax liabilities to absorb deductions and credits associated with new asset acquisitions and, in effect, sell them to firms in higher tax brackets. The Tax Equity and Fiscal Responsibility Act of 1982 put an end to the safe harbor provision.

[6]During 1985 and 1986, a number of public utilities sold their new power plants and leased them back, a primary motivation being the sale of tax benefits to higher tax bracket companies. For example, Tucson Electric Power Company sold its Springerville coal plant to a consortium of firms, including Emerson Electric, IBM, and Philip Morris, for $850 million (see "Utilities Learn It's Often Better to Rent," *Business Week,* February 3, 1986, 76).

The Lease versus Purchase Decision

In this section we consider the choice between leasing and purchasing an asset. This question has been the subject of much debate in the finance literature.[7] The basic issue has been one of measuring the costs and benefits attendant to the ownership versus the leasing of an asset. A wide array of lease versus purchase models have appeared in the finance literature; some differ from alternative models only cosmetically and others materially. Later we will examine a model that can be used in such analyses. First we must consider a set of conditions under which the use of lease or purchase is a matter of indifference to the firm. By introducing lease versus purchase analysis in this "sterile" environment (that is, where the net present value advantage of leasing is zero), we can identify the circumstances that make lease financing more advantageous than purchasing.

Irrelevance of the Lease versus Purchase Decision

In the June 1976 issue of the *Journal of Finance,* three papers appeared offering the same basic result: Under conditions of frictionless (that is, with no transactions costs) and competitive markets (both the capital and real asset markets), where all participants to a financial lease agreement face the same set of prices for funds and real assets and where lessees and lessors face the same tax rate on their income, the use of lease financing does not impact on shareholder wealth and, therefore, the lease versus purchase decision is irrelevant.[8] We will use the Lewellen, Long, and McConnell (1976) study as the basis for our discussion.

The Lewellen et al. irrelevance proof was based on a very simple proposition: *The lessee and lessor together perform the same functions that the purchasing firm performs singly. Thus, the lease versus purchase decision is of no consequence if the cash flows received by the lessor and lessee combined are no different from those of the purchaser alone.* In a competitive capital market this must be so, because if the cash flow to the purchaser is the same as that of the lessor and lessee combined, the value of the firm (purchaser) must equal the value of the lessee plus the lessor, and hence there is no gain to the lessee from using lease financing. The key consideration here, then, is that the functions performed by the purchaser are divided into two sets, one performed by the lessee and the other by the lessor. If this division of duties does not increase the value of the lessee and/or lessor such that the value of the divided set of duties exceeds that of the sum of the two components if performed by the purchaser, the lease will not contribute to the wealth of the lessee's shareholders and there will be no positive net present value advantage to leasing.

To demonstrate the above "irrelevance proposition," let us define the following terms:

NOI_t = net operating income before interest and taxes in year t

I_t = interest expense incurred by lessor or lessee firm if it purchases the asset (note that we assume for now that the lessor and purchasing firm will utilize the same amount of borrowing if either acquires the asset)

---

[7]For a survey of this literature, see Bower (1973) and Martin (1986).

[8]Miller and Upton (1976), Myers, Dill, and Bautista (1976), and Lewellen, Long, and McConnell (1976).

D_t = depreciation expense incurred in year t by the purchaser or lessor

P_t = principal payment required if purchaser or lessor acquires the asset

T = corporate tax rate on income for purchaser, lessor, and lessee

S_n = after-tax salvage value of the asset being considered for purchase or lease in year n, the terminal year of the lease (salvage value is assumed to be the same under either financing arrangement)

Using these symbols, the purchaser's cash flow for year t = n can be written as follows:

(19.1) $(NOI_n - I_n)(1 - T) + D_n - P_n + S_n.$ **Purchaser Cash Flow**

Note that depreciation expense has already been deducted from the firm's operating revenues when calculating NOI_n. Now consider the cash flow to the lessee in year t = n where R_n is the lease payment made by the lessee to the lessor in year n:

(19.2) $(NOI_n + D_n - R_n)(1 - T).$ **Lessee Cash Flow**

Depreciation expense (D_n) added back to NOI_n to determine the lessee's operating income for the lessee does not get to depreciate the asset, and NOI_n was previously defined for a firm that owns it. The lessor will receive the lease payment from the lessee, obtain the salvage value of the leased asset in year n, make principal and interest payments, and depreciate the asset. Thus, for year t = n the lessor's cash flow will equal

(19.3) $(R_n - D_n - I_n)(1 - T) + D_n - P_n + S_n.$ **Lessor Cash Flow**

Adding together the lessee's cash flow in Equation 19.2 and the lessor's cash flow in 19.3, we get

$$(NOI_n - I_n)(1 - T) + D_n - P_n + S_n,$$

which is, of course, the same as the cash flow to the purchasing firm.[9] Since the cash flow to the purchaser equals the combined cash flow to the lessee and lessor, there is *no value added* by decomposing asset ownership via lease financing. However, the simplified world described here is unrealistic, and there may be fundamentally sound reasons for utilizing financial leasing, as we will see in the next section.

Potential Advantages of Lease Financing

In the preceding section, we demonstrated that if the purchasing firm (potential lessee) and the lessor have the same tax status, borrow and lend at the same rate of interest, and have similar expectations regarding the salvage value for a piece of equipment, there is no reason to believe that there will be any advantage to leasing over purchasing. In this summary statement, we have identified the factors that

---

[9]The cash flows for any year t would produce the same result, including t = 0 when the asset is acquired. In that year, the purchaser has a cash flow of $-A_0$ (the initial cash outlay required to acquire the asset), while the lessee has no cash flow and the lessor a cash flow of $-A_0$.

might lead a firm to use leasing rather than purchasing. Leasing may be advantageous if one of the following conditions holds:

1.   *The lessee firm is in a lower corporate tax bracket than the lessor.* In the extreme case, the lessee may have suffered operating losses such that its loss carryforwards are sufficient to offset its taxable income for several years to come. Here the lessee would be unable to take advantage of the investment tax credit on the purchase of new assets and to utilize the depreciation and interest expense deductions from its federally taxable income. By leasing the asset from a lessor that could take advantage of these tax savings (and with which they might be shared through negotiation of the lease payments), the lessee can at least partially utilize the tax incentives associated with asset purchase.[10]

2.   *If the lessor has an economic advantage over the lessee firm in borrowing in that its borrowing costs are lower than the lessee's, lease financing may provide a way for the lessee to tap a lower-cost source of financing.* Basically, this argument centers around the role of the lessor as a financial intermediary. One might conjecture that the lessor, because of its diversified set of investments, may be able to seek financial arrangements at lower cost than the lessee. However, there seems to be no reason for the lessor to provide this financing to the lessee only through a lease. For example, the same borrowing cost advantage argument might be made for any financial intermediary who provides term loan financing for new equipment purchases.

3.   *The lessor may, due to specialization, have a more precise notion of the salvage value of a particular piece of equipment than the lessee.* This could lead the lessor to place a higher salvage value estimate on the leased asset than would the lessee, in which case the lessee might benefit by leasing.

Any one or a combination of the above might provide an economic advantage for leasing over purchasing an asset. Thus, lease versus purchase decisions are relevant to the financial analyst in a world in which any one of these conditions might hold. However, before presenting a basic lease versus purchase model designed to evaluate the potential economic advantages of lease financing, we will survey some of the arguments traditionally offered in support of leasing. These purported advantages of lease financing have been widely used in the leasing industry to "sell" lease financing and have appeared in a number of finance texts. They include

1.   *Conservation of working capital.* The idea here is that with lease financing the acquiring firm need not make a down payment and thus can conserve its cash. Two observations should be made here. First, although it is true that leases generally do not require an initial down payment (as is the case where

---

[10]Probably the best-known example of tax considerations being an important motive for lease financing is the purchase of an aluminum reduction mill by Anaconda in 1976. Anaconda had suffered substantial losses resulting from the nationalization of mining interests in Chile and could not take advantage of the tax incentives associated with purchasing the plant. Thus, Anaconda arranged to lease the plant.

the funds are borrowed), the lessee essentially is borrowing the full cost of the use value of the asset when the lease is used. In other words, the lease represents 100 percent financing of the asset's use value; thus, although the lessee does not make a down payment, it incurs a larger liability, akin to simply borrowing the down payment if it purchased the asset and financed the purchase 100 percent by borrowing. The second point is that with the lease the lessee finances only the "use value" of the asset, since its salvage value remains with the lessor (although the lessee may acquire a purchase option upon termination of the lease). Thus, with lease financing the lessee does not necessarily receive the salvage value, whose present value can be thought of as the equivalent of a down payment. The only way in which this purported advantage becomes real in an economic sense is where the lessee is able to obtain more financing or better terms via a lease than it could by borrowing or otherwise.

2.   *Ease of obtaining credit.* It is sometimes suggested that firms with poor credit ratings can obtain lease financing more easily than they can normal purchase financing (that is, loans or equity). One possible explanation for this phenomenon lies in the ease with which a lessor can reclaim leased property (to which it retains title) upon default of the lessee as compared to a creditor in a similar situation. To the extent that the lessor's security position is superior to the lessee's, this might be a real economic advantage of lease financing, which comes from economies of contracting and use of the legal system. However, note that rational lessors, like rational creditors, will charge risk premiums for lack of creditworthiness. The point here is that there may be some valid reason for lower risk premiums when a lease contract is used.

3.   *Flexibility and convenience.* It has been argued that leasing involves less bother and expense to the lessee than purchasing/owning an asset. The economic component of this argument relates to who can perform the functions associated with purchasing, financing, and maintaining an asset at lowest cost. If the lessor has some scale or scope economies in the purchase of equipment, maintenance of accounting and tax records, and resale of equipment, leasing may be advantageous. However, it is not necessarily true that lease financing is more flexible or convenient to use than purchasing. Note too that leasing can offer a means of obtaining the services of an asset that entails reduced administrative costs to the firm's management; that is, frequently a firm's asset acquisition policies are more stringent than its rental policies, and therefore management may find that for small items the convenience of bypassing the paperwork associated with purchase more than compensates for the possibly higher costs of leasing.

Each of these purported advantages of leasing may have economic substance in any particular circumstance; however, the financial analyst must perform a cost comparison between purchasing and leasing to ascertain their presence.

Comparing the Costs of Leasing versus Purchasing an Asset

Simply put, the financial analyst who compares the cost of leasing to purchasing an asset must determine the net wealth impact of purchasing and compare it to the corresponding impact of leasing. This can be accomplished by estimating the net present value of purchasing the asset as described in Chapter 11, estimating the net present value of leasing the asset's services, and then selecting the alternative with the larger NPV. Mathematically, the lease purchase decision involves analyzing the following objective function:

$$\max[\text{NPV}(P), \text{NPV}(L)],$$

where NPV(P) is the net present value of purchasing the asset using the firm's optimal mix of debt and equity securities (the capital structure problem was discussed in detail in Chapters 12 and 13) and NPV(L) is the net present value of the asset if lease financed.

The finance literature has taken a slightly different approach to the solution of the lease versus purchase problem, but the end result is the same. This procedure is outlined in Figure 19.1. The basic difference is in its use of the concept of the *net advantage of leasing (NAL),* defined as follows:

(19.4) $$\text{NAL} = \text{NPV}(L) - \text{NPV}(P).$$

As we will see shortly, NAL generally is evaluated independently of the calcula-

Figure 19.1   Lease versus Purchase Analysis

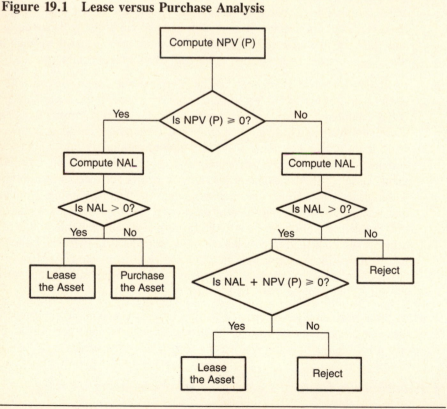

tion of NPV(L); that is, we first calculate NPV(P) and NAL and then "indirectly" calculate NPV(L) using Equation 19.4.

Following the algorithm found in Figure 19.1, we first evaluate NPV(P). If the net present value of purchase is positive, the asset's purchase will, of course, increase shareholders' wealth. Note that when NPV(P) > 0, we move down the left-hand side of the figure. However, leasing may offer an even larger wealth increase, in which case NAL will be positive. If this is the case, the asset should be leased. Returning to the top of the figure but this time assuming that NPV(P) is negative, we still want to evaluate the NAL, because a very favorable set of lease terms could produce an NAL sufficient to reverse the negative net present value of purchasing. In this instance, we move down the right-hand side of the figure. If NAL $> |$NPV(P)$|$ we observe, using Equation 19.4, that

$$NPV(L) = NAL + NPV(P) > 0.$$

Therefore, the asset should be leased even though its purchase would produce a negative net present value.

To operationalize the above model, we need only provide appropriate definitions for NPV(P) and NAL:

(19.5) $$NPV(P) = \sum_{t=1}^{N} NCF_t(1 + k)^{-t} + S_N(1 + k_S)^{-N} - A_0,$$

where NCF_t is the annual after-tax cash flow produced by ownership of the asset — that is, $NOI_t(1 - T) + D_t$, using the terminology defined earlier; N is the holding period for the asset (which, for simplicity, we will assume is the same as the lease term); k is the weighted average cost of capital for the project's financing mix; S_N is the after-tax salvage value estimated for the asset by the purchasing firm; k_S is the required rate of return estimated for the salvage value, which may or may not be the same as the cost of capital for the project, k; and A_0 is the purchase cost of the asset.

The net advantage of leasing (NAL), as defined in Equation 19.4, represents the present value of the cash flows that "differ" between leasing and purchasing. For example, with leasing there is no initial outlay, A_0; thus, the first cash flow in the NAL equation is a positive A_0. Similarly, with leasing the lessee must pay the after-tax rental payments, $R_t(1 - T)$, where T reflects the lessee's marginal income tax rate. In addition, the lessee does not get the depreciation tax savings associated with the asset's ownership, $D_t T$, and the firm may utilize more financial leverage than it would if it purchased the asset. This latter consideration means that by leasing the firm forfeits the benefits of any interest tax savings associated with using financial leverage, TI_t, where I_t corresponds to the interest expense for year t that it would incur in financing the asset's purchase. Note, however, that if leasing is used there is no equity financing such that the transaction involves 100 percent nonowner or leveraged financing. Hence, with a financial lease the firm may utilize more financial leverage than would be warranted if it purchased the asset. To reflect the loss of the tax savings on the "excess" use of financial leverage where the asset is leased, we use $T\Delta I_t$ to represent the tax savings on the interest and ΔI_t for the borrowing that now is forgone because the lease "overused" its quotient of leveraged financing.[11] Thus, we define NAL as follows:

$$(19.6) \qquad NAL = A_0 - \sum_{t=0}^{N} \frac{R_t(1 - T) + D_tT + T(I_t + \Delta I_t)}{(1 + r)^t} - \frac{S_N}{(1 + k_S)^N}.$$

In this formulation we have used the lessee's borrowing rate, r, as the discount rate for the relatively certain cash flow differences between leasing and purchasing (that is, the after-tax lease payments, depreciation tax savings, and interest tax saving opportunity loss associated with leasing). These cash flows are all contractually set (save the tax rate) and thus subject to relatively little risk. Further, the real risk of loss to the lessee is the potential loss of tax savings if the lessee becomes bankrupt prior to the end of the lease agreement and thus unable to reap the full benefits of these savings. Since the risk of lessee failure is also reflected in the cost of borrowing, we have adopted this rate as our proxy for the market's required rate of return on these cash flows. Some of the cash flows may begin immediately (t = 0), such as the rental payments, while others may not begin until t = 1. Note that the lessor faces a net present value advantage of leasing equal to the negative of Equation 19.6. However, although the terms appear to be the same, the two NPVs may differ due to the circumstances faced by the lessee versus the lessor. The possibility of different tax rates, equipment acquisition costs, and expected salvage value provides the source of an expected net present value to the lessee *and* the lessor.

Exercise 19.1: Lease versus Purchase Analysis

A. B. Spinks, Inc. is a regional publishing company located in Browning, Texas. The company utilizes two offset printing presses in its operations. One of the presses was purchased 10 years ago when the company was founded and is now being considered for replacement. The other press was bought only three years ago and is presently considered to be in good working order and expected to provide service for another three to five years. However, following a recent breakdown it became apparent that the older press could no longer be repaired at an economical cost; in fact, in its present condition its scrap value is just enough to pay for its removal from the premises.

The RX1 press has been identified as the most appropriate replacement. It will cost $60,000 and can be depreciated over a five-year period at 15, 22, 21, 21, and 21 percent for years 1 through 5, respectively. The asset has an estimated salvage value of $5,000 at the end of five years and is expected to generate operating

---

[11]We will assume here that a dollar of lease financing is equivalent to a dollar of debt. This results in the inclusion of lost interest tax savings in Equation 19.6 equal to the interest that would be owed on a loan equal to the full purchase price of the leased asset. See Ofer (1976) for a discussion of the problem of assessing the debt capacity displaced by lease financing.

income (before depreciation expense) of $25,000 per year for the first two years of use and $22,500 for years 3 through 5. The firm faces a marginal tax rate of 40 percent and estimates the required rate of return for investing in the press at 18 percent.

In addition to the purchase alternative, the seller of the press has offered to lease it for an annual payment of $12,500 (made at the beginning of each of the next five years, with the corresponding tax savings realized at the end of each year). The firm estimates that it could borrow the necessary funds at 10 percent but would finance only roughly half the purchase by borrowing if it purchased the press.

1. Analyze the net present value of the press. Should the press be purchased? (You may ignore the leasing alternative for now.)

Solution.   See Table 19.2.

2. Does the leasing alternative offer a positive advantage over purchasing?

Solution.   Yes, the net advantage of leasing is $519.06. Thus, the asset should be leased.

Leases and Options

Financial lease contracts frequently contain option components. For example, the lessee may have the option to renew the lease at the end of its original term or cancel it prior to the end of the contract period. The cancellation option is associated with operating rather than financial leases. With an operating lease the lessee makes periodic rental payments, which in turn give the lessee use of the asset until the next payment is due. The lease is canceled by simply returning the asset to the lessor and failing to make the lease payment. The cancellation option is valuable because the lessee gets all the benefits associated with the lease were it not cancelable and has the option to terminate the lease under the conditions set forth in the contract.[12]

Financial leases frequently contain options to purchase upon completion of the lease term— that is, the lessee may purchase the leased asset for a price that is set at the signing of the lease contract. We can think of the value of the purchase option as a European call option with an exercise price equal to the purchase price, X.[13] Thus, the payoff for a purchase option in a financial lease contract maturing in year T can be expressed as follows:

$$\max(S_T - X, 0),$$

---

[12]Copeland and Weston (1982) discuss the evaluation of cancelable operating leases.

[13]Chapters 15 and 16 discuss option pricing theory and applications, respectively.

Table 19.2 Lease versus Purchase Analysis for A. B. Spinks, Inc.

Capital Budgeting Analysis

	Year 1	Year 2	Year 3	Year 4	Year 5
Estimated revenues	$25,000.00	$25,000.00	$22,500.00	$22,500.00	$22,500.00
Less: Depreciation	9,000.00	13,200.00	12,600.00	12,600.00	12,600.00
Earnings before taxes	16,000.00	11,800.00	9,900.00	9,900.00	9,900.00
Less: Taxes (40%)	6,400.00	4,720.00	3,960.00	3,960.00	3,960.00
Estimated income	9,600.00	7,080.00	5,940.00	5,940.00	5,940.00
Cash flow (NI + Depreciation)	18,600.00	20,280.00	18,540.00	18,540.00	18,540.00

Project cost: $60,000.00
Salvage: $5,000.00
Estimated net present value: $4,235.78

Net Advantage of Leasing Analysis

	Year 0	Year 1	Year 2	Year 3	Year 4	Year 5
Rental payments	$12,500.00	$12,500.00	$12,500.00	$12,500.00	$12,500.00	$ 0.00
Less: Tax savings on rent	0.00	(5,000.00)	(5,000.00)	(5,000.00)	(5,000.00)	(5,000.00)
Depreciation tax savings	0.00	3,600.00	5,280.00	5,040.00	5,040.00	5,040.00
Interest tax savings	0.00	2,400.00	2,006.89	1,574.46	1,098.79	575.56
Total	$12,500.00	$13,500.00	$14,786.89	$14,114.46	$13,638.79	$ 615.56

Net advantage of leasing: $519.06

Analysis of Interest and Principal

Year	Payment	Interest	Principal	Balance
0	$ 0.00	$ 0.00	$ 0.00	$60,000.00
1	15,827.85	6,000.00	9,827.85	50,172.15
2	15,827.85	5,017.22	10,810.63	39,361.52
3	15,827.85	3,936.15	11,891.70	27,469.82
4	15,827.85	2,746.98	13,080.87	14,388.95
5	15,827.85	1,438.90	14,388.95	0.00

where S_T represents the value of the leased asset at the end of the lease term and X the asset's purchase price. Of course, S_T is unknown at the time the lease contract is signed; thus, the valuation of the call (purchase) option involves valuing a risky asset. In Chapter 15, we used a "spanning" argument to value the call option on a share of common stock; that is, we argued that by combining a riskless bond and shares of the underlying stock, we can produce the same end-of-period payoff as the option. Thus, since the bond and the stock have observable (known) current prices, we can determine the value of the option spanned by these two securities. The problem that arises in using this concept here is that the salvage value of the asset is unknown since there generally is no active secondary market for it. Further, the lessee can affect the value of the asset through the quality of care and maintenance given to it over the lease term. This "deterioration" in value of the leased asset over the lease term (due to use) produces a problem for the valuation of the purchase option similar to that created by the payment of cash dividends for a share of common stock.[14] Thus, the valuation of the purchase option on a leased asset is complicated by the fact that the asset is not traded and its value deteriorates with use over time (at a rate that is, at least partially, under the lessee's control). However, even if we find valuing the purchase option difficult, option pricing theory provides us with a means for "characterizing" an important element in the valuation of financial lease contracts.

Summary

The analysis of lease financing has been fodder for debate in the finance, accounting, and economics literature for over 30 years. Part of the intrigue surrounding this form of financing relates to the fact that its analysis requires simultaneous consideration of the investment and financing decisions. In other words, traditional analyses of the investment or capital budgeting decision assume that the cost of funds related to the sources of funds for the investment are known and need not be considered beyond their impact on the cost of capital. With financial leases, however, the investment's acceptability depends partly on the form of financing chosen — purchase or lease. Thus, financing obviously "interacts" with the investment decision. Further, the traditional weighted average cost of capital formulation of the net present value of an investment (see Chapter 11 for more details on alternative net present value models) is not easily adapted to lease financing, which generally involves no equity funding.

Although the lease versus purchase decision is easily shown to be a matter of indifference to the firm's shareholders under a set of idealized circumstances (perfect and frictionless capital markets, equal borrowing rates and tax rates for all firms), we saw that violations of these assumptions generate much of the lease financing undertaken by U.S. firms. The primary motivation for leasing large-ticket acquisitions is tax considerations and for small-ticket items the reduced organizational costs associated with acquiring the leased asset's services.

---

[14]Lee, Martin, and Senchack (1982) provide an in-depth discussion of these issues and even offer an example using Geske's (1978) option pricing model, which incorporates stochastic dividends.

Study Questions

19.1   Distinguish between a financial lease and an operating lease.

19.2   Define the following:
  a. Leveraged lease
  b. Direct lease
  c. Sale-and-leaseback agreement
  d. Net lease
  e. Net-net lease

19.3   How does the tax code impact on the motivation to use financial leasing?

19.4   A number of theorists have argued that where capital markets are frictionless and lessees are rational, leasing offers no net present value advantage over purchasing. Demonstrate this irrelevance proposition.

19.5   Why might leasing offer an economic advantage over purchasing?

Study Problems

19.1   In the spring of 1987, Tim Shaver decided he had to acquire a new delivery truck for his furniture manufacturing firm. The new truck would make the total delivery fleet four. In the past, Tim had leased his delivery vehicles for a five-year term in an effort to conserve his working capital, which was severely strained due to the rapid growth of his business. However, as a result of a very good 1986, Shaver felt that purchasing was a viable alternative this year. He utilizes an 18 percent required rate of return on investments in his business and a borrowing rate for intermediate-term financing of 10 percent. For analytical purposes, we will assume a 40 percent tax rate.

The new delivery vehicle (a tractor and trailer complete with sleeper for long-distance hauling) will cost $95,000, and for analytical purposes we will assume a zero salvage value after five years. The asset will be depreciated over a five-year term using ACRS depreciation rates (15, 22, 21, 21, and 21 percent). The estimated net operating savings (before depreciation) based on acquiring the truck are $50,000, $35,000, $40,000, $20,000, and $15,000 for years 1 through 5, respectively.

Shaver has also sought out a lease bid (net lease) calling for annual lease payments of $20,000 beginning immediately and payable at the beginning of each of the next five years. Due to uncertainty over the investment tax credit, Shaver has decided not to consider it in his analysis.
  a. What is the net present value of the purchase option?
  b. What is the net advantage of leasing over purchasing the asset? What action should Shaver take?

19.2   R. L. Jamison Printing is a small print shop operating in a Chicago suburb. The firm offers copying services to individuals and small businesses in its immediate area on a contract and walk-in basis. The firm was started four years ago by Jamison in an effort to build up some equity in

a business that he could sell in approximately 10 years to support his retirement expenses. The print shop uses six copy machines of varying degrees of sophistication, and Jamison is considering the acquisition of a
new model that will copy, reduce, and collate pages. Jamison estimates
that the new machine will generate annual revenues before depreciation
of $7,000 over the next five years. The machine will be depreciated using
ACRS rates (see Problem 19.1) toward a zero estimated salvage value in
five years. The vendor has also offered to lease the copier for a pre-tax
rental of $4,000 per year for each of the next five years, with rental
payments due at the beginning of each year.

a. If the firm uses a tax rate of 40 percent and a required rate of return of
   18 percent in analyzing new investments, should it purchase the
   copier? (You may ignore the investment tax credit in your analysis.)
b. Are the offered lease terms sufficiently favorable to entice Jamison to
   lease rather than purchase?
c. How would your answer to part b be affected if the rental rate were
   $5,000 per year?

19.3   P.B.C. Publishing, Inc. is a regional publishing company specializing in
        legal and technical manuals used by lawyers, engineers, and other profes-
        sionals. The company was started by Bill and Cathy Longley of Burkbur-
        net, Texas, in 1978. Both are lawyers with a very successful practice.
        However, they had decided to establish their printing business chiefly as a
        way to publish some of their own materials and then found that profes-
        sional engineers and accountants needed a similar service. The company
        employs a professional editor (Roy McGinty) and has contracted its print-
        ing with Lonestar Press. However, the firm is currently considering the
        acquisition of a "desktop" publishing system comprised of a sophisticated
        microcomputer, laser printer, software, and offset printer costing $50,000.
        The Longleys estimate that the printing system will generate annual net
        revenues (gross revenues less operating expenses) before depreciation
        expense of $20,000 for each of the next five years. Also, the system will
        be depreciated using ACRS rates (see Problem 19.1) toward a zero esti-
        mated salvage value in five years. The vendor has also offered to lease
        the system for a pre-tax rental of $12,000 per year for each of the next
        five years, with rental payments due at the beginning of each year.

        a. If the firm uses a 40 percent tax rate and a 15 percent required rate of
           return in analyzing new investments, should it purchase the printing
           system? (You may ignore the investment tax credit in your analysis.)
        b. Are the lease terms offered sufficiently favorable to entice the Long-
           leys to lease rather than purchase?
        c. How would your answer to part b be affected if the rental rate were
           $20,000 per year?

19.4   Calculate the annuity payments on an installment loan for $4 million that
        carries an interest rate of 12 percent compounded monthly and requires
        36 monthly payments.

19.5   In the spring of 1988 Jim Richards decided to sell his house. The house
had a market value of $125,000 and an assumable mortgage with an un-
paid balance of $100,000 and 25 years remaining to maturity. The mort-
gage carried a rate of 9 percent, while comparable new loans required a
rate of 12 percent. Furthermore, if the buyer assumes the mortgage the
required assumption fees would be only $300 as compared to $750 if a
new mortgage is created. How much value does Jim's assumable loan
(the rate remains at 9 percent with assumption) add to his home?

References

Paul F. Anderson and John D. Martin, "Lease vs. Purchase Decisions: A Survey of Current Practice,"
Financial Management 6 (Spring 1977): 41–47.

Thomas H. Beechy, "The Cost of Leasing: Comment and Correction," *Accounting Review* 45 (October
1970): 769–773.

———, "Quasi-Debt Analysis of Financial Leases," *Accounting Review* 44 (April 1969): 375–381.

Harold Bierman, Jr., "Analysis of the Lease-or-Buy Decision: Comment," *Journal of Finance* 28 (September 1973): 1019–1021.

——— and Jerome E. Hass, "Capital Budgeting under Uncertainty: A Reformulation," *Journal of
Finance* 28 (March 1977): 119–129.

——— and Seymour Smidt, *The Capital Budgeting Decision,* 4th ed. (New York: Macmillan, 1980).

Richard S. Bower, "Issues in Lease Financing," *Financial Management* 2 (Winter 1973): 25–34.

———, Frank C. Herringer, and J. Peter Williamson, "Lease Evaluation," *Accounting Review* 41
(April 1966): 257–265.

C. Robert Carlson and Donald H. Wort, "A New Look at the Lease-vs.-Purchase Decision," *Journal of
Economics and Business* 26 (Spring 1974): 199–202.

Robert A. Clark, Joan M. Jantorni, and Robert R. Gann, "Analysis of the Lease-or-Buy Decision:
Comment," *Journal of Finance* 28 (September 1973): 1015–1016.

Albert H. Cohen, *Long Term Leases—Problems of Taxation, Finance and Accounting* (Ann Arbor,
Mich.: University of Michigan Press, 1954).

Kerry Cooper and Robert H. Strawser, "Evaluation of Capital Investments Projects Involving Asset
Leases," *Financial Management* 4 (Spring 1975): 44–49.

Thomas E. Copeland and J. Fred Weston, "A Note on the Evaluation of Cancellable Operating
Leases," *Financial Management* (Summer 1982): 60–67.

R. Conrad Doenges, "The Cost of Leasing," *Engineering Economist* 17 (Fall 1971): 31–44.

Frank J. Fabozzi and Uzi Yaari, "Valuation of Safe Harbor Tax Benefit Transfer Leases," *Journal of
Finance* 38 (May 1983): 595–606.

M. Chapman Findlay III, "Financial Lease Evaluation: Survey and Synthesis," *Financial Review*
(1974): 1–15.

Julian R. Franks and Stewart D. Hodges, "Valuation of Financial Lease Contracts: A Note," *Journal of
Finance* 33 (May 1978): 657–669.

R. Geske, "The Pricing of Options with Stochastic Dividend Yield," *Journal of Finance* (May 1978):
617–625.

Richard A. Grimlund and Robert Capettini, "A Note on the Evaluation of Leveraged Leases and Other
Investments," *Financial Management* (Summer 1982): 68–72.

Robert W. Johnson and Wilbur G. Lewellen, "Analysis of the Lease-or-Buy Decision," *Journal of
Finance* 27 (September 1972): 815–823.

———, "Reply," *Journal of Finance* 28 (September 1973): 1024–1028.

Wayne Y. Lee, J. D. Martin, and A. J. Senchack, "The Case for Using Options to Evaluate Salvage
Values in Financial Leases," *Financial Management* (Autumn 1982): 33–41.

Baruch Lev and Yair E. Orgler, "Analysis of the Lease-or-Buy Decision: Comment," *Journal of
Finance* 28 (September 1973): 1022–1023.

Wilbur G. Lewellen, Michael S. Long, and John J. McConnell, "Asset Leasing in Competitive Capital Markets," *Journal of Finance* 31 (June 1976): 787–798.

Peter Lusztig, "Analysis of the Lease-or-Buy Decision: Comment," *Journal of Finance* 28 (September 1973): 1017–1018.

John D. Martin, "Leasing," *Handbook of Corporate Finance*, E. Altman, ed. (New York: Ronald Press, 1986).

————, J. William Petty, Arthur J. Keown, and David F. Scott, Jr., *Basic Financial Management* (Englewood Cliffs, N.J.: Prentice-Hall, 1979).

J. J. McConnell and J. S. Schallheim, "Valuation of Asset Leasing Contracts," *Journal of Financial Economics* (August 1983): 237–261.

M. Miller and C. Upton, "Leasing, Buying and the Cost of Capital Services," *Journal of Finance* (June 1976): 761–786.

G. B. Mitchell, "After-Tax Cost of Leasing," *Accounting Review* 45 (April 1970): 308–314.

Stewart C. Myers, "Interactions of Corporate Financing and Investment Decisions — Implications for Capital Budgeting," *Journal of Finance* 29 (March 1974): 1–25.

————, David A. Dill, and Alberto J. Bautista, "Valuation of Financial Lease Contracts," *Journal of Finance* 31 (June 1976): 799–819.

Stewart C. Myers and Gerald A. Pogue, "A Programming Approach to Corporate Financial Management," *Journal of Finance* 29 (May 1974): 579–600.

A. H. Ofer, "The Evaluation of the Lease versus Purchase Alternatives," *Financial Management* 5 (Summer 1976): 67–74.

G. David Quirin, *The Capital Expenditure Decision* (Homewood, Ill.: Irwin, 1984).

Rodney L. Roenfeldt and Jerome S. Osteryoung, "Analysis of Financial Leases," *Financial Management* 2 (Spring 1973): 74–87.

William L. Sartoris and Ronda S. Paul, "Lease Evaluation — Another Capital Budgeting Decision," *Financial Management* 2 (Summer 1973): 46–52.

Lawrence D. Schall, "Asset Valuation, Firm Investment, and Firm Diversification," *Journal of Business* 45 (January 1972): 11–28.

————, "The Lease-or-Buy and Asset Acquisition Decisions," *Journal of Finance* 29 (September 1974): 1203–1214.

Bruce D. Smith, "Accelerated Debt Repayment in Leveraged Leases," *Financial Management* (Summer 1982): 73–80.

Richard C. Stapleton, "Portfolio Analysis, Stock Valuation and Capital Budgeting Rules for Risky Projects," *Journal of Finance* 26 (March 1971): 95–117.

Richard F. Vancil, "Lease or Borrow — New Method of Analysis," *Harvard Business Review* 39 (September/October 1961). Reprinted in Leasing Series, *Harvard Business Review*, Cambridge, Mass. n.d., 79–93.

James C. Van Horne, *Financial Management and Policy*, 6th ed. (Englewood Cliffs, N.J.: Prentice-Hall, 1983).

J. Fred Weston and Thomas E. Copeland, *Managerial Finance*, 8th ed. (Hinsdale, Ill.: Dryden Press, 1986).

Chapter 20

International Finance Theory[1]

The field of international finance deals with the identification and analysis of phenomena originating in the world economy and their effects on the financial decisions of individual investors and corporations. Topics range from exchange rate determination and arbitrage conditions to the effectiveness of commercial policies in controlling the balance of payments. In this and the next chapter, we focus on the key issues surrounding these financial decisions and attempt to determine how the international environment differs from the purely domestic one, the implications of these differences for the various economic agents in foreign countries, and how these agents adjust their behavior to allow for these differences. In this chapter, we deal primarily with the fundamental positive theory of international finance — the size and efficiency of the international securities market, the degree of integration among the various domestic security markets, risk factors unique to the international financial system, and equilibrium conditions. In Chapter 21, we review the empirical evidence on the theoretical structure developed in this chapter and its implications for practitioners in the field of international finance — that is, normative theory. We discuss issues such as the advantages and disadvantages of international diversification, exchange risk hedging, project financing, and capital budgeting in this context.

---

[1]Chapters 20 and 21 were written by Glenn Boyle, Ph.D. student at the University of Texas, and are included here with his permission.

Much of the material in these two chapters is less technical and rigorous than that in previous ones. The reason is that the study of international finance is at an earlier stage of development than its domestic counterpart. Many important problems in domestic finance remain unsolved, and this has inhibited the spread of research into the international sphere. Nevertheless, an impressive body of literature on international capital market theory has evolved; unfortunately, however, it has had little practical impact. At the other extreme is a substantial body of institutional knowledge and normative theory that has not yet been linked to any positive economic theory. This chapter attempts to synthesize these two approaches. We have used rigorous arguments wherever possible, keeping in mind that rigor can never be a proper substitute for relevance.

The International Economic Environment

Definitions

Before beginning our study of international finance, we will briefly describe some of the more important components of the international financial system. Some of these are more relevant than others for the purposes of this chapter, but a basic familiarity with each is essential for any student of international finance.

Exchange Rates.   The *exchange rate* is simply the price at which one national currency can be exchanged for another. This most commonly means the number of units of domestic currency required to buy a single unit of foreign currency — in other words, the price of foreign currency. Thus, a dollar/Deutschmark exchange rate of 0.4 means that a U.S. resident will have to pay $0.4 in order to acquire 1 DM. An exchange rate expressed in this manner is known as a *direct quote*. Alternatively, the exchange rate can be expressed as an *indirect quote,* representing the units of foreign currency available for one unit of domestic currency or, simply, the reciprocal of a direct quote. In almost all countries, exchange rates are expressed as direct quotes. This convention often confuses students confronted with an exchange rate depreciation or appreciation. An exchange rate *depreciation* (or *devaluation* of the domestic currency) is said to occur when the domestic currency's value falls relative to the foreign currency — that is, a unit of domestic currency provides fewer units of foreign currency than previously. This is just another way of saying that the number of units of domestic currency needed to buy a unit of foreign currency — the domestic currency price of foreign currency or direct quote exchange rate — has risen. In other words, exchange rates expressed as direct quotes *rise* following an exchange rate depreciation and not fall, as many initially believe.

The *spot exchange rate* is the rate at which domestic currency can be exchanged for foreign currency at a moment in time. The *forward exchange rate* is the rate at which a contract can be signed today to exchange domestic for foreign currency at some specified future date. Under certain conditions (to be discussed later), the forward and future spot exchange rates may be linked through *interest arbitrage,* wherein the difference between them equals the interest rate differential plus or minus transactions costs.

An Institutional Note: Foreign Exchange Transactions

Two types of transactions generally can be carried out in the foreign exchange market — spot and forward. A *spot transaction* involves the buying and selling of foreign exchange at the existing spot exchange rate for immediate delivery. For instance, suppose a U.S. citizen arranges to purchase a painting from a British citizen for the sum of £500 and that the exchange rate ($/£) is 1.5. The U.S. citizen must obtain £500 from the foreign exchange market at a cost of $750.

A *forward transaction* involves the formation of a contract for the buying and selling of specified amounts of foreign exchange at a fixed future date where the exchange rate at which the transaction will take place — known as the *forward exchange rate* — is established at the time the contract is written. However, payment and delivery are not required until the contract matures. To illustrate, suppose that a U.S. importer has arranged to import 100,000 drachmas' worth of olives from Greece in 6 months. Because he is uncertain of the level of the spot exchange rate at that time, he covers himself by buying drachmas forward — that is, he enters a contract under which he agrees to buy 100,000 drachmas in 6 months at the forward rate of 0.2. This ensures that he will pay exactly $(0.2)(100,000) = \$20,000$ in 6 months, when it is time to purchase the olives. Had he been prepared to buy the drachmas on the spot market, the dollar value of his outgoings could have taken on any number depending on what the spot rate turned out to be in 6 months.

An important issue is the relationship of the forward exchange rate to the spot rate at any time. If the forward rate exceeds the spot rate, forward exchange is said to be selling at a *premium;* if the spot rate exceeds the forward rate, forward exchange is said to be selling at a *discount*. In the olives example, if the spot rate at the time the forward contract was made was 0.15, the forward currency was selling at a premium.

In general, the forward premium or discount is given by the following formula:

$$\text{Forward premium or discount as a percentage} = \frac{\text{Forward rate} - \text{Spot rate}}{\text{Spot rate}} \times 100.$$

Exchange Rate Systems.   A *strict exchange control system* is one in which currencies are nonconvertible and the government sets the exchange rate. This does not necessarily let individuals carry out their desired transactions. Foreign exchange is sold only under certain conditions, and individuals generally are required to sell all of their foreign exchange to the government.

In a *fixed exchange rate system*, currencies are freely convertible and transactions take place at given prices (exchange rates). The government then buys or sells foreign currencies in order to maintain the given exchange rates.

A *flexible exchange rate system* is one in which currencies are freely convertible and transactions take place at market-determined prices (exchange rates). In other words, exchange rates adjust to equalize the supply of and demand for the various currencies.

These divisions are not always as clear-cut in practice. Many countries operate under fixed or flexible exchange rates but are subject to some degree of exchange control—that is, currencies are only partially convertible.

An Institutional Note: The Balance of Payments

The *current account* is a record of all flows of goods and services among countries. Included in the current account are items such as exports, imports, tourist expenditures, dividend and interest income flowing to and received from abroad, and insurance and shipping payments and receipts. For an individual country, the current account balance is the difference between current inflows (such as export receipts, foreign tourist expenditures, and dividend and interest income from foreign sources) and current outflows (such as import receipts, tourist expenditures abroad, and dividend and interest payments to foreign sources).

The *capital account* is a record of all asset transactions between a particular country and the rest of the world. Included are items such as borrowings from abroad, purchases of securities from abroad, the drawing down of a foreign bank account, and direct foreign investment. For an individual country, the capital account balance is the difference between capital inflows and capital outflows.

The *balance of payments account* for any given country is simply the sum of the current and capital account positions. Under a flexible exchange rate system, wherein exchange rates adjust to eliminate excess supply of and demand for various currencies, the balance of payments for each country must equal zero. To see why this is so, consider a two-country world initially in long-run equilibrium with each country having a zero balance of payments. Now suppose that some exogenous shock takes place that causes one country's residents to attempt to increase their purchases of the other country's goods and services. This tendency, if left unchecked, clearly would create a balance of payments deficit. However, in order to pay for the increased imports, residents of the first country must obtain a greater quantity of the other country's money supply. In the process, the relative supply and demand positions of the two currencies—and, hence, the exchange rate (their relative prices)—will change. This will continue until the excess demand has been eliminated, that is, until individuals in the first country no longer want to obtain additional foreign currency, which in turn implies that they no longer wish to purchase additional foreign goods and services, thereby quashing the tendency toward a balance of payments deficit. In short, the exchange rate adjusts so as to make foreign goods and services relatively more expensive (cheap) and thereby eliminate any excess demand (supply) that might arise. The implication here is that under a flexible exchange rate system, the capital account balance must (in equilibrium) be equal to, and opposite in sign from, the current account balance.

Under a fixed exchange rate system, this may or may not be the case depending on exactly how we define the balance of payments. In the above scenario, the exchange rate would not adjust; hence, the planned increase in import consumption could take effect, resulting in a balance of payments deficit. However, the question as to how the additional foreign currency (or means of payment) is obtained remains. Typically, individuals obtain it from the government, which in turn borrows it from abroad. It is these latter capital flows that, if included, ensure that the total balance of payments always equals zero. This is due simply to the fundamental premise of "no free lunch." Any purchase from a foreign country must be paid for; thus, any imbalance in the current account must be offset by a like imbalance on the capital account in order to obtain the funds necessary to allow the current account imbalance. Note, however, that the private sector balance of payments need not equal zero under a fixed exchange rate system and, hence, do not require offsetting capital and current account positions. However, any total imbalance on their part is offset by official government transactions. Thus, under a fixed exchange rate system, excess supply of or demand for the various currencies is accommodated by currency flows rather than by exchange rate adjustments.

Size and Accessibility to International Securities Markets

From the standpoint of U.S. residents, the study of international finance would be of little interest if international securities markets were particularly small relative to U.S. markets or if U.S. investors had little or no access to them. If the first condition were true, the entire set of opportunities faced by U.S. residents would be little or no different from the purely domestic set of opportunities. Consequently, uniquely international phenomena would scarcely affect the optimal financial behavior of U.S. individuals and firms. If the second were true, these uniquely international phenomena would again become irrelevant from the viewpoint of U.S. investors.

Ibbotson, Carr, and Robinson (1982) analyzed the relative sizes of the U.S. and non-U.S. equity and bond markets. Their results are set out in Figure 20.1. Interestingly, while the United States easily has the largest single-country bond and equity markets, the total market value of its securities is less than 50 percent. For equities, the U.S. market comprises almost 57 percent of the world market but for bonds alone less than 40 percent. Clearly the non-U.S. securities markets are large enough to significantly expand the investment opportunity set faced by U.S. investors. Hence, the size factor indeed contributes to the relevance of international finance. As far as the accessibility of international markets is concerned, the regulations governing flows of U.S. dollars are extremely liberal. Moreover, even when there do exist factors that discourage U.S. investors from investing in a foreign security market (such as differential taxation), they can enter it indirectly by purchasing shares in U.S. multinationals operating in that country.

Figure 20.1   Size of World Equity and Bond Markets at the End of 1980 in Billions of U.S. Dollars (World Total = $5,289.9 Billion)

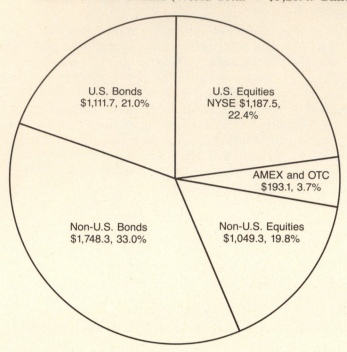

Source: R. Ibbotson, R. Carr, and A. Robinson, "International Equity and Bond Returns," *Financial Analysts Journal* 38 (1982).

This latter argument, however, should not be pushed too far. Some studies have argued that multinational stocks are poor substitutes for foreign stocks with respect to capturing gains from international diversification. For instance, Jacquillat and Solnik (1978) showed that U.S. multinational stock returns are much more highly correlated with the U.S. market than the foreign market of operation. Hence, little of the U.S. market systematic risk becomes diversifiable in an international context simply by purchasing multinational stocks. Nevertheless, the very existence of U.S.-based multinational corporations — and, therefore, U.S. direct foreign investment — represents one of the most important reasons for studying international finance.

Hence, the study of international finance is justified because U.S. investors have access to nondomestic markets, these are sufficiently large to significantly expand the opportunity set they face, and many U.S. firms operate directly in foreign markets. Having established this, we must now identify some of the more important phenomena encountered by U.S. investors who decide to take the opportunity to access international security markets.

Exchange Risk

Exchange risk is a major source of uncertainty for individuals and firms engaged in international business transactions. It can be defined simply as the riskiness of international investments due to unexpected changes in exchange rates. For instance, the value to a U.S. investor of any intertemporal cash flow streams equals the sum of their discounted dollar values. However, when in an international environment the values of these cash flows in dollar terms may become risky even though their foreign currency values are certain. To see this, consider a U.S. investor holding $1 of a British risk-free bond at an initial exchange rate of 1.0. On a risk-free security, this investor requires a nominal return of 10 percent. Now suppose that the value of the pound unexpectedly declines during the year and the exchange rate ($/£) appreciates to 0.75. In such a case, the return to the U.S. investor will be only $(0.75)(0.1) = 7.5$ percent.

The above example demonstrates the notion of exchange rate riskiness of nominal returns. However, whether real returns are subject to the same additional riskiness is not clear. For instance, if exchange rate changes simply reflect changes in the relative purchasing powers of currencies and nominal interest rate differentials simply reflect exchange rate changes, the investor may incur no additional risk through investing internationally than he or she would if confined to a purely domestic environment. These are complex issues that will become clearer in later sections. For now, we define exchange risk simply as a positive probability of the exchange rate changing and, hence, a like probability of the domestic currency value of a foreign currency–denominated investment changing.

The obvious question, then, is to ask why the exchange rate might change. To answer this, recall that the exchange rate is simply the relative price of two currencies and, as such, reflects the relative supply of and demand for each. Hence, anything that changes this relative supply and demand will cause the exchange rate to change. As currency is a purely nominal commodity, nominal as well as real phenomena could cause this relative supply and demand to change. Thus, an increase in the U.S. money supply will, other things equal, create an excess supply of U.S. dollars and therefore cause the price of the dollar relative to other currencies to fall; that is, the exchange rate (as perceived in the United States) will rise. Moreover, whenever the real supply/demand relationship for an internationally traded good is disturbed, movement back to equilibrium requires an adjustment in the exchange rate. Thus, a U.S. investor holding securities of firms domiciled in a country that exports, say, coffee is subject to exchange risk as defined above in two ways. First, if the money supply of the coffee-exporting country increases, the U.S. dollar, as we have seen, will appreciate and the dollar return to the U.S. investor will be less than it would have been in the absence of such a change. Second, a real disturbance, such as the dumping of coffee on international markets by another coffee exporter, would lower the world price of coffee. As the demand for any currency is a derived one — in this case, from coffee — this would reduce the demand for the currency of the original coffee exporter and, hence, reduce the value of its currency. Again the dollar return to the U.S. investor would be less than if the dumping had not occurred.

It is important to note that all of this represents exchange risk only insofar as that risk is transmitted in an international environment through the exchange rate. As we have seen, exchange risk resulting from both nominal and real phenomena occurs because of their effects on the underlying relative supply of and demand for national currencies. It is this supply and demand — the environment within which the firm or investor operates — that is risky rather than the exchange rate per se.

Political Risk

Aliber (1978) defines *political risk* as "the uncertainty that investors have about changes in laws and regulations that national authorities apply to the transfer of funds across national borders and the ownership of assets within their jurisdictions by foreign firms and residents" (p. 46). Every government has the power to control the flow of funds into and out of its jurisdiction and can thereby restrict loans, investments, and repatriation of profits, dividends, and capital. Moreover, each can use its powers to expropriate privately owned assets within its jurisdiction or refuse to pay debts to foreigners. All these factors contribute to the political risk faced by any firm or investor operating in a foreign country.

Political risk clearly has important implications for the financial behavior of firms and investors. If securities are priced according to their systematic risk, the price of a security in a given market reflects its systematic risk in that market. Hence, given some degree of nonintegration in the international financial markets (an issue to be discussed in Chapter 21), an asset's price will reflect its systematic risk in the relevant segmented market. Hence, a U.S. investor considering the purchase of an asset denominated in Nicaraguan cordobas will find that the asset is priced according to its systematic risk in the relevant market set for Nicaraguans. However, since the market set for Nicaraguans is unlikely to be the same as that for Americans, the asset's systematic risk, from the U.S. investor's viewpoint, may differ from that faced by the Nicaraguan investor. This matter is itself important and will be discussed further in a later section. For now, in order to focus more closely on political risk, let us assume that the asset's systematic risk is the same for both the U.S. and Nicaraguan investor in the absence of political risk. If political risk affects both investors equally, there is no problem—the U.S. investor expects to receive his or her required return. Generally, however, the political risk is more likely to have a disproportionate effect on non-Nicaraguan investors. Even here, though, the U.S. investor will expect to receive his or her required return if the political risk is nonsystematic or diversifiable. If, however, political risk is both disproportionately weighted against foreign investors and systematic from their viewpoint (for instance, if any political action is likely to be directed at European as well as U.S. investors), a disincentive to invest internationally clearly exists.

The situation from the firm's viewpoint is similar. Firms are concerned with where to invest and how to finance that investment. Consider a U.S. multinational wishing to finance a project in a foreign country where there is an element of political risk. The firm can choose to raise the funds in either the U.S. or foreign securities market (assuming that no offshore market exists). If the political risk represents systematic risk for the U.S. investor but not for the foreign investor, the firm will prefer to borrow in the foreign market and thereby lower its cost of financing the project. However, even if this cost is the same in both countries, the existence of political risk may induce the firm to raise the money in the foreign market. First, doing so would minimize its exposure to losses from expropriation; that is, if expropriation took place, the foreign government would, as the new owner, be obliged to repay any debts, thereby freeing the firm from any further financial obligation. Second, if the relevant political risk is in the form of exchange controls—constraints on repatriation of dividends and capital—the firm will prefer to raise the necessary funding in the foreign country, as this would directly minimize its exposure to the political risk. In the above example, a U.S. firm could reduce its exposure to Nicaraguan political risk by borrowing funds in Nicaragua.

The major point of all this is that firms investing abroad can reduce country-specific political risk by borrowing in the country where the investment is to take place. Consequently, interest rates in those countries may be higher than can be explained solely by anticipated changes in exchange rates. (This concerns the notions of interest rate parity and the Fisher open hypothesis, to be discussed more fully in the next section.)

Efficiency of Foreign Security Markets

An important consideration for U.S. firms and investors is the relative efficiency of foreign security markets. While a firm may prefer less efficiency, which implies the possibility of earning excess returns, this will certainly not be true for an individual international investor. In general, U.S. investors have far less information about foreign securities than do foreigners. This is unimportant if the foreign markets are efficient. Efficiency implies that all securities are priced fairly on the basis of all available information. Those individuals with additional information earn a return commensurate with their expenditure on obtaining information rather than an excess return resulting from exploiting unusually superior information. In such a case, U.S. investors can rely on foreign investors to keep security prices in the foreign market fair. If, however, the foreign market is inefficient, U.S. investors are at a disadvantage relative to more knowledgeable foreign investors.

As outlined in Chapter 10, market efficiency typically can be defined in three ways: (1) weak-form, (2) semistrong-form, and (3) strong-form efficiency. Weak-form efficiency tests of foreign security markets have tended to show that price changes exhibit greater serial correlation in those markets than in U.S. markets. However, the overall conclusion is that such departures from randomness are insignificant after allowing for transactions costs and, thus, gains from trading strategies based on past prices generally are not possible.

Tests for semistrong-form efficiency have tended to concentrate on testing CAPM-like relationships. This immediately implies a joint hypothesis of the particular equilibrium risk-return relationship used and market efficiency. Hence, one may (erroneously) reject efficiency when the model is in fact wrong. Such tests also necessitate identifying a benchmark or market portfolio. The practical difficulties of achieving this in a purely domestic context are well known. In an international setting, the task becomes even more complex. In order to be valid, tests of superior performance must compare portfolio with benchmark results for the same range of securities. In other words, it is of little use, insofar as establishing market efficiency is concerned, to conclude that a particular portfolio in a foreign country outperformed the benchmark portfolio when some of the securities in the portfolio were excluded from the benchmark portfolio. All of this makes testing of the efficiency of individual markets very difficult. As a result, there appears to be no credible evidence of consistently superior performance in foreign security markets.

Finally, all of the above difficulties may actually be irrelevant. Roll (1977) showed that such efficiency tests may be meaningless. Using efficient set mathematics, he showed that a tautological linear relationship exists between the ex-post return on an asset and its beta. This implies that if any ex-post efficient portfolio is chosen as the benchmark, all portfolios must lie on the security market line. If an ex-post inefficient portfolio is chosen, the ranking of any two portfolios can be reversed by choosing another ex-post inefficient portfolio. In other words, such tests of semistrong-form inefficiency may not make sense in themselves.

International Parity Conditions: Theory

Up to this point, we have focused on defining and describing important concepts and phenomena unique to the international financial environment. Armed with this knowledge, we can now turn our attention to the equilibrating forces at work in the international economy. These fundamental forces are described by what is known as the *pure theory of international parity* — a set of theories embodied in the writings of Keynes, Cassel, and Fisher. We will examine each of these in turn. In Chapter 21, we will review the empirical evidence on the validity and applications of these theories.

The Law of One Price and Purchasing Power Parity

The *law of one price* essentially states that identical assets or goods must sell at the same price at the same time in the same market. If they do not, arbitrage will take place until this relationship holds. The most general form of the law of one price is

(20.1)
$$|P_i - eP_i^*| \leq T,$$

where P_i = domestic price of good (or asset) i
P_i^* = foreign price of good (or asset) i
e = current exchange rate, or price of foreign currency in units of domestic currency
T = financial magnitude of market imperfections such as taxes, tariffs, and controls or institutional realities such as transactions costs or transport costs

To see why this relationship must hold, suppose that $P_i = \$5$, $P_i^* = \pounds 7$, $e = 1$, and $T = \$1$ — in other words, Equation 20.1 is violated. In such a case, individuals could purchase good i for $5 domestically, pay $T = \$1$, and then sell it abroad for £7, which, when converted back into domestic currency, yields an arbitrage profit of $1. Note that when stated in this form there is a range of relative prices, P_i/P_i^*, that can occur for a given e; that is, goods and assets need not sell at the exact same exchange rate–adjusted price in each country. For instance, in the situation described above, the permissible difference in exchange rate–adjusted prices is given by

$$-1 \leq P - eP^* \leq 1;$$

that is, the U.S. price can be as much as $1 above or $1 below the foreign price (expressed in terms of U.S. currency). The existence of such a range simply reflects the fact that transactions costs will make arbitrage unprofitable unless the single-currency values of each good become sufficiently divergent.

Suppose, however, that we make two additional assumptions:

1. Financial markets are perfect; there are no controls, transactions costs, taxes, and so on.

2. Good markets are perfect; international shipment of goods can take place freely, instantaneously, and without cost or tariff.

In this case, T = 0 and the range of allowable differences in single-currency prices becomes

$$0 \leq P - eP^* \leq 0;$$

that is, the range degenerates to a single point. Here Equation 20.1 clearly simplifies to

(20.2) $$P_i = eP_i^* .$$

The law of one price is a statement about the prices of an individual good or asset in each country and the equilibrium exchange rate between their currencies. In contrast, *purchasing power parity theory* describes average commodity price levels (as measured by, say, the consumer price index) in each country and the equilibrium exchange rate between their currencies. We have seen that if conditions 1 and 2 above hold, the law of one price as described by Equation 20.2 must hold. Suppose too that at least one of the following two conditions is valid:

3. There is a single consumption good common to everyone.

4. The same commodities appear in the same proportions in each country's market basket.

Then the following relationship must hold:

(20.3) $$P = eP^*,$$

where P = domestic price level and P* = foreign price level. This relationship is known as the *absolute* version of purchasing power parity because it concerns price levels. Note the importance of assumptions 1 through 4 in deriving it. If 1 or 2 did not hold, there would be an inexact relationship between the prices of individual goods as described by Equation 20.1. In such a case, P − eP* could take on a range of values. If neither 3 nor 4 held, Equation 20.3 would not necessarily be true even if the law of one price was valid.

A simple example may help explain why. Suppose there are just two goods, A and B, and the law of one price holds for each. In country 1, $P_A^1 = 6$ and $P_B^1 = 9$. The equilibrium price of country 2 currency in units of country 1 currency, e, equals 1.5. But now suppose that preferences in country 1 are such that 40 percent of residents' consumption expenditure goes to A and 60 percent to B, while in country 2, 60 percent of consumption expenditure goes to A and 40 percent to B. The price levels in each country, then, are calculated as follows:

$$P^1 = (0.4)(6) + (0.6)(9) = 7.8$$

$$P^2 = (0.6)(4) + (0.4)(6) = 4.8$$

$$\text{but } 7.8 \neq (1.5)(4.8) = 7.2 .$$

Hence, purchasing power parity cannot be derived as a theoretical proposition if neither 3 nor 4 holds. In the real world, of course, neither 3 nor 4 is likely to be satisfied, as the typical consumption basket for any country includes nontraded goods and services as well as those traded internationally.

If the absolute version of purchasing power parity holds, we must also have

(20.4) $$\frac{e_1}{e_0} = \left(\frac{P_1}{P_0}\right)\left(\frac{P_0^*}{P_1^*}\right) = \frac{1 + I}{1 + I^*},$$

where the subscripts represent the respective time periods and I and I^* are the domestic and foreign country's inflation rate, respectively. Subtracting 1 from both sides of Equation 20.4, we get

(20.5) $$\frac{e_1 - e_0}{e_0} = \frac{I - I^*}{1 + I^*} \approx 1 - I^*,$$

which is the usual approximation for purchasing power parity.

A less restrictive form of purchasing power parity is known as the *relative* version. This states that the rate of change in the equilibrium exchange rate is proportional to the difference between the rates of change in the domestic and foreign price levels. This is essentially the relationship described by Equation 20.5. For convenience, it is usually stated as

(20.6) $$\frac{\dot{e}}{e} = \frac{\dot{p}}{p} - \frac{\dot{p}^*}{p^*},$$

where the dots refer to rates of change. The absolute version of purchasing power parity is a sufficient, but not necessary, condition for the relative version to hold.

Purchasing power parity theory implies that changes in price level relationships cause changes in the equilibrium exchange rate. It does not, however, rule out the possibility of the exchange rate changing even when there has been no movement in the price level relationship. As we saw earlier, the exchange rate can change as the result of real or structural disturbances as well as nominal ones. Thus, it may be possible for real shocks, such as oil discoveries or changes in import demand, to generate short- or long-run deviations from purchasing power parity.

Solnik (1978) provided one view of the direct link between exchange risk and purchasing power parity. In particular, he showed that the exchange rate between any two countries will change following a real disturbance as long as the consumption baskets in the two countries are not identical, regardless of the net exporting position of each in the affected good. He considered the example of the Japanese, who consume more sake than wine, and the French, who consume more wine than sake. Wine and sake are assumed to be the only goods in the world, and there are no barriers to trade or transactions costs. Solnik then proposed that some exogenous shock occurs that reduces the supply of wine and, therefore, forces up its price. If inflation is held constant in both countries, the prices of the initial consumption baskets in each must remain the same following the shock. But with a higher price of wine, there must be a fall in the price of sake. Since the French hold a higher proportion of their consumption bundle in wine than do the Japanese, the fall in the price of sake must be greater in francs than in yen. But if we assume perfect markets, goods arbitrage will ensure that the price of sake, after adjustment for the exchange rate, is the same in both France and Japan. Hence, the price of yen in terms of francs must fall. Consequently, an unexpected real disturbance can bring about changes in the exchange rate and thus contribute to exchange risk. This is clearly a deviation from purchasing power parity. Each country's price indices remain unchanged, but the exchange rate moves. These deviations constitute real exchange rate risk. Their extent depends on such factors as the size of the foreign trade sector relative to the economy and changes in exchange controls. If the foreign trade sector is very small, overall price level changes may indicate very little about the country's international competitiveness and, hence, the equilibrium exchange rate. The greater the changes in exchange controls — and, hence, in any other such barrier to international payments — the greater the possible deviation from purchasing power parity.

All this aside, we are really interested in the extent to which purchasing power parity exists as a real-world phenomenon. As we will see, the empirical evidence suggests that deviations from purchasing power parity — or at least the absolute version of it — are the norm rather than the exception. The theory has attracted some heavy criticism. Much has been made of the fact that arbitrage is neither instantaneous nor costless and that the law of one price need not hold for nontraded or even traded goods. Samuelson (1974) has even argued that the conditions necessary for purchasing power parity to hold are so restrictive that they destroy its empirical content.

Interest Rate Parity

The *interest rate parity theorem* relates interest rates on similar assets denominated in different currencies to the forward exchange rate premium. The only assumption required for deriving this condition is that financial markets be perfect with no transactions costs or controls. In such a case, arbitrage will bring about the following relationship:

$$\text{(20.7)} \qquad \frac{1 + r_i}{1 + r_i^*} = \frac{F}{e}, \qquad \text{[IRP]}$$

where F equals the forward exchange rate and r_i and r_i^* the domestic and foreign interest rate on riskless asset i, respectively. Equation 20.7 is known as the interest rate parity theorem or, alternatively, the theory of forward exchange rates. It basically states that in the absence of financial market imperfections, exchange rates and interest rates adjust until a $1 riskless investment anywhere in the world will earn the same return. In other words, the proportionate differential between the forward and spot exchange rates must equal the interest rate differential measured over the same time interval, or riskless arbitrage opportunities will exist. To see this, suppose that an investor has \$1 to invest. If the investor chooses to invest in the foreign security at a known interest rate r_i^*, he or she can purchase $1/e$ units of foreign currency now and at the end of the period have $(1 + r_1^*)/e$ units of foreign currency. Alternatively, the investor could enter into a contract now to buy foreign exchange at rate F at the end of the period. Investing the \$1 in the domestic security at the known interest rate r_i will yield $(1 + r_i)$ units of domestic currency, or $(1 + r_i)/F$ units of foreign currency, at the end of the period. Since all relevant variables are known at the beginning of the period, these two values must be equal in equilibrium; that is:

$$\frac{1 + r_i^*}{e} = \frac{1 + r_i}{F}$$

or

$$\frac{F}{e} = \frac{1 + r_i}{1 + r_i^*}.$$

The assumption of perfect financial markets is important for the same reason as for purchasing power parity: If transactions costs or taxes existed, interest rate differentials over and above those warranted by the forward premium could endure because the transactions costs or taxes would more than offset the possible arbitrage profits. Aliber (1973, 1978) has added a further dimension to this by arguing that political risk in the form of a positive probability of future capital controls can lead to deviations from interest parity, even in the presence of perfect markets. This is in contrast to deviations caused by existing controls, which violate only our perfect markets assumption. A positive probability of future capital controls adds an element of risk to the situation despite the fact that r_i, r_i^*, F, and e may all be known with certainty. In such a case, one may well expect that the interest rate differential will reflect a risk premium in addition to the forward premium. This, of course, is an issue that can only be determined empirically; as such, we will return to it in Chapter 21.

The Fisher Open Hypothesis and Forward Parity

The *Fisher open hypothesis* proposes a relationship between observed nominal interest rates on similar assets in two countries and the expected rate of change in the exchange rate between the two countries. If financial markets are perfect and the future is known with certainty, the following relationship is hypothesized to hold:

(20.8) $$\frac{1 + r_{io}}{1 + r_{io}^*} = \frac{E(e_1)}{e_0},$$ [FOH] where r_{io} = observed interest rate on asset i from time 0 to time 1 in the domestic country

r_{io}^* = observed interest rate on asset i from time 0 to time 1 in the foreign country

e_0 = current spot exchange rate

$E(e_1)$ = currently expected spot exchange rate for time 1

This is the Fisher open hypothesis or proposition. The rationale for it is similar to that for interest rate parity: Investors hold assets denominated in currencies that are expected to depreciate only if interest rates in those countries are sufficiently high to offset the capital loss from the anticipated depreciation of the currency; conversely, investors hold assets at lower interest rates in countries whose currencies they expect to appreciate.

The assumption of perfect foresight is important in arriving at this hypothesis. If investors can predict the future exchange rate only with error, Equation 20.8 reduces to a statement that they are prepared to accept the same expected return on a risky contract as on a riskless one. Hence, if we drop the assumption of certainty, the question of a risk premium becomes important. Of course, whether such a risk premium exists can be verified only empirically; thus, we will return to this issue in our discussion of the empirical evidence on the parity theorems in Chapter 21.

The Fisher open hypothesis is often confused with the interest rate parity theorem. The above discussion should have clarified the distinction between them, namely that interest rate parity is, in principle, riskless, while the Fisher open hypothesis is vitally integrated with the notion of risk. Thus, interest rate parity must always hold in perfect financial markets (because it is an arbitrage condition), while the Fisher open hypothesis need not, due to the possibility of risk premia.[2]

Note that if financial markets are perfect and the investor operates in a certain environment, Equations 20.7 and 20.8 are both hypothesized to hold. But the left-hand side of each equation is the same and, hence, so are the right-hand sides. Thus, we must have

(20.9) $$F = E(e_1).$$ [FRP]

This is known as the *forward rate parity hypothesis* and states that under the above conditions, the forward rate equals the expected future spot rate. This hypothesis has inspired a great deal of empirical work and, as we will see, has been used (erroneously) to determine the efficiency of the foreign exchange markets. The interrelationships among the interest rate parity, Fisher open, and forward rate parity hypotheses are summarized in Figure 20.2.

---

[2]Recall, however, the work of Aliber noted earlier, which argued that interest rate parity need not hold even when financial markets are presently perfect if there is some non-zero probability of them becoming imperfect in the future.

Figure 20.2   Interrelationships among the Interest Rate Parity, Fisher Open, and Forward Rate Parity Hypotheses

If financial markets are perfect, riskless financial arbitrage becomes impossible. This is sufficient for the interest rate parity (IRP) hypothesis to hold. Moreover, under certainty it is also sufficient for the Fisher open hypothesis (FOH) to hold. Combining these two hypotheses gives the forward rate parity (FRP) hypothesis. Hence, the conditions sufficient to ensure the two former hypotheses are sufficient to ensure the latter hypothesis as well.

Assumptions

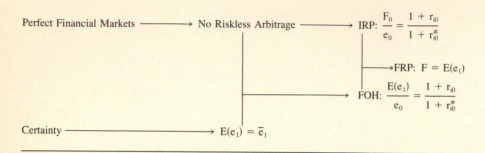

The Fisher Open Hypothesis: A Mathematical Overview

The Fisher open hypothesis can be derived from the investor's utility-maximizing behavior. Consider a representative investor in a one-period framework choosing optimal levels of consumption now (time 0) and in the future (time 1). Assume that the only available assets are a domestic riskless bond paying a certain return, r, and a foreign riskless bond paying a certain return (in foreign currency), r^*. In addition, the investor receives an endowment income (Y_0, Y_1) and has a utility function $U(C_0, C_1)$. The investor's problem is to choose the values of (C_0, C_1) that will maximize $U(\cdot)$ subject to the following conditions:

$$C_0 = Y_0 - S - e_0 S^*$$

$$C_1 = Y_1 + S(1 + r) + e_1(1 + r^*)S^*,$$

where S and S^* are the domestic and foreign currency value of investment in domestic and foreign currency, respectively, and e_i is the exchange rate at time i, $i = 0, 1$.

Equivalently, the investor solves the following problem:

$$\max_{S, S^*}\{U[Y_0 - S - e_0 S^*, Y_1 + (1 + r)S + e_1(1 + r^*)S^*]\}.$$

The first-order conditions are

(i) $$-U_1 + (1 + r)U_2 = 0$$

(ii) $$-e_0U_1 + e_1(1 + r^*)U_2 = 0,$$

where U_i represents the derivative of U with respect to its ith argument, evaluated at the optimal levels of S and S*. Solving (i) and substituting into (ii) gives us

(iii) $$\frac{e_1(1 + r^*)U_1}{1 + r} = e_0U_1,$$

which implies that

(iv) $$\frac{e_1}{e_0} = \frac{1 + r}{1 + r^*},$$

which, under the assumption of perfect foresight, is simply Equation 20.8, the Fisher open hypothesis.

To see the importance of the perfect foresight assumption in arriving at this hypothesis, let us suppose it does not hold. Then e_1 becomes a random variable whose value is uncertain to all investors at time 0, and the investor's problem becomes

$$\max_{S, S^*}\{E[U(Y_0 - S - e_0S^*, Y_1 + (1 + r)S + e_1(1 + r^*)S^*)]\},$$

where E denotes the expectations operator. The first-order conditions are

(v) $$E[-U_1 + (1 + r)U_2] = 0$$

(vi) $$E[-e_0U_1 + e_1(1 + r^*)U_2] = 0.$$

Now note that (v) implies

(vii) $$E(U_2) = \frac{E(U_1)}{1 + r}.$$

Expanding (vi), we obtain

(viii) $e_0E(U_1) = (1 + r^*)E(e_1U_2)$

$$= (1 + r^*)E(e_1)E(U_2) + \text{Cov}(e_1, U_2) \text{ by the property}$$
of covariances

$$= (1 + r^*)\left(\frac{E(e_1)E(U_1)}{1 + r}\right) + \text{Cov}(e_1, U_2) \text{ by (vii)}$$

$$= \left(\frac{1 + r^*}{1 + r}\right)E(e_1)E(U_1) + (1 + r)\text{Cov}(e_1, U_2).$$

Clearly, we obtain the Fisher open hypothesis only if $\text{Cov}(e_1, U_2) = 0$.

Summary

The field of international finance deals with the identification and analysis of phenomena originating in the international economy and their effects on the financial decisions of individual investors and corporations. Among the most important of these phenomena are exchange risk and political risk. The former represents the domestic currency riskiness of international capital flows due to the possibility of exchange rate changes; the latter constitutes the domestic currency riskiness of international capital flows due to the threat of expropriation or the imposition of exchange controls.

An important consideration for international investors is the degree to which foreign security markets are efficient. The evidence suggests that the majority of those markets conform to a weak form of efficiency, while tests for semistrong efficiency are frustrated by inadequate methodology.

A consistent body of theory has been developed to explain the equilibrium relationships among interest rates, inflation rates, and exchange rates. This has come to be known as the pure theory of international parity and is embodied in the hypotheses of purchasing power parity and the law of one price; interest rate parity; Fisher open parity; and forward parity. Purchasing power parity deals with the equilibrium relationship between domestic and foreign price indices and the exchange rate; the law of one price focuses on the same relationship for single goods or assets; interest rate parity is concerned with the relationship between interest rates in different countries and the forward exchange rate premium; Fisher open parity involves the link between domestic and foreign interest rates; and forward parity follows directly from the other conditions, deriving the forward rate as an unbiased estimator of the future spot rate.

Study Questions

20.1   Identify and explain the differences between the various exchange rate systems.

20.2   State and explain the interest rate parity theorem. What assumptions are needed to derive this theorem? Explain why these assumptions are necessary.

20.3   Describe and explain the purchasing power parity theorem. What assumptions are needed to derive this theorem? Explain why these assumptions are necessary.

20.4   Derive the Fisher open hypothesis from an investor's utility-maximizing decision in a world of perfect foresight and where the only securities are a domestic riskless bond and a foreign riskless bond. Suppose that there is a third country that has a riskless bond available. How will this alter things — will the Fisher open hypothesis still hold for the original two securities? Will it hold for the domestic security and the new foreign security?

20.5   Suppose that we allow for the possibility of investors making wrong guesses about the future — that is, we drop the assumption of perfect foresight. Explain intuitively why we might not expect the Fisher open hypothesis to hold.

References

R. Z. Aliber, *Exchange Risk and International Corporate Finance* (London: Macmillan, 1978).

————, "The Interest Rate Parity Theorem: A Reinterpretation," *Journal of Political Economy* 81 (1973): 1451–1459.

T. G. Copeland and J. F. Weston, *Financial Theory and Corporate Policy* (Reading, Mass.: Addison-Wesley, 1983).

I. Fisher, *The Theory of Interest* (New York: Macmillan, 1930).

R. Ibbotson, R. Carr, and A. Robinson, "International Equity and Bond Returns," *Financial Analysts Journal* 38 (1982): 61–83.

B. Jacquillat and B. Solnik, "Multinationals Are Poor Tools for Diversification," *Journal of Portfolio Management* 4 (Winter 1978): 8–12.

D. R. Lessard, *International Financial Management: Theory and Application,* 2d ed. (New York: Wiley, 1985).

————, "Principles of International Portfolio Selection," in *International Finance Handbook*, ed. I. H. Giddy and A. M. George (New York: Wiley, 1983).

R. Roll, "A Critique of the Asset Pricing Theory Tests," *Journal of Financial Economics* 4 (1977).

P. A. Samuelson, "Analytical Notes on International Real Income Measures," *Economic Journal* 84 (1974): 595–608.

A. Shapiro, "What Does Purchasing Power Parity Mean?" *Journal of International Money and Finance* 2 (1983): 295–318.

B. Solnik, "International Parity Conditions and Exchange Risk," *Journal of Banking and Finance* 2 (October 1978): 281–293.

Chapter 21

International Finance:
Evidence and Applications

In Chapter 20, we developed a fundamental body of theory of how the international financial system operates. In this chapter, we build on that groundwork in two ways. First, we examine the empirical work investigating the real-world validity of this body of theory. We then turn our attention to the actual problems — albeit at an abstract level — that practitioners in the international finance fields face. In particular, we discuss how their optimal choices may change as a result of the empirical shortcomings of the theoretical structure developed in Chapter 20.

International Parity Conditions: Empirical Evidence

In Chapter 20, we developed relationships that, under certain conditions, we can expect to exist in international financial markets as a result of these markets' self-equilibrating tendencies. The conditions necessary for deriving these relationships obviously are wildly unrealistic. However, positive economic thought would dictate that this is irrelevant if the relationships themselves prove empirically valid. This is clearly important to our understanding of investor behavior. For instance, if the Fisher open hypothesis proved empirically valid, the nonexistence of a risk premium would be implied, which is contrary to our usual notion of investor behavior in an uncertain world. This, in turn, would suggest that financial theory should treat investors *as if* they were risk neutral. Thus, the nature of the scientific method is revealed: Theories are developed, tested against real-world data, and ical data. . . . Exchange rate changes substantially alter the relative . . . prices of most . . . domestic and foreign manufactured goods. . . . Moreover, these relative revised to capture empirical realities. In this section, we briefly overview some of the evidence on the parity conditions developed in Chapter 20 and note its importance for our understanding of international financial markets and investors' behavior therein.

Purchasing Power Parity

Most of the evidence on purchasing power parity during the last decade suggests that the theory is certainly invalid in the short run and is doubtful, or at least open to interpretation, in the long run. For instance, Dornbusch (1980a) stated, "Most students of purchasing power parity conclude that the theory does not hold up to the facts except in a very loose and approximate fashion." Isard (1977) concluded, "In reality, the law of one price is flagrantly and systematically violated by empir-

price effects seem to persist for at least several years and cannot be shrugged off as transitory" (p. 942).

The negative nature of this evidence has led to further work on purchasing power parity. The failure of the postulated relationship to hold empirically has encouraged researchers to refine the theory to make it better fit the facts.[1] For instance, Roll (1979) developed an efficient market version of purchasing power parity under uncertainty. This simply claims that the best prediction of next period's real exchange rate is the current spot rate or, equivalently, all information relevant for predicting next period's real exchange rate should already be impounded in the current spot rate, and no other variable should improve on this prediction.

Roll's work, as well as Adler and Lehmann's (1982), has tended to support the efficient market version of purchasing power parity. Roll (1979) stated, "With a few significant exceptions, there is little evidence of disequilibria, nor of slow adjustment of prices to a long-run parity. Indeed the general impression for most countries, and for all of the largest trading nations, is a very rapid adjustment of less than one month's duration" (p. 174).

Among the more condemning recent studies of purchasing power parity are those by Dornbusch (1980a, 1980b) and Frenkel (1981). Dornbusch calculated divergences in rates of price and exchange rate movements during the 1970s and concluded that purchasing power parity fails to occur in either the short or long run. Frenkel employed a somewhat more elaborate analysis using two-stage least squares econometric methods. The equation he tested was the following:

$$(21.1) \qquad \ln(e_t) = a_0 + a_1 \ln\left(\frac{p_t}{p_t^*}\right) + \varepsilon_t.$$

[1] Empirical testing of the usual purchasing power parity relationship is also subject to econometric problems. In "Econometric Problems in Testing Purchasing Power Parity: A Mathematical Overview," we briefly discuss these difficulties and the adjustments that have been made in an effort to overcome them.

Frenkel's results for any regression involving the U.S. dollar contained no evidence supporting the purchasing power parity hypothesis. In contrast, the regressions not involving the U.S. dollar conformed much more closely to the theory. Frenkel advanced several possible reasons for this difference. First, transport costs made it more likely that purchasing power parity would hold among neighboring European countries than between any of those countries and the United States. Second, changes in commercial policies and nontariff barriers to trade were more stable within Europe than between Europe and the United States during the 1970s. Third, there appeared to have been significant changes in the equilibrium exchange rate between the U.S. dollar and the European currencies during the same period. This last effect seems particularly important insofar as it captures the relative price, or real, causes of exchange rate movements discussed earlier. In the presence of differing national consumption preferences, changes in relative prices can bring about a change in the equilibrium exchange rate even if each country's price level remains the same (see the example attributed to Solnik in Chapter 20). Roll (1979) claimed that the reason for the lack of empirical support for the traditional purchasing power parity hypothesis is that "on average, . . . relative price change effects on exchange rates dominate the observed differences in inflation rates."

In support of the purchasing power parity hypothesis, Frenkel (1977, 1980) found that during the floating-rate period of the 1920s, the doctrine was much more reliable. Aliber (1978) examined data on 50 countries during the 1950 to 1975 period. He found that the deviations from purchasing power parity over a period of five years or more were sufficiently small to support the validity of purchasing power parity. The deviations were largest (1) for the countries whose currencies appreciated relative to the dollar and (2) during the 1970 to 1975 period. In analyzing the data on the 15 most important U.S. trading partners over the same period, Aliber found that over a one-year time interval consumer prices deviated from purchasing power parity by less than 10 percent in 52 percent of the cases observed, while over a five-year time interval such deviations occurred in 72 percent of the cases. For wholesale prices, the corresponding deviations occurred in 49 percent and 75 percent of the cases, respectively.

Overall, then, the empirical evidence suggests that purchasing power parity may well have been valid prior to the 1970s but deteriorated sharply during that decade. Frenkel (1981) attempted to explain this phenomenon by postulating that "news" is among the major influences on exchange rates. Hence, in periods dominated by "news" (supposedly the 1970s), exchange rate movements are expected to be large and erratic. Aggregate price indices, however, are expected to vary less widely, as they reflect the prices of less durable goods and services, which are likely to be less sensitive to the news that alters expectations of the future. As a result, periods dominated by "news" are characterized by large deviations from purchasing power parity.

Several studies have described the implications for international financial theory of the failure of purchasing power parity to hold. Fama and Farber (1979) showed that the existence of both purchasing power parity and perfect financial markets ensures that residents of all countries will receive the same real return on a security regardless of their differing inflation risks. If purchasing power parity fails to hold, this result cannot be expected to obtain. In a similar context, purchasing power parity and perfect financial markets ensure that all investors will hold identical portfolios (as the real returns on assets with the same risk are equalized across countries). Given this, Grauer, Litzenberger, and Stehle (1976) showed that assets will be priced in a common context and were able to derive an international version of the capital asset pricing model. Deviations from purchasing power parity will, therefore, cause investors to hold different portfolios according to their nations of residence and, hence, render the derivation of such a model impossible. Finally, Adler and Dumas (1983) noted that deviations from purchasing power parity render the real gains from international diversification indeterminate due to the fact that they will differ for everyone.

Interest Rate Parity and the Integration of Capital Markets

The evidence on the empirical validity of interest rate parity is at least as confusing as that for purchasing power parity. The overall impression appears to be that the relationship holds well between some countries and/or during some time periods.

The evidence on the validity of the relationship in short-term Eurocurrency markets is overwhelming. Aliber (1973), Marston (1976), and Roll and Solnik (1977) found that interest rate parity holds almost identically in these markets. (Note that here we are talking about the actual Eurocurrency markets and not the markets for individual European country securities.) Otani and Tiwari (1981) reached a slightly different conclusion. They examined the effects of capital controls on interest parity. They hypothesized that in a market without capital controls, deviations from interest rate parity will be randomly distributed around a mean of zero, while in markets with significant capital controls, deviations will be serially correlated. They found that deviations from interest rate parity in the London (Eurocurrency) market were randomly distributed around a mean of zero, while those in the Tokyo market differed from zero significantly and, moreover, could be attributed to capital controls in Japan. Hence, their evidence suggests that the existence of capital controls causes the interest rate parity relationship to break down empirically as well as theoretically.

Dooley and Isard (1980) tested Aliber's (1978) hypothesis that a non-zero probability of future changes in capital controls can, like existing capital controls, cause deviations from interest rate parity. They concluded that although most of the deviations from interest rate parity in the German market (April 1970 to October 1973) were caused by existing capital controls, there was some evidence in support of Aliber's hypothesis. Frenkel and Levich (1977) used weekly data for 1962 to 1975 and, after explicitly allowing for transactions costs, concluded that there are no forward arbitrage opportunities.

What do these studies suggest about the empirical validity of interest rate parity theory? The prevailing view is that the theory works well in highly integrated markets, such as the Eurocurrency markets. In others, deviations from interest rate parity can be largely attributed to transactions costs, taxes, and other forms of controls.

The degree to which the international financial system is integrated has generated a great deal of interest among researchers. The existence or absence of capital market integration has important implications for financial theory and decisionmaking. For instance, investors' holding of purely domestic portfolios in a completely integrated world capital market suggests their willingness to incur diversifiable risk. Moreover, the advantages of international diversification differ according to the degree of integration among capital markets. A perfectly integrated world capital market implies that all securities will be priced in a common context and, hence, justifies the formulation of an international CAPM. Finally, capital market integration is consistent with the efficient market hypothesis insofar as it implies there are no excess profits to be made via arbitrage across markets.

Tests for capital market integration often have been closely linked to tests of interest rate parity. To understand why, recall that in our derivation of the interest rate parity relationship in Chapter 20, we required only the assumption of perfect financial markets, or capital market integration. Hence, tests of interest rate parity can be interpreted as tests of capital market integration, at least in the case of riskless asset markets. Consequently, the studies by Aliber (1978), Roll and Solnik (1977), Marston (1976), and Otani and Tiwari (1981) discussed above can be interpreted as providing various degrees of support for capital market integration. However, the Dooley and Isard study (1980) suggests that no clear-cut relationship exists between interest rate parity and capital market integration due to the effects of future political risk on the interest rate parity relationship. For instance, failure to empirically validate interest parity could just as easily mean that investors expect to be exposed to some form of capital controls in the future despite the fact that capital markets may be perfectly integrated at present. For this reason, among others, researchers have developed other methods to test for capital market integration. We will first overview the evidence with respect to equity markets and then turn our attention to bond markets.

One approach is to simply calculate correlation coefficients among equity returns in various countries. One such study (although not specifically investigating capital market integration) is that of Ibbotson, Carr, and Robinson (1982). The authors found high degrees of correlation within various blocs. For instance, Germany, Switzerland, and the Netherlands exhibited a great deal of comovement, as did the United Kingdom, France, and Belgium. The United States, Canada, Australia, Hong Kong, Singapore, and the Netherlands also appeared to form a bloc. Hence, one could argue that capital market integration was at a high level within these blocs.

A second approach is to develop and test an international extension of the CAPM. Solnik (August 1974) was the first to develop and test an international asset pricing model (IAPM). He derived a relationship similar in form to that of the CAPM:

(21.2)
$$E(r_i) - R_i = B_i[E(r_m) - R_m],$$

where r_i = risky return on security i
   R_i = risk-free interest rate for the country in which security i is located
   r_m = risky return on the world market portfolio
   R_m = average (or world) risk-free rate calculated with world market portfolio weights
   B_i = measure of international systematic risk for security i

Solnik (September 1974) then tested for capital market integration by comparing the empirical results from Equation 21.2 with those from a purely domestic CAPM. As 21.2 performed slightly better than the latter, he concluded that assets are best regarded as being traded in international markets and, hence, as evidence of capital market integration. Grauer, Litzenberger, and Stehle (1976) linked tests of the IAPM more directly to tests of capital integration by deriving a relationship similar to Equation 21.2 but using the assumption of perfectly integrated capital markets. Hence, tests of their IAPM are direct tests of capital market integration. Stehle (1977) found some evidence to support the integration hypothesis using this methodology.

A third approach is to derive the efficient investment sets for various capital markets. Obviously the existence of identical efficient sets is strong evidence in favor of integration over segmentation. Not surprisingly, the evidence on a global basis is far from conclusive. Levy and Sarnat (1970), for instance, found that the efficient sets for U.S. and Israeli investors are completely different; conversely, Biger (1979) found that those for the major industrialized countries are roughly similar.

There are, however, serious problems with all of the above methodologies. First, the empirical testing is all done with ex post data, whereas the theory is all ex ante. As Kohlagen (1983) put it, this means that "the tests are not only of the maintained hypothesis, but also of the existence of a risk premium and of the rational nature of expectations." Second, Roll (1977) suggests that the notion of testing the CAPM (and, therefore, the IAPM) is fraught with difficulties. In particular, he notes that the exact nature and composition of the true market portfolio must be known in order for the CAPM to be testable and, more important, the tautological relationship between the expected security returns and their betas makes ex post tests of the CAPM meaningless. Clearly, since the IAPM is simply a variant of the CAPM, these criticisms also apply to the IAPM. Third, Solnik (1977) points out that even if the first two problems could somehow be ignored, the distinction between integrated and segmented capital markets cannot be made merely by looking at relationships among asset prices or returns. As noted by Ibbotson, Carr, and Robinson (1982), strong correlations may simply be the result of common underlying economic factors, such as partnerships in trade, geographical proximity, similar economic bases, or international shocks, and have nothing to do with integration or segmentation of capital markets. While zero correlation almost certainly implies segmentation, strong correlations are consistent with either integration or segmentation, and changing correlations therefore indicate nothing about the degree to which capital market integration is changing.

On the topic of bond markets, an often quoted study is that of Logue, Salant, and Sweeney (1976). They developed a methodology consistent with the CAPM that involves factor analysis of rates of return on assets across international markets. They claim that the more closely rates of return across international markets are linked to an "international" factor, the more integrated are these markets. Thus, perfect market integration requires that rates of return across international markets be fully explained by a single international factor, while perfect market segmentation requires that a separate country factor explain each country's assets' rates of return. The authors analyzed returns on quarterly uncovered interest rates on medium- to long-term government bonds for many of the OECD countries over the 1958 to 1973 period and found evidence for significant, but by no means complete, market integration. Kohlagen (1983) noted that their approach could be improved and updated and, consequently, carried out similar tests for the 1973 to 1979 period. He failed to find any evidence of an international factor for short-term bonds, but for long-term bonds such a factor seemed to exist. Kohlagen noted, however, that such analyses are at best questionable. As in the case of equity markets, correlations among rates of return have no necessary implications for integration, while the same problems related to the testing of the CAPM still apply. Most important, according to Kohlagen, is the problem of using ex post data to test ex ante theory. The only way to test for integration using ex ante returns is to test for interest rate parity because, in markets for which forward cover can be obtained, such returns are directly observable. Since tests for interest rate parity in the short-term Eurocurrency markets indicate that these markets are perfectly integrated, Kohlagen concluded that this analysis of ex post data on short-term, uncovered rates of return in European markets says nothing about the degree of integration therein. He reasoned that because investors are free to take covered or uncovered positions, and the covered opportunities occur in integrated markets, the only possible conclusion is that the uncovered opportunities also occur in integrated markets. Consequently, the fact that ex post returns suggest no integration is simply a manifestation of the differences between ex post and ex ante returns due to exchange rate gains or losses.

Note that the above conclusion has caused us to come full circle. As noted above, Kohlagen has suggested that one can determine the extent of capital market integration by testing for interest rate parity in markets where forward cover can be obtained, while no such test is possible in markets where it cannot (for example, those for long-term assets). Recall, however, that we began this section on capital market integration by showing that tests of interest rate parity alone did not constitute a valid test of present capital market integration due to the effect of future changes in capital market integration on the interest rate parity relationship.

Where, then, does all this leave us? As Kohlagen (1983) put it, "Not very far, unfortunately" (p. 128). Studies pursuing this topic may be able to extend our knowledge of the extent of capital market integration. (Note, however, that Kohlagen claimed that ". . . future work in this area is equally unlikely to generate any more useful empirical tests" [p. 113].) As things presently stand, perhaps the best summation has been made by Ibbotson, Carr, and Robinson (1982): "Since international investment occurs, markets cannot be totally segmented. But, interest rates and equity returns . . . appear to differ substantially from country to country. We view the world market as partly segmented and partly integrated" (p. 82).

The Fisher Open Hypothesis, Forward Parity, and Efficiency of the Foreign Exchange Market

The Fisher open hypothesis concerns the relationship between expected changes in the spot exchange rate and the interest rate differential. Hence, it should not be confused with interest rate parity unless the forward rate equals the expected spot rate; this distinction has not always been observed in the literature (see, for instance, Aliber [1978, ch. 6]).

Recall that in our derivation of the Fisher open hypothesis in Chapter 20, we noted that unlike with interest rate parity, risk or uncertainty plays an integral part. This implies that in order for Equation 20.8 to hold empirically, a risk premium cannot exist and the foreign exchange market must be efficient. To see why the efficiency notion is important, note that Equation 20.8 simply says that interest rates and exchange rates will adjust until expected yields across opportunities are equalized — that is, there are no unexploited profit opportunities. But this is simply one definition of market efficiency; to put it another way, note that we can write Equation 20.8 as

$$(21.3) \qquad E(e_1) = \frac{e_0(1 + r_{io})}{1 + r_{io}^*} .$$

This says that the best predictor of next period's spot rate is the current spot rate multiplied by the interest rate differential. In other words, all information relevant for predicting next period's spot should already be impounded in the current adjusted spot rate and no other variable should be able to improve on this; that is, trading on the basis of publicly available information at time 0 will yield no positive profits, as this information has already been considered by the market as a whole. Consequently, Equation 21.3 says that the foreign exchange market is efficient.

These factors, in turn, have important implications for the empirical testing of the Fisher open hypothesis. Failure to verify the relationship empirically — that is, if deviations from Fisher open parity are systematic — may imply that a risk premium exists, foreign exchange markets are inefficient, or both. Also, there is no way to distinguish between these competing hypotheses, since any tests of the Fisher open hypothesis are, by necessity, a joint test of no risk premium and market efficiency.

One study on the empirical reliability of the Fisher open hypothesis that recognizes these problems is that of Cumby and Obstfeld (1981). Essentially, their approach was to assume efficiency and attribute any systematic deviations from Fisher open parity to the existence of a risk premium. They noted that Equation 20.8 could be rewritten as

$$(21.4) \qquad E_t \ln(e_{t+1}) - \ln e_t = \ln(1 + r_{it}) - \ln(1 + r_{it}^*) \approx r_{it} - r_{it}^* ,$$

where ln denotes a natural logarithm. They made two assumptions: (1) the expected value of e_{t+1} at time t is based on the true probability distribution underlying the events affecting financial markets, and (2) the foreign exchange market is weakly efficient. The former assumption means that we can write the actual future spot rate as being equal to the sum of its expected value at time 0 and a zero-mean forecast error:

$$(21.5) \qquad \ln e_{t+1} = E_t \ln(e_{t+1}) + \varepsilon_t , \qquad E(\varepsilon_t) = 0 .$$

Further, combining the latter assumption with Equation 21.5 implies that the error term is randomly distributed around a zero mean and, hence, is serially uncorrelated.

Next, substituting 21.5 into 21.4, we obtain

(21.6) $$\ln e_{t+1} - \ln e_t - r_{it} + r_{it}^* = \varepsilon_t .$$

All variables on the left-hand side of Equation 21.6 are observable ex post. Hence, given assumptions 1 and 2 above, Cumby and Obstfeld tested the Fisher open hypothesis by ascertaining whether or not the error term was serially uncorrelated over time.

These authors tested for Fisher open parity between London Eurodollar deposits and various other London Eurocurrency deposits and employed two statistical tests — a Q-test and a likelihood-ratio test. They found that Fisher parity could be rejected at the 5 percent level or higher in virtually every case and interpreted this as evidence of foreign exchange risk premiums. As our previous discussion indicated, however, their findings do not rule out the possibility of foreign exchange market inefficiencies.

The concepts of market efficiency and risk premiums are also closely intertwined with tests for forward parity. Some researchers (for instance, Giddy [1976] and Kohlagen [1974, 1976]) have interpreted foreign exchange market efficiency as requiring that forward exchange rates be unbiased predictors of future spot exchange rates, that is, that forward parity holds. It should be clear by now, however, that such an interpretation totally ignores any notion of risk.[2] The work of Cumby and Obstfeld noted above shows that the existence of risk premiums is completely consistent with market efficiency; hence, the failure of forward parity to hold does not indicate market inefficiency.

Two studies that have examined the questions of forward parity, risk premiums, and foreign exchange market efficiency are those of Frenkel (1981) and Levich (1982). Frenkel tested the following equation (on data from the 1970s):

(21.7) $$\ln e_t = a_0 + a_1 \ln F_{t-1} + \varepsilon_t .$$

If the residuals, Σ_t, are serially uncorrelated, the current forward rate encapsulates all currently available information on next period's spot rate. Hence, no excess profits can be gleaned from a trading rule based on forward exchange

---

[2]These and other authors have argued that risk aversion cannot cause the forward rate to differ from the expected spot rate, as this would imply that one party is paying a premium for reducing risk while the other is receiving a premium for doing so. This argument follows from a straightforward application of Jensen's inequality. Let the spot (forward) exchange rate from the domestic viewpoint be designated as S(F) and that from the foreign viewpoint as S*(F*). Note too that S* = 1/S and F* = 1/F. In keeping with the risk premium hypothesis, suppose that we have

$$F > E(S) .$$

This implies that

$$\frac{1}{F} < \frac{1}{E(S)} .$$

But, by Jensen's inequality, $1/E(S) < E(1/S)$. Hence, we have $1/F < E(1/S)$ or $F^* < E(S^*)$. In other words, the existence of a risk premium on one side of the market implies the existence of a risk discount on the other side. Note, however, that this crucially depends on everyone having the same expectations. If domestic residents have a different set of expectations from foreigners', there is nothing inconsistent about the idea of risk aversion causing the forward rate to differ from the expected spot rate.

rate time series data. Therefore, the foreign exchange market can be said to be (weakly) efficient. Moreover, if forward parity holds, $a_0 = 0$ and $a_1 = 1$. Frenkel found that the hypothesis of no autocorrelation in the residuals cannot be rejected and, hence, neither can market efficiency. In addition, F-statistic tests on the joint hypothesis of $a_0 = 0$ and $a_1 = 1$ indicated that the hypothesis cannot be rejected for the three exchange rates considered (dollar/pound, dollar/franc, and dollar/DM).

To further test for efficiency, Frenkel ran the following regression:

(21.8) $\ln e_t = a_0 + a_1 \ln F_{t-1} + a_2 \ln F_{t-2} + \varepsilon_t .$

If the market is efficient, $a_2 = 0$. Frenkel found that the estimated coefficients on $\ln F_{t-2}$ indeed do not differ significantly from zero. Moreover, the residuals still show no evidence of autocorrelation.[3]

Levich compared the performances of professional forecasters with that of the forward rate. The rationale for this was as follows: If the foreign exchange market is efficient, the forward rate reflects all currently available information on the future spot rate; then, if forecasters can consistently outguess the forward rate (the forward rate being a systematically biased predictor of the future spot rate), this may be an indication of market inefficiency. Levich indeed found that some forecasters outperform the forward rate with a consistency not easily explained by chance. However, he (correctly) concluded that this says very little about the efficiency or inefficiency of foreign exchange markets. To say that the forward rate should reflect all currently available information on the future spot rate is to say just that; it does not mean that the forward rate cannot reflect additional phenomena, such as a risk premium. Holding an open foreign exchange position involves risk, and to the extent that it is nondiversifiable, holders of this risk will demand a risk premium and, conversely, be prepared to pay a premium to reduce it. Consequently, the forward rate may include a risk premium, and therefore we would expect professional forecasters to do a better job of predicting the future spot rate than the forward rate does. The profits earned by following these advisory service forecasts may represent only the fair return for accepting exchange risk rather than an excess return from exploiting market inefficiencies.

What, then, can we conclude about foreign exchange market efficiency, Fisher open parity, and forward parity? As we have noted, firm conclusions are difficult to draw due to the joint nature of any conceivable test. Few people, however, would disagree with Frenkel (1981) that "the behavior of the foreign exchange market during the 1970s has been broadly consistent with the general implications of the efficient market hypothesis" (p. 9). If we accept this conclusion, the available evidence suggests that we must reject the Fisher open hypothesis and forward parity as empirical realities — most likely because of the existence of risk premiums.

---

[3]Frenkel noted that the OLS estimation procedure that he utilized is inappropriate if E_t and $\ln F_{t-1}$ are interdependent. He conducted a separate test showing that the assumption of independence between E_t and $\ln F_{t-1}$ is not unreasonable and from this concluded that his use of OLS estimation was justifiable.

Normative Issues in International Finance

Thus far, we have concerned ourselves with positive international financial theory — the theory of "what is." Having established this base, we are now in a position to consider normative international financial theory — the theory of "what should be." The material presented here is by no means exhaustive; the careful reader already will have formulated the adjustments to optimal behavior required for operating in an international environment. Our intent here is simply to provide examples of arguments advanced by researchers for optimal behavior by individuals and firms in the international environment and, wherever possible, relate them explicitly to the issues discussed in the previous section. We begin by discussing the advantages and disadvantages of international diversification; from there we turn to firm hedging policy, financing policy, and capital budgeting techniques.

Advantages and Disadvantages of International Diversification

Diversification of one's portfolio across assets in different countries yields benefits similar to those of diversifying across assets in different industries within a single country. A decline in the value of one country's assets may be offset by a rise in the value of another's. Thus, for a given level of risk (expected return), the internationally diversified investor will be able to achieve a higher (lower) level of expected return (risk) than one who holds only domestic securities.

It is important to realize that these benefits of international diversification are in no way related to successful speculation or investors' ability to concentrate their portfolios in a country they perceive as likely to do better than others in the short run and to successfully switch as their expectations change. As we have seen, the evidence on the efficiency of foreign capital and exchange markets suggests that investors will be unable to achieve this consistently.

In order for international diversification to be beneficial, it must yield either lower risk or higher expected return. The extent to which either occurs depends on the degree of integration among capital markets. If capital markets are perfectly integrated, the relevant market, from the investor's viewpoint, is the world market. Capital market theory says that the investor should hold the world market portfolio, for otherwise he or she incurs diversifiable risk with no compensation. Hence, in a perfectly integrated world capital market, the benefits of international diversification occur solely from risk reduction — the elimination of diversifiable risk. At the other end of the spectrum, suppose that capital markets are initially perfectly segmented. Some small degree of integration then occurs. In such a case, the investor still benefits in the manner described above, that is, from the elimination of risk that is systematic in a purely domestic sense but diversifiable in an international context. Moreover, the investor can gain in a more fundamental manner as the efficient frontier shifts: Investment opportunities that were previously unavailable appear. Hence, the investor may also be able to obtain higher expected returns. Insofar as the evidence reviewed in the preceding section suggests that world capital markets are neither perfectly integrated nor perfectly segmented and are (possibly) becoming more integrated, real-world gains to international diversification would appear to incorporate a combination of these benefits.

Logue and Rogalski (1979) isolated two potential gains from international diversification — beta gains and alpha gains. Beta gains essentially are those realized from the elimination of diversifiable risk. Alpha gains, in contrast, occur when securities in one market are mispriced relative to those in another, allowing investors to realize excess profits. Ibbotson, Carr, and Robinson (1982), for instance, have suggested that past low levels of U.S. investment may have led to underpricing in those markets and, hence, to the possibility of capturing excess returns therein. However, due to the evidence on the efficiency of foreign securities markets, such possibilities seem to be short term at best; hence, most researchers prefer to emphasize the beta gains of international diversification.

The above advantages are, of course, equally relevant for the portfolio management of both individual and corporate investors. However, there is an additional financial motive for a corporation to diversify its operations: To the extent that world capital markets are segmented and, therefore, investor diversification is limited, international investment by the corporation may actually reduce its systematic risk. Hence, investors will require a lower rate of return on that firm's stock and, consequently, the firm may be able to undertake projects that otherwise would be undesirable. Note, however, the importance of nonintegration in world capital markets. Perfect integration would imply that individuals could achieve portfolio diversification just as easily as firms and, hence, would no longer be prepared to accept a lower rate of return on the firm's equity. Put another way, the absence of market imperfections would mean that corporations would not lower their systematic risk by taking on overseas projects. But because such imperfections appear to be the rule rather than the exception, the value of international operations to the corporation seems considerable.

Not all aspects of international diversification are favorable, however. The above gains from reduced risk and/or increased expected returns may be offset if the risk increases and/or expected return decreases resulting from (1) exchange risk and (2) political risk are high enough.

We fully explored the notion of exchange risk in Chapter 20. Here, we concentrate on the extent to which this risk is more apparent than real and its effective deterrence to international diversification.

First, note that if Fisher open parity (or interest rate parity for assets on which it is possible to obtain forward cover) holds, exchange risk becomes a nonevent. In the long run, exchange rate losses are offset by exchange rate gains; hence, in the long run the international investor is subject only to the business risk faced by the purely domestic investor.[4] Of course, the evidence discussed in the previous section suggests that these theorems are, at best, empirically unproven.

Second — and closely related — international investors are concerned primarily with the riskiness of their returns in the currency of their country of residence. For example, a U.S. resident with investments in France is unconcerned with their riskiness in terms of francs. On the assumption that all utility is consumption based and given that the investor undertakes all consumption in the United States, he or she is concerned only with how the riskiness of the franc

---

[4]Strictly speaking, this is true only if investors are risk neutral.

returns translates into riskiness of dollar returns. (Note the close connection of this argument to the parity theorems: If the latter hold, the riskiness of dollar returns exactly equals the riskiness of franc returns.) More formally, the following can be shown to closely approximate the true relationship:[5]

$$(21.9) \qquad \text{Var}(R_t) = \text{Var}(R_t^*) + \text{Var}(e_t - e_{t-1}) + 2 \, \text{Cov}(R_t^*, e_t - e_{t-1}),$$

where R_t = period t rate of return in domestic currency (dollars)

$\qquad R_t^*$ = period t rate of return in foreign currency

Clearly, then, if foreign currency returns are negatively correlated with movements in the exchange rate, exchange risk is considerably reduced, the third term on the right-hand side of Equation 21.9 moves counter to the second term, and, hence, the effect of this latter term (the exchange risk) is negated. Solnik and Noetzlin (1981) have found evidence to suggest that such a negative correlation indeed exists. Similarly, exchange risk is seen to be less of a problem with respect to real returns; that is, although volatile inflation may make for highly risky real returns in foreign currencies, offsetting changes in exchange rates will reduce the riskiness of real dollar returns. (Note that this is closely related to the notion of purchasing power parity.) Finally, note that exchange risk can be substantially hedged by either simultaneously borrowing in the foreign currency or selling it in the forward market.

Political risk (discussed in Chapter 20) also has implications for investors' diversification behavior. First, note that if interest rate parity fails to hold due solely to the Aliber (1978) hypothesis, political risk, at least for those assets for which forward cover is obtainable, may be viewed as a fair gamble insofar as investors' ex ante returns on foreign securities are adjusted for it. The interest rate parity condition reduces to

$$(21.10) \qquad \frac{1 + R_i^*}{e} = \frac{1 + R_i}{F} + \text{Risk premium}.$$

Hence, investors can be compensated for the political risk they bear and, therefore, international diversification in these assets need entail no increase in risk for a given level of expected return.

---

[5]The ex post gross rate of return in dollar terms equals the ex post gross rate of return in foreign currency multiplied by the exchange:

$$1 + R_t = e_t(1 + R_t^*)$$

or

$$\frac{1 + R_t}{1 + R_t^*} = e_t.$$

Therefore,

$$\frac{R_t - R_t^*}{1 + R_t^*} = e_t - 1,$$

from which, with the appropriate choice of units, the following approximation can be gleaned:

$$R_t - R_t^* = e_t - e_{t-1}.$$

Equation 21.9, then, follows immediately.

For those securities on which forward cover is unobtainable (or if the Aliber hypothesis is incorrect), the key issue is whether political risks are properly reflected in security prices. This will depend on whether domestic and foreign investors are equally subject to the foreign market's political risk—which, in turn, will depend on the nature of the political risk. If this risk takes the form of controls, international investors will, in all probability, bear a greater share of the risk and, hence, security prices may not reflect political risk. If the political risk takes the form of revolution or nationalization, all investors may share the risk equally and market efficiency will determine whether or not political risk is reflected in security prices. As we have seen, the evidence indicates that foreign security markets are broadly efficient. Finally, to the extent that the political risk is nonsystematic, international investors can diversify it away.

In conclusion, then, it seems that many of the disadvantages of international diversification disappear when viewed more closely due to the ability to either diversify them away, hedge against them, or determine exactly what does and does not entail risk. As international capital markets become more integrated the remaining disadvantages should decrease, thereby increasing the net gains from international diversification even more.

Exchange Risk and Corporate Financial Policy

In the first section, we analyzed the effects of exchange risk on investor portfolio management. As we noted there, however, the corporation is subject to exchange risk in the operations sphere as well as in its portfolio management. We define *exchange risk* in this sense as the variability in the firm's value—as measured by the present value of its cash flows—due to unanticipated exchange rate changes. Although some of the firm's cash flows arise out of its portfolio dealings, we are more concerned here with its operating cash flows.

Given that the firm is subject to exchange risk in this manner, two central questions emerge: (1) whether the firm should actively manage foreign exchange risk and, if so, (2) how it should proceed to achieve this end. We will focus primarily on question 1, as the issues raised there provide a good overview of modern financial theory. However, we will briefly discuss traditional approaches to managing exchange risk and outline more recent proposals.

Dufey and Srinivasulu (1984) have reviewed the arguments for and against corporate management of foreign exchange risk. The issues they view as central to the management decision are described in the following paragraphs.

Purchasing Power Parity. If purchasing power parity holds, exposure to exchange risk is nonexistent. Exchange rate changes are simply compensation for price level changes. For instance, a U.S. firm with a subsidiary in Greece loses nothing when the drachma depreciates relative to the dollar, as the depreciation will have been induced by a higher rate of inflation in Greece. Hence, when the subsidiary remits dollars to the parent company, the decline in the dollar value of each drachma is offset by their increased number.

Dufey and Srinivasulu (D&S) point out a number of shortcomings in this argument. First, as we have seen, purchasing power parity does not seem empirically valid. Second, even if purchasing power parity holds, the law of one price may not. Hence, if the net price of the subsidiary's output rises at a lower rate than the overall price level, the parent firm is subject to exchange risk. Third, even if both purchasing power parity and the law of one price hold, the prices of the firm's specific inputs and outputs may change in relation to each other, subjecting the firm to risk. For instance, the firm is concerned with the price of its output relative to the prices of its inputs. If the prices of its imported inputs rise at a sufficiently higher rate than the price of its output, the firm will suffer a reduction in its net cash flow.

A simple example will help to illustrate this. Suppose we have a firm that produces good 1 for sale in the domestic market and imports good 2 from a foreign market for use as an input. Let P and P*, P_1 and P_1^*, and P_2 and P_2^* denote, respectively, the domestic and foreign price levels, prices of good 1, and prices of good 2. Initially, let e = 1.1. One possible scenario under purchasing parity and the law of one price is given by the following:

$$P = 110 = (1.1)(100) = eP*$$

$$P_1 = 11 = (1.1)(10) = eP_1^*$$

$$P_2 = 5.5 = (1.1)(5) = eP_2^*.$$

The firm's net cash flow, then, is 5.5. Now suppose that during the ensuing period, the foreign price index rises by 10 percent while the domestic price index remains the same. Purchasing power parity now requires that

$$P = 110 = (1)(110) = eP*.$$

But at the new exchange rate of 1, there are an infinite number of possibilities that satisfy the law of one price for goods 1 and 2, depending on the foreign inflation rates specific to those goods. One possibility is given by

$$P_1 = 10 = (1)(10) = eP_1^*$$

$$P_2 = 6 = (1)(6) = eP_2^*.$$

In this situation, the foreign price of the output good remains the same while that of the input good rises. By the law of one price, a similar situation occurs in the home country and, thus, the firm's cash flow is reduced.

Systematic Risk and Exchange Risk Management. We argued above that exchange risk does, in general, exist. The problem now becomes one of deciding what, if anything, the firm should do to manage or control this risk.

One argument against doing anything is derived from modern asset pricing theory. This postulates that the only risk that matters in determining the price of a security is the systematic risk. Then, to the extent that exchange risk is nonsystematic, investors can diversify it away themselves and, hence, there is no value to the firm of managing it. In addition, if the risk is systematic and the contracts the firm undertakes in order to manage this risk are priced according to their systematic risk, nothing will be added to the value of the firm. In other words, the contracts are viewed simply as correctly priced. Hence, the firm's equity will remain correctly priced assets and its value unchanged — it will simply move along the security market line.

However, D&S point out that where costs of financial distress are present, total variability of net cash flows is important since this increases the probability of bankruptcy, which in turn increases the firm's cost of funds and lowers its value.

The Modigliani/Miller (MM) Theorem.   Another argument against corporate management of exchange risk is that there is simply no need. Whatever the firm can do, so can the investor; thus, the corporate decision is irrelevant. This is clearly analogous to the domestic MM theorem. Nevertheless, real-world phenomena such as size restrictions, structural barriers, and differential information may result in the corporation's being better able to effectively manage exchange risk than the individual. Hence, it will be in the interest of the firm's shareholders to manage the exchange risk.

Fisher Open Parity and Market Efficiency.   Opponents of corporate exchange risk management argue that forward exchange markets (that is, hedging vehicles) provide only fair gambles. Over time, an uncovered firm will experience offsetting exchange gains and losses and, hence, be in exactly the same position as the hedged firm. This is clearly just another way of saying that Fisher open parity holds. A similar argument is that excess returns are impossible in forward exchange markets due to their efficiency; hence, firms should not hedge.

With respect to the first argument, we have seen that the Fisher open hypothesis most likely is not empirically valid. Even if it is, this argument implicitly assumes risk neutrality. Moreover, D&S note that the inability to earn excess returns is irrelevant; the objective of hedging is to achieve a desired risk-return trade-off, not excess returns. Reducing the total variability of cash flows for a given level of expected return is important to economic agents such as managers, bank regulators, shareholders, and creditors.

Heterogeneous Consumption Preferences.   Another argument against corporate management of exchange risk runs as follows. Individual utility ultimately is derived from consumption, not nominal wealth. Hence, it is the consumption bundle that should be protected against exchange risk. But shareholders are a diverse group, with heterogeneous consumption preferences; thus, attempts by the firm to hedge consumption bundles, especially nontraded goods such as domestic real estate, will be both costly and impossible. Hence, it should make no attempt to do so.

D&S suggest that as a practical matter, individuals and firms should manage exchange risk according to their respective comparative advantages — that is, firms should hedge their cash flows and individuals their consumption bundles.

Forward Rate Uncertainty.   If the firm's planning horizon is longer than the maturity of the forward contract, it is uncertain about what future forward rates will be and, hence, hedging via the forward market will also involve risk. Consequently, the firm will gain little by managing exchange risk. Two counterarguments, however, can be made. First, when the firm's planning horizon is the same as the maturity of the forward contract, the firm faces no uncertainty about its cash flows. Second, as we will soon see, management of exchange risk is not restricted to forward contracts.

What can we conclude, then, about the appropriateness of corporate exchange risk management? In a perfect world with no transactions costs, taxes, differential information, and so on, there would be no reason for a firm to engage in such activities. However, various real-world phenomena may extract a heavy cost from firms that fail to do so. Thus, a brief examination of the alternatives open to firms with respect to exchange risk management is in order.

The following techniques are those most commonly used by U.S. multi-national corporations:

1. Purchasing of forward cover

2. Borrowing in foreign currency

3. Minimizing foreign cash and marketable securities levels

4. Maximizing delays in meeting accounts payable

5. Invoicing exports in dollars and imports in foreign currency

6. Tightening trade credit in foreign currency

Cornell and Shapiro (1983) note, however, that there are several problems with these methods. First, if a devaluation of the foreign currency is unlikely, firms using these methods will incur costs with little likelihood of return. Second, if a devaluation is expected, the cost of using these techniques as a defense will rise prohibitively.

Cornell and Shapiro argue that because exchange risk affects all facets of a firm's operations, its management should be the responsibility of divisions other than the financial one. Specifically, they argue that the specialized knowledge of marketing and production executives give firms a comparative advantage in the markets in which they operate; hence, they should be able to profitably allow for exchange risk in their own nonfinancial decisions.

A more recent financial innovation for dealing with exchange risk, advocated by Giddy (1983) and Agmon and Eldor (1983), is the *foreign exchange option*. This is a contract that conveys the right to buy or sell a designated quantity of a foreign currency at a specified exchange rate during a specific period under stated conditions. Hence, it is simply the foreign exchange equivalent of the security options described in Chapter 15. Its major advantage over other forms of hedging, such as forward contracts, is that it involves a right, but not an obligation, to buy or sell a specified amount of foreign exchange. Thus, if an expected foreign currency devaluation does not occur, or if a proposed transaction involving foreign currency falls through, the firm can simply choose not to exercise the option, whereas it would be locked into a forward contract.

The Financing Decision of a Multinational Corporation

The question of how a firm should finance its expenditures is of great interest to academicians and practitioners alike. For a firm operating within the confines of a single country, the choice typically is one of instruments and timing. These issues were fully covered in Chapter 12. In this section, we identify the factors that make the financing decision of a multinational corporation more complex. First, we overview the factors unique to the multinational corporation; next, we briefly summarize one approach the literature suggests for solving its financing problem.

The usual assumption is that the firm wishes to maximize the market value of its shares. As the shares' value is determined by the present value of the firm's expected after-tax cash flows, it immediately follows that these are what the firm attempts to maximize. Hence, it wishes to finance its expenditure in a manner that will achieve this. This clearly involves the question of optimal capital structure. We covered this contentious issue fully in Chapter 12 and thus will largely ignore it here in favor of the unique aspects of multinational financing—specifically, the choice of currency in which the firm will raise its funds. This is important because of (1) exchange risk and (2) differing tax systems. Even to the extent that the parity theorems hold, firms' after-tax costs of debt may differ across countries because their tax rates differ from that of the marginal market investor. Moreover, some countries treat the tax realization of exchange rate gains and losses in an asymmetrical manner, while others tax interest expenses at a rate different from exchange rate gains and losses. For all of these reasons, the after-tax costs of borrowing may differ across countries and, hence, must be considered by the firm in making its financing decisions.

It is not always necessary that the currency the firm chooses to borrow be obtained from the country that issues it. If the two can be separated, the firm will wish to choose the country that will minimize its after-tax costs of debt. This suggests that to the extent that tax systems are not indexed for inflation, firms will prefer to borrow in high inflation, high nominal interest rate countries as long as interest expenses and exchange rate gains and losses are treated equivalently. (Note that strictly speaking this is true only insofar as the Fisher open hypothesis holds. If it does not, the expected exchange rate gains may be insufficient to offset the high nominal interest rates; thus, given a symmetric tax system, the firm may prefer not to finance in the high inflation, high nominal interest rate country.)

Many countries withhold—in the form of a tax—varying percentages of dividend and interest payments to foreign investors. This leads these investors to demand a higher before-tax return. Consequently, the firm, in attempting to minimize the cost of financing its expenditure, has two options: (1) It can issue debt in those countries whose investors are least subject to the withholding tax due to the nature of their respective bilateral tax treaties with the country of the issuing firm, or (2) it can establish an offshore finance subsidiary in a tax-haven country and thereby avoid the withholding taxes its own country imposes.

Another factor that multinational financing strategists must consider is the need to diversify and broaden the firm's financing base. First, this will eliminate the need to depend on any one source of funds. Second, it will allow the firm to enhance its fund of international economic and financial information, thereby facilitating the decisionmaking process. Third, it will familiarize a wider range of investors with the firm's name, thereby making it easier to obtain future financing and enhancing its prospects of foreign sales of its product.

Differing government economic policies also contribute to the complexity of the multinational financing decision. Restrictions on interest rates, limitations on foreign investment, and investment subsidies are all policies commonly pursued by governments that can cause the cost of funds to the multinational to differ from country to country.

Obviously, exchange and political risks are also important factors for the multinational to consider in making its financing decision. Changes in exchange rates will determine the period-by-period actual burden of interest payments when the firm issues debt in a foreign country. Political risk, whether in the form of controls or expropriation, will influence the multinational's financing decision by providing an incentive to minimize its exposure to it.

The astute reader may be wondering to what extent any of the above phenomena are truly relevant to the multinational financing decision. After all, modern financial theory tells us that only systematic risk is relevant; the firm gains no benefit from eliminating risks that are diversifiable by individual investors. Hence, the above factors, to the extent that they represent nonsystematic risk, should be unimportant to the firm. However, Lessard and Shapiro (1984) and, as we saw earlier, Dufey and Srinivasulu (1984) argue that total risk is meaningful for multinational financial decisionmaking. This is because these nonsystematic risks can have adverse effects on the expected level of the firm's cash flow, particularly for small firms having less diversified cash flows. This, in turn, has important implications for a firm's ability to gain credit, raise money, develop strong relationships with suppliers, customers, and employees, and take appropriate long-term views of its future prospects. All of these will adversely affect the firm's value. Consequently, management may attempt to reduce these risks despite their diversifiable nature. (We have already seen how such a scenario provides a rationale for managing exchange risk.)

Lessard and Shapiro (1984) have suggested a three-pronged strategy for attacking the multinational financing problem. They distinguish between passive financing strategies, which assume no special information on the part of the firm and, therefore, that all financing options are fairly priced, and active financing strategies, which involve trying to exploit perceived bargains. They suggest that multinationals concern themselves first with the passive strategies of (1) minimizing taxes and (2) managing exchange and political risks. Once it has made the optimal decision on the basis of these criteria, only then should the firm attempt to further improve its position by pursuing an active strategy, such as exploiting financial market distortions.

Thus, a multinational operating under this plan might, for instance, first attempt to determine the financing option that best fits the two passive criteria. This would involve (1) locating the currency and/or country with the most favorable tax system in terms of treatment of interest payments and exchange gains and losses and (2) considering exchange and political risk. To the extent that interest rate and Fisher open parity do not hold, the firm will tend toward currencies it expects will devalue. If political risk is large, the firm will try to reduce its exposure by raising capital from the host government and an international consortium, thereby giving the host country an incentive not to interfere.

Once the firm has reached the optimal decision subject to all these criteria, it can then attempt to find "bargains" that will lower its expected financing costs without significantly increasing its risks. Government policies are important factors here. For instance, capital markets with restricted access often have relatively low interest rates. Hence, firms operating in these markets can borrow at these rates and, to the extent they are available, lend in offshore markets.

To summarize, the pursuit of passive strategies leads to an optimal combination of financing costs and risks on the assumption that all financing options are fairly priced. To the extent that all options are not fairly priced—and, therefore, that bargains exist—the multinational must make a trade-off decision to determine whether the lower costs brought about by such active strategies will be sufficient to offset the increased risks incurred.

Capital Budgeting for the Multinational Corporation

The capital budgeting process typically consists of (1) estimating expected or most likely after-tax cash flows and (2) discounting those cash flows at an appropriately determined cost of capital in order to determine their net present value. If the latter proves positive, the investment should be undertaken. In principle, the international capital budgeting process follows exactly the same path. However, the effects of exchange and political risk, differing tax systems, government controls and incentives, and differing rates of inflation all serve to complicate the problem faced by a multinational corporation considering a project recommended by a foreign subsidiary.

Given the above description of the usual capital budgeting process, the most important issues in international capital budgeting are

1.   What implications, if any, does operating in an international environment have for estimating after-tax cash flows?

2.   What implications, if any, does operating in an international environment have on the selection of the appropriate discount rate?

For question 1, the fundamental issue is whether cash flows should be measured from the viewpoint of the foreign subsidiary or of the parent company. If the former, the capital budgeting problem simply reduces to its usual form; if all variables are to be estimated in the currency of the country in which the project is to take place, there is no need to worry about exchange rate changes, exchange controls, differential taxes, and so on. This approach cannot, however, be justified on a theoretical basis. A project's value is determined by the net present value of its cash flows to the original investor—the parent firm. Thus, to the extent that the foreign subsidiary's cash flows cannot be repatriated back to the parent firm, they are inappropriate for use in valuing the project. Further, even without additional uncertainty, such as exchange/political risk and differing inflation rates, the cash flows of a foreign subsidiary obviously can vary significantly from those the parent firm actually receives due to exchange controls, tax regulations, and third-party effects (whereby the foreign subsidiary's project affects the cash flows of some other division of the multinational).

Shapiro (1983) recommends that this problem be separated into three parts:

1.   The foreign subsidiary calculates the estimated cash flows solely from its own viewpoint.

2.   The parent company adjusts these to domestic cash flows by preparing best estimates of the size and timing of their remittance.

3. The parent company adjusts these cash flows by allowing for third-party effects.

Such a system, while conceptually simple, is obviously exceedingly difficult to put into practice. One must be able to estimate exchange rate changes, inflation rate differentials, and third-party effects and have an extremely sound knowledge of exchange, tax, and investment regulations in each country in addition to the usual requirements for successful capital budgeting.

If purchasing power parity holds, we can simplify matters somewhat. Let e_t denote the exchange rate at time t from the parent company's perspective. Then purchasing power parity implies

$$(21.11) \qquad \frac{e_t}{e_0} = \frac{(1 + I)^t}{(1 + I^*)^t},$$

where I = annualized inflation rate in the parent firm's country
    I^* = annualized inflation rate in the foreign subsidiary's country

The value of the foreign subsidiary's cash flows to the parent firm is given by

$$(21.12) \qquad V = \sum_{t=0}^{T} \frac{RCF_t(1 + I^*)^t e_t}{(1 + \rho)^t},$$

where RCF_t = real value of the cash flows in foreign currency at time t
    ρ = appropriate nominal discount rate
    I^* = foreign country's inflation rate

Rewriting Equation 21.11 and substituting into 21.12 yields

$$(21.13) \qquad V = e_0 \sum_{t=0}^{T} \frac{RCF_t(1 + I)^t}{(1 + \rho)^t} = e_0 \sum_{t=0}^{T} \frac{RCF_t}{(1 + \rho_{real})^t}.$$

Consequently, the capital budgeting problem in an international context can be reduced to one of obtaining estimates of real foreign currency cash flows and a real discount rate. The resulting value is converted into domestic currency by using the current exchange rate. Hence, even though the cash flows are (correctly) evaluated from the parent firm's viewpoint, we can treat them from the foreign subsidiary's viewpoint, thereby allowing us to ignore many of the uniquely international problems. In other words, the international capital budgeting problem reduces to the usual capital budgeting problem as long as purchasing power parity holds.

With respect to the discount rate issue, the traditional approach to capital budgeting is to use the firm's weighted average cost of capital. This is known to have severe limitations even in a purely domestic context, as discussed in Chapter 13. In an international context, such a measure is fraught with still more problems. First, it is difficult to attach any meaning to a weighted average cost of capital when that average is obtained from several (possibly segmented) markets. Moreover, if the rate is calculated only from the domestic market, it may completely fail to represent the cost of capital, perhaps due to the necessity of raising capital in a foreign country as the result of exchange controls therein.

One way to avoid this problem is to adopt the adjusted present value (APV) approach of Myers (1978). This method removes the effects of financing in project evaluation. A project's APV is given by

$$(21.14) \qquad APV_j = \sum_{t=0}^{T} \frac{NCF_t}{(1 + \rho_j)^t} + \sum_{t=0}^{T} \frac{TS_t}{(1 + r)^t},$$

where NCF_t = nominal after-tax cash flows at time t

      TS_t = value of tax shields at time t

      ρ_j = required rate of return on project j if all equity financed

      r = before-tax cost of debt

In an international setting, of course, this still leaves the problem of select-ing the appropriate ρ_j. Modern financial theory suggests that investors will receive a risk premium only on systematic risk; that is, the appropriate discount rate is determined by the project's systematic risk. But to calculate this, the firm must first establish the relevant market portfolio from the viewpoint of the investors from whom it wishes to raise capital. For if the relevant market were a purely domestic one, the adoption of a foreign project would provide diversification pos-sibilities for the investors. In other words, the shareholders would receive a risk reduction that they themselves would be unable to obtain and, hence, would be prepared to pay a premium for it. On the other hand, if the relevant market were the world, no such diversification advantages would arise and investors would not be prepared to pay any premium. In other words, the choice of relevant market— and, therefore, the determination of the project's systematic risk—depends on the integration of world capital markets. This has the important implication that to the extent world capital markets are imperfectly integrated, multinational corporations will be able to take on foreign projects at a lower cost of capital than would a purely domestic corporation. In fact, Shapiro (1983) advocated that managers of U.S. multinationals use the U.S. market portfolio as the benchmark for establish-ing a project's systematic risk (thereby implying the existence of the above advan-tages) for three reasons: (1) Foreign and domestic projects would be evaluated in a common context; (2) There is no readily available world market portfolio; and (3) The relatively low levels of international diversification achieved by U.S. investors imply that the relevant market portfolio, from their viewpoint, is the U.S. market's.

Finally, recall that in earlier sections we argued that nonsystematic risk is important to the multinational firm because of the adverse effect that variability in cash flows could have on the firm's ability to raise credit and other long-term mea-sures. The above discussion on the appropriate discount rate, however, addressed only systematic risk. Incorporating these uniquely international risks into the capi-tal budgeting framework therefore requires that either the cash flow estimates or the discount rate be adjusted. Both Lessard (1981) and Shapiro (1983) argued against the latter approach, claiming that it results in biases and is extremely arbi-trary because it is impossible to say whether the discount rate should be raised by 5 or 10 percent when the firm is faced with possible expropriation. Moreover, in-sofar as these uniquely international risks are actually unsystematic, there is no theoretical basis for adjusting the discount rate. Instead, Shapiro advocated that cash flow estimates be adjusted by either charging against each year's cash flows a premium for political and international economic risk insurance or altering each cash flow estimate to allow for the specific effect of each possible risk.

Eiteman and Stonehill (1979) suggested a slightly different approach: adjust-ing cash flow estimates until they bear a risk equivalent to that of a given domestic project and then discounting these estimates by the project's cost of capital. It appears, however, that such an approach is operationally intractable.

Econometric Problems in Testing Purchasing Power Parity: A Mathematical Overview

At the beginning of the chapter, we noted that tests of the traditional version of purchasing power parity have tended to indicate that the theory does not adequately represent reality, at least in the short run. Moreover, we found that a major cause of divergences from purchasing power parity is changes in relative prices. From this we can show that testing the purchasing power parity hypothesis — that changes in price levels cause offsetting changes in the equilibrium exchange rate — invites econometric problems that tend to encourage rejection of the hypothesis even when it may in fact be true. In other words, the usual method of testing for the existence of purchasing power parity does not adequately capture the true nature of the hypothesis and, hence, is an invalid vehicle for rejecting or accepting it.

The traditional version of purchasing power parity as described by Equation 20.5 is usually tested using the following regression:

(i)
$$I_t - I_t^* = a_0 + a_1 \frac{e_t - e_{t-1}}{e_{t-1}} + \varepsilon_t,$$

where the hypothesis is that $a_0 = 0$ and $a_1 = 1$. However, the OLS estimator, $\hat{a}_1$, will be biased if $[(e_t - e_{t-1})/e_{t-1}]$ and Σ_t are interdependent. But Σ_t will largely reflect intertemporal changes in relative prices, which, as we have seen, will correlate with changes in the exchange rate. Hence, $\hat{a}_1$ is a biased estimator of a_1. Moreover, Roll (1979) has noted that in large samples, $\hat{a}_1$ will converge to

$$\hat{a}_1 = 1 - \text{Cov}\left[\frac{e_t - e_{t-1}}{e_{t-1}}, \varepsilon_t\right].$$

Thus, even if the maintained hypothesis of purchasing power parity — that changes in price levels cause offsetting changes in the equilibrium exchange rate and, therefore, $a_1 = 1$ — is true, $\hat{a}_1$ will be less than 1, causing us to reject the hypothesis. Consequently, the use of equations such as (i) are inadequate tests of purchasing power parity.

As noted in the first section, Roll attempted to resolve this problem by postulating an efficient market version of purchasing power parity. This involved running the following regression:

(ii)
$$S_t = a_0 + a_1 e_{t-1} + \sum_{i=1}^{K} a_{i+1} S_{t-1} + \omega_t,$$

where $S_t = e_t(1 + I_t^*)/(1 + I_t)$ and the hypothesis is that $a_0 = 0$, $a_1 = 1$, and $a_{i+1} = 0$. To see this, note that these values of a_i give

(iii) $E(S_t) = e_{t-1}$,

which is just the definition attributed to Roll (1979), given for the efficient market version of purchasing power parity earlier.

The use of (ii) instead of (i) should result in an unbiased estimate of a_1, as e_{t-1} and ω_t should be uncorrelated. Hence, equations like (ii) allow us to adequately capture the true nature of the purchasing power hypothesis.

Summary

This chapter demonstrated that the empirical validity of the body of theory developed in Chapter 20 is, at least in the short run, called into doubt due to the existence of real-world phenomena such as risk premia, differential tax systems, exchange controls, inefficient and nonintegrated markets, and consumer heterogeneity. The failure of these parity conditions to hold exactly complicates the financial decisions of individuals and corporations. Nevertheless, the advantages of international diversification appear to outweigh the disadvantages due to the ability to either diversify away or hedge against the shortcomings. If purchasing power parity held and the firm were risk-neutral, there would be no need for it to ever manage exchange risk. However, since neither of these conditions is likely to hold, hedging of exchange risk offers distinct advantages to the firm.

Finally, the uniquely international phenomena greatly complicate the financing and capital budgeting decisions of the multinational firm. If markets are perfect and the international parity conditions hold, many of these difficulties are reduced. However, as the planning horizons of corporate managers are usually by necessity shorter than the time period over which these conditions appear to hold, such simplifications are typically not possible.

Study Questions

21.1   Suppose that statistical tests indicate a high degree of correlation between ex post security returns in countries A and B. Does this imply that the capital markets of countries A and B are integrated? Explain why or why not. How would your conclusions be altered had the correlations been near zero?

21.2   It is February 1987. The directors of XYZ Brewing Company are considering whether to establish an affiliate brewery in France in an attempt to wean the French away from wine. Due to French laws and regulations, they will be locked into the brewery for 20 years if they decide to go ahead. Having read this chapter, they feel justified in assuming that purchasing power parity will hold for a time period of that length. They have undertaken several consumer research surveys and feel confident that the demand for their product will be stable in real terms; thus, regardless of French inflation during the ensuing 20 years, they expect annual cash flows to be 1 million January 1988 francs, and the risk of these cash flows compels them to require a real return of 5 percent. (If undertaken, the project would begin in January 1988.) The current exchange rate is 0.12 and is expected to remain at that level through January 1988. The cost of the brewery is $500,000. Should XYZ undertake this foreign investment?

References

M. Adler and B. Dumas, "International Portfolio Choice and Corporation Finance: A Survey," *Journal of Finance* 38 (1983): 925–984.

M. Adler and B. Lehmann, "Deviations from PPP in the Long Run: A Random Walk?" (Working paper, Columbia University, 1982).

T. Agmon and R. Eldor, "Currency Options Cope with Uncertainty," *Euromoney* 14 (1983): 227–228.

R. Z. Aliber, *Exchange Risk and International Corporate Finance* (London: Macmillan, 1978).

———, "The Interest Rate Parity Theorem: A Reinterpretation," *Journal of Political Economy* 81 (1973): 1451–1459.

N. Biger, "Exchange Risk Implications of International Portfolio Diversification," *Journal of International Business Studies* 10 (1979).

T. G. Copeland and J. F. Weston, *Financial Theory and Corporate Policy* (Reading, Mass.: Addison-Wesley, 1983).

B. Cornell and A. C. Shapiro, "Managing Foreign Exchange Risk," *Midland Corporate Finance Journal* 1 (1983).

R. E. Cumby and M. Obstfeld, "A Note on Exchange-Rate Expectations and Nominal Interest Differentials: A Test of the Fisher Hypothesis," *Journal of Finance* 36 (1981): 697–703.

M. P. Dooley and P. Isard, "Capital Controls, Political Risk, and Deviations from Interest-Rate Parity," *Journal of Political Economy* 88 (1980): 370–384.

R. Dornbusch, "Exchange Rate Economics: Where Do We Stand?" *Brookings Papers on Economic Activity* (1980a): 143–185.

———, "Monetary Policy under Exchange Rate Flexibility," in *The Functioning of Floating Exchange Rates: Theory, Evidence and Policy Implications*, ed. D. Bigman and T. Taya (Cambridge, Mass.: Ballinger, 1980b).

G. Dufey and S. L. Srinivasulu, "The Case for Corporate Management of Foreign Exchange Risk," *Financial Management* 12 (1984): 54–62.

D. K. Eiteman and A. Stonehill, *Multinational Business Finance* (Reading, Mass.: Addison-Wesley, 1979).

E. F. Fama and A. Farber, "Money, Bonds and Foreign Exchange," *American Economic Review* 69 (1979): 639–649.

J. Frenkel, "Exchange Rates, Prices and Money: Lessons from the 1920's," *American Economic Review* 70 (1980): 235–259.

———, "Flexible Exchange Rates, Prices and the Role of 'News': Lessons from the 1970's," *Journal of Political Economy* 89 (1981): 665–705.

———, "The Forward Exchange Rate, Expectations and the Demand for Money: The German Hyperinflation," *American Economic Review* 67 (1977): 653–705.

——— and R. Levich, "Transactions Costs and Interest Arbitrage: Tranquil versus Turbulent Periods," *Journal of Political Economy* 85 (1977): 1209–1226.

I. Giddy, "The Foreign Exchange Option as a Hedging Tool," *Midland Corporate Finance Journal* 1 (1983): 32–42.

———, "An Integrated Theory of Foreign Exchange Equilibrium," *Journal of Financial and Quantitative Analysis* 10 (1976): 883–892.

F. Grauer, R. Litzenberger, and R. Stehle, "Sharing Rules and Equilibrium in an International Capital Market under Uncertainty," *Journal of Financial Economics* 3 (1976): 233–256.

R. Ibbotson, R. Carr, and A. Robinson, "International Equity and Bond Returns," *Financial Analysts Journal* 38 (1982): 61–83.

P. Isard, "How Far Can We Push the Law of One Price?" *American Economic Review* 67 (1977): 942–948.

S. W. Kohlagen, "The Foreign Exchange Markets: Models, Tests, and Empirical Evidence" (Federal Reserve Bank, 1976, Mimeographed).

———, "The Forward Rate as an Unbiased Predictor of Future Spot Rates" (University of California, 1974, Mimeographed).

———, "Overlapping National Investment Portfolios: Evidence and Implications of International Integration of Secondary Markets for Financial Assets," in *Research in International Business and Finance*, vol. 3, ed. R. G. Hawkins and R. M. Levich (Greenwich, Conn.: JAI Press, 1983).

D. R. Lessard, "Evaluating International Projects: An Adjusted Present Value Approach," in *Capital Budgeting under Conditions of Uncertainty*, ed. R. L. Crum and F. G. J. Derkinderen (Martinus Nijhoff, 1981).

——— and A. Shapiro, "Guidelines for Global Financing Choices," *Midland Corporate Finance Journal* 2 (1984).

R. M. Levich, "Evaluating the Performance of the Forecasters," in *The Management of Foreign Exchange Risk*, ed. R. Ensor (London: Euromoney Publications, 1982).

H. Levy and M. Sarnat, "International Diversification of Investment Portfolios," *American Economic Review* 60 (1970).

D. E. Logue and R. J. Rogalski, "Offshore Alphas: Picking Countries Instead of Stocks," *Journal of Portfolio Management* 5 (1979).

D. E. Logue, M. Salant, and R. J. Sweeney, "International Integration of Financial Markets: Survey, Synthesis, and Results," in *Eurocurrencies and the International Monetary System*, ed. C. H. Stern, J. H. Makin, and D. E. Logue (Washington, D.C.: American Enterprise Institute, 1976).

R. C. Marston, "Interest Arbitrage in the Eurocurrency Markets," *European Economic Review* 8 (1976).

S. C. Myers, "Procedures for Capital Budgeting under Uncertainty," *Industrial Management Review* 20 (1978).

I. Otani and S. Tiwari, "Capital Controls and Interest Rate Parity: The Japanese Experience, 1978–81," *I.M.F. Staff Papers* 28 (1981): 793–815.

R. Roll, "A Critique of the Asset Pricing Theory Tests," *Journal of Financial Economics* 4 (1977).

———, "Violations of Purchasing Power Parity and Their Implications for Efficient International Commodity Markets," in *International Finance and Trade*, vol. 1, ed. M. Sarnat and G. P. Szego (Cambridge, Mass.: Ballinger, 1979).

——— and B. Solnik, "A Pure Foreign Exchange Asset Pricing Model," *Journal of International Economics* 7 (1977).

A. Shapiro, "International Capital Budgeting," *Midland Corporate Finance Journal* 1 (1983): 26–45.

B. Solnik, "An Equilibrium Model of the International Capital Market," *Journal of Economic Theory* (August 1974): 500–525.

———, "An International Market Model of Security Price Behavior," *Journal of Financial and Quantitative Analysis* (September 1974): 537–554.

———, "Testing International Asset Pricing: Some Pessimistic Views," *Journal of Finance* 32 (1977).

——— and B. Noetzlin, "Optimal International Asset Allocation: Lessons from the Past," *Journal of Portfolio Management* 7 (1981).

R. Stehle, "An Empirical Test of the Alternate Hypotheses of National and International Pricing of Risky Assets," *Journal of Finance* 32 (1977): 493–502.

Appendix

Mathematical Compendium

The Mathematical Compendium is a concise survey of results from linear algebra, calculus, optimization, probability, statistics, and stochastic processes that will help the reader understand the mathematics used in the text. The results appear as clear statements with simple, illustrative examples but usually without proofs. The organization is as follows:

1. Notation and symbols

2. Linear algebra

3. Calculus

4. Optimization

5. Probability and statistics

6. Stochastic processes

Notation and Symbols

Sets and Functions

The symbols $x \, \varepsilon \, X$ means that X is a *set* and x is an *element* of X. If X is a set, $\{x \, \varepsilon \, X : P(x)\}$ is the set of elements in X for which the sentence $P(x)$ is true. The following notation applies to sets $A, B, C, \ldots$

- A $\subseteq$ B means that each element of A is an element of B; we write or say "A is a subset of B."

- A $=$ B means that A $\subseteq$ B and B $\subseteq$ A; we write or say "A equals B."

- A $\cap$ B $= \{$x: x ε A and x ε B$\}$; this is the *intersection* of A and B.

- A $\cup$ B $= \{$x: x ε A or x ε B$\}$; this is the *union* of A and B.

- A$\setminus$B $= \{$x: x ε A and x is not an element of B$\}$; this is the *complement* of B in A.

An *ordered pair* of elements (a, b) — one from A and one from B — means a distinct set for which order matters; that is, $(a, b) = (c, d)$ if, and only if, $a = c$ and $b = d$. (Note that for sets $[a, b] = [b, a]$, order does not matter.)

A $\times$ B $= \{(a, b)$: a ε A and b ε B$\}$ denotes the set of ordered pairs of elements of A and B. This can be extended to ordered n-tuples $(a_1, a_2, \ldots, a_n)$, where $a_i \varepsilon A_i$ and $A_1, \ldots, A_n$ are sets. The set of all ordered n-tuples is $A_1 \times \ldots \times A_n$. In the case where all A_i are equal to A, we write A^n for the set of all ordered n-tuples of elements of A.

A function f defined on a set A with values in a set B, denoted f: A $\to$ B, is a subset of A $\times$ B such that if (x, y) and (x, z) are both elements of f, then $y = z$. In other words, for each x element of A, there is a unique element y of B for which (x, y) is in F. Thus, we can denote y by $f(x)$ without ambiguity. The set A is called the *domain* of f and the set $f(A) = \{y \varepsilon B$: for some x ε A, $f(x) = y\}$ is called the *range*.

If f: A $\to$ B and g: C $\to$ D with B $\subseteq$ C, the composite function h: A $\to$ D, denoted h $=$ gf, is defined by $h(a) = g[f(a)]$ for all a ε A.

Real Numbers

The set of *real numbers* is denoted R; thus, R^n denotes the set of ordered n-tuples of real numbers, called n-space. Special subsets of R are the following intervals:

$$[a, b] = \{x \varepsilon R: a \le x \le b\}$$

$$(a, b) = \{x \varepsilon R: a < x < b\}$$

$$(a, b] = \{x \varepsilon R: a < x \le b\}$$

$$(a, +\infty) = \{x \varepsilon R: a < x\}$$

The first is called a *closed interval*, with endpoints a and b. The second is called an *open interval*, with endpoints a and b. The intervals $(-\infty, b]$, $[a, b)$, and so on are defined similarly.

Linear Algebra

Definitions of Terms and Matrix Operations

A *matrix* is an ordered rectangular array of real numbers. Following are some examples:

$$\begin{bmatrix} 2 & 6 \\ 4 & -1 \end{bmatrix} \quad \begin{bmatrix} 2 & 6 & -1 \\ 4 & -1 & 3 \end{bmatrix} \quad [2] \quad \begin{bmatrix} 6 \\ 3 \\ 1 \end{bmatrix}$$

$$[6 \quad 1 \quad -10] \quad \begin{bmatrix} 1 & 0 \\ 0 & 1 \end{bmatrix}$$

The size of a matrix A is the ordered pair of positive integers denoted r × c (read "r by c"), r being the number of rows and c the number of columns of A. The above examples have the following sizes, reading left to right and top to bottom: 2 × 2, 2 × 3, 1 × 1, 3 × 1, 1 × 3, and 2 × 2. (A matrix of size 1 × 1 is usually identified with the number that is its only element. Such matrices are real numbers, but in linear algebra they are called *scalars*.) The elements of a matrix are the numbers used to define it. An element a of a matrix A is said to be in the (i, j) position or to have coordinates (i, j), if a is in the ith row and the jth column. The notation $A = [a_{ij}]_{m,n}$ means that A is a matrix of size m × n and a_{ij} is in the (i, j) position of A for $1 \le i \le m$ and $1 \le j \le n$. Two matrices are equal if they are the same size and have equal corresponding elements.

The sum of two matrices $A = [a_{ij}]_{m,n}$ and $B = [b_{ij}]_{m,n}$ of the same size is the matrix $C = [c_{ij}]_{m,n}$ whose elements are obtained by adding elements of corresponding positions of A and B. Thus, $c_{ij} = a_{ij} + b_{ij}$ for all i and j. For example,

$$\begin{bmatrix} 2 & 6 \\ 4 & -1 \end{bmatrix} + \begin{bmatrix} -1 & 8 \\ 1.2 & 10 \end{bmatrix} = \begin{bmatrix} 1 & 14 \\ 5.2 & 9 \end{bmatrix}$$

Subtraction is performed in the same manner.

Scalar multiplication of a matrix $A = [a_{ij}]$ by a scalar s is defined such that the product sA is the matrix obtained by multiplying each element of A by s:

$$sA = [sa_{ij}].$$

For example,

$$2\begin{bmatrix} 2 & 6 \\ 4 & -1 \end{bmatrix} = \begin{bmatrix} 4 & 12 \\ 8 & -2 \end{bmatrix}$$

The product of two matrices $A = [a_{ij}]_{m,n}$ and $B = [b_{ij}]_{n,p}$ is the matrix $C = [c_{ij}]_{m,p}$ defined by

$$c_{ij} = \sum_{k=1}^{n} a_{ik}b_{kj} \quad \text{for } i = 1, 2, \dots, m \quad \text{and} \quad j = 1, 2, \dots, p.$$

For example,

$$\begin{bmatrix} 2 & 6 \\ 4 & -1 \end{bmatrix} \begin{bmatrix} 1 & 4 & 0.5 \\ 8 & -1 & -0.5 \end{bmatrix} = \begin{bmatrix} 50 & 2 & -2 \\ -4 & 17 & 2.5 \end{bmatrix}$$

The product AB is defined only when the number of columns of A is the same as the number of rows of B. Thus, AB may not equal BA because BA is not defined. In fact, even if AB and BA are both defined, they may be of different sizes as in the last two examples above. Hence, there is no possibility for AB = BA unless A and B are of the same size and are square. A matrix is square if its size is (r, c) and r = c. However, even square matrices A and B of the same size may not satisfy AB = BA. If two matrices A and B satisfy AB = BA, they are said to *commute*.

The special matrix I_n, which is of the size (n, n) and contains all zero elements except for those in the diagonal positions (i, i) that are equal to 1, is called the *n-by-n identity matrix*. It satisfies $I_nB = B$ and $AI_n = A$ for all A and B for which the products are defined. A matrix is said to be *invertible* if there is another matrix B such that $AB = BA = I_n$ for some n. B is unique when it exists and is called the *inverse* of A and denoted A^{-1}.

Matrix Notation and Solutions to Simultaneous Linear Equations

Matrices can be used to write systems of simultaneous linear equations in very compact notation. For example, the system

$$a_{11}x_1 + a_{12}x_1 + \cdots + a_{1n}x_n = b_1$$

$$\begin{matrix} \cdot & & \cdot & \cdot \\ \cdot & & \cdot & \cdot \\ \cdot & & \cdot & \cdot \end{matrix}$$

$$a_{n1}x_1 + a_{n2}x_1 + \cdots + a_{nn}x_n = b_n$$

can be written AX = B, where

$$A = [a_{ij}]_{n, n}, \qquad X = [x_i]_{n, 1}, \qquad \text{and} \quad B = [b_i]_{n, 1}.$$

The system is solved by finding A^{-1} (if it exists), because $A^{-1}AX = A^{-1}B$ and $A^{-1}AX = I_nX = X$ and, thus, $X = A^{-1}B$. For example, the system

$$3x_1 + 2x_2 = 8$$

$$5x_1 + x_2 = 4$$

can be written AX = B, where

$$A = \begin{bmatrix} 3 & 2 \\ 5 & 1 \end{bmatrix}, \qquad X = \begin{bmatrix} x_1 \\ x_2 \end{bmatrix}, \qquad \text{and} \quad B = \begin{bmatrix} 8 \\ 4 \end{bmatrix}.$$

For this example,

$$A^{-1} = \begin{bmatrix} -\dfrac{1}{7} & \dfrac{2}{7} \\ \dfrac{5}{7} & -\dfrac{3}{7} \end{bmatrix}$$

and

$$X = A^{-1}B = \begin{bmatrix} 0 \\ 4 \end{bmatrix}$$

Hence, the solution to the system is $x_1 = 0$ and $x_2 = 4$. It is not necessary to spend a lot of time inverting matrices to solve linear equations; computer programs do this quite nicely in most cases.

For 2-by-2 matrices,

$$A = \begin{bmatrix} a & b \\ c & d \end{bmatrix},$$

we can calculate A^{-1} if $ad - cb \neq 0$:

$$A^{-1} = (ad - cb)^{-1} \begin{bmatrix} d & -b \\ -c & a \end{bmatrix}.$$

More Definitions

The *transpose* of a matrix A is the matrix $B = A^T$, obtained from A by interchanging its rows and columns. For example,

$$\begin{bmatrix} 6 & -3 & 8 & 0.2 \\ 9 & 18 & 0 & 39 \end{bmatrix}^T = \begin{bmatrix} 6 & 9 \\ -3 & 18 \\ 8 & 0 \\ 0.2 & 39 \end{bmatrix}$$

A matrix is *symmetric* if it is equal to its transpose.

Let $A = [a_{ij}]_{n,n}$ be a square matrix and $X = [x_i]_{n,1}$. Then X^TAX is a real valued function of the n coordinates of X; it is called the *quadratic* form associated with A. A symmetric matrix is called positive *semidefinite* if $X^TAX \geq 0$ for all X. A positive semidefinite matrix A is called *positive definite* if $X^TAX = 0$ only when $X = 0$ (this last 0 denotes the matrix of the same size as X but having all zero entries).

Summary of Matrix Operations

The following rules are valid so long as the sizes of the matrices are such that the operations are defined:

- $A + B = B + A$
- $A + (B + C) = (A + B) + C$
- $s(AB) = (sA)B$
- $A(BC) = (AB)C$
- $A(B + C) = AB + AC$

- $(B + C)A = BA + CA$
- $(A^T)^T = A$
- $(B + C)^T = B^T + C^T$
- $(AB)^T = B^T A^T$
- $IA = A$ and $BI = B$ where I is an identity matrix
- $(A^{-1})^{-1} = A$ if A is invertible
- $(A^T)^{-1} = (A^{-1})^T$ if A is invertible
- $(AB)^{-1} = B^{-1} A^{-1}$ if A and B are invertible
- $A^T = A$ if A is symmetric

Vector Spaces

A *vector space* is a set V equipped with two operations, scalar multiplication and vector addition (sX is in V for all real numbers s and all $X \; \varepsilon \; V$, and $X + Y$ is in V for all $X, Y \; \varepsilon \; V$), that satisfy the following axioms.

Addition

A.1. There is a distinct element — zero (denoted 0) — of V such that $X + 0 = X$ for all vectors X in V.

A.2. For all vectors X, Y in V, $X + Y = Y + X$.

A.3. For each vector X in V, there is a unique vector, denoted $-X$, such that $X + (-X) = 0$. (We usually write $X - X = 0$.)

A.4. For all X, Y, Z in V, $X + (Y + Z) = (X + Y) + Z$.

Scalar Multiplication

S.1. $s(X + Y) = sX + sY$ for all real numbers s and all X and Y in V.

S.2. $1(X) = X$ and $0X = 0$ for all X in V. Here 0 denotes both the real number zero and the zero vector of V referred to in A.3.

S.3. $s(tX) = (st)X$ for all real s and t and all X in V.

Examples

1. Let R^n denote the set of matrices of size (n, 1). This is the set of column vectors $X, X^T = [x_1, \ldots, x_n]$. With vector addition taken to be the typical matrix addition and scalar multiplication defined as usual, R^n is a vector space.

2. Let V be a vector space and W a non-empty subset of V such that
    a. $X + Y$ is in W if X and Y are in W
    b. sX is in W if X is in W and s is a real number
    Then, with the same operations as V, W is a vector space. We say that W is a *subspace* of V.

3. Let X be a vector in R^n. Let $W = \{sX: s \text{ a real number}\}$; that is, W is the set of all multiples of X. W is a subspace of R^n.

4. If $X_1, \ldots, X_n$ are vectors in a vector space V, the set of vectors having a representation as a linear combination $c_1X_1 + \ldots + c_nX_n$ of the $X_1, \ldots, X_n$ form a subspace of R^n. This is called the subspace *spanned* by $X_1, \ldots, X_n$ and denoted $\langle X_1, \ldots, X_n \rangle$. If $X_1, \ldots, X_n$ are elements of a subspace W of V, they are said to span W if $\langle X_1, \ldots, X_n \rangle$ = W. Sometimes *generate* is used in place of *span*.

A vector space V is said to be *finite dimensional* if it contains a finite set $X_1, \ldots, X_n$ such that $\langle X_1, \ldots, X_n \rangle$ = V. The dimension of a finite dimensional vector space equals k if V has a spanning set of k elements and no $k - 1$ vectors span V. A subset $X_1, \ldots, X_n$ of a vector space V is *linearly dependent* if some linear combination $c_1X_1 + c_2X_2 + \ldots + c_nX_n$ equals zero with at least one c not equal to zero.

The following three statements about a finite set of vectors $X_1, \ldots, X_n$ in a vector space V are equivalent. Let W = $\langle X_1, \ldots, X_n \rangle$.

1. W is minimally generated by $X_1, \ldots, X_n$ in the sense that if one of the vectors is deleted from $X_1, \ldots, X_n$, the resulting set will not generate W.

2. If a linear combination of the $X_1, \ldots, X_n$ is zero, that is,

$$c_1X_1 + c_2X_2 + \ldots + c_nX_n = 0,$$

each of the scalars $c_1, \ldots, c_n$ is zero.

3. Each element Y of W has a unique representation as a linear combination of the $X_1, \ldots, X_n$. In other words, if $Y = c_1X_1 + c_2X_2 + \ldots + c_nX_n$ and $Y = a_1X_1 + a_2X_2 + \ldots + a_nX_n$, then $c_1 = a_1, c_2 = a_2, \ldots, c_n = a_n$.

When $X_1, \ldots, X_n$ satisfies one — and, hence, all — of these conditions, we say that $X_1, \ldots, X_n$ are *linearly independent*. A linearly independent generation set is called a *basis* of the space it generates. Also, any generating set contains a basis: We simply delete, one by one, elements from $X_1, \ldots, X_n$ until the resulting set satisfies 1.

Examples

1. Consider the vector $e_1, e_2, \ldots, e_n$ in R^n where e_i denotes the n-by-1 matrix with all zero elements except in the (i, 1) position where 1 appears. For any vector $X = [x_1, \ldots, x_n]$ in R^n, we have $X = x_1e_1 + x_2e_2 + \ldots + x_ne_n$. This means that $e_1, \ldots, e_n$ span R^n. Also if $c_1e_1 + c_2e_2 + \ldots + c_ne_n = 0$, all of the $c_1, \ldots, c_n$ are zero. This means that $e_1, \ldots, e_n$ satisfies statement 2 above; thus, $e_1, \ldots, e_n$ forms a basis of R^n, called the *standard basis* of R^n.

2. Let $I = [a, b]$ be an interval and V the set of all functions defined on I and having values in R. Addition and scalar multiplication are defined in the familiar way. The sum of two functions f, g: $I \to R$ is the function f + g defined in terms of f and g by $(f + g)(x) = f(x) + g(x)$ for all $x \varepsilon I$. Similarly, scalar multiplication of f ε V by a ε R is defined by $(af)(x) = af(x)$ for all $x \varepsilon I$. V is interesting mainly for its subspaces. The polynomial functions, $p_n(x) = x^n$ for all $x \varepsilon I$, usually — albeit somewhat ambigu-

ously — are denoted 1, x, x^2, x^3, ... They are independent and form a basis for the space $P[a, b]$ of polynomials on $[a, b]$. P is an example of a vector space that is not finite dimensional.

3.   The set of continuous functions defined on $I = [a, b]$ is a subspace of V from example 2, because the sum of two continuous functions is continuous and a scalar multiple of a continuous function is continuous. This subspace is denoted $C[a, b]$. Since $P \subseteq C[a, b]$ and P are not finite dimensional neither is $C[a, b]$.

If $A = [a_{ij}]$ is an n-by-m matrix, the rank of A is the dimension of the subspace of R^m generated by the n rows of A. It can be shown that this equals the dimension of the subspace of R^n generated by the m columns of A. It follows from the properties of a basis that the rank of A is the maximum number of linearly independent rows (or columns) of A.

Geometry in R^n

The inner product of two vectors X and Y in R^n is defined as the scalar $X^TY = x_1y_1 + x_2y_2 + \ldots + x_ny_n$. (Often the inner product is written XY, especially when the only matrices in sight are vectors.) The angle θ between X and Y is defined implicitly by $\cos(\theta) = X^TY/(|X||Y|)$. The two vectors are said to be *orthogonal* (perpendicular) if $\cos(\theta) = 0$ (or, equivalently, $X^TY = 0$). If $W \subseteq R^n$, then $W^\perp$ denotes the set of vectors orthogonal to every element of W:

$$W^\perp = \{X \ \varepsilon \ R^n \,|\, X^TY = 0 \text{ for every } Y \ \varepsilon \ W\}.$$

Properties of the Inner Product.   Let X, Y, Z ε R^n and a, b ε R.

1. $X^TX = |X|^2$

2. $(aX)^TY = a(X^TY)$

3. $X^T(Y + Z) = X^TY + X^TZ$

4. $X^TY = Y^TX$

5. $|X + Y|^2 = |X|^2 + |Y|^2 + 2X^TY$

6.   If $W \subseteq R^n$, then $W^\perp$ is a subspace of R^n.

7.   If $W \subseteq R^n$, then $W \subseteq W^{\perp\perp}$ and $W = W^{\perp\perp}$ if W is itself a subspace.

8.   If $V \subseteq W \subseteq R^n$, then $W^\perp \subseteq V^\perp$.

Example.   In deriving the arbitrage pricing model (see Chapter 9), we observed that the no-riskless-arbitrage principle could be stated geometrically as:

$$\text{if } X^TB = 0 \quad \text{and} \quad X^TU = 0, \quad \text{then} \quad X^TM = 0.$$

From this property we concluded — without proof — that M must be in the span of B and U. We can now prove this. Let W be the subspace spanned by U and B,

$$W = \langle U, B \rangle,$$

and let V be the span of M,

$$V = \langle M \rangle.$$

Now the no-riskless-arbitrage assertion,

$$\text{if} \quad X^TB = 0 \quad \text{and} \quad X^TU = 0, \quad \text{then} \quad X^TM = 0,$$

written in terms of V and W, means

$$\text{if} \quad X \,\varepsilon\, W^\perp, \quad \text{then} \quad X \,\varepsilon\, V^\perp$$

or

$$W^\perp \subseteq V^\perp$$

because

$$W^\perp = \{X \,\varepsilon\, R^n \,|\, X^TB = 0 \quad \text{and} \quad X^TU = 0\} \quad \text{and} \quad V^\perp = \{X \,\varepsilon\, R^n \,|\, X^TM = 0\}.$$

By property 8, it follows that

$$V^{\perp\perp} \subseteq W^{\perp\perp}.$$

Moreover, by property 7, $V = V^{\perp\perp}$ and $W = W^{\perp\perp}$. Hence, $V \subseteq W$; that is,

$$\langle M \rangle \subseteq \langle U, B \rangle.$$

Thus, M is in the span of U and B; in other words, M is a linear combination of U and B, $M = y_0U + y_1B$. This is just what we needed to show for the arbitrage pricing model in Chapter 9.

Calculus

Limits and Sequences

A *neighborhood* U in R of a point x_0 is an open interval that contains x_0. A *deleted neighborhood* of x_0 is a set of the form $U - \{x_0\}$, where U is a neighborhood of x_0. Let f be a function defined in a deleted neighborhood of x_0. The following are standard definitions that describe what may happen to f(x) as x approaches x_0:

1.
$$\lim_{x \to x_0} f(x) = L$$

means that L is a real number and for every $\epsilon > 0$ there exists $\delta > 0$ such that

$$|f(x) - L| < \varepsilon \quad \text{whenever} \quad 0 < |x - x_0| < \delta.$$

2.
$$\lim_{x \to x_0} f(x) = +\infty$$

means that for every $M > 0$ there exists a $\delta > 0$ such that $f(x) > M$ whenever

$$0 < |x - x_0| < \delta.$$

3.
$$\lim_{x \to x_0^+} f(x) = L$$

means that L is a real number and for every $\varepsilon > 0$ there exists a $\delta > 0$ such that

$$|f(x) - L| < \varepsilon \quad \text{whenever } 0 < x - x_0 < \delta.$$

Other, analogous definitions characterize still more possibilities for the behavior of f near x_0. The limit symbols suggest the nature of f near x_0. Some others are

$$\lim_{x \to x_0} f(x) = -\infty, \qquad \lim_{x \to x_0^-} f(x) = L, \quad \text{and} \quad \lim_{x \to x_0^-} f(x) = +\infty.$$

The last two are limits from the left, defined in analogy with C. Often it is important to know the behavior of $f(x)$ for very large values of x. This leads to our last two types of limit.

4.
$$\lim_{x \to +\infty} f(x) = L$$

means that L is a real number and for every $\epsilon > 0$ there exists an $M > 0$ such that

$$|f(x) - L| < \varepsilon \quad \text{whenever } x > M.$$

5.
$$\lim_{x \to +\infty} f(x) = +\infty$$

means that for every real number K there exists a real number $M > 0$ such that $f(x) > K$ whenever $x > M$.

Similar concepts are obtained analogously for $+\infty$ replaced by $-\infty$. The terminology "$\lim f(x) = L$ as $x \to x_0$" or "$f(x) \to L$ as $x \to x_0$" is sometimes used in place of $\lim_{x \to x_0} f(x) = L$.

Examples

1. Define the "sign function" as $\text{sgn}(x) = 1$ if $x > 0$, $\text{sgn}(0) = 0$, and $\text{sgn}(x) = -1$ if $x < 0$. Then $\lim \text{sgn}(x)$ as $x \to 0$ does not exist. By this we mean that there is no number L for which definition A is true with $x_0 = 0$ and $f = \text{sgn}$. However, $\lim \text{sgn}(x) = 1$ as $x \to x_0^+$ and $\lim \text{sgn}(x) = -1$ as $x \to x_0^-$.

2. $\lim 1/x$ as $x \to 0$ does not exist, but the limit from the left is $-\infty$ and the limit from the right is $+\infty$.

Properties of Limits. Let f and g be functions defined on a deleted neighborhood of x_0.

1. $\lim_{x \to x_0} [f(x) + g(x)] = \lim_{x \to x_0} f(x) + \lim_{x \to x_0} g(x).$

2. $\lim_{x \to x_0} [f(x)g(x)] = \left[\lim_{x \to x_0} f(x)\right]\left[\lim_{x \to x_0} g(x)\right].$

3. $\lim_{x \to x_0} [f(x)/g(x)] = \lim_{x \to x_0} f(x)/\lim_{x \to x_0} g(x).$

For the above three properties the "two out of three" result holds, meaning that if two of the indicated limits exist, so does the third, and the given relation is valid. For property 3, the limit of g must not equal zero. Also for property 3, if there is a number K such that $|f(x)| \leq K$ for all x in a neighborhood of x_0 and $\lim_{x \to x_0} g(x) = \pm\infty$, then $\lim_{x \to x_0} f(x)/g(x) = 0$.

4. If p(x) is a polynomial, then $\lim_{x \to x_0} p(x) = p(x_0)$. For instance, $\lim_{x \to 3} (x^2 + 5) = 3^2 + 5 = 14$.

5. If $\lim_{x \to x_0} f(x) = L > 0$, then $\lim_{x \to x_0} f(x)^c = L^c$.

An *infinite sequence* is a function $a: N \to R$. We always write a_k instead of $a(k)$ for a particular value of a. When the entire function is referenced, we list its values: $a_1, a_2, a_3, \ldots$, often denoted $\{a_n\}_{n=1}^{\infty}$. The fact that a sequence converges to L, written

$$\lim_{k \to +\infty} a_k = L,$$

means that L is a real number and for every $\varepsilon > 0$ there exists an integer $M > 0$ such that $|a_k - L| < \varepsilon$ whenever $k > M$.

Methods used for sequences generally are the same as those used for working with $\lim f(x)$ as $x \to \infty$. Further, all of the properties of limits reviewed above carry over to limits of sequences.

An *arithmetic progression*, $a, a + d, a + 2d, \ldots$, is one in which there is a common difference, d, between consecutive terms. In this case, $a_n = a + (n - 1)d$ and $\lim a_n = \pm\infty$ as $n \to \infty$ according to whether d is positive or negative, and $\lim a_n = a$ as $n \to \infty$ if $d = 0$.

A *geometric progression*, $a, ar, ar^2, ar^3, \ldots$, is one in which the ratio between consecutive terms is a constant. In such a case, $a_n = ar^{n-1}$ where $r \neq 0$ is the common ratio for the progression, and $\lim a_n = 0$ as $n \to \infty$ if $|r| < 1$.

A *series* is a sequence whose terms are sums of a given sequence $a_1, a_2, a_3, \ldots$. The notation we use is $\sum_{k=1}^{\infty} a_k$ to refer to the series whose terms are $s_1 = a_1, s_2 = a_1 + a_2, s_3 = a_1 + a_2 + a_3, \ldots, s_n = a_1 + a_2 + a_3 + \ldots + a_n, \ldots$. When the partial sequences of partial sums (s_n) converges to S, we say that the series *converges* to S and write $\sum_{k=1}^{\infty} a_k = S$.

Properties of Series.   The following are important properties of series:

1. $$c \sum_{k=1}^{\infty} a_k = \sum_{k=1}^{\infty} ca_k$$

2. $$\sum_{k=1}^{\infty} a_k + \sum_{k=1}^{\infty} b_k = \sum_{k=1}^{\infty} (a_k + b_k)$$

3. If $\sum_{k=1}^{\infty} a_k$ converges, then $a_k \to 0$ as $k \to \infty$.

4. The partial sums $s_n = a + ar + ar^2 + \ldots + ar^{n-1}$ of a geometric progression (called a *geometric series*) are given by

$$s_n = \frac{a - ar^n}{1 - r}.$$

Since $ar^n \to 0$ as $n \to \infty$ if $|r| < 1$, the geometric series converges provided the common ratio has an absolute value of less than 1:

$$\sum_{k=0}^{\infty} ar^k = \frac{a}{1 - r} \quad \text{if } |r| < 1.$$

5. The harmonic series $\sum_{k=1}^{\infty} 1/k$ diverges to $+\infty$. (Unfortunately, the terminology "converges to $+\infty$" is used to mean exactly the same thing: The partial sums increase without limit.)

6. The binomial theorem states: If $|x| < 1$,

$$\sum_{k=0}^{\infty} C_{a,k} x^k = (1 + x)^a,$$

where $C_{a,k} = [a(a - 1)(a - 2)\ldots(a - k + 1)]/k!$ and a is any (not necessarily integral) real number.

7. If $\sum_{k=1}^{\infty} |a_k|$ converges, so does $\sum_{k=1}^{\infty} a_k$ and

$$\left| \sum_{k=1}^{\infty} a_k \right| \leq \sum_{k=1}^{\infty} |a_k|.$$

Continuity

A function f at a point x_0 is said to be *continuous* at x_0 provided that for every $\varepsilon > 0$ there exists a $\delta > 0$ such that $|f(x) - f(x_0)| < \varepsilon$ whenever $|x - x_0| < \delta$. Graphically, this means that a function f is continuous at x_0 provided that as x approaches x_0 the point $[x, f(x)]$ on the graph of f approaches $[x_0, f(x_0)]$. In other words, as x approaches x_0, $f(x)$ is defined and approaches $f(x_0)$; there is no break in the graph of $f(x)$ at $x = x_0$. In terms of limits,

$$\lim_{x \to x_0} f(x) = f(x_0).$$

A function f is continuous on a set S if it is continuous at x for every x in S.

Properties of Continuous Functions. The following properties of continuous functions can be established from the properties of limits:

1. $f(x) + g(x)$, $f(x)g(x)$, and $f(x)/g(x)$ (where $g(x) \neq 0$) are continuous at x_0 if $f(x)$ and $g(x)$ are continuous.

2. All polynomials and exponential functions are continuous. In addition, any rational function is continuous at any point at which its denominator is not zero.

3. If f is continuous at x_0 and g is continuous at $y_0 = f(x_0)$, then $h(x) = g[f(x)]$ is continuous at x_0. For example, $f(x) = x^2$ is continuous and $g(y) = 10y$ is continuous; hence, $h(x) = g(x^2) = 10x^2$ is continuous.

4. If f is continuous on [a, b], its range is a closed interval (or, perhaps, a single point).

5. If f is continuous on [a, b] and f^{-1} exists, then f^{-1} is continuous — that is, the inverse of a continuous function is continuous.

Example. At what annual interest rate would an investment of \$50 immediately and \$100 six years hence accumulate to \$300 ten years from now?

Solution. Let i be the unknown rate. The equation of value is

$$50(1 + i)^{10} + 100(1 + i)^4 = 300$$

or

$$(1 + i)^{10} + 2(1 + i)^4 = 6.$$

Let $f(i) = (1 + i)^{10} + 2(1 + i)^4$. Thus, f is a continuous function of i for all i:

$$f(0) = 3 < 6 \quad \text{and} \quad f(0.2) \approx 10.34 > 6.$$

By property 4, f[0, 1] is a closed interval. It contains $f(0) = 3$ and $f(0.2) > 6$ and thus contains 6; that is, there is a solution between $i = 0$ and $i = 0.20$ because $f(0) < 6$ and $f(0, 2) > 6$. Lacking better information, we would calculate $f[(0 + 0.20)/2] = f(0.10) \approx 5.52$. Since this is less than 6, we know that there is a solution between 0.10 and 0.20.

Next, we calculate f at $(0.10 + 0.20)/2 = 0.15$ and find that this is greater than 6; hence, there is a solution between 0.10 and 0.15. We continue in this way to determine a solution to as great a degree of accuracy as desired. The results of the calculations are as follows:

Step n	i_n	$f(i_n)$
0	0	3
1	0.2	10.34
2	0.1	5.52
3	0.15	7.54
4	0.125	6.45
5	0.1125	5.97

Hence, an approximate solution is $i = 11.25\%$.

This example illustrates a method of approximating solutions to equations of the form $f(x) = c$. This method is called *successive bisection*. In general terms, it says the following: If $x_0, x_1, \ldots$ is a sequence such that (1)

$$c \text{ is between } f(x_i) \quad \text{and} \quad f(x_{i+1}) \quad \text{for all } i$$

and (2)

$$x_{i+1} = \frac{(x_i + x_{i-1})}{2},$$

the sequence $x_0, x_1, \ldots$ converges to a solution of $f(x) = c$.

Differentiation

Suppose f is defined in a neighborhood of x_0. Then f is differentiable at x_0 if

$$\lim \frac{f(x) - f(x_0)}{x - x_0} \quad \text{as } x \to x_0$$

exists and is finite. In this case we label the limit $f'(x_0)$ and call it the *derivative* of f at x_0. The compact form of the definition is

$$f(x_0) = \lim \frac{f(x) - f(x_0)}{x - x_0} \quad \text{as } x \to x_0$$

or

$$f(x_0) = \lim \frac{f(x_0 + h) - f(x_0)}{h} \quad \text{as } h \to 0.$$

Geometrically $f'(x)$ is the slope of the line tangent to the graph of f at $[x_0, f(x_0)]$. When $f'(x)$ exists, the graph will be smooth at x_0. A sharp corner in the graph of f at x_0 indicates that the derivative does not exist at x_0.

There are a number of ways to denote the derivative of $y = f(x)$. $D_x f$, $Df(x)$, Df, df/dx, f', Dy, $D_x y$, dy/dx, and y' are other ways of writing $f'(x)$.

Some important differentiation formulas are

	f(x)	**f'(x)**
Power rule	cx^n	cnx^{n-1}
Linearity	$ag(x) + bh(x)$	$ag'(x) + bh'(x)$
Product rule	$g(x)h(x)$	$g'(x)h(x) + g(x)h'(x)$
	$u(x)v(x)w(x)$	$u'vw + uv'w + vuw'$
Quotient rule	$\dfrac{g(x)}{h(x)}$	$\dfrac{h(x)g'(x) - g(x)h'(x)}{[h(x)]^2}$
Chain rule	$f[g(x)]$	$f'[g(x)] \cdot g'(x)$

Example. To find the derivative of $h(x) = (x^3 + x - 1)^{3/2}$, we let $f(x) = x^{3/2}$ and $g(x) = x^3 + x - 1$ such that $h(x) = f[g(x)] = [g(x)]^{3/2} = (x^3 + x - 1)^{3/2}$, from which the chain rule tells us that $h'(x) = f'[g(x)] \cdot g'(x)$. But $f'(x) = 3/2x^{1/2}$ and $g'(x) = 3x^2 + 1$; hence,

$$h'(x) = \left(\frac{3}{2}\right)[g(x)]^{1/2}(3x^2 + 1) = \left(\frac{3}{2}\right)(x^3 + x - 1)^{1/2}(3x^2 + 1).$$

The chain rule can be used to obtain the generalized power rule: If $h(x) = [f(x)]^n$, then $h'(x) = n[f(x)^{n-1}] \cdot f'(x)$.

Exponential and Logarithmic Functions

The exponential function $f(x) = e^x$ and its inverse, the logarithm in x, are important enough to warrant reviewing some of their properties.

Properties of Exponential and Logarithmic Functions

1. $\lim\limits_{x \to +\infty} e^x = +\infty, \qquad \lim\limits_{x \to -\infty} e^x = 0$

2. $\lim\limits_{x \to +\infty} \ln x = +\infty, \qquad \lim\limits_{x \to 0^+} \ln x = -\infty$

3.   If $k > 0$,

$$\lim_{x \to +\infty} \frac{e^x}{x^k} = +\infty,$$

$$\lim_{x \to +\infty} \ln \frac{x}{x^k} = 0, \quad \text{and}$$

$$\lim_{x \to 0^+} x^k \ln x = 0.$$

4.   If $0 < b < 1$,

$$\lim_{x \to =\infty} b^x = 0 \quad \text{and} \quad \lim_{x \to +\infty} \ln b^x = -\infty.$$

5.   If $b > 1$,

$$\lim_{x \to +\infty} b^x = +\infty \quad \text{and} \quad \lim_{x \to +\infty} \log_b x = +\infty.$$

To summarize, the derivatives of exponential and logarithmic functions are as follows:

$f(x)$	$f'(x)$
$a^x \; (a > 0)$	$a^x \ln a$
e^x	e^x
$\log_b x \; (b > 0)$	$\dfrac{1}{x \ln b}$

In addition, the chain rule yields:

$e^{g(x)}$	$g'(x) \cdot e^{g(x)}$
$\ln[g(x)]$	$\dfrac{g'(x)}{g(x)}$

Implicit Differentiation

When $y = f(x)$ is given as a function defined explicitly in terms of x, it is possible to find $y' = f'(x)$ explicitly in terms of x. When a relation involving x and y is given that does not yield an explicit function of y in terms of x, we can assume that y is an "implicit" function of x and differentiate all terms with respect to x based on this assumption. This generally will lead to a formulation of y' in terms of x and y.

Example. To find y' given $x^2 + y^2 = 8$, we take derivatives term by term with respect to x: $2x + 2y \cdot y' = 0$, assuming that $y = f(x)$. The derivative of $y^2 = [f(x)]^2$ is $2f(x) \cdot f'(x) = 2yy'$. Then, solving for y' we get $y' = -x/y$. For example, $y' = -1$ if $x = 2$, $y = 2$. To find y'', we differentiate $-x/y$ using the quotient rule:

$$y'' = -\left(\frac{y - xy'}{y^2}\right) = -\left(\frac{y + \dfrac{x^2}{y}}{y^2}\right) = -\frac{y^2 + x^2}{y^3} = -\frac{8}{y^3}.$$

Again, at $x = 2$ and $y = 2$, $y'' = -1$.

Taylor Series Expansions

Suppose the values of a function $f(x)$ and its derivatives are known at one value of x — say, $x = x_0$. An example is the function $f(x) = (1 + x)^k$ for $x = 10$ percent. How can this information be used to approximate the values of $f(x)$ for values of x near x_0? If we restrict ourselves by using none of the derivatives, we might use

$$f(x) \approx a_0 \quad \text{where } a_0 = f(x_0).$$

Geometrically, this amounts to approximating the graph of $y = f(x)$ with the line $y = a_0$, which passes through the point (x_0, a_0) on the graph of $y = f(x)$. This is illustrated in Figure C.1.

The error is the distance between the graphs of $y = f(x)$ and $y = p_0(x) = a_0$. This would be satisfactory only if x were very near x_0. For example, to approximate $(1.101)^{24}$ it may be reasonable, for some purposes, to use the tabulated value $(1.10)^{24}$. However, it is very unlikely that $(1.10)^{24}$ would ever be an acceptable approximation to $(1.11)^{24}$.

More useful approximations can be obtained by using the known values of the derivatives as well as the values of the function. Using just one derivative, we might use

$$f(x) \approx a_0 + a_1(x - x_0), \quad \text{where } a_0 = f(x_0) \quad \text{and} \quad a_1 = f'(x_0)$$

because the graph of $p(x) = a_0 + a_1(x - x_0)$ is tangent to the graph of $f(x)$ at $x = x_0$. This means that the linear function $p(x)$ has the same value as $f(x)$ at x_0, and so do their respective derivatives,

$$p(x_0) = f(x_0) \quad \text{and} \quad p'(x_0) = f'(x_0).$$

Since two equations uniquely determine a linear function, there is only one linear function that satisfies these equations. Let us denote it by $p_1(x)$. The geometric properties of p_1 are illustrated in Figure C.2.

The error is the distance between the graphs of $y = f(x)$ and the Taylor polynomial $p_1(x) = a_0 + a_1(x - x_0)$.

For example, to approximate $(1.11)^{24}$ using one derivative, we would use

$$(1.11)^{24} \approx (1.10)^{24} + 24(1.10)^{23}(0.11 - 0.10),$$

Figure C.1

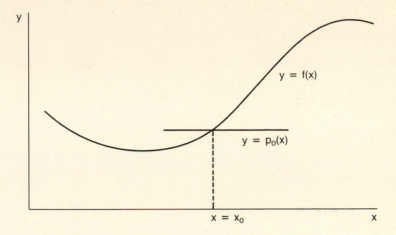

Figure C.2

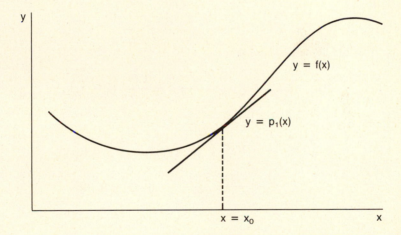

because

$$f(x) = (1 + x)^{24} \qquad \text{so } a_0 = (1.10)^{24}$$

$$f'(x) = 24(1 + x)^{23} \qquad \text{so } a_1 = 24(1.10)^{23}.$$

The right-hand side can be considered a function of x; as such, it is the simplest function having the same value at x_0 as f and the same derivative as f at x_0. If we wish to incorporate the value of $f''(x_0)$, we will naturally seek the simplest function p(x) that agrees with f at x_0 and whose first two derivatives are the same as f. The three conditions are

1. $p(x_0) = f(x_0)$

2. $p'(x_0) = f'(x_0)$

3. $p''(x_0) = f''(x_0)$

These equations uniquely determine the coefficients of a quadratic denoted p_2:

$$p_2(x) = a_0 + a_1(x - x_0) + a_2(x - x_0)^2.$$

Note that

$$p_2(x_0) = a_0 \Rightarrow a_0 = f(x_0)$$

$$p_2'(x) = 2a_2(x - x_0) + a_1 \Rightarrow p_2'(x_0) = a_1 \Rightarrow a_1 = f'(x_0)$$

$$p_2''(x) = 2a_2 \Rightarrow a_2 = \frac{f''(x_0)}{2}.$$

Therefore, a natural choice for approximating $f(x)$ for x near x_0 using two derivatives at x_0 is

$$p_2(x) = f(x_0) + f'(x_0)(x - x_0) + \frac{f''(x_0)}{2}(x - x_0)^2;$$

that is, it would be natural to use

$$f(x) \approx f(x_0) + f'(x_0)(x - x_0) + \frac{f''(x_0)}{2}(x - x_0)^2.$$

For example,

$$(1.11)^{24} \approx (1.10)^{24} + 24(1.10)^{23}(0.11 - 0.10)$$

$$+ \frac{(24)(23)(1.10)^{22}}{2}(0.11 - 0.10)^2$$

because

$$f(x) = (1 + x)^{24}, \qquad f'(x) = 24(1 + x)^{23}, \quad \text{and} \quad f''(x) = (24)(23)(1 + x)^{22}.$$

This is called the *Taylor series expansion* of f (or approximation) of order two (because two derivatives are used) at x_0. It has not only the same value as f at x_0 and the same slope at x_0, but also the same concavity; that is, near x_0, the graphs of f and the second-order Taylor polynomial have the same height, slope, and concavity. This is illustrated in Figure C.3.

The error is the distance between the graphs of $y = f(x)$ and $p_2(x) = a_0 + a_1(x - x_0) + a_2(x - x_0)^2$.

The general approximation using n derivatives is

$$f(x) \approx f(x_0) + f'(x_0)(x - x_0) + \frac{f''(x_0)}{2!}(x - x_0)^2$$

$$+ \frac{f'''(x_0)}{3!}(x - x_0)^3 + \cdots + \frac{f^{(n)}(x_0)}{n!}(x - x_0)^n.$$

Figure C.3

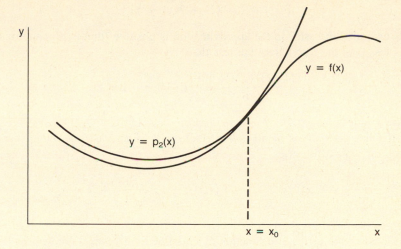

The approximating function is the polynomial of degree n, which mimics the behavior of f at x_0, at least through n derivatives. The higher the order n, the better the approximation usually is. The error $E(x)$ in the approximation depends on x (and, of course, x_0). Generally, the closer x is to x_0, the better the approximation. The most important fact about the error is that there is a value ξ between x_0 and x for which the error has the form

$$E(x) = \frac{f^{(n+1)}(x_0)}{n!}(\xi - x_0)^{n+1}.$$

In other words,

$$f(x) = f(x_0) + f'(x_0)(x - x_0) + \frac{f''(x_0)}{2!}(x - x_0)^2 + \frac{f'''(x_0)}{3!}(x - x_0)^3$$

$$+ \cdots + \frac{f^{(n)}(x_0)}{n!}(x - x_0)^n + \frac{f^{(n+1)}(x_0)}{n!}(\xi - x_0)^{n+1}$$

for some ξ between x_0 and x. This is called *Taylor's formula with remainder (or error) term*.

For example, in the approximation

$$(1.11)^{24} \approx (1.10)^{24} + 24(1.10)^{23}(0.11 - 0.10)$$

$$+ \frac{(24)(23)(1.10)^{22}}{2}(0.11 - 0.10)^2,$$

the error is of the form

$$E(0.11) = \frac{(24)(23)(22)(1.10)^{21}}{6}(\xi - 0.10)^3, \quad \text{where } 0.10 \le \xi \le 0.11$$

because

$$f'''(x) = (24)(23)(22)(1 + x)^{21}.$$

In this example, the error in the approximation is positive (that is, the approximation is less than the true value) but less than

$$\frac{(24)(23)(22)(1.10)^{21}}{6}(0.11 - 0.10)^3$$

because ξ is less than 0.11.

If f has derivatives of all orders, there will be at least one value, namely $x = x_0$, for which the series

$$\sum_{n=0}^{\infty} \frac{f^{(n)}(x_0)}{n!}(x - x_0)^n = f(x_0) + f'(x_0)(x - x_0) + \frac{f''(x_0)}{2}(x - x_0)^2 + \cdots$$

converges (to a finite value).

Consider the series as a function of x, defined wherever it converges. It can be shown that if the series converges at $x \neq x_0$, it converges at every value between x_0 and x. It follows that the set of points at which the series converges is either $(-\infty, \infty)$ or an interval centered on x_0. The endpoints of the interval may or may not be points of convergence. The distance from x_0 to an endpoint is called the *radius of convergence*.

All of the usual functions have the property that their Taylor series at x converges to f(x) if it converges at all. However, there are cases in which the series converges everywhere but converges to the function at only one point (see Gelbaum and Olmsted [1964]). We say that the Taylor series *represents* f if when it converges it converges to f. If r is the radius of convergence, for such a function we have

$$f(x) = \sum_{n=0}^{\infty} \frac{f^{(n)}(x_0)}{n!}(x - x_0)^n$$

for all x for which $|x - x_0| < r$ and the equation may or may not hold at $x = x_0 \pm r$. A sufficient condition for f to be represented by its Taylor series is that there be a number $M > 0$, which may depend on x_0, for which $|f^n(x_0)| \leq M$ for all $n = 0, 1, 2, \ldots$. For example, at $x_0 = 0$ the function $f(x) = \exp(x)$ satisfies this with $M = 1$. Hence,

$$e^x = \sum_{n=0}^{\infty} \left(\frac{1}{n!}\right)x^n = 1 + x + \frac{x^2}{2} + \frac{x^3}{3!} + \cdots.$$

The Taylor series expansions about $x_0 = 0$ are called *Maclaurin series*.

Some of the more important Taylor and Maclaurin series are as follows:

1. $e^x = \sum_{n=0}^{\infty} \left(\frac{1}{n!}\right)x^n = 1 + x + \frac{x^2}{2} + \frac{x^3}{3!} + \cdots$ for all x.

2. $\dfrac{1}{(1 - x)} = 1 + x + x^2 + x^3 + \cdots$ for all x such that $|x| < 1$.

3. $(1 + x)^a = \sum\limits_{k=0}^{\infty} C_{n,k} x^k$ for $|x| < 1$, where

$$C_{a,k} = \frac{a(a - 1)(a - 2)\ldots(a - k + 1)}{k!}.$$

4. $\ln\dfrac{1}{(1 - x)} = x + \dfrac{x^2}{2} + \dfrac{x^3}{3} + \dfrac{x^4}{4} + \cdots$, for all x such that $|x| < 1$.

5.   If f is represented by its Taylor series at x_0 with a radius of convergence r, so are f′ and ∫f with the same radius of convergence. In symbols, we have: If

$$f(x) = \sum\limits_{k=0}^{\infty} a_k(x - x_0)^k \quad \text{for } |x - x_0| < r,$$

then

$$f'(x) = \sum\limits_{k=0}^{\infty} ka_k(x - x_0)^{k-1}$$

and

$$\int_{x_0}^{x} f(u)du = \sum\limits_{k=0}^{\infty} \frac{a_k(x - x_0)^{k+1}}{(k + 1)}$$

provided $|x - x_0| < r$.

L'Hospital's Rule

A limit of the type lim f(x)/g(x) as $x \to a$ is called an *indeterminate form* if both numerator and denominator tend toward 0 or both tend toward $\pm\infty$. In this case, *L'Hospital's rule* often can be used to calculate the limit of the ratio (assuming that one exists). The rule is to replace the ratio f(x)/g(x) with the ratio f′(x)/g′(x). If the new limit exists (finite or infinite), so does the first, and they are equal.

Examples.

1.   Calculate

$$\lim_{x \to \infty} \frac{e^x}{x}.$$

Both $f(x) = e^x$ and $g(x) = x$ tend to $+\infty$ as $x \to +\infty$; thus, we cannot determine the limit by calculating each separately and dividing. L'Hospital's rule leads us to try calculating the limit of f′(x)/g′(x) = $e^x/1$. This limit is $+\infty$ and, hence, so is the first. Therefore,

$$\lim_{x \to \infty} \frac{e^x}{X} = \lim_{x \to \infty} \frac{e^x}{1} = +\infty \,.$$

2.   Similarly, we have

$$\lim_{t \to 0} \frac{(1 - e^{-0.10t})}{t} = \lim_{t \to 0} \frac{(0.10e^{-0.10t})}{1} = 0.10 \,.$$

3.   In evaluating the limit of the call option value of Chapter 15,

$$\text{call}(S, T, K) = SN(y) - Kv^TN(y - \sigma\sqrt{T}) \,,$$

where $y = [\ln(S/K) + T \ln(1 + r)]/\sigma\sqrt{T} + \sigma\sqrt{T}/2$ as K tends to $+\infty$, we encounter an indeterminate form. K tends to $+\infty$ and y tends to $-\infty$, whereas $N(y)$ and $N(y - \sigma\sqrt{T})$ both tend to 0. Hence, determining $\lim_{K \to \infty}$ call(S, T, K) reduces to determining $\lim_{K \to \infty} KN(y - \sigma\sqrt{T})$, which gives rise to indeterminate form $(+\infty)(0)$. We simplify the notation by writing $z = y - \sigma\sqrt{T}$ and noting that $z = -a \ln K + b$, where a and b are positive constants $(a = 1/\sigma\sqrt{T}, b = [\ln(S) + T \ln(1 + r)]/\sigma\sqrt{T} + \sigma\sqrt{T}/2)$.

With this notation, we have $K = \exp((b - z)/a)$ and

$$\lim_{K \to \infty} KN(y - \sigma\sqrt{T}) = \lim_{z \to -\infty} \frac{N(z)}{\exp((z - b)/a)} \,.$$

Since z tends to $-\infty$ as K tends to ∞, the limit on the right side gives rise to $0/0$. Hence L'Hospital's rule applies. Recalling that $N'(z) = \exp(-z^2/2)/\sqrt{2\pi}$, we obtain

$$\lim_{K \to \infty} KN(y - \sigma\sqrt{T}) = \lim_{z \to -\infty} \frac{\exp(-z^2/2)a}{\sqrt{2\pi} \exp((z - b)/a)}$$

$$= \frac{a}{\sqrt{2\pi}} \lim_{z \to -\infty} \frac{1}{\exp(z^2/2 + (z - b)/a)} \,.$$

Since $z^2/2 + (z - b)/a$ tends to $+\infty$ as z tends to $-\infty$, we find that $\exp(z^2/2 + (z - b)/a)$ tends to $+\infty$, so its reciprocal tends to 0. Hence,

$$\lim_{K \to \infty} KN(y - \sigma\sqrt{T}) = 0 \,.$$

Extreme Values and Curve Sketching of $y = f(x)$

Various rules and theorems are used in sketching the graph of a function. A function f is said to have a *maximum* (or *minimum*) at a point c on a set S (usually an interval or all of R) if $f(c) \geq f(x)$, or $f(c) \leq f(x)$, for any $c \varepsilon S$. The absolute maximum or minimum of a function is its maximum or minimum on its entire domain. The *extreme value theorem* says that if f is continuous on $[a, b]$, there will be points c_1 and c_2 in $[a, b]$ for which f will have a maximum and minimum, respectively, on $[a, b]$. A point is *interior* to an interval if it is not an endpoint of it. If f is differentiable on an interval and takes on its maximum (or minimum) value at x_0 in the interior of the interval, $f'(x_0) = 0$. This leads to a means of finding the extreme values: When seeking the maximum or minimum of a function f on a closed interval, check

1. The endpoints of the interval

2. The interior points of the interval where $f'(x) = 0$

3. The points in the interval at which the derivative of f does not exist

A point x_0 at which $f'(x_0) = 0$ or $f'(x_0)$ does not exist is called a *critical point*. Another way to phrase the rule is: The extreme values must occur at endpoints or critical points.

A function is said to be *strictly increasing* on an interval if $f(x_1) < f(x_2)$ whenever $x_1 < x_2$ in the interval. A *monotonic function* is one that is always increasing (or always decreasing). Sometimes a function is called *increasing* (but not "strictly increasing") if $f(x_1) \le f(x_2)$ whenever $x_1 < x_2$. In this sense, a constant function is increasing. A function is said to have a *relative* (or *local*) *maximum* at x_0 if there is an interval with x_0 as an interior point for which f has a maximum at x_0. A *relative minimum* is defined similarly.

It is useful to know intervals of increase and decrease and relative extrema when sketching a curve. If f is continuous on an interval and $f'(x) > 0$ for all x in the interval, f is strictly increasing on that interval; if $f'(x) < 0$ for all x in the interval, f is *strictly decreasing*. One way to determine relative extrema is to use the following rule: If f is increasing on some interval of the form $(x_0, x_0 + h)$ and decreasing on some interval of the form $(x_0 - h, x_0)$ with $h > 0$, then f has a relative minimum at x_0. Similarly, f has a relative maximum at x_0 if f is increasing on an interval to the left of x_0 and decreasing on an interval to the right of x_0. Note that if x_0 is a relative maximum or minimum and $f'(x_0)$ exists, $f'(x_0) = 0$.

The second derivative of a function also provides information relevant to curve sketching. A curve is said to be *concave up* (or *convex*) on an interval if it lies above any line tangent to the curve on the interval. For all x on an interval, if $f''(x) > 0$, the graph of f is concave up on it and concave down if $f''(x) < 0$. Another way to characterize a curve's being concave up or down is: A graph is concave up (down) if the line segment joining any two points on the graph lies above (below) it. A point at which the graph of a function changes from concave up to down, or vice versa, is a point of *inflection*. If $f''(x_0)$ exists and x_0 is an inflection point of f, then $f''(x_0) = 0$.

The second (and higher) derivative sometimes can be used to determine whether a critical point is a relative maximum or minimum. Suppose that $f'(c) = 0$ and $f''(c) \ne 0$. Then,

1. $f''(c) > 0$ implies that f has a relative minimum at c.

2. $f''(c) < 0$ implies that f has a relative maximum at c.

Information relevant to curve sketching also can be found from *asymptotes*, $\lim f(x)$ as $x \to \pm\infty$, and determining where $f(x) > 0$ and $f(x) < 0$.

Differentiation of Functions of Several Variables

Let f be a real valued function defined on a disk in R^2 containing (x_0, y_0). Then the partial derivative of f with respect to x at (x_0, y_0) is denoted

$$\frac{\partial f}{\partial x}\bigg|(x_0, y_0), \qquad f_x(x_0, y_0), \qquad f_1(x_0, y_0),$$

or

$$D_1 f(x_0, y_0),$$

the latter used more frequently in this text, and defined by

$$D_1 f(x_0, y_0) = \lim_{x \to x_0} \frac{f(x, y_0) - f(x_0, y_0)}{(x - x_0)}.$$

The partial with respect to y is similarly denoted and defined. To calculate $\partial f/\partial x$ for a given function $f(x, y)$, we simply hold y constant and differentiate as usual. The concept can be extended to three or more variables.

Example

If $f(x, y) = x^2 - 3xy + \ln(x^2 + y^2)$, then

$$D_1 f(x, y) = 2x - 3y + \frac{2x}{x^2 + y^2}.$$

A partial derivative will be a function of several variables; thus, a partial derivative of it may be taken. The following notation is used for second- and higher-order partial derivatives. For $f(x, y)$,

$$\frac{\partial}{\partial x}\left(\frac{\partial f}{\partial x}\right) = \frac{\partial^2 f}{\partial x^2} = f_{xx} = f_{11} = D_{11}f$$

and

$$\frac{\partial}{\partial x}\left(\frac{\partial f}{\partial y}\right) = \frac{\partial^2 f}{\partial x \partial y} = f_{yx} = f_{21} = D_{21}f.$$

For $f(x, y, z)$, we proceed in a similar manner, with the notation showing the order in which the partial derivatives are taken.

If $\partial f/\partial x$, $\partial f/\partial y$, and $\partial^2 f/\partial x \partial y$ exist and are continuous on a disk (or *ball*) in R^2 containing (x_0, y_0), the other mixed partial $\partial^2 f/\partial y \partial x$ exists and $\partial^2 f/\partial x \partial y = \partial^2 f/\partial y \partial x$. A similar result holds for functions of more variables.

There is a generalized chain rule for functions with more than one variable. If $u(x, y)$ and $v(x, y)$ are functions of two variables, $F(u, v) = f[u(x, y), v(x, y)]$ can be regarded as a function of u and v or as a composite function of x and y. The *chain rule* says,

$$\frac{\partial F}{\partial x} = \frac{\partial F}{\partial u} \cdot \frac{\partial u}{\partial x} + \frac{\partial F}{\partial v} \cdot \frac{\partial v}{\partial x}.$$

The *gradient* of $f(x, y)$ is denoted ∇f and equals $[D_1 f(x, y), D_2 f(x, y)]$. If evaluated at the point (x_0, y_0), $\nabla f(x_0, y_0)$ is also a point in R^2. Similarly, the gradient of $f(x, y, z)$ is $\nabla f = [D_1 f(x, y, z), D_2 f(x, y, z), D_3 f(x, y, z)]$ in R^3, and so on for functions of more variables. A point $P = (a, b)$ in R^2 (or R^n) can be regarded as a vector (or a directed line segment from the origin to P). (The operations of addition and scalar multiplication of vectors is reviewed in the section on optimization.) A *unit vector* is one whose distance from the origin is 1. Vectors can be added componentwise: $(a_1, b_1) + (a_2, b_2) = (a_1 + a_2, b_1 + b_2)$. In R^2, if i and j are taken to mean the unit vectors $(1, 0)$ and $(0, 1)$, respectively, then $(a, b) = ai + bj$. In R^3, if $i = (1, 0, 0)$, $j = (0, 1, 0)$, and $k = (0, 0, 1)$, then $(a, b, c) = ai + bj + ck$. If $p \varepsilon R^2$ is a vector (a, b) with length 1 (that is, $a^2 + b^2 = 1$), the directional derivative of $f(x, y)$ in the direction of p is denoted as follows:

$$D_p f(x, y) = \frac{\partial f}{\partial x} \cdot a + \frac{\partial f}{\partial y} \cdot b.$$

The *directional derivative* gives the rate of change of f in a particular direction, that is, the direction in which the unit vector p points from the origin.

Example.   Determine the rate of change of $f(x, y) = xy$ in the upward direction along the line $y = x$.

Solution: First, we find

$$\nabla f(x, y) = (y, x).$$

The vector $u = (2^{-1/2}, 2^{-1/2})$ is of length 1 in the upward direction of the line $y = x$ in R^2. Therefore, at the point (x, y), the rate of change of the function f in the direction of u is

$$D_u f(x, y) = yu_1 + xu_2$$

$$= \frac{(y + x)}{\sqrt{2}}.$$

The rate of change of f at $(\frac{1}{2}, 1)$ in this direction is

$$D_u f(\tfrac{1}{2}, 1) = (1)(2^{-1/2}) + (\tfrac{1}{2})(2^{-1/2}) = (\tfrac{3}{2})(2^{-1/2}).$$

In general, if p is a unit vector in R^n and f: $U \to R$, where f is a differentiable function defined on a ball $U \subseteq R^n$ containing x, then $D_p f(x) = [\nabla f(x)]p^T$. (The notation would be $[\nabla f(X)^T p]$ if we used column vectors to represent elements of R^n instead of row vectors.)

A function $f(x, y)$ is said to have a relative maximum at (x_0, y_0) if there is a disk in R^2 about (x_0, y_0) such that $f(x_0, y_0) \geq f(x, y)$ for any point (x, y) in the disk. A relative minimum is defined similarly. If partial derivatives exist at a relative maximum or minimum, they equal zero there.

Relative extrema for a function of two variables sometimes can be found by the two-variable analog of the second-derivative test. Suppose that $z = f(x, y)$ has continuous partial second-order derivatives defined on a disk containing (x_0, y_0). Let

$$\Delta = \left[\left(\frac{\partial^2 z}{\partial x^2} \right) \left(\frac{\partial^2 z}{\partial y^2} \right) - \left(\frac{\partial^2 z}{\partial x \partial y} \right)^2 \right] \Bigg|_{(x_0, y_0)}.$$

If $\partial z/\partial x = \partial z/\partial y = 0$ at (x_0, y_0), we have the following results:

1. If $\Delta > 0$ and $(\partial^2 z/\partial x^2) > 0$, f has a local minimum.

2. If $\Delta > 0$ and $(\partial^2 z/\partial x^2) < 0$, f has a local maximum.

3. If $\Delta < 0$, f has neither a local maximum nor a local minimum.

Note that

1. The test says nothing when $\Delta = 0$; in fact, there could be a maximum, a minimum, or neither.

2. The number Δ in the test is called the *Hessian* of f at (x_0, y_0).

Example 1. Determine the relative maximum or minimum of

$$f(x, y) = y^2 + x^2 y + x^4.$$

Solution: If f has a relative extreme value at (x, y), then $\partial f/\partial x$ and $\partial f/\partial y$ must vanish at (x, y). Thus, to find extrema of f we start with simultaneous solutions of

$$\frac{\partial f}{\partial x} = 2xy + 4x^3 = 0$$

and

$$\frac{\partial f}{\partial y} = 2y + x^2 = 0.$$

The only solution is $(0, 0)$. The Hessian is

$$\Delta(x, y) = \left(\frac{\partial^2 f}{\partial x^2}\right)\left(\frac{\partial^2 f}{\partial y^2}\right) - \left(\frac{\partial^2 f}{\partial x \partial y}\right)^2 = (2y + 12x^2) - (2x)^2 = 4y + 20x^2.$$

Hence, at $(0, 0)$, $\Delta = 0$.

The above test provides no information. Since f can be rearranged to $f(x, y) = [(y + x^2/2)^2 + 3x^4/4]$, then clearly $f(x, y) > 0 = f(0, 0)$ for all $(x, y) \neq (0, 0)$. Thus, f has an absolute minimum at $(0, 0)$ even though $\Delta = 0$ at $(0, 0)$.

Example 2. Determine the relative extrema of

$$f(x, y) = x^2 + y^2 + x + y + xy.$$

Solution: We start by solving the following system of equations:

$$\frac{\partial f}{\partial x} = 2x + 1 + y = 0$$

$$\frac{\partial f}{\partial y} = 2y + 1 + x = 0$$

The only solution is $x = y = -\frac{1}{3}$. The Hessian is a constant,

$$\Delta(x, y) = (2)(2) - (1)^2 = 3 > 0.$$

Hence, at $(-\frac{1}{3}, -\frac{1}{3})$ f has a local minimum, since $\Delta = 3 > 0$ and $\partial^2 f / \partial x^2 = 2 > 0$.

Finding extreme values of f over a subset of its domain is demonstrated in the section on optimization.

Antiderivatives and Integration

If $F'(x) = f(x)$, then F is an *antiderivative* of f. If c is a constant and $F(x)$ is an antiderivative of f, then so is $G(x) = F(x) + c$. Another way of saying that F is an antiderivative of f is: $\int f = F$, or $\int f = F + c$, or $\int f(x)\,dx = F(x) + c$; this is also called an *indefinite integral*, with $f(x)$ being the *integrand*.

The *fundamental theorem of calculus* gives the link between integration (limits of sums) and antidifferentiation. It is this theorem that makes antidifferentiation so important. On its own, the equation $\int f(x)\,dx = F(x) + c$ means no more or less than the differential equation $F'(x) = f(x)$. Before defining integration, let us translate the rules of differentiation into rules for antidifferentiation:

$f(x)$	$\int f(x)\,dx$
$ag(x) + bh(x)$	$a\int g(x)\,dx + b\int h(x)\,dx + c$
$x^n \ (n \neq -1)$	$\dfrac{(x^{n+1})}{(n+1)} + c$
$\dfrac{1}{x}$	$\ln|x| + c$
e^x	$e^x + c$
a^x	$\dfrac{a^x}{\ln a} + c$

An antiderivative can always be checked by differentiating. The *definite integral* of a function $f(x)$ from a to b is the "signed area" between the graph of the function and the x-axis from a to b. If f is negative, the signed area is taken as negative and will cancel with a positive signed area. Thus, the definite integral, strictly speaking, is not the "area under the curve."

The definite integral is defined as a *limit*. Let f be a function defined and bounded on $[a, b]$. By a *partition* of $[a, b]$, we mean a finite set P of numbers $x_0 < x_1 < \cdots < x_n$ such that $a = x_0$ and $b = x_n$. By a Reimann sum of f, corresponding to P, we mean a number $S(P, f)$ given by

$$S(P, f) = f(t_0) \cdot \Delta x_0 + f(t_1) \cdot \Delta x_1 + \cdots + f(t_{n-1}) \cdot \Delta x_{n-1},$$

where t_k is a point in the interval $[x_k, x_{k+1}]$ and $\Delta x_k = x_{k+1} - x_k$ for $k = 0, 1, \ldots, n - 1$. By definition, f is integrable on $[a, b]$ if there is a number, denoted

$$\int_a^b f(x)\,dx,$$

such that for every $\varepsilon > 0$ there is a partition P_ε of $[a, b]$ such that

$$\left| S(P, f) - \int_a^b f(x)\,dx \right| < \varepsilon$$

whenever P is a partition of [a, b] such that $P_\varepsilon \subseteq P$. The definite integral is sometimes called the *Riemann integral* and is denoted

$$\int_a^b f(x)\,dx\,.$$

Suppose that for each n, P_n denotes the partition $\{a, a + \Delta x, a + 2\Delta x, \ldots, a + n\Delta x = b\}$ where $\Delta x = (b - a)/n$. If the function is integrable, then, by using the partitions $P_1, P_2, \ldots$, we can calculate the integral of f as the limit of an infinite sequence. The summation notation used is defined as follows:

$$\sum_{k=0}^n y_k = y_0 + y_1 + y_2 + \cdots + y_{n-1} + y_n\,.$$

The definite integral, then, is

$$\int_a^b f(x)\,dx = \lim S(P_n, f) \quad \text{as } n \to \infty$$

$$= \lim \sum_{k=0}^{n-1} f(a + k\Delta x)\,(\Delta x) \quad \text{as } n \to \infty$$

$$= \lim \sum_{k=1}^{n} f(a + k\Delta x)\,(\Delta x) \quad \text{as } n \to \infty$$

where, in computing $S(P_n, f)$, we can take $t_k = x_k$ or x_{k+1} and $\Delta x = (b - a)/n$. It is worth noting that

$$\sum_{k=0}^{n-1} f(a + k\Delta x)\,(\Delta x)$$

represents the sum of the "areas" of n rectangles, each with base Δx and heights $f(a), f(a + \Delta x), \ldots, f[a + (n - 1)\,(\Delta x)]$:

$$A_0 = f(a)\,(\Delta x)$$

$$A_1 = f(a + \Delta x)\,(\Delta x)$$

$$\cdot$$
$$\cdot$$
$$\cdot$$

$$A_k = f(a + k\Delta x)\,(\Delta x)\,.$$

One of the most important results of calculus, the fundamental theorem of calculus, links the definite integral of f with antiderivatives of f and demonstrates the importance of being able to find antiderivatives.

Fundamental Theorem of Calculus. Let f be a function continuous on [a, b]. If F is differentiable and satisfies $F'(x) = f(x)$ for all $a < x < b$, then

$$\int_a^b f(x)\,dx = F(b) - F(a).$$

Example 1. Evaluate

$$\int_1^3 x^2\,dx.$$

Solution: Since the derivative of $F(x) = x^3/3$ is $F'(x) = x^2$, we can evaluate this integral by means of the fundamental theorem:

$$\int_1^3 x^2\,dx = F(3) - F(1) = 3^3 - 1^3 = 26.$$

The fundamental theorem sometimes is written in the following form:

$$\frac{d}{dx}\left[\int_a^x f(t)\,dt\right] = f(x).$$

Thus, if

$$F(x) = \int_a^x f(t)\,dt,$$

then $F'(x) = f(x)$. By the chain rule, we then see that if

$$G(x) = \int_a^{g(x)} f(t)\,dt,$$

then $G(x) = F[g(x)]$ and, hence, $G'(x) = F'[g(x)]g'(x) = f[g(x)]g'(x)$.

Some important rules of integration are

1. $\displaystyle\int_a^b f(x)\,dx = \int_a^c f(x)\,dx + \int_c^b f(x)\,dx.$

2. $\displaystyle\int_a^a f(x)\,dx = 0.$

3. $\displaystyle\int_a^b f(x)\,dx = -\int_b^a f(x)\,dx.$

4. $\displaystyle\int_a^b kf(x)\,dx = k\int_a^b f(x)\,dx.$

5. $\displaystyle\int_a^b [f(x) + g(x)]\,dx = \int_a^b f(x)\,dx + \int_a^b g(x)\,dx.$

6.   If $f(x) \le g(x)$ for all x in [a, b], then

$$\int_a^b f(x)\,dx \le \int_a^b g(x)\,dx .$$

7.   If $m \le f(x) \le M$ for all x in [a, b], then

$$m(b - a) \le \int_a^b f(x)\,dx \le M(b - a) .$$

8.   *Mean value theorem for integrals:* If f is continuous on [a, b], there is a number c in [a, b] such that

$$\int_a^b f(x)\,dx = f(c)\,(b - a) .$$

In this case,

$$f(c) = \frac{\displaystyle\int_a^b f(x)\,dx}{b - a}$$

is called the *average value* of f on [a, b].

Optimization

Introduction

Many financial models lead to a function $f: D \to R$ defined on a subset $D \subset R^n$ that is to be maximized or minimized subject to some constraints. For example, an individual's investment decision (see Chapter 2) might lead to maximizing his or her utility function,

$$u(x_0, x_1) = x_0^2 x_1 ,$$

which measures the individual's preference for current x_0 versus future x_1 consumption. The choices are constrained by inequalities $x_0 \ge 0$, $x_1 \ge 0$, and an equation that, for illustrative purposes, we take to be

$$x_1 + 0.014x_0^2 - 0.4x_0 - 100 = 0 .$$

The abbreviated way to write this problem is

maximize $u(x_0, x_1) = x_0^2 x_1$

subject to $x_1 + 0.014x_0^2 - 0.4x_0 - 100 = 0$

and $x_0 \ge 0, \qquad x_1 \ge 0.$

We use two methods for solving such a problem: (1) the substitution method and (2) the Lagrangian method.

Substitution Method

Step 1. Solve the constraint for one variable in terms of the other. In this example, we solve $x_1 + 0.014x_0^2 - 0.4x_0 - 100 = 0$ for x_1 in terms of x_0:

$$x_1 = -0.014x_0^2 + 0.4x_0 + 100 .$$

Note that the positive value of x_0 that corresponds to $x_1 = 0$ is $x_0 = 100$. Thus, the two inequality constraints correspond to two constraints on x_0: $0 \le x_0 \le 100$.

Step 2. Substitute the result of step 1 into the function to be maximized, eliminating one of the variables. Let us call the resulting function of one variable f. In the example we eliminate x_1, obtaining the utility as a function of x_0 alone. In effect, we have replaced the original two-variable, constrained problem with a one-variable problem unconstrained except that $0 \le x_0 \le 100$:

$$f(x_0) = u(x_0, x_1)$$

$$= u(x_0, -0.014x_0^2 + 0.4x_0 + 100)$$

$$= x_0^2(-0.014x_0^2 + 0.4x_0 + 100)$$

$$= -0.014x_0^4 + 0.4x_0^3 + 100x_0^2 .$$

Step 3. Solve the one-variable problem with the techniques of ordinary calculus. The solution is either a zero of the derivative or an endpoint of the interval [0, 100]:

$$f'(x_0) = (-0.014)(4)x_0^3 + (0.4)(3)x_0^2 + 100(2)x_0$$

$$= x_0(-0.056x_0^2 + 1.2x_0 + 200)$$

and

$$f''(x_0) = -0.168x_0^2 + 2.4x_0 + 200 .$$

The zeros of $f'(x_0)$ in [0, 100] are $x_0 = 0$ and $x_0 = 71.4$, which, according to the second-derivative test, are, respectively, a local minimum and a local maximum. It follows, then, that the optimal choice is $x_0 = 71.4$ and $x_1 = -0.014(71.4)^2 + 0.4(71.4) + 100 = 57.1$.

Lagrangian Method

Step 1. Introduce a new variable, λ, called the *Lagrange multiplier* of the problem. It multiplies the equality constraint, and the result is added to the function to be maximized. The new function is called the *Lagrangian* of the problem and denoted $L(x_0, x_1, \lambda)$. In this example, it is

$$L(x_0, x_1, \lambda) = x_0^2 x_1 + \lambda(x_1 + 0.014x_0^2 - 0.4x_0 - 100) .$$

Step 2. Solve the problem of maximizing L, subject only to the inequality constraints $x_0 \ge 0$ and $x_1 \ge 0$. At a point where $x_0 > 0$ and $x_1 > 0$, the partial derivatives of L must be zero. Therefore, the second step is to calculate the partials of L with respect to x_0, x_1, and λ:

$$\frac{\partial L}{\partial x_0} = 2x_0x_1 + \lambda(0.028x_0 - 0.4)$$

$$\frac{\partial L}{\partial x_1} = x_0^2 + \lambda$$

$$\frac{\partial L}{\partial \lambda} = x_1 + 0.014x_0^2 - 0.4x_0 - 100.$$

Step 3. Solve the system of equations obtained by setting each partial derivative of L equal to zero. In this example, the system to solve is

$$2x_0x_1 + \lambda(0.028x_0 - 0.4) = 0$$

$$x_0^2 + \lambda = 0$$

$$x_1 + 0.014x_0^2 - 0.4x_0 - 100 = 0.$$

We can use the second equation to eliminate λ from the first. This gives an equivalent set of two equations:

$$2x_0x_1 - x_0^2(0.028x_0 - 0.4) = 0$$

$$x_1 + 0.014x_0^2 - 0.4x_0 - 100 = 0.$$

For those solutions having $x_0 > 0$, this is the same as

$$x_1 - x_0(0.014x_0 - 0.2) = 0$$

$$x_1 + 0.014x_0^2 - 0.4x_0 - 100 = 0.$$

Subtracting the first equation from the second yields an equation that x_0 must satisfy in any solution having $x_0 > 0$:

$$0.028x_0^2 - 0.6x_0 - 100 = 0.$$

The positive solution of this equation is $x_0 = 71.4$ and, consequently, $x_1 = 57.1$ as before.

Substitution Method versus Lagrangian Method. The substitution method does not apply very often, which is why other methods were developed. This is because the constraints cannot always be solved easily. Even when solving is possible, the Lagrangian method usually is more efficient because the process of differentiation generally simplifies a function (for example, the derivative of a quadratic is linear). Further, in Lagrange's method the equations to be solved are the derivatives set to zero plus the constraints. Since an explicit, or closed-form, solution is unnecessary, the system of equations usually is solved numerically on a computer. Finally, the Lagrangian method can be extended to incorporate inequality constraints.

Mathematical Details

The mathematical details presented here are taken from Luenberger (1969, Chapter 7), to which the interested reader is referred. We have specialized Luenberger's account to functions defined on a subset of n-space. This means that our problems have solutions that are n-vectors.[1]

Let $f: D \rightarrow R$ be a function defined on a subset D of n-space R^n. Suppose that f has partial derivatives $D_1f(x_0), D_2f(x_0), \ldots, D_nf(x_0)$ at $x_0 \varepsilon D$; that is, f has a gradient $\nabla f(x_0) = [D_1f(x_0), D_2f(x_0), \ldots, D_nf(x_0)]$ at x_0. The linear function mapping R^n into R is defined by

$$\delta f(x_0; h) = h^T[\nabla f(x_0)]$$

$$= h_1D_1f(x_0) + h_2D_2f(x_0) + \ldots + h_nD_nf(x_0)$$

is called the *differential* of f at x_0. This contains no more information than the gradient, but it is in a form convenient for presenting these results. Note that where $n = 1$ such that f is defined on a subset of the real line $(-\infty, \infty)$, the differential is simply

$$\delta f(x_0; h) = hf'(x_0),$$

considered as a function of $h \varepsilon (-\infty, \infty)$. Note that $f'(x_0) = 0$ if—and only if— the differential $\delta f(x_0; h) = 0$ for all h. For larger values of n, the condition $\delta f(x_0; h) = 0$ for all $h \varepsilon R^n$ is equivalent to $D_1f(x_0) = 0$ for each $i = 1, \ldots, n$.

This form of the notion of differentiability generalizes to functions defined on subsets of linear spaces, while the gradient does not. The more general concept is called the *Frechet differential* of f at x_0, defined as follows. Let D be an open subset of a normed linear space V and $f: D \rightarrow R$ a function mapping D into R. Note that since D is open, all the vectors sufficiently near x_0 are also in the domain D of f. The Frechet differential of f at $x_0 \varepsilon D$, if it exists, is a linear mapping $\delta f(x_0, *): D \rightarrow V$, which satisfies the following condition:

$$\frac{|f(x_0 + h) - f(x_0) - \delta f(x_0; h)|}{|h|} \rightarrow 0 \quad \text{as } |h| \rightarrow 0.$$

Note that where $V = R$ and $W = R$, the usual differential is the Frechet differential, since $|f(x_0 + h) - f(x_0) - \delta f(x_0; h)|/|h| = |f(x_0 + h) - f(x_0) - hf'(x_0)|/|h| = |[f(x_0 + h) - f(x_0)]/h - f'(x_0)|$ tends to zero as h does. Similarly, for higher values of n, the Frechet differential is the usual one.

For the remainder of this section, D denotes an open subset of a normed linear space V and $f: D \rightarrow R$ is a function mapping D into R and $x_0 \varepsilon D$.

Theorem 1. If f has a local minimum or maximum at $x_0 \varepsilon D$ and is Frechet differentiable at x_0, then $\delta f(x_0; h) = 0$ for all $h \varepsilon V$.

---

[1]In some areas of finance, there exist optimization problems for which the solution is a function defined on an interval [a, b]. The models describing the interaction between a principal and an agent are examples, because the contracts between them often are represented by a set of functions. In this case, we are forced to consider the optimization of functions defined on sets of functions and replace n-space with a linear space of functions, that is, the set of functions differentiable on a given interval [a, b].

In view of the previous remark concerning the case of $V = R^n$ and $V = R$, we see that this is a generalization of the fact that the partial derivatives $D_i f(x_0)$ equal zero if f has a maximum or minimum at x_0. Points at which the differential vanishes are called *stationary points*.

Now we consider k constraints given by Frechet-differentiable functions $g_j : D \rightarrow R$, $j = 1, \ldots, k$. We are seeking to maximize (or minimize) f(x) subject to the constraints $g_j(x) = 0$ for all j. We combine the constraint equations with f to form the Lagrangian

$$L(x, \lambda_1, \lambda_2, \ldots, \lambda_k) = f(x) + \lambda_1 g_1(x) + \lambda_2 g_2(x) + \ldots + \lambda_k g_k(x).$$

In the earlier example, we saw that a local extremum satisfying the constraints was a stationary point of the Lagrangian. This gave, in turn, a system of equations to solve involving the derivatives of the constraints. In the current notation, the equations are

$$\delta f(x; h) + \lambda_1 \delta g_1(x; h) + \lambda_2 \delta g_2(x; h) + \ldots + \lambda_k \delta g_k(x; h) = 0 \quad \text{for all } h \; \varepsilon \; V$$

and the constraints $g_j(x) = 0$ for all j. In order to solve for the λ_i, we need linear independence of the differentials. This turns out to be sufficient in the general case as well. To formalize this, we define a regular point of the system of constraints, $g_j(x) = 0$ for all j, to be any point x_0 for which the linear mappings $\delta g_j(x_0; *) : V \rightarrow R$ are linearly independent (in the space of all linear mappings $V \rightarrow R$).

Theorem 2. If x* is a local maximum or minimum of f subject to the constraints $g_j(x) = 0$ for all $j = 1$ to k and if x* is a regular point of the constraints, there are values of $\lambda_1, \ldots, \lambda_k$ for which x* is a stationary point of the Lagrange function:

$$L(x, \lambda_1, \lambda_2, \ldots, \lambda_k) = f(x) + \lambda_1 g_1(x) + \lambda_2 g_2(x) + \ldots + \lambda_k g_k(x).$$

This tells us that the points at which f attains its local extreme values are among those satisfying the functional equation

$$\delta L(x, \lambda_1, \lambda_2, \ldots, \lambda_k; h) = 0 \quad \text{for all } h \; \varepsilon \; V x R^k.$$

In the case where we are dealing with $V = R^n$, this reduces to the vector equation $\nabla L = 0$, which in turn is equivalent to the n + k scalar equations,

$$\frac{\partial L}{\partial x_i} = 0 \quad \text{for } i = 1, 2, \ldots, n$$

$$\frac{\partial L}{\partial \lambda_j} = 0 \quad \text{for } j = 1, 2, \ldots, k.$$

Optimizing Quadratic Forms

Consider the problem of minimizing an arbitrary quadratic form subject to linear constraints:

minimize $x^T A x + B x$

subject to $Cx = D$,

where A is a symmetric positive definite n-by-n matrix, B is a 1-by-n vector, C is k-by-n, and D is k-by-1.

The mean-variance portfolio selection problem is of this type. Here the investor seeks to minimize the portfolio variance $\sigma^2(x) = x^T\Sigma x$, where Σ is the covariance matrix of the returns on n given assets. The portfolio must satisfy the following two constraints:

$$x^T e = 1 \quad \text{where } e^T = 1,1,1,\ldots,1$$

and

$$x^T M = \mu \quad \text{where } M^T = (m_1, m_2, \ldots, m_n) \text{ is the vector}$$
$$\text{of expected returns on the given assets}.$$

In the current framework, we would let $B = 0$, $A = \Sigma$, $D^T = (1, \mu)$ and C the 2-by-n matrix having e^T as its first row and M^T as its second.

Now we return to the problem of minimizing an arbitrary quadratic form subject to linear constraints. In terms of the notation of Theorem 2, $f(x) = x^T Ax + Bx$ maps $D = R^n$ into R. The constraint functions are $g_i(x) = C_i x - d_i$, where C_i is the ith row of C and d_i is the ith element of D. The differentials are

$$\delta f(x_0; h) = 2(Ax_0 + B)^T h \quad \text{for all } h \; \varepsilon \; R^n$$

and

$$\delta g_i(x; h) = C_i h \quad \text{for all } h \; \varepsilon \; R^n \quad \text{for } i = 1, \ldots, k.$$

The requirement that the constraints have a solution as a regular point will be satisfied if C has rank k, which we will suppose. Then Theorem 2 shows that for any solution x* of the constrained problem, there will be Lagrange multipliers for which the function

$$L(x, \lambda_1, \lambda_2, \ldots, \lambda_k) = f(x) + \lambda_1 g_1(x) + \lambda_2 g_2(x) + \ldots + \lambda_k g_k(x)$$

will have a stationary point at x*. This being the case, we must have

$$\delta f(x^*; h) + \lambda_1 \delta g_1(x; h) + \lambda_2 \delta g_2(x; h) + \ldots + \lambda_k \delta g_k(x; h) = 0 \quad \text{for all } h \; \varepsilon \; V$$

or, equivalently,

$$2(Ax^* + B)^T h + \lambda_1 C_1 h + \lambda_2 C_2 h + \ldots + \lambda_k C_k h = 0 \quad \text{for all } h \; \varepsilon \; R^n.$$

This means that

$$2(Ax^* + B) + \lambda_1 C_1^T + \lambda_2 C_2^T + \ldots + \lambda_k C_k^T = 0,$$

since it is orthogonal to every vector h of R^n. Rearranging these matrices gives

$$2Ax^* + B = -(\lambda_1 C_1^T + \lambda_2 C_2^T + \ldots + \lambda_k C_k^T)$$

$$2Ax^* + B = -C^T(\lambda_1, \lambda_2, \ldots, \lambda_k)^T = -C^T\lambda,$$

where $\lambda = (\lambda_1, \lambda_2, \ldots, \lambda_k)^T$. Also, of course, x* satisfies the constraints $C_i x^* = d_i$ for all $i = 1$ to k or $Cx_0 = D$. We now use the assumption that C has rank k to eliminate the λ_i. Since A is positive definite, it is invertible; hence,

$$x^* = -\left(\frac{1}{2}\right)A^{-1}(C^T\lambda + B).$$

Substituting in the constraints $Cx^* = D$ for x^*, we get

$$D = Cx^*$$

$$2D = -CA^{-1}C^T\lambda - CA^{-1}B$$

$$CA^{-1}C^T\lambda = -2D - CA^{-1}B.$$

Now, because C has rank k and A is invertible, $CA^{-1}C^T$ also has rank k. Since it is of size k-by-k and of rank k, it too is invertible. This gives the multipliers

$$\lambda = -(CA^{-1}C^T)^{-1}(2D + CA^{-1}B),$$

which we can now substitute into

$$x^* = -\left(\frac{1}{2}\right)A^{-1}(C^T\lambda + B)$$

in order to find x^*.

When minimum variance portfolios are to be found, $B = 0$, A is the covariance matrix (usually denoted Σ or C), $D^T = [1, \mu]$, and the other part of the constraint,

$$C = \begin{bmatrix} 1, 1, \ldots, 1 \\ m_1, m_2, \ldots, m_n \end{bmatrix},$$

has rank $k = 2$ if — and only if — there are two assets with different expected returns, which is a mild requirement. This approach to the problem is similar to the development given by Roll (1977). The formula for the multipliers becomes

$$\lambda = -\left(C\Sigma^{-1}C^T\right)^{-1}(2D),$$

and the formula for x^* becomes

$$x^* = -\left(\frac{1}{2}\right)\Sigma^{-1}(C^T\lambda).$$

Now we can describe the formal solution of the mean-variance portfolio problem. Given n assets with expected returns $m_1, m_2, \ldots, m_n$, at least two of which are different, and covariance matrix Σ, which is positive definite, we proceed as follows:

1.   Calculate Σ^{-1}.

2.   Calculate

$$H = \begin{bmatrix} 1, 1, \ldots, 1 \\ m_1, m_2, \ldots, m_n \end{bmatrix} \Sigma^{-1} \begin{bmatrix} 1, 1, \ldots, 1 \\ m_1, m_2, \ldots, m_n \end{bmatrix}^T.$$

3.   Calculate H^{-1}.

4.   Calculate $[\lambda_1, \lambda_2]^T = -2H^{-1}[1, \mu]^T$.

5.   Calculate

$$x^* = -\left(\frac{1}{2}\right)\Sigma^{-1}\begin{bmatrix} 1, 1, \ldots, 1 \\ m_1, m_2, \ldots, m_n \end{bmatrix}^T \{-2H^{-1}[1, \mu]^T\}$$

$$= \Sigma^{-1}\begin{bmatrix} 1, 1, \ldots, 1 \\ m_1, m_2, \ldots, m_n \end{bmatrix}^T H^{-1}[1, \mu]^T.$$

The nature of the set of points (σ^2, μ) for which σ^2 is the variance of the optimal portfolio x^* is obtained by determining $\sigma^2(x^*)$ as a function of μ. We label the entries in the 2-by-2 matrix H as follows:

$$H = \begin{bmatrix} a & b \\ c & d \end{bmatrix}.$$

[margin note: $H^{-1} = \dfrac{\begin{vmatrix} d & -c \\ -b & a \end{vmatrix}}{ad - bc}$]

Now we have

$$\sigma^2(x^*) = x^{*T}\Sigma x^*$$

$$= x^{*T}\left[\left(-\frac{1}{2}\right)C^T\lambda\right]$$

$$= \left(-\frac{1}{2}\right)(Cx^*)^T\lambda$$

$$= \left(-\frac{1}{2}\right)D^T\lambda$$

and

$$\lambda = -\left(C\Sigma^{-1}C^T\right)^{-1}(2D)$$

$$= -2H^{-1}D. \quad \checkmark$$

Hence,

$$\sigma^2(x^*) = \left(-\frac{1}{2}\right)D^T\lambda$$

$$= \left(-\frac{1}{2}\right)D^T(-2H^{-1}D)$$

[margin note: is this correct?]

$$= D^T H^{-1}D$$

$$= \frac{1}{ac - b^2}[1, \mu]\begin{bmatrix} c & -b \\ -b & a \end{bmatrix}\begin{bmatrix} 1 \\ \mu \end{bmatrix}$$

$$= \frac{c - 2b\mu + a\mu^2}{ac - b^2}.$$

Now we see that so long as the parameters of the distribution of the n assets (that is, their means and covariances) remain unchanged, the factors a, b, c, and d will not change either. Thus, the variance $\sigma^2(x^*)$ of the optimal portfolio is a quadratic function of the investor's required return, μ. The graph of a quadratic is a parabola and is determined by the coefficients. In finance, it is traditional to plot μ on the vertical axis (even though we think of it as the independent variable) and $\sigma^2(x^*)$ on the horizontal axis. Since H is positive definite, a, c, and $ac - b^2$ are positive; hence, the parabola opens to the right. Its leftmost point is its minimum. This is the minimum variance regardless of the value of μ. It occurs at the value of μ for which

$$\frac{\partial \sigma^2(x^*)}{\partial \mu} = 0 .$$

This value of μ is b/a and the corresponding variance $1/a$.

This method (finding Σ^{-1}, H^{-1}, and so on) gives insight on the nature of the relationship between σ^2 and μ. However, it may not be the best way to calculate the portfolio x^* itself, especially if Σ is changing from time to time. This is because matrix inversion is time consuming and may be inaccurate when the coefficient matrix is nearly singular. However, once H^{-1} is obtained, it is not necessary to recalculate it until the parameters of the distributions have changed.

For calculating portfolios of three or more assets on a computer, it may be more practical to use an iterative procedure based on the equations

$$2\Sigma x^* + C^T \lambda = 0$$

and

$$Cx^* = D .$$

We would regard this as a system of $n + 2$ equations in $n + 2$ unknowns, the n coordinates of x^* and the 2 coordinates of λ. The matrix equation of this system is

$$\begin{bmatrix} 2\Sigma & C^T \\ C & 0 \end{bmatrix} \begin{bmatrix} x^* \\ \lambda \end{bmatrix} = \begin{bmatrix} 0 \\ D \end{bmatrix}$$

where the zero in the coefficient matrix represents a 2-by-2 matrix of zeros. Because C has rank 2 and Σ rank n, the new coefficient matrix has rank $n + 2$ and, hence, a solution exists. We recommend one of the widely available computer programs (most of which are based on an iterative procedure or Gaussian elimination rather than matrix inversion) for solving these linear equations. Readers who have microcomputers with spreadsheet programs can write an iterative procedure with which to easily solve this system for as many as 20 assets. The λ is obtained simultaneously with the x^*. Having λ makes calculating the resulting variance easy:

$$\sigma^2(x^*) = \left(\frac{1}{2}\right) D^T \lambda .$$

Then one could find points on the parabola that is the graph of the relationship between $\sigma^2(x^*)$ and μ by running the program for several different values of μ.

Thus, it would not be necessary to find Σ^{-1} or H and, as needed, one could simply update the covariance matrix.

Probability and Statistics

Probability Spaces

A *probability space* consists of a triple (Ω, Φ, P) where Ω is a non-void set whose elements represent "outcomes" or "states of the world" that might occur; Φ is a collection of events, that is, a set of subsets of Ω; and P is a mapping from Φ to $[0, 1]$ that gives the probability $P[E]$ for each event $E \ \varepsilon \ \Phi$. By definition, the triple (Ω, Φ, P) must satisfy the following conditions:

1. The events ϕ and Ω belong to Φ and $P[\phi] = 0$ and $P[\Omega] = 1$.

2. If an event E is in Φ, its relative complement, $E^c = \Omega \backslash E$ is too.

3. If $A_1, A_2, \ldots$ is a sequence of elements of Φ, then $\cup_{i=1}^{\infty} A_i$ is too. Moreover, if the sequence is pairwise disjoint, then

$$P\left[\bigcup_{i=1}^{\infty} A_i\right] = \sum_{i=1}^{\infty} P[A_i].$$

By definition, the sequence $A_1, A_2, \ldots$ is *pairwise disjoint* if, for all i and j, $A_i \cap A_j = \phi$. Disjoint events are also called *mutually exclusive* events.

The collection Φ in the definition is called a σ-*algebra* or an *event space*. The function P is called a *probability measure*, and $P[A]$ is thought of as the probability that A will occur. $P[A \cup B]$ is the probability of A or B, $P[A \cap B]$ is the probability of A and B, and so on. Because

$$\left[\bigcup_{i=1}^{\infty} A_i\right]^c = \bigcap_{i=1}^{\infty} A_i^c,$$

then, because of conditions 2 and 3 above, the intersection of a sequence A_1, $A_2, \ldots$ of events of Φ is also in Φ. Events E for which $P[E] = 0$ are *null events*; their probability of occurrence is zero. If E is an event for which $P[E] = 1$, then E is a *sure event* and is said to occur almost surely or with a probability of 1.

If Ω is a finite or countable set, Φ is always taken to be the set of all subsets of Ω. In this case, it is sufficient to give the values of P on the elements of Ω, since by condition 3 the value of $P[E]$ for a subset E of Ω will then be given by $\Sigma P[\{x\}]$, where the sum is over the elements of E. Also, $P[x]$ is always written for the correct but more cumbersome symbol, $P[\{x\}]$.

Often it is necessary, or simply convenient, to allow subsets of the real numbers R as spaces of outcomes. For example, it may be convenient to allow any real number as the possible random return r on a share of stock over the next year. In such cases, it is natural to focus on the events $r \ \varepsilon \ (a, b]$, $r \ \varepsilon \ (-\infty, c]$, and so on for various real numbers a, b, and c. The smallest σ-algebra containing all such intervals $(a, b]$, $(-\infty, c]$, and so on is called the σ-*algebra of Borel sets*.

Conditional probabilities are defined as follows: The probability of A given B, where $A, B \ \varepsilon \ \Phi$ and (Ω, Φ, P) is a probability space, is defined as

$$P[A \mid B] = \frac{P[A \cap B]}{P[B]}$$

provided that $P[B] > 0$. ($P[A \mid B]$ is not defined for $P[B] = 0$.) For a fixed non-null event B, the function $P_B: \Phi \to [0, 1]$ defined by $P_B[A] = P[A \mid B]$ is a probability measure. In other words, (Ω, Φ, P_B) is a probability space.

Two events, A and B, are said to be independent if

$$P[A \cap B] = P[A]P[B].$$

Note that if B is not a null event, A and B are independent if — and only if — the probability of A given B is the same as the probability of A; knowing B adds no knowledge about the probability of A. If B is a null event, so is $A \cap B$; that is, $P[A \cap B] = 0$ if $P[B] = 0$ and, therefore, both sides of the equation are zero.

Properties of Probability Space.   Let (Ω, Φ, P) be a probability space and $A, B, C, A_1, A_2, \ldots$ events.

1. $0 \le P[A] \le 1$, $P[\phi] = 0$, and $P[\Omega] = 1$.

2. $P[A \cup B] = P[A] + P[B] - P[A \cap B]$.

3. $P[A^c] = 1 - P[A]$.

4.   If $A \subseteq B$, then $P[A] \le P[B]$.

5.   If $A_1, A_2, \ldots$ are pairwise disjoint, then

$$P\left[\bigcup_{i=1}^{\infty} A_i\right] = \sum_{i=1}^{\infty} P[A_i].$$

6.   If $A_1 \subseteq A_2 \subseteq A_3 \subseteq \ldots$, then $P[\bigcup_{i=1}^{\infty} A_i] = \lim P[A_i]$ as i tends to $+\infty$.

7.   If $A_1 \supseteq A_2 \supseteq A_3 \supseteq \ldots$, then $P[\bigcap_{i=1}^{\infty} A_i] = \lim P[A_i]$ as i tends to $+\infty$.

8. (Ω, Φ, P_B) is a probability space where $P_B[A] = P[A \mid B]$. (Thus, 1 through 7 remain valid with P replaced by P_B. For example, 5 says that if $A_1, A_2, \ldots$ are pairwise disjoint, then

$$P\left[\bigcup_{i=1}^{\infty} A_i \mid B\right] = \sum_{i=1}^{\infty} P[A_i \mid B].$$

9.   *Law of total probability:* If $A_1, A_2, \ldots$ are pairwise disjoint and $\bigcup_{i=1}^{\infty} A_i = \Omega$, then

$$P[B] = \sum_{i=1}^{\infty} P[A_i]P[A_i][B \mid A_i].$$

10.   *Bayes' rule:*

$$P[B \mid A] = \frac{P[B]P[A \mid B]}{P[B]P[A \mid B] + P[B^c]P[A \mid B^c]}.$$

Examples

1. *A single coin toss:* A coin toss has exactly two results: H and T. Let $\Omega = [H, T]$. Then $\Phi = \{\phi, \Omega, [H], [T]\}$ has four elements that represent, respectively, the following events: neither H nor T occurs; either H or T occurs; H occurs; and T occurs. A probability measure P is determined as soon as P[T] or P[H] is set, since $P[T] + P[H] = P[\Omega] = 1$. If the coin is fair such that $P[T] = P[H]$, there is only one choice: $P[T] = 0.5$.

2. *Two coin tosses:* Take $\Omega = [H, T]$ from example 1 and build a new space $\Omega \times \Omega = ([H, T], [H, H], [T, H], [T, T])$. Φ is the set of all 16 subsets of $\Omega \times \Omega$. Define $P[(x, y)] = \frac{1}{4}$ for all $(x, y) \, \varepsilon \, \Omega \times \Omega$. This choice of P models independent tosses. For example, the events A = $\{[H, T], [H, H]\}$ and B = $\{[H, T], [T, T]\}$, which correspond, respectively, to a head on the first toss and a tail on the second, are independent because $P[A] = \frac{1}{2}$, $P[B] = \frac{1}{2}$, and $P[A \cap B] = P\{[H, T]\} = \frac{1}{4}$.

Random Variables

A *random variable* is a function $X: \Omega \rightarrow R$, where (Ω, Φ, P) is a probability space, which satisfies the following condition:

- For each $x \, \varepsilon \, R$, the set $\{\omega \, \varepsilon \, \Omega: X(\omega) \leq x\}$ is an event in Φ.

This condition provides for the probability of events such as $X \leq x$, which is shortened notation for $\{\omega \, \varepsilon \, \Omega: X(\omega) \leq x\}$; that is,

$$P[X \leq x] = P[\{\omega \, \varepsilon \, \Omega: X(\omega) \leq x\}].$$

Using the definition of a probability space, it can be shown that

- For each Borel set B, the set $\{\omega \, \varepsilon \, \Omega: X(\omega) \, \varepsilon \, B\}$ is an event in Φ.

This means that P[B] is defined not only when B is an interval but for any Borel set B.

When Ω is countable, we always take Φ to be the set of all subsets of Ω; thus, the defining condition is satisfied by any function $X: \Omega \rightarrow R$.

If X is a random variable defined on (Ω, Φ, P), each of the sets $\{\omega \, \varepsilon \, \Omega: X(\omega) \, \varepsilon \, B\} \, \varepsilon \, \Phi$ by definition. But Φ usually contains many other sets as well. The collection of all such events corresponding to Borel sets B is itself a σ-algebra, which we denote $\Phi(X)$; it is called the σ-*algebra generated by X*.

In many applications it is possible to suppress the underlying probability space of a random variable $X: \Omega \rightarrow R$ by shifting to its distribution function, $F: R \rightarrow R$, defined by

$$F_x(x) = P[X \leq x]$$

for each $x \, \varepsilon \, R$. The distribution function $F: R \rightarrow R$ (we drop the subscript if no confusion will result) of a random variable X always satisfies the following properties; conversely, it can be shown that if a function satisfies these properties, it is the distribution function of some random variable.

Properties of Distribution Functions

1.   *Increasing:* If $s \leq x$, then $F(s) \leq F(x)$.

2.   *Right continuous:* As $s \to x^+$, $F(s) \to F(x)$.

3.   *Asymptotic to 1 at $+\infty$:* As $x \to +\infty$, $F(x) \to 1$.

4.   *Asymptotic to 0 at $-\infty$:* As $x \to -\infty$, $F(x) \to 0$.

Two special classes of distributions will suffice for all of our needs: continuous and discrete. A random variable X is of the *continuous* type if its distribution function F is a continuous function. If F is also differentiable, X (or its distribution) is said to be absolutely continuous and $f(x) = F'(x)$ is called the *probability density* of X. The probability that $X \leq x$ is the integral of f over $(-\infty, x]$:

$$F(x) = \int_{-\infty}^{x} f(s)\, ds \, .$$

The random variable X is of the *discrete* type if F is a step function with (at most) countably many steps at real numbers $x_1 < x_2 < \ldots$. Let $p_1 = P[X \leq x_1]$, $p_2 = P[x_1 < X < x_2], \ldots$. Then the probability $X \leq x$ becomes a (possibly infinite) sum,

$$P[X \leq x] = \sum p_i \, ,$$

where the sum runs over those indices i for which $x_i \leq x$.

The developments of the theories of discrete distributions and continuous distributions are parallel. In most cases, simply replacing sums with integrals, or vice versa, is all that is required. That being the case, we will use one notation for convenience,

$$F(x) = \int_{-\infty}^{x} dF(y) \, ,$$

with the understanding that it is the usual integral from calculus if the distribution is absolutely continuous and a discrete sum if the distribution is discrete.

The mean of a random variable X is given by

$$E[X] = \int x\, dF(x) \, ,$$

with the integral interpreted as the usual calculus integral if X is absolutely continuous and as a discrete sum if X is discrete. The limits of integration $-\infty$ to $+\infty$ are understood. In general, the expected value of $u(X)$, where $u(x)$ is an integrable function defined on the range of X, is given by

$$E[u(X)] = \int u(x)\, dF(x)$$

with the analogous interpretation of the integral.

At times it is necessary to consider several random variables simultaneously; for now we will consider only two, X and Y, defined on the same probability space (the general case is reviewed in the next section). The joint distribution function is given by

$$F(x, y) = P[X \leq x \text{ and } Y \leq y],$$

and the expected value of u(X, Y), where u(x, y) is an integrable function defined on the range of (X, Y), is

$$E[u(X, Y)] = \int u(x, y) \, dF(x, y),$$

which we naturally interpret as an iterated integral if X and Y are both continuous, a double sum if both are discrete, and a sum of integrals if one is discrete and the other continuous.

Examples of the common distributions are given at the end of this section.

Properties of Expectations. Let X, Y, Z be random variables and a, b ε R.

1. $E[aX] = aE[X]$.

2. $E[X + Y] = E[X] + E[Y]$.

3. If $P[X \leq Y] = 1$, then $E[X] \leq E[Y]$.

4. *Definition of variance:* $Var[X] = E[(X - E[X])^2]$ (usually denoted $Var[X]$ by σ^2).

5. *Definition of moments:* The kth moment of X about a is $E[(X - a)^k]$. An important special case is $a = 0$, denoted $\mu^k = E[X^k]$. (Usually the first moment, $E[X]$, is denoted μ.)

6. *Tchebychev's inequality:* $P[|X - \mu| \geq c\sigma] \leq 1/c^2$.

7. *Jensen's inequality:* If u is twice differentiable and $u''(x) \leq 0$ for all x (on an open set containing the range of X), then

$$E[u(X)] \leq u(E[X]).$$

8. *Approximation to E[u(X)]:* If X is concentrated near its mean, then

$$E[u(X)] \approx u(E[X]) + \left(\frac{\sigma^2}{2}\right) u''(E[X]).$$

(The symbol $\approx$ means that the quantities are approximately equal; how good the approximation is must be investigated in each application. It is exactly correct if u is a polynomial of degree two. It can be very poor but is good if X is concentrated near its mean.)

9. *Definition of covariance:* $Cov[X, Y] = E[XY] - E[X]E[Y]$.

10. $Cov[aX, Y] = a \, Cov[X, Y]$.

11. $Cov[X, Y + Z] = Cov[X, Y] + Cov[X, Z]$.

12. $Cov[X + Y, X + Y] = Var[X] + 2\,Cov[X, Y] + Var[Y]$.

13. *Cauchy-Schwartz inequality:* $\{E[XY]\}^2 \leq E[X^2]E[Y^2]$.

Examples of Distributions

Name	Density	Mean	Variance
Uniform	$f(x) = \dfrac{1}{(b - a)}$ on $[a, b]$ $f(x) = 0$ elsewhere	$\dfrac{(a + b)}{2}$	$\dfrac{(b - a)^2}{12}$
Normal	$f(x) = \dfrac{\exp\dfrac{-(x - \mu)^2}{2\sigma^2}}{\sigma\sqrt{(2\pi)}}$ for all x	μ	σ^2
Exponential	$f(x) = \left(\dfrac{1}{\mu}\right)\exp\left(\dfrac{-x}{\mu}\right), x \geq 0$	μ	μ^2
Binomial	$f(x) = C_{n,x}p^x(1 - p)^{n-x}, x = 0, \ldots, n$ where $C_{n,x} = \dfrac{n!}{(n - x)!\,x!}$ $f(x) = 0$ elsewhere	np	$np(1 - p)$
Poisson	$f(x) = \dfrac{e^{-\mu}\mu^x}{x!}, x = 0, 1, \ldots$	μ	μ

Sequences of Random Variables

Let $X_1, X_2, \ldots, X_n$ be random variables defined on the same probability space (Ω, Φ, P). The *joint cumulative distribution function (cdf)* F of $X_1, X_2, \ldots, X_n$ is defined by

$$F(x_1, x_2, \ldots, x_n) = P[X_1 \leq x_1, X_2 \leq x_2, \ldots, X_n \leq x_n].$$

The joint cdf is defined on R^n and has properties analogous to the cdf of a single random variable. The joint cdf also gives the cdf of each single random variable in the sequence. The cdf F_i of X_i is called the *marginal cdf* and is obtained by letting each $x_j (j \neq i)$ tend to $+\infty$ in the above definition. The $X_1, X_2, \ldots, X_n$'s are said to be *independent* if F factors into the product of its marginals; that is, they are independent if

$$F(x_1, x_2, \ldots, x_n) = F_1(x_1)F_2(x_2) \ldots F_n(x_n),$$

where $F_1(x_1) = P[X_1 \leq x_1, X_2 \leq +\infty, \ldots, X_n \leq +\infty]$
$F_2(x_2) = P[X_1 \leq +\infty, X_2 \leq x_2, \ldots, X_n \leq +\infty]$

$\cdot$

$\cdot$

$\cdot$

$F_n(x_n) = P[X_1 \leq +\infty, X_2 \leq +\infty, \ldots, X_n \leq x_n]$

As in the one- and two-variable cases, we consider only random variables that are discrete or absolutely continuous. If $u(x_1, x_2, \ldots, x_n)$ is an integrable function defined on the range of $X = (X_1, X_2, \ldots, X_n)$, the expected value of $u(X)$ is given by

$$E[u(X)] = \int u(x_1, x_2, \ldots, x_n) \, dF(x_1, x_2, \ldots, x_n),$$

where the integral is interpreted as a sum of multiple integrals of the usual type.

Let $\mu_i = E[X_i]$ and $E[X] = (\mu_1, \mu_2, \ldots, \mu_n)$, where X denotes the n-vector of values of $X_1, X_2, \ldots, X_n$. The covariance matrix of X is the n-by-n matrix C_x, defined by

$$C_x = E[(X - E[X])(X - E[X])^T].$$

The (i, j) element of C_x is $E[(X_i - \mu_i)(X_j - \mu_j)] = \text{Cov}(X_i, X_j)$. From the properties of the covariance, it follows that C_x is symmetric and positive semidefinite. It is positive definite if it is invertible or, equivalently, it has rank n. An important instance of a positive definite covariance matrix occurs when the Xs are uncorrelated but each has a non-zero variance σ_i^2. In this special case, C_x is a diagonal matrix with zeros off the main diagonal and the σ_i^2 running down the diagonal.

More on Conditioning

Earlier we described how conditioning on a single event works. Conditioning on an event B of a probability space (Ω, Φ, P) gives rise to a probability measure $P_B(E) = P(E \cap B)/P(B)$ in such a way that (Ω, Φ, P_B) is also a probability space. A random variable X will have a distribution function relative to P_B, as in the previous section, which is denoted $F(x \mid B)$. The measure P_B and distribution function $F(x \mid B)$ are related by

$$F(x \mid B) = P_B[X \leq x].$$

The mean, variance, and so on of this distribution are called the *conditional* (on B) mean, variance, and so on of X. More precisely, the random variable that has $F(x \mid B) = P_B[X \leq x]$ as its distribution function is called *X conditioned on B* and denoted $X \mid B$. Using these terms, we have

$$E[X \mid B] = \int x \, dF(x \mid B).$$

Further, all of the properties of the expectation operator $E[X]$ reviewed in the preceding section carry over to conditional (on B) expectations.

In some financial models, conditioning on a σ-algebra is required. This is a difficult concept to develop with mathematical rigor. There is such a presentation in Laha and Rohatgi (1979), to which we refer readers prepared for a graduate-level probability text. In this section we simply list the results we have used, especially those in Chapter 10. A random variable X defined on (Ω, Φ, P) conditioned on a σ-algebra $Y \subset \Phi$ similarly gives rise to random variables $E[X \mid Y]$,

Var[X|Y], and so forth, which satisfy properties analogous to those of the usual expectations operator. The following is a summary of some of the results from Laha and Rohatgi.

Properties of Conditional Expectations.   The random variables X, Y, Z, . . . are defined on the same probability space (Ω, Φ, P) and have finite expectations. Y is a σ-algebra, $Y \subset \Phi$.

1.   If for each b the event $X \le b$ is an event in Y, then

$$E[X|Y] = X$$

(that is, if Y contains all the relevant information on X, conditioning on Y does not change X).

2. $E[aX + bY|Y] = aE[X|Y] + bE[Y|Y]$.

3.   If for each b the event $X \le b$ is an event in Y, then

$$E[XY|Y] = XE[Y|Y]$$

(again, since Y contains all the relevant information on X, conditioning on Y does not change X).

4.   If $Y_1 \subset Y_2$ are σ-algebras, $Y_1 \subset Y_2 \subset \Phi$, then

$$E[X|Y_1] = E[E[X|Y_1]|Y_2] = E[E[X|Y_2]|Y_1].$$

5.   If X and Y are independent in the sense that for each b and each $E \, \varepsilon \, Y$ the events $X \le b$ and E are independent, then

$$E[X|Y] = E[X].$$

6.   If the variance of X is finite, then

$$E[(X - Y)^2] \ge E[(X - E[X|Y])^2]$$

with equality if — and only if — $Y = E[X|Y]$.

7. $Var[X] = E[Var[X|Y]] + Var[E[X|Y]]$.

In Chapter 10, we present a financial market model that uses the terms "securities" and "information" without giving a precise definition. The securities are sequences of random variables defined on a probability space (Ω, Φ, Pr).[2] The price at time t is denoted P_t for $t = 0, 1, 2, \ldots$. If it is necessary to discuss two or more securities at the same time, we will use an additional subscript; for example, $P_{j,t}$ denotes the price of the jth security at time t. Thus, the mathematical model of a security is simply a sequence of random variables $P_t: \Omega \to [0, \infty)$ defined on the probability space (Ω, Φ, Pr).

The σ-algebra Φ has all the information necessary for dealing with the security at any time, since by the definition of a random variable each of the sets

---

[2]The battle for the symbol P has been won by the security's "price." We will use P for security prices and Pr for the probability of an event depending on the context.

$\{\omega \, \varepsilon \, \Omega \, | \, b \le P_t(\omega) \le a\}$ must be in Φ for all a and b, $-\infty \le b < a \le \infty$, and all t = 0, 1, 2, ... Indeed, the rigorous definition of *information* as used in Chapter 10 is given in terms of σ-algebras: The information available at time t is a σ-algebra ($\Phi_t \subset \Phi$) containing all events that might occur at times $\{0, 1, \ldots, t\}$ and affect the price of some security. In other words, Φ_t is the σ-algebra generated by the random variables $P_{j,s}$ where s = 0, 1, 2, . . . , t and j = 1, 2, ...

The σ-algebra $_m\Phi_t$ of information used in calculating expectations of future values (such as the expected value of P_{t+1}) is a subset of Φ_t. In some models, it may be appropriate to distinguish market information from full information; hence, in general, $_m\Phi_t \ne \Phi_t$. To distinguish values based on this information, we would write $E[P_{t+1}|_m\Phi_t]$ rather than $E[P_{t+1}|\Phi_t]$. However, in most of Chapter 10 we assume that $_m\Phi_t = \Phi_t$.

The key properties of the information σ-algebras, or information sets Φ_t, are as follows:

1. $\Phi_0 \subset \Phi_1 \subset \Phi_2 \subset \ldots \subset \Phi.$

2. $\Phi = \bigcup_{t=0}^{\infty} \Phi_t.$

3. P_t is measurable with respect to Φ_t for all t = 0, 1, ...

Stochastic Processes

Introduction

A *stochastic process* is a set of random variables X_t defined on a common probability space (Ω, Φ, P) and indexed by time t. For example, in the multiperiod setting of Chapter 10, security prices form a stochastic process. The values of $X_t(\omega)$ define the path the process takes given that the state of the world is $\omega \, \varepsilon \, \Omega$. The graph of $X_t(\omega)$ as a function of t is called the *sample path* of the process given that ω occurs. Sometimes we use the notation $X(\omega, t)$ or simply $X(t)$ in place of $X_t(\omega)$.

The process may be defined for only t = 1, 2, . . . or for an interval such as t $\ge$ 0. A process that is defined for only a finite or countable set of times is a *discrete time process*. The only other processes we will consider are *continuous time processes* — those for which the process is defined on an interval. An example is shown in Figure C.4.

The set of values that the process $\{X_t\}$ takes is called the *state space* and is usually denoted S:

$$S = \{x \, \varepsilon \, R: \quad \text{for some } \omega \, \varepsilon \, \Omega \text{ and some time t, } X_t(\omega) = x\}.$$

The state space usually is either a countable set or an interval (possibly unbounded). The first is referred to as a *discrete state space* and the second as a *continuous state space*.

For a state s ε S, the first passage time to s is defined as the greatest lower bound of the times t for which $X_t(\omega) = s$ for some $\omega \, \varepsilon \, \Omega$. It is denoted T_s:

$$T_s = \inf\{t \ge 0: X_t = s\}.$$

A state a is called an *absorbing state*, and the value a is said to be an *absorbing*

Figure C.4

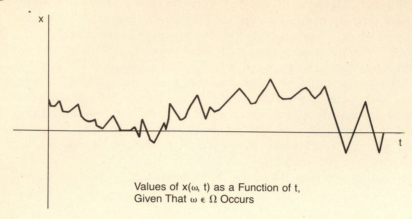

Values of x(ω, t) as a Function of t,
Given That $\omega \in \Omega$ Occurs

---

barrier, if the process almost certainly stays at a once it reaches it. In other words, the state a is absorbing if for each t and s $\geq$ t,

$$P[X_s = a \mid X_t = a] = 1.$$

We will consider only processes with discrete or continuous state spaces and only discrete or continuous time. The four possible combinations are illustrated in the following section.

Examples

Discrete Time and Discrete State Space: The Simple Random Walk. In this example, the times are n $= 0, 1, 2, \ldots$ and the state space is the set of all integers. A bug is at 0 at time n $= 0$. At each later time t $= 1, 2, \ldots$, a fair coin is flipped. If a head occurs, the bug jumps one unit to the right; if a tail occurs, it jumps one unit to the left. The state of the system (or process) at time n is the bug's position. More formally, we let $X_0 = 0$ and for each n > 0 we let Z_n denote a binomial random variable that is 1 with probability $\frac{1}{2}$ and -1 with probability $\frac{1}{2}$. The state at time n is

$$X_n = X_0 + Z_1 + Z_2 + \ldots + Z_n$$

$$= X_{n-1} + Z_n.$$

The common probability space (Ω, F, Pr) is not usually specified explicitly, because even in this simple case it is quite complex and adds little to our understanding of applications of stochastic processes (at least at this stage).

Continuous Time and Discrete State Space: The Poisson Process. In this example the times are t ≥ 0 and the state space is the set of all nonnegative integers. The process is denoted N(t) and should be considered as the number of events of interest that occurred in the time interval (0, t], for example, the number of claims reported to an insurance company or number of customers to enter a store. Such a process N(t) is said to be *Poisson* with rate λ if the following are satisfied:

1. $P[N(t + \Delta t) - N(t) = 0 | N(t)] = 1 - \lambda \Delta t + o(\Delta t)$.

2. $P[N(t + \Delta t) - N(t) = 1 | N(t)] = \lambda \Delta t + o(\Delta t)$.

The symbol $o(\Delta t)$ denotes a function of Δt that tends toward zero faster than Δt; that is, $o(\Delta t)/\Delta t \to 0$ as $\Delta t \to 0$. It can be shown that Poisson processes have the following properties:

1. Let T_k denote the time of the kth event, that is, the first passage of time from $N(0) = 0$ to k. Then the times $T_1, \ldots, T_k$ are independent and identically exponentially distributed with parameter λ.

2. $N(t + h) - N(t)$ has a Poisson distribution with parameter λh.

Discrete Time and Continuous State Space: Lognormal Prices. The random returns of sets of assets at discrete times $0, 1, 2, \ldots$ are often modeled with continuous distributions. For example, it is commonly assumed that an asset's return R_k over the period labeled k to k + 1 is normally distributed with mean μ_k and variance σ_k^2. The corresponding prices $P_0, P_1, P_2, \ldots$ are given by $P_k = P_0 \exp(R_1 + R_2 + \ldots + R_{k-1})$ and are lognormally distributed. It is often assumed that the returns are independent and identically distributed.

Continuous Time and Continuous State Space: Cash Balances. The problem of determining the optimal cash balances for a firm to hold often is approached by modeling the cash balance X(t) at time t in continuous time $t \geq 0$ because it is easier to solve than the corresponding discrete time model and cash balances usually are almost continuously observable anyway. Let x be the value of the fund at time 0. A common specification for X(t) is

$$X(t) = x + \mu t + \sigma Z(t),$$

where Z(t) is a standard *Brownian motion*. By this we mean that Z is a continuous time stochastic process such that Z satisfies the following:

1. For any finite set of times $t_1 < t_2 < t_3 < \ldots t_n$, the random variables $Z(t_2) - Z(t_1), Z(t_3) - Z(t_2), \ldots, Z(t_n) - Z(t_{n-1})$ are independent.

2. For all $h > 0$ and all $t, Z(t + h) - Z(t)$ normally is distributed with mean 0 and variance h.

3. For each $\omega \ \varepsilon \ \Omega$, the sample path $X(\omega, t)$ is a continuous function of t.

From 1 and 2 it follows that the cash balance X(t) normally is distributed with mean

$$E[X(t)] = x + \mu t$$

and variance

$$Var[X(t)] = \sigma^2 t.$$

Continuous Time Stochastic Modeling

Continuous time stochastic modeling is very important in finance, as a survey of recent issues of academic journals would reveal. Therefore, we devote the remainder of this section to a review of this setting, although analogous results often hold for discrete time models. Throughout this section $Z(t)$, $t \geq 0$ denotes a standard Brownian motion. Its underlying probability space is $(\Omega, \Phi, \mathrm{Pr})$. In many models, the information available at time t, derived solely from observing $Z(s)$ for $s \leq t$, is represented by the σ-algebra $F(Z(s): s \leq t)$ generated by the family of random variables $\{Z(s) \mid s \geq t\}$. With time, there may be more information available; that is, there may be processes other than Z observable. We model this evolution of information as an increasing collection of σ-algebras $\{F_t \mid t \geq 0\}$. Since we are thinking of F_t as the information available to us at time t, it must contain the information embodied in the family of random variables $\{Z(s): s \leq t\}$ and be independent of that contained in the family $\{Z(s) - Z(t): s > t\}$. In terms of σ-algebras, this means that $F(Z(s): s \leq t)$ is contained in F_t and the σ-algebras F_t and $F(Z(s) - Z(t): s > t)$ are independent.

Stochastic Differential Equations

The ordinary differential equation, where $a(x, t)$ is a continuous function of x and t,

$$dx = a(x, t)\, dt, \quad t \geq 0$$

is formally equivalent to an integral equation

$$x(t) = \int_0^t a[x(s), s]\, ds \,.$$

The stochastic differential equation, in which a and b are continuous functions,

$$X(t) = a[X(t), t]\, dt + b[X(t), t]\, dZ(t) \,,$$

is analogously equivalent to an integral equation

$$X(t) = \int_0^t a[X(s), s]\, ds + \int_0^t b[X(s), s]\, dZ(s) \,.$$

But the difference is that the integrals are random variables. The first integral is called a *path integral*. For each $\omega \; \varepsilon \; \Omega$, the value of the path integral is simply the usual integral of the continuous function $a[X(\omega, s), s]$ over the interval $[0, t]$. The second is the *Ito integral* and is defined as the limit of the random variables

$$\sum b[X(s_i), s_i][Z(s_{i+1}) - Z(s_i)] \,,$$

where $0 = s_0 \leq s_1 \leq s_2 \leq \ldots s_n = t$. The limit is in the sense of mean square convergence and is taken as the $\max\{s_{k+1} - s_k: k = 0, 1, \ldots, n - 1\}$ tends toward zero. There is not space to go into more detail here. The book by Malliaris has a complete development.

When X is obtained in this way, it is said to satisfy the above stochastic differential equation. The function a is called the *drift coefficient* and b the *diffusion coefficient* because of the following relationships:

$$\lim_{s \to t^+} \frac{E[X(s) - X(t) \mid X(t) = x]}{s - t} = a(x, t)$$

and

$$\lim_{s \to t^+} \frac{E[\{X(s) - X(t)\}^2 \mid X(t) = x]}{s - t} = b(x, t)^2.$$

Ito's Formula

Now we come to *Ito's formula,* the most frequently quoted result in financial applications of stochastic integration. It is a generalization of the chain rule of ordinary calculus: If $dX(t) = a(t) \, dt$ and $f(x, t)$ has continuous partial derivatives, the composite function $Y(t) = f[X(t), t]$ has the differential $dY(t) = \{a(t)D_1 f[X(t), t] + D_2 f[X(t), t]\} \, dt$. The subscripts denote partial differentiation with respect to the first and second arguments of f. Of course, the ordinary chain rule can be stated in more general terms; for example, we could plug in a smooth function for the second argument as well as the first. However, the stochastic analog of this form is the most useful one for financial applications. Ito's formula is the following:

- Let f: $R \to [0, \infty) \times R$ be a continuous function having continuous partial derivatives $D_1 f$, $D_2 f$, and $D_{11} f$ and X(t) a process satisfying the stochastic differential equation

$$dX(t) = a[X(t), t] \, dt + b[X(t), t] \, dZ(t).$$

Then the process $Y(t) = f[X(t), t]$ satisfies the stochastic differential equation

$$dY(t) = \left\{ a[X(t), t]D_1 f[X(t), t] + D_2 f[X(t), t] \right.$$

$$\left. + \frac{b[X(t), t]^2}{2} D_{11} f[X(t), t] \right\} dt + D_1 f[X(t), t]b[X(t), t] \, dZ(t).$$

Often the variables X and t are suppressed and another notation for the partial derivatives used. In this case, the formulas appear as follows:

$$dX = a \, dt + b \, dZ$$

$$dY = \left[a \frac{\partial f}{\partial x} + \frac{\partial f}{\partial t} \left(\frac{b^2}{2} \right) \frac{\partial^2 f}{\partial x^2} \right] dt + b \left(\frac{\partial f}{\partial x} \right) dZ.$$

Example 1. Let $f(x, t) = x^2$ for all x and t. Then $f_1(x, t) = 2x$, $f_{11}(x, t) = 2$, and $f_2(x, t) = 0$ for all x and t. Let $X(t) = Z(t)$, a standard Brownian motion; thus, $a(t) = 0$ and $b(t) = 1$ for all t. Then Ito's formula gives the differential for squared Brownian motion $Y(t) = X(t)^2$:

$$dY = [f_2 + af_1 + (b^2/2)f_{11}] dt + bf_1 dZ = dt + 2Z dZ.$$

Example 2. Let $f(x, t) = e^{cx+kt}$ for all x and t, where c and k are real constants. Then $f_1 = cf$, $f_2 = kf$, and $f_{11} = c^2 f$. Again let $X(t) = Z(t)$, a standard Brownian motion. The differential of $Y(t) = e^{cZ(t)+kt}$ is, according to Ito's formula,

$$dY(t) = \left\{ kf[Z(t), t] + \left(\frac{1}{2}\right) c^2 f[Z(t), t] \right\} dt + cf[Z(t), t] dZ(t)$$

$$= \left[kY(t) + \frac{c^2 Y(t)}{2} \right] + cY(t) dZ(t).$$

This shows that Y solves the stochastic differential equation $dY = Y[(k + c^2/2) dt + cdZ]$, which is sometimes written $dY/Y = (k + c^2/2) dt + cdZ$.

For a financial version of this example, we consider a bond whose value $S(t)$ is thought to satisfy a stochastic differential equation $dS(t) = a(t) dt + b(t) dZ(t)$ in which the drift term $a(t)$ is proportional to $S(t)$, $a(t) = \mu S(t)$ and the diffusion term $b(t)$ is proportional to $S(t)$, $b(t) = \sigma S(t)$ for all t with μ and σ known real constants. This is, in fact, a frequently used model of bond prices. By comparing $dS/S = \mu dt + \sigma dZ$ with $dY/Y = (k + c^2/2) dt + cdZ$, we see that if we set $c = \sigma$ and $k = \mu - \sigma^2/2$, we will obtain the solution of the bond price stochastic differential equation within a multiplicative constant, $S(t) = S(0) \exp[\sigma Z(t) + (\mu - \sigma^2/2)t]$. To reiterate: If $S(t)$ satisfies $dS/S = \mu dt + \sigma dw$, subject to an initial condition $S(0) = s_0$, then $S(t) = s_0 \exp[\sigma Z(t) + (\mu - \sigma^2/2)t]$. $Z(t)$ is log-normally distributed; hence, we can calculate its means $E[S(t)]$ and covariances $Cov[S(t), S(s)]$.

Example 3. Let $dX(t) = b(t) dZ(t)$; that is, $X(t) = \int_0^t b(s) dZ(s)$. Apply Ito's formula with $f(x, t) = x^2$. Since $f_1 = 2x$, $f_2 = 0$, $f_{11} = 2$, and $a = 0$, the differential of $Y(t) = f[X(t)] = [\int_0^t b(s) ds]^2$ is $dY(t) = [f_2 + af_1 + (b^2/2)f_{11}] dt + bf_1 dZ = b(t)^2 dt \rightarrow b(t)[2X(t)] dZ(t)$. In the integral form, $Y(T) - Y(0) = \int_0^T b(t)^2 dt + 2\int_0^T b(t)X(t) dw(t)$. Since $Y(T) = [\int_0^T b(t) dw(t)]^2$ and $X(t) = \int_0^t b(s) dZ(s)$, we obtain a formula for the square of the integral:

$$\left[\int_0^T b(t) dZ(t) \right]^2 = \int_0^T b(t)^2 dt + 2 \int_0^T b(t) \int_0^t b(s) dZ(s) dZ(t).$$

Taking expectations gives us the second moment of $\int_0^t b(t) dw(t)$ in terms of the expectation of b:

$$E\left[\left(\int_0^T b(t) dw(t) \right)^2 \right] = E\left[\int_0^T b(t)^2 ds \right] = \int_0^t E[b(t)^2] ds.$$

The same idea applied with $f(x, t) = x^{2m}$ can be used to obtain bounds on $E[(\int_0^T b(t) dw(t))^{2m}]$.

References

T. M. Apostol, *Mathematical Analysis,* 2d ed. (Reading, Mass.: Addison-Wesley, 1977).

B. R. Gelbaum and J. M. H. Olmsted, *Counterexamples in Analysis* (San Francisco: Holden-Day, 1964).

P. G. Hoel, S. C. Port, and C. J. Stone, *Introduction to Stochastic Processes* (Boston: Houghton Mifflin, 1972).

S. Karlin and H. M. Taylor, *A First Course in Stochastic Processes* (New York: Academic Press, 1965).

————, *A Second Course in Stochastic Processes* (New York: Academic Press, 1981).

R. G. Laha and V. K. Rohatgi, *Probability Theory* (New York: Wiley, 1979).

S. Lang, *Linear Algebra* (Reading, Mass.: Addison-Wesley, 1966).

D. G. Luenberger, *Optimization by Vector Space Methods* (New York: Wiley, 1969).

T. G. Malliaris, *Stochastic Methods in Economics and Finance,* Advanced Textbooks in Economics, Vol. 17 (North Holland: Elsevier).

R. Roll, "Critique of the Assets Pricing Theory Tests I," *Journal of Financial Economics* 7 (March 1977): 129–176.

Subject Index